Guerrilla Warfare
in Civil War Missouri,
Volume III,
January–August 1864

BY BRUCE NICHOLS
AND FROM McFARLAND

*Guerrilla Warfare in Civil War Missouri, Volume I,
1862* (2004; paperback 2012)

*Guerrilla Warfare in Civil War Missouri, Volume II,
1863* (2007; paperback 2012)

*Guerrilla Warfare in Civil War Missouri, Volume III,
January–August 1864* (2013)

*Guerrilla Warfare in Civil War Missouri, Volume IV,
September 1864–June 1865* (2013)

Guerrilla Warfare in Civil War Missouri, Volume III, January–August 1864

Bruce Nichols

McFarland & Company, Inc., Publishers
Jefferson, North Carolina

All maps are by the author unless otherwise noted.

LIBRARY OF CONGRESS CATALOGUING-IN-PUBLICATION DATA

Nichols, Bruce, 1951–
Guerrilla warfare in Civil War Missouri, Volume III,
January–August 1864 / Bruce Nichols.
  p.   cm.
Includes bibliographical references and index.

ISBN 978-0-7864-3813-6
softcover : acid free paper ∞

1. Missouri—History—Civil War, 1861–1865—Underground movements.
2. Guerrillas—Missouri—History—19th century.
3. Guerrilla warfare—Missouri—History—19th century.
4. Confederate States of America. Army—History—19th century.
5. Missouri—History—Civil War, 1861–1865—Commando operations.
6. United States—History—Civil War, 1861–1865—Underground movements.
7. United States—History—Civil War, 1861–1865—Commando operations.
  I. Title.
E470.45.N535 2014   973.7'478—dc22   2006027132

BRITISH LIBRARY CATALOGUING DATA ARE AVAILABLE

© 2014 Bruce Nichols. All rights reserved

*No part of this book may be reproduced or transmitted in any form
or by any means, electronic or mechanical, including photocopying
or recording, or by any information storage and retrieval system,
without permission in writing from the publisher.*

Cover art © 2014 PicturesNow.com

Manufactured in the United States of America

*McFarland & Company, Inc., Publishers
Box 611, Jefferson, North Carolina 28640
www.mcfarlandpub.com*

In memory of my beloved parents,
Chester and Edith Nichols,
who gave me life and the love of learning

Table of Contents

Preface 1

Introduction 6

ONE
Winter 1864 in Southeast Missouri 9

TWO
Winter 1864 in Southwest Missouri 29

THREE
Winter 1864 in Northeast Missouri 36

FOUR
Winter 1864 in Northwest Missouri 41

FIVE
Missouri Guerrilla Warfare Changes During Early 1864 56

SIX
Spring 1864 in Southeast Missouri 68

SEVEN
Spring 1864 in Southwest Missouri 90

EIGHT
Spring 1864 in Northeast Missouri 109

NINE
Spring 1864 in Northwest Missouri South of the Missouri River 123

TEN
Spring 1864 in Northwest Missouri North of the Missouri River 145

ELEVEN
Summer 1864 in Southeast Missouri 154

TWELVE
Summer 1864 in the St. Louis Area 179

THIRTEEN
Summer 1864 in Southwest Missouri 190

Fourteen
June Through Mid-July 1864 in Northeast Missouri   212

Fifteen
Mid-July Through August 1864 in Northeast Missouri   229

Sixteen
Before the Insurgency Ignited: June Through Early July 1864 in Northwest Missouri North of the Missouri River   262

Seventeen
Before the Insurgency Ignited: June Through Early July 1864 in Northwest Missouri South of the Missouri River   281

Eighteen
The Premature Insurgency That Failed During July 1864 in Northwest Missouri North of the Missouri River   304

Nineteen
Renewed Guerrilla Operations During August 1864 in Northwest Missouri North of the Missouri River   333

Twenty
Supporting the Insurgency: Mid-July Through August 1864 in Northwest Missouri South of the Missouri River   350

Afterword   387

Notes   393

Bibliography   447

Index   456

Preface

This work is an in-depth study of all known guerrilla operations in Missouri from January through August 1864—part of the darkest, most traumatic, terror-filled period in the history of the state. This military history covering these eight months represent the huge southern guerrilla and Confederate recruiting effort behind Union lines in the Show-Me State that preceded Confederate Major General Sterling Price's regular army invasion of the state in September and October that year.

When I initiated active research for my work on guerrilla warfare in Missouri in the middle 1980s, I envisioned one rather full volume covering this topic in enough detail to add something useful to the body of knowledge. When I began to analyze the vast quantities of material I amassed in several years, I discovered one volume could not contain this work. Fortunately, the seasonal nature of Missouri's guerrilla war allowed me to divide my study of this topic into either yearly or seasonal periods without loss of too much transition.

I deliberately chose to begin this overall project with the first day of the year 1862, and from that came my *Guerrilla Warfare in Civil War Missouri, Volume I, 1862*. My long study of this topic convinced me that both northern and southern armies of the conflict spent the year 1861 fighting to see whose military would occupy the state. The nature of guerrilla or irregular warfare is the secret, clandestine, or hidden resistance to an established power. The word "guerrilla" literally means "little war," and that was just about how the Union and Confederate high commands regarded the warfare in Missouri after the northern forces ejected the southern ones in early 1862. Not until the winter of 1861 and 1862 were most Missouri southerners finally convinced that the Union military was the occupying power and their own military was about to be an army in exile. With that realization, a large number of men of southern sympathy began to seek ways to attack the despised Yankee occupation of their state. Therefore, although there were some southern guerrilla actions during 1861, these were mostly local incidents, and the main military actions were the contests between the southern and northern regular forces. Only with the expulsion of the southern Missouri State Guard from its native soil in early 1862 did guerrilla warfare become the dominant form of fighting in Missouri. *Guerrilla Warfare in Civil War Missouri, Volume II, 1863*, traced evolutions in Missouri guerrilla and counter-guerrilla operations during 1863. This third volume is part of the continuing study of that form of fighting for the first eight months of 1864.

An in-depth study of the protracted guerrilla warfare in Missouri has value for a variety of applications. I have empathy for descendants searching for their ancestors' roles in this strange form of war so far removed from the more familiar active theaters of regular warfare. These family researchers often know the "who" of their search while the "when," "where," and especially the "why" elude their grasp. Those searchers find their first great hurdle just finding which resources they need to use to begin the hunt, and I intend this work to introduce some of those resources. I also intend this book for enjoyable reading and the discovery of a troubled although neglected period of our nation's history. Just about the only thing most Americans can recite from their education about guerrilla warfare in Civil War Missouri is the leader Quantrill, and if they can remember that he raided Lawrence, Kansas, they don't recall anything beyond that. A more somber reason to study Missouri guerrilla warfare during that terrible war is the value our citizens can derive from the study of thousands of men and many women who resisted a Federal occupying force with some success for over four years. Even if their logistics and technology are relics of the past, how Missouri southern irregulars not only managed to survive overwhelming numbers but even kept the offensive for long periods of time may have current applications. The guerrillas of the 1860s did not call themselves "terrorists," but terror and intimidation were among their greatest weapons in a war fought mostly with the grim, mutual understanding that prisoners would not always be taken.

Speaking of terms, in this work, as in the earlier ones about 1862 and 1863, I use the labels "guerrilla," "bushwhacker," "irregular," and "partisan" all interchangeably to mean the same thing. I qualify such combatants as "southern," "Rebel," or "Confederate" to ensure the reader knows these are combatants of southern sympathy, since there was no need of northern guerrillas in a state under the occupation of northern troops. In some instances where I identify guerrillas who seemed to have no allegiance except robbery and personal gain I use such terms as "renegades" or "freebooters." I resist the temptation to borrow from biased period sources such names for southern guerrillas as "bandits," "robbers," "outlaws," and similar epithets since such words do not accurately portray these southerners' warrior status. Similarly, I call northern combatants who forsook their duty and disgraced their uniform to plunder and murder "renegades" or even "jayhawkers," the term particularly applied to some Kansas troops who engaged in revenge and plunder raids into western Missouri. "Jayhawker" may be a present-day admired and honored term to Kansans, but in terms of guerrilla warfare in Missouri of the 1860s it meant something much more sinister. A term I use sparingly is "massacre," which in military subjects means "an unwarranted, indiscriminate, merciless, and needless slaughter of a group of human beings," often unable to defend themselves. The "needless" aspect of a massacre implies that the victims were unarmed, as with disarmed prisoners, and no longer a threat to the other side who held them, and that to harm them would be inhumane. Others use this term all too freely to mean a variety of things. In Missouri during the Civil War, the "no quarter" nature of guerrilla warfare complicated issues about what could and could not rightfully be called a "massacre." Many southern military men returned from the South to Missouri many hundreds of miles behind Union lines and sought to enlist fellow southern men and bring them back to the Confederate army, and these I call "recruiters" to distinguish them from the guerrillas. This distinction is sometimes hard to make since southern recruiters used local bushwhackers as security forces, and men who at times during the war acted as recruiters seemed to act at other times as guerrillas. The Confederate government and military freely used their own term "partisan rangers" to protect the status as legitimate combatants of both their guerrillas and recruiters, but Missourians made limited use of that term. The Union military leadership disputed such a loose granting of legitimacy to what they considered "brigands," "thieves," "assassins," and the like, and was always loathe to recognize as lawful combatants southerners who wore no uniforms, refused most of the time to face combat in the open, and who seemed to answer to no rightful chain of command. Therefore, period sources reflect this confusion of terms to the southerners who fought in guerrilla warfare. Northern combatants I call "Union," "Yankees," or "Federals," although I reserve this last term for northern troops on active status in federalized units and not local militia or home guards. Wherever possible, I make distinctions in this work between the different types of northern militia in the bewildering array of militia that Missouri northern authorities authorized at different times during the war. This is not only for historic precision, but to show the reader how the different training, leadership, and experience levels of these different units affected their conduct in the field.

I divided Missouri into four parts for this study, using the same lines of division along major rivers and along the borders of counties less active in guerrilla warfare that I used in the 1862 and 1863 books. I made exceptions on occasion, as in cases where a moving guerrilla operation spilled over my arbitrary boundary into another quadrant of the state. Of course, my purpose is to allow the reader to follow logically a military action as it progresses, so as not to allow a fleeing bit of history to escape the mind's capture. When the text involves individuals or actions described in other parts of the book, I often mention the chapter number to assist the reader fit one part to another. I caution readers that guerrilla war is not continuous, but episodic in its nature. Its starts and stops with a jerky pattern of isolated killings, skirmishes, raids, and the like separated by breaks or lulls. This "incident" nature of guerrilla war makes it difficult to write and also challenging to read.

For most location descriptions I use county designations, since most period records used them too, and their boundaries have changed little to the present day. I included my own general use maps for each region showing county lines, towns and some villages, major rivers, and railroads; to help the reader visualize aspects of this warfare.

For sources, I relied mostly on period sources such as the U.S. War Department's *The Official Records of the Union and Confederate Armies*, those surviving issues of local daily and weekly newspapers, journals, letters, and some specific military unit records written during the war, such as those in Broadfoot Publishing Company's new *Supplement to the "Official Records of the Union and Confederate Armies."* I also used skirmish summaries and northern unit histories from Frederick Dyer's landmark *A Compendium of the War of the Rebellion*, as well as separately published specific unit histories and memoirs of both sides. Another vital resource that I used extensively are the histories of the 114 Missouri counties that included local Civil War material, particularly the large number published not long after the war between the 1880s and the First World War. These local accounts are not always accurate, and some are flavored with wishful thinking, cover-ups, self-vindication, and the like, but they generally tend to provide accurate names of participants, correct unit designations, precise names of locations, and many other details otherwise difficult to find.

I also used many of the fine secondary works available on this topic, and I categorize them into two groups. There are those written within a few years of the war when participants were still alive to give their accounts, but most of these suffer from a bias of the author either toward the northern or the southern viewpoint. I found I could work through the bias and still use such works if I had several corroborating accounts of the same event. The second category of good secondary works I used is that of those written in the last several decades, especially since the 1940s. These show considerably less bias and can draw on a wider range of sources than those written just after the war, but, unfortunately, were also penned without the benefit of actual participation in the events described. These more modern works usually give helpful citations of their source material, too. There are too many of all categories of secondary works to list here, so I cite these in the notes and the bibliography.

Where I had multiple sources on an event or topic I was forced to make delicate judgments about which resource was more correct, but I tried to list most resources in the notes for those who wish to delve further in certain topics. I usually refrained from detailing the rationale for such value judgments for the sake of time and space. Despite my best efforts there will be some error in this work, and I take full responsibility for all mistakes.

I drew on a combination of education and life experiences to compose this work. My formal academic education toward a teaching degree in social studies and a master of arts degree in American history, both from Central Missouri State University (now the University of Central Missouri), combined with my formal military education as a U.S. Army military intelligence officer gave me disciplined training to produce a scholarly work. This book is, in a way, an extension of my master's thesis, "The Civil War in Johnson County, Missouri," on which noted Missouri Civil War historian and author Dr. Leslie Anders was my advisor. My twenty years experience as a reserve officer in the Army in the specialties of counterintelligence and psychological warfare ably demonstrated to me the need for high levels of accuracy and research applied to real-world situations. This has been complemented by my simultaneous 22 years of experience striving for technical accuracy and attention to detail as a cartographer for a government agency. Those same standards continue in my current work these last nine years as an intelligence analyst for the Department of Defense, and I am careful to keep my job and my hobby separate. Another hobby I have pursued for many years is amateur genealogy which has instilled in me a need to balance fairness with precise research in order to portray real individuals accurately in their environment without judging them.

There are several institutions and individuals who rendered assistance to the production of this book. I am grateful to the help given me by the St. Louis Public Library, the St. Louis County Library, the State Historical Society of Missouri at Columbia, the Western Historical Manuscripts Collections at both Columbia and St. Louis, and the Missouri Historical Society of St. Louis on numerous occasions. Among the individuals I wish to acknowledge are Clark Kenyon of Camp Pope Bookshop of Iowa City, Iowa, who was helpful particularly with scarce source material as well as publishing and copyright issues; the late Bob Younger, and Mary Younger and Andy Turner of the former Morningside Books of Dayton were generous with many illustrations; Connie Langum, historian at Wilson's Creek National Battlefield and her staff for help with photographs of Missouri Civil War personalities; Terry Harmon of Granite City, who generously provided numerous new and out-of-print publications and period photographs over a number of years; Thomas R. Rose of Columbia, Missouri, for his generous help with period newspaper research, especially with determining headlines; John Russell, M.D., of Cape Girardeau whose excellent genealogy tools and expertise came to my rescue identifying obscure people of the 1860s on a number of occasions; Glenn Hunt regarding her ancestor Cole and Miller County guerrilla chief Wiley Shumate, Dr. Thomas Sweeney, and advice and leads about period photographs; Thomas Bowen and Charles Orear for the use of period photographs; and several other Civil War descendants and collectors cited in the text, notes, and bibliography for what they shared with me. Among the numerous Missouri Civil War historians who encouraged me and shared knowledge are Carolyn Bartels, John Bradbury, Jr., Dr. Leslie Anders, Bryce Suderow, Jim Thoma, Tom Pearson, Jim McGhee, Terry E. Justice, Kirby Ross,

Homer Ficken, Rose Mary Lankford, and Bob Owens. I am unable to list all the relatives, friends, co-workers, friends in the Army Reserves, and friends at church who not only encouraged me but helped to hold me accountable to finish various parts of this project. I also owe many thanks to my wife Pat and our son Andy and daughter Anna, for their long-suffering, encouragement, and support in the production of this series of books. Pat was also particularly helpful assisting me with graphic technology for all the illustrations. This work also reflects my gratitude to the state of Missouri for giving me a wonderful family, a worthwhile home, and many fine friends and neighbors.

The story continues—and ends—in *Guerrilla Warfare in Civil War Missouri, Volume IV, September 1864–June 1865*.

Introduction

Guerrilla warfare in Missouri as evident during 1864 had been under way and evolving for three years in what had become a "backwater" of the Civil War. There are two things the reader should understand to predicate any reading of guerrilla warfare in Missouri: (1) that this form of warfare at least in Missouri was fought to the death because the standard evolved during spring 1862 that no prisoners would be taken on either side; (2) guerrillas were strongly motivated to fight such a war against great odds, even to the death. That "to the death" part happily and humanely closed in the spring of 1865.

No Quarter

The professional Union military leadership in Missouri initiated what has been called the "no quarter" rule in guerrilla warfare during the early weeks of 1862, evidently without consideration of the eventual consequences. Professional American military officer training in the decades preceding the Civil War failed to prepare senior Union authorities how to deal humanely with partisan warfare. They studied Napoleonic warfare, and Napoleon dealt harshly with the partisans he encountered in Spain and Russia. Now, these officers were faced with secession within their own beloved country and all that entailed—rebellion, treachery, treason. Internal rebellion is the most heartbreaking form of warfare. It evokes the strongest of emotions, and those same emotions tend to obscure reason. The problem of dealing with Missouri partisans came to the fore during the fall of 1861 and early winter of 1861/1862 when thousands of southern recruits riding to southwest Missouri to join the Rebel army carried out numerous acts of sabotage against the railroad infrastructure operated by the Union military in Missouri. The northern military had from the outset been careful to control water and rail transport in the state in a vain effort to contain rebellion and also keep those means of transport for their own use. The result of the sabotage was a lot of nuisance repairs to culverts and bridges, but there were tragic instances where trains derailed and a number of innocent civilians were killed and injured. As a result, the then commander of the Department of the Missouri, Major General Henry W. Halleck, ordered in March 1862 the execution on the spot of any guerrillas caught burning railroad bridges. Captured "bridgeburners" convicted of such a crime were sentenced to death on the presumption that they were criminals endangering innocent lives and not worthy of being treated as southern combatants. Abraham Lincoln personally intervened to reduce such sentences and appealed for calmer heads in Missouri, but a dangerous precedent had been set. With the expulsion of the southern Missouri State Guard from southwest Missouri by spring 1862, many southern men in the state began to oppose the occupying Yankees with guerrilla tactics. Southerners recalled with pride how during the Revolution patriots such as the men under General Francis "Swamp Fox" Marion resisted the British in the Carolinas with guerrilla tactics and helped bring about victory. Union authorities could envision only that their troops were being attacked by men "who pretended to be peaceful citizens by day but would shoot soldiers in the back by night." They soon extended beyond the railroads the directive that armed Rebels captured not wearing uniforms or not providing proof that they belonged to an established Rebel unit should be executed in the field after a "drumhead" court-martial conducted by the officer in charge. Previous to such orders, combatants on both sides regarded their prisoners as fellow Americans and tended to release them on written parole with the understanding that they could later be exchanged. In other words, there were rules and laws pertaining to regular warfare mutually followed by both sides. Guerrilla warfare did not neatly fit such rules of warfare, and northern officers had little experience or patience with it. Unfortunately for all concerned, cooler Union heads did not prevail, and the order to execute all captured guerrillas in arms and not in uniforms was upheld in Missouri. The predictable result was that if guerrillas were ordered to be executed when they fell into Yankee hands, the reverse became the practice, too. By summer 1862, partisan warfare throughout Missouri acquired the deadly "no quarter" aspect that made every single farmyard skirmish and country lane ambush a desperate combat to the death. When Union soldiers were uncertain about a prisoner's status they faced the choice to execute anyway or send the captive to prison to await military tribunal. The prisoner languished in prison until the tribunal would get to his case months later and await the verdict that he was either a regular soldier and fit to be exchanged and live, or that he was a guerrilla and face an execution. The desperation of waiting for such a decision led such captives to seek any means to escape, and the prisons could hardly hold them. Guerrilla warfare in Missouri was fought under this cloud of desperation, and there was little chivalry to it.

What Motivated the Guerrillas?

There are a number of motives that compelled hundreds and perhaps thousands of Missouri men to face great odds by opposing the Union occupation as guerrillas knowing they faced death if they fell into Yankee hands.

ANGER. Many Missourians felt anger enough to oppose their own government that had either caused or permitted the following list of complaints specific to Missouri:

- the suspension of civil rights;
- occupation of Missouri by tens of thousands of Yankee troops;
- extremism of abolitionists and the emotional issue of freeing the slaves;
- ruthless Kansas jayhawker raids on western Missouri communities;
- the introduction of northern troops from other states into Missouri;
- use of thousands of recent German immigrants in St. Louis as Union troops and the depredations by some of them on duty in Missouri;
- the sensational southern press in Missouri and the squelching of it by Union authorities;
- harsh northern military measures such as the draft, impressing private property for military use, recruiting black men, control of all traffic on waterways, mandatory enrollment of all men of military age into the Enrolled Missouri Militia, foraging, enforcement of civil law by U.S. Army provost marshals, and the like.

Many of the above acts were those of lawless and criminally minded men using northern service as a pretense for personal gain or revenge. Many of the above were the desperate acts of the northern authorities to stamp out a rebellion in their midst. With hindsight, we can say that a number of the above acts were mistakes. To many southern Missouri men they spelled out tyranny and compelled many to fight as either regular Confederate military or in their home regions against the Union occupation as guerrillas. Anger is a strong motivator.

BITTERNESS. Many joined various bushwhacker bands out of the bitterness of a personal experience. Some felt compelled to fight in reaction to having a family member or friend abused or killed unjustly by someone representing the northern side. The protracted Kansas/Missouri border conflict from the 1850s affected many Missourians personally. Hostility, revenge, and bitterness scarred many.

HOPE. The hope of a Rebel overthrow of the tyranny of the Union occupation of Missouri helped to encourage the southern cause. That is partly why the southern military kept sending a steady stream of recruiters far behind Yankee lines to keep hope alive that some day the southern army would return. Southerners took encouragement that these recruiters and the guerrillas operated with some success in spite of all the northern troops could do to stop them. Such hope motivated many.

DESPERATION. Many men joined guerrilla bands out of desperation that they would be killed or imprisoned by northern authorities unless they did so. Men who returned from the southern army disgusted with what they had seen of war discovered to their horror that they were marked by local officials as incorrigible Rebels and would not be left in peace. The threat of draft by the Union side and the mandatory enrollment of all Missouri military age men in the Enrolled Missouri Militia forced hundreds of men to join the southern guerrillas to avoid such forced northern service. Desperation is an unpredictable incentive, but an incentive nevertheless.

EXCITEMENT. There were also men of the daredevil type who became bushwhackers just for the excitement of the experience. There were always young men seeking adventure and there were many in this border state on the frontier's edge who were already considered to be living on the edge of the law. Many of these preferred a life of daring and action to that of peaceable citizens, and fighting as guerrillas gave legitimacy and prestige to their adventures. People noticed them and considered them to be special. Seeking a life of excitement has always been a strong inducement to young men.

KEEPING FAITH WITH COMRADES. As is universal with most combatants, the initial motivations often were supplanted by another strong one—that of not disappointing soldiers in their same group. The above inducements often took second place to not wanting to let down comrades when in harm's way. The need to keep faith with their fellow fighters is a very powerful urge that sometimes transcends common sense.

ONE

Winter 1864 in Southeast Missouri

The winter weather during January and February 1864 was severe enough throughout Missouri to limit guerrilla activity, this was not the case in the southeast quadrant of the Show-Me State. The ice, snow, and cold here were no less treacherous to man and beast than in other parts of the state, but the tempo of irregular war continued at about the same pace as it had in autumn 1863. The dogged determination of a variety of local Rebel leaders in this region and the same attitude of Union commanders here was responsible for the continuation of the activity level even into the heart of the winter when guerrilla warfare all but stopped in other parts of Missouri. The question of which side would achieve complete mastery over the other in southeast Missouri continued in deadly small actions in spite of the weather.

Freeman and Others During January and February 1864 Actions in South-Central Missouri

As in earlier seasons, the main Rebel activity in south-central Missouri in early 1864 was attacking the Union use of the main wagon road between the two large bases at Rolla and Springfield. This was particularly true about that stretch of the road marked by steep hills and deep ravines in west Phelps County and Pulaski County in south-central Missouri where guerrilla attackers and ambushers had the advantage. In 1863 the Federals had established small cavalry posts along this stretch of the road and even small cavalry posts in towns some miles south of this vital road in Texas and Dent Counties in an attempt to keep the determined Confederate guerrillas from attacking the vulnerable wagon trains, stagecoaches, and couriers. War was often fought to the death here with prisoners not always taken as Rebel leaders continued to funnel small squads of bushwhackers north toward this main road and Union leaders struggled with limited numbers of cavalrymen to stop them.

Unit records of Company D, 2nd Wisconsin Cavalry proudly attest that sometime during January and February 1864 a ten-man patrol of this unit from the small garrison at Little Piney Creek in west Phelps County managed to kill a guerrilla sub-chief named Tom Brown they had been hearing about for some weeks. The scant history also mentioned that the troopers captured one of Brown's men, but gave no other details.[1]

The small Yankee garrison at Houston, county seat of Texas County, was intended to give early warning against a large-scale Rebel attack against one of the larger posts like Rolla or against the main wagon road to the north. But to survive against the constant threat that a large Confederate force could surprise and overwhelm them the little

Guerrillas shooting at freight wagons (Charles C. Coffin, *Marching to Victory*, 1888, p. 423).

Houston post had to send out frequent patrols just to protect itself. The constant patrols wore down both troopers and horses, so in mid-winter these patrols had difficulty mustering enough healthy troopers and mounts to do any good.

That is why Sergeant Dugan led only a five-man patrol from Company G, 5th Cavalry MSM out from Houston between January 4 and 8. The sergeant's patrol captured Jacob Rustin and John Inman of south Texas County, both known in this area as bushwhackers. The patrol also discovered the horses the pair had been riding were stolen from local northern sympathizers. The patrol report stated that some time after their capture Rustin and Inman attempted to escape and the troopers had to shoot them dead. The Federal pronouncement in Missouri since early 1862 was that southern combatants captured armed but not wearing Confederate uniforms were in violation of the rules of war and subject to execution, in spite of official Confederate protests that such combatants had legitimacy as "partisan rangers." Of course, southern bushwhackers retaliated in kind to the extent that prisoners were not often taken in Missouri guerrilla fighting, and prisoners taken were not sure of their ultimate fate at their captors' hands. As a result, even the smallest brush skirmish in Missouri was most often fought to the death. Therefore, Sergeant Dugan's two captives may or may not have actually attempted to escape, but they were dead nevertheless.[2]

The ranking Confederate commander in south-central Missouri this winter was Colonel Thomas Roe Freeman of Crawford and Phelps Counties before the war. During 1863 Freeman directed his cavalry commands as guerrillas against Union forces in south-central Missouri attacking Union shipping on the main wagon road west of Rolla, and in 1864 he was still dedicated to this same mission. His cavalry regiment was reorganized this January officially as "Freeman's Cavalry Regiment," consisting of 11 companies containing about 800 Missourians and Arkansans from this region. In spite of this new official status Colonel Freeman still directed these cavalrymen as he always had—in small groups infiltrating past Union patrols to attack Union logistics on the main wagon road in Phelps and Pulaski Counties.[3]

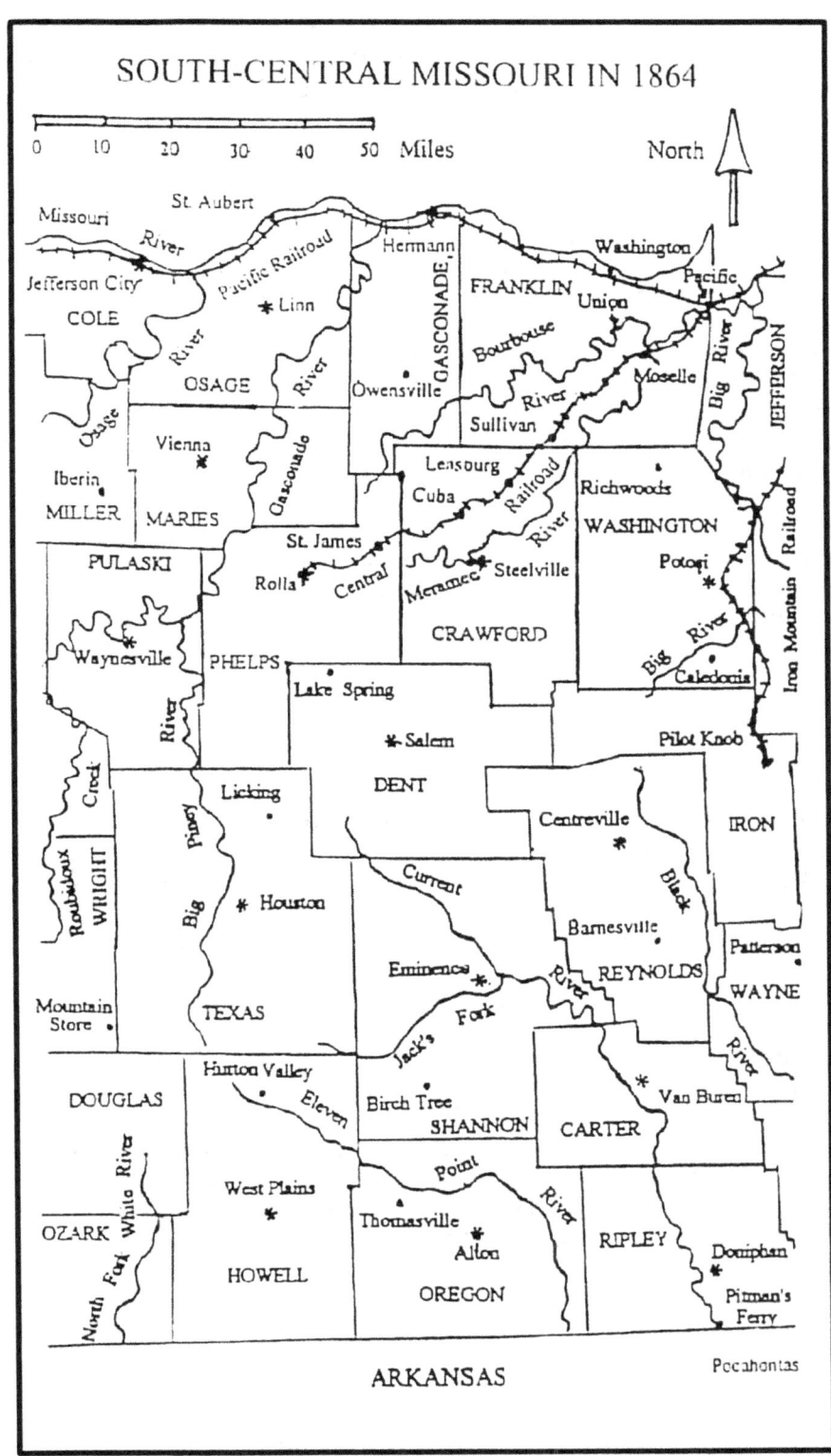

On January 22 an unidentified Union patrol killed one of Colonel Freeman's lieutenants and four enlisted men on Frederick's Fork, southeast Oregon County. The patrol then hurriedly carried back to their base that information plus the word that Freeman and 400 of his men were camped in that vicinity. Supporting this patrol's report, Union prison records attest that northern troops captured a Confederate Private Samuel M. Anderson January 25 in Oregon County and later passed Anderson along to one of the St. Louis area prisons.[4]

A Union spy identified only as "J. B." from the small Houston, Texas County, garrison rode across three counties between January 26 and February 3 probably to follow up the previous reports and verify exactly what Rebel forces were in the area. "J. B." first encountered Confederate Captain George Evans with some of his irregulars in Shannon or Howell County. The spy later claimed that next he encountered Confederate Colonel William O. Coleman with 20 men and a Campbell with about 100 irregulars at a place he gave only as "Ash Flats." "J. B." may have confused Rebel Colonel Thomas Freeman for another Confederate regimental commander Coleman, prewar from Rolla, since this is the only report that places Coleman in this region this season. The spy later reported that this colonel said he was expecting 75 more men to join him on the nearby Eleven Points River probably in Oregon County as soon as they obtained horses, and then they would raid Yankee logistics miles to the north on the Rolla to Springfield Road. This southern colonel then rode with the men he had to Alton, county seat of Oregon County, where he heard the startling report that Union troops south at Batesville, Arkansas had just captured his horse herd and he rode south to investigate, leaving the spy behind in Oregon County. "J.B." near Thomasville, northwest Oregon County, next connected with Captain Evans again and a Captain McCulloch each of whom had about 30 guerrillas. These two small companies rode north across Texas and Dent Counties on their way to harass and attack Union forces. Confederate forces commonly gathered for raids in Oregon, Shannon, and Howell County assembly points, since these were so far removed from Union bases and snooping patrols. It was common during the Civil War where Americans sided against Americans for both sides to employ spies against each other since men's actual loyalties were often difficult to verify. Based on the surge of fresh guerrilla attacks during the next several days, the spy's report about Rebels riding to attack the isolated Union units was correct.[5]

One of these groups of guerrillas committed a series of depredations during the first eight days of February in Phelps County. On February 1 seven bushwhackers took 47-year-old Virginia-born stone mason Robert W. Wade away from his house in south Phelps County and mortally wounded him with several shots. Wade told witnesses before he died that his attackers oddly told him that "the Southern army can never get back into Missouri, and we are going to have revenge." Wade was a southern man, having lived in Virginia and Texas, but was known as a northern sympathizer in his community. Just outside the large town of Rolla on the evening of February 3 several bushwhackers fired about 20 shots at six men who were in the act of retiring for the night. Nobody was hit by the fusillade of shots, two of the startled residents ran to town to get help, but the pursuit was ineffectual. On the next day seven miles from Rolla four guerrillas held up and robbed a Union Army private who was working for the Rolla provost marshal office delivering a subpoena a few miles outside of town. The Rebels took the private's horse, weapons, papers, and uniform, but spared his life. On February 6 guerrillas stopped and robbed a stagecoach one mile west of the village of Little Piney. They stripped a soldier on the coach of his uniform and money but allowed him

Stagecoach (Charles C. Coffin, *Building the Nation*, 1888, p. 392).

to proceed on his way. Perhaps it was these busy bushwhackers that same day that attacked and took the lunches from a group of civilian laborers working for the Union Army quartermaster corps eight miles south of Rolla. On February 8 ten guerrillas wearing Union uniforms attacked a group of northern sympathizers leading their teams to Rolla, killing one of them and mortally wounded another. The same group also attacked and took the lunches of a group of men repairing the road. On February 9 the Salem garrison sent out a patrol of 5th Cavalry MSM tracking the guerrillas that robbed the soldier serving the subpoena. They were successful in tracking the robbers, noting that the guerrillas camped nights in sink holes and caves, but lost the trail after the cavalrymen got close enough that the bushwhackers dispersed and set the woods afire to finally baffle the trackers. None of the other pursuits of the Phelps County attacks got even that close. The effect of these large numbers of guerrilla assaults in rapid succession was pandemonium and the cavalry stationed in the immediate area seemed helpless to prevent them. As was common in much of Missouri by this time of the war, Rebels found it practicable to take Federal uniforms in order to get close enough to

Three Rebel scouts (The Werner Company, *The Story of American Heroism*, 1896, p. 441).

their victims to assure they could master them. The fact that these raiders spared the lives of captive Yankee soldiers tends to identify them as regular Confederate soldiers acting as irregulars rather than guerrillas. The Rolla commander, Lieutenant Colonel Eppstein of the 5th Cavalry MSM, noted in his report that the raiders often took food from their victims, conjecturing that they had no other way to obtain it in this war ravaged area. Possibly, these busy Confederates confronted victims daily simply to obtain food for their own subsistence.[6]

Meanwhile, another batch of bushwhackers was committing a series of similar attacks further west along the main wagon road in Pulaski County. On February 2 eighteen Rebels robbed two freight wagons and tore down about 500 yards of telegraph line along the main road only 1.5 miles west of the landmark California House Inn in central Pulaski County. First Lieutenant Uriah Bates and 8 or 10 troopers of 5th Cavalry MSM from the nearby Waynesville garrison rode out in pursuit, and tracked the raiders to their campsite near D. I. Lowe's house along Roubidoux Creek in north Texas County a few miles south of Waynesville. Although outnumbered, Lieutenant Bates' patrol attacked at sunrise on February 3 as the Rebels were eating breakfast killing seven at no loss to themselves. The remaining Confederates fled for their lives into the brush, and Bates' patrol lost their trail in the thick vegetation. The Federals captured six horses, recovered all the stolen goods, and learned from one of the mortally wounded guerrillas before he died that their leader was Frank Smith, well-known as a bushwhacker in the area.[7]

Union troops escort arson victims to safety (Frazar Kirkland, *The Pictorial Book of Anecdotes of the Rebellion*, 1888, p. 506).

On February 7 west of Waynesville some bushwhackers took as prisoner Private F. L. Kelton of 5th Cavalry MSM. Private Kelton's comrades never discovered what happened to him after this, and his company's record sadly comments that "nothing has been heard of him since."[8] Perhaps Kelton's captors were the same Rebels who that same day fired on a stagecoach on the main road west of Waynesville. Lieutenant Bates led another patrol north to the Gasconade River, then tracked the coach shooters south to the Roubidoux Creek where the tracks indicated that the wary bushwhackers split up to foil their pursuers.[9]

Also on February 7 miles to the south, Lieutenant William F. Boyd and his patrol of 33 troopers of 5th Cavalry MSM from the Houston garrison patrolling in Howell County found information about a large body of Rebels in the area. They learned this from a Mr. Judd whom the guerrillas had recently beaten, so the angry Judd told Boyd that Rebel leader Captain George Evans and 84 men were waiting in ambush for them ten miles from Thomasville, northwest Oregon County. The lieutenant wisely asked for reinforcements. When fifty more troopers from Houston with one cannon arrived on February 9 Lieutenant Boyd set off to find Captain Evans' force of Confederates. By February 10 the guerrillas heard about the large force riding toward them and moved, but the Federals shot and killed one of three Rebel scouts they encountered in southwest Oregon County and later killed two others. That night Captain Evans' command attempted to overwhelm the Union camp with volley fire, but the veteran Yankees did not panic, formed ranks, and returned the volleys. Boyd's troopers suffered no losses from this fire, and Evans' casualties, if any, were unknown. On February 11 the Union force burned a house they found to contain barrels of salt, guns, and gunpowder for the Rebels. As the building burned another barrel of gunpowder hidden under the floor exploded with a startling bang. Later that day Lieutenant Boyd's large force killed two Rebels, then later discovered one of the dead was William Lamb, Confederate Colonel Thomas R. Freeman's brother-in-law. Boyd learned from a captive that Colonel Freeman himself "with a strong force" was close by and the Yanks prepared a defensive position in case the southerners attacked that night as they had the night before. On February 12 Boyd realized Freeman was seeking to move away from him and avoid a fight. While riding to find the Rebels Boyd's patrol killed two who may have been Freeman's scouts. The Federals remained on patrol a few more days but accomplished little more than to assist some families of northern sympathy to move out of the area. They did hear that notorious guerrilla Bill Coats was camping along the Big Piney River in Texas County, but they failed to find him.[10]

Meanwhile, other guerrillas were attacking traffic along the main road in Pulaski County, and one attack was well-documented both in Union Army reports and newspapers. On the morning of February 12 about twenty well-mounted Rebels dressed in Federal uniforms overwhelmed the stagecoach escort of nine troopers of 5th Cavalry MSM four miles west of the California House inn, robbed the westbound stage and passengers, and escaped the resulting pursuit. In the initial gun battle the guerrillas killed one trooper, captured another, and wounded three others, while two of their own men were wounded. After the battered escort retreated, one of the lady passengers shamed the Confederates into sparing the life of their captive who they had already beaten with the flat side of a saber. The effrontery of this lady did not prevent the raiders from taking all the luggage of the passengers, their cash, the stage horses and harness, and the Union Army correspondence for the Springfield post. The Rebels released the passengers-four ladies and two men-who had to walk for help. One of the passengers may have recognized one of the raiders as Joe Craig of nearby Lebanon, and they commented that the Rebels seemed to be Confederate soldiers. General Sanborn, the district commander at Springfield, was incensed that the Rebels were reading his mail and all orders from the St. Louis department headquarters, and replied to the reports that this area needed to be "cleaned out" even if the military in that neighborhood had "to put a man under every bush." The men of the 5th were not only upset by this defeat and concerned about the welfare of their captured comrade, but furious that their dead comrade had been shot fifteen times by the Rebels. Their duty escorting the stagecoaches on this vulnerable stretch of road made them little more than targets for the wily guerrlllas.[11] A few days later along the main road in east Pulaski County this same Rebel band robbed six wagons containing civilian merchandise intended for Springfield stores.[12]

Guerrilla actions over the next several days took place south of Phelps and Pulaski Counties. The Union commander at Salem, Captain L. E. Whybark of 5th Cavalry MSM, reported that "old man McCarty" living in the Dent County countryside fought off three guerrillas who came to his door the evening of February 13, killing one. Census reports of this county seem to indicate this home defender was 50-year-old Jesse McCarty who had a large family in Franklin Township of south Dent County.[13] A Union spy in either east Douglas or Howell County looking for Rebels found more than he wanted when thirty guerrillas of Colonel Freeman's command captured him. He managed to escape after a time and reported to the Houston garrison that these bushwhackers had spoken of riding north to raid the main road in Phelps or Pulaski Counties.[14] Lieutenant W. T. Chitwood's patrol of 8th Cavalry MSM from the Lebanon garrison searching for guerrillas in south Texas County killed two riding together in the headwaters of the Big Piney River there on February 18. Not far away they discovered and attacked a camp of ten more, killing two, wounding one, and capturing two of their horses. Chitwood's patrol later reported that in each instance they found with these dead Rebels plunder taken from the aforementioned stage robbery near California House Inn on February 12.[15] Captain Whybark at Salem on February 18 reported to higher authority that he heard Colonel Freeman and his executive officer, Lieutenant Colonel Joseph B. Love, with hundreds of their soldiers were on the Frederick's Fork in southeast Oregon County burning out the families of men of northern sympathy. The men had already left the region for their own safety in the past, and now the Rebels were burning their homes, forcing their destitute families to seek shelter at Union military garrisons in the region.[16]

The Phelps County area had been quiet for a few days, but nine guerrillas dressed in U.S. uniforms demanded food from Mrs. Ellen Brookshire a few miles from Rolla on February 23. Mrs. Brookshire was at first fooled by the uniforms into thinking these were Union soldiers, but they informed her of their true identity and made her feed them anyway. The following day Mrs. Brookshire reported her encounter to Federal authorities at Rolla, as required by current Union rules, but she seemed deliberately vague about details. For their own preservation, rural inhabitants often maintained a certain level of neutrality toward both sides.[17]

The month of February ended in war-ravished Pulaski County with more guerrilla incidents. On the evening of February 26 guerrillas from hiding fired upon the stagecoach both as it entered and later left Waynesville, wounding one passenger and one of the escort's horses.[18] First Lieutenant Uriah Bates and his patrol of eight veteran guerrilla-hunters of 5th Cavalry MSM learned probably from an informant that well-known local bushwhacker Burt Woods with as many as thirty guerrillas was five miles south of Waynesville, and they promptly rode to intercept the Rebels on February 29. They encountered these bushwhackers in the process of making prisoners of two local men of northern sympathy near Spring Creek in east Pulaski County and promptly attacked despite their smaller numbers. Success favors the offensive in guerrilla warfare and Bates' attacking patrol yelling like fiends unnerved the bushwhackers who scattered into the woods. The Federals suffered no loss, but killed two of the southerners, and rescued the two grateful civilians.[19]

The obvious determination of Confederate leaders such as Colonel Freeman and local bushwhackers to eject the Yankees from south-central Missouri, and the equal persistence of the Union cavalry to hold this region promised a violent spring here.

Reeves, the Bolins, and Others in the Eastern Ozark Hill County During January and February 1864

Parts of the far southeast corner of Missouri that normally were hotbeds of guerrilla activity in all weather were silent in the winter months of January and February 1864 while actions persisted in three main arenas that normally were the scene of only occasional fighting. Federal efforts to subjugate the swampy "Bootheel" appendage of

Missouri that jutted into Arkansas may have been successful after two years of fighting, for that war-torn region was quiet this winter, except for Union patrols. Sam Hildebrand, the vengeful one-man-retaliation force, may not have staged a raid into southeast Missouri this season, both according to his own postwar journal and the absence of his famous name in Union Army records and newspapers. Occasionally during the war Confederate guerrillas would pass through those hilly, wooded counties just south of St. Louis known for large populations of northern sympathy-but that area was quiet this winter, too. Instead, the action this winter centered around the Bolin brothers in the Bollinger and Cape Girardeau County area; local guerrillas in the Mississippi County area near the "Bootheel"; and Confederate Colonel Tim Reeves and his men in the rugged hills of Wayne, Carter, Ripley, and Butler Counties.

Brothers Nathan and John F. Bolin, prewar of Cape Girardeau and Stoddard Counties, did much throughout the war to organize and lead southern guerrilla actions against northern interests in the far southeast corner of Missouri. They were responsible for bringing the wounded and grieving Sam Hildebrand into the bushwhacker fold in summer of 1862 as well as many others; they raided settlements of northern sympathy in 1862 and 1863; and they conducted daring attacks like the deadly Round Ponds fight in August 1863 which all served to challenge the Union military's hold on this corner of the state.

The Bolin brothers evidently led the eleven guerrillas that attacked four northern sympathizers at the Daniel Crites home near Dallas in south-central Bollinger County on December 27 as 1863 was drawing to a close. Crites was a member of the local 56th Enrolled Missouri Militia (EMM) and with his three companions fought for their lives when the bushwhackers laid siege to his house. The Rebels suffered three of their members severely wounded but killed two of Crites' companions and wounded a third, then robbed the house and quickly left. A few days later the Union commander of the Cape Girardeau garrison about eighteen miles to the east wrote about this fight "in Dallas 4 citizens fought and killed 2 of Bolin's men." Perhaps this officer received information that two of Bolin's men wounded in the fight succumbed to their wounds.[20] Rudimentary war records show that elements of the 3rd Cavalry MSM fought a skirmish somewhere in Bollinger County on January 14. Parts of this regiment were stationed west and northwest of here at this time, so perhaps a patrol from one of those garrisons fought some of the Bolin guerrillas in Bollinger County on January 14.[21] On February 3 guerrilla chief John F. Bolin and 35 guerrillas were on Holcomb Island a few miles southwest of Clarkton in Dunklin County taking fifteen farm wagons loaded with corn toward Jones Ferry to cross the St. Francis River to Rebel forces on the Arkansas side. While Bolin's men were encumbered with the slow-moving wagons Captain Samuel Shibley's patrol of 2nd Cavalry MSM from Bloomfield, Stoddard County, rode up and attacked Bolin's detail, killing seven, and capturing eight, without loss of Union life. The Yankees also destroyed the ferry to prevent other Rebels from taking scarce food and forage across the river. The victorious Federals were delighted to find gang leader John F. Bolin himself was one of their prisoners, and they triumphantly took him with the others to jail facilities at the large Union post at Cape Girardeau, two counties away.[22] Bolin was a determined southerner who hurt the northern cause in southeast Missouri deeply for over three years and personally killed a number of Union servicemen. Many soldiers of the Cape Girardeau garrison were incensed that he had been brought alive into custody in violation of standing orders to kill known bushwhackers on the spot. Bolin's confession to his captors about how he killed Yankees in the Round Pond fight the previous August 1 did little to calm the unrest. This unease

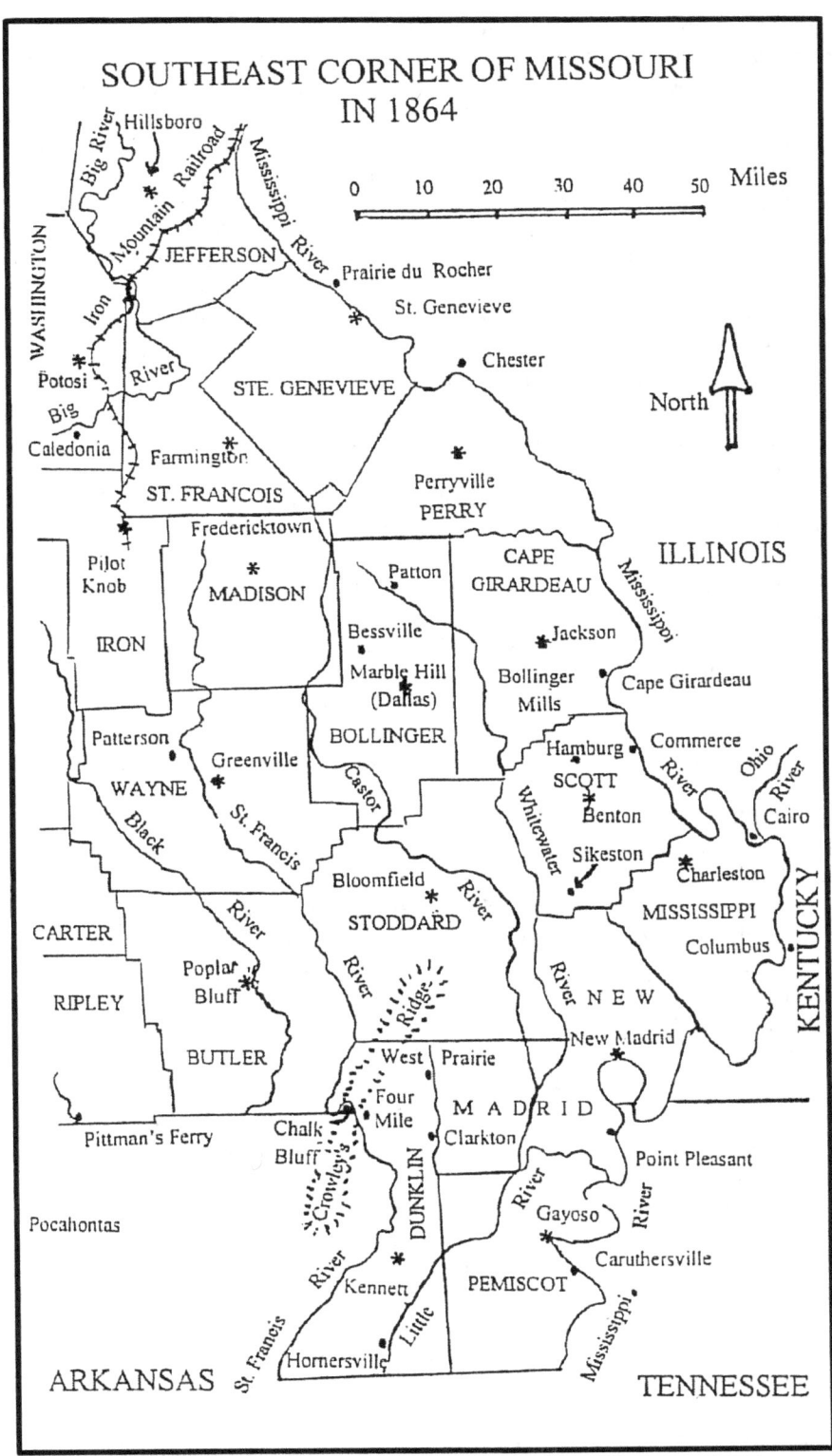

erupted into violence during the night of February 5 and 6 when a large mob of soldiers and civilians ignored the shouts of officers, broke into the jail, and hanged John F. Bolin to death. Before the hanging, the Cape Girardeau commander, Colonel John B. Rogers, had been asking his boss, district chief Brigadier General Clinton B. Fisk, how to try Bolin for his crimes. After receiving a spot report about the hanging, General Fisk sardonically replied to Rogers that "it will hardly be necessary to give Bolin a trial." Even with the death of John Bolin, his brother Nathan still commanded southern guerrillas in this district, and was still a potent threat to the Yankees.[23]

Throughout this winter a small but determined guerrilla band, mostly led by Vernon Campbell, kept Mississippi and Scott Counties in an uproar. By early January Company I of 2nd Cavalry MSM moved its garrison from the larger base at Cape Girardeau to the Mississippi County seat at Charleston just to squelch these bushwhackers, and promptly killed one of them. Colonel Rogers at Cape Girardeau also thought his men finally managed to kill the notorious Sam Hildebrand earlier, but Hildebrand himself would later prove this to be untrue.[24] These troopers from Charleston managed to kill another guerrilla January 20, too.[25] The guerrillas struck back February 15 when a patrol of this same regiment grew careless while searching Vernon Campbell's house a few miles southwest of Charleston. Mrs. Campbell told the Yankees that the men were not present, and they had searched the house before, so they were not expecting four bushwhackers including two of the Campbells to ambush and kill two of the troopers inside the house. The remainder of the patrol chased the Rebels into the thick brush where in another ambush two more of the northerners were severely wounded. They found a guerrilla's hat covered with blood, so at least one guerrilla was probably wounded. Mrs. Campbell was ordered "to leave the country" for her treachery, and the battered patrol burned the Campbell house.[26] Another Union patrol somewhere in Mississippi County on the evening of February 25 exchanged shots with bushwhackers wounding one of them and killing one Rebel horse and wounding another at no Federal loss.[27]

To the west in the rugged hill county of Wayne, Carter, Ripley and Butler Counties, the Civil War during the first two months of 1864 was merely a continuation from 1863 of the personal war fought mostly between Confederate Colonel Timothy Reeves and his irregulars and Captain William T. Leeper and his troopers of the 3rd Cavalry MSM. Before the war North Carolina-born Timothy Reeves was a determined Baptist minister who founded a number of churches in this region, and postwar he continued this activity for a number of years as though the war was only an interruption of God's work. Reeves was about 43 years old in 1864, and brought the same fervor into his service for the Confederacy and proved himself over and over again to be a dedicated and imaginative foe. Captain Leeper was one of those extremists whose mania to restore the severed Union overrode the morality inherent in the oath he took as an officer in the United States Army. Leeper was honored as a man whose dedication to his cause helped southeast Missouri to remain loyal to the Federal cause, but he resorted to ruthlessness including murder to accomplish that end. Perhaps if he had not commanded his company in such isolated villages so far from regimental command his superiors could have kept him better in check. However, his reports to proper authority clearly showed his propensities and those officers showed little inclination to curb Leeper's excesses. This is an indicator that the Union military in Missouri by this time in the awful guerrilla war was turning more and more to radicalization to finally stamp out the persistent bushwhackers and Confederate recruiters in this region and other such hot spots across Missouri. That such unlikely antagonists as Reverend

Reeves and Captain Leeper could both survive the war and enjoy life as peaceful citizens is all the more remarkable considering the cunning and wiles they both employed to destroy each other throughout the war.[28]

The winter weather in early January was certainly as bad in this region as the rest of the state, since Captain Leeper complained on January 11 that "snow and ice had been so bad that my scouts cannot travel far." Nevertheless, the progress of the war was more important than suffering, danger, and inconvenience to many of the veteran combatants of both sides in southeast Missouri. In that same report Leeper crowed to a higher headquarters that four of his men that he had sent a few days before had managed to kill three guerrillas of a Tucker's band that had been bothering him since the previous autumn.[29] Much of the guerrilla war in the hills of this part of the state was not well recorded except in a few distant newspaper accounts, local folklore, and Captain Leeper's blustery reports. Another of Leeper's missives on January 29 bragged about the exploits of Captain Abijah Johns and his patrol of Company A, 3rd Cavalry MSM out of the Patterson, Wayne County, garrison. Captain John's patrol about January 22 through 25 chased Confederate Colonel Timothy Reeves and some of his Rebels into the Cherokee Bay Swamp between the Black and Current Rivers near present-day Neelyville, southwest Butler County. Johns reported killing 4 Rebels, but the report also told how Reeves' men were seasoning or smoking pork and beef in that area to supply their future food needs. Local folklore of this area tells how Rebels made a secret base on Coon Island inside the Cherokee Bay Swamp, and that sometime during the war Captain Johns and his Yankees captured and perhaps killed Confederate George Thannisch of Reeves' regiment near Martinsburg, east Ripley County, who was taking a wagon load of food and supplies toward the secret camp. Perhaps this was that occasion. In this same report Leeper revealed his acceptance of the "total war" concept in frightening reality when he wrote "guerrillas cannot stay in this or any other part of the State without friends, and their friends will have to be exterminated also." Sadly, there were many instances of the killing of seemingly innocent residents in this corner of Missouri indicating that Captain Leeper and others put these sentiments into action.[30] Another patrol by First Lieutenant R. Kelley of the 3rd from the Patterson garrison killed two more Rebels near Greenville, central Wayne County about January 25.[31] Area guerrillas refused to be conquered, however, for on January 30 or 31 one squad of them lost one member killed skirmishing with Federals in north Wayne County or south Iron County and cavalry was chasing another squad on the Black River either in Butler County or west Wayne County. One of these parties abducted and perhaps killed the Wayne County sheriff. Captain Leeper theorized that these raiders were from Confederate Colonel Freeman's command then in Oregon County, possibly staging a demonstration to take pressure off of the hard-pressed Colonel Reeves.[32] Captain Leeper reported February 6 that his men had killed two more guerrillas in the region and the two squads of hard-riding Rebels had ridden out of the area. He happily reported that area citizens were arming themselves to resist future such southern raiders. Later in 1864 citizen groups all over Missouri would be ordered to organize and be given firearms for self-defense, so these in the southeast quadrant were ahead of a future practice.[33] Union Captain Johns reported to higher command at the large Pilot Knob base in Iron County that one of his patrols from Patterson in late February in south Butler County attacked Rebel wagons carrying corn and firearms killing two bushwhackers and destroying the wagons and cargo. Apparently, this cargo was also intended to supply the secret southern base at Coon Island.[34] It was obvious that Union troops in this hilly country could not bring the Rebel irregular troops to a decisive defeat, and that these Confederates were cautious not to give their enemies such an opportunity.

In fact, the active southern guerrillas across southeast Missouri this winter conducted harassing attacks against patrols, logistics, and isolated units of Yankee troops. Union soldiers here were facing veteran guerrillas who combined daring and initiative with careful planning and execution so as to remain in their operational areas until larger Confederate forces may hopefully come to deal with the "blue coats." One advantage that the northern soldiers enjoyed that was becoming more and more scarce for the southern ones was the dwindling supplies available to keep men and horses combat effective. A proficient Union supply system shipped logistical needs into this area by railroad and wagon, but gradually the guerrillas' friends and supporters were leaving the region voluntarily or not, while three years of almost constant warfare was denuding the countryside of food and forage the bushwhackers needed for sustainment. More and more the southern irregulars were forced to take their sustenance from their enemies, military and civilian, which meant that the "knights of the brush" had to raid and fight more frequently just to remain combat effective. With this significant and growing vulnerability guerrillas in southeast Missouri were facing a bleak future unless they could get help.

The Hidden War in the St. Louis Area During January and February 1864

Throughout the war southern sympathizers and secret Confederate operatives conducted a clandestine form of warfare in the St. Louis area to further the southern cause and weaken the northern one, but this winter this activity all but stopped. One noticeable change was that the sabotage of river transport supporting the Union cause in St. Louis stopped abruptly after early October the previous year. These riverboat arsonists employed by the Confederacy took a tremendous toll of destroyed Union vessels along the Mississippi River levee in the city during September and early October 1863. Significantly, Union guards and detectives were unable to arrest the perpetrators. However, the whole city was alerted, guards and sentinels increased, and riverboat docking procedures changed to make these valuable vessels harder for saboteurs to target. The flow of Rebel smuggling of mail, medicines, firearms, uniforms, and other supplies from the many southern sympathizers in St. Louis seemed to slow this winter, too-or at least Union concerns seemed to arrest such smugglers at a slower rate. There had been enough publicized arrests for this activity in recent months, revealing a veritable army of detectives and informants across St. Louis, that even determined smugglers may have stopped the practice—at least here. Even the flow of southern sympathizers banished to the South by Union authorities seemed to stop this winter, perhaps because of the severe weather.[35]

One cryptic mention appears on Union records this winter of a woman or two women arrested and incarcerated in military prison, but with no explanation of the reasons or circumstances. A "Miss Lizzie Hardin" was arrested in St. Louis January 13 and sent to the former Lynch's Slave Market now called Myrtle Street Military Prison, with the notation that she was released by order of the Missouri Provost Marshal General five days later on January 18. Oddly enough, there is also an entry in such records that a "Mary (Lizzie) Harens Aka Hardin" was arrested in St. Louis January 29 and sent to the same Myrtle Street Prison, with the notation that she was released about

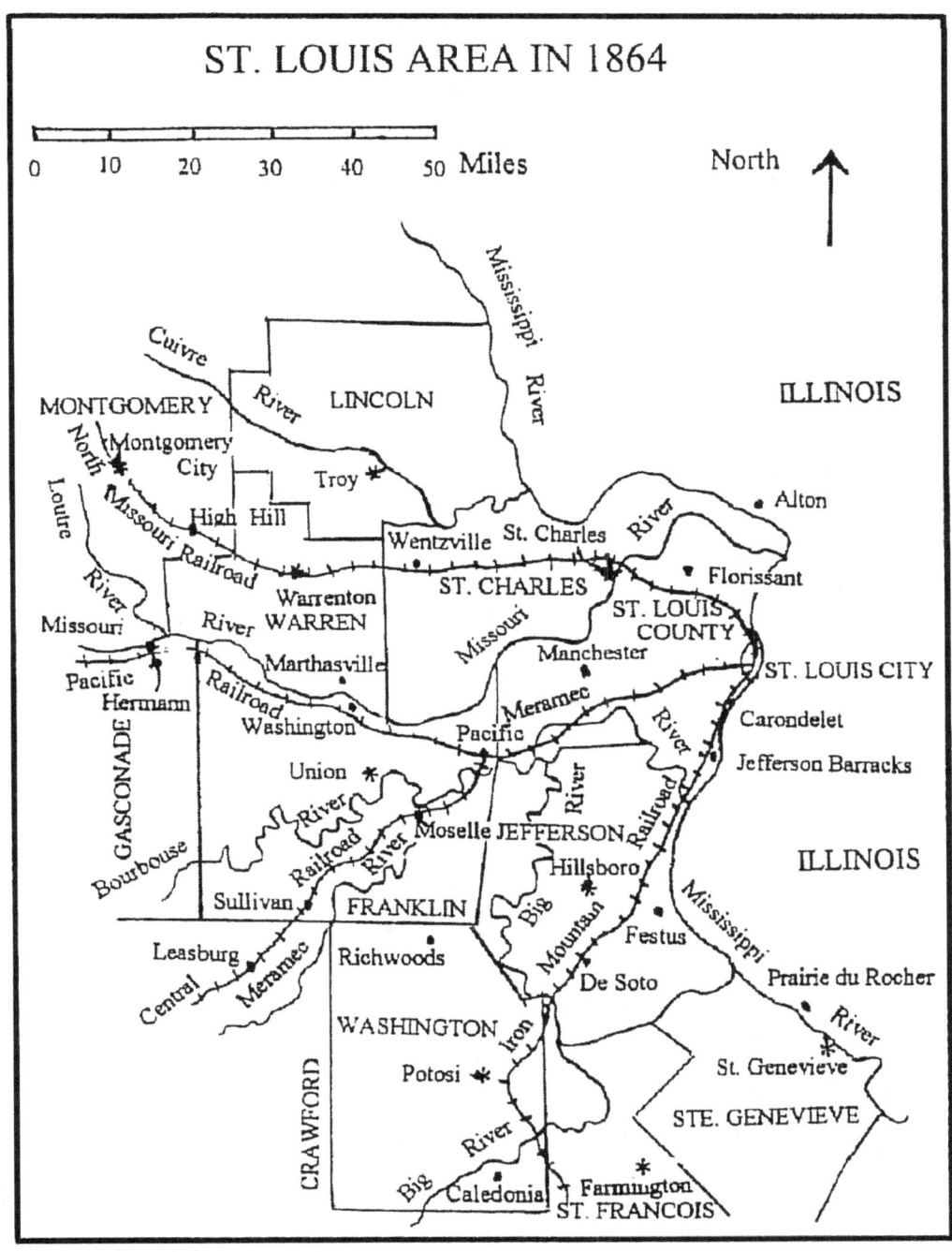

one month later on February 29. These prison records were full of errors and even duplicate or near duplicate entries, but these two entries seem to have too many differences to be anything but two separate entries for the same woman arrested, incarcerated in the same military prison, and released at two separate times. She could have been considered guilty of such varied crimes as "disloyal speech," sewing uniforms to be sent to Confederate soldiers, carrying secret mail to or from the Rebel army, or aiding escaping southern prisoners[36]

St. Louis Area Military Prison Escapes During January and February 1864

The several Federal military prisons of the St. Louis area became the unhappy home of southern military and civilian prisoners captured or arrested across Missouri and the region. It cannot be emphasized too much that these places of incarceration may have seemed adequate institutions to house military and political prisoners by 19th century standards, but they were in reality dangerous to the health of their inmates and often deadly. Even Federal military inspections of these dreaded facilities offered a glimpse of the horror that lay within.

The flagship of the Union prison fleet of the St. Louis area was, at least in numbers, the condemned former state penitentiary at Alton, Illinois, just up the Mississippi River a short distance from St. Louis. This leased Federal facility was condemned for Illinois state use in the 1850s because of flooding and sanitation problems, but the Union military was able to place more prisoners in this foreboding, four-story, 256-cell, stone structure than in any of the other military prisons in the St. Louis area.[37] In a catalog of sorts of the Union military prisons dated 7 December 1863 the Department of War reported of the Alton installation that it housed 1,550 prisoners, had 29 deaths during November, had 119 inmates listed as sick, "is too well crowded" and

Gratiot Street Military Prison (Galusha Anderson, *The Story of a Border City During the Civil War*, 1908, p. 189).

"needs a new wall," referring to how some of the exterior prison wall was propped up in places. This December report also stated that the prisoners "...are comfortably quartered and well supplied with good, warm bedding." Also,

> the prisoners are well supplied with an abundance of food, which is well prepared and cooked. A sutler is allowed to sell to them. The sanitary condition of this prison is very good. It is cleanly and well kept and under good discipline.... The garrison, commanded by Colonel [George W.] Kincaid with his regiment [37th Iowa Infantry Regiment], 450 strong, is sufficient....[38]

Surgeon Augustus M. Clark on 17 and 18 February 1864 rendered a more realistic inspection of the Alton, Illinois military prison for the War Department. He found there:

- 1,757 prisoners (instead of the estimated capacity of 800);
- 125 in the sick hospital (50 of those with smallpox), with 109 more sick restricted to their quarters;
- "hospital [and all prison] clothing washed outside prison";
- water supplied from the Mississippi River "conveyed in barrels in one six-mule wagon";
- "sewerage—by one main sewer into river," the latrines "in close proximity to hospital" and "in a filthy and most offensive condition";
- the kitchen—"in great disorder and miserable police," "much cooking and messing is done in prison quarters";
- and "three female prisoners now confined in a damp, half-underground room, only partitioned off from an open cellar," "an outrage on humanity."

Surgeon Clark bemoaned that the "dead house," the building to house the dead awaiting burial, was merely an open shed. He noted that the total number of sick for the month of January was 1,882, and that there were 92 deaths that month. He also noted that there were 107 cases of smallpox in January, resulting in 28 deaths. Clark noted that smallpox patients with their bedding and clothing were moved to a small facility on an island in the river opposite the prison to prevent the spread of the disease, and, if they recovered, were issued new clothing and bedding upon their return to the main facility. The Alton prison was not a healthy place.[39]

The Union Gratiot Street Prison in downtown St. Louis was formerly the McDowell Medical College. The Federals confiscated this large, brick-walled, brick building when Dr. Joseph McDowell and his family and slaves abruptly moved to the deep South at the war's outset. Although the college's new masters converted lecture halls, cadaver room, and examination room into dormitory space for the prisoners, Gratiot Street Prison could not house nearly as many prisoners as the Alton prison. Ironically, they found they could not properly use the facilities even as a hospital, and rented an adjoining building outside the college proper for housing the sick-using contract doctors to treat them by 1864.[40]

The War Department catalog of Federal military prisons dated December 7, 1863, counted at Gratiot Street Prison "382 rebel prisoners of war and 114 citizens held under military orders." This glowing report extolled the "abundant supply of good food," "good facilities for cooking," "abundant supply of pure water" and "well policed" and clean building and yards, but complained "there is a great lack of personal cleanliness among the prisoners." Further, the report gave the contradictory comment that "the prisoners are generally in good health, though there are a large number on hand sick." The report admitted that in November 15 died with 119 being designated sick that month.[41]

Once again, Surgeon Augustus M. Clark in his 20 February inspection revealed the reality of Gratiot Street Prison for the War Department. He described the facility as a main building with two wings and two dwellings on the grounds. Further he found:

- 125 patients in a hospital where the bedding, clothing, and persons were "foul," and "in bad police";
- the entire prison and especially the hospital is "unventilated," with windows being kept closed;
- baths in the basement, but "apparently but little used," with none in the hospital;
- sewerage: latrines in yard "insufficient in number and size, and ... in very foul condition";
- the kitchen, "is in better condition than any other part of the prison";
- "whole building requires repair, especially north wing, which is in a dilapidated and apparently dangerous condition." Surgeon Clark attributes much of the building's condition and the dank, humid atmosphere in the prison to the staff's use of fire hose flooding each room to wash "the rubbish and debris into the hall, where a large portion of water finds its way ... into the rooms beneath. The bedding and blankets are left in the bunks, and by the time the washing is over are about as wet as the floor." Use of red-hot stoves created a constant "fetid steam" or mist throughout the facility. Clark noticed an exterior wall of the building bulging dangerously toward falling and displaying signs that it had been propped to prevent its collapse. He noted that prisoners facing tribunal on very serious charges were kept locked in strong rooms on the second floor. Surgeon Clark noted in January 347 prisoners were reported as sick and 30 died.[42]

The smallest of the three Union military prisons in the St. Louis area was the Myrtle Street Prison, which formerly had been Lynch's Slave Market on Myrtle Street. Housing secessionists in what had been slave holding cells was a form of ongoing abolitionist local joke, but this two- story brick building just a few blocks from the Gratiot Street Prison was no laughing matter to the prisoners brought through its doors. This small-capacity prison was closed several times during the war, but lack of space at the other facilities led Union authorities to re-open it for limited periods of time.[43] Again, doctors made two inspection tours of Myrtle Street Prison in February 1864. They found fifty civilian prisoners, including two females, and 104 military prisoners in rooms and strong rooms on the two floors. The overall impression of one visitor was one of "unqualified condemnation," noting "it is overcrowded and extremely filthy in every part, and its keeper, a civilian, is utterly unqualified for his post." One doctor was particularly horrified that "no attempt has been made here to secure proper ventilation." The other doctor added that "all light is excluded from the strong rooms, and air is admitted through a few auger holes in the floor and roof. These do not communicate with the external air, but with the spaces between the floors. The means of cooking and bathing and the water supply are inadequate." These inspectors were particularly incensed that the latrines were in each room where the prisoners also ate their meals. In short, the former owners of the slave market seemed to have devised this facility to intimidate the slaves housed there before the war to keep them manageable, and the place's wartime operators did little or nothing to lessen that affect on the prisoners they kept here.[44]

One activity of the hidden guerrilla war throughout the war was the steady flow of escaping southerners from the several military prisons in the St. Louis area. The Union military had to divert men from other duties to guard and service these prisons, and when any of the inmates escaped, northern troops had to be employed to try to recapture them. The escapes were a form of rebellion against the Federals, and therefore, a part of guerrilla war. The suffering of these prisoners was more acute this season because their prisons did not fully protect them from the bitter weather or from disease. In fact, these hazards motivated some of the incarcerated southerners to try to escape more than ever.

One of the first recorded prison escapes of 1864 was the breakout of at least two prisoners of war from one of the St. Louis area prisons on January 6. Union prison records state that Confederate Private John T. Ridgeway of the 4th Missouri Regiment had been captured in Greene County on 8 January 1863, perhaps during General John S. Marmaduke's raid there about that time. Perhaps he celebrated the passing of one year in Union captivity by freeing himself. The prison record of Private Riley Everett of the 10th Missouri Regiment states that he was captured at Little Rock, Arkansas on 10 September 1863, and that he escaped one of the St. Louis area prisons the same day as Private Ridgeway. Maybe they escaped together, and they may have had company. The scant prison record does not reveal their fate.[45]

Of course, some escape attempts failed, and two of those were recorded in January, too. Prisoner of war Captain Griffin Frost in his journal recorded that on the evening of January 9 some of the enlisted POWs in the "lower quarters" of the Gratiot Street Prison, formerly the McDowell Medical College, tried to break out in some manner. The Union troops guarding the prison detected their effort and several of those involved were made to wear "ball and chain" thereafter.[46] Captain Frost's journal also reveals that prisoners W. Parker and Stephen Kerrick made some kind of attempt to escape the Alton Military Prison across the Mississippi River at Alton, Illinois, about the third week of January, but were caught in the act.[47]

Union Colonel William Weer of the 10th Kansas Infantry Regiment had just taken command of the Alton prison and his men assumed the guard duties, and all this escape activity upset him greatly. On January 19 he wrote to headquarters requesting "the services of a few skilled detectives" to come to Alton and "fathom whatever plot might be existing among the prisoners." He reluctantly admired the prisoners' "wonderful ingenuity," but still wanted to ferret out the various escape plots then in work. The 10th Kansas would remain at work guarding the Alton prison until April.[48]

No escape attempt is recorded yet for prisoner of war Captain John Thrailkill, who had been captured recruiting for the Confederacy in northwest Missouri in July 1863, but Union authorities at his St. Louis tribunal passed down his sentence on January 23. They took issue that Thrailkill had been captured "under arms" even though he was in full Confederate uniform so far behind Union lines. These factors may have swayed the officers to declare the POW as a guerrilla and deserving of a death sentence, but mitigating circumstances caused them to instead decide for a sentence of life in prison for the captain. Those circumstances were that when captured Thrailkill was attempting in good faith to convince his captors to join the Confederate command he was recruiting before they revealed they were actually Union militia in plain clothes and he was under arrest. In effect, he proved himself to be a legitimate Confederate recruiter and not a bushwhacker—a vital distinction in Civil War Missouri where captured bushwhackers faced a death sentence and captured Rebel regulars did not. Still, facing the rest of his life working at hard labor in any of the St. Louis area hellhole prisons was not a good prospect for this Holt County Missourian, and, after the tribunal's sentence he began looking in earnest for a way to escape. Five months later on 28 June 1864 Captain John Thrailkill would achieve this goal and his freedom and soon after become a noted and accomplished guerrilla leader in central Missouri. Most Confederate recruiters captured behind Union lines in Missouri were considered POWs and subject to exchange. If the tribunal had so regarded Captain Thrailkill and he were exchanged, perhaps he would have returned to his regular command with the Rebel army and not bedeviled the Union forces in Missouri as a skillful, motivated leader of guerrillas. Of course, this is conjecture.[49]

POW Captain Griffin Frost recorded a botched escape at the Alton, Illinois, prison February 3. At one in the morning that day ten or twelve prisoners were trying to dig their way out under the wall from inside an outbuilding when a guard heard them. At least their plan was well-founded, for 35 POWs at the same prison used this idea to break out in one of the war's largest mass escapes on July 25 or 26, 1862. A difference was that the 1862 escape owed part of its success to the bribery of a Union guard, which this 1864 group may not have accomplished.[50]

At least five prisoners of war escaped from one of the St. Louis area military prisons on February 17, although few details of this remain. Three of these escapees had been captured at Vicksburg when it fell the previous July 4, one captured at Little Rock, Arkansas, in September, and one captured in Barry County of southwest Missouri also in September. This event is indicated in the individual records of the escapees as recorded in the Union military prison ledgers, and only in the "remarks" column noting the same date of escape for all five men. It is possible that others broke out with them and the clerk may have neglected to note it in this column of his ledger. The record does not reveal other details including whether or not they evaded recapture.[51]

The frequency of the escapes and escape attempts show the determination of the prisoners to escape. That so many of their attempts were detected and thwarted by their guards indicates that the Union military was learning to become more efficient jailers of the thousands of military prisoners in their care in the St. Louis area this winter.

Two

Winter 1864 in Southwest Missouri

The extreme cold of the winter of 1863-1864 probably accounted for the reduced guerrilla activity level in the southwest quadrant of Missouri, compared to the rapid pace of warfare here throughout the previous two years. The ease of crossing the prairies and the lack of wide rivers to cross meant that this region was the best overall avenue of approach for southern irregular forces—Confederate recruiters and guerrilla—trying to infiltrate Union lines to reach other parts of the state. So, the fewer Rebels passing through here during January and February 1864 would normally have indicated less guerrilla activity later in those parts of the state, too. That would prove true in some places of the state but not in others during the year 1864.

Reduced Action in the Far Southwest Corner

There were just a few events related to guerrilla warfare in January and February 1864 in the extreme corner of the state that winter in McDonald, Barry, Newton, Jasper, Lawrence, Dade, and Barton Counties. This was in stark contrast with the heavy tempo of fighting here during the previous two winters. This part of southwest Missouri was primarily covered in grassy prairie intersected by occasional wooded creek bottoms, and most of the residents by this late in the war had left after facing the rigors and dangers of many months of almost constant warfare.

At sunrise on January 23 veteran guerrilla fighter Captain Milton Burch and his patrol of 30 troopers of the 8th Cavalry Missouri State Militia (MSM) from Neosho, Newton County, surprised 10 guerrillas at a house. This skirmish occurred at Cowskin Bottom at the very southwestern corner of McDonald County—the most southwestern county in the Show-Me State. The Rebels ran for their lives from the house into the nearby brush, but the cavalry killed two of them at no apparent loss to themselves. One of the dead was a Union deserter, Corporal Wessel Harden Talifaro, who absented himself from the 6th Kansas Cavalry the previous June.[1]

A sad fact of Missouri's guerrilla war was that on occasion undisciplined Union troops themselves wreaked havoc on the rural people already suffering from guerrilla depredations. This tended to stiffen southern sympathy and less northern support among the victimized populace. The Union general of this part of Missouri, district chief Brigadier General John B. Sanborn stationed at nearby Springfield, ordered his provost marshal on February 11 to investigate alleged atrocities and misbehavior in Dade and Lawrence Counties evidently of local militiamen quartered at the village of Melville in east-central Dade County. The provost marshal was so ordered to investigate various

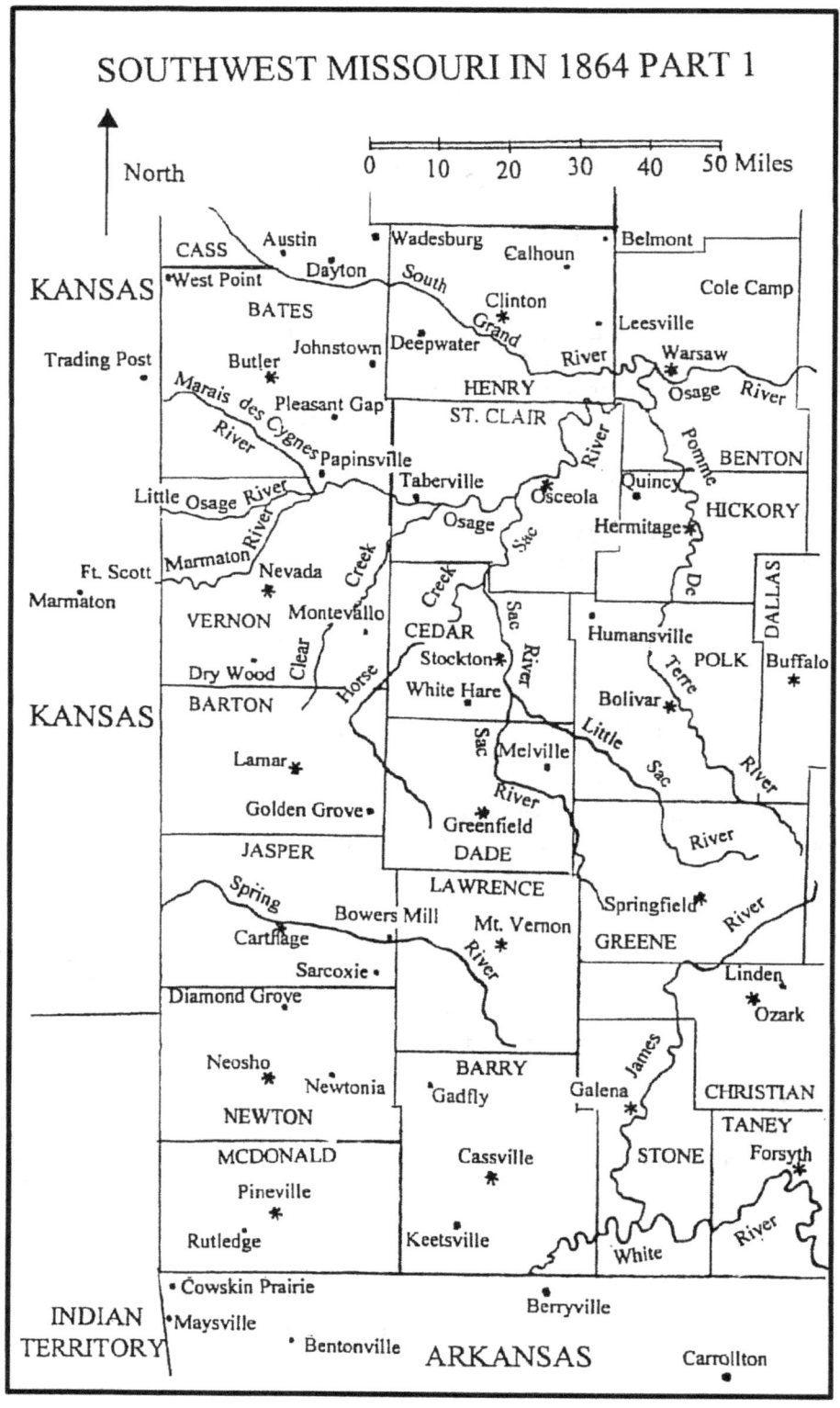

accusations about depredations over the previous six months including Union officers plying their men with liquor, troops intimidating local inhabitants, northern troops vandalizing a schoolhouse, and local officials ignoring all of this. General Sanborn recommended his official investigate if justice may be better served if the resulting trials be held in the Lawrence County seat of Mt. Vernon, since the culprits seemed to be local militia from Dade County. The Union misbehavior was all the more harmful since Dade County had been victimized by Yankee deserters turned renegade the previous year. Further, Dade County was home to noted bushwhacker Kincheon West and his dedicated band. Some of these guerrillas' family members were victims of northern lawlessness, and the bitterness this created motivated some locals to continue giving aid to the band.[2]

An unidentified southern bushwhacker band of six terrorized northern settlements along Canville, Big, and Hickory Creeks in Allen County, Kansas and western Newton County, Missouri on February 29. That morning on Canville Creek in Allen County the marauders mortally wounded Dr. William W. Hill with a bullet to his hip, then rode east to Big Creek in northwest Newton County where Mrs. Martha Freeman "went away with them." This wording in the report gives the impression that Mrs. Freeman joined the raiders of her own choice, but that may not be the case.[3]

A Quiet January and February on the Springfield Plateau of the Western Ozarks

The hilly, tree-covered area east of the far southwest corner was the scene for only a few small actions this winter. This area was dominated by the large Union garrison at Springfield, the largest town in this part of Missouri. The mounted Yankees of this garrison and other smaller ones patrolled back and forth through the cold hills looking for the few southern guerrillas who remained to challenge northern control of this part of the state. The antagonists did not always record the isolated shooting scrapes that resulted, and the scant accounts remaining are often void of details.

A case in point was a possible skirmish in this sub-region sometime in late December 1863 or early January 1864. Union trooper Wiley Britton, then stationed at distant Fort Scott miles to the north, recorded in his journal that he heard Federal troopers of the 8th Cavalry MSM engaged the bushwhackers about December 24 near the border, bested them, and chased the survivors a long distance. Trooper Britton recorded these few details in his postwar history, claiming that he heard the defeated guerrillas were none other than notorious west-central Missouri bushwhacker Captain William Clarke Quantrill and a portion of his band. Another northern reporter wrote only that a patrol of the 8th Cavalry MSM out of their garrison at Forsyth, Taney County, patrolled in late December and the first two days of January along the border, but did not mention any such action. Further, Quantrill and his men are well-documented to have been wintering in north Texas at this time, and were definitely not in southwest Missouri.[4]

In early January some Union troopers of 5th Kansas Cavalry Regiment were making nuisances of themselves to the locals near Urbana, northwest Dallas County. Inhabitants of this neighborhood appealed to General Sanborn at Springfield that these Kansans were "taking forage and other things" without paying. Records of the 5th reveal that Companies L and M were indeed garrisoned at this time not far from Urbana at Lebanon, Laclede County, so the accusation may have merit. General Sanborn had

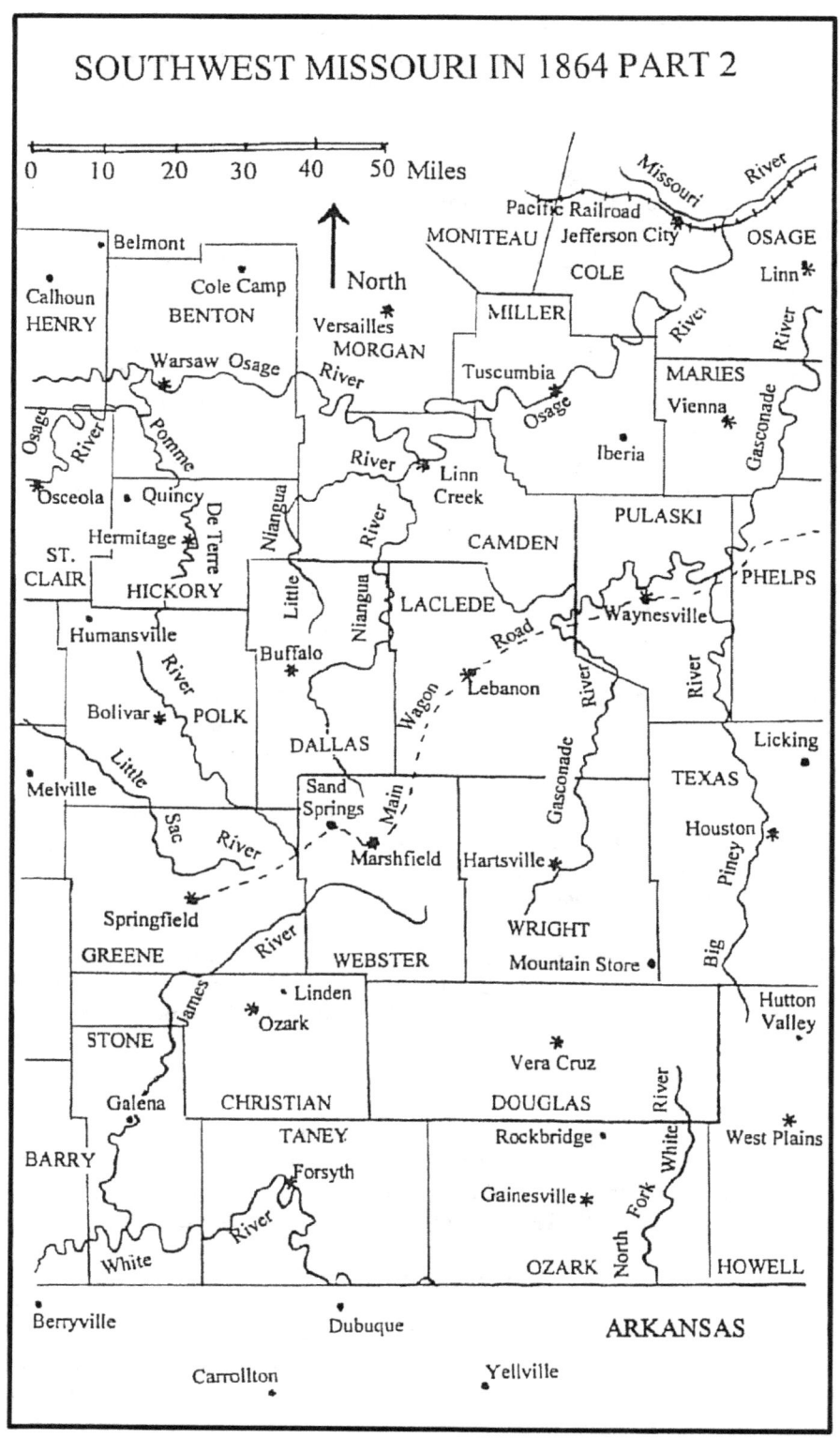

officers investigating similar accusations against several small garrisons of Union cavalry in his district, and this may have resulted in these two companies of the 5th Kansas Cavalry being transferred out of southwest Missouri later in January. Perhaps the Kansans could find no Rebels to fight in Dallas County, and some of the troopers adopted the common winter soldiers' pastime of getting into trouble.[5]

Union Colonel Ratliff B. Palmer, commander of the local 73rd Enrolled Missouri Militia Regiment (EMM), on February 24 had more serious accusations against northern cavalry garrisoned this winter in the county seat towns of Lebanon, Laclede County, and Waynesville, Pulaski County. Palmer was hearing that patrols from these garrisons were lately killing people in nearby Wright County, and that the enlisted men as well as their officers at the Lebanon station were demoralized and frequently drunk. The colonel attributed the demoralization among the soldiers at Lebanon to the eight businesses in that town that were selling liquor. Union army troop reports indicated that the Lebanon garrison at this time involved mostly men of the 8th Cavalry MSM while the Waynesville troopers belonged to the 5th Cavalry MSM, and these garrisons were protecting the main supply road to Springfield from guerrilla attack. Lieutenant Colonel Joseph A. Eppstein of the 5th Cavalry MSM replied to Colonel Palmer that the Wright County killings were actually authorized Union patrols correctly killing guerrillas as they found them. Further, Eppstein took issue with Palmer's attack upon the character of his soldiers and reminded the militia colonel that "the insufficiency of troops" in this area was more responsible for troop misbehavior. In sum, it seems Lieutenant Colonel Eppstein was telling Colonel Palmer that he had better check his facts before he made accusations against someone else's overworked soldiers doing their best to fight a desperate war.[6]

Winter War in the Osage River Basin

The advent of the fourth year of war in those counties around the Osage River was bleak, too. Like the area further south, war devastation caused many residents to move away. Further, the Union military forcibly depopulated Bates County and the northern half of Vernon County as part of the hated District of the Border General Orders Number 11. The purpose of the order was to deny the southern guerrillas sanctuary neighborhoods they had been using to raid Kansas settlements, and to prevent them from receiving aid and encouragement from southern sympathizers. The sad irony of this was that Federal inability to stop ruthless Kansas jayhawker raids on these Missouri border counties earlier in the war had turned many former loyal northerners into angry southern sympathizers. Since September and October 1863 thousands of these sad exiles were scattered across western Missouri dependant on the charity of friends and relatives, many of them in the throes of poverty this winter living hand-to-mouth in towns and villages or near Union military garrisons.

One sign of the breakdown of civil order in much of Missouri during the war was the vandal destruction of valuable county records as well as the clever means responsible citizens took to spirit away the records until civil law would return. Parties unknown carried away the county papers of Vernon and Cedar Counties earlier in the war, and Union troops patrolling from Forth Smith found them hidden in the mountains of northwest Arkansas on January 19. This announcement of the discovery, carried in at least one Missouri newspaper, implied that the Federals would safeguard the books and papers until they could be returned to Cedar and Vernon Counties later.[7]

A guerrilla camp in the thick reeds near a river (Charles C. Coffin, *Redeeming the Republic*, 1889, p. 45).

The well-known "brother against brother" Civil War theme came to light in southwest Missouri during a skirmish somewhere in Cedar County February 8. Lafayette "Pete" Roberts of near Stockton in south Cedar County had identified with the southern cause since the beginning of the war, and in early 1864 he began operating as a guerrilla chief in his home region. A mounted patrol of the local militia of Company D, 26th EMM from the Stockton area this day found and pursued five of Roberts' men, killing two, wounding a third, and capturing another. The St. Louis newspaper picked up the story in which the two dead men were noted as known Rebels in that area, but the captured man made this small skirmish a human interest story. This Confederate was Lieutenant Samuel Thomas Deardorf of the Rebel 2nd Missouri Cavalry Regiment who hailed from this same neighborhood. While being chased Lieutenant Deardorf drew careful aim with his firearm on one of the militia pursuers closest to him when he recognized his own brother, who evidently was Private Reuben D. Deardorf of the 26th. Rather than shoot his own family member the lieutenant promptly threw up his hands and allowed his brother to capture him and take him to the nearest Union garrison in Bolivar, Polk County, as a prisoner of war. Indeed, Yankee military records show Deardorf listed as a POW in one of the St. Louis prisons with the notation that he was captured February 8 in Cedar County.[8]

A patrol of 20 troopers of the 3rd Wisconsin Cavalry worked hard to eliminate a known bushwhacker haven in west Vernon County during two days in late February and early March 1864 while the guerrillas were away from this region. For much of 1863 local guerrillas used a patch of ground between the east and west forks of Big Drywood Creek as a fortress and hideout. The Wisconsin men found this hideout unmanned this time and torched off all the thick vegetation. They returned a few days later on March 6 and took away parts of a grist mill that the guerrillas had erected there some time in the past.[9]

The relative quiet of the entire southwest Missouri region during the heart of this particularly cold winter indicated that very few southern irregulars remained in this area of operations. The few that remained kept to their shelter in dugouts, caves, and isolated buildings until such time as the weather would warm. After three years of grueling warfare both sides realized the quiet of January and February 1864 was only a respite for the bitter winter, and when it eased the fighting would return as before.

Three

Winter 1864 in Northeast Missouri

Most of the southern guerrillas and Confederate recruiters left the northeast quadrant of Missouri and went south to warmer places like Arkansas before the onset of winter 1863–1864. Experience in earlier winters of the war taught them that operating surreptitiously out-of-doors this far behind Union lines was just too hard on men and horses, and secret operations indoors were simply too dangerous for the southern sympathizers that would support them. However, a few Rebel guerrillas continued to operate on a limited basis in northeast Missouri during January and February 1864. Much of the guerrilla actions of northeast Missouri the previous year took place in the counties lining the Missouri River, but the few such incidents this winter occurred in the interior counties north of these and in a three-county area not far to the north and west of St. Louis.

January and February Actions in Macon, Linn, and Chariton Counties

There were several incidents this winter in Macon, Linn, and Chariton Counties in the interior of northeast Missouri. About mid January a newspaper correspondent near Springfield, Missouri discovered that a number of families of southern sympathy of southwest Missouri were moving from that war-ravaged region to resettle north of the Missouri River in more tranquil areas. He specifically named the Ira Wainscot and the Rans Stewart families of Polk County as having moved to Macon County, and intimated that there were others. It is uncertain what affect these southern families had on their new neighborhoods.[1]

Gunfire disturbed the Bottsville neighborhood of southwest Linn County the evening of January 23. That night five local northern sympathizers robbed the homes of North Carolina–born, 77-year-old Seth Botts, Sr., and middle-aged, Tennessee-born Seth Botts, Jr., near Bottsville in southwest Linn County. At the senior Botts' home the robbers got $25, but at his son's house they encountered resistance. Seth, Jr. took a bullet in his wrist but he managed to seriously wound one of the raiders, Garret A. Anderson, a veteran of the Union 23rd Missouri Infantry. Anderson's fellow night riders abandoned their wounded comrade at Seth, Jr.'s home, where the Botts did what they could to treat the man's wound, while Anderson gave his fellows' names to the Botts in his anger at being abandoned. A small patrol of 9th Cavalry MSM happened along and left two troopers to guard Anderson while the remainder attempted to track the others. Meanwhile, the four raiders summoned a mob of 20 southern sympathizers from the nearby town of Laclede who rode to Botts' home, shot at the troopers, and took Anderson away. Later, a patrol of the 9th at Laclede encountered gunfire but still arrested ten men identified as the initial robbers and part of the rescue mob. A military tribunal at the district headquarters in Macon City later convicted these men, although several were released a few weeks later. A number of them had served in various Yankee units earlier in the war, a factor which may have convinced the tribunal to show leniency. This whole episode seems to have originated from the jealousy of northern men for their wealthy southern neighbors.[2] A cryptic Union military record states that part of the 9th Cavalry MSM perhaps from the Macon City garrison fought a skirmish somewhere in the area February 12, but gave no other details. Perhaps this was the patrol that arrested the Botts robbers and rescuers in Laclede.[3]

On February 26 another patrol from Macon City probably of the 9th Cavalry MSM on the Chariton River in either Macon or Chariton County captured a Dabney Santon who confessed to having been part of Captain Ingram's or Ingraham's guerrilla band in this area the previous summer. Santon also admitted to taking part in the raid on St. Catherine in southeast Linn County August 18 and named other members of the raiding party. The patrol used this information to arrest one of the named men.[4] During this period Rebel guerrilla leader Captain Clifton D. Holtzclaw remained hidden in the Linn County town of Linneus attended by a small group of dedicated southern sympathizers. Holtzclaw led Howard County southerners in the Missouri State Guard in the early months of the war, suffering wounds and capture. He returned to this region to recruit behind Yankee lines in spring 1863, and in September that year Union troops under suspicious circumstances shot and killed his father allegedly while trying to arrest the man at home. This and his many war adventures served to strengthen Captain Holtzclaw's resolve, even when family members were killed in the Confederate army on distance war fronts. In a few weeks Holtzclaw would emerge from hiding to continue guerrilla warfare in this region.[5]

Pulliam's and Cobb's Bands in Pike, Lincoln, and Montgomery Counties

Captain John Drury Pulliam was one of Confederate recruiter Colonel Sidney D. Jackman's more stalwart fighting commanders throughout 1863 in the Missouri River counties of northeast Missouri, and one newspaper article said he was back in mid–February of 1864. The reporter wasn't sure it was Pulliam, but reported that "a man calling himself Capt. Pulliam is prowling through Pike and Lincoln counties, robbing citizens of horses, firearms, clothing, & etc. Sometimes he is represented as having forty or fifty men with him, sometimes not more than four or five." Guerrilla bands and Confederate recruiters were forced to take what they needed from isolated farms in Missouri during the war, because this far from Confederate lines they had no other way to obtain mounts, weapons, wearing apparel, and even subsistence. Not much is known about Captain Pulliam's background, and, in similar fashion, there are few remaining sources that tell about his shadowy work for the South in this region during 1864.[6]

Just as Captain Pulliam's background seems hazy, guerrilla chieftain Alvin Cobb's life and exploits survive in several records. Kentucky-born Cobb was a large man, six feet tall and about 180 pounds, with shoulder length hair and a full, bushy beard—about 45 years old in 1864. His most imposing features included the hook he wore on his left

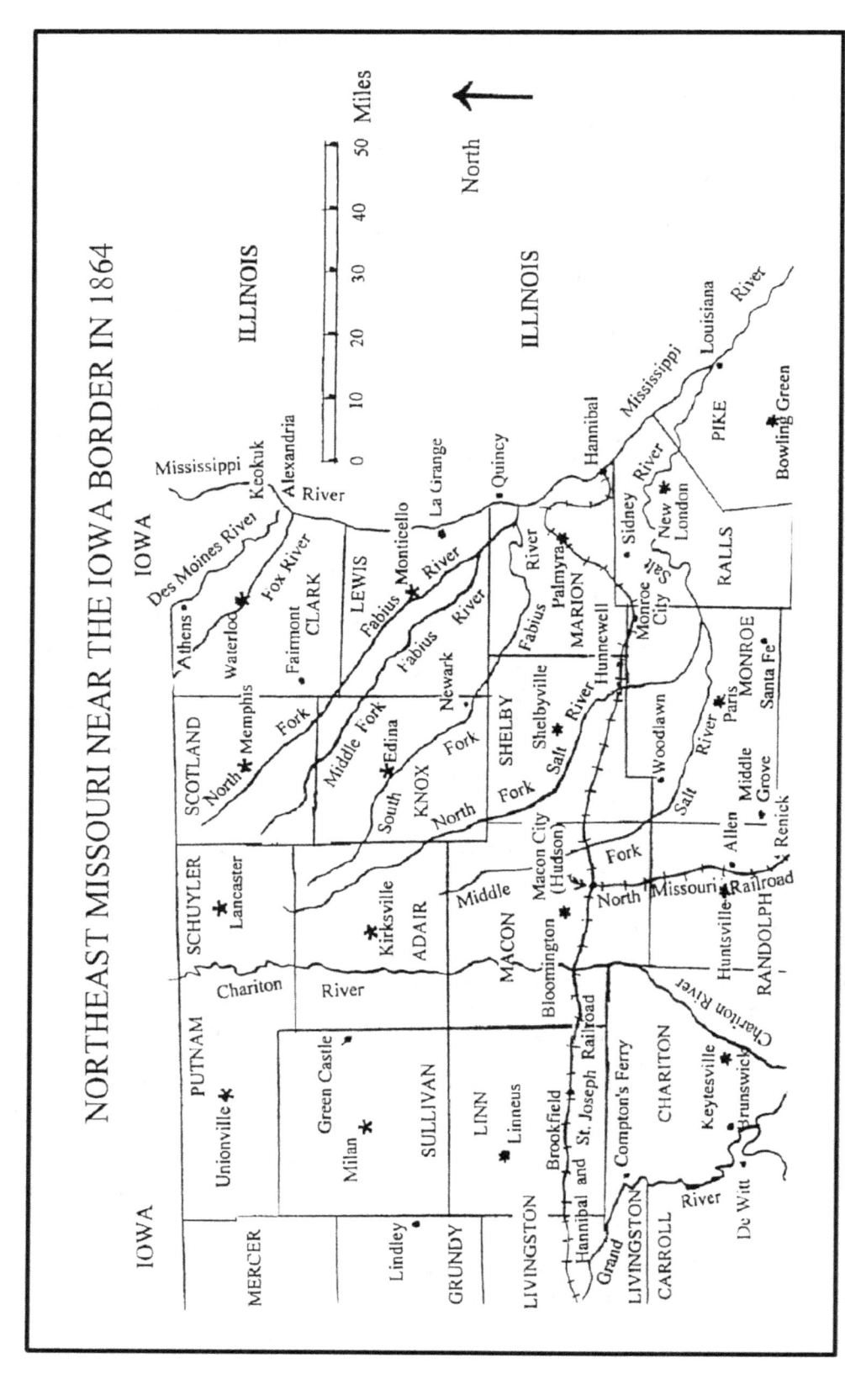

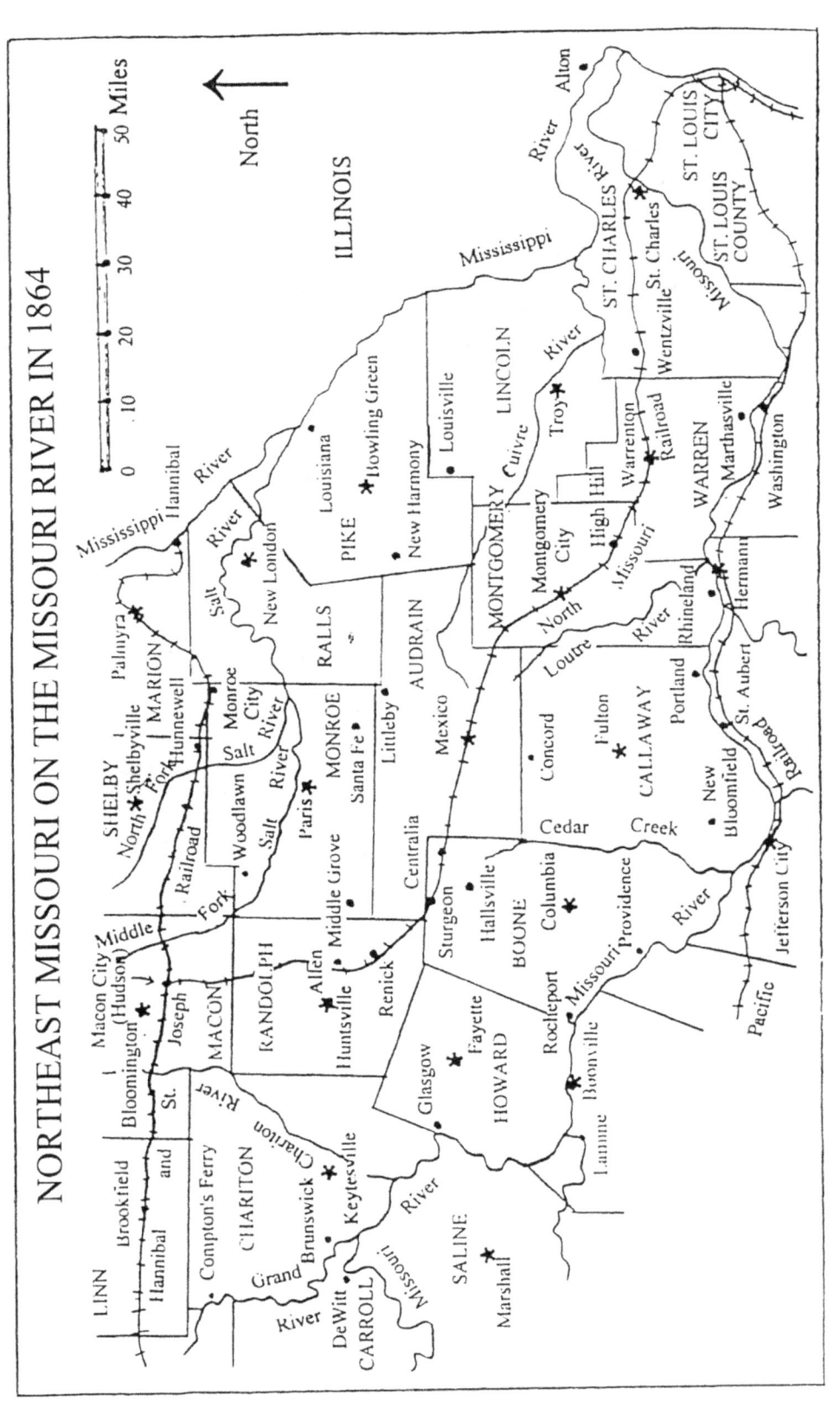

hand-he lost the hand and part of his forearm in a pre-war shooting accident-and his severe expression and gray piercing eyes. He traveled prewar in the Rocky Mountains, but had settled in Montgomery County to farm and raise a family in the 1840s. He was a champion for the South early in the Missouri conflict, shooting up a passing buggy carrying two Union officers in 1861. His band raided heavily in Callaway, Montgomery, and Warren Counties during much of 1862, but he operated with fewer men and in a more subdued manner over a larger part of this region in the summer and autumn of 1863. Alvin Cobb seemed to chafe under the Confederate restrictions of regular warfare, and favored bushwhacker tactics to fight his war for the South. He held the reins of his horse in his hook and favored a short rifle and several large revolvers probably of the "Army" or .44 caliber type as his personal weapons.[7]

During the evening of February 25 two men saw Cobb near Todd's Mill seven miles from Wellsville in northwest Montgomery or northeast Callaway County, and later excitedly but accurately described him to Union authorities-hook, "a very heavy beard," "stout build," and all. The two witnesses said this man was accompanied by over 100 riders, but they must have been mistaken about that number. That same night five guerrillas stopped at a house near Williamsburg in northeast Callaway County. This was part of Cobb's favorite operating area during 1862 and 1863.[8] This brief appearance seems to have been Cobb's last act in Missouri's war, for the Montgomery County history reported that he fled with his family to the Indian Territory perhaps not long after this. Maybe he was only back in his old war area to gather up his family and leave. After the war he reportedly moved to Oregon, and a former Confederate saw him in California at one time, too.[9] Missouri Civil War newspapers contributed to rumors back home about Confederates away in the army, and in the coming summer Columbia's *Missouri Statesman* reported that elements of the Rebel army probably in Arkansas hanged to death "Capt. Cobb of Montgomery county" for robbing civilians "and other crimes."[10] The local county history account cited above is probably more correct than the period newssheet, but Alvin Cobb remains a man of mystery.

As spring 1864 approached other southern bushwhackers and recruiters would not find the war so discouraging in northeast Missouri, and would soon return to this region with new hope and determination.

Four

Winter 1864 in Northwest Missouri

The winter weather of January and February 1864 was in some measure worse in the northwest quadrant of the state than other corners of the Show-Me State. Parts of this region were in higher latitudes and closer to polar air masses and the winter storms that roared in off the Great Plains. The *St. Joseph Weekly Herald* noted for posterity in that city on New Year's Day 1864 that "the thermometer stood 25 degrees below zero." The winter cold froze even the great Missouri River in this region and it remained frozen between January 1 and February 6 according to a Platte County historian living at the time.[1] What otherwise would have been an obstacle to travel was then crossable on foot for participants of all sides of guerrilla war. The tempo of guerrilla warfare in this quadrant of the state continued in spite of the ice, snow, and frigid winds. A great difference in the winter version of this hidden war was that it operated in fits and starts in localized areas as all people tended to limit outside efforts in such weather. Therefore, guerrilla warfare events appeared as isolated incidents here and there and now and then during this season.

Jayhawkers, Bushwhackers, and the "Paw Paw Militia" in Platte and Buchanan Counties During January and February 1864

The destructive Kansas Jayhawker raids that plagued the western border counties in earlier years continued this winter in northwest Missouri north of the Missouri River. Not only were these small-scale raids from Kansas border communities destructive in the theft and damage of personal property, but they steadily eroded public confidence in the Union and the Federal government to put a stop to them and increased sympathy and occasionally outright support for the Rebel cause. Such raiding earlier in the war seemed to be calculated to inflict punishment on Missouri southerners for instigating the war, but border renegades and outlaws by this time of the war had taken over such raiding primarily to take plunder back to Kansas to sell for money. They were aided at times by being able to cross over the frozen Missouri River that otherwise served as an obstacle to their cross-border raiding.

One such Jayhawker raiding party at night during early January 1864 took six horses and mules from Henry Lower's farm nine miles north of Rushville in west-central Buchanan County. The thieves crossed back over the Missouri River three miles above Geary City, Kansas with their booty. The angry Mr. Lower with the assistance of a detective from Atchison, Kansas looked in vain for either the perpetrators or the

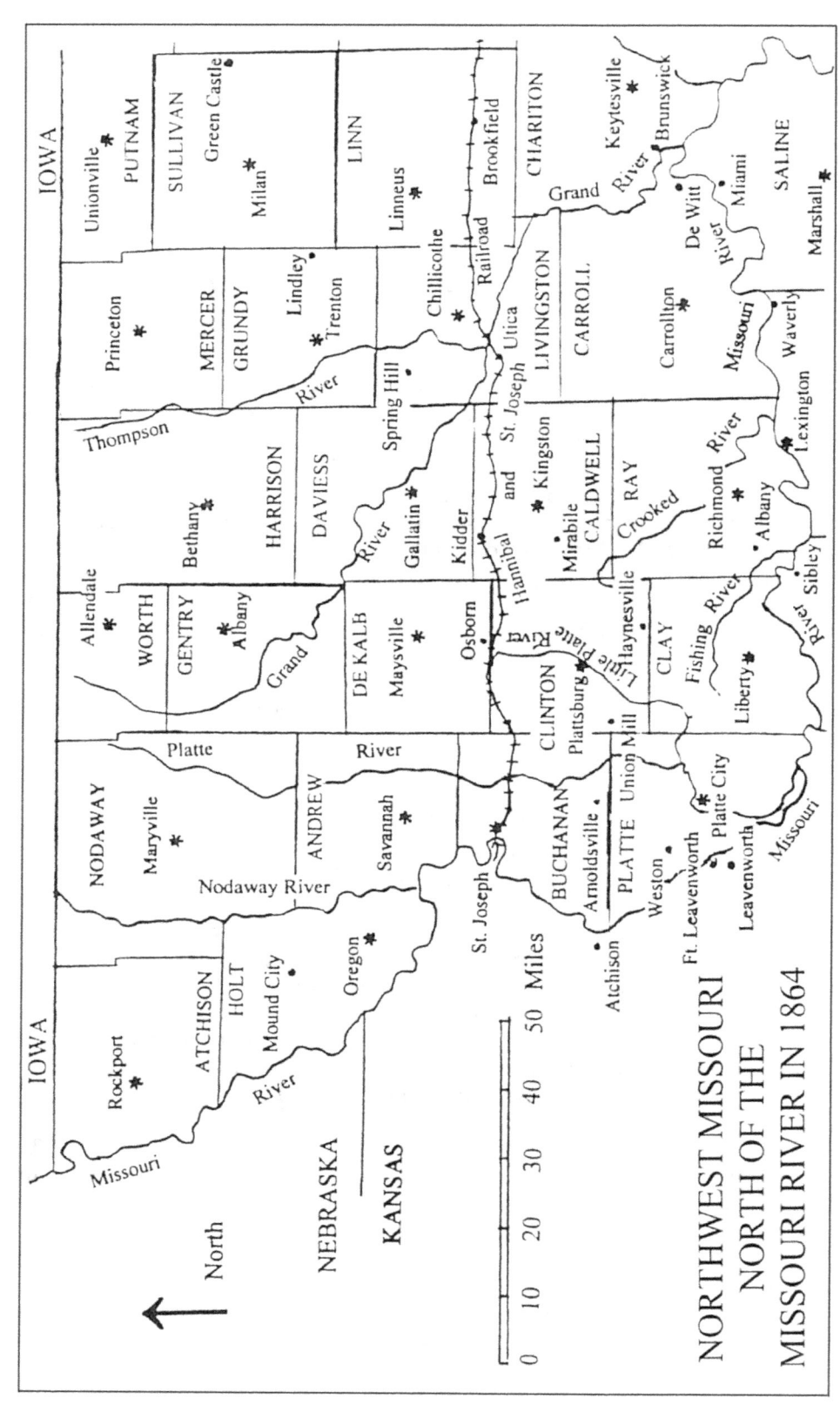

NORTHWEST MISSOURI NORTH OF THE MISSOURI RIVER IN 1864

purloined stock for several days. These raiders often had the assistance of Kansas border communities and even Kansas soldiers who helped hide the fruits of crime and give bad leads to pursuers.[2]

Guerrillas were active here on occasion. Nebraska City in the far southeast corner of Nebraska Territory just across the Missouri River from the far northwest Missouri corner had been publicized in Missouri newspapers during 1863 as a haven for Missouri refugees of southern sympathy.[3] Among three former Missouri bushwhackers then living in self-exile in or near Nebraska City was G. Byron Jones who had been active in the southern cause in Platte and Buchanan Counties earlier in the war. Jones sent one of his two companions to Buchanan County, Missouri in a two-horse sleigh to bring to him his wife, then living in a house there. The man found the house and packed Mrs. Jones and her belongings into the sleigh, unaware that the local 81st Enrolled Missouri Militia was watching the house for just such an eventuality. The militiamen apprehended the pair and made the guerrilla lead them back to also capture the other two just across the border near the village of Wyoming, Nebraska. The existing record fails to name two of them, except to mention that one had ridden with Quantrill in the past. The militiamen knew Byron Jones well since he had even been a member of this same militia company the previous year, but had been kicked out of the unit for being too much of a Rebel. Jones was eventually tried for a number of his actions as a Confederate recruiter and agent provocateur and sent to prison.[4]

In fact, the 81st and its sister regiment, the 82nd Enrolled Missouri Militia, during 1863 in this region had purposely recruited men of known southern sympathy including returned Rebel soldiers because able-bodied northern sympathizers there were in short supply. The state militia apparatus and some local residents were desperate to raise these units primarily to counter the pesky Jayhawkers who haunted this area with their nocturnal raiding. The numerous critics of this questionable program gave these militiamen the derisive nickname of "Paw Paw Militia," and warned repeatedly in the press and the legislature that these unreliable men were going to rise up sooner or later and turn on the northern sympathizers of this area. When some of these critics heard that this prisoner Jones had been a former member of the "Paw Paw Militia" despite his record as a notorious Rebel they renewed their dire warnings that these southern men would eventually turn on their leaders. Later in 1864 these vocal soothsayers would be proven right in a bloody insurgency in this area. But that was months away, and, for now, some defenders of this program saw the capture of these three as simple proof that the "Paw Paw Militia" of the 81st and 82nd regiments were fulfilling their oaths as Yankee troops, despite the Rebel background of many of the members and the criticism.[5]

As if to remind these critics of the reason for the "Paw Paw Militia," Jayhawkers in late January robbed the Charles A. Perry farm one mile from the village of Weston, west Platte County, taking three horses and two mules. Perry himself pursued the robbers to Kansas and somehow recovered his animals. How Perry, a trader with a large family, managed to achieve such a task when others could not was not recorded.[6]

Jayhawker and Northern Depredations in Holt and Gentry Counties in the Far Northwest Corner of Missouri

A band of about 30 Jayhawker raiders crossed the state border and robbed two houses on January 24 in south Holt County. They shot and killed one homeowner when he refused to open his door to them, and then escaped. Locals knew enough of this band to admit its members were men formerly from Missouri and some men from Nebraska Territory.[7]

The far northwest corner of Missouri seldom experienced guerrilla warfare during the war, but even in the dead of winter there were incidents evidently of northern aggression or depredations against southerners. Some northerners were impatient with the progress of the war and were concerned that Rebel recruiters would return in secret to sign up southern men, as they had months before in some locations. On occasion, small bands of these toughs would strike out on their own to make sure known southern men in their midst realized they were not welcome to remain.

Three such men in late January or early February near Atlantus in west Gentry County attacked George Finley's home. They shot through the windows, broke down the door, then wounded Finley's son seriously in the thigh. With the family now cowed, the raiders took about $100 or $200 cash from the house and left. Local officials pressed one man they suspected of being part of this robbery. The suspect confessed, named his accomplices, and all three faced justice for the crime.[8]

These bullies were not always caught for their brutality. On February 21 one such group near Graham in northeast Holt County murdered a returned Rebel, Lewis Garnett, at his door by shooting him in the head despite the presence of his large family in the house. The murderers then searched the home for alleged proof of Garnett's disloyalty, leaving in glee when they found $300 in Confederate money. Lewis Garnett had indeed served in Missouri Rebel forces during 1861 and at the Elkhorn Tavern or Pea Ridge battle in March 1862, but the Confederate Army discharged the middle-aged private in March 1863 for being "over age." When Garnett returned home, he gave a loyalty oath and bond at the Union headquarters in St. Joseph as required by martial law, and apparently lived as a peaceable citizen tending to his own business up to the time of his murder by this mob. Perhaps the $300 was part of his pay when he left military service that he kept as a souvenir of that chapter of his life.[9]

Jayhawkers, Guerrillas, and False Alarms in Clay, Ray, and Carroll Counties Along the North Bank of the Missouri River During January and February 1864

Hill's Landing Jayhawker Raid Night of 19 and 20 January

The severe cold in this region on the nights of January 19/20 and 20/21 assisted Jayhawker raiders to cross the frozen Missouri River to raid two villages on the north bank. One unidentified group crossed on foot from northeast Lafayette County the night of January 19/20 to raid Hill's Landing in south-central Carroll County. The 1881 history of that county recorded that these men robbed at least ten homes in and near the riverbank village taking in all $490, jewelry, watches, bed clothing, men's and women's and even children's clothing, and four horses before walking back across the ice to Lafayette County. Militia probably of the 65th EMM from nearby Carrollton pursued and first recovered the four stolen horses, which must have been skittish about crossing the ice and broken away from the raiders. On the southern bank the militiamen tracked the robbers five or six miles before they turned back—perhaps afraid of an ambush on this unfamiliar ground.[10]

Mysterious Missouri City Raid Night of 20 and 21 January

The raid the following night on Missouri City some miles to the west does not seem to be the work of the same band, but the identity of these raiders has been a mystery since it occurred. During the previous week a man identifying himself as "Major Sanders of the Federal Army" was staying in Richfield, southeast Clay County, with his wife, identified as the daughter of refugees from the depopulated area defined by General Orders Number 11 of the previous autumn. Military officers in nearby Kansas City and Clay County met this "Major Sanders" as he traveled around the area and grew suspicious about his claim that he was from one of the Kansas regiments. On the night of January 20/21 this "Major Sanders" with 30 or 40 men in civilian dress and Union uniforms riding horses with the "U.S." brand crossed the frozen Missouri River from Jackson County and rode into the small riverbank village of Missouri City, southeast Clay County. The mysterious leader informed the village local militia commander, Captain George S. Story of 82nd EMM, of their desire to take custody of a prisoner Coil held there, but Captain Story explained that Coil was in jail in Liberty, the Clay County seat, a few miles away. At this point "Major Sanders" and his group made the captain and his few militiamen their prisoners, partly because the militiamen were reluctant to fire on what appeared to be fellow Union soldiers. The riders then raided the B. W. Nowlin store of about $2000 in goods and a local resident of $50. Residents noted later it seemed odd that the raiders robbed residents of both sympathies in the war, something guerrillas did not usually do. At one point during the raid Captain Story broke away from his captors and ran into the darkness with bullets whizzing past his ears. The robbers placed their loot in gunny sacks across their saddles, rode back across the frozen river, and no more was ever heard from them. Captain Story and his men were not actually harmed, the robbers escaped pursuit, and area authorities were never able to correctly identify the mysterious "Major Sanders," as Kansas authorities said they had no such officer. As will be detailed later, just across the Missouri River in Jackson County elements of the 11th Kansas Cavalry stationed at the south bank village of Sibley were apprehended for "jayhawking" in rural Jackson County on January 19. There is no proof that "Major Sanders" and his riders were from that regiment, but it appears at least that "Sanders" and several of his men had previous military experience.[11]

Guerrilla Depredations Near Bogard's Mound in Late January

Sometime in late January 1864 three unidentified guerrillas raided the home of a Union trooper, Daniel T. Glover of the 2nd Missouri Cavalry Regiment ("Merrill's Horse"), near Bogard's Mound in north Carroll County while he was away with his regiment. The bushwhackers demanded money first from Glover's wife, ransacked the house, then burned the place. Guerrilla leader Jim Ryder of this region had been around in November and appeared again the following spring, so perhaps this was his work. Also, Confederate recruiter and guerrilla Captain Clifton Holtzclaw spent part or all of this winter in hiding in nearby Linneus, Linn County, so perhaps some of his men remained in the area and performed this depredation.[12]

Escaping Slaves This Winter

Slavery was still in effect in Missouri until January 1865, but slaves had been escaping in groups to free-state Kansas from farms and plantations in central and west central Missouri for months. Civil institutions to stop slave runaways were not fully functional because of wartime restrictions, and Union troops found such work distasteful

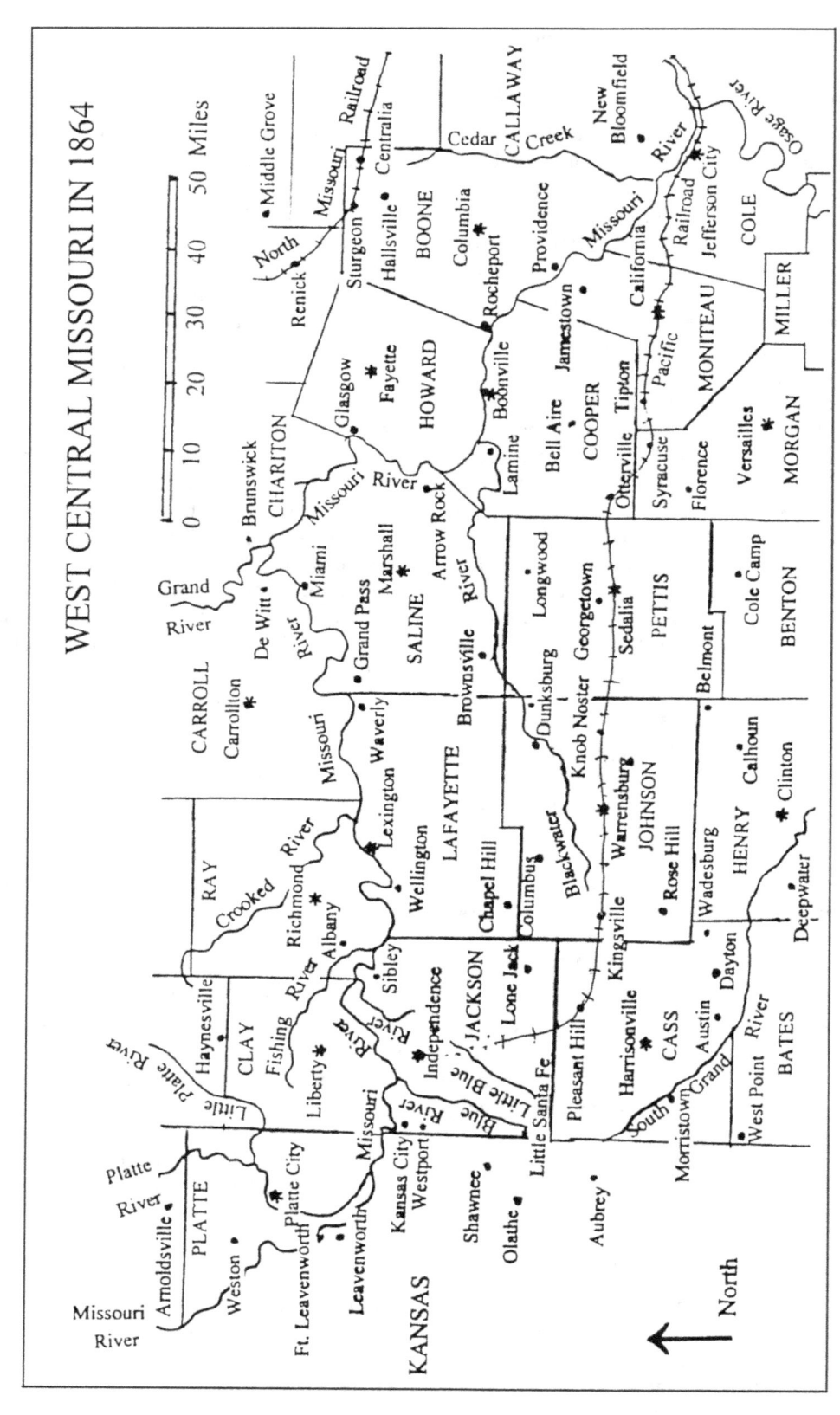

in the extreme. Slave-owners were forced to take their own actions to prevent slaves from running away and to recover escapees, and they employed armed men to carry out their wishes.

Clay County Battle Between Escaping Slaves and Slave Catchers About 25 January

Confrontations between slave-catchers and slave escapees were not normally part of guerrilla warfare, but one such conflict produced unexpected results and demonstrated the widespread anxiety in the Kansas/Missouri border communities at this point in the war. About January 25 or 26 an armed band of escaping slaves happened upon an armed band of slave-catchers in the southwest corner of Clay County along the north bank of the Missouri River, and a fierce gun battle ensued. The results of the gunfight itself were not recorded, but the sound of the shooting created problems in nearby Wyandotte, Kansas a short distance to the west. Residents of this small border community heard the rapid firing and mistook it for a guerrilla raid on the town. Visions of the much-publicized lurid details of Quantrill's Lawrence, Kansas raid of the previous August came instantly to mind and the townspeople panicked in large numbers. There was much running around, ringing the town's alarm bell, and mobilizing the local militia before the residents discovered the true nature of the shooting. Such false alarms occurred frequently along the border settlements after the Lawrence raid, and a number of them were recorded in local newspapers and even in Union army records. This kind of disorder and unease was a propaganda victory for the bushwhackers' bravado, and a reminder to the Union troops that in spite of all their efforts they were unable to fully drive the guerrillas from this region.[13]

Somewhere near Missouri City, southeast Clay County, on February 16 Sergeant James H. Hampton of the local company of 82nd EMM ("Paw Paws") went to the James Harris farm to arrest Harrison "Doc" Harris for reasons not recorded. The sergeant did not find the man he sought, but became involved in a pistol fight with one of "Doc" Harris' younger brothers and killed the man. The Liberty newspaper carried Sergeant Hampton's account that the younger Harris pulled a revolver on him and that he was forced to shoot to defend his own life.[14]

Isolated Violence in Saline and Cooper Counties of Central Missouri During February 1864

The strong Union military presence in the central part of the state guarding the state capital at Jefferson City and the new Pacific Railroad there usually meant this part of the state suffered less from guerrilla warfare, even though there were large numbers of southern sympathizers living here. However, a couple of violent acts occurred in Saline and Cooper Counties in February 1864. These may simply be acts of crime and not guerrilla warfare, but locals believed otherwise.

Sometime in February 1864 one or two miles from Marshall, central Saline County, parties unknown murdered two area residents perhaps for the money they displayed earlier buying supplies and paying taxes in town. Christopher Faber was aged 71, born in Pennsylvania and operated a prosperous farm not far from town. John Dawson, age 45 and born in Missouri, was the caretaker of the vacant Sweet Spring resort where he made a modest living. Their bodies were found by the wagon in the road, and the authorities noted that the contents of the wagon were not disturbed nor were the dead men's pockets rifled. These men had no known enemies, there were no known guerrilla activities in this area at this time, but Union troops were drilling in Marshall that day. A number of residents suspected, but had no proof, that soldiers in town had seen the men's cash, followed their wagon down the road, and waylaid them.[15]

In early February middle-aged Hugh W. Miller, brother of Circuit Court Judge George W. Miller of Boonville, disappeared. Nobody had any knowledge what happened to Miller, who lived east of Pilot Grove in central Cooper County. About a month later at a forest called McGee's Grove not far from Pilot Grove locals found Miller's remains, but this discovery did not solve the mystery of his disappearance. Authorities noted a killer delivered great blows to the front and back of Hugh Miller's head, perhaps with an ax, so at least they knew how he died. Locals believed guerrillas killed Miller, but no reasons for this remain, and there did not seem to be any guerrillas in this area at the time.[16]

Even these isolated incidents emphasize how peaceful this area in the center of Missouri remained this winter compared to continued guerrilla war in other parts of the state. Although these isolated violent acts do not so indicate, later in 1864 this quiet portion of the state would be the scene of intense guerrilla warfare.

January and February 1864 Actions of the Blunt and the Returned Shelby Cavalry Guerrilla Bands in West-Central Missouri

Two veteran bands of bushwhackers conducted guerrilla warfare during the winter of 1863-1864 in west-central Missouri. In early October 1863 when Captain William C. Quantrill led about 400 area guerrillas and some Confederate recruiting units south with him to winter in the South he left in his operating area trusted lieutenant Andy Blunt with about 40 men to carry on while the rest were gone. Experience with the two previous winters in this region convinced the bushwhackers that the problems inherent in feeding and hiding guerrillas in this war-ravaged region were only workable with smaller numbers of men in the cold weather months. The lack of foliage in the plentiful woods and brush lots in winter gave the Union military the advantage of greater visibility and robbed the guerrillas of concealment. For food and forage the remaining "knights of the brush" were more dependent for their subsistence in winter on the generosity of their numerous civilian sympathizers. The forced depopulation of parts of Jackson and Cass Counties under the hated General Orders Number 11 in autumn 1863 was specifically intended to deny guerrillas that very support by their sympathizers. The result of the depopulation was not as severe for the bushwhackers as was intended, but the guerrillas had to use more creative means to keep themselves and their horses fed this winter.

Mysterious Andy Blunt and His Small Band This Winter

Andy Blunt, the chieftain of one of the two bushwhacker bands, was a mystery even to the guerrillas who rode with him. Journalist and postwar guerrilla interviewer John N. Edwards in his 1877 book *Noted Guerrillas* wrote of Blunt: "No one knew his history. He asked no questions and he answered none. Some say he had once belonged to the cavalry of the regular army ... that he wished to find isolation." Edwards put forth one version told by the bushwhackers that Blunt was a private in the 2nd U.S. Cavalry in New Mexico Territory where he killed a sergeant and/or a lieutenant and fled to the Missouri frontier where he assumed a new identity.[17] Warren Welch was perhaps a leader of the second guerrilla band active in this region this winter, and he heard third-hand what may be a telling clue about Blunt's pre-war background. After Blunt was killed in early March Union troopers of the 2nd Colorado Cavalry came to view the body at a Jackson County farm. The farm inhabitants overheard one of the Coloradoans to remark that he had fought alongside the dead man in Colorado Territory before the war in "several hard places." He also said the man now known as Blunt was "a brave man and a good fighter."[18] The Union intelligence apparatus was ever perplexed about the leaders of the west-central guerrillas, and could only surmise that Andy Blunt's real name was Henry Starr, son of a judge who lived in the eastern edge of Kansas eight miles southwest of Westport. Guerrilla sources give no such indication, and they may have planted this tidbit to deliberately mislead the Yankees.[19]

Whatever Blunt experienced in earlier life, he displayed evidence of military experience as well as great fighting skill and courage to the west-central guerrillas who held him in awe for his readiness to kill. He was wounded and captured by Federals in an early Quantrill skirmish known as "the Lowe cabin fight" in Jackson County on April 16, 1862. The Union officer there barely stopped his troopers from shooting the captive out-of-hand and placed Blunt in a hospital. Andy Blunt later escaped and returned to Quantrill.[20] Guerrilla memoirs took care to note that later in 1862 Captain Quantrill used Blunt as an executioner to kill captives on at least three occasions.[21] By some accounts, when Quantrill traveled to Richmond, Virginia during winter 1862–1863 in an attempt to obtain a colonelcy he took only Andy as his traveling companion.[22] During summer 1863 Quantrill had faith enough in Blunt to send him as expedition leader to bring back recruits from the large population of southern sympathizers in Saline County. By August 1 Blunt brought back about 100 of the Saline County men, and he led them in the Lawrence Raid a few days later.[23] Therefore, when Captain Quantrill left Andy Blunt behind this winter in charge of about 40 men, he was leaving a capable, proven leader and fighter.

Guerrilla Group of Returned Confederate Cavalrymen

The second guerrilla band in west-central Missouri during the winter of 1863–1864 appears to have been a group of returned Rebel soldiers, many of whom wore Union uniforms; but their identity and mission are as mysterious as Andy Blunt's early life. The Federals mistakenly believed this band was led by well-known Quantrill sub-chief George Todd, but there is ample evidence that Todd was wintering in Texas with Quantrill. Union leaders did note that these blue-uniformed horsemen were mostly armed with Sharps breechloaders, which was a characteristic of Shelby's brigade at this time.[24] There is only one guerrilla memoir from this group by Warren W. Welch, but, sadly, Welch not only fails to name his comrades, but his postwar account also fails to clarify why these 30 men left the celebrated Shelby's "Iron Brigade" and rode all the way through Yankee lines back to their home area in the Jackson County area of west central Missouri. Warren Welch's account strongly implies that this band of 30 consisted of what the Union called "returned Rebels," that is, Confederate soldiers who for one reason or another left the southern army and returned home. Welch recounted that this band arrived by horseback in the Jackson County area to discover they missed Captain Quantrill and about 400 others who set out on their ride south only five days before. Since Quantrill and company set out about October 1, 1863, this band of southern cavalrymen must have arrived in west-central Missouri about October 5 through 8. This corresponds roughly to the movement toward the north of a stealthy guerrilla band through Jasper, Vernon, and Bates Counties in late September and early October. Welch

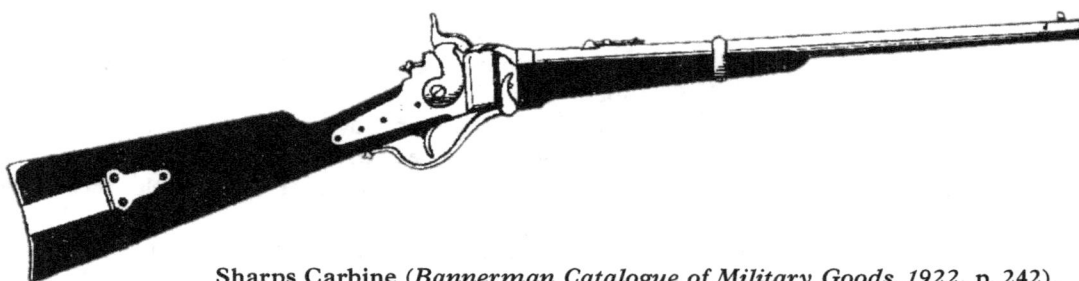

Sharps Carbine (*Bannerman Catalogue of Military Goods, 1922*, p. 242).

acknowledges meeting Andy Blunt and his 40 guerrillas who were remaining in west-central Missouri to continue operations that winter.[25]

Studying the scanty remaining military records provides clues about the identities of this second band of "returned Rebels," but fails to identify their purpose in returning home. Welch's record identifies him as Second Lieutenant "W. W. Welsh" of Company C, 2nd Missouri Cavalry Regiment (formerly called 12th Missouri Cavalry and "the Jackson County Regiment"). Since most members of the 2nd were Jackson County men, perhaps all 30 members of this band were deserting regular service with Colonel Joseph Shelby to fight as irregulars against Yankee atrocities back home. Indeed, Welch's record states he deserted his unit as of August 10, 1863.[26] By about middle September men of this regiment in the Confederate Army in Arkansas would have learned from newspapers and letters about the suffering of the refugees ejected from Jackson, Cass, Bates, and Vernon Counties by the hated General Orders Number 11. They would have also learned that Union General John Ewing's District of the Border allowed Kansas troops to operate in west-central Missouri where they occasionally committed depredations on the residents. Another "returned Rebel" apparently of this band was Private Jacob "Jake" Wedington from Company A also of the 2nd. Wedington with a few men conducted operations in deserted Cass County against Yankees of the 6th Kansas Cavalry and 9th Kansas Cavalry during October 1863. Strangely, his military record does not reflect an absence from his regiment and indicates that he was on active duty with the 2nd during January and February 1864. This evidence seems to indicate that Wedington rode with Warren Welch and the 30, operated a few weeks around his Morristown, Cass County, home about October 1863, and then alone or with a few comrades rode back to Arkansas and rejoined his regular unit.[27] Wedington's record raises the possibility that these 30 soldiers were sent by lawful military command back home for some purpose. Were these soldiers sent back home to recruit? Were they sent to augment other guerrillas operating in their home area? Other members of the Confederate 2nd Missouri Cavalry operated as guerrillas with Quantrill earlier in the war, and several of them would leave the 2nd and operate in this area as guerrillas later in 1864.

A January 1864 newspaper article raises the possibility that these 30 were sent or rode on their own to west Missouri to assist the General Orders Number 11 refugee families to find safe places to live in less war-torn neighborhoods north of the Missouri River. The correspondent for a St. Louis newspaper in Springfield, Missouri on January 25 wrote of his recent discoveries of large-scale movement of southern families:

> During a recent trip to North Missouri I had a favorable opportunity of learning what had become of a large portion of the missing citizens of this part of the state. I saw on the road many families going from Southern to Northern Missouri. I learned from the persons themselves ... that they are the families of rebels.... I know, also, of a few families of rebels from

War refugee families sometimes have difficulty finding a place to live (Walter B. Stevens, *Centennial History of Missouri*, vol. II, p. 565).

> Lafayette and Johnson counties, now living in the western part of Davies [County].... I was told by persons living on the road between Sedalia and Lexington that more than a hundred rebel families (the females and the children) passed over that one road to North Missouri.[28]

Indeed, Welch's memoir lists several fights this band of "returned Rebels" fought with Union troops, but none of them seems to have taken place earlier than middle January 1864. It seems reasonable to assume that these 30 combat veterans were doing something besides combat during October, November, and December 1863 after they arrived back in their home area in early October. Could they have been specifically detailed, perhaps at company or regimental level, to return home on the humanitarian mission of assisting their own and their comrades' families to find new, safe homes and then return to their unit? The newspaper article specifically implies men were noticeably absent from these traveling family groups. Further, there does not seem to be documentation to show such a humanitarian mission. However, such a humane quest could explain why so many combatants from a unit high in esprit and morale like Shelby's brigade rode back home from that distinguished military unit but did not conduct any known combat actions in the midst of their enemy for about three months.

Poorly Recorded Skirmishes During January 1864

The frequent skirmishes of these two bushwhacker bands during January and February 1864 are poorly reported in the existing record, and what facts survive do not always identify which of the two bands was involved in which incident. Examinations of what evidence remains seems to indicate that Blunt's band operated primarily in Lafayette County while the "returned Rebel" soldier band favored the Jackson County area. During October, November, and December Union patrols killed, seriously wounded, or captured nine or ten of the guerrillas probably of Blunt's band mostly in Lafayette County.[29]

The first known incidents of guerrilla war in this region for 1864 took place in Lafayette County. Lieutenant Colonel Bazel F. Lazear of the 1st Cavalry MSM wrote home to his wife January 13 and mentioned that elements of his regiment "had a little skirmish" on January 11 near Lexington, but that he had not heard details.[30] Also on January 13 the 1st's regimental commander, Colonel James McFerran, wrote Lazear that he had ordered Company G to move from Lexington to Columbus, north-central Johnson County, because of depredations men of that company were alleged to have committed in and near Lexington. Colonel McFerran also ordered an investigation into these acts.[31]

In mid–January patrols of the 1st Cavalry MSM began to find evidence that guerrillas had moved back into Jackson County. A Company G patrol out from Lexington January 15 near Pink Hill, northeast Jackson County, found a recently abandoned guerrilla camp with the campfires still burning and called for assistance. First Lieutenant James Couch brought a Company C patrol out to this area from Warrensburg in response to this summons. His men found and chased Andy Blunt's band until dark January 16 when the guerrillas scattered to throw off pursuit. It was at this point that Lieutenant Couch's scouts brought in word that a second guerrilla band, which may have been the "returned Rebel" band, was nearby at Round Prairie. Warren Welch in his memoir wrote that at Round Prairie with 15 other guerrillas he attacked a forage-gathering detail, probably of the 1st Cavalry MSM, and drove the troopers away. Couch's patrol came to the rescue only to find the bushwhackers gone and the wagons standing abandoned but not harmed nearby. Welch specifically mentioned Lieutenant Couch in his memoir and remarked that the guerrillas were not aware "three loads of commissary" were left near the scene, or they would have burned them. The forage gatherers suffered a bad scare, but were not hurt. Welch wrote that the Rebels suffered no harm, and were delighted to have chased off veteran Union cavalry. The nearby Kansas City newspaper issued a short bulletin on January 20 stating that they had heard that the guerrillas "killed six of the soldiers, burned the wagons and drove off the mules," but this was only a hasty first report from the field.[32]

Depredations by Union 11th Kansas Cavalry in Mid-January

The Union local command was diverted from guerrilla issues over the next few days with Jayhawker troubles. A portion of Lieutenant John W. Ridgway's command of 11th Kansas Cavalry Regiment garrisoned at Sibley, northeast Jackson County, seems to have gone berserk in mid–January. These 50 or 60 Kansas cavalrymen ostensibly rode into the countryside to gather forage for their horses, but instead turned to liberating slaves and robbing rural families in Clay Township, northwest Lafayette County. The Kansas troopers took money and jewelry but also took wagons and teams in which to transport the slaves they forcibly freed from farms. The victims were at a loss to know what to do since they were under the impression that even the Kansas troops represented law and order, so for a while Union authorities did not know about the jayhawking depredations still underway. On January 19 two of the victims, Strother Renick and James Musselman, rode to Lexington to get help. Not knowing which Union troops would listen to them, Renick and Musselman ignored the Lexington military commander there, and instead told their story to a local man—Richard C. Vaughn, who happened to be a brigadier general in the EMM. General Vaughn telegraphed district commander, Brigadier General Egbert Brown, to personally inform him of the jayhawking by the 11th Kansas. General Brown immediately sent a large force of the 1st Cavalry MSM to western Lafayette County to stop the raiding, where the Missouri troops discovered the Kansas troops had ridden back into Jackson County. The troopers of the 1st at first had a difficult time getting statements from the victims of the Kansas raiding, as most of the remaining inhabitants of west Lafayette County were hiding in the brush in fear for their lives from the Jayhawkers. The troopers did recover some of the stolen stock and a wagon and composed a detailed report of the thefts by January 22. The troops of the 11th Kansas Cavalry were moved to Kansas a few days later. Meanwhile, for a while General Brown confused the reports about the actions of the new guerrilla band in Jackson County with the marauding 11th Kansas Cavalry and may have lost an opportunity to deploy troops against the new "returned Rebel" band.[33]

Increased Bushwhacker Activity in Late January and February

With two guerrilla bands of about 30 members each now operating in Jackson and Lafayette Counties as of middle January, the pace of guerrilla actions increased noticeably. Lieutenant Couch's patrol of 1st Cavalry MSM reported small groups of bushwhackers all over northeast Jackson County where his men fired on three guerrillas and captured their mounts.[34] Lieutenant Colonel Lazear of the 1st reported that six or seven irregulars fired on his couriers in Greenton Valley in west Lafayette County January 24. He may have been skeptical about earlier reports that these men were under George Todd, as he laconically stated in his report that he could not learn who was the bushwhacker leader.[35] On February 3 Captain Charles Coleman with all or part of Company D, 9th Kansas Cavalry fought a skirmish in the rugged Sni Hills, and afterwards reported in apparent exaggeration that there must have been 100 of the guerrillas.[36] Guerrilla Warren Welch briefly mentioned one skirmish about this time at a placed called Elm Hollow where 60 mounted Yankees attacked six of the bushwhackers resulting in the killing of one of the southern mounts.[37] Welch next wrote about 400 Kansas cavalry fighting with 16 of his comrades mortally wounding one guerrilla at the cost of seven Kansans killed.[38] Perhaps these reports by either side are actually describing the same actions, but there is not enough detail for careful matching.

Between February 6 and 10 a combined Kansas patrol of several companies of the 5th and 9th Kansas Cavalry led by Captain Charles F. Coleman had a series of running fights with bushwhacker groups of 10 to 40 all through the hollows of the Sni Hills. Coleman did not state any Union casualties and only mentioned one Rebel wounded, but the captain concluded that he had chased the bushwhackers out of the Sni Hills.[39] A diarist living near Lexington heard secondhand that about this same time "some US soldiers and Indians" burned a couple of farmsteads near the Sni Hills, so perhaps this same Kansas cavalry force—whose units often contained a few native Americans—burned dwellings, barns, and corn cribs to deny their use to the guerrillas.[40]

Dick Yager and a Small Group of Guerrillas in Cass County

A Union detective reported that about February 21 well-known Westport guerrilla Dick Yeager or Yager with five or six others stopped at a house near the Grand River in Cass County and that later Yeager and his companions also stopped at a house south of Lawrence, Kansas, stating that they intended to raid wagon trains moving freight along the Santa Fe Trail in eastern Kansas. Yeager was present in this region weeks later in May 1864, so perhaps he was here as the report said at this time, too, although there were no reports of such raids on the famous trail. Since Yeager was a freighter in this region before the war he was ideally suited to such an undertaking.[41]

54 Guerrilla Warfare in Civil War Missouri, January–August 1864

After February 21, 1864, for the rest of the month the skirmishing was almost daily in its frequency in this part of west-central Missouri. In the northwest corner of Johnson County near Blackwater River First Lieutenant Walter B. Hamilton's patrol from Company D of the 4th Cavalry MSM from Warrensburg at eight in the morning of February 22 drove 20 allegedly of Andy Blunt's band through the scrub wounding one Rebel at the cost of Lieutenant Hamilton severely wounded.[42]

Blunt's Attempt to Break a Guerrilla Out of Lexington Jail Night of 21 and 22 February

That same night Blunt and a few of his men put into effect a desperate scheme to break one of his men, Otho Hinton, out of Union confinement at Lexington. Federals had been holding Hinton as prisoner since his capture a few days before Christmas, and Blunt set up an elaborate plan to free Hinton by force at the time when three guards—Sergeant John Kincaid, Private John R. Burns, and Private William Sabins of 5th Provisional EMM—were to take Hinton in shackles to Mrs. Reid's house in town that night to eat supper. Blunt had bribed Privates Burns and Sabins with money and having attractive 24-year-old Annie Fickel of Greenton romance the younger Sabins. Union troops killed Fickel's younger brother Joe, one of Quantrill's guerrillas, the previous April, and she wanted to do what she could for the cause. Blunt had even enlisted elderly Mrs. Reid to step out of the room precisely at 7:00 pm when the escape would take place. Blunt sprung his ambush unaware that Private Sabins had confessed his part to his superiors who set up an ambush of their own. The Federals brought in a dozen militiamen from Johnson County under Captain Daniel W. Johnson to keep Blunt and his conspirators from discovering the surprise awaiting them near Mrs. Reid's house. Precisely at 7:00 o'clock as Mrs. Reid left the room prisoner Hinton picked up his shackles and reached for the door assuming that Private Sabins would disable the sergeant according to the plan. Of course, Private Sabins was now operating on a different plan and Sergeant Kincaid shot Otho Hinton dead before he could wrench open the door and escape to freedom. Sabins remained with Sergeant Kincaid, but the confused Private Burns, who had been in southern service earlier in the war, ran into the night to join Andy Blunt waiting near the house. The hidden militiamen then sprang their trap shooting Burns to death and wounding guerrilla leader Blunt in the leg. Blunt shot to death one of the militiamen and barely escaped Lexington with another of his

Shackles intended to restrict a prisoner's movement (*Bannerman Catalogue of Military Goods, 1922*, p. 334).

men and sought medical help with a family of southern sympathy nearby. Union authorities arrested old Mrs. Reid and the attractive Miss Annie Fickel for their parts in the botched escape.[43]

Later the same night as the Hinton escape attempt the bandaged and frustrated Andy Blunt with a few of his men rode to Arthur G. Young's house five miles from Lexington and took away and murdered two Union soldiers he had been informed were staying there for the night. The unfortunate soldiers were Westport, Jackson County, men, Private Elsy F. Sanders of Company B, 6th Kansas Cavalry, on furlough and his friend, former Private Thomas Mockbee, who had been discharged from the same company a few months before with a disability. Evidently, Blunt wanted their killing to be a last word to the Yankees about the night's tragic events.[44]

The rest of February was filled with a string of skirmishes in the region. Patrols of the Union 1st and 4th Cavalry MSM from the Warrensburg garrison conducted operations probably in north Johnson County and Lafayette County between February 22 and 24, but left few details.[45] On February 23 Captain Milton Burris and his patrol of 19 troopers of Company I, 1st Cavalry MSM, near the Sni-A-Bar Hills on February 23 mortally wounded two guerrillas of Blunt's band in a skirmish while several other bushwhackers escaped into a dense thicket.[46] On February 27 at 9:30 in the evening five or six guerrillas a mile or two east of Independence took as captive an Irishman and a black man from a family there. Later that night the Irishman managed to escape from his captors. This enraged the southerners to the extent that they shot and severely wounded the black man and left him for dead.[47] As the month of March 1864 approached with the hope of spring and warmer weather this increasing tempo of guerrilla actions forecast a violent year of guerrilla warfare in west-central Missouri, especially when Captain Quantrill and the balance of the bushwhackers returned from wintering in the South.

FIVE

Missouri Guerrilla Warfare Changes During Early 1864

Both sides in the guerrilla war of Missouri, but especially the northern side, used the relative calm of winter and spring seasons to make adjustments in commanders, tactics, and plans before the onset of the faster pace of renewed bushwhacker violence returned in the spring. Similar changes took place to some extent during the cold season in both 1862 and 1863, and 1864 was no exception.

Changes in Command

A number of high-ranking personalities important to the conduct of guerrilla warfare in Missouri changed in the early months of 1864. These new leaders would attempt to imprint their own stamp on the conduct of the "backwater" war stubbornly sputtering on in Missouri.

Union Major General John M. Schofield was replaced as the commander of the Department of the Missouri January 30, 1864—a troublesome duty he had filled twice during the war. This second time he commanded the irksome department since May 24, 1863, and evidently took on the job a second time because President Lincoln appreciated his moderate stance, midway along the continuum of the fractious Missouri northern politicians. Further, 32-year-old New York–born General Schofield gave up an enviable position leading troops in the field in obedience to higher command's desire to place him back as commander of this thankless department. Therefore, being released from command of the north's effort to conquer Missouri's determined, bothersome guerrillas and returning to a combat command was actually a favor to Schofield and perhaps a reward for a ticklish job done well. Schofield, on the very day he stepped down as head Missouri general, offered himself and his aides to General Grant and asked for orders to his next assignment away from the Show-Me State.[1]

Schofield's successor in the "hot seat" fighting guerrillas in Missouri was Major General William S. Rosecrans, 44 years old and born in Ohio. "Old Rosy," as his men called him, had led the Union Army of the Cumberland in defeat at the Battle of Chickamauga the previous September. For this debacle and other goofs Rosecrans was relieved from that command in October 1863, and had been languishing in that "never-never land" of unemployed Yankee generals waiting in the wings for another chance to prove themselves. Since command of the Department of the Missouri was primarily an administrative job more than a field command, and Rosecrans had proven adept at the first and inept at the second, naming him commander of the irksome Missouri department seemed a perfect fit. Besides, "Old Rosy" bore more of the radical political stamp compared to Schofield's moderate stance, and that fit better to the growing ascendancy of the radical northern party in Missouri. It must have perturbed Missouri's moderate northern governor, Hamilton B. Gamble, if he had not been so ill at the time of the appointment to notice Rosecran's politics. However, Provisional Governor Gamble by his order granted to the newcomer general a tremendous gift that had been withheld from all the previous commanders of the Department of the Missouri—Federal control of all Missouri state militia. This included both the active-duty Missouri State Militia and the occasionally active-duty Enrolled Missouri Militia. Previously, these forces had been carefully kept under state control with some Federal help with weapons, subsistence, ammunition, and other help. Gamble and the General Assembly had grown tired of the frustration of paying huge sums to maintain these "private armies," and had reached the stage where they gladly handed over the reins and the bills to the U.S. Department of War. General Rosecrans was a religious man—a devout Catholic since his cadet days at West Point years before—which was undoubtedly viewed well by the large number of Catholics in Missouri, especially in St. Louis. He was known to be bright and applied his mind to problems, and new ideas might just bear fruit in the tired bush war in Missouri, too.[2]

Also in January the Union command in Missouri decided the experiment of combining Kansas and Missouri troops on Missouri soil had led to atrocities and failed to prevent or stop the horrendous Lawrence, Kansas raid of August 1863. So, they disbanded the controversial District of the Border. The changes meant that Kansas troops were sent back to Kansas, and could no longer operate on Missouri land without permission from Missouri generals. The Missouri counties that were formerly part of the Department of the Border reverted to the Department of Central Missouri with headquarters then at Jefferson City. General Schofield began this process on January 8 while he still commanded the Department of the Missouri, and General Rosecrans followed through in March 1864 by making the former District of the Border

Union Major General William S. Rosecrans was commander of the Department of the Missouri for most of 1864 (National Park Service collection at Wilson's Creek National Battlefield, historian Connie Langum).

commander, Brigadier Thomas Ewing, Jr., the commander of his District of St. Louis, which covered about the southeast quadrant of the state. Ewing was a bright officer whose leadership brought results, but the controversies of his hated General Orders Number Eleven which forced depopulation of three-and-a-half Missouri border counties and the Kansas dislike of him for failing to stop Quantrill and 450 Rebel irregulars from raiding Lawrence in August had "worn out his welcome" along the Missouri-Kansas border. Transferring Ewing away from this controversy and disbanding his District of the Border helped to mend political fences.[3]

On January 31—the very next day after General Rosecrans officially replaced General Schofield as commander of the Department of the Missouri—Missouri's northern governor since the start of the war died suddenly of pneumonia. Back in summer 1861 Provisional Governor Hamilton B. Gamble took over in that role when properly elected, pro-southern Governor Claiborne Fox Jackson fled the state capital ahead of the arrival of Federal troops. Gamble, in his sixties, struggled to govern a state torn asunder from internecine warfare as he charted a course of moderate politics. Gamble's moderate stance entailed reaching out to the secessionists in an effort to persuade them to return peaceably to the Federal fold. Union Major General Schofield, as commander of the Department of the Missouri, shared many of Gamble's attitudes about the conduct of the war in Missouri, and they worked well together. The dual frustration of not seeing southerners come back to the northern viewpoint in large number while seeing the radical northern party grow in strength and numbers as the war dragged on wore heavily on Gamble. Politically, he was fighting a losing battle with the radicals, who stood for tough treatment of the secessionists to mend the broken country by force. Hamilton Gamble's death came about when he injured his arm in December 1863 falling on ice-covered steps to his residence in St. Louis. His associates and relatives failed to realize the seriousness of his injury, and his weakened condition led to the pneumonia that claimed his life after a relatively short illness.[4]

Lieutenant Governor Willard P. Hall took over as provisional governor to complete the remainder of Gamble's term. Just a few months before, Hall had been an Enrolled Missouri Militia brigadier general attempting to keep law and order in northwest Missouri as the district chief headquartered at St. Joseph, his hometown. He shared Hamilton Gamble's moderate political goals, but found them more and more difficult to employ in the face of the fast-growing radical northern throng of politicians who were taking control of the General Assembly at Jefferson City. Now that radical-bent William S. Rosecrans had taken command of the Department of the Missouri, the new provisional governor's moderate tendencies faced even more oppos-

Provisional Governor Hamilton B. Gamble (Perry S. Rader, *The Civil Government of the United States and the State of Missouri*, 1898, p. 351).

Governor Gamble's tombstone in Bellefontaine Cemetery in north St. Louis (author's photograph).

ition. Forty-three-year-old, Virginia-born Hall was to serve as Missouri governor only about one year, and his political limitations were mostly the reason for his short term.[5]

There was a notable change in a key Confederate leadership position that affected guerrilla warfare in Missouri, too, in early 1864. On March 16 Confederate Major General Sterling Price replaced Major General Theophilus Holmes as commander of the District of Arkansas. The significance of this change was that 54-year-old, Virginia-born Price was as dedicated to the cause of a free, southern Missouri as he was a free, southern Confederacy. Beginning in 1862 General Price, called "Old Pap" by his men, sent literally scores of Missouri southern officers miles behind Union lines into Missouri as Confederate recruiters, and many such behind-enemy-lines recruiters went into Missouri

Confederate Major General Sterling Price of Missouri (John R. Musick, *Stories of Missouri*, 1897, p. 246).

again in 1863 and 1864, although in fewer numbers. Sterling Price was a popular Missouri politician, serving in state politics during the 1830s, 1840s, and 1850s, and was even Missouri governor for several years in the 1850s. Now during the war "Old Pap's" chief cause was to free Missouri from the yoke of Yankee oppression that had been in charge there since the northern forces forced the southern Missouri army out of their home state in early 1862. He spoke vehemently to any Confederate official or general who would listen about the need to send a large-enough southern force into the Show-Me State to literally rip the state out of the control of the Federals, which evoked little sympathy with Confederate high command. The Rebel policy-makers felt such a plan had limited chance of success at best, and at worst would deprive the struggling Confederacy of thousands of irreplaceable combat veterans better utilized in other struggling theaters of war. Despite such forebodings, as commander of this region, General Price was now in a position to at least look for an opportunity to lead his forces back into Missouri.[6]

On April 14 Department of the Missouri commander Rosecrans acquired from the War Department an

Union Major General Alfred Pleasonton (National Park Service collection at Wilson's Creek National Battlefield, historian Connie Langum).

able second-in-command, 39-year-old, Washington D.C. native Major General Alfred Pleasonton. Pleasonton was something Rosecrans was not—a cavalry expert, having in 1863 led the entire cavalry of the Army of the Potomac back in the Eastern Theater. Since early in the war it was cavalry more than infantry that fought the regular and the irregular warfare throughout Missouri, particularly in guerrilla warfare. In fact, the U.S. War Department sent Pleasonton to command General Rosecrans' cavalry forces and use them to hold the state for the Union. Alfred Pleasonton was known for his pride and stubbornness, which got him into trouble in the Army of the Potomac. So, like his new boss, Pleasonton was given another chance "out west" to redeem himself.[7]

General Rosecrans' Changes

General Rosecrans may have sensed that he was placed in command of the Department of the Missouri because, as a sideshow to the rest of the war, the lowly guerrilla war in Missouri had fallen into complacency and neglect. The dirty little war was perhaps drying up under Federal military control in 1863 and drawing little national press attention until Quantrill's startling Lawrence raid in August. That Captain Quantrill somehow patched together from little sub-bands of guerrillas and even passing Confederate recruiting commands a force of about 450 southern raiders and destroyed Lawrence, Kansas, killed well over 150 men and boys, and brought all but a few of his raiders safely back to Missouri shocked the nation. This tragedy implied that the Union military there missed something and certainly underestimated bushwhacker potential for spectacular surprises. General Schofield, Rosecrans' predecessor, took determined action after the Lawrence raid to prevent another such raid from west-central Missouri, but now Rosecrans in early 1864 put his mind to work on the Missouri guerrilla problem.

The new Missouri commander selected a strange topic for his first changes. Just a few days after taking his office, Rosecrans endeavored to stop organized religion from supporting rebellion. It rankled American sensibilities for the U.S. Army to pick on religion to solve its problems, and even President Lincoln had personally intervened earlier in the war when the Union military in Missouri jailed preachers for uttering secessionist rhetoric from the pulpit or closed down churches for refusing to display the U.S. flag.[8] On the other hand, it certainly rankled Union soldiers in Missouri that certain preachers and members of their congregations gave encouragement to the enemy. General Rosecrans was probably aware of these earlier skirmishes between church and state, and that the Yankee military usually lost these contests.

However, as a deeply religious man, Rosecrans certainly recognized the power that preachers and congregations could wield. On February 12, less than two weeks after he took command, Rosecrans' headquarters issued a circular to his troops to report disloyal preachers, especially those of the Methodist Episcopal Church South denomination that had a history of disloyal activity in the state. Further, the circular stated that this denomination's Bishop Edward R. Ames would act upon such complaints and replace disloyal pastors with loyal ones.[9] About three weeks later on March 5 Rosecrans' office issued an order seeking to prevent religious gatherings from "concocting treason or injuring the national cause." This order required "every member of an ecclesiastical convention, or anyone participating in such a convention" in the state must take a prescribed oath of allegiance to the United States.[10] Earlier in the war Rosecrans's superiors all the way to the White House would have quickly censured such blatant interferences of the state in the affairs of religion. War weariness and the growing northern radicalism in early 1864 perhaps played a part in the Union failure to stop these violations of American rights. The official records seem to show no correction of the new Missouri commander for these measures.

Major General Rosecrans also applied his intellect to concocting new tactics to defeat the Missouri guerrillas in early 1864. On February 26 Rosecrans queried his southwest Missouri district chief, Brigadier General John B. Sanborn, about the feasibility of using pack-mule trains to carry supplies for Union operations in the field. His reasoning was that using pack mules instead of wagons would enable troops to avoid the roads and better follow bushwhackers to their remote hideouts.[11] Secondly, the new provisional governor, Willard A. Hall, wrote out of his recent experience as district chief of far northwestern Missouri to Rosecrans on March 11 about the necessity of arming loyal citizens to defend themselves against guerrillas:

> For the last year the robbers were the only class of people who were thoroughly armed, and the people unarmed were at their mercy, and those scoundrels were encouraged in their depredations by the defenseless condition of the people. There is no remedy for this but to

Secretary of War Edwin M. Stanton remained active in Missouri's Union command issues throughout 1864 (Underwood and Clough, eds., *Battles and Leaders of the Civil War*, vol. 2, p. 119).

permit the people to bear arms.... As the ruffians cannot be disarmed, let peaceable citizens have the means of defending thernselves.[12]

Governor Hall was not the only voice for creating civilian posses or militias for self-defense, but his support to the concept added credibility. Rosecrans also campaigned with the War Department starting in March 1864 to employ "disciplined, well-officered troops from other States," "to insure impartiality in quieting local troubles." Secretary of War Edwin M. Stanton may have earlier crystallized his new department chief's thinking on this when he wrote on March 5 "it is a good plan to have troops in your command who are strangers to the troubles there." "Old Rosy" was quick to realize that many of the personal animosities that fed Missouri's brand of guerrilla warfare originated from using Union troops in their home areas where they acted on old quarrels and hatreds. Ironically, knowledge of the local people had been an advantage of the Enrolled Missouri Militia program, but lack of proper training and supervision in many localities failed to prevent atrocities. Some of the Iowa and Indiana troops proved the wisdom of impartial troops from out-of-state earlier in the war and Rosecrans was proven correct later this year by the use of Colorado, Illinois, and Minnesota soldiers in Missouri.[13]

Rosecrans' inspector general, Randolph B. Marcy, made some recommendations March 29 after visiting troops all over the state. He agreed that stationing troops near home was an invitation to depredations. He pointed out that the lack of a realistic prisoner-of-war policy in Missouri and the "no quarter" result had turned guerrilla warfare in the state to a desperate struggle that served no purpose. Unfortunately, this sad state of affairs had been in effect too long to stop it entirely. The inspector general also offered ideas to prevent overworking cavalry troopers and their mounts. Marcy suggested troopers desist from racing and excessive galloping to spare their animals and that mail stages and wagon trains requiring cavalry escorts limit their number of trips between garrisons.[14] In spite of this idea exchange, these innovations mostly addressed the periphery of the problems of fighting a guerrilla war.

On June 28, 1864, General Rosecrans advanced the thinking of self-defense for communities as recommended to him by Governor Hall and others earlier that spring by setting the principle to law. His timing was based primarily on the immediate need to create new forces to resist the bushwhackers, who were back in large numbers in several parts of the state this summer. On that day he instituted Department of the Missouri General Orders Number 107, which called for each county to hold public meetings and organize one or two companies of about 100 men each from the remaining ranks of the existing local Enrolled Missouri Militia units for defense of their own communities. Rosecrans recognized that he did not have enough troops to defend every community from attack by bushwhackers, so this measure empowered the citizens themselves to organize their own defense. Using the authority the state of Missouri granted Rosecrans months before, these new Provisional EMM Companies when activated for nearby emergencies fell under control of the Federals who armed and sustained these troops, although the state paid them. Some local communities had really already been employing citizen posses to deal with isolated guerrillas, and now it was legal. Having local self defense forces on the job also meant that Federal troops could "go on the offensive" against Rebel threats in their areas and use fewer troops to defend towns and villages. Local communities across the state reacted positively to Rosecrans' order, minutes of G.O. Number 107 meetings began appearing in Missouri newspapers by the first days of July 1864, and local communities formed 62 different Provisional Enrolled Missouri Militia Companies across the state. Both citizenry and Union authorities welcomed this new program as a step away from martial law and a step closer to prewar civil law and eventual peace.[15]

Changes by General Brown in Central Missouri During the Late Winter of 1863–1864

Like his new commander, Brigadier General Egbert G. Brown of the District of Central Missouri at Jefferson City initiated changes to the way his soldiers conducted guerrilla warfare during late winter 1864. New York-born Egbert Benson Brown, age 47, was involved in the northern cause in Missouri since the early days in 1861, had commanded the 7th Missouri Infantry Regiment, and lost the use of his arm fighting against Confederate General Marmaduke's southwest Missouri raid in January 1863 at the Battle of Springfield.[16] His district and those nearby had expended much effort during 1863 to tailor forces and tactics to drive out the bushwhackers, but, in spite of some successes, the flexible guerrillas defied all efforts and doggedly remained in west-central Missouri. Captain William C. Quantrill's daring August 1863 Lawrence, Kansas raid was a notable example of such bushwhacker resilience. Of course, Brown's district was part of the operating area of the Quantrill family of guerrilla bands—a daunting force that, if combined, counted three to four hundred riders. Therefore, it was gravely important to the general to evaluate current tactics and seek better ways to counter the Rebels already on the scene and the larger number coming in the spring.

What may have prompted General Brown's thought process was the requirement to reply to a list of probing questions from the Missouri General Assembly also in Jefferson City. The legislators asked him about a list of citizens Brown's subordinate commanders had perfunctorily tried by military tribunal and executed without allowing the accused full due process. Further, the legislators wanted Brown to comment about the depredations that lawless militiamen and even citizen posses committed over the previous months in his district. Just by investigating these incidents, the Missouri General Assembly put the general on notice that even under martial law they were partners with the Federal government in quelling secession and that they would not permit either a military dictatorship or anarchy in his district. Although he sent a detailed reply to the

General Assembly February 10, the process of seeking answers to these queries probably helped General Brown evaluate the problems of 1863 and crystallize his thinking about improvements for 1864.[17]

One of the first areas for improvement Brown sought was what to do with towns in his district, or how should population centers and vital infrastructure like railroads be protected while using scarce troops to take the fight to the guerrillas? Nervous town and village dwellers continually begged for troops to be stationed in their communities to afford protection against guerrilla raiders and to prevent depredations by ill-disciplined Union troops and renegades. Further, construction of the Pacific Railroad progressed through General Brown's district this winter, and that vital line of communication must be protected. The ear-

Union Brigadier General Egbert B. Brown photographed earlier in the war (National Park Service collection at Wilson's Creek National Battlefield, historian Connie Langum).

lier practice of parceling out the available cavalry in small towns throughout the district in effect tied those troops to the protection of all those "burgs" and allowed the bushwhackers to roam the countryside at will, dodging the occasional Yankee patrol. Worse yet, the guerrillas' superior intelligence network enabled the southerners to mass enough force on occasion to harass or even defeat a single detachment and then retire before General Brown could send reinforcements to help. In essence, the goal should be to defeat the guerrillas where they could be found with offense and avoid the defensive posture inherent in protecting population centers and infrastructure.

General Brown's solution to the issue of protecting towns and railroads while simultaneously "carrying the fight to the enemy" was in several parts. One of his regimental commanders, Colonel James H. Ford of the newly arrived 2nd Colorado Cavalry, on February 13 suggested using infantry to guard towns and vital infrastructure, leaving the cavalry to do what cavalry does best—use their inherent mobility and shock action to find and chase the guerrillas. Brown appreciated the suggestion and sent several companies of the newly arrived 9th Minnesota Infantry Regiment to Warrensburg, Johnson County, to carry out the mission of guarding the town and railroad construction underway nearby.[18] The next day General Brown ordered towns and villages in his district to provide their own protection by organizing citizen guards which he would arm.[19]

General Brown also sought to retain the offensive on his side and place the Rebels on the defensive. The general realized that the key to protecting populated places from guerrillas was to keep tracking and attacking the bushwhackers so that they would be too busy for town raiding. He ordered troops in the Kansas City sub-district to keep "constantly on the move," particularly in known guerrilla sanctuary areas, patrolling daily by horse and even with foot patrols using "citizen guards and scouts" to navigate heavily vegetated areas and even footpaths.[20]

General Brown also realized that many rural residents of the border region were more sympathetic to the Rebels because the Rebels lived among them and defended them against the dreaded Kansas Jayhawker raiders. He knew that he would have to summon the rural people back into the fold of civil law and show them that their Federal government could function in their defense. Therefore, he ordered Colonel Ford to help refugees living in the towns to resettle the rural neighborhoods and seek to restore civil law, while being cognizant of "bitterness and personal hatreds." Further, he ordered Colonel Ford to help "allay passions that have grown out of border warfare" by working closely with Kansas troops. Perhaps Brown's thinking on this point was that Kansas troops would be less likely to commit depredations against civilians if Missouri troops were close by.[21] Perhaps, that is partly why on February 16 General Brown moved his district headquarters closer to the border from Jefferson City to Warrensburg.[22]

The breaking up of the Missouri River ice after February 6 may also have reminded General Brown how throughout 1863 guerrillas attacked Missouri River shipping. On February 14 he ordered that all steamboats navigating the Missouri River bulletproof their pilot houses and engine rooms. Further, he empowered his subordinate commanders of the posts along the Missouri River at Jefferson City, Lexington, and Kansas City to enforce this order.[23]

The overall aim of General Brown's changes was to take the Union troops in his district off the defensive and force the bushwhackers to look more to defend themselves. He gambled that Kansas troops would stop their depredations against Missouri residents if Missouri soldiers worked closer with them. He sought to deny guerrillas their areas of sanctuary, and to eventually turn the rural inhabitants against the "knights of the bush." Brown's ideas of arming loyal civilians and empowering them in their own defense against guerrillas was premature, but would later be implemented with success. He also gambled that keeping guerrillas on the defensive and moving would keep them from raiding populated places and force them out in the open where veteran Federal cavalry could fight them on more favorable terms. This gamble would not always work, but the principle had merit. General Brown also gambled that he could implement these improvements before the bulk of the bushwhackers returned to this area from the South this spring. Events would prove that Brown was not an effective gambler.

"Price's Army Is Coming"

The year 1864 seemed to be the culmination of the fervent desire of Missouri southerners, civilian and military, to finally see General Sterling "Old Pap" Price return with his army to rescue the Show-Me State from the Yankees. Southerners expressed this hope since Federals expelled Price and his army from southwest Missouri in early 1862. A Union soldier writing to a St. Louis newspaper back in January 27, 1862, learned this from disgruntled southern sympathizers in Moniteau County, Missouri and wrote "some deluded rebels have faith in the 'second advent' of Price's victories," referring to Price's 1861 battle accomplishments at Wilson's Creek and Lexington.[24] Colonel Jo Shelby's celebrated Missouri raid just the previous October, as it cut through the Union militia deep into the heart of the state and then cut its way back south to Arkansas, proved that a large, fast-moving, well-led, trained southern force could possibly beat the Union troops garrisoning Missouri. General Price himself encouraged the hope of southern Missourians when he wrote to two Confederate colonels January 3,1864, who were deep behind Yankee lines recruiting southern men secretly into Confederate service:

> I am glad to believe that the Southern people of Missouri are, as you state, consistent in their loyalty to the Confederacy, and anxious for an opportunity to take up arms in its support.... If those Missourians who still remain at home would but emulate the example of those gallant men who have fought so gloriously for the independence of Missouri.... If they, instead of waiting until the Confederate States can send into the State an army able to maintain itself there, would manfully braving every danger and bidding farewell to ease and selfish indulgence, come to this army and place themselves by the side of their brave kindred and neighbors here, the Confederacy would soon send into Missouri an army capable of maintaining itself there for the rest of the war.[25]

General Price was like other Missourians in the Confederate army west of the Mississippi River who kept in touch with their friends and families via a secret mail network throughout the war. Knowledge that such a secret mail existed frustrated the Federals who occasionally captured the secret couriers but could never eradicate the entire network. In April 1863 Brigadier General James G. Blunt of Kansas Union troops complained of this to his commander: "a regular correspondence by rebel mail is carried on between here and the rebel army."[26] The southern guerrillas in Missouri benefited from the secret mail, too, as it kept them in touch with the regular Confederate military. In late 1864 Union Colonel John F. Phillips bemoaned this practice: "These guerrillas beyond all question are recognized by and are in constant communication with the trans-Mississippi rebel army. They are the mediums of communication through which these families correspond with their friends South."[27]

The clandestine southern correspondence between Missourians at home and in the Confederate army kept lit the flickering candle of hope that someday General Price would bring back his army and seize Missouri from the Yankees. In late March 1864 Union General Odon Guitar poetically noted these rumors that seemed to grow as the warm weather of spring approached: "The season for sensation reports is near at hand; it comes with the swelling buds and opening blossoms, and on every breeze freighted with their rich fragrance will be borne rumors of untold thousands rallying to the clansman's call."[28]

Just a few days later on April 3 Lieutenant Colonel Francis T. Russell at Columbia wrote with concern to General Rosecrans about the rumors that had all the southern folk in his area excited:

> All sort of stories are set afloat of rebel prospects, invasions, and that Price is coming, and etc. Sympathizers look and act bolder and have increased confidence.... [It] excites serious fears. To my mind it is clear that there is some mischief coming, although I cannot make it out. They are counting on an invasion or an insurrection. So very marked is the change that it is founded on something generally known to them in which they confide.[29]

Brigadier General Fisk on May 1 wrote to Rosecrans a shorter version of this Federal worry by saying "we must expect and prepare for trouble. Rebellion in Missouri is not dead, but sleepeth."[30] Major General Rosecrans himself later summed up this surge in secessionist confidence:

> Rebel agents, amnesty oath-takers, recruits, sympathizers ... and traitors of every hue and stripe had warmed into life at the approach of the great invasion. Women's fingers were busy making clothes for rebel soldiers out of goods plundered by the guerrillas; women's tongues were busy telling Union neighbors "their time was now coming."[31]

Indeed, in the spring of 1864 actual preparations for such an invasion were underway in the Confederate army in Arkansas, although the actual raid would not begin until September. General Price's superior, Lieutenant General Edmund Kirby Smith, on May 19 directed Price to begin gathering supplies and intelligence preparatory for his great endeavor back to Missouri.[32] In June "Old Pap" sent trusted officers back into forbidden Missouri to obtain this intelligence, begin to raise recruits, and spread the word of what was coming.[33]

The rumors, preparations, and especially the fervent hope combined to make guerrilla warfare in Missouri throughout spring, summer and fall of 1864 a growing crescendo attacking the Union troops and support network to prepare for the long-expected return of General Price and his army. In many ways, this made 1864 perhaps the most desperate year of the guerrilla war here.

Six

Spring 1864 in Southeast Missouri

Spring 1864 in the southeast quadrant of Missouri saw guerrilla and anti-guerrilla activity across the entire region. Less affected by cold weather than other parts of the state in the winter, the secret warfare here grew in intensity and numbers this spring season. In the swampy "bootheel" appendage into Arkansas large Union forces swept through bogs chasing local bushwhackers, but had difficulty stopping Sam Hildebrand, Vernon Campbell, and Nathan Bolin as their bands openly defied Federal force. Union cavalry stationed in Mississippi County sent patrols into the swamps and this season began to take a toll on local Rebels who began to assert themselves here in the winter. The war was much the same in the hill country north of the "bootheel," too. Sam Hildebrand rode through this area every few weeks, but like local guerrilla chief Francis Valle, he moved carefully and was always on the watch for Federals. Union cavalry this spring sent a large patrol across the Mississippi River to the town of Prairie du Rocher in Illinois where they surprised and defeated John Highley's Missouri band and killed him. In the hilly eastern Ozarks region west of this area both the Union 3rd Cavalry MSM and Confederate Colonel Tim Reeves kept spies and scouts out all the time looking to catch each other in a weak moment. Both sides would surge forward if the reports were favorable, but neither could bring the other to a final defeat. The south-central Missouri area west of this was quiet for a change this spring as Confederate Colonel Thomas R. Freeman evidently pulled his men back into northern Arkansas to refit and avoid a large Federal expedition in March. An exception was Phelps County bushwhacker chief Bill Wilson who began to operate this spring on home ground familiar to him. In late spring several guerrilla bands intent on riding through Federal lines back to their own operating areas infiltrated through southeast Missouri, occasionally skirmishing with Union patrols as they rode steadily back to the north with local militia hunting for them. The quiet guerrilla war in the St. Louis region continued with some secret southern operations hiding from Federal detectives, while Confederate prisoners of war continued to escape in small numbers from the prisons there.

"Bootheel" Actions During March–May 1864

Although the swampy "bootheel" appendage of southeast Missouri that jutted into Arkansas was quiet during the winter of 1863-1864, Rebel guerrillas made it come alive again during the following spring. The "bootheel" is delineated by Arkansas to the south; the St. Francis River on the west; the Mississippi River on the east; and the

Swamp of southeast Missouri at night (Chancey R. Barns, ed., *Switzler's Illustrated History of Missouri*, 1877, p. 186).

wooded hill country of Wayne, Bollinger, and Cape Girardeau Counties to the north. From those hills flow the Castor and Whitewater Rivers that join in New Madrid County to form the Little River which flows on south into Arkansas between the St. Francis and Mississippi Rivers. These several rivers help to feed the extensive swamps that covered this lowland area, which were drained and turned into productive cropland several years after the war. This boot-heel shaped appendage of Missouri consists of Dunklin, Pemiscot, New Madrid, Stoddard, Scott, and Mississippi Counties, which had large populations of southern sympathy during the war. Many men of these families joined regular Confederate forces while a number of them also fought their war as irregulars or bushwhackers. This spring the bands of Vernon Campbell in Mississippi County, Bulge Powell in Pemiscot County, and Nathan Bolin in Dunklin County, along with the passing raiding band of Sam Hildebrand fought a determined guerrilla war to assert to the Federals that they had a fight on their hands in this corner of Missouri.

Campbell's Band Victimizes Mississippi County Resident During March

In James Bayou Township of south Mississippi County March 3 guerrilla leader Vernon Campbell with 8 other bushwhackers rode up to 63-year-old Judge Haly W. Molder's yard, ordered the elderly jurist to surrender, and shot him dead with 27 bullets. The assassins then rifled the house taking firearms and money and scattered the dead man's papers. Campbell's band then made two other men present swear not to divulge the guerrillas' identity to authorities under penalty of death and rode off. Nearby, the band stopped at John Claycomb's house and robbed him of $30 and "all his clothes," as the local newspaper reported.[1] About three weeks later on March 22 four bushwhackers, perhaps of the same band, rode into the Molder yard and demanded Judge Molder's widow give them money. When she hesitated, the quartet stripped off the woman's outer clothing and took $100 that the grieving widow had hidden in her stocking. They then took a mule and left.[2] Obviously, the war in Mississippi County had grown personal.

Hildebrand Attacks Small Groups of Yankees in Scott County Area During March

Also in March 1864, the vengeful guerrilla Sam Hildebrand with fifteen riders traveled through the "bootheel," too, according to the memoir he wrote just after the war. From his base usually in Greene County, Arkansas, Hildebrand with a small number of men often traveled through this region on his way back to his familiar hill country haunts further to the north. His memoir claimed he captured and hanged nine Federal soldiers somewhere near Whitewater River in either Scott or Cape Girardeau County, although neither Union military records nor regional newspapers back his claim. The guerrilla referred to these Federals as "McNeal's men," and, indeed, the 2nd Cavalry MSM which Brigadier General John McNeil had commanded earlier in the war was stationed in several nearby garrisons. Hildebrand also wrote that near Benton, central Scott County, he captured five more Union troops but released four and only killed one of them. Hildebrand's memoir indicated he occasionally released captive Yankees if they came from southern families or seemed sympathetic to the plight of southern people of this region.[3]

The Union forces were not totally inactive during this time. A small patrol of 2nd Cavalry MSM under Captain Samuel Shibley sent out from the Bloomfield, Stoddard County, garrison probably in the same county on April 1 rode onto three guerrillas "in the act of robbing a Union man's house." The patrol killed one of the bushwhackers and captured the others. The prisoners stated they were part of Confederate Colonel Solomon G. Kitchen's command, and that one of them was from Douglas County, Missouri, many miles to the west, and the other was from Illinois.[4]

Major Rabb's "Bootheel" Expedition in Early April

At the nearby Union base at New Madrid, New Madrid County, the commander, Major John W. Rabb, 2nd Missouri Light Artillery Regiment, sought a way to stop these depredations in the "bootheel." He waited impatiently to take the field until early April because the post's cavalry, three companies of 1st Missouri Cavalry Regiment, were away on furlough as reward for re-enlisting. The remainder of his New Madrid garrison was mostly artillerymen of his regiment, generally inexperienced in guerrilla warfare—as events would prove. When the furloughed troopers returned, Major Rabb was disappointed to discover that their mounts were worn out, but he sent all three companies to the field anyway. The major's orders to the cavalry senior officer, Captain Valentine Preutt, were to ride at their own speed to see what guerrillas they could find in the "bootheel," while Major Rabb and a force of his artillerymen would deploy by river steamer to the northeast corner of Arkansas and march north on foot toward the cavalry. Captain Preuitt and his men rode their tired horses through Pemiscot and Dunklin Counties killing thirteen Rebels, capturing five others, and wounding more, at the loss of three troopers slightly wounded. Some of the guerrillas they encountered belonged to Bulge Powell's band. This cavalry portion of the expedition was the successful part.[5]

The part of the expedition executed by Major Rabb and his cannoneers in the northeast corner of Arkansas was not as successful. Although Rabb had no horses he placed 200 of his artillerymen aboard the steamer *Silver Moon* April 5 and deployed them on foot at two places in Mississippi County, Arkansas, south of Pemiscot County to surprise whatever Rebels were in the area. The problem with this plan is that these Federals were on foot while area Rebels were generally mounted, so the southerners recovered from their surprise quickly and prepared one of their own. One party of 100

Union soldiers on foot sweep through swampland looking for Rebels (Charles C. Coffin, *Freedom Triumphant*, 1890, p. 317).

artillerymen under Captain William C. F. Montgomery deployed from the river steamer just south of the Missouri border and had no real difficulty, but Major Rabb and the other 100 cannoneers ran into trouble in heavily wooded swampland north of Osceola, Arkansas. Much of the reason was that these artillerymen were used to manning the large cannons at the fortifications at New Madrid, and probably had not experienced field operations in some time. Major Rabb's party killed five or six mounted Rebels riding along a road April 7. That night this group camped near a house in the swamp even though the occupants told them they were southerners and their son was in the guerrillas. The man of the house also obligingly warned Rabb that area bushwhackers would attack the Yankees at daylight, but his timing was off. At two o'clock that morning of April 8 Rebel irregulars infiltrated past the sentries and Major Rabb awoke facing a southern officer armed with a shotgun who quietly demanded the surrender of his force. Rabb instead pulled his revolver and the two officers fired upon each other, initiating a general melee in the darkness. Rabb afterward could not estimate Rebel casualties, since the guerrillas recovered their dead and wounded from the scene, but his own included a lieutenant killed outright and three mortally wounded, plus six other wounded. The next day Major Rabb's battered group had to pack the wounded several miles through the swamp on foot to the agreed rendezvous with the steamer *Darling* which took Rabb's thoroughly chastened artillerymen back up the Mississippi River to New Madrid.[6]

MSM and EMM Combine to Pursue Campbell's Band in Mississippi County

Major Rabb's expedition south of New Madrid County did nothing to stop the guerrillas in Mississippi County, so Union troops of the 2nd Cavalry MSM and 79th Enrolled Missouri Militia in that area took matters in their own hands between April 14 and 20. Local militiamen of Colonel Henry J. Deal's 79th used their knowledge of the area and began patrolling through the swamps, killing or wounding one or two guerrillas at a time in two or three actions. Local bushwhackers were confident that the swamp was their sure refuge, and had grown careless. Men of Captain James A. Ewing's and First Lieutenant Robert C. Calvert's Company I, 2nd Cavalry MSM stationed in Charleston noticed that the EMM were having success and they volunteered first on foot patrols into the bogs and later on horseback. They also began to shoot at fleeing guerrillas. The culmination of these actions took place April 20 when the MSM and the EMM working together tracked eleven bushwhackers to a house and killed six of them before the remainder fled. The combined Union forces failed to catch leader Vernon Campbell, but they did manage to kill at least fourteen guerrillas in the several days' effort, which did lessen bushwhacker activity in the county.[7]

Troopers Pursue Rebels Across Stoddard County in Early May

Twenty unidentified, mounted southerners rode past the Stoddard County seat of Bloomfield with its Union garrison about three in the morning of May 6 heading south, probably to rejoin Confederate forces in Arkansas. The Rebels were hoping to evade Yankee detection by riding past in the dark, but Lieutenant Harvey M. Toney and his patrol of 2nd Cavalry MSM from the Bloomfield station pursued for 25 miles and killed two of the riders, probably in north Dunklin County or west New Madrid County. The dead men were Private Harrison Whitson of the Confederate 5th Missouri Cavalry from St. Luke, Stoddard County, and Private Hollas Saddler of the Confederate 2nd Missouri Infantry from Cape Girardeau County. One of the two was carrying in his pocket a paper written by the New Madrid Union garrison in December testifying that this southerner had taken oath not to bear arms against the United States. Colonel John B. Rogers, commander of the 2nd Cavalry MSM at Cape Girardeau, mentioning the dead man's paper in his report, wryly commented that "as the bullet missed the pocket it failed to protect him."[8]

Bolin and Union Cavalry Play Cat and Mouse in May

These twenty riders from May 6 may have been on their way to join Nathan Bolin's guerrilla band, for Bolin and a reported fifty Rebels crossed the St. Francis River from Arkansas into south Dunklin County south of Hornersville on May 10 to raid in the "bootheel." Perhaps Nathan desired to have revenge for his brother John's lynching by a mob in Cape Girardeau February 5 while being held there as a prisoner of war. Colonel Rogers at Cape Girardeau ordered troops of his regiment from Charleston and Bloomfield to find and destroy this new threat, but Bolin adroitly hid his men in the swamps until the Federals grew tired of searching and returned to base. On May 16 Colonel Rogers heard that part of Bolin's band was at Sikeston, south Scott County, and directed troops from the same two garrisons to that vicinity, but the guerrillas once again hid themselves until the troopers of 2nd Cavalry MSM tired of searching and headed back. The cavalry had hardly left when Bolin put his men back into motion, rode to the village of Hamburg in north Scott County, and raided this center of northern sympathy. The raiders burned the Catholic Church and some other buildings, took some booty, and promptly returned to hiding in the swamps. Naturally, the Union cavalry could find no trace of Bolin's band in the dense vegetation around Hamburg. It is difficult to determine what Nathan Bolin's men did next, but they definitely remained in hiding and may have split into two groups. The Confederates realized that the Union Colonel Rogers at Cape Girardeau was in command of this area, and they may have attempted to isolate him from his outlying posts by severing the telegraph lines near his headquarters. Bushwhackers cut the line near Charleston, Mississippi County in late May, passed the word that "they intended to keep it down." Federals found and killed three guerrillas May 26 who had cut the telegraph line near the Cape"—one of them after the troopers chased him into the swamp through water three feet deep. It appears Bolin took part of his band back across the Arkansas border about this time.

On May 28 a patrol of the 2nd Cavalry MSM from Bloomfield killed a Rebel Captain Watson, perhaps of Bolin's band, at Gum Slough in Dunklin or Pemiscot County. Not far away that same day observers reported seeing Nathan Bolin with about twenty riders on Horse Island, near the Arkansas border. Based on this raid's seemingly limited objectives, and the manner in which Bolin allowed his men to be seen and then skillfully hid, this appears to have been a nuisance raid intended perhaps to demonstrate guerrilla superiority of will and skill over the Yankee cavalry.[9]

Spring 1864 Actions in the Hills North of the "Bootheel": Valle, Highley, Hildebrand, and a Federal Raid into Illinois

The hilly region north of the "bootheel" and south of the St. Louis area, had been relatively quiet since the previous summer, but guerrilla war reappeared here in spring of 1864. This is the area covered by Cape Girardeau, Bollinger, Madison, Perry, Ste. Genevieve, St. Francois, Washington, and Jefferson Counties that was home to a population full of southerners but was also controlled by large numbers of determined militiamen of the controversial EMM program. The Federals were mindful of the defense of the Iron Mountain Railroad and holding the Mississippi River safe for their shipping, so they also kept active duty regular cavalry in a few posts throughout this area.

Valle Raids a Riverboat Near Perry County on 12 March

Francis Valle of Perry County had been active in the secessionist movement since 1861 when he was active in the southern Missouri State Guard, was captured and imprisoned in 1862, and returned briefly to his home region in March 1864 to conduct guerrilla operations once again. He was definitely in the area and was perhaps the leader of a band of guerrillas from the Perry County area and Illinois who attacked the river steamer identified as the *C. E. Hillman* on the Mississippi River forty miles north of Cape Girardeau March 12. The Cape Girardeau commander, Colonel John B. Rogers, succinctly stated what happened: "A party of thieves from Missouri crossed the river about 40 miles above here and robbed a trading-boat, and killed one man and unmercifully abused women and children. There were joined by a band of thieves from on the other side, who assisted in the outrage." Colonel Rogers begged for a chance to cross into Illinois and root out the guerrillas there, but, Illinois was a Union state with its own law enforcement ability and nothing came of his request.[10]

Unidentified Guerrillas Raid Caledonia on 19 March

During the evening of March 19 a band of 15 to 20 unidentified "knights of the bush" broke into a store in Caledonia, southeast Washington County, and carried away goods worth about $1300. Some of the burglars may have had families in the region as the stolen merchandise included such unlikely items as children's shoes and sewing thimbles. Sam Hildebrand and the men who rode with him were known to rob isolated country stores in this area throughout the war, but Hildebrand's memoirs written just after the war do not indicate his band reached this far north during their March 1864 expedition in southeast Missouri.[11]

Valle Band Members Scout Saint Genevieve for Possible Raid

Northern sympathizer John H. Kenner from the Rozier Mills area near the Ste. Genevieve/Perry County line complained to Union military authorities that Francis

Valle with about 25 guerrillas during the last days of March stole horses from northerners, threatened them, and forced some to swear oaths to the Confederacy. Kenner also told the Union military that residents of the county seat of Saint Genevieve recognized individual members of Valle's gang looking around the town. Francis Valle of Perryville, Perry County, was bold enough to return to his home area even for a brief time, probably to recruit for the Confederate army.[12]

Union 3rd Cavalry MSM Invades Illinois at Prairie du Rocher

It is a serious matter for the militia of one loyal state to invade the territory of another, but the Union authorities of southeast Missouri authorized just such a raid from Missouri into Illinois in early April 1864. For months their concern had been growing about Missouri guerrillas seeking sanctuary among residents of southern sympathy in Illinois and merchants there selling war materials with little regard for their intended use. Union troops learned that local guerrillas led by John Highley of St. Francois County, Missouri were using the Illinois village of Prairie du Rocher, Randolph County, as a base. The area Union command sent Captain Henry B. Milks and a raiding party from his Company H, 3rd Cavalry MSM from their Farmington, St. Francois County, garrison by boat across the Mississippi River to the Illinois village on April 6. Captain Milks briefed his men on the delicacy of their operation and warned them emphatically not to harm the persons or property of the Illinois citizens unless absolutely necessary. As Milks and his troopers charged into Prairie du Rocher bushwhackers in some buildings fired upon them and then fled to the river bluff behind the town. The cavalry pursued as guerrillas on top of the bluffs sniped at them. In the fight three guerrillas died, including leader John Highley, and one Union trooper was badly wounded. Captain Milks' men seized some guerrilla firearms from homes they had been using in the village and commandeered a buggy to bring the wounded trooper back to the boat. After the raid, village men sent a letter to the Union leadership complaining that the Missouri militia stole several items in the village. Captain Milks was temporarily arrested, perhaps to mollify outraged Illinois leaders, but was released after evidence revealed the charges against the raiders were fabricated by men known to be sympathetic to the southern cause. During the Prairie du Rocher raid, Milks and his troopers captured a bushwhacker named Buck Perkins and brought him back to Farmington for questioning. At the Union provost marshal's office there April 9 a member of the 33rd Enrolled Missouri Militia pulled out a pistol and murdered the unarmed prisoner, evidently without redress.[13]

An Ambitious Hildebrand Raid Through at Least Six Counties in late May

In his autobiography written soon after the war Sam Hildebrand recounted an expedition he took with nine other guerrillas in late May 1864. Sam's version said his small band rode through Stoddard, Scott, Bollinger, St. Francois, Washington, and Cape Girardeau Counties on this ambitious patrol festooned with lots of escapades. Sadly, few of the encounters Hildebrand remembered can be verified with other sources. Early in this expedition he captured a German immigrant in the Union service whose broken English presented an obstacle to communication which the guerrillas overcame by killing the man. Hildebrand operated alone in the dense brush of Pike Run in north St. Francois County attempting to assassinate certain northern militiamen known for cruelty to southerners. Sam, a noted marksman, was unable to get a clear shot from his hiding places and gave up the effort after several attempts. He also wrote how on this patrol his band robbed the store of F. E. Abrret, who he called "Albright," near Potosi in southeast Washington County. In his narrative Hildebrand described how he robbed this store over a year before, so it must have been a worthwhile endeavor for him to repeat it. On the last part of his expedition in the Cape Girardeau County area Sam described how he captured and then released some troopers of Colonel John L. Beverage's regiment, the 17th Illinois Cavalry. Hildebrand may have confused the chronology of his escapades on this point, since this regiment's war record indicates it did not serve in this part of Missouri until 1865. On May 25 unidentified bushwhackers did capture and release two Union dispatch riders in either south Iron County or the northwest corner of Wayne County, as described in the next section, and this may very well have been Hildebrand.[14]

Colonel Reeves Versus 3rd Cavalry MSM in the Eastern Ozark Hill Country During Spring 1864

The rugged Ozark hills in Ripley, Oregon, Carter, Reynolds, Iron, Butler, and Wayne Counties during March through May of 1864 seemed to be the personal battleground between the veterans of Confederate Colonel Timothy Reeves' southern irregulars and several companies of the Union 3rd Cavalry Missouri State Militia. Neither side could summon enough combat power at the decisive time and place to push the other out of the heavily wooded hills of this region for long, so most of the actions here this spring were the parried thrusts one side or the other made looking to catch the other in a weak moment. This spring the troopers of the 3rd (which were re-designated from the 10th Cavalry MSM earlier in the war) were stationed at the main Union base for this region at Pilot Knob in Iron County and also at smaller one-company garrisons at Patterson, Wayne County; Centerville, Reynolds County; Arcadia, Iron County as well as two companies further to the east.[15] The Confederate irregulars of Colonel Reeves primarily based in well hidden camps in the marshland of Ripley and Butler Counties. They were always ready under pressure to scoot south into Arkansas during heavy Yankee expeditions, and then ride back into this hilly region as the Union efforts waned. In this manner the Rebels operated as a mobile force never totally dependent upon an established base. Guerrilla scouts remained active most of the time looking for Union vulnerabilities, and with short notice, area Rebels could gather for a sudden strike against an isolated patrol or small garrison and then fade back into the hills before Federals could pursue.

Federals Learn of Combined Rebel Force in Oregon County in Mid-March

The Union cavalry's intelligence network, if it could be dignified with such a name, was inferior to that of the southerners, and its exaggerations and errors produced a level of constant paranoia to the Union bases isolated from each other in the deep woods. A frantic report from Lieutenant Colonel John N. Herder, newly commanding at Pilot Knob, to his regional commander in St. Louis, Brigadier General Clinton B. Fisk, on March 14, 1864, is typical both of exaggerated claims about Confederate strength and actions and exasperation with the lack of reliable intelligence:

> Captain Johns [Abijah Johns of 3rd Cavalry MSM], at Patterson, telegraphs Freeman [Colonel Thomas R.]. Crandall [Colonel Lee], Dick Boyce [Boze], and Barnes [Charles] are at Eleven Points River, Oregon County, robbing and burning; their men are scattered

all through that country in small gangs. Colonel Joslyn [John J. of 1st Missouri Cavalry], just returned from below, tells me, from an interview with Captain Johns, that these banditti are at least 500 to 600 strong, and becoming troublesome, killing Union men, women, and even children without discrimination. Something ought to be done speedily. Not knowing yet how far my command extends, I did not know whether I could operate against them and asked your advice.[16]

Freeman and Crandall were the commanders of irregular regiments that operated primarily in south-central Missouri and frequently bivouacked in Oregon and Shannon Counties. Dick Boze seems to have been a subordinate to Colonel Freeman and is somewhat of a legend in south-central Missouri; Charles Barnes seems to have been a subordinate of Colonel Tim Reeves, but both men often conducted independent operations. It is entirely possible that not all of these commands and personalities were actually present in this area at this time. The report-writer himself, Lieutenant Colonel John N. Herder, of the 1st Infantry MSM, was new as commander of the large Union base at Pilot Knob, since the previous one, Colonel Richard G. Woodson of the 3rd Cavalry MSM, was dismissed from the service February 27. Being new in this position and having to take over from a predecessor who left suddenly could partly explain the uncertainty apparent in his March 14 letter.[17]

In the truth offered by hindsight, the Confederates in question numbered only a

Hunger was an unwelcome visitor to homes across Missouri during the war ("The Effect of the Rebellion on the Homes of Virginia," *Harper's Weekly*, New York, 24 December 1864, p. 824).

fraction of the "500 to 600"—perhaps as few as 100—and they were probably commandeering foodstuffs and forage from area farms in that vicinity. They may have killed a farmer or two who refused their demands or resisted conscription into their ranks, and probably burned a few homes of families whose men were away serving in Union ranks. The purpose of such burning was to force people of northern sympathy to leave the countryside for larger towns and thereby reduce the danger of informants in the Rebels' favorite base areas. There were very few documented cases of Confederate combatants, regular or guerrilla, killing women or even children in Missouri during the war, but the emotional strain of a brutal civil war between two sides of the same nation fed such inflammatory statements. Women and children of men away serving in both armies died on isolated farms during the war, because raiding by both sides of the food stocks of such families left them susceptible to starvation and disease.

Wilson's March Cavalry Expedition Through Five South-Central Missouri Counties

General Fisk's reply March 15 to Lieutenant Colonel Herder's frantic report reminded the nervous Pilot Knob commander that Major James Wilson's cavalry expedition leaving Pilot Knob the next day would clarify this situation and hopefully chase away the Rebels, too. Indeed, Major Wilson's large patrol of 100 troopers of 3rd Cavalry MSM in nine days between March 16 and 25 did not disappoint. Wilson led the force through Reynolds and Oregon Counties into Arkansas almost to Pocahontas, then returned to base via Ripley, Carter, and Wayne Counties. On March 18 a side patrol of 20 troopers at Spring Creek probably in Oregon County had a fire-fight with 8 or 10 Rebels in an old house. The southerners held their fire until the patrol was close to the building, then fired a volley which killed one trooper and wounded another before escaping out the back to scramble out of reach down a bluff. The ambushers left their horses behind to effect their escape. On March 20 the Union force's advance fought two skirmishes. In the first, they found and charged a Rebel conscripting party killing eight, mortally wounding another, and capturing several southerners at no northern loss. That same afternoon the advance guard shot and killed a man running from a house at their approach. Near Pocahontas March 22 the expedition's advance exchanged volleys with a Confederate Captain Payton and his band of guerrillas then charged them killing eleven and pursued the rest in a horserace over several miles before they dispersed. In all the large patrol rode over 300 miles, killed 21 Rebels, and captured eleven others at the loss of one Federal killed and one wounded. Major Wilson determined that the Rebels were dispersed in several small groups over Oregon County under Captains Payton, Long, and [George] Evans, while larger southern units were several miles south well inside Arkansas. He also discovered that Colonel Reeves with about ninety riders was then fifteen miles southeast of Pocahontas. Major James Wilson was one of the most aggressive Federal officers of southeast Missouri, and this trait would result in his death later in the year.[18]

Johns' 3rd Cavalry MSM Strikes Out at Reeves' Rebels in Wayne County Area

Wilson's ambitious patrol in March seemed to bring peace to these hills for some weeks until Colonel Tim Reeves led his 90 or 100 irregulars north on a surge in early May. Captain Abijah Johns, the commander of the small Patterson, Wayne County, garrison, led 50 troopers of his Company A of 3rd Cavalry MSM out to find Colonel

Reeves' men Sunday May 8. Somewhere in the hills Johns' command found and evidently surprised the wily Baptist preacher's band, based on the casualty figures from the fight. Captain Johns afterward reported his men killed twelve Rebels at the loss of one of his noncommissioned officers killed and several Union horses dead.[19]

Large Two-Pronged Union Expedition into Arkansas in Mid-May

The regional Union command decided that a bigger push now against the weakened force of Confederates would help chase them back into Arkansas, so they devised a two-prong expedition from Pilot Knob and Patterson. Captain Johns and much of his Company A, 3rd Cavalry MSM rode south from Patterson between May 16 and 25 while Captain Herman J. Huiskamp with 46 troopers of the 6th Missouri Cavalry rode south from Pilot Knob between May 10 and 25. Captain Johns' command fired upon seven men across the Black River about May 17, then after crossing the river found and destroyed a cache of Confederate medicines that would be worth thousands of dollars on the commercial markets. On May 18 troopers of the 3rd Cavalry MSM in Cache Swamp exchanged shots with elusive but determined Rebel skirmishers, killing two and wounding one, then captured a secret Confederate mail carrier and his mail. That night at Gainesville, Arkansas, Captain Huiskamp's Pilot Knob patrol met and merged with Captain Johns' men. Later that same night guerrillas severely wounded Captain Johns with a shot that shattered his left arm and another that slightly wounded his hip. The officers of the now-combined force noted that guerrillas evidently of Colonel Reeves' and Colonel Solomon G. Kitchen's commands were numerous in the Gainesville area, but did not attempt any organized resistance against the Federal expedition. Colonel Kitchen prewar was a Stoddard County, Missouri judge and state senator. As the horses and troopers were worn down and hungry from the expedition and Captain Johns needed medical attention, the two parts of the expedition re-entered Missouri through Stoddard County and rode back to their respective posts by May 25.[20]

Just as the two parts of this Federal expedition arrived back at Patterson and Pilot Knob, unidentified guerrillas on May 25 captured two Union troopers on horseback carrying dispatches between the two posts in either south Iron County or the northwest corner of Wayne County. The bushwhackers took the troopers' horses and weapons, but released the captives to find their way to the nearest garrison on foot. One of the few guerrilla chiefs in southeast Missouri known to release enlisted Union captives was the seemingly unconquerable Sam Hildebrand, and, indeed, in his memoir Hildebrand told of releasing captive Union cavalrymen about this time in the region.[21]

Gun Duel Between Two EMMs and Two Guerrillas in Iron County in Late May

Perhaps it was a couple of Sam Hildebrand's guerrillas that got into a gun battle with two truculent militiamen within a few miles of Pilot Knob also about May 25. David Meloy of the 47th Enrolled Missouri Militia from Farmington, St. Francois County, and Joseph Armstead of the 54th Enrolled Missouri Militia from near St. Clair in central Franklin County were riding together when attacked by two mounted bushwhackers. Meloy and Armstead were armed with shotguns while the southerners had two revolvers each. The militiamen prevailed when they badly wounded one of the guerrillas as his partner escaped into the brush. Colonel John F. Tyler, commanding at Pilot Knob, sent a patrol to the site that night which captured the two guerrillas' horses. Tyler enthusiastically wrote about this incident: "Mr. Meloy and Mr. Armistead deserve great credit for their promptness and courage in the matter ... if the Union men would defend themselves as these have done, stealing would soon die out in my command."[22]

Spring 1864 Actions in South-Central Missouri Involving Bill Wilson, Dick Kitchen, and Others

South-central Missouri, scene of some of intense guerrilla warfare in 1863 and through the winter in early 1864, was strangely quiet during the spring of 1864. The chief Confederate commander here, Colonel Thomas Roe Freeman of Phelps and Crawford Counties, and his regiment of irregulars were pushed south into Arkansas partly by Major James Wilson's aggressive expedition of 100 troopers of 3rd Cavalry MSM through Reynolds, Carter, Oregon, and Ripley Counties in the last two weeks of March 1864, as described earlier. Freeman may also have wanted to retire further south to rest and refit his battered command, members of which had been so hungry as to steal food from civilians during operations in Shannon, Phelps, and Pulaski Counties in February. Besides, his mounted men had been actively fighting Yankee patrols in this area for weeks this winter, and probably needed a respite. The Lebanon garrison sent a patrol of Union 8th Cavalry MSM southeast through Texas and Oregon Counties and over the Arkansas line between March 17 and April 1 to find what Rebels in that region may threaten south-central Missouri. The patrol encountered numbers of guerrillas in Arkansas including those under Colonel Solomon Kitchen and Captains B. Chambers and G. W. Evans, and had several fights with them. The patrol also heard that Colonel Freeman with a large number of Rebels was then at Pocahontas, farther to the east.[23]

Bill Wilson of Phelps County Begins His Guerrilla War

Local guerrilla bands led by Bill Wilson in Phelps County and other bushwhackers riding north through this area provided most of the excitement in south-central Missouri this spring. The story of Bill Wilson of rural Phelps County is similar to that of infamous Sam Hildebrand of a few counties to the east. That is, local folklore claims Wilson took little part in the war until local Union militia named him a suspect for guerrilla acts in the area and burned his house and harassed his family. Like Hildebrand, Bill Wilson took the vengeance trail and set out to repay the Federals for brutalizing him and his. Either alone or with a few friends and neighbors Wilson used his great hunting skills and prowess with firearms to conduct a private war against small Yankee patrols and couriers in Phelps County during 1864.[24]

There was a small, unidentified band of bushwhackers active in the Phelps County area during March and April 1864. The Rolla wartime newspaper reported that during the evening of March 13 horse thieves shot to death elderly Mr. Davis at his home on Spring Creek north of Rolla. Davis heard a noise at his stable and took a gun to investigate when he met his fate.[25] Local legend states that in late March or early April a small, unidentified group of guerrillas killed a few Union cavalrymen six miles southwest of Rolla near the mouth of Little Beaver Creek and took some of the Federal mounts. The legend continues that local Union authorities attributed this killing to Bill Wilson and that led to his arrest, the burning of his house, and his escape shortly thereafter. Available Union military records reveal no such killing of cavalrymen at this time, but the mouth of Beaver Creek a few miles south of Rolla is very close to Wilson's home near the present-day village of Vida.[26]

Rolla historian Dr. John F. Bradbury, Jr. in the early 1990s discovered Union military reports from the garrison of Rolla in the National Archives that mention what apparently is the beginning of Wilson's career as a bushwhacker. On April 11 the Rolla commander, Lieutenant Colonel Joseph A. Eppstein of the 5th Cavalry MSM, wrote his superiors about the encounter a Sergeant Gee, on recruiting duty for the 11th Missouri Cavalry, had near the Lenox farm on the Salem-Rolla Road about eight miles southeast of Rolla April 5, 1864. Sergeant Gee, who lived in this area before the war, that day met a man wearing a Union uniform at that location and was surprised to recognize him as "Wilson, a well known Bushwhacker and Marauder." This Wilson told Gee in picturesque terms how he despised the Union cause and what he would do to Federal soldiers, but that he knew Gee from before the war and therefore spared his life and allowed Sergeant Gee to proceed without harm. Lieutenant Colonel Eppstein also wrote how he sent a patrol that searched in vain for Wilson at that location and then searched Wilson's home neighborhood with orders to bring the man in dead or alive, but also without success. This evidence seems to indicate that Bill Wilson was already known as a local bushwhacker by April 5.[27]

Wilson's Band Attacks Two Union Couriers on 7 April

This same April 11 report from Lieutenant Colonel Eppstein also detailed an attack April 7 by four guerrillas in Federal uniforms upon two dispatch riders of the 5th Cavalry MSM riding from Salem toward Rolla near the location described by Sergeant Gee in his experience two days before. These six combatants exchanged a number of shots at close quarters killing Private Vincent Smith's horse and capturing both of the dispatch riders. The bushwhackers then took their two prisoners a short distance off the road, took their uniforms and weapons, and shot them both. Their captors left the pair for dead, but Private Smith regained consciousness with a bullet in his head, and painfully made his way to a home some distance away where he received help and the farmer summoned his comrades. He described in detail what he encountered. Private Smith's companion's body, that of Private Andrew Sparrow, was later found where the guerrillas left him. Since this attack two days after Sergeant Gee's encounter with Bill Wilson took place near the same location with guerrillas also dressed in U.S. uniforms, it seems likely that this April 7 attack involved Wilson, too. The attack on the two dispatch riders may very well be the same attack upon Union cavalrymen at the mouth of Beaver Creek mentioned in local Phelps County lore that led to the Union military naming Bill Wilson as a dangerous bushwhacker. Lieutenant Colonel Eppstein's report excludes the fact that his command warned Bill Wilson's family to leave for the South within five days. A newspaper correspondent for a St. Louis newspaper in Rolla noted this fact, but omitted what the Federals threatened to do if the Wilsons failed to leave by the deadline.[28]

Wilson's Band Victimizes Area Residents in Mid-April

A second report that Dr. Bradbury discovered at the National Archives in the early 1990s pertinent to Bill Wilson was an April 18 report from the Rolla Union base's chief of scouts, Thomas Maxwell. The chief scout told how Bill's family lived at the head of Little Piney Creek, how his family and brother Napoleon Wilson offered that Bill remained in the area so that he could come home some nights, and that he had with him about 15 or 20 men. Thomas Maxwell also narrated that about mid-April guerrillas, probably Wilson's men, robbed Sarah Bond, a widow who lived in the same township as the Wilsons, of a sorrel mare and about $200 or $300 in gold and silver. This same gang went to rob James Mathews, who lived just across the county boundary in Pulaski County. Mathews queried the rough-looking men, then ran into the brush near his house to escape. The bushwhackers shot after the fleeing homeowner, but failed to hit him. When the raiders went to elderly Mr. Lewis' home and demanded his money, he refused initially. The robbers hanged Mr. Lewis for a while until he reluctantly surrendered his cash, then left without harming him further. If this band was under Bill Wilson's leadership, their robbing money from elderly neighbors hardly fits the folklore image of Wilson as a Robin Hood hero fighting outnumbered against the evil Yankees.[29]

Federal Reverses in Arkansas Lay Southeast Missouri Open to Rebel Horsemen in May

As warm weather returned to south-central Missouri in late spring, other bands of guerrillas traveled through this region on their way back from wintering in the South to their chosen operating areas. Further, in May the ill-fated Union Red River campaign ended badly for the Federals in Louisiana along with Union Major General Frederick Steele's Camden Expedition in south Arkansas. Therefore, the Federals withdrew from Louisiana and General Steele led his battered force north to Little Rock. These twin northern disasters freed thousands of Confederate troops who advanced north to threaten Steele's recovering force. Things looked grim for the Federals in the Trans-Mississippi West in May 1864.[30] The ripple effect from this catastrophe affected all Yankees across Arkansas as worried commanders pulled back isolated garrisons before the now-unencumbered Rebel troops could overwhelm and capture them. Yanks ordered their Batesville base closed May 11 and ordered the larger Jacksonport garrison evacuated May 22. This development in essence emptied northeast Arkansas of bluecoats, and jubilant Confederates filled the void.[31] Some of them ventured further north into Missouri. Between May 12 and 16 two bands of unidentified bushwhackers, one of twelve riders and the other of thirty, passed east of Rolla heading north. Guerrilla chieftain Andrew Jackson "Dick" Kitchen with about 25 men rode back into this area in late May arriving near Jack's Fork in south-central Shannon County. Before the war Kitchen was a laborer in Phelps County and was returning to operate on home ground. Union patrols reported that bushwhackers by then were already scattered around in groups as small as three or four. Small units that size were better able to find food and forage in this war-ravaged region.[32] On May 27 a larger group of Rebels of about forty riders headed north not far from the California House Inn in central Pulaski County perhaps on their way to northeast Missouri.[33]

Spring 1864 Guerrilla Actions of Traveling Rebel Bands in Counties South of the Missouri River

The counties just south of the Missouri River in southeast Missouri had such large populations of northern sympathy and aggressive local militia throughout the war that southern guerrillas and Confederate recruiters learned to avoid traveling through this area. Furthermore, the Union military kept careful guard on the Pacific and Iron Mountain Railroads in this section to prevent Rebels from disrupting these vital transportation links. For these reasons the war seldom came to Osage, Maries, Gasconade, Crawford, and Franklin Counties. However, the Federal reverses in Arkansas during May, as mentioned earlier, removed Union troops from northeast Arkansas. This allowed several fast-riding guerrilla bands to run the gauntlet of militiamen here this spring in order to take a more direct course of travel to their preferred operating areas north of the Missouri River. Occasionally, these Rebel riders and their Union pursuers collided in furious fire-fights.

The band of about 30 Confederate riders that rode past the large Union base at Rolla about May 12, as reported earlier, created an uproar in this normally quiet area as they rode on north. A combined Union patrol of sixteen men of the 1st Infantry MSM and a detachment of local 63rd EMM came across this band six miles northeast of Cuba, north-central Crawford County, about 1 pm May 13. The Rebels had dismounted to have lunch, and the attacking Yankees scattered the southerners into the brush, killing two Confederates. The northerners also gained a few captured horses and a variety of items strewn on the ground such as firearms, blankets, and about 100 letters of the secret Rebel mail intended for families of southern sympathy from friends and relatives in the Confederate Army in Arkansas. The Confederates who lost their horses had no choice but to replace them from the stock of local farmers, creating a spate of stolen horse reports across the area soon after this encounter. The Union command at Rolla was of the opinion that this Rebel band was bound for a destination north of the Missouri River in northeast Missouri.[34]

A local man, John Goddard, wrote in his diary about events later the same day as the Cuba fight that militiamen were "hunting horse thieves. [who] stole two of old Duvall's horses last night. No trace of them yet." Goddard seemed caught up in the excitement of hearing about the hunt for the Confederates, whom he called "horse thieves" because they were desperately commandeering horses to escape from the pursuing militia. For May 14 Goddard wrote "heard from them horse thieves. The militia found them on the Little Burbase [Little Bourbouse Creek in south Gasconade County and Franklin County]. They fired on the Federals first. Did no execution. They fired several rounds on both sides. Was one thief killed." Goddard's diary seems to be the only source for this skirmish in which one Rebel lost his life on May 14.[35]

Passing Rebel Horsemen Rush Through Hermann to Cross River in Mid-May

About 25 of the guerrillas who fought the militia near Cuba May 13 and fought militia again on the Little Bourbouse Creek May 14 later that same day raced through Hermann to cross the Missouri River into northeast Missouri. These Rebels probably knew the German-American town of Hermann was staunchly pro-Union and had an active militia, for they did not linger in town. The residents may have seemed threatening as the Confederates fired at residents, mortally wounding the area provost marshal, Captain Charles C. Manwaring, with a shot in the head. As the Rebels dashed out of Hermann members of the local 34th Enrolled Missouri Militia, ran for their own horses and gave pursuit for some distance into Montgomery County north of the river. The pursuit by the Hermann militia was so close that the guerrillas were forced to abandon their horses and disperse into the woods and brush. The Columbia, Boone County, newspaper reported that some black men captured one of the raiders, murdered him with gunshots, and dropped his body into the river. Hermann had become a haven for escaped slaves from the region, and many of them held the Confederacy in bitter contempt.[36]

Union Pursuit of Passing Rebel Groups

About this time or a few days later four guerrillas from one of the passing bands robbed E. Gibler's store on Little Bourbouse Creek in southwest Franklin County. An area resident, Gert Goebel, mentioned this robbery in a letter to the Union military the following month. It was Mr. Goebel's belief that these four were soon after caught and executed in the field by infantrymen from one company of the 10th Kansas Infantry Regiment that he stated was guarding railroad facilities not far away. Goebel referred to his hearing about four men "found in the woods, each with a hole in his head." This prompted him to state "the presence of a company of the Tenth Kansas Regiment on the southwest branch also tends to mollify the warlike propensities of our rebels, because they have a very distinct sensation in what peculiar manner these Kansas boys are wont to settle accounts with bushwhackers." The 10th Kansas was at this time assigned in St. Louis performing guard and escort duties, but one company could have been sent to help guard railroad facilities here. However, there seems to be no collaborating account about four of the southern riders being killed to verify Mr. Goebel's account.[37]

Meanwhile, other Rebel riders were trying to ride through Franklin County to the Missouri River. Local Union authorities reported that seven of the guerrillas robbed Biddle's Store ten miles north of Sullivan in central Franklin County the night of May 23/24, but no report survives to state what was taken. These four were evidently part of the band of twenty or more Confederates who resorted to buying horses and saddles in southwest Franklin County with "greenbacks" instead of seizing them, according to the commander of the Union 55th Enrolled Missouri Militia Regiment from that area. Perhaps this cash came from Biddle's Store. The guerrillas were all wearing U.S. uniforms and coolly told passersby and horse sellers that they were part of Union Major General Frederick Steele's troops from Arkansas. These riders thus escaped further violence in their ride across the rest of Franklin County and evidently crossed the Missouri River into northeast Missouri where they had friends to assist them.[38]

Neither Side Shoots as Tired Rebel Horsemen Ride Through Vienna

There was yet another unidentified guerrilla band of between 12 and 20 riding north through Maries County. This smaller bunch was first reported riding east of Rolla about May 12, as mentioned earlier. Union authorities next heard about them when they rode through the Maries County town of Vienna at 4:00 the morning of May 14. Startled local residents were not sure if this Rebel band headed north or west after they left town, but noted that their horses were "much jaded." That seems to have been the last heard of these riders for several days, so perhaps they found a secluded place to rest themselves and their tired horses. Patrols sent out from Jefferson City could not find these elusive horsemen.[39]

Passing Rebel Horsemen Capture and Kill Second Wisconsin Troopers in Maries County

It seems that the southern band riding through Maries County lingered there several days and found a tempting target to strike on May 26. On that day Sergeant LeGrand Carter's patrol of 2nd Wisconsin Cavalry rode out from Rolla north to near Lane's Prairie, east-central Maries County, to bring back horses left there earlier by guerrillas. Suspecting no trouble, the patrol found some of the horses and the sergeant with four troopers rode about a mile away where more of the horses were supposed to be, leaving the other six guarding those already obtained. When the sergeant and the four cavalrymen failed to return after a long while and a search revealed nothing, the six remaining patrol members returned to base to summon help. A larger force of the regiment returned May 27 and was guided by civilians to the bodies of Sergeant Carter and the four men who had been with him. The civilians told the cavalry that a mounted force of about fifteen men in Federal uniforms were in the neighborhood on May 26 claiming to be U.S. troops from Jefferson City. A boy working in a nearby field on May 26 saw the two groups of cavalry meet on the road, heard the larger group order the smaller one to halt, and then escorted them a distance away. Soon he heard shots, then silence. Nearby residents later explored where the boy heard the shots and found Sergeant Carter and the other four troopers dead in a nearby woods. The horrified Wisconsinites studied the bloody corpses for a while to determine what had happened. From what they could observe, the guerrillas had been making the troopers exchange the guerrillas' worn Federal uniforms for their own fresher ones when the captives decided to make a fight of it even though unarmed and outnumbered. The half-clothed bodies were all shot four or five times, and some bore knife wounds, too. They also bore defensive wounds, as one had a broken arm and some of the four had scraped knuckles. Earlier in the war southern sym-

Guerrillas captured and killed Sergeant LeGrand Carter of the 2nd Wisconsin Cavalry with four of his troopers in Maries County on 26 May (private collection, courtesy of John F. Bradbury).

pathizers fought in the Lane's Prairie neighborhood, so it is possible that these guerrillas were befriended and aided by sympathetic residents, which may explain why these guerrillas remained in this area for several days. The identity of these guerrillas, like the other groups that rode through this region in May, has never been determined.

About this same time one of the St. Louis newspapers printed what appears to be a twisted version of this story of the five killed Wisconsin soldiers in Maries County. The *Union* wrote about a company of unidentified Federal troops that happened upon fourteen horses hitched outside a cave in Maries County. Six of the Yanks died in an ambush when they got too close, and the remaining northerners prepared a long siege to wait out their trapped quarry. Realizing there was no escape, the Rebels under a flag of truce tried to surrender if the soldiers would agree to treat them as prisoners of war, but the Yankees refused. The newspaper article left the siege under way with no resolution, and there seemed to be no follow-up story to detail its outcome. Maries County was the setting for very few actions during the war, and to have two skirmishes there about the same time, involving about the same number of Federals killed, and involving finding untended guerrilla horses involves too many coincidences. Add to that the St. Louis paper offered no identity of the Union troops, no identification of even a general location in the county, no date of occurrence, no corroborating resource, and it appears that the *St. Louis Union* fell victim to an unreliable source for this story.[40]

The Hidden War This Spring in the St. Louis Area

If the guerrilla war outside of St. Louis featured action and shooting, its version inside that city was quiet and concealed. Most of this war in the spring of 1864 featured Rebel prisoners trying to escape the several St. Louis area military prisons in various, ingenuous ways and southern sympathizers working behind the scenes to smuggle mail and *materiel* to Confederate forces further south.

Foiled Escape Attempt at Gratiot Street Prison and Successful One at Alton in March

March 1864 was particularly quiet until the last days of the month. Fellow prisoner Captain Griffin Frost noted in his diary that a number of his fellow "students" at the McDowell Medical College, now called "Gratiot Street Prison" by the Federals, were captured by their jailers the night of March 26/27 trying to dig through the prison wall into the Christian Brothers Academy next door. Perhaps these unidentified prisoners' version of quiet warfare was just a little too noisy for a still night.[41] Captain Frost noted with glee in his diary a few days later the news he heard that "a number of prisoners" had escaped from the Alton, Illinois military prison nearby. Haphazard Union prison records seem to show two of the escapees on this March 30 break included a guerrilla named Cushman transferred from Columbus, Kentucky and a Hiram Withers transferred from Rolla. Both men had strong motive to escape since proven guerrillas faced a death sentence and Withers was already sentenced to be shot.[42]

Federal Prison Inspector Tries Without Success to Get Better Facilities

Union Surgeon Augustus M. Clark submitted his health and safety inspection report March 29 of his findings at both Gratiot Street and Myrtle Street Prisons. Clark

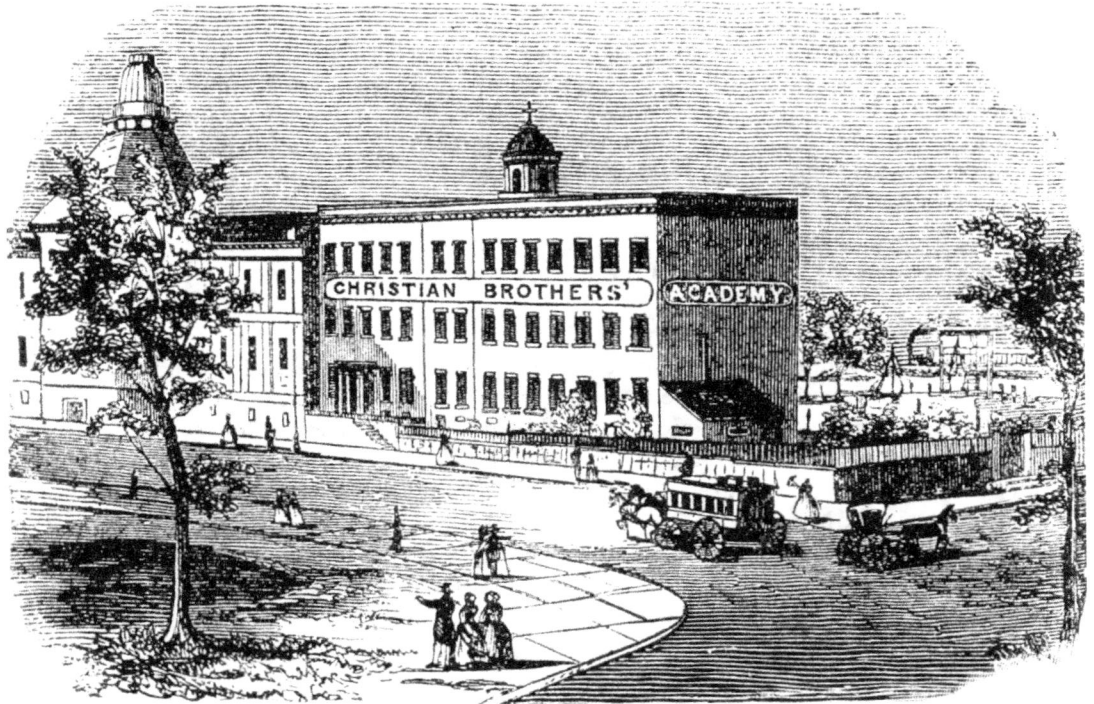

Gratiot Street Military Prison is to the left of Christian Brothers' Hospital (Walter B. Stevens, *Centennial History of Missouri*, vol. 2, 1921, p. 2).

commented that the structural problems he noted at the Gratiot Street institution earlier were "being patched up," but that the Missouri commanding general, Major General Rosecrans, felt the installation had deteriorated too much to save. Rosecrans would try for months to convince his superiors they should erect a more suitable prison just a few miles south at the Jefferson Barracks facility, but he would lose that battle. The Federals would continue to use the former medical college on Gratiot Street until the war's end. Surgeon Clark duly noted that Gratiot Street had 520 prisoners when he visited and that Myrtle Street had 163. The inspector wrote that the Myrtle Street prison was "still greatly overcrowded," but that the military had taken his earlier advice and replaced the ineffective civilian who had operated the place with a Union officer. Clark was more concerned with the disease hazard at these prisons, especially smallpox. He wrote that medical personnel found two new cases March 27 and two more on March 28, making 43 smallpox cases for the month at both prisons. He commented that such cases were taken to a small hospital on Quarantine Island in the Mississippi River three miles south of the city. He noted that 144 prisoners were then in hospital care from both prisons, and that three hospital patients had physically escaped while 22 had escaped life on earth in the month of February 1864.[43]

Alton Commandant Neglects Prisoners During Battle of Wills with Doctor

Surgeon Clark next inspected the Alton Military Hospital, submitting that report March 31. He noted gladly that there were at the time of his visit only five smallpox cases there, and those patients were in convalescence. Clark spent the rest of his report furiously reporting that the commandant at Alton, Colonel William Weer of 10th Kansas Infantry, was engaged in a battle of wills with the head doctor there who was defying him about Weer's refusal to remedy sanitary matters at the prison. During this prolonged argument Colonel Weer refused to sign food provision orders for the prisoners at hospital for five days earlier in March. Fortunately, humanity prevailed, and the prison mess hall evidently sent meals to the hospital without the knowledge of the commandant. Doctor Clark wrote a scathing report on this matter, thus singling out Colonel Weer for close scrutiny in the near future. The brutally factual reports from honest inspectors like Clark went far to preserve health and protect some life at these installations for not only prisoners but the guards as well.[44]

Alton Prison Escapes in Early April

Evidently, some of the prisoners at Alton were disappointed with Colonel Weer's hospitality, too, as several escaped April 4, as recorded later by Captain Frost down the river at another prison. The escapees included a citizen of Pike County, William O. White, and Confederate Captain M. V. B. Moseley of Colonel John Q. Burbridge's command. Union forces captured Captain Moseley May 5 the previous year in Montgomery County, Missouri as a spy and Rebel recruiting officer. Since the Federals seemed to acknowledge Moseley's rightful military rank and position in prison records, he may not have been facing a death sentence, as Union tribunals usually sentenced to spies. However, escaping from such a notorious prison as Alton was certainly motive enough for any prisoner held there.[45]

Capture Rebel Lieutenant from Louisiana in St. Louis

On April 9, Union authorities arrested in St. Louis Confederate First Lieutenant Thaddeus A. Ripley of Colonel Rob Wheat's Louisiana "Tigers" Infantry Battalion.

When arrested, First Lieutenant Ripley may have passed himself as the higher rank of captain, perhaps hoping to get better treatment at the hands of his captors. Being captured not in uniform well behind Union lines on business he would not divulge went badly for Ripley at his tribunal, for Department of the Missouri General Orders Number 85, June 6, 1864, sentenced him to hard labor for the remainder of the war. Fellow prisoner Captain Griffin Frost noted in his journal on June 9 that "Thad Ripley" was chained to several other prisoners known to be notorious or troublesome to the Union authorities. Obviously, First Lieutenant Ripley was in St. Louis on some nefarious business such as a secret Rebel mail ring or smuggling.[46]

Union troops arrest a suspect in the street (Frazar Kirkland, *The Pictorial Book of Anecdotes of the Rebellion*, 1888, p. 126).

Prison Inspections Reveal Problems

A Lieutenant Colonel John F. Marsh reported his general inspection findings of Gratiot Street Prison and Myrtle Street Prison also on April 9. Lieutenant Colonel Marsh wrote that the former prison housed 515 prisoners, the latter housed 169, and 28 prisoners were at that time kept in the smallpox hospital on the island in the Mississippi River. He found the financial accounts of these prisons in disarray and blamed the provost marshal-general of the Department of the Missouri for not monitoring the books. This inspector was not impressed with the guards from the 7th and 10th Minnesota Infantry Regiments, finding their quarters dirty and the men "inattentive and careless." He did note, however, that no prisoner had escaped from either of these two prisons since February 1864. Marsh found that "the health, clothing, food, and shelter of the prisoners is satisfactory," but "the economy and discipline" of both facilities needed improvement. He admitted that the hospital was well managed, and smallpox was "gradually disappearing." Lieutenant Colonel Marsh felt Gratiot Street Prison needed cleaning, "especially the latrines."[47]

If Inspector Marsh was displeased with the two prisons in downtown St. Louis, he was far more critical of Alton Military Prison in his April 13 report of his general inspection there. Colonel Weer lost his chance to make a good first impression since Marsh found the man drunk when he arrived. The inspector made some choice remarks about Weer being unfit to command and not suitable to even hold the position of officer. He liked the garrison of 10th Kansas Infantry a bit better, writing that they were "quiet and orderly," but "deficient in discipline and efficiency" and also "careless." The guards merited those last two criticisms because Marsh pointed out four prisoners had already escaped in April. Lieutenant Colonel Marsh pointed out that since the guard force lived in tents some distance away from the prison, their officers should not be leasing a building for their quarters, but should live in camp with the men—a tradition in the U.S. Army. He found the cells "filthy," but the "health, clothing, and food of the prisoners is entirely satisfactory." The inspector found the prison hospital to be "clean and the patients well cared for," even if the location near the latrines was ill advised. He wrote that there were 509 Rebel prisoners there when he inspected and 142 other Union prisoners."[48]

Surgeon Augustus M. Clark returned to inspect health and safety at Alton Military Prison again just a few days after Lieutenant Colonel Marsh's general inspection, because of the severe inadequacies Clark had discovered there on his previous health and safety inspection at the end of March. He was incensed to find that Colonel Weer was drunk again, and had not even considered the recommendations Clark made earlier, so his even-more scathing report dated April 23 got immediate action, especially coming on the heels of Marsh's more recent criticisms. The Union command relieved Colonel Weer and his regiment of their duties at the prison and sent Brigadier General Joseph T. Copeland to take command and the 13th Illinois Cavalry Regiment from Benton Barracks in St. Louis to garrison the place and guard the prisoners.[49]

The next known prison escape took place May 6 from Alton Military Prison when James A. Jamison of Dent or Phelps County somehow managed to get away. Jamison had been incarcerated in St. Louis area facilities for over a year, and when he returned to his home area he joined Bill Wilson's small guerrilla band in Phelps County, as shown in Chapter Eleven. Jamison became known as one of the most daring of Wilson's bushwhackers and it would have been better for the Union cause in the Phelps County area if Jamison had not escaped.[50]

Federals Intercept a Dangerous Shipment of Eggs at St. Louis Levee

The Department of the Missouri Provost Marshal General, J. P. Sanderson, received a tip this spring that a firm would be sending a disguised arms shipment from St. Louis to Memphis labeled as "eggs" that was destined for the Rebel army. Between May 8 and May 11 detectives watching cargo being loaded on river steamers at the St. Louis levee spotted the tell-tale label and, sure enough, discovered hidden in the shipment 204 one-pound cans of rifle gunpowder, 10,000 percussion caps, and three bags of shot. It was then an easy matter to arrest the shipper of the contraband war *materiel*.[51]

Prison Escapes and Arrivals at Alton During May

The Alton Military Prison records tell of various authorized arrivals and unauthorized departures throughout May 1864. On May 10 Confederate Private John H. McDaniel of the 1st Missouri Cavalry escaped from the Alton Military Prison perhaps to carry on his war someplace else. The scant Union military record of McDaniel's escape does not comment how he accomplished the deed.[52] Just the following day Confederate surgeon Dr. William S. Wright was transferred to the same prison for the remainder of the war. The doctor had been caught February 13 over a year before at a home in St. Louis smuggling secret Rebel mail, uniform material and medicines to the Confederate army. A military tribunal had long before imposed a severe sentence on Dr. Wright, but President Lincoln personally interceded and commuted Wright's sentence for imprisonment at Alton only as long as the war would last.[53] The prison records at Alton recorded another escape May 16, this time of a Confederate Private Moses Fornshill.[54]

The steady comings and goings of prisoners and smugglers continued to circulate through the St. Louis area while the Union military and its detectives struggled to stop the secret war that was quietly fought in the large river city. Summer 1864 promised to bring more adventures of this kind to St. Louis.

Seven

Spring 1864 in Southwest Missouri

The prairie-covered southwest quadrant of Missouri had been a frequent battleground throughout the war to the extent much of it was vacant and fallow by the spring of 1864. Even though the lack of deep river obstacles and the ease of riding through grasslands made southwest Missouri a natural avenue of approach for Rebels riding to and from the state, the logistics of horse feed was a problem with the landscape. Namely, the absence of farmers growing grain that horses could eat was a real problem to the mounted military of both sides. To overcome this feed shortage, riders either had to bring their own or feed their mounts on grass that was only high enough for horses to eat between approximately April and December of the year. It may seem fantastic that the progress of a war was suspended for a few weeks because of a grass and grain shortage, but that seems to have been the case here this spring. A hopeful newspaper correspondent in east Jasper County during mid–April 1864 looked forward to the advent of the grass when he wrote "a great many families are expected when grass rises." The words of this witness gave evidence that grass grew late this spring.[1] The severe winter of 1863-1864 had exhausted local supplies of forage to the extent that the Union cavalry stationed in this region had to ship most of its horse feed by into the region by railroad and wagon. Of course, guerrillas operating in this area could not duplicate this logistics feat, but the aggressive Federal campaigns of the past had reduced local bushwhacker bands in southwest Missouri by 1864 anyway. Therefore, this part of the Show-Me State in the spring of this year became merely a conduit for fast-riding southerners to cross to reach their favored operating grounds further to the north and northeast. Much of the military operations here this season involved Federal cavalry looking for traveling Rebel bands and chasing them on their northbound treks.

Few March 1864 Actions in the Prairie Region on the Kansas Border

The late spring this year seemed to keep the vast grassland along the Kansas border quiet through most of March. There were just a few isolated incidents.

Sometime during March a few guerrillas attacked a small Union army wagon train going from Lawrence County to Fort Scott somewhere near Lamar, Barton County. There was no mention of a military escort and the bushwhackers attacked the civilian teamsters, shooting to death Thomas W. Allison of Lawrence County, a Smith, and a Hightown. This area was so isolated in March 1864 that no record of this event seems to have been made until the following month, and one newspaper said of this killing then that the dead included "a one-armed boy fourteen years old, an old man eighty-four years old, and a man some twenty-five." The military must not have suspected guerrillas in the area to have sent out a supply train without an escort.[2]

Indeed, at this stage of the war in the border states lawless renegades robbed and killed for self gain and booty, and were often mistaken for southern irregulars. The accomplished Confederate cavalry general, Joseph O. Shelby, on May 19 in Arkansas warned his subordinate commanders to distinguish between their own men and such outlaws and keep their men under proper discipline so they were not a burden to the local population. Shelby went so far as to direct his commands that "you will send details under good officers to arrest all bands of jayhawkers, whether Southern or Union, who may be committing outrages upon the citizens. In all cases where the proof is sufficient ... you will cause them to be shot." By this phase of the war deserters from both armies hardened by their war experiences and embittered by the waste of war were a new part of the equation of guerrilla war, and they occasionally influenced local actions.[3]

Confederate Brigadier General Joseph O. Shelby of Missouri (Eugene M. Violette, *A History of Missouri*, 1918, p. 375).

During early March about 45 guerrillas rode north through Polk and Hickory Counties, creating a stir. A St. Louis newspaper picked up the report that this bunch forced two local men to help them navigate through this area, but later released these involuntary guides unharmed. The article also wrote that these Rebels "killed a stray soldier of a Kansas regiment" as they passed through, but there does not seem to be any identification of this unfortunate soldier. Several southwest Missouri men served with Kansas regiments during the war, and occasionally they came home on furlough.[4] Union Captain William B. Ballew commanding the garrison of Company K, 7th Cavalry MSM at Quincy, northwest Hickory County, about this same time reported to his headquarters that he was investigating a report that someone saw about 15 bushwhackers riding near the county seat of Hermitage, central Hickory County, about eight or ten miles away. These were probably part of the same band, but there seem to be no reports documenting the continued movement of this large band in this area.[5]

Benton Gann, Pony Hill, Clements, and Others from March Through Mid-April 1864 in the Osage River Basin

The counties on both sides of the wide Osage River were the scene of many of the guerrilla actions of southwest Missouri during the winter of 1863-1864, and there were a number of incidents here during March 1864, too. As mentioned before, the hated Union General Orders Number Eleven had depopulated Bates County and the north half of Vernon County during the autumn of 1863 in a vain attempt to deny support for guerrillas. Bushwhackers operated there anyway, so it seems the suffering inherent in forcing the occupants to leave their homes and businesses was not worthwhile. Therefore, effective March 8, the commander of the Central District of Missouri, Brigadier General Egbert B. Brown, ordered that some of the exiled residents could return to these forbidden lands, provided they could show proof of their loyalty to the U.S. government. Some could argue that this exception to the depopulation order was a tacit admission that the policy was unsuccessful.[6]

About March 16 or 17 witnesses reporting seeing small numbers of guerrillas near Rockville, southeast Bates County. Three bushwhackers looking for horses stopped at the home of the Long family, and others were seen reconnoitering the countryside from on top of a mound. Perhaps the loyal citizens were not the only ones moving back into Bates County.[7]

This small band of bushwhackers evidently remained in this area for several days, taking what they needed by force from local farmers. When oppressed residents decided that this band was not just traveling through and demonstrated the intention to remain, some of them decided to resist in a manner the guerrillas would respect, and this led to an episode of demonstrated border bravery. On March 26 farmer Archibald Colson in Deepwater Township, southwest Henry County, seriously wounded one of three "knights of the bush" with shotgun fire, and he sent a neighbor to summon the cavalry from nearby Germantown. Sergeant John W. Barkley with a patrol from Company E, 1st Cavalry MSM responded and was able to catch up to the guerrilla trio because the wounded man was too badly hurt to ride his horse. The three bushwhackers took refuge in a house and Sergeant Barkley's patrol besieged them there during the night of March 26/27. At one point during that night several other guerrillas attempted to break the siege and rescue their comrades, but the cavalry drove them off. Seeing the futility of their situation and desiring to obtain medical help for their wounded man, the guerrillas reluctantly surrendered to Sergeant Barkley in the early morning hours of March 27. Back at Germantown, Company E commander, Captain Joseph H. Little, fed and then interrogated the prisoners, who at first claimed to be returned Confederate Army veterans Captain A. D. Jones and two of his men. Captain Little would be obligated to send these men to military prison if they could prove their status as captive regulars, whereas current Department of the Missouri regulations required local commanders to execute prisoners if sufficient evidence proved they were guerrillas. The U.S. Army overcoats these prisoners wore and the U.S.-supplied Remington revolvers and accouterments they possessed proved their claim to be false. Furthermore, local citizens rode to Germantown and were able to identify other items the prisoners had taken from area families. Captain Little sent the perhaps mortally wounded captive to the regimental surgeon at Clinton for treatment, but convicted the other two as bushwhackers and executed them there at Germantown on March 28. Before they died, the condemned men confessed their true identities as Benton Gann of the Oliver Gann family of Lafayette County and George Herold of Cass or Bates County, and faced the firing squad bravely. Captain Little wrote in admiration of their courage facing their fate:

> They refused to give any useful information; said their trial had been fair and that they were not afraid to die, which boast they made good. They calmly walked to the grave, looked contemptuously on the detail assembled, said they were ready, quietly folded their arms, kneeled down, and met death with a dauntlessness worthy a better cause.

The consensus at the Union district headquarters was that these guerrillas and their comrades were among the 20 or so bushwhackers that lived through the winter in the

Remington revolvers were number two in sales behind Colt's during the war years (Schuyler, Hartley, and Graham, *Illustrated Catalogue of Arms and Military Goods,* 1864, p. 142).

Lafayette County area, miles to the north, under Andy Blunt; but left no proof to this claim. What impressed Captain Little, other than the bravery of the condemned men, was the willingness of common citizens to fight back against veteran irregulars. The captain awarded one of the captured Remington revolvers to Sergeant Barkley and another one to citizen Archibald Colson, for their fearlessness facing a well-armed and deadly foe.[8]

Pony Hill was a notorious bushwhacker of Vernon County, where he was a roustabout and brawler even before the war. During summer 1863 Hill rode with former sheriff Henry Taylor's band of guerrillas in the area. In late March 1864 residents of northwest Vernon County reported to Union troops stationed nearby that they had seen Pony Hill, but the patrol of 3rd Wisconsin Cavalry sent out from their camp near the ruins of Balltown March 28 to investigate failed to find the man.[9] The Wisconsin cavalry sent another patrol of eleven men under Second Lieutenant George M. Ellis the next day to watch major road crossings and search woods and brush for a sign of the elusive Pony Hill and any of his companions. Ellis' patrol followed paths in the woods and came upon about seven bushwhackers sleeping in their camp March 30. Second Lieutenant Ellis and his sergeant were riding first on the pathway and fired a few shots as the campers scrambled into the brush leaving behind six horses and saddles, bedding, and camp equipment. The Wisconsin troopers did not seem to know if Hill was one of the fleeing men.[10]

The Union commander at Warsaw, Benton County, wrote his superiors about the success of one of his patrols April 5 or 6. A sergeant led 10 troopers of Company A, 7th Cavalry MSM from there to the southeast corner of Benton County "to hunt out some robbers who have infested that portion of the county for some time." The patrol captured two bushwhackers. There seems to be no surviving information about these guerrillas who operated at the junction of Benton, Hickory, and Camden Counties during late March and early April 1864, but perhaps these were some of those 45 or so bushwhackers who rode through Polk and Hickory Counties in early March, as described earlier.[11]

The Union forces in this region captured a bushwhacker named Clements in southwest Henry County April 13 and executed him at the Germantown garrison April 15. Before he died, Clements confessed that the two guerrillas executed there March 28,

Benton Gann and George Herold, were comrades of his, and that there were about ten of this band left in the west Henry County and Bates County area. He also told his captors that the surviving members often rested in a camp along Deer Creek 20 to 30 miles west of Germantown. The garrison commander who ordered Clements' death was First Lieutenant William L. Hardesty of Company E, 1st Cavalry MSM. In his memoir dictated years later in 1923 bushwhacker Harrison Trow claimed that a year later about May 7, 1865, guerrilla band leader Archie Clements in Benton County looked for and murdered "a Federal militiaman named Harkness" for killing his brother and burning the home of their mother earlier in the war. Possibly, Trow was referring to revenge for this April 15, 1864, execution of Clements by First Lieutenant Hardesty's command.[12]

Spring 1864 Action on the Springfield Plateau of the Western Ozarks

There were a few guerrilla actions in the hilly, tree-covered area east of the prairie lands during spring of this year. The Federals maintained in this area the large regional base at Springfield and a few smaller posts both to protect military traffic on the main wagon road between Springfield and Rolla and to watch for southern incursions in this region. The formidable Union presence of these garrisons and the mounted patrols they deployed around the countryside discouraged Confederate incursions into this rolling country.

An unusual battle took place in the brush five miles southeast of Springfield, Greene County, during the last half of March, probably about March 20 to 23, 1864. The Springfield newspaper reported that residents about 10 or 12 miles southeast of town saw ten or twelve suspicious riders heading toward Springfield. Some of the citizens, who may have been local militiamen, suspected trouble, grabbed firearms, saddled their horses, and followed the unidentified riders. As the locals rode along their numbers grew, and they concluded the men they were following were bushwhackers. This band of irregulars stopped in dense brush about five miles southeast of town and the citizens attacked. They then chased the guerrillas for some distance in a running fight through Clay Township, southeast Greene County, in which they mortally wounded one southerner and may have wounded one or two more before the shadowy riders escaped from the makeshift posse. The posse itself suffered no loss. The escapees in their panic killed a local man, Elijah Hunt, and wounded a Dodson whom they encountered in their flight. The dying Rebel appears to have been Private William W. Fulbright of Campbell Township, who had served the southern cause since 1861, and whose military record at Missouri State Archives testifies that he "was sent on a scout to Springfield, MO where he was captured & killed." Fulbright told his captors that his leader was Lewis Brashears, known by some of them as a Clay Township resident before the war. Brashears' record shows that he was a Confederate lieutenant serving with Fulbright in Captain James McSpadden's Company C of the 3rd Missouri Cavalry Battalion (CSA), that had been recruited of men from the region around Springfield. The newspaper article failed to identify the mission of these Confederates, but it may have been to scout Yankee strength at their Springfield base. Although local military tried to track the Rebels, no other record of contact with them in southwest Missouri remains. It is notable that this band rode so boldly across Greene County since the large number of Union troops at Springfield as well as the large number of northern sympathizers who lived nearby usually seemed to deter Rebels from approaching this area except with great strength or stealth. Since Second Lieutenant Brashears had been away on other war fronts he may have underestimated the danger posed to his command in approaching Greene County in such an open manner.[13]

The Union garrison at Forsyth, Taney County, sent out Second Lieutenant Andrew C. C. McElhannon with 40 troopers of the 8th Cavalry MSM to the Arkansas border between May 1 and 5 where they chased and fought with small numbers of bushwhackers. Residents told the lieutenant about a large guerrilla camp hidden in the hills near Bee Creek in south-central Taney county. When the patrol found the camp they chased and killed three bushwhackers guarding the place, Campbell, Williams, and Parkes, then destroyed the camp. The troopers rode only a short distance before they saw and chased more Rebels who escaped by scattering into the hills. Over the next three days Second Lieutenant McElhannon's patrol roamed over both sides of the Arkansas border along Bee and Bear Creeks chasing small numbers of guerrillas but only got close enough to capture one.[14]

About this same time the Union quartermaster department at Springfield supplied a large number of farmers from Barry, Stone, Taney, Christian, Lawrence, and Greene Counties with seed corn in order for them to plant a crop. Both Federal and Rebel troops passing through had taken so much of their crop, that they did not have enough to even plant without substantial help this year, and starvation loomed. Obviously, the Union military wanted to keep local farmers on their farms and avoid having more refugees parked in the towns and outside Union bases relying on U.S. subsistence.[15]

In late May guerrillas of Confederate Colonel John Charles Tracy's command

So many war refugees crowded into towns that the Union military often fed them (Charles C. Coffin, *Redeeming the Republic*, 1889, p. 201).

took needed supplies from rural families of Ozark and Douglas Counties and killed some men who opposed them. Before the war Colonel Tracy lived in Lafayette County far to the north. The Federals also heard that Confederate Colonel Thomas R. Freeman was recovering from a wound near the North Fork of the White River near the Arkansas border with a bodyguard, but there seems to be no confirmation of this report. In fact, another report said that Freeman was convalescing from a wound on Crowley's Ridge in northeast Arkansas at this time.[16]

Late April 1864 Hard Trip of Quantrill and Todd's Band Heading North Across Southwest Missouri

The spring of 1864 through middle-April brought only scattered guerrilla combat to the southwest quadrant of Missouri, but a rush of different bushwhacker and Confederate recruiting commands heading north through here throughout the second half of April brought a flurry of activity to this previously quiet region. Many of these mounted southerners had previous bitter experience trekking across this grassland during the previous two years with the Federal cavalry in hot pursuit. They learned some life-saving tactics that helped them cross this deadly, long gauntlet avoiding contact with the Yanks. Among these techniques were speed of movement; avoidance of gunplay unless absolutely necessary, and then, if necessary, overwhelming firepower to discourage bluecoats; use of advance, rear, and flank security to prevent surprise; designation in advance of knowledgeable guides and safe resting places hosted by sympathetic residents; use of concealment for rest stops (such as tree-lined creek bottoms); and reliance on well-selected, manageable horses. The guerrilla groups had learned to wear U.S. uniforms when they traveled long distances to throw off suspicion and attract the unwary, although the Confederate recruiting teams generally rejected such a subterfuge. They knew if Union cavalry caught them wearing enemy uniforms—and capture was always a strong possibility—they would face execution instead of later exchange. Many veteran Confederate recruiters had by spring 1864 already been caught, imprisoned, and exchanged one or two times. However, since bushwhackers were already facing execution if captured under Department of the Missouri regulations, such niceties did not deter them from wearing Union blue, and they could obtain Union uniforms in Missouri a lot easier than Confederate gray ones.

Many of the Union troopers and leaders were veterans at hunting fast-riding Rebels, but the odds did not all favor the pursuers. Not knowing when the Rebels would be coming, all Union garrisons had to keep sending out alert and often far-reaching patrols or scouts in order to spot passing Rebel riders. Over time, these efforts tended to wear down horses, and to a lesser extent, also the men. Furthermore, such isolated garrisons required constant logistics support, and the cavalry had to escort those coming and going. Also, active Union army posts necessitated timber details, couriers, and a number of other noncombat needs that tended to use up horses and fatigue troopers. Union posts relied on the telegraph to overcome this disadvantage and cover great distances, but Rebels moving over long distances commonly cut the telegraph wires. As a result, the Union cavalry in southwest Missouri pursued passing Rebel groups, but were not always able to close with them to attack.

Captain William C. Quantrill and George Todd with anywhere from 40 to 70 riders rode into southwest Missouri ahead of the other large groups of Rebels traveling north. In his 1910 book William Connelley evidently quoted Sylvester Akers' memory

Quantrill's guerrilla group suffered through frequent rains and flooded creeks returning to Missouri in early spring 1864 (Charles C. Coffin, *Marching to Victory*, 1888, p. 469).

of this very hard trek back north from north-central Texas. Connelley indicated that Quantrill and Todd left Texas sooner than they wished because of trouble with Quantrill's lieutenant Bill Anderson and difficulty with the Confederate command there. Quantrill's hasty departure from Texas and the late spring and lack of grass for the horses combined to make the trip north a grueling endurance test for even veteran band members. Connelley wrote about this trek north that "there was little food for man or beast in the country ridden through and all suffered. The streams were bank-full and the horses had to swim them bearing their riders."[17]

Quantrill's April ascent to west-central Missouri from Texas this year was radically different from this same trip exactly a year before. In April of 1863 much of this same group took their time on the trip north and, with their blue uniforms, seemed to make sport of deceiving Yankee militiamen and killing them. They left a trail of bodies behind them and some of their postwar memoirs had exciting stories to relate. What little their autobiographies told about the trip north during April 1864 was the suffering of horses worn down from lack of grass and the frequent rains which drained the energy of the soaked riders.[18]

The guerrillas' recounted memories from this trip were mostly about what they encountered before they got to Missouri. They were dismayed in the Indian Nations to discover the body of their comrade Bill Bledsoe that they buried in October had been dug up and ravaged by wild animals over the winter. They sadly reburied his gnawed bones and continued north.[19] One of those in the group later told fellow veteran John N. Edwards that also in the Indian Nations they used the Yankee uniforms they wore to deceive and killed five Indians serving as Union soldiers.[20] In his memoirs John McCorkle related another incident of this trip that reveals wearing the other side's uniforms did not always bring about the desired result. Near the Neosho River in the northeast corner of the Indian Nations the guerrillas suddenly encountered a small number of fellow bushwhackers from that neighborhood who retreated into the brush when they saw the blue uniforms. Accompanying Quantrill's men on their way back to west-central Missouri was veteran Confederate recruiter Colonel Jeremiah Vardaman Cockrell of Johnson County, Missouri. Colonel Cockrell was traveling in his uniform as a Confederate colonel, and he approached the skittish locals to convince them they were on the same side. The frightened men thought this Rebel officer coming toward them was a Yankee trick and badly wounded Cockrell with a bullet in the shoulder. The locals were sorry when they learned the colonel was legitimate, but he still had to nurse his wounded shoulder for the rest of the trip.[21]

Guerrilla memoirs from this group are strangely silent about the part of their trip through Missouri, their home state, probably because their lack of forage and food and the rainy weather reduced them basically to survival level. About the time Quantrill's traveling group rode through Newton County unidentified raiders tortured septuagenarian Jonas Weems and his middle-aged son at their home on Indian Creek southeast of Neosho, Newton County. To get the men to reveal where they hid their money the thieves applied hot coals to the men's legs, feet, and faces, but the Springfield newspaper article about this travesty fails to reveal if the robbers succeeded. The Weems men were born in southern states, and may have thought their southern roots would protect them from bushwhackers. Perhaps their tormentors were renegades who felt no affiliation with either side of the war, and not some of the passing Quantrill men.[22]

Some details of the Quantrill men's trip north through southwest Missouri come from Yankee sources. The Union military at the Springfield base reported April 22 that a group of guerrillas were at Horse Creek, northwest Dade County, and this was probably Quantrill and company. The Federals attempted to direct cavalry from Greenfield and Melville to intersect with these riders, but they failed to find them.[23] On April 25 Union scouts from Fort Scott learned this band was still riding north through about east Vernon County and the commander at the fort sent out this warning on April 27 when word of this arrived: "Seventy men, supposed to be rebels from their dress, horses, and accouterments, passed north 30 miles from this place on the 25th."[24]

Quantrill and Todd's band crossed the wide Osage River near Papinsville, southeast Bates County April 26 and continued heading straight north along the Bates and St. Clair County line. Historian Albert Castel quoted from guerrilla Frank Smith's memoir about crossing the Osage River that "Quantrill and Todd went over first, then lit fires on the bank to guide the others." The guerrillas had so far escaped the Union patrols looking for them, possibly because of the rain and gloom, but one source indicated that they suffered an attack after crossing the Osage River. A Union sergeant of the 3rd Wisconsin Cavalry stationed a few miles west of Papinsville heard after the fact that Union cavalry caught up to the exhausted bushwhacker band perhaps north of the Osage and killed 15 of them. This death toll appears to be an exaggeration, but it is entirely possible that northern troops watching the Osage River carefully for the coming guerrillas did manage to shoot at them. Indeed, the self-appointed guerrilla chronicler, Confederate Major John N. Edwards, in his 1877 *Noted Guerrillas* does give one indication that Quantrill and Todd's band encountered trouble in St. Clair County. Although not dated, Edwards mentions an episode of the war when Quantrill member James Morris was recovering from wounds lying in the woods along Blackwater River in northwest Pettis County when he was discovered by Federals. Edwards mentions the detail that Morris received his wounds in St. Clair County, and the only time this season Quantrill's and Todd's men were there was during this trek north. A company of the Union 60th EMM lived in St. Clair County and patrolled their home area aggressively during this part of the war, but, like most EMM units, kept little record of their achievements. Perhaps they shot up some passing guerrillas and did not think it worthwhile to ride several miles to the nearest Union post to report.[25]

On April 27 the weary, travel-worn bushwhackers rode to some part of Johnson County where Quantrill had them disperse with the agreement to rendezvous at a set time and place a few days hence after some scouting. Many of their horses were dead by this time, and a number were of little use after their ordeal, so all but a few of the men needed time to refit and recover.[26]

Late April and Early May Easy Ascent of Colonel Dorsey's Recruiting Command Northeast Across Southwest Missouri

Coming only a few days behind Quantrill's ill-starred group, Confederate Colonel Caleb Dorsey's recruiting command of about 112 to 125 riders enjoyed a less harrowing trip north on their way to northeast Missouri. In their favor, they did not have as far to ride, and they were probably better prepared for the trip. Oddly, Federals mistakenly believed that Confederate Colonel Sidney Drake Jackman, who had successfully recruited in northeast Missouri almost under the noses of Union troops there throughout 1863, was leading this group back to repeat his feat for 1864. In truth, Jackman was commanding his own troops in northern Arkansas during this time, but just his name alone seemed enough to shake up the Federals in Missouri.[27] Perhaps Colonel Dorsey even dropped Jackman's name in passing just to unnerve the Yanks. To their credit, the bluecoats knew Dorsey himself was along, but they failed to grasp that Dorsey was actually the commander of this group of riders. Dorsey, about thirty years old from Pike County, was a highly successful Confederate recruiter in his own right, having served the southern cause in Missouri since 1861. He recruited hundreds of southern men of northeast Missouri during 1861 and 1863, and was now on his way back with help to repeat the feat in 1864. He was captured early in 1862 and spent some months in the Alton, Illinois military prison before exchange, which may account for his desire to avoid capture again.[28]

Colonel Dorsey and his men were masters at avoiding capture. They determined that the best approach to avoid apprehension by Union forces was to avoid attention, too, for this group of over 100 horsemen was only reported by Union authorities a few times as they rode halfway across Missouri to the northeast quadrant. The Union commander at Clarksville, Arkansas, east of Fort Smith, first reported that Dorsey's recruiters were riding into Missouri. He reported April 25 that "Colonels Jackman, Dorsey, and Parker passed this post this morning, going north to Missouri, with 112 men, mostly officers for rebel army. They intend passing all points quietly." Except for the mention of Jackman, this officers dispatch was accurate as to Dorsey's numbers, tactics and intentions.[29] Actually, Dorsey's command may have been further north than this report indicated, since the Springfield, Missouri garrison that same day reported that 100 guerrillas were at Cowskin Prairie at the extreme southwest corner of McDonald County, and that "Jackman and his command, about 125 men" passed Carthage, Jasper County, the night before. It seems that these riders moved so fast that the Federals were confused as to where they were. The Springfield commander, Brigadier General John B. Sanborn, repeated the error that this band of southerners was led by Jackman in his report April 28, but added "he evades all posts and public roads and commits no depredations, and has moved since crossing the Arkansas [River] about 40 miles a day." Unfortunately for the northern cause, General Sanborn also wrote that "there are rumors that Jackman's design is to rob banks at Boonville and other towns."[30] The Jefferson City Union command miles away to the northeast misread or misunderstood Sanborn's report for they telegraphed Boonville, county seat of Cooper County, to warn them that Quantrill and his bushwhackers were on their way to raid their town and rob their banks, which, understandably, created a panic in town. Businessmen placed their money on a ferryboat that anchored out in the middle of the Missouri River at night to keep it from raiders, and the Tipton telegraph operator wired the Boonville postmaster not to send mail toward Tipton in case it would fall into Rebel hands. Guards were placed in the streets that night and merchants boxed up their goods and horses and sent them across the river for safekeeping. A day later cooler heads prevailed and Boonsville residents realized the whole affair was a false alarm. The Boonville newspaper editor, writing of the fiasco on May 7, unwittingly compounded the error of the whole panic when he wrote "it may be proper to add that Quantrill is nowhere in Missouri. The newspapers report him on Red River in Texas." Quantrill at that time was only 75 miles away to the southwest in about Henry County, and, if he read this report, would have enjoyed this gaffe along with the rest of the account of Boonville townspeople panicking. It would seem that all Colonel Caleb Dorsey had to do to throw Missouri into pandemonium was to ride across the state with 112 to 125 Confederate recruiters. The real irony of this situation is that Colonel Dorsey and his riders actually were riding toward Cooper County on their way to northeast Missouri at the time the newspaper article was written.[31]

Meanwhile, Union authorities were attempting to determine the true course of Dorsey's group. On May 3 the Warrensburg commander reported that the band (still led by Jackman, he wrote) was on Horse Creek in Cedar County, and, since Quantrill's band passed that point a few days before, he concluded this group would probably continue to follow Quantrill's path.[32] Of course, Colonel Dorsey was on his way back to recruit on his home ground of northeast Missouri, and had already veered in that direction. The details of how and where his group crossed the mighty obstacle of the Osage River probably in Benton or Camden County seems to have been lost to history. These riders next appear about May 20 spread across Cooper County in small groups where for several days they had been quietly stealing horses to replace their worn-out mounts. A Cooper County official, A. H. Thompson, attempted to raise the alarm several times, but was rebuffed by Union officers still embarrassed from the false alarm that Boonville was about to be raided a few days before. The frustrated official's pleas were greeted like the fairy tale about "the boy who cried 'wolf'" and ignored by officials! Colonel George H. Hall, commander of 4th Cavalry MSM, even endorsed Thompson's pleading letter back to district headquarters with the remarks "respectfully returned, with the information that the matters and things stated by Mr. Thompson are not facts. There are no bushwhackers in Cooper County." Of course, Colonel Hall was correct. They were not bushwhackers. They were Confederate recruiters![33] In fact, Union authorities in the region were confounded by other panics and false rumors that bedeviled their attempts to find out where the Rebels really were located. On the north side of the Missouri River a stagecoach driver from Glasgow, Howard county, a few days before brought to Randolph County the false rumor that Colonel Sydney D. Jackman with 200 Rebels was nearby. Never mind that the colonel and his troops were really in northern Arkansas at that moment. The Randolph County newspaper later reported that merchants closed stores and citizens armed themselves for an attack expected at any minute until Union officers interceded and brought back calm and reason.[34] Through this environment of panic and rumor Colonel Dorsey and his men simply went about the business of refitting themselves after their long, stealthy ride, infiltrated in small groups across Cooper and Moniteau Counties and crossed the Missouri River back into their chosen recruiting area. By the time Union officers finally believed Mr. Thompson and the poor farmers who were missing horses, it was too late to take action. Ironically, the Union district command ordered the same Colonel Hall that rebuked Mr. Thompson to take steps: "Major General Rosecrans reports that Jackman's [sic] men in small bodies are reported returning through Cooper and Moniteau Counties. You will please have the roads watched on the old routes."[35] Colonel Caleb Dorsey and his men had safely ridden halfway across Missouri through a veritable comedy of Union errors to return to their assigned area in the northeast part of the Show-Me State and resume recruiting for the Confederacy.

Late April and Early May Return of West's, Marchbanks', and Taylor's Guerrilla Bands to Their Southwest Missouri Operating Areas

Beginning in late April 1864 some bands of southwest Missouri's own bushwhackers began to return to their favorite operating areas after spending the winter away. These included the groups under Dade County's Kincheon West, Vernon County's Captain William Marchbanks, and Vernon County's Henry Taylor. They rode back into the region at the same time as other groups of southerners passed through on their way to more distant destinations. This variety of Rebel irregulars confused the Union leaders, and the contradictory reports made it easier for these bushwhackers to evade the harried Union patrols.

Guerrilla chieftain Kincheon West did not enjoy an easy return to southwest Missouri in late April 1864 as his band rode in the direction of Dade County, their customary operating area. West had made the Indian Nations a haven since area Union militia had driven him away from southwest Missouri the previous summer, and he was intent on repaying the militia in kind with his return. As his band of about forty

Missouri farmers working in a grain field (Underwood and Clough, eds., *Battles and Leaders of the Civil War*, vol. 2, p. 419).

rode back into Missouri through Jasper County April 27 or 28 they happened upon farmers of southern sympathy threshing winter wheat north of Carthage. The guerrillas killed three of the farmers, seized the horses and mules these fellow southerners needed for the threshing, and also confiscated supplies the farmers recently bought at Fort Scott with what little money they had. The farmers' protests about preying on their own kind fell on deaf ears, but West perked up when he learned that Captain T. J. Stemmons and a number of his company of 7th Provisional Enrolled Missouri Militia had been guarding the threshing operation earlier in the day and were staying nearby. The realization that Yankee militia was assisting southern residents return to peaceful pursuits should have impressed "Kinch" West, but he was only thinking of carrying on his private war. One year before local militia murdered West's father and two of his brothers at their Dade County home because Confederate veteran Kincheon had recently recruited his own guerrilla band.[36] As West and company left with their booty he told the farmers to tell Captain Stemmons that he only had two weeks to live before he would personally kill him. As Stemmons shortly heard about the robbery and West's threat, he decided to act fast and catch West and his band while they were out in the open encumbered with all the stolen livestock and supplies. As Stemmons wrote afterward "as soon as I heard of the robbery I hurried to Cave Springs and borrowed thirteen men from Captain [Green C.] Stotts and set on the bushwhacker's trail." Stemmons and his men caught up to the guerrillas near Preston in northeast Jasper County, and in a long running fight the militia killed five guerrillas including another of West's brothers and wounded several bushwhackers including Kincheon himself before darkness ended the chase. One of the militiamen was killed, but they punished the guerrilla band to the extent that West and his remaining men were inactive for a few weeks.[37]

Captain William Marchbanks' guerrilla band, originally from northern Vernon County and Bates County, came to the notice of the Federals in early May. They may have been in the area a few days earlier, but Union scouts of the 2nd Colorado Cavalry Regiment first reported Marchbanks by name with 60 to 100 riders near Pleasant Gap in southeast Bates County May 3.[38] Captain Marchbanks enlisted in the southern cause early in the war in the southern Missouri State Guard of 1861 where he attained his captaincy and fought in several battles. During 1862 and 1863 he was sometimes in regular Confederate service and sometimes led his own guerrilla band in his home area. He led his men south to Arkansas about December 1863 where the captain and some of his men evidently served with Joseph Shelby's brigade before returning back to their home area in spring 1864.[39] On May 7 Union troopers of 3rd Wisconsin Cavalry rode to the Papinsville area of southeast Bates County looking for eighteen guerrillas supposed to be near there, but found nothing. If that report was true, those Rebels were probably Marchbanks' men, too.[40] Two separate patrols of the 2nd Colorado Cavalry operating in Bates County reported the evening of May 8 that two groups of 25 bushwhackers both crossed the Osage River near Papinsville heading toward Pleasant Gap and the Grand River. Since the total number of Rebels approximated the number Marchbanks was reported to have at this time and he operated in this neighborhood often in 1863, these were possibly also his men. There were so many groups of southerners moving in the region about this time that it is difficult to distinguish which is which. However, Union district headquarters at Warrensburg learned Quantrill and Todd with perhaps 100 men recently arrived in the region from their long ride from Texas and scattered their men across Johnson, Lafayette, and Jackson Counties preparing to commence hostilities soon. A newspaper correspondent at Lexington on May 7 wrote to a St. Louis newspaper correctly that Quantrill, Todd, and Confederate recruiter Lieutenant Colonel Jeremiah Vardaman Cockrell with 100 men recently arrived and dispersed in the brush.[41]

Some local militias were trying to stem the tide of returning Rebels across this region, but they were nearly powerless to stop the larger groups and could only attack small numbers of bushwhackers. North of the Osage River a Captain J. A. Wells operated a small company of Union citizen guards in Henry County at this time. Wells' company during the first week of May 1864 managed to capture a lone guerrilla in Bogart Township, northwest Henry County. These northern men stated the captive belonged to a band headed by a man named Teague, and this was perhaps the same bunch that had been operating in the Henry County area for a few weeks, as described earlier. Many Henry Countians joined the Confederate army throughout the war, so guerrillas could probably get support and sustenance from a number of sympathizers there. The establishment of local citizen guards, armed by the Federals, was a new phenomenon in 1864. This much publicized program provided self defense for northern sympathizers who had earlier been in Union service and feared for their safety from southern neighbors and passing guerrillas.[42]

Local Union militia organizations further south were active in early May, too. Near Newtonia, Newton County, on May 5 or 6 Lieutenant Oscar Wear and another militiaman of the 7th Provisional Enrolled Missouri Militia chased down and killed a well-known local southerner, Dr. W. C. Adams. Dr. Adams had on his farm horses and mules he had allegedly stolen from Union units in the area.[43]

The acting Yankee provost marshal at Springfield bemoaned the sad state of affairs in McDonald County at the far southwest corner of the Show-Me State. He wrote on May 14 that the county "is still infested by outlaws, and nearly all the loyal people long since abandoned their homes, and but a few have returned; a small portion of the county only is under cultivation." Indeed, many of the southern groups traveling through southwest Missouri entered the state across war-torn McDonald County this spring, partly because there were fewer enemies to oppose them and report their passing.[44]

About mid–May the guerrilla band of former Vernon County sheriff and Nevada merchant Captain Henry Taylor rode back into Vernon County to continue operations. As this group of 50 or 60 bushwhackers crossed unfamiliar terrain near present-day Pittsburg, Kansas along Cow Creek in east McGee County on May 14 they forced 90-year-old Indiana-born Jacker Manly to guide them against his will and then shot him to death. As Taylor's band crossed the state boundary into Barton County, Missouri, they released a younger man they had also forced to accompany them as guide, and the released captive told the Manly family where to find their man's body for burial.[45]

Henry Taylor's guerrilla band marked their return to Vernon County on May 15 and 16 with intense action and hard riding, but they discovered the Federals were full of fight. During the early morning hours of May 15 the band of about 50 or 60 raided farms of northern sympathizers near Dry Creek, southwest Vernon County, taking along a few men as prisoners. They surrounded the house of noted Union scout Josiah C. Ury at daybreak, captured him and his father Lewis, and lined up their eight prisoners with the promise that they would execute them soon. Earlier, five troopers of 3rd Wisconsin Cavalry garrisoned on the West Fork of Dry Wood Creek to the west, not far from present-day Garland, Kansas, heard about trouble in the neighborhood and rode to investigate. As the Wisconsin troopers encountered evidence of the guerrilla raiding, they sent two of their number back to their post to summon help, and the three remaining cavalrymen rode on toward trouble to see what they could do. This stalwart trio happened to ride into the Ury barnyard as the guerrillas were making the Ury women prepare breakfast for the band and the eight concerned captives were lined up awaiting their sure death. For reasons best known to themselves, the three Wisconsin troopers decided that offense was their best option in the face of so many of the enemy, and they charged into the Ury barnyard shooting at the very surprised bushwhackers. The eight condemned northerners scampered away to safety except Lewis Ury who was mortally wounded in his thigh by one of his captors. Henry Taylor and his men naturally assumed the three shooting Yankees were only the vanguard of a blue-coated column bearing down on them, left the Ury farm in a cloud of dust, and sought refuge to the east in the brush of Cedar Creek. No record remains that details Taylor's casualties at the Ury farm.[46]

The bushwhackers did not rest long, because a Union pursuit of troopers of 3rd Wisconsin Cavalry from nearby posts and Colorado and Kansas troopers from Fort Scott—about 100 in all—soon chased them from Cedar Creek east to Clear Creek. Somewhere along Clear Creek in Dover Township Captain Taylor's hard-pressed guerrillas formed a line of battle which two companies of the 15th Kansas Cavalry charged, knocking several Rebels from their saddles. Taylor attempted to reform this line, but thought better of it and instead led his battered band away south along Clear Creek with the jubilant Union force chasing for about ten miles until the southerners scattered in the brush. Total casualties from this cavalry action were between three and five guerrillas killed and a number wounded, and three Kansas troopers wounded.[47]

Bill Anderson's Conspicuous Ascent Through Southwest Missouri

Unlike some of the earlier Rebel groups who rode with stealth and speed through southwest Missouri avoiding Yankee contact to reach operating areas miles to the north, Captain Bill Anderson's collection of former Quantrill bushwhackers moved deliberately and menacingly, occasionally daring Union troops to come out and fight them as they passed. Most of Anderson's about eighty guerrillas dressed in Union uniforms and enjoyed giving out false information about their identity and plans to citizens they passed in order to confuse Union leadership and confound pursuing northerners.

Even though Quantrill and George Todd had left Texas almost a month before Anderson's men, this group seemed in no hurry to return to west-central Missouri. Historian Wiley Britton in the 1890s wrote that these eighty-or-so bushwhackers lingered in the northeastern corner of the Indian Nations resting their horses on the newly emerged spring grass while watching for small patrols and supply details passing between Fort Scott and Fort Gibson that they could pounce.[48]

Anderson's blue-clad riders first appeared in Missouri May 15 or 16 near Pineville, McDonald County. A Union scout from Cassville, Barry County, reported one of the

Rebels camped at White Rock Prairie near Pineville said they were fifty men altogether and hoped to leave for Johnson County about May 19. The scout heard about or saw another thirty riders who crossed the main road near Keetsville, west Barry County, heading toward Pineville. Johnson County, Missouri was the destination for Captain Quantrill two weeks earlier, so perhaps while wintering in Texas Quantrill and his lieutenants discussed heading for that county when they returned to Missouri.[49]

On May 18 Anderson's group boldly rode north through Newton County, bypassing Newtonia and Neosho in the central part of the county. Union scouts watched them, one counting 75 riders and the second reported eighty men in the band. Anderson was oblivious to the pandemonium that followed his deliberate daylight ride through Newton County. Union Captain James M. Ritchey's Yankee garrison of 7th Provisional EMM at Neosho prepared for trouble by firing their rifle muskets in order to clean them and reload. A lady passing by later reported to the Union garrison at Mount Vernon over in Lawrence County that there were 160 of the Rebels and she distinctly heard heavy shooting, not realizing the cause of the firing she heard. Inexperienced, excited militia officers reported a variety of exaggerated claims about the bold body of horsemen to Brigadier General John B. Sanborn's district headquarters at Springfield, and even the regular Union officers at the base required a day or two to sort out the true eyewitness reports from the wild ones. Mounted militiamen were sent here and there over a four county area in response to all the exaggerated reports, all the while Anderson's men calmly continued north without a shot fired at them in anger or otherwise. This changed when they rode into Jasper County. The bushwhackers dressed in blue robbed residents along the Spring River east of Carthage that night of May 18, and passed within two miles of the Carthage garrison of fifty men of 7th Provisional Enrolled Missouri Militia. The confident raiders even sent a note in to Captain Phillip Rohrer challenging him to bring his garrison out and fight them. Amazingly, after some deliberation Captain Rohrer and his men actually sallied forth from their protection to the prairie, but Anderson's men had already left. Considering how terribly lethal this heavily armed, veteran group of bushwhackers had become by this time in the war, the militiamen were indeed fortunate that Anderson had only been toying with them. Another close call for area militia took place the next night on Dry Fork in east Jasper County. Captain T. J. Stemmons and six members of the local 7th PEMM set out an ambush along the road for local guerrillas and fired with revolvers and one shotgun on Anderson's riders as they rode through the killing zone. The night was very dark and neither Stemmons nor the bushwhackers realized the size of the force that opposed them. The militia captain saw one of the guerrilla leaders reel in his saddle and drop his firearm, but he could not tell if his men's shooting damaged the guerrillas more than that. The wounded bushwhacker shouted some choice epithets at the militia, but the guerrillas rode off toward the north without investigating more about their ambushers. When Captain Stemmons later discovered he had fired upon Bill Anderson's band that night on the road, he was amazed the guerrillas did not kill every man of his little squad.[50]

At daybreak on May 20 Anderson's band rode into the remnants of Lamar, the county seat of Barton County. Guerrillas had burned parts of Lamar earlier in the war and Quantrill's band, including some of the men now riding with Anderson, had also attacked the place unsuccessfully November 5, 1862. The defense of Lamar was in the hands of First Lieutenant George N. Alder and about 40 men of the 7th PEMM, but their command had not properly informed them of guerrillas in the area, and when the bushwhackers attacked Alder and about half of the garrison was away on a patrol. In fact, many of the remaining militiamen of the garrison ran for their lives when they saw the eighty irregulars ride in, and only nine of them under Sergeant Jeffrey Cavender were able to reach the ruins of the Barton County courthouse where their Springfield rifle muskets and ammunition were stored. Anderson's Rebels quickly laid siege to the small defense force, and Sergeant Cavender's men turned back two mounted charges and kept the guerrillas away with a lively fire for several hours. The militiamen inside the ruined courthouse remained under cover so the guerrillas could not determine how many there were of them, and a couple of ladies brought buckets of water to the defenders to enable them to remain at their shooting positions. At 10:30 that morning the guerrillas realized they would have to pay too dear a price to conquer the ruined courthouse fortress and left town in disgust. Their bravery knew no limits, but they were not so stupid as to rush one more time across an open courthouse square into the fire of accurate riflemen shooting from the safety of loopholes cut into masonry. Anderson failed to recall this lesson in September of 1864 in Howard County with loss. Southern losses were not recorded from this May 20 fight, but several men were killed and wounded, which the band carried away. The Union side had one man killed at the start of the fight.[51]

After the abortive Lamar attack, Anderson's riders employed elaborate ruses to disguise the fact that they were intent on heading slightly northeast through St. Clair County and eventually west Johnson County. The band still riding north split into two groups and members of one bunch told citizens they passed that they were under command of a "Captain Conan" and would re-unite at Warsaw, Benton County, May 23 with another band led by a "Greer." Their deception went too far when they also claimed at Warsaw they would all come under the direct supervision of Confederate Brigadier General John S. Marmaduke himself! The Fort Scott commander, Colonel Charles W. Blair, in charge of the column riding south to find and fight the bushwhackers from Lamar, took note of these various stories from the residents he encountered and passed them along to his superiors with the wry comment "I give it as it comes," and "I give you the information for what it is worth." Colonel Blair's southbound force evidently passed to the west of Anderson's northbound guerrillas by a few miles and missed them.[52] It seems Bill Anderson conducted the rest of his band's trip north in less conspicuous fashion than their conduct in southwest Missouri, since Union intelligence reports hardly mentioned their progress after this. Anderson's seventy-something riders crossed the wide Osage River at or near Taberville in west St. Clair County the evening of May 21 then turned almost straight north as they quickly rode through west Henry County and western Johnston County May 22 back into their familiar operating area for another season of guerrilla warfare.[53]

Isolated Guerrilla Actions in Southwest Missouri in Late May 1864

After the passing of Bill Anderson's bushwhacker band on their ascent through the region toward their west-central Missouri operating area, there were other actions in southwest Missouri involving smaller number of guerrillas. Some of these were also passing through on their way north, but others were local southwest Missourians returning to this region for a new fighting season.

About the time Bill Anderson's riders made their conspicuous trek north though southwest Missouri an unidentified smaller body of guerrilla riders passed almost unnoticed through north-central Greene County, just a few miles north of the large Union base at Springfield. These Rebels secured the services of Union Enrolled Missouri Militiaman 21-year-old Joseph Cooper at his home near Cave Springs. Either these bushwhackers took Cooper along by force or mislead him by disguise to guide them on their way north from his hometown. The only trace these riders left of their passing was the horribly mutilated corpse of young Cooper in the south part of Polk County. This was an ominous harbinger of more mutilations of dead by both sides in the guerrilla war in Missouri throughout 1864. These unidentified bushwhackers probably rode north through Polk County to Henry County, since Union intelligence reports said there were large numbers of southern guerrillas in parts of that county about May 23 and 24.[54]

The same Captain T. J. Stemmons whose squad of 7th Provisional EMM had somehow survived ambushing Bill Anderson's guerrilla band a few days before was involved in one fight near Carthage, Jasper County, about this time. At a house near town Stemmons and his men shot up two southerners who had formerly been members of Major Thomas R. Livingston's hard-hitting local guerrilla body earlier in the war. The militiamen left Gabe McDaniel and Ferd Ozment for dead, but they were mistaken. McDaniel was certainly dead, but Ozment somehow recovered from his terrible wounds and later escaped from the Jasper County area.[55]

In late May Colonel John D. Allen, commander of the 7th Provisional EMM, ordered his scattered militiamen to assemble on Neosho, Newton County, to thwart a reported attack on that town, leaving a number of garrison towns undefended for a few days. Captain Henry Taylor and twelve of his guerrillas took advantage of the militia's absence from the war-torn town of Lamar at two in the morning of May 28 and burned ten houses there, leaving very few buildings left standing. The women and children left in town could offer no resistance to Taylor and his men. The fires consumed county records as well as personal possessions and household goods. The district Union commander, Brigadier Sanborn, ordered Colonel Allen to send militiamen back to guard what remained of Lamar when he heard about Taylor's arson there, and he was irked to discover that the threatened attack on Neosho was merely a rumor.[56]

Meanwhile, at Neosho, troops

A town burns (Charles C. Coffin, *Drum-Beat of the Nation*, 1887, p. 391).

of the 8th Cavalry MSM on May 29 heard about guerrillas robbing farms along Indian Creek in southwest Stone County, many miles to the southeast. The Neosho commander sent Captain John R. Kelso and thirty troopers of the 8th who arrived in the area on the morning of May 30. Near a guerrilla Waitman's house on Mill Creek, Kelso's patrol found and killed two bushwhackers. The troopers crossed the Arkansas boundary and near Butler's Creek found and destroyed a hidden tanyard. On May 31 Captain Kelso's patrol chased a Lieutenant McGee's small guerrilla band near Honey Creek, killing two and wounding two of the Rebels. After the chase the Federals returned to the bushwhacker camp and destroyed it, then returned back to Missouri and their Neosho base, having evidently suffered no loss to themselves.[57]

It is surprising, therefore, that even though southwest Missouri was largely depopulated in the spring of 1864, it was still a battlefield that season of passing guerrilla and Confederate recruiting bands and its own local bushwhacker bands returning from a winter somewhere else. Although regular Confederate forces were far removed from this corner of Missouri, large numbers of southern irregulars managed to cross it with a fearful amount of mounted, veteran combat power-mostly intended for the northwest and northeast parts of the Show-Me State. This region's own guerrilla groups of Kincheon West, William Marchbanks, and Henry Taylor brought a local surge of southern energy back to battle-weary southwest Missouri that gave promise that the coming summer of 1864 would be action packed here as previous ones had been.

EIGHT

Spring 1864 in Northeast Missouri

Guerrilla actions during the spring of 1864 throughout northeast Missouri were small, seemingly isolated incidents widely spread across this quadrant of Missouri. Some were acts of resistance against Union military presence here by southern men who had remained hidden and mostly inactive throughout the bitter cold winter that recently ended. Other incidents involved a few brave Rebels who traveled through Union lines to return to this region from wintering in the South during this spring of 1864. A few identified guerrilla leaders here, like Captain John Drury Pulliam and Captain Clifton D. Holtzclaw, had served the previous year here with the ambitious Confederate recruiting command of Colonel Sydney D. Jackman. Others were individual Rebel soldiers returned home from the war, who for a variety of reasons re-entered the war as bushwhackers in their home neighborhoods. The tempo of their combined actions would increase as warm weather returned to make a bold statement to the Union military that the southern will to resist in northeast Missouri was still evident.

Captains Holtzclaw and Pulliam and Others Operating from the Missouri River Counties of Boone, Howard, and Chariton

The most guerrilla actions this spring took place in and near the Missouri River counties of Boone, Howard, and Chariton primarily as a carryover from the intense Confederate recruiting Colonel Sidney D. Jackman performed here with his wide-ranging recruiting command during 1863. That this area was the center of deep-seated, well-hidden Rebel activity was in large part due to the determination and expertise of two of Jackman's officers, Captains Clifton D. Holtzclaw and John Drury Pulliam, who had remained in this region in hiding throughout the long winter. Both of these leaders had Howard County roots, but many of their men were from Boone, Linn, and surrounding counties, and this led to actions this spring across at least six counties. The operations security that Captain Holtzclaw and Captain Pulliam maintained in all their actions here was so effective that after a while the Union military believed Colonel Jackman was still in personal command, even though he obviously commanded his own troops in northern Arkansas this spring. The Rebels picked their actions carefully since their numbers were few at first, partly to prevent the Union military from discovering their whereabouts and concentrating forces against them.

The first action of March in this part of the northwest quadrant was initiated by Union forces, though not in an official capacity. Three times during the first week of

March black Union soldiers on furlough in Boonville, north Cooper County, raided across the Missouri River into Howard County. These black men had formerly been slaves in Howard County and they brought back family members out from under slavery back to the Union garrison in Boonville to live free. Each time they seized wagons, stock to pull them, and loaded them full of relatives, furniture, tobacco, and anything else of value to help finance their new free life. It was rumored around Boonville that northern authorities even permitted and perhaps encouraged white soldiers to accompany these raids to ensure that the black soldiers and their family members remained safe. Even though slavery was still the law in Missouri, for months there had been a steady flow of fugitive slaves fleeing through the countryside toward free-state Kansas or the safety of Federal garrisons, to which Union leaders seemed to pay little regard.[1] The black soldiers' raiding in Howard County did not seem to produce reactions from the guerrillas in the region, perhaps because they were still scattered about the region in hiding awaiting warmer weather.

At least four unidentified bushwhackers raided a couple of homes in the southern tip of Chariton County about six miles northwest of Glasgow, Howard County, the evening of March 16. The raiders took blankets, gunpowder, and shot from James Page, but they mortally wounded Baptist minister A. T. Hite when they robbed his home. The thieves may have heard that Reverend Hite recently sold stock and were upset when he did not surrender the money right away. Neighbors nearby wondered if these same guerrillas had also burned a tobacco barn a few days earlier. The killing of this minister created quite a stir in the region, as the incident was reported in at least four area newspapers. Hite's widow later offered a reward for the identity of the robbers, which led to the April 1864 capture of a man named Briggs in Sullivan County.[2]

On March 25 near Renick, southeast Randolph County, three troopers of Company C, 9th Cavalry MSM scouting in the area captured two local men, John T. Lewis and Solomon Lewis, armed with revolvers. Both men were previously Union soldiers in the 1st Provisional Enrolled Missouri Militia, but Solomon deserted from active duty near this same village the previous June and joined Confederate Colonel Caleb Perkins' command in the area. John Lewis, surprisingly, at the time of his apprehension was a fellow trooper of the 9th Cavalry MSM, but in Company G, stationed in nearby Sturgeon, and, after this incident, finished his service obligation and was mustered out at war's end. John's service seems not to have been marred by this arrest with a known Union deserter and Confederate, perhaps because Solomon Lewis was a relative. The available record fails to record Solomon's fate after this arrest.[3]

Another patrol of 9th Cavalry MSM in south Chariton County, the morning of March 26 captured a Confederate deserter and guerrilla, Green Irvin, and took him to Union authorities at the nearby village of Brunswick for questioning. There, Irvin revealed (1) he was 20 years old and raised in Saline County, (2) had robbed a Chariton County man named Grotjohn at Bowling Green Prairie the previous summer, (3) after that he had gone south to join Confederate Brigadier General John S. Marmaduke's

Colt's Revolving Rifle (Schuyler, Hartley, and Graham, *Illustrated Catalogue of Arms and Military Goods,* 1864, p. 134).

Black men having returned to bring their families out of slavery (Charles C. Coffin, *Drum-Beat of the Nation*, 1887, p. 365).

command, (4) deserted Marmaduke's command while near Pilot Knob in southeast Missouri in fall of 1863. Irvin then stated (5) he had ridden back north of the Missouri River where he was caught. Union soldiers took Irvin to Macon City, where his fate does not seem to have been recorded, but he was probably executed as a guerrilla.[4]

The provost marshal of the northeast district, Colonel William F. Switzler, wrote to Major General Rosecrans March 30 that small groups of armed Rebels had crossed the Missouri River mostly into Boone County during the previous few days. In light of this and "the rapid approach of the bushwhacking season" Switzler pleaded that a company of Federal cavalry be stationed at Columbia to keep watch over Boone and Callaway Counties. Indeed, all of northern Missouri north of the Missouri River as of February 29 was protected only by 27 Federal officers and 587 enlisted soldiers-not counting Enrolled Missouri Militia men, compared to several times that many in other districts of the state. Whatever else it achieved, Colonel Switzler's plea did not result in more troops being sent to north Missouri, as by April 30 there were only 32 officers and 560 enlisted men-not counting EMM-stationed north of the Missouri River.[5]

At eleven in the evening of April 6, an intruder tried to smash his way into a home where Captain William A. Skinner of the 46th EMM was staying at Allen, east-central Randolph County. The young man loudly tried several doors and window shutters without success, causing Captain Skinner to fire warning shots from his revolver and Colt revolving rifle to deter the young man. Finally, when the intruder tried to bash his way through a side door with a large plank the captain fired another bullet through the door which struck the unknown man in the neck. The intruder died several hours later leaving no identification nor indication why he attempted so stubbornly to force his way into the house.[6]

Between April 8 and 11 up to 35 bushwhackers evidently of Captain Holtzclaw's band conducted a series of raids on communities of south Linn County and west Chariton County to inaugurate the start of the guerrilla season for 1864 in this area. During the night of April 7/8 six or eight of these guerrillas robbed four homes of northern sympathizers in the railroad town of Brookfield, south-central Linn County. The victims recognized three of the robbers as members of Holtzclaw's group and who were local Linn County residents. Indeed, Captain Holtzclaw himself spent part of the preceding winter hiding in Linneus, the Linn County seat. The raiders seized cash, horses, horse equipment, clothing, firearms, and ammunition then quickly rode out of town. Guerrillas of Holtzclaw's band robbed some of the same families several times previously during the war. Sergeant Thomas J. Wesly of Company H, 9th Cavalry MSM organized a pursuit from the town of Laclede consisting of four soldiers and seven citizens and set out for north Chariton County based on information Lieutenant Colonel Daniel M. Draper of his regiment sent to him by telegraph from the Union district headquarters at Macon City. Meanwhile, a few of the Brookfield raiders rode to the small community of Porche's Prairie, west-central Chariton County, and on the evening of April 10 robbed several families of northern sympathy there, and shot to death Private John Smith, a discharged trooper of the 9th Cavalry MSM. About 9 pm the evening of April 11 Sergeant Westy's patrol had a meeting engagement with the guerrillas at Elk Creek, northwest Chariton County and killed one of the bushwhackers' horses at first fire. The rest dispersed immediately with the northerners in pursuit. Two of the Rebels jumped their horses into Elk Creek and may have drowned, but in the dark it was impossible to verify these men's fate. When the chasing was over Sergeant Westy held three prisoners at no loss to his patrol. Besides the captives—William Hickman, William Hines, and Jackson Bazier—the patrol captured five horses, six shotguns, three Colt revolvers, three Federal overcoats, three Federal uniform coats, and one U.S.-issue saddle.

Sergeant Westy's superior, Lieutenant Colonel Draper, later reported that Hickman had guided the guerrillas in the Porch's Prairie raid, that members of the 9th Cavalry MSM had wounded Hines in fighting during June 1863, and Bazier was a known member of Holtzclaw's band. For a while on April 10 and 11 the guerrillas held discharged Union veteran of 18th Missouri Infantry William D. Vice as prisoner and guide, and he counted at various times 35 different men riding with this band in these raids. Vice made no statement that Captain Holtzclaw himself was riding with them, however. The Rebels had bragged to Vice "that they would have possession of the State before next fall and stop the draft." This last statement was perhaps another of the frequently heard veiled threats that Confederate Major General Sterling Price would be leading his army in Arkansas to invade Missouri and seize it from the occupying Union troops sometime this year. The various Union officers who wrote about these Linn and Chariton raids attributed overall command of these guerrillas incorrectly to Colonel Jackman, then operating against Union troops in northern Arkansas. Colonel Jackman had operated so efficiently and masterfully against Union troops in this region for several months during 1863 that they refused to believe that he was no longer conducting guerrilla warfare in their midst. A few days later Union officers in this region correctly assigned Rebel leadership roles to Captain Clifton D. Holtzclaw, but mistakenly mangled Captain J. Drury Pulliam's name to "Pullman" and added a third imaginary officer by the name of "Frost" to the Rebel leadership team.[7]

Isolated Guerrilla Depredations in Chariton, Randolph, and Monroe Counties During Last Half of May

A few guerrilla activities in these several counties during the last half of May 1864 were a signal that bushwhackers there were getting set for an action-filled summer of fighting again. During the evening of May 16 two unidentified guerrillas robbed the farm of Thomas Ward in Richmond Township of central Howard County of a horse, a rifle, a revolver, and $15. Perhaps the robbers were equipping a new recruit in their ranks.[8]

On May 20 a guerrilla named Wilkie and an unidentified bushwhacker called on Elder C. M. W. Phillips at his blacksmith shop next to his home in Clark Township, northeast-central Chariton County. Phillips had been a chaplain for the local 35th EMM earlier in the war, and happened to be working on a pistol in his shop when the two men called for him to come to the door. The callers were evasive about naming their business with Phillips, so he opened the door with the pistol and mortally shot one of the guerrillas with it when they demanded his surrender. The second bushwhacker immediately shot Elder Phillips dead with a shot to his head. Later in the day the surviving Rebel returned with three comrades and pulled Phillips' body into the yard where this "knight of the bush" kicked and stomped the corpse in a fit of anger over the death of Wilkie. When Mrs. Phillips loudly objected, the southerners used abusive language to her and threatened harm to her, then set fire to the Phillips home and left. Mrs. Phillips was able to extinguish the flames.[9]

That night somewhere in Randolph County six bushwhackers entered the home of Esquire Conrad, seized his two horses and two shotguns. They inquired for Conrad's son, who had been in the militia earlier in the war, but could not find him at the house. They left with their booty and did the Conrads no further harm.[10]

While riding on the public road about two miles south of Paris, central Monroe County, middle-aged farmer Blake Minor on May 24 refused the demand of a roadside guerrilla to surrender his horse and simply rode on. The infuriated Rebel shot Minor's horse in the neck, but fled after the farmer returned the fire, wounding the would-be robber in the arm.[11]

Quiet Advent of Colonel Dorsey's Recruiting Command

About the last days of May 1864 Confederate Colonel Caleb Dorsey and his recruiting command of about 112 veteran Rebels crossed the Missouri River into Boone and Howard Counties in small groups from Cooper and Moniteau Counties, after having spent the previous three or four weeks avoiding the Union military as they rode up through southwest Missouri, as described in Chapter Seven. Colonel Dorsey of Pike County was an accomplished behind-Yankee-lines recruiter for the Confederacy since 1861. He brought large numbers of northeast Missouri southerners to the Rebel army on several occasions after having recruited them in a deliberate but secretive fashion mostly in Pike, Lincoln, Audrain, St. Charles, Warren, Montgomery, and Callaway Counties. Dorsey and his recruiters were most likely heading back into that region this time, too.[12] During the night of May 26/27 some guerrillas took a couple of horses and saddles near the village of Renick, southeast Randolph County. A band of bushwhackers, estimated from 20 to 40, raided a store in the town of Allen, east-central Randolph County, the next night. They took about $175 worth of clothing from the store, but did not ask for cash. Perhaps these raiders were part of Colonel Dorsey's recruiting command that arrived in the region about this time. Whatever the identity of these bushwhackers, the North Missouri Railroad ran through both villages, and the Union district headquarters at Macon City was only 25 miles further north on the same line. These raiders did not seem to fear the Yankee district command would send troops down the line quick enough to catch them, and indeed, the Union military at Macon City did not send reinforcements fast enough to harass these raiders.[13]

A strange encounter took place the evening of May 27 at the bridge over Hinkson Creek about one mile south of Columbia, in Boone County. Unidentified soldiers probably stationed at Columbia overheard a conversation at the bridge between Jim Washington, a black man who lived in the area, and some guerrillas who were contracting Washington to sell pistols to them. The soldiers heard enough to learn this group was discussing something harmful to themselves, so they fired some shots at the small group severely wounding Jim Washington. The bushwhackers escaped into the darkness, and the wounded Washington told the soldiers that he had been talking to Captain Tom Todd, a well-known local guerrilla leader. Part of the reason was unusual in that black citizens of Boone County did not commonly seek out guerrillas, who bore increasing malice against slaves and former slaves as public debate increased throughout 1864 about slave emancipation in Missouri.[14]

Ramseys, Briscoe, and Others in Spring 1864 Actions in the Callaway County Area

There were a few determined bushwhackers that operated in the east edge of Boone County and in Callaway and Montgomery Counties during the spring of 1864. These guerrillas operated locally, for the most part, and did not roam too far from their home area when they could help it. This had been their practice through much of 1863 and perhaps earlier. This spring the more well-known of these veteran irregulars included brothers Barton J. and Joel Franklin "Frank" Ramsey from Franklin County across the Missouri River and John F. Briscoe from Warren County just to the east. At least during 1863 these three murdered men of northern sympathy, especially men they felt had informed the authorities about them. They also took what they needed from northerners. Frank Ramsey had been one of the leaders in a band of about 15 bushwhackers that raided the German-American settlement at Rhineland in south Montgomery County 26 May 1863. Local militia shot down and killed fellow guerrilla leader Joe Cole December 1 near Portland, southeast Callaway County, but the loss did not seem to affect the Ramseys and John Briscoe a few months later.[15]

During the evening of March 8 a small local militia patrol stopped at a house four miles east of Williamsburg, east-central Callaway County. The guard left outside the house reported that later six or eight unidentified riders stopped for an instant in front of the house and then galloped off at a high rate of speed, as if they had seen some signal warning them the militiamen were there. An official of the local Union provost marshal's office at nearby Wellsville, northwest Montgomery County, wrote about this encounter and the strong southern feeling in that neighborhood: "they [the militiamen] report that there is nothing to be found out from the citizens, who are all rebels, and do not deny that they would go in the brush, but, on the contrary, boast of it."[16]

There is a brief mention of area southern guerrillas in this area during early May 1864 in a letter from a northern sympathizer of Danville, Montgomery County, to the Union district commander May 10. The letter writer, L. A. Thompson, told of three well-armed bushwhackers under the leadership of a man named Prig hanging around

Williamsburg since late April or early May. The trio took three horses from a northern sympathizer named Miller who lived a mile south of the village. Thompson also heard from another northerner that John Briscoe and at least one of the Ramsey brothers with other guerrillas were seen near the town of Portland, southeast Callaway County, also in early May.[17]

These small numbers of bushwhackers seemed to await only a strong catalyst to ignite their irregular style of war once again. That catalyst consisted of about 25 veteran bushwhackers who on May 14 galloped through Hermann, crossed the Missouri River, and scattered into this region with the militia from Hermann in pursuit, as described in Chapter Six. One of these Rebels evidently stole a horse from James Craig in southwest Montgomery County that night. Craig tracked the man riding his horse to near Williamsburg, but he was reluctant to pursue further because of that town's reputation as a "Rebel town." Meanwhile, another eight armed bushwhackers on May 15 crossed to the north side of the Missouri River at Coal Creek, three miles west of Hermann and disappeared into the brush of south Montgomery County near Rhineland. This made about 33 heavily armed, experienced guerrillas were suddenly thrust upon this two-county area. That same day four guerrilla in Union uniform or four Yankee soldiers robbed a southern sympathizer named Tatum of his cash six miles north of New Florence, in north-central Montgomery County. On May 16 one lone bushwhacker stopped at the Baker farm seven miles east of Danville in central Montgomery County, forced the family to feed him, and then rode in a southerly direction. About this time fifteen armed guerrillas robbed a store in Readsville, east-central Callaway County, taking little but tobacco and whiskey. The newspaper editor in Fulton was of the opinion that these raiders were part of the bunch that raced through Hermann on May 14, and he was probably correct. On the evening of May 17 five guerrillas heavily armed with shotguns and pistols forced their way into a store in Hallsville, northeast Boone County. These intruders stated to the startled store owner that they were part of the band that raced through Hermann three days before, but, surprisingly, they took nothing and rode off into the night. Perhaps just their imposing presence was all they wished to impart to the startled village. Basically, since all these Rebels crossed the Missouri River into Montgomery County May 14 and 15, they were all over the Callaway County area like an angry swarm of hornets. All this activity greatly upset local northerners and awed the small detachment of Enrolled Missouri Militia nearly into inactivity. These Rebels repeatedly appeared out in the open as is trying to assert their presence in the region and daring the Union military to come fight them. A few days later Confederate Colonel Caleb Dorsey's command of 112 Rebel recruiters would also ride through this area and begin recruiting here over the summer, further overwhelming limited numbers of Union troops in this part of northeast Missouri.[18]

Guerrilla Onslaught and Kansas Backlash During April and May 1864 in Pike County

Pike County, Missouri, had a large southern population and contributed many brave southern men, such as Colonel John Q. Burbridge and his brothers, to the southern cause during the previous three years of the war. Now, during late April and May 1864 a large number of unidentified southern guerrillas operated from sanctuaries across the Mississippi River in Illinois and sanctuaries offered by southern residents in Pike County to victimize and intimidate northern sympathizers in this county. This was reminiscent of a bushwhacker violence surge in Pike County one year before during spring 1863 which Union militia had brutally put down. Pike County remained quiet for several months after this the previous year until the autumn of 1863 when Confederate Colonel Caleb Dorsey quietly recruited Pike County southerners and others and successfully carried many of those recruits back to the southern army in Arkansas.[19] The residents of Pike County in May 1864 had no way of knowing that Colonel Dorsey was already riding with his recruiting command back to the region around Pike County to recruit for the Rebel army this summer, as stated earlier. Meanwhile, before Dorsey returned, a new surge of bushwhacker violence broke out in spring 1864, supported by southern civilians in Illinois and Pike County, and it seemed all but unstoppable to both the militia and local northern residents. Then, members of the notorious "jayhawker" regiment, the 7th Kansas Cavalry, set about in a few days in late May and early June to blunt this southern resurgence in a direct, bloodthirsty manner.

This intimidating guerrilla movement began in late April 1864, in a seemingly innocuous way. Local Union authorities captured and incarcerated three local guerrillas in the jail at the county seat of Bowling Green, central Pike County. A local Union official from the provost marshal's office wrote that two of these "are the worst bushwhackers and thieves that Missouri has ever produced," but did not name them. About April 22 or 23 when the prisoners' comrades or friends attempted to break them out, Bowling Green citizens united to repulse this effort and kept the trio in jail. The same official wisely pointed out that "the citizens are not prepared to keep any force from coming in."[20]

About mid–May three or four armed bushwhackers near Frankford, in northwest Pike County near the Ralls County line, robbed a Mr. Griffith of several hundred dollars. These Rebels may have been based close to Griffith's neighborhood where they could have heard from friends that this man had such a sum of money on hand.[21]

The Union command structure must have refused local requests to send a few troops to Pike County, and the bushwhackers struck again at the vulnerable residents. Only garbled details of a large-scale guerrilla raid on Pike County survive in sketchy newspaper reports from St. Louis and Howard County, rather far removed from the scene. These conflicting accounts reported that a gang of either 20 or 70 bushwhackers crossed the Mississippi River from their sanctuary in the tangles of Calhoun County, Illinois evidently on Friday night May 20, and, in a fast-paced crime spree, stole about fifteen horses and some ammunition from a number of farms between Louisiana and Bowling Green. When the raiders reached middle-aged William Kindrick's farm about eight miles south of Spencerburg, west-central Pike County, they called Mr. Kindrick from his home, but he answered with gunfire, according to the Howard County newspaper. One of Kindrick's shots wounded one of the raiders in the shoulder, but the Rebels' answering fire wounded one of his sons in the thigh. The St. Louis paper assured its readers that young Kindrick's wound was "not dangerous." Meanwhile, citizens formed a posse and pursued the horse thieves as far west as Spencerburg, recovering five horses. The St. Louis newspaper article mentioned an unconfirmed rumor that the posse also captured three bushwhackers.[22]

The raiders evidently re-crossed the Mississippi River with most of their booty. The guerrillas had learned that as long as they behaved themselves across the river in Illinois they could hide out there between raids relying on support and subsistence from Illinois residents sympathetic to the South. This tactic worked especially well if their only opposition during the raids continued to be citizen posses and not actual Yankee troops. For the rest of the war Missouri Union authorities would be cooperating with Illinois officials to ferret out hiding Missouri Confederates and bring them back to the Show-Me State for tribunals.

If the Union command gave little attention to guerrillas in Pike County before, they reacted to this interstate raid with great concern and action. Major General Rosecrans had been partly diverted from affairs in northeast Missouri by the traveling groups of Rebels streaming north through south Missouri, but suddenly on May 28 he realized that the few troops he had trying to keep control of north Missouri were insufficient to handle the growing numbers of bushwhackers and Confederate recruiters active there. Rosecrans directed the northeast district commander at Macon City, Brigadier General Clinton B. Fisk, to order the Enrolled Missouri Militia for several counties to active duty to handle the problem, and specifically named Pike County. General Fisk was aware of the problem as he told his boss that "squads of villains are constantly drifting through our lines south of the river [the Missouri River], and crossing to this side." At the same time Fisk ordered a subordinate to "send a scout of 50 men into Pike County on a mission of extermination of thieves and guerrillas.... Don't take any prisoners of the class named. Kill them wherever you find them in their hellish work." Fisk wrote to Lieutenant Colonel Daniel Draper of his staff to "be prepared for lively work and give the rascals no quarter."[23]

Unnamed Union officials back in St. Louis took General Fisk's strong words seriously and unofficially sent him just the right soldiers to root out the southerners in Pike County giving aid, support, and intelligence to the bushwhackers. Part of the 7th Kansas Cavalry, reputed earlier in the war to be one of the most offensive of the jayhawker units along the Missouri and Kansas border, was for a few days waiting in depot in St. Louis for the rest of the regiment so they could be sent on to another war front. There were still enough "hard cases" in this notorious regiment by May 1864 to qualify for "special duty" with no questions asked, and what happened over the next six or seven days before the 7th Kansas Cavalry shipped out south to Memphis was not entered into the war record of any of its companies or the regiment. Some northern sympathizers in Pike County gave the Kansans a kill list of 52 southern citizens of the county, and the troopers energetically murdered at least seven or eight from the list at their rural homes. A St. Louis newspaper article about this episode described these atrocities by Union troops as taking place during the week of 29 May through 4 June 1864, and detailed how several Kansans came for newspaper editor James Monaghan at his place of business. The outnumbered editor cut some of his assailants with a jackknife, but Monaghan suffered several injuries himself and they wrecked his office. A number of other southerners including a prominent attorney promptly moved to St. Louis for their safety, whereupon the visiting Kansans returned to their unit and shipped out to Memphis in early June.[24]

Guerrilla Warfare and the Illinois and Iowa Connections of the Knights of the Golden Circle in Lewis, Marion, Shelby, and Clark Counties

There were large southern populations in the Missouri counties of Marion, Lewis, and Clark along the Mississippi River upriver from embattled Pike County. After remaining rather quiet during 1863, secessionists here renewed their war activity in the spring of 1864.

On March 8 five unidentified armed men in civilian clothes, professing to be returned Confederate soldiers, forced their way into five homes of northern sympathizers in the area around LaBelle, west Lewis County. At gunpoint, these intruders threatened the inhabitants of the homes to surrender money, firearms, horses, and clothing, and even hanged two men for a while to force their compliance. One man they also threatened and accused of informing on his southern neighbors to the authorities. The bushwhackers had things their own way with the first four homes they invaded, but when they broke into the fifth home looking for Union recruiting officer William Winsell that official shot at them, badly wounding one of the guerrillas. Although the southerners fired their pistols at Winsell, he managed to escape and they dragged their wounded comrade from the house, leaving a horse and overcoat behind in their haste. The residents of the invaded homes reported that they did not recognize the guerrillas as men who had lived in that area.[25] A few days later on March 19 unidentified guerrillas burned the home of a Joseph Ingersoll in Marion County just south of Lewis County, probably because he was a staunch northern sympathizer.[26]

The guerrillas who occasionally appeared in these counties in the far northwest corner of Missouri also had an important Illinois connection, as did southerners in Mississippi River counties just to the south. Like Rebels who raided in Pike County, as described earlier, some of these Missouri southerners found they could live longer and avoid capture better if they actually lived off the charity of southern sympathizers on the Illinois side and only came over to Missouri when they deemed it important to do so.

On the evening of March 29 eight very irate citizens of the Canton area of east Lewis County started tracking five guerrillas who had just burgled and robbed a few homes in that area and escaped across the river from Gregory's Landing, southeast Clark County, to Illinois. At daylight on March 30 the citizen posse caught up to the bushwhackers on the Illinois side and opened fire, wounding one guerrilla and capturing three. Of the three captives, one was from Kentucky and supposedly once a member of Confederate Colonel John Hunt Morgan's command; one was from Illinois, and the third was Indiana-born, mid-twenties Thomas McCalister of the carpenter James McCalister family of Monticello, central Lewis County. Evidently, these raiders did not realize that some of their Missouri victims would be angry enough to follow them across the Mississippi River into Illinois and shoot them up.[27]

Gunfight at Hunnewell in Shelby County on 18 April

The little railroad town of Hunnewell in the southeast corner of Shelby County near the Marion County line endured a classic shootout April 18 that would have done justice to the Old West. On that day Captain James Foreman, the superintendent of the Monroe County poor farm, tracked two stolen horses to Hunnewell. The thieves appeared to be three bushwhackers "armed to the teeth" inside the grocery in town, and Captain Foreman, who was also commander of Company D of the local 70th Enrolled Missouri Militia Regiment, telegraphed to the district Union headquarters at Macon City and obtained prompt permission to deal with the robbers himself. Foreman obtained the help of five other citizens, all armed, and they entered the grocery and attempted to capture the trio of guerrillas. The three southerners began shooting at once and a fierce gun battle ensued for a few tense moments. One of Foreman's helpers, a Mr. Eazel, and the guerrilla named Maupin shot each other to death; a second unidentified guerrilla shot another posse member, Benedict J. Durbin, a part-time soldier in the 70th EMM, through the body and managed to escape from Hunnewell. The third guerrilla, Andrew Snyder supposedly from Iowa, shot Captain Foreman twice in one arm and in the back, then ran out of the grocery and hid in a railroad car on a siding. Snyder had dropped his pistol while running, so he surrendered quietly when confronted, and the battered posse sent him to district headquarters at Macon City. The Union soldiers at Macon City tried Snyder by tribunal and executed him on 29 April. The badly wounded posse member, Durbin, died of his wound about a month later, leaving behind a large family.[28] The growing frequency of citizen posses chasing and doing battle with heavily armed guerrillas was a strong indicator that civilians in many parts of Missouri were willing to take a larger role in restoring law and order in their communities, and that civil law may someday replace martial law in the war-weary Show-Me State. Missourians could not know in May 1864 that milestone was still a year away.

A particularly ruthless band of three guerrillas from northwest Missouri was at large in the part of Illinois across from Marion and Lewis Counties, Missouri during April and early May. This small band had on 11 December 1863 robbed a store in Caldwell County, Missouri, killing the owner and another man; then fled to Illinois; were captured in Quincy, Illinois during the winter; but escaped. Union Lieutenant Colonel A. J. Swain of the 65th EMM at Chillicothe, Livingston County, heard these bushwhackers were still at large in the Quincy region of Illinois and traveled across Missouri with several men to find and apprehend these fugitives. Swain and his men used detective work to learn the hiding place of the dangerous trio; captured them near

One of the guerrillas hid in a boxcar on a siding ("View of the Stations on Grant's Military Railroad," *Harper's Weekly*, 24 December 1864, New York, the Patrick's station, p. 821).

Mt. Sterling in Brown County, Illinois; and brought them back to jail in St. Joseph by May 11. Unfortunately, a few days later this trio and other prisoners broke jail and got away into the countryside. These three desperadoes were James Nave, allegedly of Livingston County; Nicholas Weldon of Daviess County; and William Stone of Platte County.[29]

When left to their own devices, American soldiers tend to deal with their concerns in a direct manner, and a group of furloughed Union soldiers in Clark County conducted a campaign of terror against southern sympathizers and collaborators between May 21 and 26. The three-year Federal regiments formed in spring of 1861 reached the end of their tour of duty in spring 1864, and many of these veterans were sent home for 30-day furloughs as an inducement for re-enlisting. As a distant Howard County newspaper explained this violence, many of these soldiers in the Clark County area bore a grudge against the citizens of Athens in the northeast corner and set fire to several buildings there and left. Citizens extinguished the fires, but the furloughed soldiers returned, re-lit the fires, and destroyed four stores belonging to alleged southern sympathizers. A battle at Athens on 5 August 1861 was the first fight of the Civil War for several of these Yanks of the 21st Missouri Infantry Regiment, and they still considered the town a hotbed of secessionist support. Now that these men had consummated this part of their three-year-old "unfinished business," they next threatened to burn the town of Alexandria. Some enterprising locals believed the threat to the extent that on the day given for the burning they drove thirteen empty wagons near Alexandria with which to carry away the plunder they expected to ransack from the burning town. The veterans failed to carry out their threat, much to the relief of the Alexandrians, but, instead, ransacked the store in nearby St. Francisville belonging to Maryland-born Robert McKee.

The Union district command was aghast that fellow Union soldiers were seemingly running amuck in three Mississippi River towns on the east edge of Clark County, until somebody explained that the violence was actually a beneficial operation against secret Rebels. Northern sympathizer William Bishop of Alexandria confidentially explained to General Fisk's office that:

> This place appears to be one of the principal [sic] points for ingress and egress for disloyal persons to and from Illinois and Iowa. Many of the worst class of our citizens have taken refuge in Illinois and Iowa, and almost hold possession of the counties of Lee, in Iowa, and Hancock, in Illinois. I am credibly informed that powder, shot, and etc. is purchased both in Iowa and Illinois and brought into this State; one individual gives as much as 50 kegs per week. That the Knights of the Golden Circle exist, and are well organized, throughout all this section I have no doubt. You can assure the general commanding that no effort shall be spared on my part to effect the object desired.

It would appear that informed northerners in this area may have directed these angry veterans to perform violence in order to expedite the cleaning out of secret Rebel suppliers and conspirators. These northerners intended to damage the "underground railroad" the South had established here to funnel their own fugitives to sanctuaries just outside the Missouri border and badly needed war supplies from Illinois and Iowa into Missouri so it could be sent to the southern army in Arkansas. In spite of the damage the secret Knights of the Golden Circle organization suffered from Union detectives, informants, and spies perhaps this "Copperhead" society did function just enough in this corner of Missouri to set up a successful supply and fugitive network. That could explain how so many southern guerrillas found asylum just over the river in Illinois.[30]

More Spring 1864 Depredations by Furloughed Union Soldiers in Putnam, Sullivan, Linn, and Knox Counties

While the Union command had been desperate for more troops to handle the growing numbers of southern irregulars in northeast Missouri this spring, they did not appreciate the volunteer help large numbers of furloughed Yankee regulars gave them in parts of this region. A number of these were "uninvited guests to the party" and set about righting the secessionist wrongs near home before returning to the war front.

Union soldiers of the 18th Missouri Infantry Regiment were also given 30-day furloughs at home for re-enlisting at the end of their three-year term of service, and a number of them brought their own version of war to southerners living in their neighborhoods. On March 26 Brigadier General Odon Guitar, the district commander of northeast Missouri at Macon City, proved he was a man of few words when he said "in simple terms, these men have inaugurated a reign of blood and terror in Putnam and Sullivan Counties." General Fisk informed General Rosecrans that during the week of March 20 through 26 "at Unionville [county seat of Putnam County] they shot and killed 3 peaceable citizens and mortally wounded the fourth. They also shot at and drove out of town a large number of other citizens, killing a fourth man at another point in the county." What incensed these veterans was while they were away risking their lives on distant war fronts southern sympathizers in their home communities were enjoying the comforts of peace while giving encouragement and aid to secessionist belief and even bushwhackers that could harm northern families. Several of the 18th Missouri Infantry veterans consumed great quantities of alcoholic beverages, and in some cases this led them to shoot at men they only suspected of being disloyal. Civil court was in session in Unionville during some of this wanton violence, and some of the court officers were northern sympathizers who refused to step in and quell the madness,

Union Brigadier General Odon Guitar was commander of the District of Northeast Missouri during early 1864 (private collection; courtesy of the late Bob Younger and Mary Younger and Andy Turner).

and even seemed to encourage some of the veterans' excesses. In one tragic instance, the infantrymen ordered a reverend of the Methodist Episcopal Church South to leave town, and while he was riding away on his horse to get away from the abusive veterans one of them fired a haphazard, careless shot in his direction which struck the minister a mortal wound in his back. Another more fortunate victim of the veterans' violent spree came away with no wounds to his body but seven bullet holes in his clothing. Violence finally subsided when officials and officers the truculent veterans knew and respected made repeated and persistent appeals. Throughout the area the rumor passed that these veterans had a list of 18 southerners they targeted for retribution, and indeed, they killed several men of southern sympathy.

Having seemingly slaked their bloodlust, the veterans of the 18th Missouri Infantry behaved themselves for the most part until the thirty days of furlough drew to a close in late March 1864 and it was time to travel from Putnam County across Sullivan County to catch the train at Laclede, Linn County, and return to military duty. The 1882 history of Linn County wryly commented that men of the 18th "on their return to take the cars at Laclede ... passed through this county and committed serious depredations on the people, Unionists and Confederates," but omitted the details. Linn County had become notorious earlier in the war for the number of its men who joined the bushwhacker ranks, and even at this time several of them rode with Confederate Captain Clifton D. Holtzclaw. This reputation may have moved the Yankee veterans to atrocities as they passed by.[31]

In April 1864 it was Knox County's turn to feel the wrath of returned veterans on furlough—this time from the 21st Missouri Infantry Regiment. On April 14 some drunken veterans from the 21st torched the house of a returned Rebel, Rice McFadden, in Colony Township in the northeast part of the county. McFadden himself hid nearby, saddened to see his house burn to the ground, but wise enough not to show himself to the drunks. The soldiers acted in ignorance that McFadden's son served in Company D of their own regiment. Dr. Anders, who detailed this incident in his 1975 history of the 21st, mentioned an editorial battle that took place after the arson between two local newspapers in neighboring Lewis County. The small-town editor of the Canton *Press* condemned the act as cowardice and hinted that the soldiers were persuaded to fire the house by local civilians. The editor of the LaGrange *National American* fired back in his paper so boldly as to name four soldiers who burned McFadden's house with the retort against the Canton paper that the soldiers should not be blamed for burning a Rebel's house.

A few days later unknown miscreants who were perhaps rampaging 21st soldiers robbed and burned the store in Colony of southern sympathizer Thomas A. McMurry. Later, locals found the body of a Mr. Cody northwest of Edina, the county seat. The rumor spread that soldiers killed Cody to keep others from learning the identity of the McMurry store raiders. When the 21st Missouri Infantry members finished their furloughs and returned to duty, many were understandably sad to see them depart, but others were relieved.[32]

Even after the soldiers finished their furloughs and left northeast Missouri to return to their units there were many bushwhackers lurking in neighboring Illinois this spring as well as plenty more on the Missouri side. This, plus a number of Confederate recruiters operating in northeast Missouri, meant that this region would see a violent summer of 1864.

NINE

Spring 1864 in Northwest Missouri South of the Missouri River

The Union military in the northwest quadrant of the state awaited the arrival of spring with all its new leaves to hide the guerrillas in the woods and brush with great uncertainty and concern. After all, the previous two springs of 1862 and 1863 had brought back from the South large numbers of guerrillas originally from this region fresh from a winter of resting and refitting and highly motivated to attack the Yankee soldiers in irregular warfare. These spring returns of hundreds of well-mounted, well-armed bushwhackers about April and May signaled the beginning of a new guerrilla fighting season that tested the Federals in every way possible and lasted until the return of cold weather in October or November. The new chief of the Department of the Missouri, Major General William S. Rosecrans, showed cocky confidence to the General-in-Chief of the U.S. Army, Major General Henry W. Halleck, 2 March 1864 when he wrote "I have pretty well mastered the situation in Missouri."[1] One of his predecessors, Major General Samuel R. Curtis, now head of the Department of Kansas, ten days later was more cautious in his advice to one of Rosecrans' subordinate generals, Brigadier General Egbert B. Brown, head of Rosecrans' battle-worn District of Central Missouri. Curtis wrote Brown:

> I do not myself suppose there are many bushwhackers now assembled at anyone place, but, as you say, we may all expect them when the leaves are out. But even now the news of small squads created much anxiety among the people who have been scourged by Quantrill's raids, which, as you know, spring out of apparently quiet localities or from the hills where only 10 or 20 had been seen at any one time. It is best, therefore, to be as watchful and wary as possible.

Major General Samuel R. Curtis commanded Union troops in Kansas during 1864 (Underwood and Clough, eds., *Battles and Leaders of the Civil War,* vol. 1, 1887, p. 315).

[Major General Franz] Sigel once said to an officer in my room, "We better consider the rebels all have good guns and shoot very straight." So I always think myself; we better regard our foes as pretty well prepared to strike us if the least opportunity occurs.[2]

Just such cooperation as this discourse between the general in charge of Kansas and one of the Missouri commanders indicated one improvement in the Union approach to the expected return of the southern irregulars. They planned to coordinate their forces between them better to face the bushwhackers with more unity of command then they had in the past.

Actually, General Brown had done all he could to prepare west-central Missouri for the expected spring onslaught of the returning bushwhackers. He had implemented many changes to the Union tactics and practices of this area as detailed in Chapter Five. Further, his aggressive pursuit of those guerrillas still present in this region early this spring was steadily cutting down their numbers.

March 1864 Disintegration of the Andy Blunt Guerrilla Band in Lafayette County

Captain William C. Quantrill left his operating area in the very capable hands of trusted Andy Blunt with 40 men the previous October, but constant Yankee pressure all winter bore fruit during March 1864 against the band in Lafayette County. Perhaps the Federal-ordered depopulation of much of Jackson and Cass Counties under the hated General Orders Number 11 the previous autumn convinced Blunt to operate from neighboring Lafayette County this winter, since the guerrillas still had many friends and sympathizers still living there. The desire of Blunt and his men to keep picking away at the Yankees all through the winter, rather than finding good hiding places and waiting for Quantrill to return in the spring, worked against the southerners during March. The disintegration of Blunt's band before March had been gradual and not visible to all observers. Throughout the winter, every now and then, Yankee patrols would kill or wound one of the bushwhackers, until by March Blunt had lost about ten men and even been wounded himself. In March the attrition rate increased at an increasing rate.

A typical guerrilla harassment of the important river town of Lexington took place the evening of March 2. Several bushwhackers chased a Union quartermaster just inside the town limits for sport that evening, and it seemed to have the desired result. Both the townspeople and the Federal troops were thrown into confusion, and the guerrillas simply rode away. That night they raided the nearby farm of John Catron taking a horse, cash, and firearms.[3]

Tragedy struck the Blunt guerrilla band March 7. Andy Blunt and about 15 of his men near Oak Grove in the southwest corner of Lafayette County were flushed from their camp by Captain F. W. Ferman's patrol of 1st Cavalry MSM and scattered. The rest of the band managed to escape without harm, but Blunt and James H. Waller ran directly into Captain Milton Burris' patrol from the same regiment nearby. In the shooting that followed Blunt was killed and Waller was wounded but escaped. Postwar guerrilla chronicler John N. Edwards later claimed that at the time of his death Blunt was recovering in camp from a wound he received February 22 in his unsuccessful attempt to break band member Otho Hinton out of jail in Lexington, and that a woman who lived nearby informed the Federals of the camp location.[4]

Blunt's body seemed to attract as much attention in death as the man did in life.

As was their custom, Captain Burris' patrol left Andy Blunt's lifeless body where it fell. Within hours local residents evidently carried the corpse to the nearby home of a Mr. Welch, reputed to be away in the Confederate army, because a patrol of Company K, 2nd Colorado Cavalry passing through on patrol stopped at the house and viewed Blunt's remains lying on a plank in one of the rooms. Private Joseph Hays of this patrol attested to this and named himself as a witness in a letter he wrote to the Kansas City newspaper March 9. As written in an earlier chapter, one of the Coloradoans passed the comment that he had served with the deceased prewar out west in the army fighting Indians, and that he was brave and a good fighter when he knew him. Some of the people living in the house later passed this remark to bushwhacker Warren Welch who stopped by later to pay his respects, and Welch recorded it in his memoirs. In fact, this house either belonged to Warren Welch or his kinsmen, as his home was in the Oak Grove neighborhood, too. This comment by the Colorado trooper was one of the few clues west-central Missouri guerrillas ever had as to Blunt's life before the war, because in life the man flatly refused to reveal his true name and origins to his comrades. Oddly, the captain of another Yankee patrol passing this area March 19 noted in his patrol report that he "saw the body of Captain Blunt, the rebel bushwhacker." How could Blunt's body still be visible ten days later when it received attention from the locals hours after death? Union Brigadier General Brown, the district commander, commented on April 5 that certain guerrillas were "under the sod, except the fellow Blunt, who has been left to rot, not being considered worthy of burial." General Brown's vitriolic remark seems to imply that some Union officer—perhaps him—ordered the locals not to bury the dead enemy's corpse. Perhaps somebody resented the honors apparently rendered to the dead man lying on the plank in Welch's house and ordered the body to be placed back on the ground as a warning to southerners what fate lay in store for bushwhackers.[5]

Incredibly, on the day after his chief was killed, one of Blunt's men married the daughter of a local judge in east-central Lafayette County. Perhaps James W. Wilkenson was not aware of Andy Blunt's death in southwest Lafayette County on March 7 since he was at the opposite end of the county. Two of Wilkenson's comrades kidnapped the Reverend Moses B. Arnold in central Pettis County and on March 8 the abducted minister married Wilkenson to the daughter of Judge F. R. Gray. The excitement involved in kidnapping the minister and exchanging wedding vows in the middle of a war zone probably appealed to the guerrilla mystique.[6]

Captain Ferman's patrol of 1st Cavalry MSM in the same area captured a guerrilla camp March 9, killing a guerrilla, Robert Cartnel. The following day the Federals took away the gunpowder, lead, and formed bullets and burned the camp. Ferman estimated the camp had housed about 20 bushwhackers, so the camp had belonged to either Blunt's band or the guerrilla band of the returned Rebel cavalrymen such as Warren Welch.[7]

Sometime during the week of March 13 through 19 another patrol of 1st Cavalry MSM found the new bridegroom, James Wilkenson, in west-central Missouri on the Davis Township farm of his father-in-law, Judge Gray, and killed him. Perhaps the Federals heard about the guerrilla wedding and watched the place to see if the new husband would make an appearance.[8]

Blunt's old band was dwindling at a rapid rate in March 1864. Already this month they lost their brave leader and perhaps two men with James H. Waller wounded. As recorded in the previous chapter, some Lafayette County bushwhackers about mid-March appeared in Henry County, two counties to the south, and began guerrilla operations there. Some of those men had Lafayette County and Quantrill connections, and Union officers believed they were some of the same bunch that was operating in Lafayette County a few weeks before. Apparently, a large portion of the remainder of Blunt's former band rode out of Lafayette County, crossed through west Johnson County, and began to conduct warfare in Henry County.[9]

Noticeably, Lafayette County was quiet from middle March until the end of the month—perhaps because most of Blunt's former men had moved their operations south to Henry County. On March 30 another of the 1st Cavalry MSM patrols found a faint trail in the brush near Greenton, west Lafayette County. The veteran cavalrymen followed the trail and killed the convalescent James H. Waller and wounded two other bushwhackers who escaped. Perhaps these two had been tending Waller, who was still recovering from his March 7 wounds. When reporting his death, the Lexington newspaper wrote that Waller had earlier boasted of killing 14 men during the infamous Lawrence raid the previous August.[10]

In the two previous years, small numbers of west-central Missouri guerrillas had trickled back to this area throughout the winter and early in the spring, but not this year. The harshness of this particularly winter and the cold, wet spring discouraged southerners from returning, and the many Missouri guerrillas wintering in northeast Texas really enjoyed their sojourn there. They enjoyed each other's camaraderie, thrilled to the dance halls and saloons, and had lots of fun to take their minds off the hard fighting they endured in Missouri during 1863, and expected to encounter in 1864. Although a few bushwhackers may have ridden back to this region in late winter and early spring, the first large group to return was that led by Quantrill and George Todd in early May, as described in Chapter Seven. Therefore, the disintegration of the Andy Blunt band in Lafayette County in March left a hole that was not readily filled.

Guerrilla Hunter Team, Beal Jeans, Shelby's Troopers, and Limited Guerrilla Action in the Jackson County Area During March and April 1864

Unlike the previous two years, there were only sporadic guerrilla actions in Jackson County during March and April 1864. Union information indicated the capable Richard Yeager with five or six others rode back into this area in February, if the Yankees' information was accurate this time. Some of the 30-or-so Rebel cavalrymen from Shelby's brigade that rode into this area for unknown reasons back in October were still at large, although over the winter a number of them returned to General Shelby's command in Arkansas. These soldiers were looking after southern interests, undoubtedly, but perhaps not with the burning desire to pick fights with the Yanks as other groups had done in previous spring seasons.

A special Union chief of scouts, Benjamin F. Allen, accompanied by up to 15 hand-picked enlisted troopers, encountered eight guerrillas near Fire Prairie Creek, northeast Jackson County March 13. The Union fusillade of shots that followed killed a Rebel horse and wounded a second one. When the shooting stopped, the bushwhackers had fled and Allen's party picked up a Rebel rifle or carbine dropped on the ground. Detective Allen afterward tersely wrote in his report "we followed them all night," picked up some Union reinforcements at a nearby camp and continued tracking the same group. After some hours they managed to capture three men and turned them in at the nearest Union camp. Allen's group continued their long patrol over several counties of west-central Missouri through early May with varied results. Evidently, the employment of special bushwhacker "hunter/killer" teams was another new tactic the Union military was using this year. A small team like Allen's proved to be effective while guerrilla numbers were short this spring, but could be in trouble when the larger groups of Rebels returned to this area in a few weeks.[11]

The Union military in Jackson County intensified their guerrilla search efforts in middle March based on an intelligence report forwarded from an unidentified source to Major General Rosecrans. Rosecrans was proving to be a skittish commander of the Department of the Missouri, and he issued frequent alarms. However, he was determined the Federals in Missouri would suffer from no more catastrophes such as Quantrill's Lawrence, Kansas raid and the Baxter Springs, Kansas reverse of the previous year. His information this time was that Confederates in Jackson County were preparing for an outbreak on March 20, possibly with help from recruits from Platte County across the Missouri River. Evidence would prove Rosecrans was at least partially correct, but the real irony of his report was that four months later the very insurrection he feared would break out but in Platte County assisted by Rebels from Jackson County, not the other way around.[12]

Large patrols of the 1st Cavalry MSM scoured the hilly, brush-choked ravines of east Jackson County and west Lafayette County even on foot between March 19 and 30 with some results. The troopers tore their uniforms crashing through bramble patches, occasionally shooting at one or two fleeing guerrillas, and finding a number of older bushwhacker hideouts and campgrounds. Since the leaves were not out yet in trees and bushes the Federals had more success finding such hidden places than they would in a few weeks. Major Alexander W. Mullins of the 1st Cavalry MSM was happy to report that his troops found no indications of large numbers of Rebels in this area. However, an informant near Bone Hill told the cavalry that Confederate Lieutenant Colonel Beal G. Jeans, formerly of the Confederate Jackson County Cavalry Regiment or 12th Missouri Cavalry, spent the winter in this area recruiting for the South. Jeans led this regiment at the Battle of Newtonia in Newton County 29 September 1862, just after the regiment joined Colonel Jo Shelby's

Union Major General William S. Rosecrans by spring 1864 seemed less than sure he could hold Missouri with the troops he had on hand (J. Henry Haynie, *The Nineteenth Illinois*, 1912, p. 192).

cavalry brigade. Earlier, in 1861, Jeans had served as a lieutenant in the Missouri State Guard in the Jackson County area. Just a few days later one of the Union patrols wounded one Rebel as he escaped into the brush and they captured two horses. They found evidence that one of the horses belonged to Lieutenant Colonel Jeans and that he was likely the fleeing man they wounded. So, the informant's report was correct. Since the Confederate troopers still in the area at this time were part of Jeans' old unit, perhaps part of their mission here was to assist their former commander to recruit. There seems to be no more information about Lieutenant Colonel Jeans in this area, so perhaps he concerned himself with healing his wounds and left the area.[13]

There was even less guerrilla activity in the Jackson County area during the month of April, indicating perhaps that aggressive Yankee patrolling made a difference. Union patrols mostly of the 2nd Colorado Cavalry occasionally skirmished with small numbers of bushwhackers here during April, but greater violence in neighboring Johnson and Lafayette Counties to the east indicated that many guerrillas had moved there for a time.[14]

A sad notice printed several times this spring in the Kansas City paper indicated this region was still a dangerous place. The family of Douglas County, Kansas miller and apple peddler Orville Denison appealed to the public for any word of middle-aged Orville who disappeared in the Jackson County and Clay County area during April. The notice indicated one of Orville's sons died in Union service and a second son was still serving at the time, affirming that Denison was probably a devout northern sympathizer working in a part of Missouri widely known for its southern sentiments. Mr. Denison's trip alone selling apples in an area known for bushwhacker activity was foolhardy to the extreme, and he was sure to be suspected as a northern spy—which he may have been. That this peddler hailed from near Lawrence, hated by southerners as being a hotbed of abolitionist expression and northern sympathy, may have been too much temptation for some violent southerner who stood to gain a wagon, team, some cash, and a load of apples for murdering this Kansan.[15]

Gann's Guerrillas and Return of Quantrill's and Todd's Men in Johnson and Lafayette Counties During April and May 1864

It was more than just irony that so little guerrilla activity took place in Jackson County while Johnson and Lafayette Counties witnessed almost daily warfare during April and May 1864. Historian Albert Castel wrote that as Captain Quantrill and George Todd returned to the region in late April they concluded that Jackson County, their old headquarters, was too well patrolled and watched by the Federals and chose Lafayette County as better suited to conduct their bushwhacker operations.[16] Bands of bushwhackers returning from their winter stay in the South finished their long horse ride in Johnson County to avoid the strong Federal presence just to the west in Jackson County, so the violence level grew in Johnson County also in April and May.

During the first few days of April Second Lieutenant Albert L. Gooding was leading a patrol of 2nd Colorado Cavalry from their garrison near the Sni-A-Bar Hills at the junction of Lafayette, Jackson, and Johnson Counties. At some point on the patrol Gooding suddenly encountered a lone guerrilla a few feet away who got off the first shot. As the Rebel's pistol bullet cut harmlessly through the lieutenant's coat, the startled officer emptied his own revolver into the southerner, killing him instantly. While Gooding reloaded his pistol and congratulated himself on being alive, his men searched the dead man and found on him papers belonging to a Lawrence, Kansas merchant. This seems to prove that this bushwhacker had taken part in Quantrill's great Lawrence raid the preceding August.[17]

The Union military in Lafayette County believed that after the death of guerrilla leader Andy Blunt in March the bushwhackers in this area were led by one of the sons of Sni-A-Bar area farmer Oliver C. Gann. Oliver's son Benton was captured and executed as a guerrilla by Federals March 28 two counties to the south at Germantown, as mentioned in Chapter Seven, but Oliver had other sons of military age. A patrol of 1st Cavalry MSM killed a guerrilla with the unlikely name of "Fear" in early April near Republican Church, near present-day Higginsville in south-central Lafayette County, and Major Alexander W. Mullins of that regiment stated his opinion in his report that Fear was one of Gann's band.[18] About April 10 an informant told the Federals that he saw guerrilla leader Gann and another bushwhacker riding in northwest Johnson County toward the Sni-A-Bar Hills, but this area was quiet for the next several days.[19]

Pending the arrival of large numbers of guerrillas from their winter sojourn in the South a few days later, by April 20 just a few of them remained active in Lafayette County. On the night of April 20/21 four bushwhackers launched their own attack against the newly formed Union citizen guard of the county. They killed a Mr. Atkinson who had been made lieutenant of this force probably in Washington Township, south-central Lafayette County, and broke into citizen guard captain and farmer Charles Ewing's home eight miles southwest of Lexington. If the guerrillas desired to show the vulnerability of the citizen guards, they brutally demonstrated that at Ewing's. The quartet, included a Wilson and a Wilhite, broke through the door and stormed up the stairs toward the family sleeping quarters. As Charles Ewing advanced against the intruders firing his shotgun his wife carrying their small child dashed into the line of fire in her panic to prevent the assassination of her husband. In the confusion, Charles' shotgun blast shot off the child's foot. The Rebel quartet, intent on their own mayhem, shot Mr. Ewing through the back, the bullet passing through one of his lungs. This left Charles Ewing, the new captain of the county's citizen guard and a former Rebel soldier earlier in the war, severely wounded. As the Ewings struggled to treat their own wounded, the raiders stole several items from the farm including between 100 and 200 pounds of flour and escaped west to the Sni-A-Bar Hills. Such callous cruelty was steadily eroding support of the inhabitants of Lafayette County for the bushwhackers, but also demonstrated the terrible cost of openly opposing them.[20]

Captain Quantrill and George Todd with seventy-something riders reached west-central Missouri in late April after a grueling trek from Texas that featured scant food for themselves and scant grain or grass for their mounts in rainy weather most of the way, as narrated in Chapter Seven. As they crossed the Grand River near Dayton, southeast Cass County, April 27 they captured and took with them as prisoner a Union Sergeant P. Russell from a regiment not familiar to them. The introduction to west-central Missouri of the 2nd Colorado Cavalry, the "Mountain Boomers," was another innovation of the Yankees to fight the guerrillas. This cavalry regiment was created from the consolidation of the veteran 2nd and 3rd Colorado Infantry Regiments that had previous experience not only on the frontier in the wilds of their home state but fighting guerrillas in Missouri, too. Some of the 2nd Colorado Infantry had been at Lawrence when Quantrill's force overwhelmed the place the previous August, and the regiment aggressively took part after that in the weeks-long dragnet in west-central Missouri scouring the region for the hiding bushwhackers. The 3rd Colorado Infantry had experience the previous summer in southeast Missouri, so they were no strangers to guerrilla fighting, either. Confederate veteran and the guerrillas' self-appointed chronicler, John N. Edwards, wrote postwar in uncharacteristic praise of this Yankee 2nd Colorado Cavalry Regiment:

> Those Colorado fellows were slashing fellows, fond of a grapple and fond of a melee. They were grave, quiet, middle-aged men, the most of them, rarely influenced by sentiment and not at all by any romantic folly. They volunteered to fight, and they did it as they would follow an Indian trail or develop a silver mine. They could be whipped, and they were whipped; but such fighting as would do for the militia would not do for them. Man to man, the best of the border knew that to drive them required close work and steady work.

Guerrilla John McCorkle mentioned the capture of Sergeant Russell, too, in his postwar memoir. McCorkle related that as they passed a Union cavalry camp near Dayton, they bluffed their way through with their own blue uniforms. Sergeant Russell bravely walked out to the passing riders, probably to check their identity, and they unobtrusively make him their prisoner so as not to alarm his comrades watching from their camp. Edwards narrated that Quantrill's and Todd's men later only reluctantly put to death Sergeant Russell to prevent him from revealing their identity and plans. They admired the man's courage and composure and inwardly wondered how many more like him were members of this new Colorado cavalry regiment that they would soon again face in battle.[21]

In the wee hours of April 28 Quantrill and Todd's weary band entered the southwest corner of Johnson County, rode past Rose Hill, and about noon passed Holden to familiar haunts east of Chapel Hill where Quantrill dispersed his men whose horses had died or were worn out from the trip. They were now back in their familiar operating area for another season of guerrilla operations. A few miles away in Warrensburg, Union district chief Brigadier General Egbert B. Brown suspected as much. He reported to his boss in St. Louis that "I am unable as yet to learn what band this is, but it moves like Quantrill's." The guerrillas were not aware that some miles south of them Union troops, probably of the 2nd Colorado Cavalry looking for their missing Sergeant Russell, killed three more of Andy Blunt's former guerrillas near Johnstown in east-central Bates County that same day. It seems to have been Blunt's mission to keep the region active with the 40-or-so guerrillas given to him when Quantrill left in early October. Now that Quantrill had returned, Blunt was dead and no more than a dozen of his men were probably left scattered in the Sni-A-Bar Hills and in Bates and Henry Counties to the south. Those few survivors of Blunt's winter command would soon hear that Quantrill was back and ride to rejoin their comrades. About 2:30 that same rainy afternoon of April 28 Captain Quantrill and George Todd with about 15 to 20 of those left who were not too weary to ride rode looked with great interest at a small Union detail led by an officer in a buggy that approached them.[22]

This spring, as in the one of the previous year, Union troops stationed in west-central Missouri grew careless from the lack of action and were surprised by the sudden advent of large numbers of bushwhackers from the South. At 2:30 this rainy afternoon of April 28 First Lieutenant James E. Couch of the 1st Cavalry MSM riding in a buggy escorted by three troopers of his regiment and two local men evidently of the citizen guard near Offutt's Knob in north-central Johnson County asked an approaching column of 15 to 20 blue-clad riders to identify themselves. The riders were in reality Quantrill, his lieutenant George Todd, and a number of their bushwhackers and they approached close enough to Couch to shoot up his detail with a sudden volume of pistol fire. Quantrill himself approached the two startled men in civilian clothes who had been riding with Couch's detail, waved his smoking revolver, told them his true identity, and demanded they tell Brigadier General Brown he said "he would kill all the damned Yankees he could find." He also stated that Brown should release four of his men the Union troops held in jail, and that he had killed those four men whose bodies lay before them for the killing of Andy Blunt. Before he rode away Captain Quantrill also told his captive audience that he had 150 men. The two witnesses could see an additional 35 or 40 other men in blue uniforms milling around a nearby house, and these two were discharged Union soldiers, so their estimate was probably correct. It seems First Lieutenant Couch and his detail had ridden right into Quantrill's band as they were organizing themselves after their long trek north from Texas. Quantrill and his men quickly rode away, and soon after the two men in civilian clothes found one of the shot troopers to be alive but badly wounded and got him to medical care. The following day Captain Jesse L. Pritchard with 49 troopers of the 2nd Colorado Cavalry near Lone Jack to the west tracked ten guerrillas of this band into the brush and chased them in a long running fight, killing one and wounding one at no stated loss to themselves. They also recovered the flag of an Indiana regiment that Quantrill's men had carried to deceive people they met while they traveled. Yes, the guerrilla war in west-central Missouri was now heating up.[23]

The buggy was a one-horse, light passenger wagon with one seat and little room for baggage or freight (Sears, Roebuck, and Company, *Fall 1900 Catalog*, 1900, p. 974).

May Actions: Yeager, Gann and Wilhite, Todd, Executions of Watkins and Hadley, Night Fight, Hopkins, and Anderson

The Union command to the west in Kansas on May 3 sent along a report to the Federals in Missouri that they heard guerrilla Richard Yeager and eighty men were camped in northwest Cass County about 12 miles southeast of the village of Little Santa Fe. There were a number of exaggerated or false Union military intelligence reports this spring as guerrillas returned to this region, and this may have been one of them. However, there were a couple of Union intelligence reports back in February that Yeager was in the region, as described in an Chapter Four, and one of those placed him near the Grand River in Cass County just a few miles south of the area mentioned in this May 3 report. The Federals were well aware that Dick Yeager guided a guerrilla raid deep into Kansas one year before, so they had a tendency to attach value to any report bearing his name. Even if Yeager was in northwest Cass County, it seems highly problematic that he would have as many as eighty men with him in such an open place as this prairie neighborhood, which had been depopulated by the General Orders Number Eleven the previous fall.[24]

Gann and a Wilhite of the former Andy Blunt guerrillas stopped and robbed a stagecoach the evening of May 3 near Tabo Creek in east-central Lafayette County about seven miles southeast of Lexington. There was a trooper on board who was returning to Company K, 6th Cavalry MSM in the Springfield area from being on furlough at home in Ray County. Gann and Wilhite took him away at gunpoint with a rope around his neck. Therefore, it was no surprise to cavalrymen of the 1st Cavalry MSM who investigated the incident to find that trooper's mutilated corpse about three quarters of a mile from the holdup site. They also found the mail the guerrillas took from the coach and tore to pieces.[25]

About a day or two later unidentified Federal troops called on the residence of town merchant Cortez Kavanaugh in Lexington Township not far from Lexington and shot him to death for the reason that they heard he was from Alabama and rumored to be "an active Southern man," according to town gossip. Evidently, troopers of the 1st Cavalry MSM garrisoned at Lexington or local EMM militiamen killed the store owner in retaliation for Gann and Wilhite's killing and mutilation of the 6th regiment trooper in the stage robbery May 3 and perhaps for their attacks on the citizen guard officers at their homes the night of April 21/22.[26]

The arrival of so many bushwhackers back to this region seemed to bring about a resurgence of violence and worry to northerners. The Union district headquarters at Warrensburg heard about 20 or 25 guerrillas passing north of town the night of May 4/5 heading northeast toward Brownsville in the southwest corner of Saline County and warned area garrisons.[27] Unidentified guerrillas robbed the Lexington-Independence stagecoach on May 5 somewhere in west Lafayette or north Jackson County.[28] Reports of moving bushwhackers blossomed from several places May 7 and created concern in Lexington since a couple of these messages seemed to indicate the Rebels were headed in that direction. Andy Blunt's band had harassed Lexington much of the preceding winter and left the many rural exiles living there in a perpetual state of paranoia. The report that day that Quantrill with large numbers crossed the Osage River heading north about three counties to the south caused great concern, even though Quantrill with over seventy men was already much closer at the time. If there were guerrillas crossing the Osage May 7 it was probably Rebel Captain Bill Marchbanks and no more than forty or fifty riders, and they had no intention of riding all the way north to Lexington! Union scouts brought the news May 7 that there were about 100 bushwhackers in east-central Lafayette County near Judge Gray's farm in Davis Township, and this was probably correct and was probably Captain Quantrill's actual band.[29] During the night of May 7/8 guerrillas near the Sni-A-Bar Hills robbed the Baugh family and two Lewis families of cash, bedding, clothing, and other items, then threatened to "shoot the women's brains out" if they made noise. They also threatened to return and kill all of these people if they reported them to the Federals. Elements of the 2nd Colorado Cavalry heard of the plight of these three families of northern sympathy, who were probably exiles from the depopulated area by the border, and escorted them to the Union garrison nearby.[30]

Meanwhile, railroad construction of the Pacific Railroad was continuing through west-central Missouri with tracks already laid into Knob Noster in east Johnson County about May 1.[31] Uninvited visitors paid a call on the camp of one of the construction crews near Independence, northwest Jackson County, the evening of May 14. George Todd and a few of his men visited with the workmen for about thirty minutes chatting freely among men that already knew the guerrilla leader. Todd informed them that he had 88 men nearby that had no fear of Federal troops, and both statements were probably correct. Indeed, even though a Union garrison was only four miles away in Independence, these Rebels seemed very much at ease and not at all fearful of attack from the Union troops. Construction crews this far ahead of track laying were probably working at grading and filling, bridge construction, and masonry culvert construction. Since Todd was a Kansas City stone mason before the war, perhaps that is where these workmen knew the man.[32] A St. Joseph newspaper reported May 24 that near Independence bushwhackers drove workmen away from the railroad site, and forced some of the tradesmen to surrender revolvers they were carrying for self protection. The Kansas City newspaper, just a few miles from Independence, repeated the story May 26, but the editor added the note that he heard of no such incident.[33]

When not visiting construction crews, bushwhackers engaged in fire fights in west-central Missouri with Federal cavalry in mid May. A small mounted patrol of 1st Cavalry MSM from Warrensburg May 15 killed one guerrilla and wounded another near the Jackson County line in west Johnson County, capturing both horses. The cavalry felled the bushwhacker that died with a pistol shot but the Rebel fought on with a bowie knife before additional shots stopped his efforts. In the man's pocket was a paper addressed to "Colonel" Quantrill from a Confederate quartermaster in Texas, Captain W. H. Wooten, perhaps dated several weeks before. This find started a round of mistaken newspaper articles across Missouri that Union troops finally killed the dreaded Quantrill, which quelled a few days later. That same day not far away another patrol of 1st Cavalry MSM also killed one bushwhacker and wounded another, who escaped.[34] On May 18 a foot patrol of 2nd Colorado Cavalry from the Sni-A-Bar garrison three miles south of Blue Springs, east-central Jackson County, flushed from the Richard Hopkins home his son Billy F. Hopkins and a Tucker who were both bushwhackers. The Coloradoans reported that they wounded one of them, but both escaped. The cavalrymen were disguised as guerrillas themselves, and as they quietly climbed over the Hopkins fence they distinctly heard children posted as lookouts call out a warning to the people inside "here are some Federals," and immediately after that two men ran out a door on the other side of the house.[35]

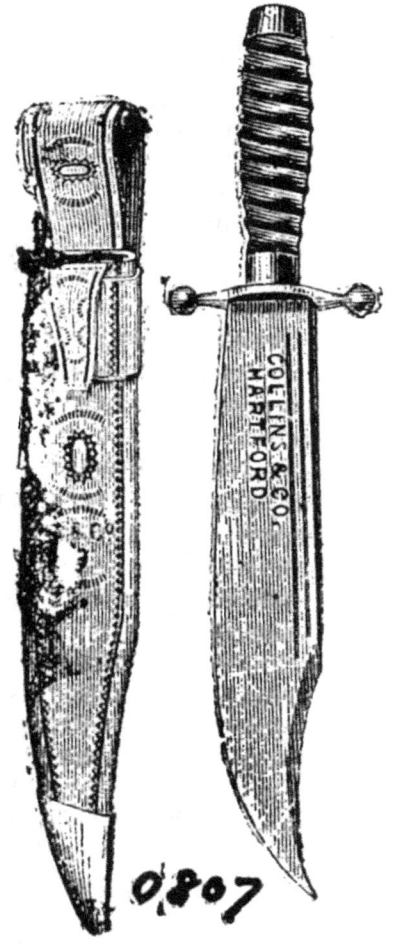

The Union military in this region executed two bushwhackers in separate incidents on May 20. During the evening of May 19 a Union patrol in east Lafayette County wounded a guerrilla and saw him suffer a bad fall from his horse while they were chasing him. During the evening of May 20 the local Union command sent Second Lieutenant James E. Teal and a patrol of 1st Cavalry MSM to find this man. Teal's patrol found and executed on the spot badly wounded 22-year-old

Bowie knife: a large single-edged hunting knife popularized by Colonel James Bowie, of Texas Alamo fame, and often carried by Confederate soldiers of the western theaters (*Bannerman Catalogue of Military Goods, 1922*, p. 184).

northeast Cass County blacksmith Benjamin Watkins. The patrol brought back to headquarters a $5 greenback they found on Watkins' body.[36] That same afternoon Union soldiers at the district headquarters at Warrensburg executed by musketry another captured guerrilla, 22-year-old New Hampshire–born former Platte County stagecoach driver Willard Francis Hadley. Facing the certainty of his approaching death, Hadley had earlier recounted in detail his war experiences to Union officers, and his confession was printed in a number of newspapers across Missouri. One newspaper correspondent ascribed as motive for Hadley's detailed confession "that he thirsted, fiend-like, for an opportunity to plunge himself still deeper in everlasting infamy." The convicted southerner described in detail his activities either leading other southern men or as a member of southern units from 1861 through his final capture and execution many adventures and misadventures in Missouri, Kansas, Arkansas, and Mississippi. As if to prove his leadership of guerrillas operating in Platte, Clay, and Ray County during 1861 and 1862, Hadley gave names of specific members of his unit killed at certain fights, but this does not necessarily prove that Hadley commanded them at those times. The prisoner's mention of being a member of Captain Silas Gordon's Platte County Confederate company for a while in 1861 is actually documented in Missouri State Archives and a Platte County history. The condemned man's narrative of being one of a number of guerrillas crossing the Missouri River to operate with Quantrill's men in late summer 1862 and taking part in the ill-fated Sibley fight October 6, 1862, matches the historic record. Hadley's detailed mention of desertions from certain Rebel units, his trouble with Confederate authority, and other unflattering actions tend to give his narrative a ring of truthfulness. However, other activities Hadley described to his questioners such as several captures and escapes seem fanciful, especially his own role in them. It is also telling that his name does not appear in several well-researched lists of west-central Missouri guerrillas. In summary, Willard Hadley's long confession is a mix of fact and fiction, and apparently an attempt by him to enlarge his own contribution to the southern cause to raise his spirits and maintain his courage facing his executioners. Brigadier General Brown, the district commander, specifically mentioned Hadley's confession to being part of the Lawrence raid of August 1863 in the execution order, as Brown seemed to have a penchant for executing men who confessed a part in that raid. Ironically, Hadley offered no proof or relevant detail that he had even taken part in the Lawrence campaign, though he may well have been part of it. He closed his long confession with this statement: "I went to war to be a terror to the Feds. No man in the country has done more than I have. I went in to rob and steal without regard to law. I thought the South had her rights trampled upon. I am now sentenced to be shot. But I feel that I have been fully avenged."[37]

The rest of the month of May in west-central Missouri was a blur of daily movement and skirmishes of the Union cavalry and the energetic, newly returned guerrillas. About midnight during the night of 20/21 May 1864 an 18-man patrol of 2nd Colorado Cavalry led by Lieutenant Albert L. Gooding came directly upon guerrilla chieftain George Todd with five bushwhackers in the middle of the road near the Sni-A-Bar Hills. Trying to identify each other in the dark, Todd gave the correct initial recognition signal to the Coloradoans who responded with the countersign. The southerners did not know the response to this and the cavalry opened fire at close range—their muzzle flashes temporarily lighting up the scene. A newspaper account states the Federals killed two guerrillas outright and seriously wounding a third, whom they quickly shot to death as he lay in the road, while Todd and the remainder made good their escape. Gooding's patrol tracked the bushwhackers the next morning 21

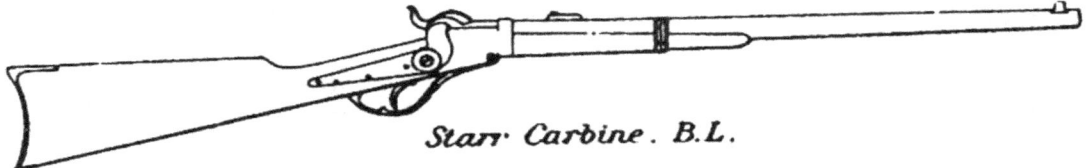

Breech-loading Starr carbines failed to work for the 2nd Colorado Cavalry in gun battles with guerrillas in west-central Missouri (United States Department of War, *Atlas to Accompany the Official Records of the Union and Confederate Armies,* 1891–1895, drawings of shoulder arms, p. 393).

May to a house in the southwest corner of Lafayette County where they were having breakfast while a neighbor boy kept lookout. The lookout gave adequate warning and the guerrillas escaped eventually to the river bottoms near Sibley, northeast Jackson County, where the cavalry lost their track again. The woman who served food to the guerrillas later identified George Todd as one of the men that ate breakfast there, but asserted that she was forced to do it. The Kansas City news article about this also stated that Todd sent word to the efficient Lieutenant Gooding that if he ever caught the officer he would burn him alive. This was clearly a threat to the lieutenant, but, from a violent man like George Todd, it was also a form of compliment to a worthy opponent.[38]

The same Richard Hopkins family that featured in the May 18 action starred in another fight May 21. The Colorado cavalry managed to capture young Billy Hopkins near the Sni-A-Bar Hills, and sent a sergeant and nine troopers to escort the prisoner in a wagon pulled by mules toward the jail in Kansas City. Bushwhacker chief George Todd did not miss much this spring, and he ambushed the Yankee detail with about 30 to 35 men near where the road crossed the Blue River, not far from Independence. The Rebels, firing from only twenty yards away in the brush, isolated the two-man advance, killing one trooper and sending the other running for his life into the brush with several southerners running after him. One of this private's pursuers seemed to be Billy Hopkins' very irate dad who fired a few epithets at the running Coloradoan as well as bullets. This private was fortunate to be able to hide and later make his way back to his comrades. The remainder of the Colorado cavalry detail were startled that in the heat of battle their Starr carbines failed to fire, and they had to ride for their lives, shooting back only with their Starr revolvers. The detail sergeant scooped up a wounded corporal and slung him across his own saddle with bushwhacker bullets cutting through the air all around him, and escaped. Todd's men welcomed Billy Hopkins back into their ranks, killed many of the mules, set fire to the wagon, and then dispersed to hide in small groups in anticipation of the Union pursuit. The losses were for the Union one killed, and one badly wounded, compared to perhaps one or two of the Rebels wounded. Before the Colorado cavalry could get the unreliable Starr carbines replaced with better

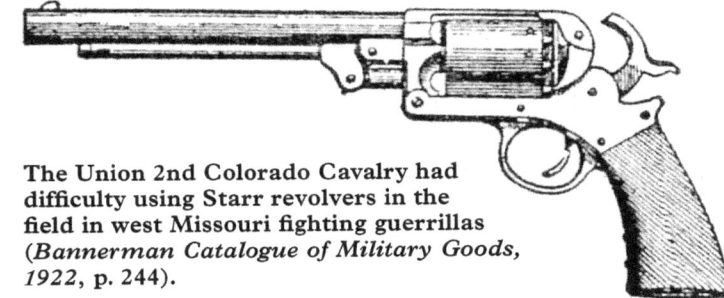

The Union 2nd Colorado Cavalry had difficulty using Starr revolvers in the field in west Missouri fighting guerrillas (*Bannerman Catalogue of Military Goods, 1922,* p. 244).

shoulder arms there would be several other instances of them failing in battle against the deadly guerrillas.[39]

The next day, May 22, Bill Anderson with about 80 guerrillas rode north into west Johnson County on their return trip from wintering in Texas, playing havoc with the newly created Union citizen guards as they went. About five in the evening four miles northeast of the village of Chilhowee 20 of Anderson's band struck Sergeant Solathel Stone's detail of four troopers of 1st Cavalry MSM and Judge Richard M. King of that neighborhood who was with the troopers. The bushwhackers killed the judge, captured the sergeant and three of his cavalrymen, while one other escaped to spread the word. Meanwhile, citizen guard captain John Taggart realized that the guerrillas were in his neighborhood south of Holden before he could muster his men to offer resistance, so he wisely scattered what men he had on hand to hide in the brush until the large bushwhacker band rode on north. There had been so many false and conflicting reports of Rebels in exaggerated numbers riding here and there this spring that no reliable warning system survived for isolated citizen guards and militia. These men fought their enemies with no warning or chance to prepare. Anderson's men also cut the telegraph line west of Warrensburg as they passed to deny the Yankees updated information on their movements, and stole a few horses from the farmers and the stagecoach company as they traveled on north. On the following day some men presumably of Anderson's band robbed the mail coach near Pleasant Hill, northeast Cass County, taking all Union Army mail from the state headquarters for May 22 and 23, and further hampering their enemy's communications.[40]

On the evening of May 25 sixteen bushwhackers evidently of Todd's band just outside Wellington, northwest Lafayette County, attacked a squad of Captain James B. Moore's Company F, 1st Cavalry MSM, killing one trooper. Without putting up any additional fight, Captain Moore and his company retreated out of harm's way. Three of the guerrillas robbed stores in the village and none of the residents offered any resistance, although seeing the example offered by the hasty departure of the Union cavalry gave the residents little inspiration to make trouble. When Brigadier General Brown heard of this, he was incensed that a whole company of Union cavalry would retreat at the advance of 16 guerrillas, and he ordered Captain Moore arrested and held for trial for cowardice in the face of the enemy. Moore must have made a good accounting for his actions, as he served faithfully through the rest of the year and was mustered out at the end of his term in 1865.[41]

As of May 26 the situation looked grim for Union forces in west-central Missouri. Captain John Ballinger of the 1st Cavalry MSM, commanding the post at Lexington, reported to district headquarters that he had reliable information that between 50 and 100 guerrillas were camped within two miles of Union citizen guard captain Charles Ewing's home only eight miles southwest of the town. He added the ominous note that he had "no men to send out." Colonel James McFerran, commander of the heavily engaged 1st Cavalry MSM holding the district headquarters at Warrensburg sent a telegram to General Brown temporarily in Kansas City that up to 100 bushwhackers were robbing homesteads along Post Oak Creek within ten miles southwest of town. Obviously, Colonel McFerrin had no troops to send since he asked the general if he was authorized to issue rations to citizen guards so that they could take to the field. At this juncture, the general ordered some of the 1st Cavalry MSM troops in Henry County to advance north into Johnson County and help, six companies of the 4th Cavalry MSM at Sedalia to advance west into Johnson County, and up to 100 troopers of the 7th Cavalry MSM to also come to help if they could be spared. By now, the Union command in this area believed between 200 and 300 veteran, well-armed, well-mounted guerrillas under Quantrill were running amuck in this district. They could not know that only twenty of Anderson's guerrillas were then southwest of Warrensburg along Post Oak Creek, and not the 100 Colonel McFerran reported. They could also not know that with Todd's 50 to 70, Anderson's 70 to 80, and perhaps up to 30 others, there were no more than 180 guerrillas in the entire west-central Missouri, and perhaps no more than 150. Still, 150 veteran, well-armed, highly motivated bushwhackers were a potent force to face for any number of Federal cavalry. As will be seen, the Union command could also not know that Todd and Anderson had by this date probably already deposed Captain Quantrill and sent him away into exile, and Captains Todd and Anderson were evidently the only active guerrilla commanders in Jackson, Cass, Johnson, and Lafayette Counties.[42]

Evidently on May 22 or 23 about five of Bill Anderson's bushwhackers separated from the main body and rode west to operate in the Pleasant Hill area of northwest Cass County between May 24 and 26. Perhaps one or more of these Rebels was from that area. It was they who robbed the stagecoach west of Pleasant Hill and took all the Union military mail from that from that vehicle May 24. About 11 in the morning of May 26 three of them captured three citizens from Pleasant Hill driving a team along the road and took them back to their camp in the brush. At camp they met two Colorado troopers guarded as prisoners by the remaining two Rebels. The bushwhackers released the civilians that night and ominously mentioned to them that they would soon kill the two soldiers they held. True enough, troopers of the 2nd Colorado Cavalry the next day found the bodies of their two comrades near the road, stripped of their uniforms.[43] There is a bare mention in Union military records that a detachment of the 2nd Colorado Cavalry fought a skirmish with guerrillas at or near Pleasant Hill the following day, May 28. Two troopers were wounded, but no other details of this action survive.[44]

About twenty of Anderson's men separated from the main body May 22 and began operating in the Post Oak Creek area southwest of Warrensburg near Chilhowee and Cornelia. It was this group that attacked Sergeant Stone's small detail May 22 and killed Judge King, and this same group robbed families along Post Oak Creek May 26. Guerrillas Bill Stewart, Marion "Gooly" Robinson, Thomas Little, and Michael Burgess were members of Anderson's band and from this area, so they were probably part of this sub-band of twenty. During the evening of May 27 this group burned the village of Shanghai ten miles southeast of Warrensburg while most of the citizen guards were away. In fact, the raiders probably targeted this town because four of its few residents had recently joined the Union citizen guards. The loss was two stores, four homes, and several other buildings leaving six families destitute. After burning the little village the guerrillas rode two or three miles away and burned another man's home and everything he had, too. It appears that the raiders had used their time in the neighborhood learning from family and friends who among their neighbors was supporting the northern side and these Rebels exacted retribution from those people.[45] A patrol of the newly arrived Company H, 7th Cavalry MSM twelve miles out from their new station at Warrensburg on May 28 "had a light skirmish with some guerrillas and returned" on May 29, according to company records. Perhaps "a light skirmish" consisted of the Yanks shooting at somebody but not hitting them, or something similar; and this perhaps took place in the Post Oak Creek area.[46]

During the evening of May 28 unidentified guerrillas took advantage of the temporary absence of the Union cavalry from their garrison at the little village of Mt.

Hope, a few miles northeast of Chapel Hill in southwest Lafayette County, and raided the place. They burned the church and two homes. The Federals had been quartered in the church and one of the destroyed homes, and the fire destroyed also a quantity of corn the Union military had stored there for horse feed.[47]

Todd and Anderson Depose Quantrill

There was a noticeable lull in the pace of guerrilla actions between May 29 and June 2, as if the west-central bushwhackers were preoccupied with a council of war or were re-organizing to operate more efficiently for the 1864 fighting season. Bill Anderson had brought back about seventy men to the area of operations May 22 and 23, completing the roster of men that the guerrillas expected to see back in this region this season.

George Todd and Bill Anderson had already emerged as the dominant guerrilla sub-leaders down in Texas the past winter, and they no longer accepted Quantrill's role as chief overseer of their separate operations. Many of Quantrill's former subordinate leaders, such as Bill Gregg, John Jarrett, Cole Younger, and Dave Poole, either became disgusted with Quantrill's band and left voluntarily or were sent away into regular Confederate units during the winter in Texas. Bill Gregg wrote his opinions that may have mirrored the feelings of others of the "older" members of Quantrill's band who had served from its infancy in 1862. Many of these original 1862 members of the band were repulsed by the growth of savagery they witnessed in the guerrilla ranks at Lawrence and Baxter Springs the previous year which continued during the winter in Texas with murders and larceny. Their self concept as patriots of Missouri was affronted by the seeking of booty they witnessed in newer band members and the spread of such dehumanizing traits as scalping Yankee dead that began after the end of the Lawrence raid. Anderson and Todd seemingly had gone beyond the "no quarter" necessity imposed on these guerrillas by the Union command in Missouri into pure blood lust and the enjoyment of killing. When pressured by the Confederate command in Texas to send some of his men into regular ranks, Quantrill choose about forty men to leave guerrilla ranks who were from the older 1862 members and keep mostly the newer, younger more savage bushwhackers who would hold up better in the deadly killing business that guerrilla warfare in west-central Missouri had become by this time in the war. A number of these men Quantrill sent to join the Confederate regulars would chafe at the lack of freedom of action, desert their new commands, and either return to Missouri or set out for new frontiers. Several, and perhaps most, would serve faithfully in their new roles as regular Confederate soldiers, however. A number of these forty men had already served in regular ranks earlier in the war. Ironically, Quantrill had chosen to keep in his command the very deadly killers that in the spring of 1864 decided he was of the "older" 1862 class, too, and had to go.[48]

The new leaders, George Todd and Bill Anderson, had several complaints about Captain Quantrill that caused them to first question and now challenge his continued leadership over them.

Part of their dissatisfaction with him could have originated with his actions the previous year. They may have resented Quantrill's absence for weeks during the summer of 1863 while he was in dalliance with his teenage lover and then wife Kate King. Although they enjoyed the freedom of command without him at the time, Quantrill's personal sabbatical showed a lack of commitment to the cause and to them.[49] Todd

Above, left: George Todd, a Canadian-born stone mason and one of Quantrill's lieutenants since 1862, with Bill Anderson deposed their leader in spring 1864 (John N. Edwards, *Noted Guerrillas,* 1877, p. 52; courtesy of the late Bob Younger and Mary Younger and Andy Turner).
Right: Bill Anderson, one of Quantrill's lieutenants for about one year, along with George Todd deposed their guerrilla chief during the spring of 1864 (*Noted Guerrillas*, p. 164).

and Anderson may have chafed under Quantrill's inactivity during the several week dragnet the Federals conducted in a desperate search to hunt down the Lawrence raiders in late August and September 1863. Such men of action would have found weeks of inactivity hiding from the very enemies they would rather be fighting to be unbearable. Perhaps they considered Quantrill's decision to "lay low" during those weeks after the great victory at Lawrence to be cowardice, too.[50] Also, at the end of their highly successful Baxter Springs battle on October 6, 1863, Anderson and Todd chafed because Quantrill would not allow them to conduct further attacks on the Union Fort Blair after the firing ceased.[51]

Bill Anderson particularly had differences with Quantrill during their winter respite in Texas. Anderson resented Quantrill's interference with his men's criminality and Quantrill's lack of solidarity with Missouri comrades when he attempted to arrest some of Anderson's men. In fact, the differences between Anderson and Quantrill drove their respective men to battle against each other. Of course, Captain Quantrill was in a quandary to remain loyal to men who had risked their lives with him in battle while at the same time obeying the orders and directives of the Confederate command in Texas that grew to dislike and distrust his lawless men. Quantrill and George Todd took 40 to 70 guerrillas loyal to them away north back to Missouri earlier than prudent in late April in order to escape both Anderson's deadly intentions and the Confederate command's discipline. Any meetings between Todd and Quantrill and the malevolent Bill Anderson back in Missouri in late May would have been testy indeed considering the hard feelings between them back in Texas a few weeks before.

George Todd had to bear resentment against Quantrill for the premature departure from Texas in late April that resulted in the miserable trip north with little food or forage in the rain nearly the whole way, as described in Chapter Seven. Of course, Quantrill was not responsible for the late grass or the heavy rains, but as overall commander he was ultimately responsible that he allowed the situation with Bill Anderson and the Confederate command to deteriorate to the point that they had to leave Texas in such haste. Further, Quantrill failed to provide adequate logistics for the trip that caused it to be almost a starvation march with many of the riders and their mounts barely able to stumble into Johnson County April 27. During the last stages of this hardship trek the guerrilla force was so debilitated that they were easy prey for any Union force that could have correctly fixed their position and attacked in force.

For a combination of these reasons both Bill Anderson and George Todd, the impetuous and volatile acting commanders of Quantrill's bushwhacker force, found it intolerable in late May for Quantrill to remain among them trying to exert some form of command. The actual date of their parting is not recorded, but this could account for the period of guerrilla inactivity between May 29 and June 2, 1864. Some memoirs say they finally fell out during a card game and others point to Todd threatening Quantrill with a pistol, and some chroniclers of the band combine the two. The split had been in the making for a long time, and Quantrill finally realized that to remain with men who no longer trusted him or his leadership was dangerous to his life and that of the few devotees he had left. Accompanied by a small number of these loyal men as bodyguards and his teenage wife Kate King, Quantrill took his small entourage far from west-central Missouri and lived several months in seclusion and inactivity hiding in Howard County in the center of the state. Modern-day historian Donald L. Gilmore in 2006 summarized the split: "in a guerrilla setting, where group dynamics and personalities reign, military talent can be overshadowed and a leader ousted through personal intrigue, as Quantrill was."[52]

Spring 1864 Central Missouri Actions: Traveling Guerrillas, Brownlee, Dorsey, and Shumate

There were a number of isolated guerrilla actions in Saline and Pettis Counties this spring. Company F records of 7th Cavalry MSM indicate that five unidentified bushwhackers attacked two troopers stationed that season at New Frankfort, northeast Saline County, about April 20. These cavalrymen were probably garrisoned in this predominantly pro-northern village to protect it from another guerrilla raid, such as the one that struck the place the previous July. No other details remain from this April 1864 encounter.[53] About this same date three other guerrillas crossing north Benton County or south Pettis County heading north may have skirmished with unidentified Union troops who killed two of them according to the confession of bushwhacker James A. Johnson captured three days later. Union troops were alerted that a lone guerrilla stole a horse and a hat April 23 from a man on Flat Creek, six miles south of Sedalia, and captured this Johnson a few miles north. After interrogation at the 7th Cavalry MSM garrison in the village of Brownsville, southwest Saline County, James A. Johnson confessed his brief career as a bushwhacker in Platte and Buchanan Counties the previous year, and explained that his companions and he were returning there from wintering in the South when beset by Union troops. Ominously, Johnson also told his captors that Confederate Colonels John Calhoun "Coon" Thornton and John H. Winston were recruiting in Platte County during the past winter. Union forces knew about

Colonel Winston, who they captured in Platte County March 22, but Colonel Thornton would give them plenty of grief there later this year. The Brownsville Union commander had Johnson shot to death the morning of April 24, in obedience to Missouri-wide regulations for local commanders to execute captured guerrillas whose guilt was proven by a tribunal they were to hold.[54] Modern-day guerrilla historians Donald R. Hale and Joanne Chiles Eakins mentioned in their 1993 book *Branded As Rebels* that on 18 May bushwhackers William Wilhite and William Martin robbed a Mrs. Hindricks in Saline County, but left no other details. The 1860 Saline County census recorded two Hendrick households, both contain ladies, and both were located in the north part of the county. Since one Hendrick family hailed from Virginia and lived in the predominantly southern Miami Township, the pair of bushwhackers probably robbed German-born Amelia Hendrick of Jefferson Township in northeast Saline County in or near the German-American enclave of New Frankfort—a target of guerrilla torment during the war.[55] Troops of the 7th Cavalry MSM executed convicted guerrillas W. H. Morris and John Bowen (or Bones) May 25 at the Union base in Sedalia. The pair from the Cass County area admitted to participating in the Lawrence raid the previous August, and Morris also said that he was part of Quantrill's band.[56]

Cooper County was the scene of considerable violence this spring from several sources. On March 9 someone near the village of Pilot Grove, west-central Cooper County, discovered the skeleton of obvious murder victim Hugh Miller in a grove of trees, and his pocketbook nearby identified his remains. The middle-aged farmer from the Pilot Grove area disappeared in early February, and his vanishing then was carried in area newspapers. Miller's skull showed fractures as if hit by an axe, but no motive was apparent. Locals conjectured that Charles Brownlee's guerrillas killed Miller in revenge for telling on them, or because his brother was a local magistrate.[57]

Brownlee's small guerrilla band was very active this spring across much of Cooper County. Pennsylvania-born attorney Charles Brownlee came to Tipton to practice law as a young man in the late 1850s, was caught up in the cry for southern rights, and led a Moniteau County company in the southern Missouri State Guard during 1861. He returned from the Confederate army in the spring of 1863 and with his men was responsible for some mayhem; Union troops captured him in Cooper County with two of his men; a local tribunal convicted the trio of being guerrillas and sentenced them for execution, but with his comrades and the help of local southerners he escaped.[58] Now, the wily, young lawyer and several followers were back in Cooper County fighting for the South as guerrillas once again. Brownlee's band robbed Seeley's Store at Round Hill, southeast Cooper County, on March 15 taking over $380 in cash and about $300 worth of boots, cloth, and domestic goods. Somebody who knew Charles Brownlee before the war later stated that they recognized him as the robber leader. A small patrol of 4th Cavalry MSM rode over from Otterville, but found no trace of the raiders.[59] Another patrol of 4th Cavalry MSM from Otterville April 2 managed to capture guerrilla James Gilmore, about ten miles south of Boonville. Gilmore admitted being a member of Lafayette Roberts' band in Dade County, but gave no explanation as to why he was so far away at the time of his capture. Gilmore was apparently part of Brownlee's band.[60] Captain William D. Blair's patrol of 4th Cavalry MSM on April 10 near Tipton in east Cooper County captured Brownlee gang member Patrick Mullins of Moreau Township, east-central Morgan County. The capture was easy since the troopers found Mullins sleeping by the road. The Federals tried the man and executed him by shooting April 23. Captain Blair's patrol on the same day they found Mullins also recovered 375 cans of gunpowder five miles south of Tipton buried in a hollow, but mostly ruined by water seepage. This gunpowder was evidently a small fraction of the large southern gunpowder hoard southerners spirited out of the Jefferson City capitol and hid around central Missouri in 1861 before Union troops occupied the region. The powder was usually well hidden, so a local resident must have informed the Federals where this cache was buried.[61] It was perhaps the Brownlee gang again that burned the homes of southwest Cooper County farmers middle-aged Dryden Starke and his son John "Jack" Starke May 7 a few miles from Otterville. Locals recorded that this Virginia-born family tried very hard to remain neutral in the war, but it seems somebody burned their homes because the Starkes tended to lean a bit on the northern side. The arson seemed to stir the Starkes to commit, because in August Jack Starke enlisted at Otterville in Company B of the Union 48th Missouri Infantry Regiment.[62]

As recorded in an earlier chapter, about the second and third weeks of May 1864 Confederate recruiter Colonel Caleb Dorsey and over 100 of his men paused several days in Cooper and Moniteau Counties to quietly take fresh horses to replace their mounts worn out from the long, rainy trip north from Arkansas. Wealthy farmer William H. Mayo of near Bell Air, west-central Cooper County, on May 14 shot at two suspicious riders who rode up to his house. Mayo thought that he may have wounded one of them, as they left hastily, leaving behind a horse and saddle. Either these were two of Brownlee's guerrillas or two of Colonel Dorsey horse-seeking Confederate recruiters.[63] An unknown sniper on May 18 in the Cooper County seat of Boonville shot and missed Captain A Harrison Thompson of the local 52nd EMM at his home. Captain Thompson was at that time a local commissioner who helped determine who was exempt from Union military service—a job that did not always make him popular. Thompson was apparently energized more than intimidated by the attempt on his life. Two days after the shot he bypassed military channels and wrote directly to Major General Rosecrans informing the general about the reports he was receiving about guerrillas in Cooper County. The bold captain wrote about bushwhackers "prowling around through the county, stealing horses and committing other depredations" and pleaded for more troops to be sent right away. Unfortunately for the captain, his letter to high command arrived just at the same time as several embarrassing false reports about Rebel raiders first here and then there, and his report was dismissed as that of just another over-imaginative rumor monger. Actually, Captain Thompson was reporting exactly the truth, for all the good it did, as he described the stealthy horse-acquiring activities of Colonel Dorsey's busy cavalrymen.[64] By May 31 Rosecrans himself finally grasped the truth that at least scattered bodies of Rebels were infiltrating through Cooper and Moniteau Counties on their way to northeast Missouri, although they had by this date probably already crossed the Missouri River. The general now knew that these were regular cavalry and not bushwhackers, but he mistakenly believed they were under Colonel Sidney D. Jackman, a nemesis to the Union cause in northeast Missouri throughout much of the previous year, and not Colonel Dorsey.[65]

Brownlee's guerrillas were not idle during this time. During the evening of May 23 at the village of Pisgah, southeast Cooper County, three masked bushwhackers roused Dr. David P. Mahan from bed and made him open his store next door. The trio took over $500 in cash and a large amount of store goods, too. That these raiders cared enough to hide their faces seems to indicate that they were local men afraid of being recognized.[66] Elements of the 4th Cavalry MSM were hunting guerrillas near Bell Air, west-central Cooper County, May 26 when they saw middle-aged farmer James M. Nichols and another local man out riding their horses. The troopers called upon the pair to halt, but Nichols' horse was startled by the yelling and ran away out of control with its rider hanging on to prevent a fall. The soldiers fired on the unfortunate farmer wounding him slightly and his horse. The cavalrymen were very apologetic for the mistake and advised the shaken and wounded riders to make their way slowly back to the main road to prevent any more mishaps. Sadly, on the way to the road another group of 4th troopers, alerted to the yelling and shooting, happened upon Nichols, mistook him for a guerrilla, and shot him to death. It was all a tragic series of misunderstandings.[67]

After a one year hiatus, guerrilla warfare returned to southern Cole and Miller Counties, a few miles south of the state capitol. Back in September 1862 the guerrilla leader and Confederate recruiter known only as "General Crabtree" was mortally wounded in this area by a small party of vengeful militiamen angry that Crabtree had robbed one of his old wedding suit. With this bushwhacker leader's death, relative quiet resumed in this area throughout the next year. Some of Crabtree's men returned to their guerrilla ways this spring joined by other southern men led by Wiley H. Shumate, a former member of the Confederate Pindall's Sharpshooter Battalion, and a man known only as "Clark."[68] On March 20, 1864, a Union patrol probably of the 4th Cavalry MSM from Jefferson City wounded John Wilcox of Shumate's band near Hickory Hill, northwest Miller County, then left Wilcox at the scene as too badly wounded to take back.[69] A few days later on March 31 First Lieutenant William C. Lefever's patrol of Company F, 4th Cavalry MSM in south Cole County captured Wilcox and this time took him back to confinement at Jefferson City. The Federals there convicted John Wilcox of being a guerrilla.[70] On April 7 Union authorities of Miller County arrested Miss Ruth Bond and Miss Sarah Bond of that county and sent them off to Myrtle Street Prison in downtown St. Louis. The simple prison ledger does not state the charges against the two Bond ladies, but does state that both gave oath and bond and were released June 21.[71]

Some atrocity stories of guerrillas are so ghastly as to be almost unbelievable. An anonymous Jefferson City correspondent wrote such a story April 18 to the St. Louis *Daily Missouri Democrat,* but did not give his source. The correspondent wrote that Shumate and Clark's small bushwhacker band tortured a German-American farmer named Kuntz 25 or 30 miles upriver from the mouth of the Osage River somewhere in Cole or Miller Counties April 12. In an attempt to coerce the farmer to tell where he hid his money the correspondent wrote that the guerrillas cut the poor man's legs repeatedly with Kuntz' own wood saw. The violence gained the southerners nothing as Kuntz fell into unconsciousness from shock and loss of blood and died soon after, taking the secret of his hidden treasure to the grave. The story was carried by a boy who lived with Kuntz and escaped frantic with terror to carry the tale. The newspaper article also stated that the guerrillas next attacked another farmer nearby and cut that man's head off because he also would not disclose under pressure where he had hidden his funds. The correspondent ended this part of his tale by stating that "all of this is vouched for by the whole neighborhood."[72] Whether Wiley Shumate and his men actually performed these depredations is questionable, but they would have other adventures in the coming summer.

Despite some reverses, the guerrilla cause in northwest Missouri south of the Missouri River gained strength this spring across much of the region. During early spring bushwhackers lost numbers and lessened their activities in Jackson and Lafayette Counties with the death of leader Andy Blunt, the disintegration of his band, and the unwillingness of remaining southerners in Jackson County to present much of a threat. With the return of Captain Quantrill and George Todd in late April southern actions against the Yankees surged, but when Bill Anderson brought his band back to the region from

Texas in May with Todd he deposed Quantrill. To them, their old leader no longer personified the dashing, don't-count-the-costs, devil-take-the-hindmost spirit they felt the guerrillas needed, and Captain Quantrill's leadership had produced disappointments in recent weeks. With Quantrill on his way to exile in distant Howard County with a handful of faithful followers, Todd, Anderson, and their men looked forward with excitement to the death and destruction they would wreak upon the hated Yankees. Meanwhile, guerrilla bands led by Charles Brownlee around Cooper County and Wiley Shumate in the Cole and Miller County area of central Missouri had brought their own version of bushwhacking to that part of northwest Missouri. This approaching summer of 1864 promised to be and became the most violent summer of the war.

TEN

Spring 1864 in Northwest Missouri North of the Missouri River

The tempo of guerrilla war increased steadily throughout the spring of 1864 in northwest Missouri north of the great Missouri River, too, but not in all parts. Union troops in Holt and Atchison County in the far northwest corner of Missouri during March captured and arrested gangs of thugs and thieves that comprised Jayhawker bands that had been the scourge of this region during previous months. During April and May guerrilla acts increased noticeably in Livingston, Clay, and Ray Counties. There were acts of violence mostly during May in the St. Joseph area and in Clinton, Andrew, and DeKalb Counties that had been relatively quiet throughout the winter. By far, the most frequent acts of irregular warfare took place in Platte County throughout the entire spring, building toward something ominous for the summer of 1864.

Mass Arrests of Jayhawkers in Far Northwest Corner of Missouri During March

Early in the spring during the first two weeks of March 1864 Union cavalry in and around the far northwest tip of Missouri captured and brought to justice large numbers of thugs, thieves, discharged soldiers, and deserters who were living in gangs in the area and preying on residents of southern sympathy. A detachment of Federal cavalry identified by the local press as part of the 7th Iowa Cavalry Regiment in early March raided hideouts of these jayhawkers in Richardson and Nemaha Counties, Nebraska and Atchison County, Missouri. The cavalry arrested about 40 men on both sides of the Missouri River border, including the clerk of Richardson County who was alleged to be "the chief of the band." A local newspaper article called these miscreants "this class of lazy, thieving, reckless, disloyal bipeds."[1] Over the next several days elements of the 9th Cavalry MSM stationed in this region of Missouri carried out their own raids on the notorious hangout of the jayhawkers, Rush Bottom by the Missouri River in west-central Holt County. About March 12 Captain William B. Kemper and his patrol of Company K, 9th Cavalry MSM from St. Joseph captured at Rush Bottom a motley group of renegades including a "Lieutenant Cunningham," a John Holley supposed to have deserted from the 4th Cavalry MSM, Corporal Michael Eastman of the 14th Kansas Cavalry who lived at Oregon in south Holt County, Private William Colton of the 58th EMM who also lived in Oregon, and two other men from Andrew County.[2] A few days later in mid–March Captain Samuel A. Hunter with his patrol of Company M, 9th Cavalry MSM from their garrison at Oregon, south Holt County, captured four more men at Rush Bottom and placed them in jail. These included at least two men

Union Captain William B. Kemper, commanding Company K, 9th Cavalry Missouri State Militia (Private collection; courtesy of the late Bob Younger and Mary Younger and Andy Turner).

who lived in south Holt County, one of them being Andrew Farmer who had been discharged from the Union 25th Missouri Infantry Regiment the previous June.[3] Even though these men were evidently misguided northern sympathizers, local Union authorities had to arrest and jail them to prevent more atrocities against residents of southern sympathy. That Union authorities took action against interests other than that of secession could be taken as a harbinger of an eventual interest in restoring civil law and true constitutional rights in this part of Missouri.

Guerrilla Actions Increase During April and May in Ray, Clay, and Livingston Counties and Jesse James Joins the War

The tempo of Guerrilla actions steadily increased in Livingston, Clay, and Ray Counties from April through May of 1864. On April 13 a shooting occurred when two local soldiers of the 65th EMM went to arrest George Burton for either not paying his commutation tax for the draft or failing to enroll in the militia as required by state law. The pair of militiamen called upon Burton at his father-in-law's house near the village of Bedford in southeast Livingston County and stated their intent to arrest him as he was working in the field. Burton convinced the soldiers to allow him to step over to the house, where they made the mistake of not accompanying their suspect to oversee his actions in the house. Therefore, when the farmer charged out of the dwelling with a double-barreled shotgun, he had the element of surprise. Burton critically wounded one with a shotgun blast to the face and wounded the second with a shotgun blast to the arm and side. With his uninjured hand the second militiaman fired a shot at the now fleeing Burton but missed.[4]

Ten or twelve guerrillas, perhaps including both notorious postwar outlaws Frank and Jesse James, crossed the Missouri River from Lafayette County to the river village of Camden, south-central Ray County, the night of May 7/8 and robbed stores and residents of about $800 worth of goods and cash. The raiders used skiffs to cross their horses over the wide river and returned to Lafayette County the same way. They kept their time in Camden short because the local militia at Richmond was only eight miles away to the north, but the raiders told their startled victims that they also had intentions to raid Richmond in the near future. The bushwhackers escaped completely, and Union authorities could only arrest the man who held their horses. After the war, Confederate veteran Major John N. Edwards interviewed many surviving guerrillas, and

Above, left: Postwar artwork of wartime photograph of guerrilla Frank James of Clay County, Missouri (John N. Edwards, *Noted Guerrillas*, 1877, p. 175; courtesy of the late Bob Younger and Mary Younger and Andy Turner). *Right:* Heavily armed 16-year-old Jesse James sat for this photograph soon after joining a guerrilla band that already had as a member his veteran bushwhacker brother, Frank James.

among the eight guerrillas he named as being part of this raid, he included not only veteran bushwhacker Frank James of Clay County, but also his kid brother Jesse, who would celebrate his seventeenth birthday September 5, 1864. The Camden raid may have been Jesse James first foray as a guerrilla. Edwards wrote that one of the drunken bushwhackers, Bill Gaw or Gaugh, accidentally shot Jesse in the face during the raid. The wound could not have been bad for the teenager was active in operations shortly thereafter.[5]

Also about May 1864 a squad of the newly activated Clay County Militia ambushed two local bushwhackers, Jim Cummins and Theodore Castle, and temporarily trapped them in a thicket in the Clay County area. Cummins described this harrowing experience in his 1903 memoir. One of the militia's bullets thudded into Cummins' leg and Castle was wounded in the hand from an earlier experience loading his own revolver. They had to abandon their horses and coats, but managed to escape through a brushy creek bed. Cummins also wrote that two other bushwhackers riding with them, Peyton Long and Jesse James, had stopped at a spring a short distance up the road and avoided the militia ambush.[6]

During the night of May 22-23 a small number of unidentified guerrillas from south of the Missouri River crossed into Ray County and stole six horses from what they thought were the pastures of northern sympathizers. As they rode with their prizes back to the mouth of Fishing River, southwest Ray County, southern residents made them aware that two of the horses they had taken actually belonged to returned soldiers of the Confederate Army. The raiders decided to turn those two horses loose so that their owners may find them, but a stallion belonging to former Union Major Abraham Allen of the hamlet of Crab Orchard got away into the darkness, too. The raiders took their three remaining purloined horses back across the Missouri River into Lafayette County, pleased with the night's efforts. With morning Abraham Allen gathered some trusted neighbors and rode after the thieves, but when he quizzed known southern men if they had seen horse thieves go by in the night, he got either denials or false leads intended to slow his hunt. Therefore, Allen felt great relief when he found his own stallion grazing among the cottonwoods at the river's edge. He wrote area Union authorities offering to organize a militia for self defense against both the bushwhackers and the large numbers of southern residents who seemed to bear him ill will.[7]

As May drew to a close a number of guerrillas crossed the Missouri River into Clay County and began to rob people traveling along the roads and steal horses. A Union captain at Independence reported that he heard as many as 200 Rebels moved across the Missouri River and began operations in Clay County, but this number was greatly exaggerated. Whatever the actual details, these developments promised a action-filled summer in Clay County.[8]

Accelerating Guerrilla Acts in Clinton and Buchanan Counties and Numerous Vengeance Attacks

The guerrilla war increased in intensity in Clinton and Buchanan Counties this spring, also. During late March near Plattsburg, county seat of Clinton County, two northern men of the area arrested local guerrilla Louis Vandevere, a former member of Joe Hart's bushwhacker band in 1863. One of the pair apprehending Vandevere was the same former Union Major Abraham Allen of Crab Orchard in Ray County who in May would complain to Union officials that area southern sympathizers seemed to wish him ill. In Allen's letter he specifically mentioned his arrest of Vandevere a few weeks before as the incident he felt incurred southern wrath against him. After his arrest, bushwhacker Vandevere confessed to having buried $400 he robbed at Plattsburg the previous year, but Allen and his partner could not find the hidden loot.[9]

When Missouri guerrillas returned to their operations area after a winter away a common first order of business was revenge against residents in their home areas who had made a stand for the northern side. Buchanan County was the scene for a number of these revenge attacks during April and May 1864.

For several nights in late April 1864 unidentified raiders committed arson, larceny, and murder in the southwest corner of Buchanan County around the village of DeKalb. They seemed to target wealthy properties for the arson and theft, since they burned not only homes but a smokehouse containing 100 butchered hogs, a distillery, and took expensive horses. The loss of the smokehouse was valued at $10,000 and the distillery loss was estimated at $5,000.[10] On the morning of May 1 unknown assassins murdered three unidentified men in this same neighborhood and rode into Platte County where the Union troops from St. Joseph failed to find them.[11]

A number of northern men and officers in DeKalb and Buchanan Counties were either found dead or disappeared and their bodies later found between May 16 and May 25. Area newspapers dutifully reported these men either as disappeared and feared dead or the grisly discovery of their bodies in issue after issue as near panic ensued among the war weary residents of this region. Officials feared another outbreak of northern night riders killing southern men that took place here the previous year after Joe Hart's guerrilla band killed two or three men of northern sympathy. District commander Union Brigadier General Clinton B. Fisk personally investigated this spate of murders and quickly reported his findings May 26 so as to allay the growing panic in the region. His findings became an incomplete history of these killings.

The first death occurred about May 16 took place when unidentified guerrillas captured Private John Christian of Company E, 87th EMM somewhere in Buchanan County, and took him to their camp 15 miles south of St. Joseph near Bretz' Mills in Jackson Township in the southeast corner of the county. One of the Rebels later revealed to Union authorities how they forced 30-year-old Private Christian to list a number of staunch northern sympathizers he knew, then callously told him they were going to kill him and then kill every man that he had named. Five of the bushwhackers, including three men who were members of the northern "Paw Paw Militia" of the 81st or 82nd EMM, then took Christian to the Platte River, shot him several times, and threw his body into the water. Someone recovered Christian's body with three bullet wounds in the head from the Platte River about May 18. General Fisk had to conclude that Private Christian was murdered by "Paw Paw Militia" of Platte County.[12]

On May 18 Captain Hamilton S. Wilson of Company C, 87th EMM left St. Joseph at four in the afternoon evidently carrying $3000 in cash on his way home to southwest Buchanan County, but was not seen alive again. Unknown parties shot the captain six times in the head and left his body a quarter mile from the road where a passerby discovered it May 25. In his quick investigation after the discovery of Wilson's body General Fisk noted that Wilson was carrying lots of cash and concluded that he was killed for the money. Fisk left unsaid the possibility that southerners assassinated Captain Wilson because he was a staunch Union officer and just happened to find and take the man's cash afterward. It is notable that Wilson lived near the village of DeKalb, where unknown assailants committed a series of arsons, thefts, and three murders three weeks before.[13]

On May 19 two Robinson brothers murdered their cousin, Union Captain James McDonald, near his home in central DeKalb County over a long-standing dispute about the sale of a mule or some cattle. The St. Joseph newspaper on May 26 spread the rumor that his murder was just another assassination of a loyal Union militia officer, marking a dangerous trend in the region. Both the Savannah, Andrew County, newspaper and the same St. Joseph newspaper responsibly printed the correct story just a few days after the event, and General Fisk mentioned the true account in his report.[14]

Just to add to the hysteria, St. Joseph people repeated a rumor that a Mr. Floyd, a miller of south Buchanan County, was also found murdered. General Fisk actually enjoyed mentioning in his May 26 report that "one party who was reported found dead with 12 bullets in his head turns out to be unhurt and at work over in Kansas."[15]

Parties unknown shot to death Union First Sergeant Harvey Bradford of Company E, 81st EMM about 12 miles south of St. Joseph about the same date as Captain McDonald's death. The first sergeant's military service record shows he was relieved from active duty March 2, so it appears he was not on active duty when killed. Locals found Bradford's bullet-riddled body the morning of May 20. General Fisk's own aide the next day excitedly telegrammed the general who was in St. Louis at the time and concluded: "Another murder yesterday.... This is the fourth murder within this week. It is the beginning of the end of the fight between the radicals and conservatives."[16]

General Fisk's stated aim was maintaining peace and order in this district, and he specifically wanted to head off another spate of northern vigilante violence that cruelly swept this area in 1863. Although Fisk was delighted to show one of the reported deaths was invented and another was an old grudge murder about livestock, the fact remained that an unidentified band of southern guerrillas in south Buchanan County coldly assassinated Captain Wilson and Private Christian of the 87th EMM and First Sergeant Bradford of the 81st EMM between May 16 and May 21. The general reported to Major General Rosecrans May 26: "I shall go to Platte [County] myself, and use all my means and power to allay the apprehensions of the people. Not over 8 bushwhackers have as yet been seen in any one place. My force are all at work. I shall organize and put on duty a military force sufficient to maintain quiet." In fact, Union militia May 27 near Taos, south-central Buchanan County, attempted to arrest John Turner, shot him dead when he ran, and found in his pocket dead Captain Wilson's own revolver. This gave Fisk and others confidence that the violence was localized and containable. Still, the St. Joseph newspaper on June 2 added a note of caution about what that editor observed to be a disturbing trend of southern resurgence this spring:

> One theory respecting these troubles is, that guerrillas and murderers have returned from Price's army, and are in the brush, recruiting men, and stealing horses and supplies. That these bushwhackers have old scores to settle with their former neighbors.... That there are guerrillas roaming in small squads near us, is probably true; but, that they number more than a handful, outside of Jackson County, and the infected district, we do not believe.

Actually, the Confederacy was growing in strength during this time, particularly in Platte County, and the general and others would have a rude awakening from that area in the approaching summer.[17]

The unexpected discovery of a large cache of hidden Rebel gunpowder near St. Joseph May 27 briefly diverted northern attention from the growing southern violence in the region. Evidently acting on a tip that the gunpowder was hidden in a neighborhood just three miles east of St. Joseph, the Union provost marshal's office discovered 23 kegs and 180 cans of the explosive secreted on the farms of "four of our first families," as General Fisk succinctly put it. At least two of the landowners, James Dysart and Lewis Gaines, were members of the local "Paw Paw Militia," which was another clue to Fisk that all was not as well in his district as he touted. Union officials arrested the quartet and theorized that this gunpowder was part of what St. Joseph secessionists assembled when they were in control of the city back in 1861.[18]

Platte County as the Center of Southern Resistance for Northwest Missouri: Winston and Gordon

That Platte County southerners were enjoying a robust resurgence, even General Fisk could partly agree, but he refused to see the signs since most of them remained hidden from observation. On March 12 Captain David Johnson and part of his Company A, 82nd EMM badly whipped a free black man, Sam Marshall, for attempting to take his Platte County family across the Missouri River to freedom in Kansas. Marshall understood what he attempted was correct and he traveled first to check with county officials at Platte City where the sheriff and Captain Johnson berated him for daring to do such a thing. Then the captain had some of his "Paw Paw Militia" escort the humbled black man out of town supposedly for his own protection where they tied him to a tree and whipped him viciously with a rawhide cord before they allowed Marshall to return to Kansas. The Union commander of Kansas, former Missouri commander Major General Samuel R. Curtis, filed an official protest about this racial cruelty to Major General Rosecrans. Missouri officials were fully aware that a large proportion of the "Paw Paw Militia" were avowed southerners, so they would not be surprised at this behavior.[19]

About March 20 unidentified guerrillas robbed the Tufts and Miller Store in or near the village of New Market, north-central Platte County. In retaliation, Union officials compelled five nearby farmers of southern leanings to pay the damages to the store owners.[20]

Illustration of a fanciful version of the real-life capture of Confederate recruiter Colonel John H. Winston at his Platte County home (Frazar Kirkland, *The Pictorial Book of Anecdotes of the Rebellion*, 1888, p. 230).

Union troops from St. Joseph and Kansas ignored the "Paw Paw Militia" units in Platte county and performed their own raid six miles from Platte City March 22 and arrested at his own home Confederate Colonel John H. Winston, who for some weeks had been recruiting for the Rebel army—even wearing his gray uniform. Union Captain William J. Fitzgerald, formerly of the 39th EMM of Platte County and then of the 16th Kansas Cavalry became suspicious when Winston's brother, Confederate Captain Samuel Winston, was captured in this neighborhood earlier in March. Fitzgerald orchestrated his own detective work without notifying the militia then in Platte County, and guided the raid of Captain William B. Kemper and some of his troopers of the 9th Cavalry MSM from the St. Joseph garrison. The Federal cavalrymen of the 9th took Colonel Winston to jail in St. Joseph where his Platte County friends had less influence to conduct a jail break. This raid was predicated three days earlier by an angry exchange of messages between the Kansas commander, Major General Curtis, and the commander of the central Missouri district, Brigadier General Egbert B. Brown. Brown was incensed that Curtis suggested intelligence told him that the Confederacy was fomenting an insurgency in Brown's Jackson County and actively recruiting a large force of southerners in nearby Platte County:

> I do not believe that there is any foundation for this report; and the part of it that recruiting is being done for the South in Platte County, and that they will concentrate in Jackson [County] and move south in a body, is so different from their usual mode of operations that it carries its own contradiction.... The commanding general may be assured that this command is on the alert.

Now, after Winston's capture, Curtis sent a curt note to his Missouri counterpart, Major General Rosecrans:

> Captain Fitzgerald, aided by your officers, has captured the rebel recruiting colonel, Winston, who I informed you was concealed in Platte City. My first information of this rebel's

presence in that place was about the 9th, and many persons there must have known of his being in the vicinity. The militia company located there seems to have been oblivious to all this.

Meanwhile, General Fisk, whose district included Platte County, had to be concerned about reports that other Confederate officers were also actively recruiting in Platte County. Generals do not like surprises, and they do not like to be criticized for them by other general officers.[21]

A normally accurate Platte County historical source reported that local guerrilla chief Captain Silas Gordon was back in the area at least long enough to stop men from the Fort Leavenworth area from stealing wood from the Platte County side of the Missouri River for a while. This account stated that about April 14 Gordon took from one wood gatherer his wagon and team, and that stopped the practice. This seems to be the only report that placed the capable Gordon back in the vicinity of his home county this season, so it is difficult to gauge if the accomplished guerrilla leader was really there.[22]

Unidentified guerrillas attempted to raid the village of Parkville in south Platte County April 14, but First Lieutenant Franklin Luthy, formerly of the 39th EMM and then of Luthy's Platte County Veteran Missouri Militia "held them at bay." The would-be raiders considered Luthy too much of a threat to continue and left empty-handed.[23]

Platte County seemed to enjoy a surprising five weeks of peace after the Parkville incident until the night of May 21/22, when eight guerrillas allegedly raided the village of Camden Point in the northeast corner of the county. This was about five or six days after a group of bushwhackers camped just a few miles north in the southeast corner of Buchanan County tortured and murdered Union Private John Christian of the 87th EMM, as detailed in an earlier paragraph. Captain W. T. Woods, commander of Company D, 82nd EMM of the "Paw Paw Militia," reported to headquarters that the eight guerrillas broke into a building in town where Woods' company had recently secured their rifle muskets that higher authority had ordered them to turn in. The burglars took away 27 rifles. It seemed very suspicious that the rifles were taken just after the company was ordered to give them up, but a skeptical investigator from district headquarters could not uncover any more facts on the matter. Even more disturbing was Captain Woods' assertion that he had received word that parties unknown were organizing eight companies of bushwhackers in that neighborhood. Subsequent actions a few weeks later would prove that Woods' astounding assertion of a secret Rebel organization being formed in Platte County was largely true. However, at this time, the captain's rumor was discounted as too ridiculous to believe, even though the Union commander of Kansas, Major General Curtis, was hearing of this, too, and tried in vain to alert the disbelieving Union high command in Missouri, as disclosed earlier in this chapter. It appeared that the Federal leaders were more concerned about the theft of 27 shoulder arms.[24]

Area newspapers were also warning about suspicious activities in Platte County. The Kansas City paper on May 26 repeated a St. Joseph article of May 24 that "serious trouble is brewing in Platte County." They reported that "the rebels are taking guns, horses, and stock from loyal men, and great fear is experienced by all true Union citizens," but gave no specifics nor named any of the victims. Such activities across Missouri throughout the war were standard methods for behind-Union-lines Confederate recruiters to arm, mount, and feed new recruits. The reporter interviewed Judge William Heren who attempted to hold circuit court at Platte County. The judge sensed great tension in the community, adjourned early without completing the docket, and hastily returned to the relative safety of St. Joseph on May 23. Unfortunately, the failure to provide specifics and a judge's indistinct suspicions failed to deter Union authorities from discounting this report as wild, unsubstantiated rumor.[25]

On May 24 two guerrillas robbed a teamster driving his wagon through Platte County on his way from Leavenworth to Liberty. They not only took his valuable team of horses, destroyed the wagon and load, but robbed the driver of his watch and money. The highwaymen left the teamster with a warning against anyone who would attempt to pursue them.[26] Unidentified guerrillas raided the village of Camden Point, northeast Platte County, on May 27, taking about $5,000 worth of goods from Thomas Hale's mercantile store there. They also drove off the Union enrolling officer and tore up the papers that he left behind.[27]

On the afternoon of May 30 the crew of the river steamer *Paragon* reported two unusual passengers to the commander of the Union provost guard at Fort Leavenworth when the vessel arrived at dockside. The Yankee guards promptly removed two apparent Rebel soldiers complete in butternut uniforms, who had evidently stopped the boat for a ride not far away. The pair gave their names and told the Federals they were from Platte County, but one had a severe bullet wound in his foot. The duo explained that they were in a skirmish with bushwhackers near Kansas City where the one was shot. The Union guards took them away into the fort to examine them further. Perhaps these men really were Confederates from Platte County who were seeking better medical care for the foot wound than they would find in their hidden rural camp.[28]

During the night of May 31/June 1 a gang of armed robbers near Weston, western Platte County, forced their way into the home of an unnamed household, tied and gagged the occupants, and took several hundred dollars in cash. The thieves threatened their victims that if they reported the theft before daylight the robbers would return and burn the house. This could be the act of jayhawkers from across the Missouri River, but such acts had become rare since the mobilization of the local "Paw Paw Militia" a few months before.[29]

The Union district commander, Brigadier General Clinton B. Fisk, was correct that Platte County was the seat of the troubles in his jurisdiction, but wishful thinking or failure to correctly interpret numerous clues led him to underestimate the danger hidden in the place. It was ludicrous for him to claim that only eight bushwhackers were active at a time there. Union leadership ignored what in hindsight was systematic arson, larceny, and murder in and near Platte County by veteran bushwhackers skilled at brutal killing. Northern leaders defended the openly southern "Paw Paw Militia" since the previous autumn while the militiamen fought against jayhawking Kansas raiders. These leaders failed to understand that the "Paw Paws" were willing to fight Kansas renegades, but were not about to oppose fellow Rebels in the form of southern guerrillas and Confederate recruiters. The opponents of the "Paw Paws" cried "wolf" much too often to the point that Federal leaders like Fisk were no longer willing to listen to their diatribes. Now "the fox was placed in charge of the henhouse," to coin a phrase, and the "Paw Paws" became, in effect, a screening force to prevent snooping northerners from learning too much about the secret Rebel force then forming in Platte County. The summer here promised disaster unless the Federals interpreted the many danger signs more accurately and/or the Rebels revealed themselves too soon. Union victories over jayhawkers in the far northwest corner of the state, southern guerrillas increasing in strength and audacity along the counties along the north bank of the Missouri River, and internecine warfare in other parts of northwest Missouri could pale in comparison to the secretly growing southern strength in Platte County in the summer months.

Eleven

Summer 1864 in Southeast Missouri

The southeast quadrant of Missouri was the scene of heavy guerrilla fighting across most of its parts in the summer of 1864. Several different guerrilla and regular Confederate units fought against Union troops in the swampy "bootheel" this season. The unstoppable bushwhacker Samuel S. Hildebrand leading small numbers of guerrillas made a number of his characteristic long patrols across the "bootheel" and through the hill country west and mostly north of it this season assassinating northern sympathizers he found loathsome and raiding small villages and isolated stores. As Colonel Tim Reeves was occupied recruiting for his regiment across the border in Arkansas, his command had small influence on the fighting this season in the hill country along the Missouri/Arkansas border. Dick Berryman and other guerrilla leaders still made trouble for the Federals here whenever they could. The south central corridor that saw some of the heaviest fighting in past seasons was comparatively quiet this summer as Confederate Colonel Thomas R. Freeman was also busy recruiting for his regiment mostly south of the state border. Frequent bushwhacker fights of local Rebels still took place mostly in Phelps, Dent, and Texas Counties. Guerrilla leaders such as Hildebrand, Peter Smith, and others were active during June, July, and August in the hilly country north of the "bootheel" and south of the St. Louis area. Some Rebel activity took place this season also in the normally quiet counties along the south bank of the Missouri River.

Summer 1864 in the Swampy "Bootheel": Guerrillas Led by Guthrie, Wright, Hildebrand, Clark, Bolin, and Others

The swamps of Missouri's southeast-most appendage, called the "bootheel" because of the map outline shape of this region resembled the heel of a boot, served to hide and protect southern irregulars throughout the war. By the summer of 1864 Union forces had learned to watch this region of mostly six counties and send in large troop expeditions from New Madrid or Cape Girardeau whenever they learned Rebels were gathering there in any numbers or a particular bushwhacker band made itself obnoxious to them. Some southern combatants made the swamps of this area their base, but others crossed through the concealment of the swamps as an avenue of approach on their way to some other part of southeast Missouri.

By early June of 1864 Confederate Brigadier General Joseph O. Shelby, the daring cavalry commander then in northeast Arkansas, directed all the southern forces in his region to concentrate on recruiting, and this affected operations in Missouri's "bootheel." The Confederate commander at Jacksonport, Arkansas, Colonel Thomas H. McCray, was obedient to General Shelby's commands, sending some inventive, dedicated men into the far southeast corner of Missouri to recruit, but especially to obtain corn meal for his growing command. This explains why a local Union militia colonel June 3 sent word to the Yankee base at Cape Girardeau that 200 Rebels were operating a grinding mill all night the night before at Patton in north Bollinger County. The incredulous northern commander sent troops to Patton who were there when they reported finding no Rebels when they arrived. Of course, the militia colonel's estimate of 200 southerners was probably too high, but his credibility with the regulars in the region had taken a blow just the same from his fanciful report.[1]

Confederate Captain Guthrie's Recruiting Drive in Early June

Actually, Confederate Captain John H. Guthrie of McCray's growing command assisted by John P. Wright and a recruiting command of about company strength were probably the men responsible for the all-night corn grinding party at Patton, and they had more in store for area Yankees in order to encourage recruiting. Resourceful Rebel recruiters behind Yankee lines knew they had to challenge local Federals in order to embolden local southern men to come in and join up. Wright and his men asserted themselves toward this goal by ambushing a detail of ten troopers of 1st Missouri Cavalry riding along the road near the large base at New Madrid, killing a sergeant and capturing three horses on June 3. That night they tore down telegraph line near Charleston, Mississippi County, and Wright even told civilians nearby that his men intended to keep the telegraph inoperative for a time.[2] On June 4 Colonel Joseph B. Rogers, commander of the 2nd Cavalry MSM and in charge of the Cape Girardeau base, issued an order to all his men that "you will not capture, under any circumstances, any man known to be a guerrilla or acting with them. They will be killed when and where found." Confederate Captain Guthrie on June 6 sent a note of protest to the Federal captain commanding the small garrison at Charleston, Mississippi County. In his note Guthrie stated he had a proper commission paper to recruit for the Confederacy and that his men were part of the Confederate army and entitled to proper treatment as prisoners of war if captured. When Colonel Rogers read of the Rebel captain's note, he sent as response "I can't see the prisoner of war part of it." Wright and five of his men rode into Sikeston the evening of June 7 where he shot to death a horse only because it wore the "U.S." brand, then he killed a black man just because of the man's race. Union Lieutenant John A. Rice and a detachment of 2nd Cavalry MSM from Cape Girardeau rode up to Wright and his men just moments later, killing two guerrillas and capturing Wright himself. Wright was not at all cowed, as he bragged to his captors about ambushing the detail of 1st Missouri Cavalry on June 3. He seemed proud, too, of tearing down telegraph line, and had the Federals look in his saddlebag where he had a roll of the wire as a souvenir. The official report states that Wright was killed soon after trying to escape, but more likely he was executed in compliance with the regimental commander's recent order reminding his troopers not to take guerrillas as prisoners.[3]

There were other southerners active in the "bootheel" during the first days of June 1864. Major Hiram M. Hiller of the 2nd Cavalry MSM, commanding at Bloomfield, Stoddard County, on June 2 or 3 reported an unidentified Rebel guerrilla body of unknown size at Cane Island in the St. Francis River, Dunklin County, at least 30 miles south of his post. Possibly, these southerners were crossing the Arkansas border there, but no other record seems to survive about this group.[4]

Sam Hildebrand in Stoddard County in Early June

On the night of June 3/4 notorious guerrilla Sam Hildebrand with one or two companions assassinated a middle-aged northern sympathizer Hicks at the man's home about seven miles from the Bloomfield Union garrison. Major Hiller reported that the bushwhackers shot Hicks working in the garden, which agrees with an account Hildebrand wrote himself just after the war telling about an event he says took place in 1863 near Bloomfield in which he shot down a Captain Hicks who tried to defend himself with a garden hoe as the bushwhacker gunned him down. In his autobiography Hildebrand claimed Hicks led a Union group following the guerrilla's wife and children as they left Missouri to join him in Greene County, Arkansas some weeks before, and that Hicks bragged about inflicting an earlier wound on Hildebrand.[5]

Captain Guthrie's group of Confederate recruiters used the knowledge of remaining Mississippi County guerrillas to find safe havens in the vast swamps of that county, but the Union regular and militia troops especially around the county seat at Charleston had learned how to fight in these swamps in bitter fighting that spring. Captain James W. Edwards and his men of Company B, 2nd Cavalry MSM used their previous experience to carefully ferret out these new Rebels in the swamps with some success. By mid June his men had killed nine of the southerners, evidently at no loss to themselves.[6]

Under pressure from the Yanks hunting them in the swamps, Captain Guthrie and his 40 Confederate recruiters rode west from the swamps of Mississippi County June 11. They killed a discharged Union soldier around noon in about north New Madrid County, then turned southwest toward Dunklin County. That evening these bushwhackers killed a Doctor Sutton at the village of Clarkton in north Dunklin County after mistaking the physician for a Union soldier. Also on June 11 some guerrillas, perhaps of the same group, attempted to ambush Lieutenant Harrison H. Byrne's patrol of 2nd Cavalry MSM from Bloomfield somewhere in this area. The cavalrymen killed two of the Rebels with no harm to themselves. Three

Swamp fighting (Underwood and Clough, eds., *Battles and Leaders of the Civil War*, vol. 1, p. 465).

separate patrols of the 2nd in this area failed to find further sign of Guthrie's 40 riders, and the Federals concluded their quarry veered back east, re-crossed the Little River in Pemiscot County, and found refuge in the swamps there.[7]

On June 18 two bushwhackers stole two horses of the 2nd Cavalry MSM near Cape Girardeau and attempted to ride them to safety. They misjudged how fast the Union cavalry could set out a pursuit which soon caught up to the fleeing pair and killed them both.[8]

Confederate Colonel Henry E. Clark's June Recruiting Drive in the "Bootheel"

One of the major Confederate recruiting commands answerable to Colonel Thomas H. McCray at Jacksonport, Arkansas was that of Ohio-born, prewar New Madrid resident Colonel Henry E. Clark, whose hidden recruiting headquarters was somewhere in Dunklin County by mid June. In a June 19 plea to Rebel units across the Mississippi River Colonel Clark begged for shoulder arms, pistols, and ammunition—especially shotgun ammunition—for his neophyte cavalrymen. At this time of the war Rebel cavalry recruits in the Trans-Mississippi West found shotguns easier to obtain and supply than carbines, and Clark confided that he had already accumulated 7,000 buckshot cartridges for his men's shotguns. Clark had recruited in the "bootheel" with success in 1862, where he was captured in October and later exchanged. He returned to this region and recruited again in 1863. Most of the men Colonel Clark recruited those two years now comprised the bulk of Colonel Solomon G. Kitchen's 7th Missouri Cavalry Regiment—also known as the 10th Regiment—which was then also located somewhere in this part of Missouri or Arkansas. Henry Clark revealed in his appeal for arms that he had already signed up over 1,000 southerners, but sent them for safety temporarily to their homes lest the Yankees detect the presence of so many troops in one place. Probably it was Colonel Clark's recruiting command that the Union military noted at Cane Island in the St. Francis River two weeks earlier. Clark had given all his men the date of July 4 to assemble together for the first time under his command there in Dunklin County. When that happened the northern forces were sure to hear about it and come in force.[9]

About four miles south of the large Union base of New Madrid on June 29 unidentified guerrillas attacked a small patrol or detail of the 1st Missouri Cavalry. Unit records for that unit indicate one trooper was wounded, and the guerrillas evidently suffered no harm.[10]

Union Lieutenant Colonel Burris' Expedition in the "Bootheel"

The rendezvous in the Pemiscot and Dunklin County area of Confederate Colonel Henry Clark's newly recruited regiment about July 4 attracted Union attention and a large expedition of 200 cavalrymen from the New Madrid and Cape Girardeau bases crashed around that area between July 5 and 10. The large Union force was led by Lieutenant Colonel John T. Burris of the 10th Kansas Infantry Regiment, who had commanded large, but mostly ineffectual task forces during 1862 in west-central Missouri against Quantrill's bushwhackers. Burris perfected his technique by July 1864 and the veteran cavalry he commanded this time produced some measure of success. None of Burris' own 10th Kansas took part, since they were working elsewhere in southeast Missouri, but elements of 1st Missouri Cavalry and 2nd Cavalry MSM performed the cavalry portion of the expedition. Lieutenant Colonel Burris even had elements of 1st Infantry MSM and 18th U. S. Colored Infantry dropped by the government-seized river steamer-now-tinclad *Huntress, No. 58* on the eastern shore of Pemiscot County where they skirmished with elusive guerrillas between July 7 and 9 and killed about eight of them before taking their vessel back to New Madrid. Meanwhile, the cavalry portion of the expedition crisscrossed the two counties for six days riding through swamps and brush tangles uncovering Rebel campsites and even crossed the St. Francis at Blue Cane Island to raid briefly at Scatterville, Arkansas. Along the way Burris reported that he encountered Nathan Bolin's and Bulge Powell's guerrilla bands and elements of what he claimed were Confederate Colonel Solomon G. Kitchen's regiment, who were probably really Colonel Clark's recruiters and recruits. The Federals also used the 1861-built Mississippi River steamer *G. W. Graham* to move much of the cavalry back to New Madrid. Burris reported no losses of his own men, but claimed his command killed in all 23 Rebels, captured 52 horses and mules, and seized a wide variety of firearms including "near 50 common rifles and shotguns, which were unfit for Government use ... and destroyed." These results appear not to have eliminated many of Colonel Clark's 1000 recruits, certainly tested their resolve, but surely made the weapons shortage Clark complained about in June more acute than ever.[11]

On July 14 near Bloomfield, Stoddard County, riders of the 2nd Cavalry MSM and some local EMM, probably of the 79th EMM, skirmished with several guerrillas resulting in a like number of casualties on each side. One of the EMM was killed and one of the Federals slightly wounded, while they mortally wounded one of the bushwhackers and slightly wounded two others. The northern troops did manage to capture "3 splendid horses and horse equipments," so it appears they finished the fight with a slight advantage, although the loss of a militiaman deprived them of a man with a thorough knowledge of the local terrain and people.[12]

Burris' Second Expedition in the "Bootheel"

The Union command of southeast Missouri was pleased with Lieutenant Colonel Burris' expedition in the "bootheel" area in early July, but concerns about Rebel recruiting commands and pesky guerrilla bands still there and nearby in that far northeast corner of Arkansas led Brigadier General Thomas Ewing, Jr., the southeast Missouri district commander, to send him back with a larger force on a longer expedition between July 18 and August 7.[13] Burris split the expedition into two parts: a guerrilla hunt in the "bootheel" between July 18 and 26; and a campaign against Rebel recruiting commands and guerrillas in northeast Arkansas between July 26 and August 7.

For the first part of the expedition Lieutenant Colonel Burris took a battalion of the 2nd Cavalry MSM and elements of the 1st Missouri Cavalry hunting bushwhackers in New Madrid, Mississippi, and Stoddard Counties for nine days. They were seeking small groups of secretive guerrillas led by Captain John H. Guthrie and a West who had been stealing horses in the area and hiding them in canebrakes. The gunboat *Huntress, No. 58* dropped one group of troopers on foot onto Island No. 8 in the Mississippi River where they found no bushwhackers but recovered 18 stolen horses the Rebels had placed on the island for safekeeping. Another detail of the cavalry near James Bayou in Mississippi County killed two guerrillas. Lieutenant Colonel Burris was satisfied his force had thoroughly scoured the three counties, having killed two bushwhackers and recovered in all 42 horses and mules.[14]

For the second and more dangerous part of the expedition Burris picked up more troopers of the 3rd Cavalry MSM under Major James Wilson and 6th Missouri Cavalry at Bloomfield. This expanded force of about 500 Missouri cavalry spent the next 12 days sweeping Pemiscot and Dunklin Counties, Missouri and Mississippi and Greene

Counties, Arkansas of any Confederate regulars and irregulars they could find. This large Yankee force chased away parts of Colonel Henry Clark's recruiting command, and those of a Colonel Cowen, a Captain Bowen, and a Captain McVeigh, as well as guerrilla bands of Polk Conyers, a Darnelle, and Nathan Bolin. Parts of the 3rd Cavalry MSM relished destroying the camps, gardens, and shelters of Bolin and Sam Hildebrand not far from Scatterville in Greene County, Arkansas about July 28 after a brief fight with the guerrillas. Part of Burris' expedition even fought pitched battles with the men of Captains Bowen and McVeigh near Osceola, Arkansas August 2, Colonel Cowen's force at Elk

Graves in the swamp (Frazar Kirkland, *The Pictorial Book of Anecdotes of the Rebellion*, 1888, p. 579).

Chute, Pemiscot County on August 4 and the following day skirmished with bushwhackers also in Pemiscot County. For Union losses of one captain of 3rd Cavalry MSM killed and a few slightly wounded, Lieutenant Colonel Burris tallied up his wins as killing in all 47 Rebels including a captain and three lieutenants, mortally wounding 6, wounding less than mortally "about 40," with 57 prisoners taken including two captains and a lieutenant. His forces also captured 230 horses and mules, over 200 firearms, and brought back to base 20 freed slaves from Arkansas. Burris also took pride that he brought no extra transportation other than his troopers' mounts on the expedition and subsisted entirely "off the enemy" for the duration of the campaign. His hope was that the damage his force inflicted on General Shelby's command in northeast Arkansas and southeast Missouri would set back that wily raider's plans for the future.[15]

Union Glimpse Into General Price's Missouri Invasion Plans

Lieutenant Colonel Burris' accomplishments in late July and early August were a blow to General Shelby's force, but only delayed both Shelby's and Major General Sterling Price's developing plans for an invasion of Missouri. Back on June 23 an informant from Glasgow in the center of the Show-Me State communicated to Union Brigadier General Fisk information he obtained from hardcore southerners that turned out later to be surprisingly accurate details of what the Confederate leaders planned in their coming Missouri invasion. Among the information were these specifics:

- Guerrillas would attempt to cripple the railroads of north Missouri to deny its use to the Yankee troops for rapid movement over great distances;
- A major goal of General Price's invading force would be to conquer St. Louis;
- Shelby was to use his veteran cavalry brigade to raid through the countryside against isolated Union units and garrisons as he did in October 1863;
- And, particularly sinister was the remark that "the leaders are in the country and are getting encouragement from residents."[16]

On July 22 General Price wrote exuberantly but in exaggeration to Missouri Governor-in-exile Thomas C. Reynolds at Marshall, Texas that "the people of Missouri are ready for a general uprising" and that "the federals have but few reliable forces in the State."[17] Just a few days later on July 27 General Shelby argued vehemently to his boss General Price for a large-scale Missouri raid.[18] On August 4 both Generals began actual planning for the invasion or large-scale raid of their home state to take place in a few weeks.[19]

New Madrid County Residents Drive Out Guerrillas

The rest of August 1864 was relatively quiet in the "bootheel" until the last few days. Unidentified guerrillas robbed rural families near Point Pleasant, southeast New Madrid County August 23, according to an article written by a New Madrid correspondent to a Kansas City newspaper. The article stated that the guerrillas afterwards rode to a place called Grosby in north Pemiscot County, where local men headed by a G. M Hayes found them in camp. The furious farmers killed three bushwhackers and mortally wounded a fourth, recovered their stolen belongings, and also recovered additional horses and mules, five .36 caliber revolvers, and carbines. The next day four southern men, claiming Confederate authority to conscript able-bodied men into the southern army, had a confrontation with a "M. Cook" also in New Madrid County and took the man's horse. Mr. Cook and a neighbor gave chase, killed one of the conscripting southerners named "Cruteban" or "Cluteban," and wounded another. These two stories seem suspicious since seemingly common farmers defeated southern combatants in each one, if the newspaper correctly stated the facts. However, members of the Confederate army were actually conscripting men in several Missouri counties along the Arkansas border as part of General Shelby's big recruiting push during this summer, and Confederate Captain John H. Guthrie's band of irregulars actually hid in the swamps of Pemiscot County this season. Possibly, the Hayes and Cook named may have been experienced militiamen of this area, and not mere farmers, untrained in warfare.[20]

Attack on the Hay Wagons Near Cape Girardeau

On the evening of August 23 two guerrillas attacked a Union army quartermaster forage-gathering detail four miles south of the large Federal post at Cape Girardeau. As the six wagons filled with hay traveled the road through a swamp, the pair of guerrillas shot at the last three wagons, killing one teamster. The bushwhackers then set fire to the hay and escaped, but did not take any of the mules. The Union Cape Girardeau commander, Lieutenant Colonel Hiram M. Hiller of the 2nd Cavalry MSM, had not heard of any sightings of guerrillas in the area, and therefore thought the ambush of the wagon train may have been "done by citizens." This attack may also have been the work of traveling guerrillas, in the manner of notorious Sam Hildebrand, whose memoirs written just after the war referred to a variety of incidents, and some near Cape Girardeau.[21]

Lieutenant Colonel Hiram A. Hiller, 2nd Cavalry Missouri State Militia, was commander of the Union garrison at Cape Girardeau (National Park Service collection at Wilson's Creek National Battlefield, historian Connie Langum).

August closed in the swampy "bootheel" region with an alarm from Lieutenant Colonel Hiller at Cape Girardeau to district chief Brigadier General Thomas Ewing, Jr. On August 31 Hiller reported that a Union officer at the Bloomfield garrison sent word that 200 guerrillas were located near Kennett in Dunklin County and "some 300 more have gone toward New Madrid." This was after Hiller on August 25 sent a glowing report that he was "not aware of a single camp either of guerrillas or Confederates in his sub-district." General Ewing had encountered wild reports in his earlier experience fighting in Missouri's murky guerrilla war, so he fired this reply to the lieutenant colonel: "If you find the guerrillas are in Dunklin County in some force, send an expedition after them. It is much better to go after them than wait for them to come." Indeed, by September 2 Ewing gathered more precise intelligence that Confederate Brigadier General Jo Shelby did indeed have such numbers of new Confederate recruits, guerrillas, and conscripts centered around the Jacksonport, Arkansas area further south, but they were not immediately threatening the "bootheel" Union garrisons.[22] Indeed, the southern leaders had higher ambitions for these and other recruits they had been gathering all summer across northeast Arkansas. In about three weeks they would aim these new troops as part of a large combined Confederate force at southeast Missouri in a desperate aim to force the Union grip to release on the Show-Me State. Ironically, this southern force would enter Missouri further west of the swampy "bootheel" through the hill country, and bypass nearly the whole "bootheel" except the Bloomfield garrison.

Summer 1864 in the Hill Country West of "the Bootheel": Light Action with Reeves Gone

The wooded hills of Butler, Ripley, Carter, Reynolds, Wayne, and Iron Counties northwest of the swamplands of the "bootheel" were not the battlegrounds of intense guerrilla warfare this summer they had been earlier in the war. The primary reason was that General Shelby had ordered Confederate Colonel Tim Reeves to strengthen his small regiment with intense recruiting among the population south of the Missouri border preparatory to a large-scale raid or invasion of Missouri later in the year. The few guerrillas that remained were mostly local men that did not have the numbers to continue a contest of the scale that Colonel Reeves had waged against the Union garrisons in this region previously. About June 19 or 20 an unidentified scout from the large Union base at Pilot Knob in Iron County found and killed a single bushwhacker perhaps of the Dick Berryman gang of Washington County operating in the headwaters of the Black River in about Reynolds County. That a veteran scout could only find one guerrilla to report demonstrates the change in the scope of guerrilla operations in these hills this summer.[23] Captain H. A. Rice of the 3rd Cavalry MSM from the Patterson, Wayne County, garrison told of a similar scarcity of his enemy near Doniphan, Ripley County. His 50-man patrol June 25 saw "two men skedaddling for the brush" six miles from town and later that day his men fired long distance shots at three guerrillas across the Current River running into the trees.[24]

Union troops were accustomed to large patrols in this area because Tim Reeves' aggressive irregulars previously were prone to pounce any group smaller in size, and had the discomforting custom of following larger bodies of Yankees looking for them to make a tactical error that would allow the Rebels a chance to attack. Second Lieutenant Warren C. Shattuck's 25-man patrol of 3rd Cavalry MSM from Patterson, between July 8 and 12 had similar experiences through Ripley and Carter Counties and across the border in Arkansas. On the Buffalo River in Arkansas they sought and killed a particular guerrilla, and on Brush Creek in northeast Carter County, Missouri killed two bushwhackers "who were shot trying to make their escape." The lieutenant also included in his report these remarks from information he gleaned from residents along the way: "We found no enemy in force nor heard of none nearer than Jacksonport, except small parties of guerrillas. All men subject to military duty are ordered to report to the Southern army, and many are obeying the order. From the information I obtained the conscripts are sent to Jacksonport."[25]

Wayne County Action in Mid-July

Guerrillas began infiltrating back into this hill country of southeast Missouri during early July in groups of varying size, and the Union forces aggressively took to the field to catch as many as they could. By middle July some guerrillas were active near the Patterson, Wayne County, garrison, according to the diary kept by a Union artilleryman, Private Edward Hansen, evidently of Battery B, 2nd Missouri Light Artillery, which was then stationed somewhere in the Rolla district. The artillerymen were either sent along with cavalry patrols for field experience or were with one or more of their guns operating in the field when this soldier made his observations. He wrote in his diary on July 19 that they were ordered to take southern men as prisoners. They obeyed this order until they discovered one of the prisoners had a hidden firearm, whereupon they hanged several. Within the few days after this event the soldier told about his force capturing seven of twelve guerrillas they cornered in "a big tobacco field." The cavalrymen present took charge of the seven prisoners, and the following morning Hansen and his artillerymen comrades saw the seven hanging on trees in the woods.[26] Private Hansen may have been part of the force including part of the 6th Missouri Cavalry led by Major Samuel Montgomery that chased one body of bushwhackers at least as far north as the west fork of the Black River in northwest Reynolds County during this part of July. There is just a mention in written record of Montgomery's patrol, so the truth is as fleeting as the riding bushwhackers. There is a tendency in Federal actions where northern troops committed atrocities to leave only a skimpy outline instead of a detailed report.[27]

Union Atrocities Against the McGee Family

On August 10 and 13 unidentified Union cavalry killed Thomas J. and Blair McGee of southern sympathy in eastern Wayne County and forced most of their surviving family members to accompany them to the Union base at Pilot Knob. Area militiamen were well aware that several McGee men joined the Confederate military in the first two years of the war, and Union troops in early February 1863 killed Thomas' son Daniel as a leader of an area guerrilla band. Some male relatives were as of August 1864 still active as guerrillas fighting against Union troops in the region. On August 10 the northerners took 64-year-old Thomas J. McGee into custody somewhere near his home in east-central Wayne County, killed the old man, and later refused to tell the dead man's distraught family the location of his body. In the late afternoon of August 13 evidently the same troops rode into the farmyard of Thomas' son, 28-year-old Blair McGee, and shot unarmed Blair to death when he attempted to run from them. The soldiers forced the grieving family members to fix the family's chickens for the cavalrymen's supper, gave the McGees a few minutes to grab some belongings, torched the house and outbuildings, and took the surviving McGee family members in their own farm wagons accompanied by their livestock to the Union base at Pilot Knob. The intent of the soldiers must have been to force this southern family to leave the region, but that was not the result. At Pilot Knob higher Union authority forced the cavalry to return the McGees to what remained of their farms, and the soldiers sold the family's livestock to passersby and pocketed the money as they traveled back to east Wayne County. In spite of this blatant brutality, the McGee family survivors remained in their home area, and the present day town of McGee in east-central Wayne County not far from the scene of these depredations is a testament to their tenacity and industry.[28]

First Lieutenant Marquis D. Smith's patrol of 3rd Cavalry MSM in Butler County sometime between August 19 and 21 killed five guerrillas who were well known as bushwhackers in that county. The Federals killed the five men, including Mancil Holder, on Cow Island, which may be an island in the St. Francis River.[29]

Even though Union troops seemed to have a strong hold on this wooded hill country at the end of summer 1864, the Confederate command down in Arkansas was already preparing the largest southern raid into Union occupied Missouri of the war. This raid of thousands of Rebel soldiers would roll right through this same region of hills in September.

Summer 1864 in South-Central Missouri: Wilson, Watson, Lenox, Coats, Kitchen, Freeman, and Others

The previously heavy volume of fighting in the south-central region of Missouri from the Arkansas border north to Phelps and Pulaski Counties was noticeably lighter this summer. The primary reason was that Confederate General Shelby had ordered Colonel Thomas R. Freeman to take what was left of his regiment south of the Arkansas border and build up its manpower again with intense recruiting this spring and summer. Earlier in the war another southern regimental commander, William O. Coleman, also bedeviled the Yankees in this region, but he no longer led his small regiment. Recently published sources revealed Colonel Coleman defied orders from higher Confederate authority to either surrender his five companies of men to another command or to recruit more to fill out his regiment, and Major General Thomas C. Hindman dismissed him from the regular Confederate service.[30] Many of Coleman's veterans, such as Bill Wilson, Dick Kitchen, Bill Coats, Bill Lenox, and others in disgust left the Confederate army and returned to their home ground to fight the Yankees. These local bushwhackers relied on friends, neighbors, and relatives to spy for them, feed them, lie for them, and patch up their wounds; and used their superior knowledge of caves, grottos, hollows, woods, and hilltops to outwit and out-hide both the regular Federals and local militiamen. These survivors were deadly enemies and very hard to catch and kill.

Actions in Phelps County Near the Missouri Central Railroad

One of the first summer actions of 1864 in this south-central region of Missouri occurred June 10 near the villages of St. James, Ratterman, and Dillon in northeast Phelps County, near the tracks of the Missouri Central Railroad. Captain George L. Herring and Lieutenant James M. Roberts of Company E, 3rd Cavalry MSM out riding near camp suddenly rode onto about 25 mounted bushwhackers dressed in Federal uniforms who were crossing the tracks. The Rebels fired into the startled pair, mortally wounding the captain while the lieutenant scrambled for cover. The guerrillas grabbed the lieutenant's horse and quickly scattered as the rest of Company E responded to the shooting and rode over to investigate. Later at Dillon, some of the troopers chased off five of the blue-clad Confederates who were setting fire to boxcars on a siding and captured three horses, including the one taken from Lieutenant Roberts. The identity of the guerrillas is a mystery to present day. Several groups of from 12 to 25 Rebels—some in Union uniforms—infiltrated through Federal lines both east and west of Rolla during the last three weeks in May. These Confederates, riding toward the north, evidently were guerrillas and regular recruiters on their way to northeast Missouri. Small numbers of unwary northern soldiers, not used to seeing guerrillas in this normally peaceful part of southeast Missouri, came to grief at the hands of these disguised Rebels, and that is what happened to these two Union officers, too.[31]

Inventive Unidentified Guerrillas in Texas, Pulaski, and Dent Counties

During the last two weeks of June and the first week of July an unidentified but enterprising band of guerrillas operated out of a base hidden on the Big Piney River in either Texas County or south Pulaski County. Captain Levi E. Whybark of 5th Cavalry MSM, commanding the Federal garrison at Salem, Dent County, could only express his frustration and begrudging admiration for the finesse of these Rebels in his description of these activities to his district commander on June 23:

> The county is swarming with bushwhackers. All seem to be going north in small squads, from 2 to 10 in a squad. They have stolen some horses and plundered a great deal this week in this county and in Texas County. They seem to have a hiding place on the [Big] Piney [River]. We can't, it seems, come up with them, as they will not fight, the brush is so thick. Their idea seems to be to divest the country of everything there is in it. There are two companies of Enrolled Militia in this county, and what few private arms they had they lost them by those fellows.[32uy]

Captain Whybark described the actions of a disciplined, experienced body of irregulars who seem to have agreed in advance to avoid combat with the Federals while they systematically took horses and private firearms especially from northern sympathizers, and particularly from EMM members in Texas and Dent Counties. Their use of the vegetation and terrain and their knowledge about the differing loyalties of the inhabitants in order to target militiamen at home indicates these were mostly local men. This tends to point to an amalgamated guerrilla band composed of several smaller groups with Confederate army experience.

Various Bands and Personalities in Phelps, Pulaski, Dent and Texas Counties

Bill Wilson and some of his men from the southwest corner of Phelps County were probably involved since they were already active in this same area during the spring. One source lists Wilson as a captain of Company D, Colonel William O. Coleman's regiment at least during 1862. The most prominent men of Wilson's band included Andrew Jackson "Dick" Kitchen, James A. Jamison, and Anthony Wright. Jamison had escaped from the dreaded Alton Military Prison May 6, as detailed in Chapter Six.[33]

Dick Watson and some of his men of Texas and Pulaski Counties may have taken part. Federals identified Watson as leading 16 guerrillas on the Big Piney River in Texas County later in July. He served during 1861 under Colonel Freeman in the southern Missouri State Guard in this area as an enlisted man, later joined the Confederate army in early 1862, and participated in a number of battles through the Vicksburg surrender.[34]

Bill Lenox and some of his men from Dent and Phelps Counties may have been part of this group. Union officials identified Lenox with up to 30 bushwhackers involved in some raiding in this area in late August 1864. Confederate records show a Private William M. Lenox served in Company D in the 10th Missouri Infantry (CSA) from May through September 1862 when at Pocohontas, northeast Arkansas with some other Lenox men Bill deserted from this military service. Andrew Jackson "Dick" Kitchen was also prominent in assisting Lenox with leadership duties.[35]

Bill Coats and some of his band from southwest Texas County may have been part of these Rebel raiders. Local records and family oral history states that Coats was active in guerrilla actions in his home area during 1864. He was company commander of Company B of Colonel William O. Coleman's regiment earlier in the war. Prominent members of his band included his former lieutenant in Company B, Thomas Yates, as well as men from the Sutton and Morris families of his neighborhood.[36]

Guerrilla Threats to the Main Wagon Road in Phelps and Pulaski Counties

Earlier in the war many of these men were part of Colonel William O. Coleman's efforts to attack Union use of the main Rolla to Springfield wagon road, particularly in Phelps and Pulaski Counties, but the disintegration of Coleman's regiment before 1864 seemed to free these men to conduct guerrilla warfare with their own goals in mind. By the way they conducted their own campaigns in 1864 and 1865, they seem to have chosen to attack both the Union cause and the Union military anywhere they could and still escape to attack it again another day. Like the notorious bushwhacker Sam Hildebrand in counties to the east, these men singled out individuals who betrayed earlier confidences as well as former neighbors and prominent citizens of northern sympathy who informed the Union military about them. It is typical of guerrilla warfare throughout the northern Ozark hills across southern Missouri and with these men that their individual battles and feats were recorded primarily in oral history and local lore but the dates of these events and the identities of their Union antagonists were not attached to the stories of their accomplishments. The lack of these details makes difficult the task of matching these often otherwise well-defined battle stories to surviving Union military records.

On July 5 the garrison of the 5th Cavalry MSM at Big Piney River near the Phelps and Pulaski County line sent a corporal's patrol south to catch a guerrilla named Pruitt who had been evading their efforts to capture him for several days. The patrol captured the man and somewhere about the southwest corner of Phelps County shot him to death when he made a break for freedom. Other patrols from the Big Piney camp found signs that a number of bushwhackers were still moving about the area, and one group of 12 even crossed the main wagon road just half a mile from the northerners' Big Piney camp on July 6.[37]

Some of the busy bushwhackers around Texas and Phelps Counties turned murderous during the week of July 17 through 23. On July 17 a guerrilla named Westlake and others for unknown reasons killed a wealthy farmer named Uri Phillips who lived about 30 miles southeast of Rolla on the Big Piney River in north Texas County, according to local correspondents to the St. Louis newspapers. One of the correspondents at Rolla reminded the readers that Phillips was well known as one of many Missourians who went to the goldfields of California during 1850, but returned home safely to marry the daughter of a prominent Rolla merchant. The same sources reported that unidentified guerrillas murdered Henry Greiser the morning of July 20 either three or seven miles north of Rolla, and gave no reason for the killing. The night before Greiser's killing miles away in the southwest corner of Phelps County unidentified bushwhackers turned out the wife and several children of Abraham Overlease and torched their home. Abraham was away serving in the Union 3rd Missouri Cavalry Regiment and not home at the time. This was in the Spring Creek neighborhood that was also home to notorious guerrilla Bill Wilson, so perhaps he was involved.[38]

Threats of Southern Invasion

About this time Confederate Brigadier General Shelby and some of his subordinate commands were still busy conscripting and rounding up deserters just south of the Missouri border. One Union spy reporting at Rolla July 20 said that Shelby was

Rural mills were popular meeting places for local men, and therefore many became the setting for guerrilla war violence (Edwin Forbes, *Life Studies of the Great Army*, 1876, "The Old Saw Mill").

personally located at Mammoth Springs, Arkansas just over the border from Oregon County, and that he had 2300 men spread in a wide pattern in small groups just south of the Missouri line. As if to prove part of this, unidentified Union troops captured a Private James W. Roberts of Shelby's command in Oregon County July 19 and sent him along to the St. Louis area military prisons. Another Union report placed Colonel Thomas R. Freeman's recruiting headquarters at Batesville, Arkansas. Having so much Confederate cavalry located close to the Missouri border made Yankee commanders uneasy, and they kept lookouts and spies busy watching for any sign that these thousands of Rebel horsemen would move north. There were too many Rebels and too few Yankee troops available for the northerners to mount an offensive and drive the Confederates back, so both sides watched each other warily while they went about their own respective missions.[39]

Between July 23 and 30 Captain George Muller and troopers of Company A, 5th (new) Cavalry MSM from Waynesville conducted a bloodless patrol to investigate guerrillas using Mill # 1 on the Big Piney River in north Texas County as a rendezvous point. They found no guerrillas, but learned that Andrew J. "Dick" Watson and 16 riders had their horses shod at the blacksmith shop of the sawmill July 23 preparing for a raid north into Maries and Miller Counties. Careful questioning of locals in the area revealed that a number of them provided food and shelter to guerrillas on a regular basis-but in most cases Captain Muller found it impossible to decide if these innocent-sounding residents provided this aid to his enemies willingly or under duress. However in two cases guilt was more obvious, and the captain arrested and took back to Waynesville a young woman of the Rodgers family and Miss Nancy George, both known to prepare and take food baskets to the bushwhackers at their hideouts. In fact, the Rodgers woman was rumored to have secretly married well-known area guerrilla Frank King. The sawmill operator, a Mr. Robinson, admitted that bushwhackers frequented his business, but he claimed to be loyal to the Union even though he maintained a protected status as a British subject. When faced with the mandatory enrollment in Missouri's EMM program, a number of Missouri men of military age claimed to be subjects of England and other nations neutral to the war in America in order to avoid the duty.[40]

Cat and Mouse Maneuvers in Phelps, Texas, and Oregon Counties

The deadly cat-and-mouse games of the Federal cavalry and the bushwhackers continued in August. Obscure records point to a skirmish between elements of the 5th (new) Cavalry MSM somewhere around Rolla August 1, but no details of the fight seem to remain.[41] Captain Richard Murphy with about 40 troopers of the 5th from Waynesville searched Texas County between August 1 and 7, concentrating on the water-powered mills as Rebel rendezvous points, but they encountered no guerrillas themselves. They learned from reliable witnesses that about 150 bushwhackers were operating out of the town of Thomasville in neighboring Oregon County, but this large band retired south ahead of the patrol to avoid contact. Near Big Piney River Murphy's patrol tracked guerrilla sub-leader Tom Yates and four men for a few miles, but lost the trail.[42] On August 4 about 50 unidentified bushwhackers captured teamster Mike Kelly riding a horse on the main road near Rolla, These Rebels took Kelly away from the road, entertained him with their horse riding skills, and, in all, treated him well. One of their two officers confided in the teamster that they were Confederate soldiers recently arrived from west Tennessee and they were proud of their fair treatment of prisoners, which may tend to explain their informality with this civilian prisoner. The officer also asked Kelly to convey to Federal authorities that if the Yanks killed their men as prisoners they would retaliate in kind, then released the teamster to go on his way.[43]

Return of Confederate Colonel Thomas R. Freeman

During the last half of August the Yanks' old enemies of south-central Missouri, Confederate Colonel Thomas R. Freeman and his regiment, began to move back into their old battle area in Oregon, Howell, and Shannon Counties. A Union spy on August 16 saw Freeman's command riding north at Eveningshade, Arkansas, south of Mammoth Spring and only about 18 miles south of the state line.[44] Confederate Major Ai Edgar Asbury confided in his postwar memoir that he had recruited two Rebel companies in Oregon and Howell Counties on the Missouri side of the border about this time, probably for Freeman's regiment. Asbury had a difficult time getting his new Missouri recruits to cross the state line into Arkansas and leave their home state they had sworn to defend. The veteran major tried every form of persuasion he knew and finally had to resort to force to get his neophyte soldiers to comply with the order to assemble with the rest of the regiment in Arkansas. Perhaps the 150 guerrilla riders in Oregon County mentioned in Captain Murphy's patrol report a few days earlier were Asbury's part of Freeman's regiment, then. Their shyness at facing Captain Murphy's patrol of 40 could be explained by the fact that they were not only untrained but mostly without firearms, as well.[45] Other Union spy and scout reporting about 29–30 August placed Freeman with 400 armed veterans and about 1000 weaponless conscripts in Oregon County itself. Union commanders across all of southern Missouri theorized that this new Confederate force would target isolated Union posts to seize in order to acquire firearms for the unarmed conscripts. The Union commander of southwest Missouri, Brigadier General John B. Sanborn, read these reports and others about lots of civilian refugees coming across the state line ahead of Freeman's large force, and ordered the commanders of his smaller garrisons to ensure that they permit no firearms to fall into enemy hands if they have to abandon their posts in the face of this new threat.[46]

Lenox and Kitchen in Phelps and Crawford Counties

Bill Lenox and Dick Kitchen with about thirty guerrillas between August 29 and 31 undertook a three day crime spree in east Phelps County and Crawford County. They began this campaign with personal business for Bill Lenox' family by raiding his father's former farm seven miles northeast of Rolla. The Tuttle-Colony family acquired the Hamilton Lenox farm, which they renamed "Union Farm," and won a Federal contract to grow hay for Union horses there. The Lenox-Kitchen band struck at three that morning and surprised the household by sneaking up to the house through an adjacent orchard. The farm overseer, a Mr. Darling, came to Missouri with his family and taken this job after having survived the Sioux Indian uprising in Minnesota. When Darling began shooting at the attackers from a window, some of them shot through a side window of the farmhouse, mortally wounding the overseer. The bushwhackers refused Darling's daughter's attempt to bring water to her wounded father until they were certain that the man was dying. Bill Lenox also told Mrs. Darling that nobody except the Lenox family should ever live on that farm, and then with his men took from the house several firearms, $30 cash, a pocket watch, and some clothing. The band then rode east and raided the Meramec Ironworks close to the Crawford County line. They forced the employees to line up while they robbed the store and then took twelve horses as they left. The Lenox-Kitchen band next raided the Crawford County seat of Steelville the morning of August 31, taking several horses. They mortally wounded a

THE IRON-MILLS.

The Lenox and Kitchen guerrilla band raided the Meramec Ironworks in Phelps County to rob the company store in late August 1864 (Charles C. Coffin, *Marching to Victory*, 1888, p. 84).

Baptist preacher there and killed five militiamen who were hurrying to town in response to the alarm.[47]

Summer 1864 Actions in the Hills North of the "Bootheel": Pete Smith, Alfred Yates, Hildebrand, Collier, Evans, Berryman, and Others

If some parts of southeast Missouri saw light guerrilla action this summer, the wooded hills north of the "bootheel" were the setting for heavy fighting by a variety of small but veteran bushwhacker bands. Some of these Rebels knew what the Yanks only suspected-that a large portion of the Confederate army in Arkansas was preparing to invade Missouri in the coming months. Perhaps they saw their role bringing irregular warfare to the Union troops in this region as keeping the enemy busy while the Confederate regulars recruited, conscripted, trained, and generally prepared for the "big push" to come. For some of the bushwhackers, the warfare they conducted was personal—a chance to bring justice to their prewar neighborhoods and settle scores with the Yankees. For others, this was grand adventure and the most death-defying excitement of their lives. Their form of war was not for the timid or for those that counted the cost.

The commanding officer at the Union base at Pilot Knob in Iron County, Colonel John F. Tyler of the 1st Infantry MSM, on June 18 crowed to his boss, district commander Brigadier General Thomas Ewing, Jr., about how ten of his unidentified, mounted soldiers bested about 50 guerrillas somewhere in Iron County. The result of this meeting engagement was one Rebel wounded and one Union horse killed.[48]

Sometime during the week of June 17 to 24 local Union troops in the Perry County area arrested southerners Frank Tucker and a Winsett as being "dishonest and dangerous," according to a Perryville newspaper. They were given a military tribunal probably at Perryville, found guilty evidently of being bushwhackers, and executed by shooting.[49]

Sam Hildebrand Rides Again

Samuel Hildebrand conducted another of his many long combat patrols into this part of southeast Missouri with nine other bushwhackers in late June and early July, with the intent to kill certain northern sympathizers and militiamen for the harm they had caused southerners. His memory of this expedition three years after the war is partially corroborated by other sources. The early part of the patrol in and around St. Francois County targeting certain members of the 68th EMM created quite a stir. The guerrilla leader wrote about capturing and killing three 68th EMM members—Henry Voges, John Zimmer, and George Hart—in the area around Farmington, St. Francois County, in retaliation for their depredations against southerners. Historian Kirby Ross uncovered a Perryville newspaper quoting an earlier *St. Louis Union* article and a later grand jury investigation that indicated that Hildebrand also tortured Hart while he was hanging the man on 27 June 1864. The bushwhackers also paid a visit to Captain Ross Jelkyll, formerly a company commander of the 68th EMM, near Farmington, but did no harm to the man and left after a brief confrontation taking a few items from the house. Kirby Ross' research into Jelkyll indicated the captain had been forced out of the 68th for demonstrated southern favoritism, and may have given Hildebrand some information that led to the other militiamen's deaths.[50] Hildebrand next told about robbing Matthias Lepp's country store six miles southeast of DeSoto in south Jefferson County. A St. Louis newspaper on July 6 printed an article about Lepp traveling to St. Louis to complain to Major General Rosecrans that Hildebrand's guerrillas a few days before took from his store about $1,000 in goods, $400 in cash, a horse, and a watch while they held guns to Lepp's head.[51] It was probably also Hildebrand's daring men that made an attempt the night of July 1 and 2 to burn the Christopher Bridge on the Iron Mountain Railroad near Lawson's Station in northeast Washington County by the St. Francois County line between present day Cadet and Blackwell. The infantrymen of the 135th Illinois Infantry guarding this critical transportation node fired on men near the bridge that night and drove them off, but Hildebrand's memoir does not mention such an event.[52]

Hildebrand did write about hiding in the Pike Run hills of north-central St. Francois County a few days until one of his men recovered from a sudden illness. Hildebrand also described killing two black men-one of them near Flat River at Westover's Mill in central St. Francois County. On the return trip to Greene County, Arkansas, Hildebrand said in Wayne County, Missouri, his band questioned but released two Union deserters, then allegedly in south Shannon County captured and brought back to Confederate justice three Rebel deserters.[53]

Pete Smith in Action in Washington, Cape Girardeau, and Bollinger Counties

During the same night that guerrillas attempted to sabotage the railroad bridge at the border of Washington and St. Francois Counties, 25 bushwhackers raided the village of Millersville in west-central Cape Girardeau County. These raiders took about $25,000 worth of goods from the stores in town.[54] Since Hildebrand was busy in the St. Francois County area at this time, these raiders were probably led by Bollinger County's own bushwhacker leader, Pete Smith, who was known to have raided some in the Bollinger County area also in early July. Smith was a farmer about 30 years old from north Bollinger County, who was a strong secessionist advocate in this area early in the war. Some sources say Peter Smith survived the war and moved to Texas for a new start, as did many of the surviving Missouri bushwhackers. Smith's second-in-command was a James Collier or Colver.[55]

Pete Smith's guerrillas killed two northern sympathizers in northwest Bollinger County area on July 3 and 4. Both Bennett Murray and Jefferson Hartle of Union Township served in Union local military units earlier in the war, which may have been the reason the bushwhackers killed them—although there could have been more involved. This may have led to a skirmish somewhere in the area around Cape Girardeau on July 4 in which three unidentified Union soldiers were killed, and two wounded for unknown Rebel loss. It seems there are no other surviving records of this fight.[56]

Alfred Yates

A notorious guerrilla was killed on July 7 near Grubbville, east Washington County. Alfred Yates of that neighborhood had earlier in the war served his cause in the Confederate army, but lately had fought against the Union as a guerrilla. Union troops had captured Yates in that area January 17, 1864, and sent him to one of the military prisons in St. Louis where a tribunal sentenced him to death for his bushwhacker acts. Yates escaped from prison June 18 before the date set for his execution, made his way back to his home neighborhood where unidentified Union troops recaptured him July 7. Knowing he faced execution anyway, Yates desperately tried to escape from the squad of soldiers taking him back to custody, forcing them to shoot him down. Yates' friends around Grubbville buried his body there July 8.[57]

Sam Hildebrand Again

Guerrilla Sam Hildebrand led another patrol of from 9 to 15 bushwhackers back to this region between middle July and the end of the month. In his memoirs, Hildebrand said he approached from the west through Butler County to ride back to Madison County, then north to his favorite Pike Run Hills where his band based in a cave along the Big River in St. Francois County and radiated from there in short strikes. His band robbed poor Mr. Lepp's store again in south Jefferson County, which was also mentioned in a St. Louis newspaper. The article said that the bushwhackers lined up the customers whereupon one man whose horse the robbers had just taken loudly protested that he was a southern man and they should give his horse back to him. One of the guerrillas retorted that if the victim was a good southern man he should accept southern money for the animal and thrust a wad of Confederate paper money into the startled farmer's hands. The loudmouth had no choice but to cram the currency—worthless in Missouri—in his pocket and keep quiet.

On July 18 or 19 Lieutenant Hugh M. Bradley's patrol of 3rd Cavalry MSM from Pilot Knob tracked Hildebrand's men in Madison and St. Francois Counties, reporting that they killed three guerrillas and captured a horse and three firearms in two separate fights, with no Federal losses. Hildebrand acknowledged that a Yankee cavalry patrol fought with his band about four one afternoon along a ridge, but he admitted to only losing one man killed. He claimed he ambushed this patrol later that afternoon and killed two troopers and captured their horses, while the remainder of the patrol retreated in terror. The truth must be somewhere in between the two versions.

These guerrillas robbed the store of Selaphian Cole six miles south of DeSoto, south Jefferson County, the night of July 21/22, taking $600 worth of dry goods and destroying "$10,000 in notes." Hildebrand's band used their Union uniforms near Castor Creek, southeast Madison County, to trick a black man into revealing his earlier aid to northern troops, and then hanged the man to death. In Stoddard County eight miles from Bloomfield the band used their blue uniforms again to fool and kill two German-American troopers of Captain William Leeper's Company L, 3rd Cavalry MSM, who were traveling in civilian clothes on furlough. Hildebrand claimed that his band next met a number of Missouri southern families, including his own, near the St. Francis River in north Greene County, Arkansas. These families had earlier been living near the guerrilla's own Greene County base a few miles away that had had been burned out by a Yankee expedition a few days earlier, and were now camped in the woods in squalor and want. This Union expedition was that led by Union Lieutenant Colonel John T. Burris in this part of Arkansas between July 18 and 26, as described earlier in this chapter.[58]

Unidentified Guerrillas Raid Washington and Iron Counties

During the evening of July 19 a band said to number 25 guerrillas raided the village of Webster in south Washington County. They killed one man, abducted two others, took $1,500 worth of goods and six horses, and departed toward the west. Federals from the large Union base at Pilot Knob in neighboring Iron County pursued and killed one of the raiders, and heard that Bob Grady was part of this band. Grady often rode with Hildebrand; but this was about the time that Hildebrand's band had their fights with Lieutenant Brady's patrol around St. Francois County, and Hildebrand's postwar journal indicated he did not have as many as 25 men this trip.[59] Perhaps it was this same unidentified bushwhacker bunch that raided the village of Middlebrook in north Iron County the night of July 21 and 22. These 15 raiders robbed this village only three miles from the Pilot Knob army base and wounded a resident, yet evaded the Union pursuit. The earlier Union withdrawal from northeast Arkansas allowed an influx of Rebel irregulars into southeast Missouri, which may account for the presence of these guerrillas. At least some of these southerners knew this area well, and this bold band escaped identification just as well as they escaped capture.[60]

James Collier

About July 20 to 24 James Collier, formerly of Pete Smith's bushwhacker band that had been operating in Bollinger County, with some men killed and robbed in his home Perry County. A news article written from Perry County describing his raiding noted that Collier favored the southern cause from the beginning of the war, but had been spared from the wrath of Union troops by some of the same residents his band was now victimizing.[61]

Pete Smith Again in Bollinger County

During the last days of July Pete Smith's band of about 15 bushwhackers ambushed Sergeant James C. Steakley's patrol of Company K, 3rd Cavalry MSM of about the same size somewhere in Bollinger County. Steakley reported that the Rebels fired from the woods only 40 yards away from his men, yet, did little damage to his patrol. His men counter-charged immediately, sweeping the ambushers in front of them. The troopers killed two southerners and captured seven horses and two revolvers, according to Union records. Historian Kirby Ross in his Hildebrand history found a more personal memoir from Sergeant Steakley. The sergeant had stark memories of this fight more than many of the others since some of the guerrillas and horses were festooned with plunder from some store or village they recently raided. One of the Rebel dead wore a new suit of clothes under his guerrilla outfit and his pockets contained five pocketbooks from robbery victims, some with the money still inside. A number of the captured horses were loaded with booty, too.

Steakley added "Sam Hildebrand was with them," although he did not state how he discovered this. Ross connected this with Hildebrand's memoir that stated after finding the southern families in dire condition after their homes were torched by Burris' expedition in Greene County, Arkansas, Hildebrand and some of his men made a special raid back into Missouri all the way to Washington County where they robbed a store to obtain not only ammunition but clothing and supplies for the guerrillas' wives and children of that Greene County camp. Loaded with such spoils could explain why these guerrillas did not defeat Sergeant Steakley's patrol at such close quarters. Steakley recalled that one of the Federal horses was killed and a trooper injured his arm during the charge when he hooked it in a grapevine which pulled him off his mount. Surprisingly, Hildebrand's own version has the Rebels more victorious in a Reynolds County ambush, but this must been wishful thinking. Hildebrand and his small band may have been using Pete Smith's Bollinger County gang as guides through that area when they encountered the Union patrol.[62]

Union Depredations in Jefferson County During August

Between August 12 and 23 Union troops in Jefferson County went on a killing spree to rid that county of a few southern men and intimidate the rest into compliance. This coincided with the arrival there of Captain R. H. Montgomery's Company E, 6th Missouri Cavalry about August 12, evidently sent to stop Rebels from using Jefferson County as a conduit between St. Louis and Arkansas and as a crossing over the Mississippi River to and from Illinois. Perhaps the killing also had something to do with the fact that notorious guerrilla Sam Hildebrand farmed in Jefferson County before the war, and Union troops wanted to punish southern men who may have given aid to Hildebrand. Immediately after the 6th arrived, Captain Montgomery reported guerrillas and smugglers were crossing the great river in the area of Rotten Rock near Selma and Rush Tower in the southeast corner of the county. Some troopers of 6th Missouri Cavalry on August 12 were detailed to escort arrested southerner James T. Mathews from DeSoto west to the railroad and on to St. Louis. The cavalrymen claimed that Mathews tried to run and they killed and buried him on the spot. The admission of burial made this story suspect, since Union cavalry as a rule did not bury their victims. They would not have burdened their mounts with shovels and picks, either.[63] It may have also been members of the 6th Missouri Cavalry who near Victoria in south Jefferson County August 15 waylaid five Rebels taking secret southern mail to St. Louis. The Union soldiers killed three of the riders, wounded and captured a fourth, while the fifth man managed to escape. Among the letters between Confederate soldiers and St. Louis area civilians was coded mail between the Confederate army in Arkansas and the St. Louis leadership of the pro-southern secret society, the Knights of the Golden Circle, also called Order of American Knights. Federal code-breakers weeks later translated the hidden messages which eventually led to the execution of southern spy James M. Utz, of Bridgton, St. Louis County.[64]

On August 23 a few troopers of the 6th Missouri stopped and killed middle-aged west Jefferson County farmer Dugeld Pitzer driving his wagon near Morris Mills four miles northwest of Hillsboro. A few days later when local authorities at Desoto arrested a Private Hurst for stealing a revolver, he confessed to being one of Pitzer's killers, which led to the arrest of several more troopers of Company E. Some residents said Pitzer was a southern man, while others claimed he was a northerner, so it appears the dead farmer did not have a reputation as a notorious southerner, which raises the questions about why the troopers killed him.[65] About this same time unknown northerners also killed Thomas Wall of Dry Creek and a Gamel both of west Jefferson County, as well as Ire Drake of Plattin Township and another Gamel both of southeast Jefferson County. This was probably the work of Company E, 6th Missouri Cavalry, too.[66] These troopers' lawlessness may have had something to do with Captain R. H. Montgomery's resigning his commission the following month.[67]

Guerrillas in St. Francois and Iron Counties in August with Hildebrand Again

The guerrilla war continued in other parts of this hilly region north of the "bootheel" during August 1864. Union Major James Wilson reported about ten guerrillas at large in St. Francois County on August 15, and about ten to twelve guerrillas about in west Iron County on August 18, but he had no information about the leaders of these bands.[68]

The intrepid bushwhacker Sam Hildebrand in his memoir described another of his long expeditions through southeast Missouri in late August and early September with four other men, so one of the two groups Major Wilson reported may have been his. Hildebrand claimed that he waylaid and killed two men of Captain Henry B. Milks' Company H, 3rd Cavalry MSM near Wolf Creek in St. Francois County about four miles east of Farmington, but historian Kirby Ross' research fails to verify two such deaths at this time from that company. The guerrilla also described how a body of Union cavalry gave lively chase to his small group in Jefferson County from whom they barely escaped with just a few bullet holes in their clothing. Their pursuers were probably the bloodthirsty Company E of 6th Missouri Cavalry that had been killing men in that area for several days, as described above. Hildebrand recognized that these Union troopers were more determined than most to hunt him down and took his small band southwest into Washington County. There, wearing Federal uniforms again allowed them to hoodwink a discharged Union soldier, whom they accompanied for a while as he entertained them with tales of the bloodthirsty Hildebrand, thinking he was traveling with Union cavalrymen. Hildebrand and his men eventually let the gullible veteran in on their joke by revealing their true identities and enjoyed the man's antics as he finally had complete realization of his predicament before they allowed him to beat a hasty retreat. The Rebels evidently felt this storyteller would do more harm to the Union cause alive with his wild exaggerations than if they killed him. Hildebrand and his small band finished this patrol by chasing a patrol of Company L, 3rd Cavalry MSM near the Black River somewhere in Reynolds, Wayne, or Butler County, killing three of them at no loss to themselves. Hildebrand's next action would be to serve as a scout during September for Confederate Major General Sterling Price's long-awaited campaign through this region that the notorious guerrilla knew so well.[69]

By the end of August a combination of Confederate regulars and guerrillas had established a hidden camp somewhere in St. Francois County, to recruit and perhaps provide guidance to the large southern force expected to pass this way the following month. Among the local southern leaders at the camp were Confederate Major Dick Berryman and former Hildebrand companions Bob Highley and Bob Grady. This southern unit Berryman and others assembled across this area later became known as Clardy's Battalion, for its commander, Major Martin Linn Clardy. Union First Lieutenant Christian Helber of this county and formerly of the local 68th EMM was also at work organizing Company F of the new 47th Missouri Infantry Regiment in St. Francois County, when he heard about the southern camp. Helber gathered the recruits on hand and attacked Berryman's camp the night of 27/28 August, sending the southerners fleeing into the darkness. The Yankee lieutenant was wounded and four Rebels were killed. Major Berryman was determined to carry out his mission and re-established his camp somewhere else in the area.[70]

As August drew to a close in this area the Union command received a report that former Confederate Lieutenant David Reed with about 15 guerrillas were "committing depredations" in Bollinger County. If this report was accurate, Reed, from east Wayne County, may have combined his guerrillas with the band of Pete Smith already there.[71]

Strong Guerrilla Action Just South of the Missouri River: Raids on Sullivan, Vienna, Leasburg, and Webster; and Rebel Recruiters Hull and Evans

Many small groups of southern guerrillas and a few Confederate recruiters passed through the part of southeast Missouri south of the Missouri River in the spring of 1864, yet a number of them remained in this normally quiet sector over the summer, too. Perhaps several of them were preparing for the great Confederate raid through this area that was coming soon. Some Confederate recruiters were active nearby encouraging southern men not already disenchanted with the cause to come enlist.

Guerrillas in Franklin County

Guerrilla Samuel King was one of the disenchanted Rebels. Earlier in the war King deserted his Confederate unit. Union troops captured and placed him in a Yankee jail at Rolla, whereupon King enlisted August 1863 in the Union 11th Missouri Cavalry. This opportunist accompanied that unit to campaign in Arkansas where he deserted again in late April 1864. In late May King stayed in south central Franklin County where he plundered households of northern sympathy. A patrol of the 7th Kansas Cavalry garrisoned at nearby Sullivan rode to this guerrilla's last reported location June 1, where they found and killed the man who had made himself obnoxious to two armies.[72] The 7th Kansas Cavalry—which had a reputation for being obnoxious itself—moved out of Sullivan on their way to Memphis a few days later, and local Union commanders were slow to send a new unit to man this post and others the Kansans occupied along the strategic Missouri Central Railroad. Five guerrillas noticed the Yankee goof and robbed a store in unguarded Sullivan the night of June 5/6. The next day Union district commander, Brigadier General Thomas Ewing, Jr., corrected this omission when he angrily ordered the commander of the Union base at Pilot Knob to "select a good company, well officered. They must exert themselves to the utmost to kill any small gangs of guerrillas prowling near the line of the [rail]road."[73]

Guerrillas in Washington and Crawford Counties

By the second full week of July 1864 Rebel irregulars began to make their presence in this area more obvious. Three armed robbers invaded the home of New Hampshire–born, lumberman Samuel Grant July 10 while he was away, held a pistol to his wife's head, and took the man's horse. This took place a few miles southeast of Sullivan in the northwest corner of Washington County. The next day the local militia of Crawford County tracked the three raiders southwest to near Cherryville in south Crawford County where they came upon the trio sleeping. The militia promptly fired into the reclining men seriously wounding all three. When conscious, the robbers gave false names and told false stories that they were deserters from this or that Union unit. Indeed, Mrs. Grant had recognized one of them as Valentine P. Summers, the relative of one of her neighbors. Summers had briefly been a member of the 11th Missouri Cavalry back in July 1863 at Rolla, but deserted the same day he was mustered into the regiment at St. Louis. It is not known if these three men were acting as southern guerrillas or merely lawless renegades at the time of their capture.[74]

Also on July 11 in the Richwoods area of north-central Washington County a number of unidentified Rebels assaulted the Rue or Rulo family's dwelling while the father and son fired a few shots at the attackers. The man and boy escaped out a back window when they realized they could not hope to beat back the number of men shooting at the front of the house. The raiders then forced an entrance, demanded the woman of the house give them money, and searched in vain for it when she explained that they had none. The attackers left empty-handed, and locals summoned Union Lieutenant Colonel Amos Maupin, formerly of the 26th Missouri Infantry but then organizing the new 47th Missouri Infantry in this area. Maupin quickly responded with a few men and tracked the house attackers north to the Bourbose River in central Franklin County before he turned back to get reinforcements. Union authorities arrested two local southern brothers named Jackson who were suspected of providing aid to this band of Rebels.[75]

The Vienna Raid of 27 July

At daylight on the morning of July 27 twenty unidentified guerrillas robbed the town of Vienna, the county seat of usually peaceful Maries County, and then rode west. As written earlier in this chapter, a subsequent Union patrol in north Texas County, about 50 miles to the south, heard from witnesses that notorious bushwhacker leader "Dick" Watson and 16 of his men several days earlier told locals they were on their way to raid in Maries County. Evidently, Watson and his men made good on their threat. A cavalry patrol of 3rd Wisconsin Cavalry from Rolla in Maries County three days later found nothing of the raiders, who probably circled to the south after the raid and were already back in the Texas County area. Why ride 50 miles to raid a town? Texas County and the counties adjacent were by summer 1864 wrecked by three years of war, while Maries County had seen little of this. It made a tempting target.[76]

Confederate Colonel Hull in the Area

On August 7 a man identified only as "J. W. Boyd" at St. James in northwest Phelps County exchanged telegrams with Rolla Union commander, Brigadier General Odon Guitar, to the effect that Boyd knew where Confederate Colonel Edmund Broady Hull was hiding in the St. James area. Hull, in his twenties from the Pike County area, was primarily a regular officer from the early days of the war, but also had experience recruiting southerners behind Union lines in Missouri. Boyd discovered a southerner in St. James who was supposed to take some supplies to Colonel Hull and he asked Colonel Guitar what to do. Guitar replied that he was sending help to Boyd by morning and for Boyd "to keep things quiet" in the meanwhile, probably so they could move troops there to capture the colonel. Evidently, nothing came of this adventure, because there was a report in October that Colonel Hull was then recruiting near his home in northeast Missouri.[77]

Although Confederate Colonel Edwin B. Hull hailed from Pike County of northeast Missouri, at least twice during the war he recruited in the Phelps County area (private collection, courtesy of Terry Harmon).

Early August Raiding in Washington County

Between August 5 and 8 four southern guerrillas committed a crime spree across Washington County. A St. Louis newspaper account identified the quartet as a George Smith from St. Louis County, another Smith, a Samuel A. Swift, and the leader was Amasi Moss. It appears that this small band was carrying secret mail from southern family members to people in the South. Although Moss' little band had a mission to deliver this mail, they brought trouble upon themselves when they strayed from this objective on other business. During the evening of August 5 they waylaid and abducted schoolteacher J. M Carroll at Green's Mills in Washington County, telling him that they were taking him to justice for informing Union authorities about southerners of his neighborhood. Two evenings later with the worried Mr. Carroll still in tow, the quartet robbed John Lewis' store two miles from Richwoods, in north-central Washington County, of about $2,000 in goods. A posse of ten Richwoods area angry citizens set out in pursuit, tracking the store robbers to the west throughout the night. On the morning of August 8 near Indian Creek 35 miles west of Richwoods the posse caught up to the Rebels who had stopped by the road to feed and rest horses and repack the stolen goods. The leader Moss escaped, but the posse killed the two Smiths, captured Samuel Swift, rescued the very relieved schoolteacher, and recovered much of the stolen loot. They also found and turned over to authorities nine letters written to persons in the South and three photographs young ladies were evidently sending to their Confederate sweethearts.[78]

Chasing Guerrillas in Crawford County

Northeast Crawford County resident John Goddard wrote in his diary about an experience he had the morning of August 20: "[S]een eight bushwhackers come to

Hinches about 11 o'clock. They did not interest me." At eight-to-one odds, the diarist was wise to keep to his own business! Hinch's was a small village on the south side of the Meramec River in northeast Crawford County. Goddard then wrote that these guerrillas rode on to Leas' store nine miles to the northwest on the Missouri Central Railroad and robbed the place of about $1000 in goods. The diarist soon after joined the local Union 63rd EMM, proving he indeed was willing to take a stand.[79]

Confederate Recruiters Raid Webster in Washington County

All the store robberies in this area this summer were an indicator that there was Confederate recruiting taking place, since new recruits needed many items that the recruiters could not supply so far behind enemy lines. As if to prove this was the case, on the morning of August 23 Confederate recruiters Captain George W. Evans and evidently Captain Seth C. Farris led a large-scale raid on the village of Webster, southeast Washington County, involving from 57 to 84 of their men. This raid seemed to have several purposes. Besides the need to outfit all their new Rebels, the two recruiters also wanted to express their outrage to the Webster residents that Union soldiers shot to death fellow Confederate and escaped POW Alfred Yates July 7 in the area, as described earlier in this chapter. They also killed a militiaman, Henry Bequette, who was hurrying through the countryside responding to an alarm given out to respond to the raiders. Besides taking large amounts of goods from stores and residents the raiders publicly stripped the clothes from a Union exemption or enrolling officer named Captain Wilborn and two other prominent Union sympathizers of the town, so as to humiliate these men. Some of the robbers also forced men, women, and even children of Webster to remove items of clothing—especially shoes—evidently so these Rebels could take them to needy southern folk living nearby. These activities seemed to be a form of retribution for the killing of Yates, and perhaps to supply such items to a number of destitute southern noncombatants who lost their meager possessions in the recent Union destruction of a Rebel refugee and guerrilla camp in nearby Greene County, Arkansas, as mentioned earlier in this chapter. Further, Evans and Farris timed the raid because some unidentified resident informed them that the local company of the Union 32nd EMM just received a shipment of firearms and rations. In fact, this local EMM company could not respond to the Rebel Webster raid and had to disperse because these very shipments were late and the militiamen were unarmed! Not only were the Confederate hopes of capturing new weapons unrealized, the EMM were spared casualties because they were unable to make a showing against this large southern force. Some of the more adventurous militia members tracked Evans' and Farris' raiders west to near Huzza Creek in neighboring Crawford County, but wisely turned back since they were few in number.[80]

The fighting continued in southeast Missouri into the fall season, but with it came a Rebel army returning back to the Show-Me State in a mad gamble to force the state out of Federal hands and back into southern ones. That Confederate force rolled first into this corner of Missouri and kept going.

Twelve

Summer 1864 in the St. Louis Area

The action-filled summer of 1864 across southeast Missouri assumed a quieter, hidden form in the St. Louis area. Rebels and southern sympathizers by this time of the war learned to conduct their activities in the city and the area around it in secrecy lest they attract the unwanted attention of some of the large numbers of Union troops training, organizing, and refitting in the heavily populated St. Louis City. This summer, secret Rebel agents conducted smuggling from the rich resources of this area toward the Confederate forces in Arkansas, as they had before. The Union provost marshal's office of the Department of the Missouri, while ferreting out some of these furtive Rebel operations, stumbled upon a secret southern society called the Order of American Knights that had a network across the Midwest that hoped to influence the national elections coming in the fall of 1864 and maybe more. Southern arsonists returned to attack Union shipping at the St. Louis levee this July after an absence of several months. Southern prisoners of the area's several prisons continued to apply their energy and intellect to novel ways of escape, with some spectacular successes as well as many failures. The Union leadership employed an aggressive prison inspection system to provide an orderly analysis to ensure they were keeping their prisoners in a humane manner.

Summer 1864 Secret Rebel Activity in the St. Louis Area Including the OAK and Rebel Guerrillas in West St. Louis County

The summer in the St. Louis area began with a quiet arrest on June 4, that evidently did not merit a notice in the newspapers. Union authorities in St. Louis arrested there Confederate Major John F. Rucker of Sturgeon, north-central Boone County. This man had been an instrumental Boone County leader for the southern cause from 1861, beginning in the Missouri State Guard and later the Confederate army. Federals had captured Rucker earlier in the war on more than one occasion, imprisoned him, and he had escaped prison once and he was also released on parole. John F. Rucker's Missouri State Archives service record states he was arrested on charges of "treason and conspiracy" and banished to Montana, so U. S. authorities may have arrested him this time for returning from banishment without permission. According to the scant prison ledger entries, Rucker spent the rest of the war mostly in the Alton Military Prison a few miles upriver from St. Louis and the Federals released him after most other southern prisoners-of-war in July 1865. Rucker returned to his hometown of Sturgeon and was active in Confederate reunions.[1]

Not all war developments in St. Louis were as benign as quiet arrests in early June 1864. On June 9 Confederate Major General Sterling Price in Arkansas sent an encouraging letter to Missouri Governor-in-exile Thomas C. Reynolds in Marshall, Texas regarding hope for wresting Missouri out of Union hands. Price told the governor that he was sending a former Missouri congressman, Colonel Samuel Woodson, to Marshall to provide Reynolds with details about "20,000 men in Saint Louis alone now armed and waiting to join me." General Price would not learn until weeks later that figure of southern secret warriors was a gross exaggeration, but southern advocates were busy in St. Louis at this time preparing to assist Price's army when it moved north to invade the Show-Me State later in the year.[2]

Thomas Reynolds was the governor in exile, but had high hopes that General Price's Confederate army would restore him to his rightful office in the Capitol at Jefferson City (Perry S. Rader, *The Civil Government of the United States and the State of Missouri*, 1898, p. 332).

The following day, June 12, Provost Marshal-General Sanderson revealed a bombshell to his boss, Major General Rosecrans. That spring Sanderson uncovered the St. Louis connection to a hidden southern conspiracy in St. Louis and parts of the Midwest which had named Missouri's Confederate Major General Sterling Price as its military commander. This secret society, founded by a Phineas Wright, had its roots in the earlier failed Knights of the Golden Circle, called itself the "Order of American Knights" (OAK), and found hope in the Peace Democrats political movement of the Midwest that was maneuvering to challenge Lincoln and the Republicans in the November 1864 national election. In late May Sanderson arrested two St. Louis leaders of the OAK— Charles L. Hunt, the Belgian counsel to St. Louis, and Charles E. Dunn, the superintendent of the St. Louis Gas Light Company. Because of Hunt's Belgian connection the group was nicknamed "the *Corps de Belgique*." Through interrogations and some undercover work the provost marshal general assembled an accurate concept of the organization not only in Missouri but in Louisville, Cincinnati, and other places in the Midwest. In truth, the OAK faltered for much the same reason as its predecessor society, the Knights of the Golden Circle. In spite of codes and elaborate recognition and authentication signs, it was impossible to keep a secret organization in a civil war within a society like the United States where both sides looked and spoke the same. Infiltration under those limitations was inevitable. Rosecrans and Sanderson had been disgraced at the September 1863 Chickamauga battle, and they seized upon Sanderson's discovery of the Missouri branch of the OAK as a bid to propel themselves back into positive light with federal authorities. Rosecrans had earlier harried his superiors with his complaining and his preoccupation with spies and conspiracies, so both the military and civilian command structure were reluctant to accept Sanderson's findings. President Lincoln sent a trusted advisor, John Hay, to St. Louis who concluded that Rosecrans' and Sanderson's proofs did not have enough validity to call the faltering

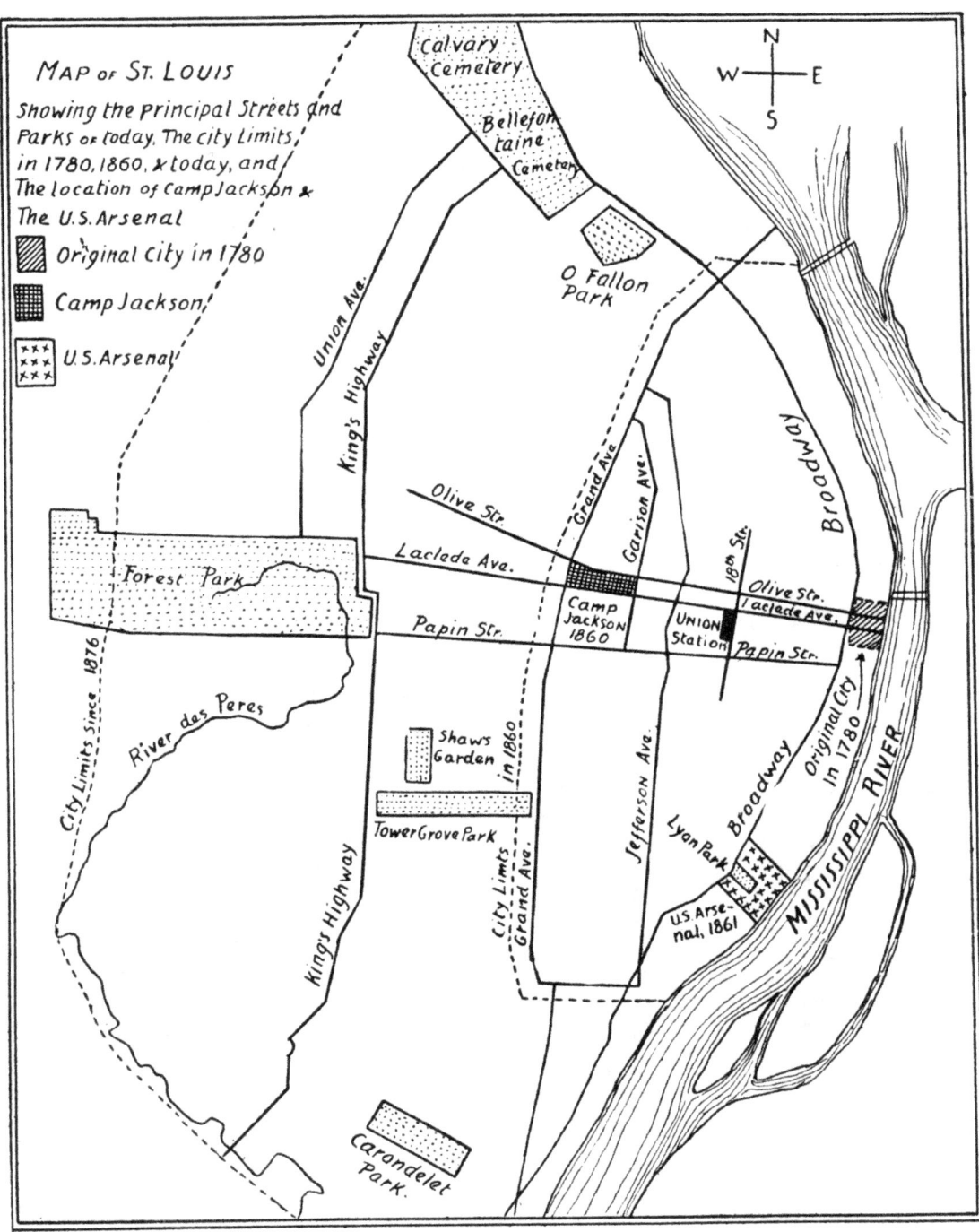

This map of St. Louis in Violette's 1918 history shows the 1780, 1860, and 1876 city limits as well as other features familiar to present-day residents (Eugene M. Violette, *A History of Missouri*, 1918, p. 349).

OAK a serious threat to the Union cause, and also sensed those officers' unrequited ambitions. As a result, the War Department ordered Rosecrans to release two of Hunt's and Dunn's associates from prison because there was not enough proof to warrant holding them as a hint to Rosecrans that they did not fully approve his chasing after conspiracies. In frustration with federal reluctance to take further action on the OAK, in July General Rosecrans released to the press Sanderson's report of his discoveries, which was used by some radical Republican leaders to discredit the Peace Democrat's election campaign then in progress. In effect, the OAK was exposed; its members scrambled to disassociate themselves from it; and the Confederate associates of it, such as General Price, soon realized the poor OAK was so infiltrated and discredited that it was of little aid to the Southern cause. If Price and Rosecrans wanted victory in Missouri over each other, they had better achieve it in battle and not in the furtive contests of spies and secret societies. In the weeks before Rosecrans publicized Sanderson's findings, the OAK's undercover operatives persevered with their secret preparations for eventual battle and continued with smuggling, sabotage, and other behind-enemy-lines activities.[3]

Guerrilla actions in St. Louis County were rare during the war mostly because of large numbers of Union troops inside the City of St. Louis, but a guerrilla action did occur on the Old Bonhomme Road near present-day University City and Olivette on July 12. A northern sympathizer, F. Phelps, traveled six-and-a-half miles west of the city that day and

Groups of southern sympathizers held secret nighttime meetings near Creve Coeur Lake in west St. Louis County during the summer of 1864 (The Werner Company, *The Story of American Heroism*, 1896, p. 76).

obtained a meal at the Woodland Diary where the proprietor questioned Phelps about his politics. While the guest ate, the proprietor left and returned with scores of mounted, unidentified, Rebel guerrillas. The proprietor and the Rebels locked Phelps in a room, where the prisoner overheard them discussing what to do with him, since they evidently suspected Phelps to be a spy. Fearing for his life, Phelps broke out of a window and ran desperately to get away. The escapee was relieved to see four of the mounted Rebels who were tracking him unexpectedly ride into a Union patrol of about a dozen troopers evidently of the 5th Cavalry MSM who opened fire on the guerrillas and killed one, according to unit records. In the excitement, Phelps kept running and sometime later brought Union Captain James Clifford and a detachment of the 1st Missouri Cavalry to the diary where they arrested a dozen diary employees Union authorities evidently later released as innocents in this affair. One of the St. Louis daily newspapers printed Phelps' story, but questioned the truth about certain details. The few existing records of this incident did not identify the guerrillas, nor did they provide any indication what they were doing so close to the city, and subsequent Union patrols were unable to find them.[4]

Later in July there were signs that southern guerrillas were still active in west St. Louis County. Unknown individuals sneaked into the Six-Mile House Tavern on the St. Charles Rock Road in northwest St. Louis County the night of July 26/27 and took a horse, the bartender's vest, money, butter, ham, and coffee without the staffs and patrons' knowledge.[5] This could have been simply the work of clever thieves, but there were other thefts that, taken together, pointed to Confederate recruits taking what they needed for military operations. Officials in west and northwest St. Louis County made Yankee authorities aware as of August 26 that unknown parties had stolen over 30 horses in that area over the previous two weeks. One official pointed out that twelve of the missing animals were government horses, told of frequent meetings near Creve Coeur Lake of groups of southern sympathizers, and hinted that "many circumstances ... have led citizens to believe it to be mainly the work of guerrillas."[6] Perhaps some of this was also the work of supporters of the secretive Order of American Knights. Indeed, on August 15 Major General Rosecrans wrote about the OAK "the secret order is tamed down but still formidable and active" and "is as formidable and potent for mischief, if occasion offers, as has been represented."[7] As if to point out the danger, Union authorities in St. Louis on August 19 hanged southerner William Jackson Livington of West Ely, Marion County, for taking notes on Yankee installations around Hannibal and St. Louis.[8] Union authorities in the St. Louis area such as Rosecrans were concerned about where all this furtive activity was leading. Were the Rebels preparing to push a large-scale raid up from their army in Arkansas into this part of Missouri?

Return of the Riverboat Arsonists to St. Louis In July 1864

Riverboat arson returned to the St. Louis levee this summer for the first time since the previous autumn with an attack on the side-wheeler *Imperial* the evening of July 10. Watchmen had noticed a suspicious man lurking around the vessel. One of them followed the stranger when he boarded the 1863-built *Imperial* and caught the man in the act of starting a fire with some combustibles in his pocket. The crew found the arsonist carried in another pocket an amnesty oath and about $200 in Confederate money. Ironically, there was another vessel with the same name that southern arsonists destroyed also at the St. Louis levee the previous September.[9]

There were other Confederate saboteurs watching for their opportunity to attack the river steamers, and they struck and achieved a great victory at four in the morning of July 15. Apparently, an arsonist managed to start a fire on the *Edward F. Dix* which burned that vessel to the waterline and spread to five other riverboats which also burned to the water's edge. The burned boats included the:

- *Edward F. Dix:* new side-wheeler; 266 feet long by 40 feet wide; completed 1864 at Madison, Indiana; rebuilt and lost about a year later on the Red River in Louisiana;
- *Glasgow:* side-wheeler of 340 tons, 208 feet long by 34 feet wide; completed 1862 at New Albany, Indiana; about to carry a government load up the Missouri River when burned; rebuilt and steamed on Missouri River and others until sank in 1873 in Red River, Louisiana;
- *Northerner:* older side-wheeler of 332 tons, 210 feet long by 33 feet wide; built 1858 in Elizabeth, Pennsylvania; operated mostly on the Mississippi River between St. Louis and St. Paul; competed in speed races prewar; evidently a total loss from the 15 July fire;
- *Sunshine:* side-wheeler of 354 tons; built 1860 in Elizabeth, Pennsylvania; prewar operated on Mississippi River between St. Louis and St. Paul; saw considerable war service and some action mostly on Missouri River; was loading to go up the Missouri River for Leavenworth and had loaded only 30 sacks of coffee on board when burned; evidently a total loss from the 15 July fire;
- *Welcome:* newer side-wheeler of 449 tons, 214 feet long by 36 feet wide; built 1863 in Shousetown, Pennsylvania; operated between St. Louis and Montana Territory and was loaded with government cargo consisting of barrels of pork and whisky, rice, soap, coffee, potatoes, etc. destined for Fort Randall and several Indian agencies; was rebuilt and operated various places until destroyed in fire at New Orleans in 1871.

St. Louis residents recalled that the horrible 1849 fire started on the riverfront, and they feared the Rebel arsonists' riverboat fires would spread to the entire city (Walter B. Stevens, *Centennial History of Missouri*, volume 2, 1921, p. 243).

Two other steamers, the *City of Alton* and *Mary E. Forsyth,* were able to make enough steam to back away from the levee and narrowly escaped the conflagration. Still, the loss of six river steamers and their 81 tons of U.S. government commissary stores was a catastrophe to Union river transport for both the Missouri and the Mississippi River systems, and a great encouragement to the battered southern cause in St. Louis.[10]

The Department of the Missouri headquarters even on the day of the fire issued General Orders Number 119 to reduce the vulnerabilities of the wooden craft at the St. Louis riverfront in the face of a determined band of wily boat burners. The chief quartermaster was charged with the responsibility to keep a tow-boat ready with a full head of steam around the clock to assist burning boats. Transports not loading were ordered to berth 100 yards apart. Small boats not belonging to anchored steamers would henceforth be banned from the harbor. The aim of these changes was more to prevent fire from spreading from one vessel to others rather than stopping arson altogether. These wooden craft had proven they could withstand all manner of projectiles short of artillery that Rebels shot at them while steaming along the rivers, but they were at their weakest when stopped at dockside.[11]

Summer 1864 in the St. Louis Area Prisons

A constant source of concern for the Federal leadership in St. Louis was the large number of enemy prisoners housed in the several St. Louis area prisons. Not only could escaped POWs damage military targets and tie up Union troops needed elsewhere, but propriety demanded that the Union military house and treat those prisoners with decency and humanity. By this time in the war the northern leaders had established a workable prison inspection system that oversaw the care of these military and civilian internees.

Union Provost Marshal Sanderson sent a letter June 6 to Colonel William Hoffman, the Commissary-General of Prisoners in Washington, telling that he had worked to correct structural problems at the Gratiot Street and the Myrtle Street Military Prisons in downtown St. Louis. He mentioned that at his direction workmen completed repairs to walls at the Gratiot Street facility that a February inspection, noted in an earlier chapter, pointed out were ready to fall down. Colonel Sanderson also wrote that he was appointing a prisons inspector to keep him better informed of the prison conditions, and assured Colonel Hoffman that prison matters were much improved. Indeed, subsequent inspections of those two named facilities reveal that he was truthful about improvements.[12]

Some Confederate prisoners of war could not wait until General Price's army marched north to rescue them, and Union guards caught seven in the act of digging an escape tunnel from Gratiot Street Prison on June 9. As chronicled by prison diary-writer Confederate Captain Griffin Frost, cellmates of convicted guerrilla A. J. Lanier were desperate to help him escape before Union guards would come to send him away to west Missouri to face execution. They lacked only about ten minutes more digging for the break-out when the guards came to get Lanier and discovered the secret project in progress. The soldiers sent Lanier to his doom and his six digging buddies, including notorious secret Rebel mail courier Absalom Grimes of Ralls County, were sentenced to be chained to posts in the prison yard for the following twenty afternoons and evenings as punishment.[13]

Provost Marshal-General Sanderson made good his intention to appoint a prison inspector as First Lieutenant Isaac Gannett of 7th Kansas Cavalry on June 11 gave an over-optimistic report of his inspection of Gratiot Street and Myrtle Street Prisons. Gannett, a Chicagoan, seemed to enjoy writing about cleanliness of the prisoners, their clothing, their bedding, and how their kitchen was "scrubbed daily," but his cheerful report contained little of substance. Gannett referred to recent escape attempts at Gratiot Street in his only reference to anything negative: "Some two or three attempts have been made in various ways of late to escape, but owing to the vigilance of the keepers and the guards [of the 10th Kansas Cavalry, he revealed] they have each time proved unsuccessful and have tended to increase the discipline and watchfulness." The lieutenant's findings about Myrtle Street Prison were as sickly sweet as those for Gratiot Street: "Myrtle Prison, in all its details, is but the rival of the Gratiot." This seems to have been Gannett's first and last prison inspection report in the existing records. He returned to Company H and the saddle and eventually mustered out of the Seventh Regiment in September 1865. Evidently, the Department of the Missouri preferred more factual and useful prison inspection reports that did not read like advertisements for resort lodging. Earlier hard-hitting reports by brave inspectors at the prisons had wrought changes in the pattern of neglect that made material progress toward safeguarding the health of both prisoners and guards, and helped slow the death rate.[14]

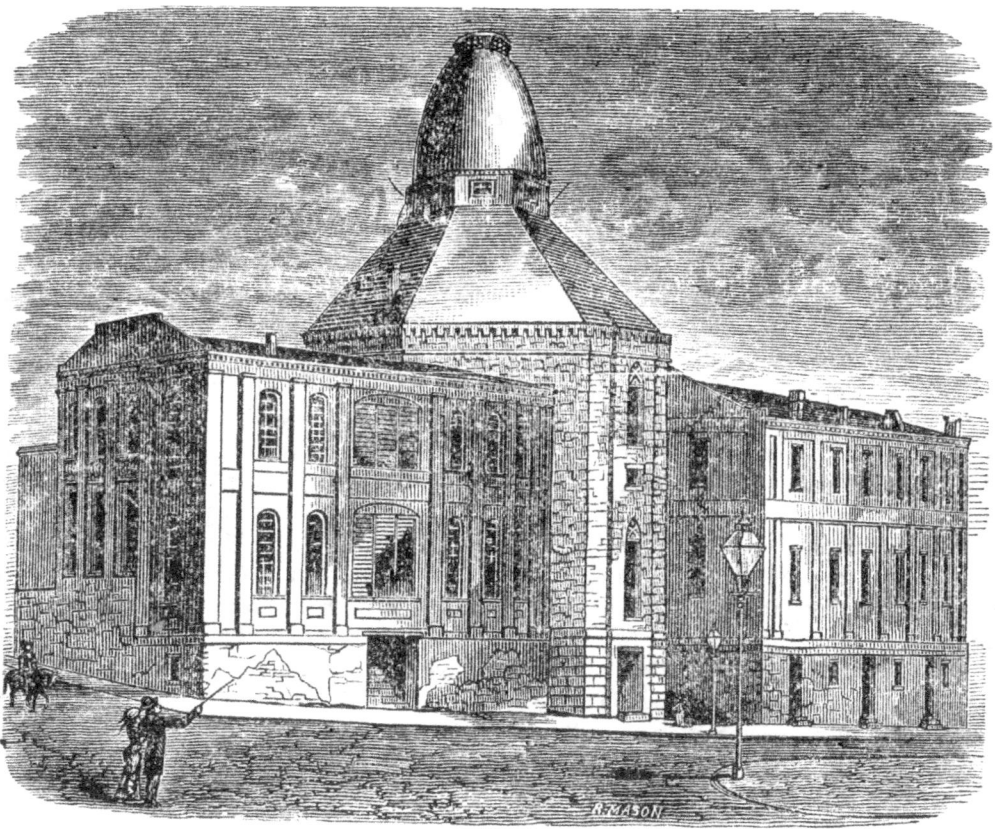

Despite Union repairs to the neglected Gratiot Street Military Prison, numbers of southern prisoners continued escape schemes this summer, and some succeeded (Joseph A. Dacus, *A Tour of St. Louis*, 1878, p. 42).

Several of the prisoners involved in the ill-fated June 9 attempt to dig out of the Gratiot Street Prison along with some others tried a more direct escape technique late in the morning of June 18 in one of St. Louis' most action-filled prison escapes. That morning guards were escorting 15 prisoners to the courtyard for exercise when the prisoners grabbed an untended axe beside the kitchen, used it to break through a door in the rear of the facility, overpowered and disarmed two guards of the 10th Kansas Infantry, then bolted for the street. Three of these prisoners, included notorious Rebel mail carrier Captain Absalom Grimes, still hobbling under the restraint of irons and chains from the earlier attempt, made good targets for the other guards who wounded Grimes twice in the leg and killed former U.S. detective L. S. Schultz from Indiana with a bullet in the heart. Also killed instantly was Private Joseph H. Colclazier of Clay County. Frantic guard shooting also wounded prisoner John Abshire and led to his recapture. The guards and other nearby soldiers scrambled through alleys and back yards pursuing the remaining escapees and recaptured most of them. Five who made good this unexpected escape were Colonel John C. Carlin of 10th Missouri Cavalry (CSA) from Marion County, Lieutenant William H. Sebring, Private Alfred Yates from Washington County, Captain Jasper C. Hill of Saline County, and citizen William M. Douglas of Chariton County. Alfred Yates traveled back to near his Washington County home where he was recaptured and killed July 7, as recounted in Chapter Eleven. Both Colonel Carlin and Lieutenant Sebring had earlier attempted to break out of this prison on the previous Christmas evening. In fact, this entire group was relegated to special security because some were facing death sentences and some had tried earlier escapes. Douglas was aided in his escape by members of the Order of American Knights in St. Louis, and he was later arrested on the railroad attempting to transport a barrel containing hidden revolvers for the OAK. Grimes survived the war in spite of his many adventures and mentioned in his 1926 autobiography that in 1878 he brought his family back to the vacant prison and solemnly showed them his cell and the escape scene where he was shot twice in the leg that June 18 back in 1864.[15]

Southern prisoners slipped away from the Alton Military Prison twice over the next several days just upriver in Illinois, as if not to be outdone by the exciting Gratiot Street Prison escape of June 18. On June 21 citizen Edward Philips somehow escaped from this prison. Union authorities arrested Philips of New Madrid County in nearby Dunklin County back in April 1862, and he probably was of the attitude that he had remained there long enough. Three southern POWs and a Union prisoner left during the night of June 27/28. Captain John Thrailkill of the 1st Missouri Cavalry (CSA), Lieutenant Robert S. Lavalle of New Madrid County, and T. M. Meador of the 7th Missouri Infantry or Cavalry (CSA) took their leave of their Union captors. The Union prisoner, Sergeant John F. Clemmons of the 10th Ohio Cavalry, also escaped that same night, probably with the other three. This was Meador's second escape from the Alton prison, as his prison ledger recorded his unscheduled departures on 27 November 1863 as well as on 28 June 1864. The Union cause in Missouri would soon deeply regret the escape of Captain Thrailkill, since he would shortly afterward lead a southern bushwhacker gang in northwest Missouri in active operations.[16]

Major Gustav Heinrichs of the 4th Missouri Cavalry Regiment (USA) was the St. Louis prisons inspector in early July. He had been the officer in charge of the investigation into the violent breakout at Gratiot Street Prison on June 18, and impressed General Rosecrans' staff with how he conducted his study of that embarrassing episode. Heinrichs' prison inspection report on July 10 demonstrated that he was "nobody's fool." About the Gratiot Street facility he gave most aspects passing grades, but noted that it was "in need of repairs." He was more critical about the Myrtle Street facility, the prewar Lynch's Slave Market. He noted the buildings there were "too small for the purpose," and complained that the prison cadre should remove the building materials stored in the prison yard. He disliked the food preparation at Myrtle Street, wrote that the cleanliness of the prisoners "could be better," and that the quarters and bedding were "somewhat in disorder." In his concluding remarks Heinrichs called for "a thorough repair of both prisons" and felt that the prison commandants be provided with more detailed guidance about their duties and responsibilities. Heinrichs' boss, Provost Marshal-General John Sanderson, in his endorsement to the inspection report, took issue with Heinrichs' comments about guidance for the prison commandants, and took the inspector's comments about building repairs to a new dimension. Sanderson recommended the command junk the existing prisons and build new facilities either at Jefferson Barracks south of the city or on Quarantine Island out in the Mississippi River (where the smallpox hospital was located). Higher command must have disliked the expense involved in building new prisons, because the Department of the Missouri had to "make do" with the existing facilities for the remainder of the war.[17]

Inspector Heinrichs submitted a weekly report July 17 that praised Gratiot Street Prison for cleanliness and for the smaller Myrtle Street Prison he noted improvements in the latrines, removal of material from the yard, and general cleanliness. He found the quarters and bedding there "somewhat in disorder," whereupon Provost Marshal Sanderson replied that the problem of the bedding will get attention. Heinrichs also noted sardonically that the soldier prisoners generally kept themselves clean, possibly in keeping with their military training, but the civilian prisoners did not. What is noteworthy here is that the Union military through this frequent inspection system was gradually improving the living conditions and health of the prisoners involuntarily entrusted to their care.[18]

Some prisoners of the Yankees still managed to find ways to take their leave without the Federals' permission. Guerrilla W.R.P. Henderson, identified in the prison ledger as belonging to "Houts' guerrillas" somehow escaped from the Alton Military Prison July 23, but he was recaptured nearby at the village of Taneyville. A short newspaper mention of Henderson's escape stated Houts' band stole horses in Jersey County, Illinois before his imprisonment, so perhaps Henderson was returning there. By this time of the war a number of Missouri southerners evading problems in their own state lived with friends in Illinois counties along the Mississippi River, and Houts' gang may have been some of these.[19] William P. Wilson of "Elliott's Guerrillas" made good his escape from a wood-cutting party of the Alton prison July 31. Confederate Colonel Joseph O. Shelby had in November 1862 ordered Captain Benjamin F. Elliott to organized a company of "guides and spies" from the 5th Missouri Cavalry (CSA), and Elliott's company had earned many honors thereafter for their tenacity and survivability fighting against Federals in Arkansas and Missouri on seemingly impossible missions. If this Wilson was of that unit, it would be small wonder he could slip away from a detail of wood choppers. Sadly, the cryptic Union prison ledger gives little information.[20]

Union Surgeon Charles T. Alexander performed detailed health inspections on two of the St. Louis area prisons in the first days of August 1864. Regarding the Gratiot Street facility, the doctor said there were 321 inmates in a facility that had capacity for 500, and, other than recommending the jailers provide the prisoners more vegetables, found the place "sufficient" and "efficient." He noted that mortality at Gratiot Street Prison was "small, ten deaths in last three months." He noted that the prevalent diseases at this prison were diarrhea, dysentery, fevers, and malaria—the first two of local origin and "probably from prison diet and confinement." Surgeon Alexander's remarks about the Alton Military Prison were more critical. He noted the facility was overcrowded with 1086 POWs, 173 citizens, and 218 Union soldier prisoners where he calculated maximum capacity for health should be no more than 1200 persons. He found the same diseases as at Gratiot Street, but felt the disease rate at Alton could be improved by "removal of offal and rubbish" to improve the poor "police of the camp" that probably led to the "tardy" rate of recovery for disease patients. Alexander also noted that there was inadequate ventilation for the stoves inside the prison.[21]

These inspections did not name the smaller Myrtle Street facility, but a local newspaper mentioned its name after an escape attempt was foiled there by one of the 10th Kansas Infantry guards the night of August 13/14. An informant tipped the Kansans that an escape was planned, so they were alert. It seems a prisoner cook, Private Charles Warner of the 1st Nebraska Infantry (USA), had become enamored with beautiful female prisoner Miss Annie Fickel of Lafayette County who Union authorities sent to this facility as a cook. She had been convicted to three years in prison for her part in a Lexington conspiracy to free a guerrilla prisoner that resulted in the 22 February death of a Union soldier, as described in Chapter Four. Warner organized a work party of six other Union soldier prisoners to help him use crude tools to dig through the prison walls to freedom for Miss Fickel and all of them. On the night in question one of the Kansas guards heard the noise of their labors and caught the digging team in the act. As a result, Warner and the other escapees had to wear ball and chain and had their terms lengthened. This was not the only time this very attractive and vivacious Rebel woman in her mid-twenties caused unintentional embarrassment to Union authorities and created unfavorable publicity. In September northern leaders sent her on to the Missouri State Penitentiary in Jefferson City where similar problems followed in her wake. Eventually, President Lincoln heard how the pretty Annie inadvertently disrupted discipline in whatever jail officials sent her. Therefore, Lincoln determined that the months of imprisonment she had served were sufficient and ordered Annie Fickel pardoned as of 30 January 1865, probably to the relief of her many supporters as well as her jailers.[22]

Meanwhile, back in St. Louis during late August and early September, this ill-fated escape attempt involving Miss Fickel was affecting leader sensibilities to produce better care for women prisoners in St. Louis. Union Assistant Surgeon J. M. Youngblood and Inspector Heinrichs, incensed that male prisoners at Myrtle Street Prison were caught digging their way towards a young female prisoner's quarters, used their offices and appeals to propriety up the St. Louis Union chain of command to champion successfully to move all the female prisoners to a new facility "opposite Gratiot Street." There had been a female prisoners' facility during 1863 for some months, but for some reason the Union authorities abandoned the practice. Now, uproar over the Annie Fickel case had helped to bring back such a badly needed facility.[23]

In his prison journal POW Captain Griffin Frost noted that a fellow inmate, Robert Graham of Audrain County, and two others successfully sawed through one bar of a window at the Gratiot Street Prison. They were partially through a second bar August 26 when another prisoner informed prison officials on them and they were caught and punished with having to wear ball and chain and placed in a more secure room.[24]

The secret war in the St. Louis area would continue with the steady repetition of prison escape attempts for as long as the Union forces held southern prisoners in these facilities. The Rebel compulsion to escape would continue to test the Union ability to keep the prisoners in their prisons.

Thirteen

Summer 1864 in Southwest Missouri

Both sides of the guerrilla war in the southwest quadrant of Missouri seemed to fight their own isolated war in the summer of 1864 little affected by events in other places. As in the earlier years of the war, various bushwhacker bands and Confederate recruiting commands crossed the prairies of this region on their way to either northwest or northeast Missouri. In all other major regions of Missouri this summer both guerrillas and Confederate regulars prepared and planned for a long-awaited return of Confederate Major General Sterling Price and large numbers of his troops from Arkansas to invade the state in the autumn and wrest it out of the hands of the Yankees. About the only part this corner of Missouri played in the preparation of Price's return were several of his recruiting teams that rode through on their way to other parts of the state. Various bushwhacker commands of southwest Missouri this season operated in their own chosen areas. The guerrilla bands of John Goode, David Rusk, and Ab Humbard in Jasper and Newton Counties, Lafayette Roberts in and around Dade County, Bill Marchbanks in north Vernon and Bates County, Henry Taylor in central Vernon County, and others operated against the Yankee cavalry and militia in much the same way they had before. A difference this summer was that several of these bushwhacker bands, such as Rusk's, Marchbanks', and Taylor's recruited for the Confederacy and sent a number of these southern men south to join with Confederate regular forces in northeast Arkansas, as commanded by Confederate authorities.

Hot Summer Action in the Far Southwest Corner: Goode, Rusk, and Humbard

The far southwest corner of Missouri was the scene of much fighting throughout the war, and the summer of 1864 certainly lived up to this standard. This far corner of the state included McDonald, Barry, Newton, Jasper, and Lawrence Counties; it was also the junction of Missouri, Arkansas, and the Indian Nations (now Oklahoma); and it was also the junction of prairie and woodlands. By this time of the war the combatants of both sides had hard-won reputations here for callousness which during this summer they seemed determined to uphold.

Goode's Band in Newton County Actions in Early June

During the morning of June 3, 1864, Union Sergeant Josiah Ruark and Private Poag of Company L, 8th Cavalry MSM, returning to garrison at Neosho, Newton County, from some detail, thought they could escape from the war for a few minutes by swimming in Shoal Creek about a mile north of town. While the two troopers were splashing in the water eight to ten guerrillas under Confederate First Lieutenant John R. Goode rode up, captured the sergeant and shot Poag to death as he endeavored to escape to the opposite bank. Goode and some of his men from this area had formerly been members of the 11th Missouri Infantry (CSA), and were in this corner of Missouri either recruiting for the regulars or assembling their own bushwhacker group. The rebels were still marveling how easily they captured Sergeant Ruark, two Yankee horses, and firearms when they encountered and captured a passing black man, too. The garrison in Neosho soon heard about the bushwhackers north of town and quickly dispatched a reaction force of parts of two companies of the 8th Cavalry under Captains Ozais Ruark and John R. Kelso. The Union force carefully tracked Lieutenant Goode's riders north for about 10 miles and crept up to them near Diamond Grove as they were feeding and resting their horses. In the shooting and running fight that followed the Federals rescued Sergeant Ruark and the black man and killed three of the Rebels. Union Second Lieutenant John T. Smith was the only northern casualty in this fight, as a guerrilla he was chasing turned in the saddle and shot him dead during the melee. First Lieutenant Goode's band would have more battles this summer, as would the Union 8th Cavalry MSM.[1]

Warnings of Northbound Traveling Rebel Groups

Union reverses this spring in Arkansas seemed to leave lightly garrisoned southwest Missouri vulnerable to infiltration by large bodies of regular and irregular Rebels from south of the Missouri border, and in early June the Federal command helplessly documented the advent of a number of these southerners into the region. Major General Rosecrans, in command of Missouri, on June 4 warned his Kansas counterpart, Major General Samuel R. Curtis, that the southerners were coming. A Union local commander at Berryville in northwest Arkansas on June 6 telegraphed that former Shelby subordinate, Major J. F. Pickler, with over 250 Rebels left Texas weeks before, and was then headed for Newtonia, Newton County, Missouri and ultimately north Missouri. The Union command in Missouri continued to receive spot reports

Federal forces in the prairie country of southwest Missouri spread out cavalry pickets watching for fast-riding bands of Rebels (Edwin Forbes, *Life Studies of the Great Army*, 1876, "A Quiet Nibble on the Cavalry Skirmish Line").

almost daily about the steady movement north of these large numbers of southerners as they rode progressively north to near Pineville, McDonald County, Missouri at the extreme southwestern tip of the state.[2]

Colonel Palmer's Rebel Group Including Roberts', Rusk's, and McCullough's Guerrillas

It was not until June 10 that concerned Union troops in southwest Missouri finally witnessed a portion of this particular northbound body of Rebels for themselves. The first Federals to encounter this large body of mounted Rebels were First Lieutenant Malcolm Hunter and his patrol of 35 troopers of Company H, 8th Cavalry MSM who saw 80 to 100 unidentified riders on the prairie twelve miles from the Neosho garrison. Hunter and his men rode toward the mysterious horsemen who then retired to the brush in a nearby creek bottom. The Federal patrol rode around the barely concealed Rebel body, and when the Rebels remained in place, First Lieutenant Hunter realized the southerners would only fight if he was foolish enough to go into the brush after them. Wisely, Hunter hurried back to Neosho and reported while the Rebel body rode on to the north into Jasper County. The Union command then sent out all available cavalry after this band, but the mysterious horsemen rode to within ten miles of Carthage, Jasper County, and seemingly disappeared. Union authorities at Mt. Vernon, Lawrence County, on June 13 apprehended two southern ladies carrying secret Rebel mail that seemed to identify the mysterious body of horsemen as a Colonel Palmer leading Lafayette Roberts of Cedar County and his guerrilla band, Indiana-born Captain David V. Rusk and Captain Edward McCullough with a portion of the late Thomas R. Livingston's former Jasper County bushwhackers, and an unidentified major. Captains Roberts and Rusk were now company commanders in Major Jesse F. Pickler's battalion, and were returning to their respective home counties to recruit. Colonel Palmer, the unnamed major, and perhaps a few other Confederate regulars traveling with the others were evidently recruiters on their way to west-central Missouri to enlist troops for their army in Arkansas.[3]

Also on June 13 the Union Neosho commander, Captain Henry D. Moore of Marshfield and commander of Company H of the 8th Cavalry MSM, confessed to his district commander that he could not stop the flow of northbound Rebels that had been bypassing his command as they trekked through Newton County. He wrote:

> I deem it my duty to inform you that quite a number of rebels are passing north for the last month. They have been passing on either side of this post, in squads of from 20 to 100, every few days. The country south of here is so sparsely inhabited, and the inhabitants about all rebels, that I can gain no information about them only from scouts. They are frequently past this post before I know anything about them.

It seems obvious from Moore's remarks that the war-ravaged condition of this part of Missouri contributed to the ability of southerners to travel through with little chance of detection.[4]

Rumors

Meanwhile, Union forces across the area pondered rumors about the newly arrived enemy. The Kansas City newspaper reported June 11 that a Union staff officer in southeast Kansas sent a telegram to Fort Scott, west of Vernon County, Missouri, about 40 half-breed Rebel Cherokee Indians dressed in Union uniforms camping on the Spring River somewhere in that corner of Kansas.[5] On June 13 the Union district commander of southwest Missouri, New Hampshire–born Brigadier General John B. Sanborn, reported to General Rosecrans that Major Pickler had claimed to have sent north over 1,200 Rebels through lightly populated southwest Missouri, but this number seems to have been an exaggeration.[6] To the north at Warrensburg, the Union district headquarters there heard that 600 Rebels attacked Neosho on June 14, but this was false.[7]

Return of Livingston's Old Band to Jasper County Area

The greatest impact to this region from this resurgence of Rebel numbers was in the Jasper County area over the next few weeks. The returning bushwhackers that used to ride with lead miner Thomas R. Livingston before his death in battle the previous July 11 set about dealing vengeance to old enemies with brutal rapidity.

County historian Ward L. Schrantz in his 1923 book about the Civil War there revealed that about this same time former Livingston member Ab Humbard and his band returned to the county specifically to conduct vengeance. His bushwhackers, like many of them at this time in the war, wore Union uniforms to fool their enemies, and used them to good advantage to ambush a small detail of the local 76th EMM four miles west of Sarcoxie. Humbard's band captured and murdered one of the militiamen and wounded three of the remainder who barely managed to elude their pursuers. Having neutralized this small group of militiamen, Humbard's newly arrived band rode through the countryside killing several men they knew to be northern sympathizers. Word of the bushwhackers' depredations brought Captain Green C. Stotts and a force of the 76th EMM that caught up to the guerrillas near Sarcoxie about a day later. Stotts' force attacked the guerrillas in a bramble thicket, mortally wounding two and giving others less serious wounds at the loss of one militiaman killed. The northerners also captured 17 of the guerrilla horses, recovered a quantity of stolen household goods, and rescued a young black girl the raiders had abducted. There seems to be no further mention of Ab Humbard during the war in this area, and no indication of his fate.[8]

Historian Schrantz also wrote about the demise of noted guerrilla Edwin "Bud" Shirley, another guerrilla evidently just returned to Jasper County. Union soldiers camped at Cave Springs, four miles northeast of Sarcoxie, heard that Shirley and fellow guerrilla Milt Norris were hiding near Sarcoxie and occasionally visited nearby homes of a couple of southern sympathizers. The soldiers watched these homes and struck when Shirley and Norris were inside eating. When the pair broke for freedom the Yanks shot Shirley to death and wounded Norris, who managed to escape. Afterwards, some of the local EMM burned the two homes. Despite his wounds and the danger, Milt Norris traveled to Carthage and told the Shirley family of Bud's death. Bud's distraught 16-year-old sister, Myra Shirley, rode to Sarcoxie wearing a gun-belt and two revolvers and boldly strode about the village swearing vengeance on the Yankees who killed her brother. Nothing came of the teenager's posturing and threats, and a few years later with a name change she became notorious as the outlaw Belle Starr.[9]

Schrantz also documented local accounts about how Union soldiers killed another noted bushwhacker, William Rader, another of the guerrillas who evidently also just returned to Jasper County. Locals suspected that Rader was responsible for one or two local killings about the time of his return. Unknown assassins killed a Union dispatch rider near present-day Golden City in the southeast corner of Barton County. and mutilated the body, and unknown miscreants murdered and robbed an elderly southern sympathizer named Robinson somewhere in Jasper County. Some of Mr.

Robinson's outraged neighbors recognized and seized Rader at Turkey Creek near present-day Joplin and wanted him to face justice for the murder, when local militiamen of the 7th Provisional EMM rode by and stopped to discover the source of the upset. At the sight of Union uniforms Bill Rader bolted out of the men's grasp and ran into the brush. The men at the scene chased Rader through the bushes and shot him dead.[10]

For the rest of June and early July across Jasper and north Newton Counties Union forces in the form of the local 76th EMM or 7th Provisional EMM and the 8th Cavalry MSM fought almost daily with the former Livingston guerrillas now led by David Rusk and Edward McCullough, as well as the bushwhackers under John Goode. Actually, the 7th Provisional EMM ceased to exist back on June 10. On that date the 7th Provisional EMM across southwest Missouri became the 15th Missouri Cavalry Regiment—a regular unit with a 20-month enlistment, and the 6th Provisional EMM in this region became the 16th Missouri Cavalry, too. On July 16 Major Milton Burch, commanding the companies of the 8th Cavalry MSM at the Neosho garrison, summarized the efforts of these units over the last several weeks in a report to his district commander, Brigadier General Sanborn. Burch mentioned the 100-or-so bushwhackers investing this area which Burch asserted "by continual scouting I have succeeded in driving from this country" adding "I think they have moved south." Major Burch also warned his general that Confederate Major Pickler and Arkansan Colonel Buck Brown with several hundred Rebels also remained to the south, probably across the border of the nearly depopulated McDonald County. After some mopping up, Burch indicated that he wanted to direct his troopers there next.[11]

Union troops baited Rebel Lieutenant Goode's band to attack what appeared to be a lightly guarded forage detail (Charles C. Coffin, *Freedom Triumphant*, 1890, p. 91).

Rusk's Band at Carthage

Mopping up is always easier to write about in a report than the harsh reality to the combatants on the ground, as the hard fighting in Jasper and Newton Counties demonstrated through the remainder of July and early August 1864. Guerrilla Captain David V. Rusk with an estimated 125 bushwhackers attacked First Lieutenant Brice Henry's detail of 25 members of 76th EMM grazing their stock just outside the town of Carthage on July 21, killing Henry and five men and carrying off eleven of the others as prisoners. These men failed to post a guard, thinking they were safe since they were in full view of the town. There were too few Union soldiers inside the town to offer any resistance to this guerrilla victory. The eleven prisoners initially sought refuge in a house and refused bushwhacker calls to surrender until they received southern assurance that they would be treated as POWs. Good to their promise, the guerrillas later released these men after taking most of their clothes and shoes.[12]

Residents would not identify local Union soldiers who committed vengeance against southerners of the Carthage area during the month of August. These unknowns killed five men of southern sympathy all in town or within two miles of it and they burned several homes of southerners. Some of this violence was backlash against guerrilla depredations in June and July.[13]

Henry Taylor's and Bill Marchbanks' Bands

Guerrilla warfare in this area did noticeably move further south with two fights in early August. On August 1 Captains Samuel E. Roberts and James M. Ritchey formerly of the 7th Provisional EMM and now of the new 15th Missouri Cavalry with 80 troopers probably from the Mt. Vernon garrison found and attacked about 30 guerrillas of the Henry Taylor and Bill Marchbanks bands of Vernon and Bates Counties. These bushwhackers had been pressured from their own operating area a few days before by other Union troops and were about ten miles east of Baxter Springs in the southwest corner of Jasper or the northwest corner of Newton County when the Federals found them. The Union cavalry chased these displaced guerrillas an estimated ten to twelve miles and killed five or six and wounded others in the long running battle. Union sources of this fight recorded that one of the Rebel dead was "Old One-Eyed Davis" of Greene County.[14]

Killing of Goode in Careful Ambush

The following day, Captain Ozias Ruark and his patrol of 40 troopers of 8th Cavalry MSM from the Neosho garrison rode into the Diamond Grove area of north-central Newton County to find and bring back forage for the garrison's horses. In that neighborhood they also found and defeated their old nemesis, Rebel Lieutenant John R. Goode. Actually, Ruark and his men were hoping the bushwhackers would make a showing and sent First Lieutenant Malcomb Hunter with wagons loaded with forage back toward Neosho with twenty of the troopers as bait. When Goode and two of his men walked into the open to see what was happening, the rest of Captain Ozias' force fired into them, killing Goode. On his body the Yanks found a roster of his men and a 30-day furlough from the 11th Missouri Infantry Regiment (CSA) dated back in January.[15]

August Fights in McDonald County

For most of the rest of August elements of the 8th Cavalry MSM from several garrisons moved the battle against the bushwhackers further south into McDonald County, as Major Milton Burch earlier told his general he would. On August 4 Major

A tense fight in the brush (Underwood and Clough, eds., *Battles and Leaders of the Civil War*, vol. 1, p. 510).

Burch sent First Lieutenant Malcomb Hunter with 80 troopers from the Neosho garrison looking for the main Rebel camp near Rutledge. Hunter did find the Rebel camp, and did not find his enemy other than a few pickets, but the Confederates certainly found him. Major J. F. Pickler with an estimated 300 Rebels attacked Hunter's men in the rear and on both flanks in the thick brush. Some of Colonel Buck Brown's Arkansas men were part of this force, but Rector Johnson led them in Brown's absence. The Federals also learned that among these Rebels were Captain David Rusk and his Jasper County guerrillas, Captain Lafayette Roberts and his bushwhackers from Dade and Cedar Counties, and others. First Lieutenant Hunter managed to keep his men together as the jubilant southerners chased them about four miles before breaking off the battle in the dense foliage. Both sides suffered casualties of three killed and several wounded, but the Federals realized Pickler's and Johnson's men were no pushovers.[16] Between August 5 and 7 Burch advanced his 175 troopers further south after the Rebels to Cowskin Creek in south McDonald County. There the Federals lost six men killed compared to perhaps one Rebel killed and some wounded, but the southerners retired in a southward direction into Arkansas.[17] By August 7 Burch's command had accumulated a number of wounded and they rode back to Neosho with the incapacitated on litters, ending the expedition. Burch reported that he had learned that Pickler was part of Confederate Lieutenant Colonel Andrew J. Piercey's unit, and with his force were some Rebels of Brigadier General Stand Watie's command.[18]

On August 13 and 14 the commander of the 8th Cavalry MSM, Colonel Joseph J. Gravely, personally led elements of his regiment from several area garrisons back to the Cowskin Creek area of south McDonald County just to ensure the Rebels had not returned after Major Burch's force departed a week before. Gravely noted the work of

Captain John Kelso on this patrol for killing a Rebel Lieutenant Baxter in a house on the morning of August 14. Baxter was carrying orders from Brigadier General Stand Watie at Fort Smith to his men in that vicinity. Captain Kelso was educated and known for having a calm, almost detached, demeanor, but he had a penchant for sometimes single-handedly tracking down guerrillas and killing them with gun or knife, to the awe of his own men. Gravely's report of this patrol and Union company records seem to indicate that the casualties from this patrol were two killed on each side.[19]

On August 21 a patrol of 8th Cavalry MSM from a garrison at Granby near Diamond Grove in north-central Newton County fought with bushwhackers probably of the late Lieutenant John Goode's guerrillas. One Union trooper was killed and another reported missing and presumed killed.[20]

Obviously, some guerrillas remained in this area in spite of hard fighting all summer. Union intelligence reports about August 14 told the Federals that Captains David Rusk, Lafayette Roberts, and their veteran guerrillas left southwest Missouri for Arkansas with some of General Watie's command. Colonel Gravely commented happily that most of the area bushwhackers had left this area "except for a few bushwhackers who hide in the bluff and caves when any Federal soldiers are near."[21] There were still guerrillas in the far southwest corner of Missouri dedicated to their cause who would continue the war in the coming autumn.

A few times during the war Confederate Brigadier General Stand Watie brought his command raiding into southwest Missouri (Underwood and Clough, eds., *Battles and Leaders of the Civil War*, vol. 1, 1887, p. 333).

Summer 1864 Fighting in the Prairies of Vernon, Barton, Dade, and Cedar Counties: Bands of Roberts, Taylor, and Marchbanks

There was fighting this summer with passing Rebels crossing the Osage Plains or Western Plains of Missouri in Vernon, Barton, Dade, and Cedar Counties. However, most of the action here was from the efforts of the guerrilla bands of Lafayette Roberts in Dade and Cedar Counties, Henry Taylor in south and central Vernon County, and Bill Marchbanks in north Vernon and Bates Counties. These were all veteran groups accustomed to the "no quarter" Missouri style of guerrilla fighting with an intimate knowledge of this area. They faced here Wisconsin and Kansas cavalrymen and, like the far southwest corner of Missouri, a mix of different types of Missouri soldiers.

Large numbers of mounted bushwhackers and Confederate recruiters used the prairies of southwest Missouri as a convenient avenue to ride to northwest and northeast Missouri throughout the war despite the efforts of the Union military to stop the practice. The Union commander of Fort Scott just west of Vernon County, Colonel Charles W. Blair of the 14th Kansas Cavalry, reported such a traveling southern group had passed through war-ravaged Montevallo in southeast Vernon County too late for him to do anything about it: "A party of 150 rebels went through Montevallo, Mo., 35 miles east of here last Wednesday [8 June], going north, on the old Boonville road, the usual route."

There appears to be no earlier corresponding Union report further south about the passing of a group this size. Maybe Blair's source exaggerated the number, or perhaps several smaller groups of traveling southerners banded together for mutual protection in sparsely populated Barton County after infiltrating past more numerous Union posts and patrols further south. Newspapers in St. Louis and Kansas City copied Colonel Blair's report, since the advent of large numbers of Rebels into Missouri was an ominous sign of more fighting to come somewhere.[22]

Taylor's Band Near Montevallo in Vernon County

Elements of 3rd Wisconsin Cavalry were patrolling around Montevallo several days later and may have heard about the 150 southerners passing from locals there, but they had Rebel concerns of their own, probably from Henry Taylor's bushwhacker band. In his diary, Sergeant James P. Mallery of Company A recorded that he was one of the ten on a patrol under Captain Robert Carpenter that on June 11 found and attacked seven bushwhackers at a house, killing one of them, and capturing four of their horses. Mallery also wrote that this patrol found six more guerrillas in the woods "with 5 girles." He made no comment about the outcome with this bunch, so it is possible that the Wisconsinites held their fire for fear of hitting the females while the bushwhackers escaped into the foliage, and Sergeant Mallery was too disgusted to enter that result in his diary. This account plus Mallery's comment about not having much to eat while around Montevallo tends to support numerous reports earlier in the war that Montevallo was famous in the region as a town of strong southern sympathy.[23] Colonel Blair's report also told about a patrol led by First Lieutenant Clark B. Willsey on June 12 that encountered 30 guerrillas at or near Montevallo who the Federals charged, scattered into the brush, killed one, and captured several horses. Perhaps these differing accounts were actually describing one action by the same patrol, but the differences of date and patrol leader say otherwise.[24]

Traveling Rebel Bands in Barton County

Second Lieutenant Joel T. Hembree of the 7th Provisional EMM at Lamar reported to Brigadier General Sanborn that a northbound band of about 100 Rebels robbed three women traveling ten miles from Lamar, central Barton County, on June 12. The Rebels took two horses, all the ladies' food, and some clothing. This particular traveling group of Confederates may very well be the same one that Lieutenant Hunter encountered on June 10 fifty miles south in Newton County, as described earlier in this chapter. Moving that far and that fast may help explain why the southerners needed horses and food. Hembree was disgusted that his company at Lamar was too small in such a vast place as the prairies of Barton County "and has effected nothing in the way of putting down the rebellion." He elaborated about his frustrations imposed by the small size of his command at Lamar:

> They are just like a stake drove down in the middle of a big road. The rebels can go on either side and we cannot help it, from the fact that we are too weak.... The rebels know our strength and condition generally, and when they pass through they go in squads of 80 to 100 men. Then when we run on them they whip us, and we have to skedaddle, which tends to encourage them rather than any other way ... if we had more men, we might kill some of those fellows going north.... We do not ask to be moved from Lamar particularly. All we ask is to be placed in a in a condition that we can do something.

To his credit, General Sanborn replied directly to this second lieutenant that he was already increasing the force at all the outposts in the western tier of counties "by calling out the entire militia force of several counties." The general also wrote that "I desire to hold both towns and counties, if possible, throughout the district. If it is found impossible, than I shall concentrate and hold what I can." [25]

Roberts' 14 June Raid on Melville

Guerrilla chieftain Lafayette "Pete" Roberts arrived back in his home area of south-central Cedar County about June 11 or 12. Roberts had served as a junior officer at age 19 in the southern Missouri State Guard during 1861, and had commanded a company in capable and aggressive Thomas R. Livingston's bushwhacker battalion in southwest Missouri probably from 1862 until Livingston's death in the Stockton, Cedar County, assault on 11 July 1863. Livingston's large band disintegrated somewhat after that. Major Jesse F. Pickler eventually took command of Livingston's former battalion and Roberts commanded Company C in it. He led a band briefly in Cedar County during February 1864 as mentioned in an earlier chapter, perhaps to recruit in his home area. On May 27 General Shelby's headquarters named him in a direct, written order as a company commander of Pickler's battalion to return to his home county and recruit, and that compelled him to return this time.[26]

Roberts wasted no time leading his band of 60 to 75 riders on a sunrise raid of the town of Melville in northeast Dade County June 14. Perhaps some of Roberts' hurry was the absence from Melville of the militia commander there, Major Wick Morgan of the newly designated 15th Missouri Cavalry, and most of his men who were then patrolling near Horse Creek to the west after Rebels reported there. This raid was particularly brutal, as the *Springfield Journal* related, "killing some three or four citizens and boys, and wounding several men, boys and negroes, and setting fire to most of the houses, after robbing them of all that they could pack off, after which they immediately left in the direction they came."

Citizens of the town, mostly women, rushed to extinguish fires as soon as the raiders left and were able to save some homes, but most buildings of the town were destroyed. About 40 area residents attempted to pursue Roberts' band, but the raiders were better mounted and too far ahead. Major William B. Mitchell and a number of his men of the 15th Missouri Cavalry and Captain Calvin S. Moore and much of his company of 6th Cavalry MSM stationed at the Dade County seat of Greenfield, about twelve miles to the southwest, quickly took up the pursuit as the Melville garrison had not yet returned from their patrol. The pursuers discovered tracking Roberts' raiders was made easier because the guerrillas had burned a number of homes along the Sac River as they rode back to Cedar County. On June 15 Major Mitchell, Captain Moore, and their men caught up to the bushwhackers near White Hare in south-central Cedar County in the act of auctioning the goods taken at Melville to each other. Mitchell's force immediately attacked, killing seven, and wounding several with Union casualties of two men slightly wounded. In their report the Yanks gleefully wrote that the pursuers recaptured "all the stolen goods" and captured 15 horses.[27]

It seems that the remainder of the large body of southerners who rode north with Captain Lafayette Roberts from Arkansas were near the border of Jasper and Barton Counties to the west of Dade County at this time. On June 16 First Sergeant R. W. Smith's detail of 30 troopers of 3rd Wisconsin Cavalry was on its way back north to their post at Dry Wood, south Vernon County, herding cattle they obtained at Carthage when they encountered a large unidentified body of Rebels. Initially, 46 southern horsemen came out of the woods shooting at the troopers who were preoccupied driving the cattle in front of them. As the cattle bounded off into the nearby timber, the cavalrymen retreated about 100 yards to a ravine where they were able to concentrate and put forth a credible defense. The first group of attackers advanced on the ravine, but as the troopers shot several of them, they retired back to the woods, where some of the Wisconsinites saw an equal number of Rebels among the trees. First Sergeant Smith sent two troopers a half mile on a flank where they found 30 more Rebels waiting to commit a flank attack upon the Yanks. Smith then realized his 30 men faced over 100 Rebels, and left the battlefield and the cattle to the southerners and rode on north to their Dry Wood base. One of the troopers was killed at first fire and Smith estimated they mortally wounded one of the Rebels and less seriously wounded three others. If the Yanks had counterattacked those Rebels who initially fired on them, they would have ridden into a clever and dangerous ambush. The participants also commented that some of the southerners fired infantry rifle-muskets of heavy caliber with skill, reluctantly admitted the enemy's conduct during the fight showed they had combat experience as regulars, and concluded that these Rebels seemed better trained than guerrillas. Based on these factors and their numbers, Smith's cattle herding detail must have encountered the recruiting body with which Lafayette Roberts and his men returned to this area.[28]

On the night of June 21/22 five guerrillas, perhaps of Henry Taylor's band, went to John Rogers' home on Drywood Creek, southwest Vernon County, and killed him as he attempted to escape to the brush, though he wounded one of his assailants. Rogers was a captain in the 6th Kansas Cavalry, and shortly before he had arrived home on a wagon train from Fort Gibson. A neighbor may have told the bushwhackers he was back home for a visit, as there were many southern sympathizers in south Vernon County. Colonel Blair, the commander at Fort Scott a few miles to the northwest, sadly commented that if Rogers had remained in the house he could have held off his attackers, since there was another man in the house and both were well-armed.[29]

Major Pickler's Recruiting Command in Area

On June 23 Colonel John D. Allen, formerly commander of the 7th Provisional EMM and at this time commander of the newly created 15th Missouri Cavalry, while investigating surprising claims of large numbers of Rebels in the region, was startled to discover the reports were very correct! Allen and his men with help from a small patrol of 3rd Wisconsin Cavalry under Captain Robert Carpenter—about 75 troopers altogether—followed the tracks of a few riders along Horse Creek for about 20 miles to an area in the junction of Barton, Vernon, Dade, and Cedar Counties. There, they saw and pursued four or five mounted Rebels for five miles who led them almost into an ambush of some estimated 150 or 200 Confederates waiting in a woods to attack! The advance guards of both forces maneuvered around each other across the prairie for several hours, but the outnumbered Federals warily refused to make any rash move. Colonel Allen noted that the Rebel skirmishers were "sharpshooters," implying they were armed with rifles. Finally, the Confederate body rode off with Colonel Allen's force following until dark, when the Yanks withdrew to keep a safe distance from this unidentified, large body of southern cavalry. The Union cavalry slept on the prairie with a large guard that night, but no Rebels approached and the following morning they discovered that the southern horsemen had ridden away. There seemed to be no casualties in this unusual meeting of two opposing forces.[30]

Union cavalrymen were surprised to encounter a large body of veteran, regular Confederate soldiers armed with rifles, and the Federals kept their distance (Charles C. Coffin, *My Days and Nights on the Battlefield*, 1887, p. 81).

This unidentified Rebel force seemed to be at least partially armed with rifles and behaved as if they would fight if a Union force discovered them, just as did the large Rebel body near Preston a few days before. These Confederates were apparently the recruiting command that first appeared as about 80 men riding north in Newton County June 10; next as about 100 riders ten miles from Lamar, Barton County, who took all the food from three traveling women on June 12; then as about 100 riders who fought with the Wisconsin cavalry patrol near Preston, north-central Jasper County, June 16; and now were at least 150 horsemen along Horse Creek at the corner of Barton, Vernon, Dade, and Cedar Counties on June 23. Lafayette Roberts' guerrilla band was able to raid Melville so easily June 14 because the Union garrison there was off patrolling along Horse Creek to the west, perhaps looking for this same body of Confederates. Nearly all the passing southern groups using the southwest Missouri prairies as avenues for rapid movement kept moving to prevent Union detection and deter Union pursuit, but this band preferred to remain in this prairie region for several days during June and July. These southerners may have already noted what Lieutenant Hembree pointed out to his general—that his small Lamar garrison was no threat to Rebels in the Barton County area. There was plentiful grass for horses here, but the area was nearly depopulated by this time of the war, and a poor place to find food for a large body of men. This acute need for food could explain why these Confederates took all the provisions from the traveling women near Lamar on June 12—uncharacteristic behavior for Confederate troops under normal circumstances, and this logistics problem was partly solved by the herd of cattle lost to this group by the Wisconsin troopers on June 16. Perhaps they were even aided by the Lafayette Roberts' guerrilla band in south Cedar County and Henry Taylor's band in south Vernon County, who were supposed to be assisting with the recruiting. The steady growth of this Confederate band between June 10 and June 23 seems to indicate that they were deliberately waiting in this depopulated, poorly patrolled area of southwest Missouri gathering in recruits from the area. They must have gambled that the thin cordon of Union cavalry watching this region would miss them if they avoided offensive action and quietly moved about.

These prairielands were quiet for the next several days, but violence erupted in several places in early July. The large Confederate band evidently grew to nearly 300 riders by then and Captain David S. Vittum's patrol of 45 troopers of 3rd Wisconsin Cavalry discovered them along Cow Creek on the Kansas side west of the junction of Jasper and Barton Counties on Independence Day. The Federals lost one horse killed but reported killing one of the Rebels and killing two of their horses. Two riders of the 15th Kansas Cavalry carrying dispatches from Fort Gibson to Fort Scott passing through this same area that day were not so fortunate. One was killed and the second was wounded when they encountered these Confederates. During the night of July 5/6 unidentified guerrillas exchanged fire with the guards of Captain Robert Carpenter's garrison of 3rd Wisconsin Cavalry at the ruins of Balltown, northwest Vernon County. Evidently, nobody was hit by the flying bullets. Colonel Charles W. Blair at Fort Scott commented on these events. Blair seemed to have information that the large Rebel body at Cow Creek was then under the personal command of Major Jesse F. Pickler, that they were sent by higher Confederate authorities into southwest Missouri to recruit, and they were working in concert with guerrilla chiefs Bill Marchbanks in north Vernon and Bates Counties and Henry Taylor in central and south Vernon County. Colonel Blair also reported that Taylor had already recruited about 200 men who were camped along Clear Creek and Montevallo in southeast Vernon County. If this were true, this is the first report indicating that Major Pickler personally was this far north of the Arkansas border and in personal command of this large band of Confederates. This also seems to shed light on the lack of offensive actions this large body demonstrated when approached by Union patrols during June. If this body contained large numbers of recruits, they would probably be mostly unarmed and untrained. The recruiters would hold the recruits in the woods or brush in case of a confrontation with Yankees and send just a few veterans out as skirmishers to keep the Federals from discovering their vulnerability.[31]

Subsequent events tended to verify two items in Colonel Blair's report. A corporal's patrol of five troopers of 3rd Wisconsin Cavalry on the afternoon of July 5 near Clear Creek and Montevallo in southeast Vernon County encountered eight guerrillas and killed one after first killing the man's horse. This skirmish tends to show at least that there were guerrillas in this area.[32] Guerrilla chief Bill Marchbanks stopped at a man's house the night of July 10/11 about four miles from Balltown. This would seem to indicate that Marchbanks' bushwhackers were the ones who exchanged shots with the Union guards at Balltown a few nights before.[33]

Pickler's Band Raids Barnesville, Kansas

It was inevitable that the large numbers of Rebels along the border would sooner or later raid on the Kansas side. During the evening of July 11 about 20 guerrillas raided farms and ran off stock in northeast Bourbon County west of the Vernon County line. About eight o'clock the riders attempted to raid the town of Barnesville. They rode within three miles of the Union post named "Fort Lincoln," but met an unexpected obstacle. A number of alerted citizens of this community gathered with firearms in a log house and held their fire until the bushwhackers rode almost up to the building before shooting. They killed three of the raiders and captured their horses, and the remainder escaped into Vernon County. Union troops from Potosi, Kansas and Fort Scott pursued and one patrol discovered a Rebel camp and captured three more horses.[34] During the afternoon of July 18 guerrillas stole horses from farms along Indian Creek between Potosi and Barnesville, Kansas. Union troops from Mound City pursued, but there is no further record to tell what came of this.[35]

Death of Major Pickler

Union troops of the 1st Arkansas Cavalry in Benton County, south of McDonald County, Missouri, on July 17 or 18 killed Rebel Major Jesse F. Pickler during combat with part of his battalion. Either Pickler returned to that area subsequent to Colonel Blair's information that he was on Cow Creek, Kansas July 5, or Blair was mistaken about him being there at all. Since Major Pickler was commander to both David V. Rusk's company in Jasper County and Lafayette Roberts' Cedar County company, it is unknown what effect his death had upon their orders from General Shelby to recruit in their home counties.[36]

The Mayfield Girls Near Montevallo

On July 22 or 23 Lieutenant Davis' patrol of 3rd Wisconsin Cavalry from the Fort Curtis (Balltown) garrison in northwest Vernon County found a guerrilla camp near Montevallo, wounded several Rebels, and captured between 12 and 15 horses. That was not all the Wisconsinites captured. At the time the patrol assaulted the camp some local young ladies were visiting, and the Federals arrested four of them for "being found in company with the bushwhackers."

One girl escaped on the way back to Balltown, but the Union troops sent sisters Sallie and Jennie Mayfield and Nancy Burrus along to Fort Scott and later to Kansas City where Miss Burrus took the oath to the United States and the Federals released her. The Mayfield girls were of a determined Rebel family of Vernon County and would not take the oath. Officials sent them to St. Louis where they spent time first in Gratiot Street Prison and then were transferred to the female prison at the corner of 7th and Chestnut Streets where they both escaped on 19 October. This intrepid pair made their way to Morgan County where their mother was living and remained with her for the rest of the war.[37]

Rebel Raiding Along Kansas Side of Border

It appears in late July that the large body of recruiters and new recruits was still operating with varying amounts of stealth in lightly settled southeast Bourbon County, Kansas near Cow Creek west of Vernon County, Missouri. An uncertain number of guerrillas raided the town of Barnesville one hour before sunrise on July 31, and the nearest Union post at Mound City ordered up the area militia to deal with the Rebels, since there were few soldiers in the area available to go. The Kansas City newspaper of August 5 reported 120 guerrillas raiding along Cow Creek again, referring to this incident.

The paper also claimed this bunch was reputed to have "one piece of light artillery," although this seems to be the only mention of such a piece of ordnance in Confederate hands in this region at this time. Earlier this summer scores of southern sympathizing EMM in the Platte County area north of Kansas City conducted an insurrection that overwhelming Union forces squelched there, and this article claimed that also near Cow Creek was a second body of "several hundred" of these "turncoat" EMM who had fled here to save their lives from Union revenge. If there were still large numbers of southern men in southeast Bourbon County area in late July, raiding was probably a necessity to provide subsistence.[38]

Taylor's Guerrillas on Clear Creek in Vernon County

Union patrols continued to ride to the Clear Creek area of south-central Vernon County looking for members of Henry Taylor's guerrilla band and recruits known to camp there.

An unidentified patrol of ten troopers from Fort Scott August 7 rode onto five bushwhackers in the woods there and scattered them, except for one anonymous Rebel. This man determined to make a battle to the death and accounted well for himself with a carbine and two revolvers until the hard-pressed patrol finally felled him with 15 bullets. When the shooting ended, the patrol had killed three bushwhackers with losses to themselves of two wounded.[39]

Rebel Recruiters Withdraw to Arkansas in Mid-August

This prairie region grew relatively quiet for the remainder of August until the last days of the month. Another unidentified patrol from Fort Scott in the Clear Creek area made a fortuitous capture on August 27 or 28 of a Rebel named Jackson. This prisoner vehemently claimed that the guerrillas conscripted him against his will four weeks before. To prove his good intentions Jackson led the patrol back to his bushwhacker camp occupied by 19 very surprised southerners. The Federals fired into the campers killing two outright and wounding two of those fleeing with shots in the back. Jackson informed the Yanks that one of the wounded men was Bob Marchbanks, younger brother of guerrilla chief Captain Bill Marchbanks. Bob Marchbanks was a captain himself in southern service earlier in the war, but was captured and had taken the oath not to bear arms against the United States government. After the patrol took Jackson back to Fort Scott, the prisoner told Colonel Blair the locations of several guerrilla meeting places and tactics, and the latest news Jackson had heard through bushwhacker contacts about the progress of some of the west-central Missouri bands and southern forces in Arkansas. Colonel Blair wrote of his remarkable interview with the talkative Jackson that he learned a lot "that I hope to make useful."[40]

This prairie region grew quiet again toward the end of summer. Major Jesse F. Pickler, the battalion commander for Lafayette Roberts and David V. Rusk, was dead, as was guerrilla leader John R. Goode. Roberts himself with Bill Marchbanks and their guerrillas and some recruits, left southwest Missouri for Arkansas about mid–August, probably as a result of orders from General Shelby's headquarters to all the recruiters of this region to come back in with whatever men they had collected by that time. At the end of August it seems the only guerrilla band possibly still operating in this area seems to have been that of Henry Taylor in central and south Vernon County.

Summer 1864 in the Osage River Basin: Marchbanks', Potter's, and Beck's Bands

Guerrilla warfare was sporadic this summer in the basin of the wide Osage River. Some of the guerrillas and Confederate recruiting commands that passed northbound through the prairie region to the south also passed through this mixed prairie and woodland terrain, but they made little impact as they passed. Most elements of the Enrolled Missouri Militia in this region were not on active duty this spring and early summer to report and oppose southern riders. Some guerrillas who returned to the Osage River basin reveled in the lack of opposition and set out to settle old scores, particularly with the local militiamen of the 60th EMM who were responsible for killing and capturing so many southern combatants in this area during 1863. Some of these bushwhacker bands included Bill Marchbanks' command which operated in north Vernon County and most of Bates County, a Doctor Beck who led a smaller guerrilla band in northeast Henry County in early June, and there were other unidentified bands in the region.

Guerrillas Hunt Militia in St. Clair County

Local militiamen in St. Clair County escaped from a guerrilla group hunting them at home only by running for their lives (Frazar Kirkland, *The Pictorial Book of Anecdotes of the Rebellion*, 1888, p. 342).

The summer began in this region with bushwhackers hunting down militiamen of the 60th Enrolled Missouri Militia in sparsely settled St. Clair County. Major Andrew J. Pugh of this regiment at Osceola, the county seat, reported that about June 6 guerrillas took two unidentified members of Captain Morton Anderson's Company E from their rural homes and murdered them nearby. The same raiders attempted to kill other members of Company E, but those men barely managed to escape. In his report Major Pugh bemoaned the lack of any Union troops stationed in St. Clair County to the point that county officials kept their records at Sedalia, miles to the northeast, in order to prevent their destruction. Pugh acknowledged that in some parts of the county families of northern sympathy had to live and work together for self protection from bushwhackers.[41]

Marchbanks' Guerrillas Along Osage River

Further to the west, First Sergeant Carmi B. Vaughan led 40 troopers of the 2nd Colorado Cavalry from their Harrisonville, Cass County, garrison on a long mounted patrol between June 8 and 19 carefully searching for guerrillas on both sides of the Osage River in southern Bates and northern Vernon Counties. Vaughan's large patrol sustained itself by bringing their provisions with them packed on a wagon pulled by six mules, since large portions of this area were depopulated either by General Orders Number 11 the previous autumn or by voluntary flight of residents. They obtained corn to feed their horses from the 3rd Wisconsin Cavalry post at Balltown and from an operating mill in the area. On June 9 Vaughan's patrol ambushed six guerrillas riding by two miles east of Papinsville, southeast Bates County, and chased them in a running fight, killing two and wounding two others. The Federals suspected another drowned in a slough, as the bushwhacker's horse swam out of it without the rider. The Coloradoans collected clothing, calico, coffee, about $250 in Confederate money, and other odds and ends that the fleeing Rebels discarded to speed their flight. The patrol leader thought these bushwhackers were led by a Potter who had lately been raiding on the Kansas side, but in all likelihood these were probably members of Captain Bill Marchbanks' local band. The patrol camped in deep woods or thickets at night for security, and often remained hidden by pathways and roads to ambush any passing guerrillas. Vaughan later reported they found signs that about 60 riders passed this area not long before. They carefully searched reputed bushwhacker havens such as the island in the Marais des Cygnes River and other locations made notorious in guerrilla battles over the previous two years, but from tracks they found Vaughan admitted that the Rebels kept scouts watching their progress and avoided this large patrol after the Federals' initial success on June 9. On June 17 on Miami Creek, south-central Bates County, the patrol found a camp of a few guerrillas who saw the Federals and rode away, but the Coloradoans fired on a picket reading a book who managed to escape although wounded. The Federals destroyed all the camp equipment the southerners left behind, and noted "a euchre deck dealt out" in the hastily abandoned camp. In his report, First Sergeant Vaughan bemoaned their unreliable carbines that missed fire at several critical moments on the patrol allowing Rebels to escape who otherwise would have been casualties. He also suggested that he could have maneuvered better and kept better security if he had carried his provisions on pack animals and not had to lug along a bulky wagon that restricted his cross-country movement and added to his security problems. Vaughan acknowledged that the enemies his patrol faced "were well armed, splendidly mounted, and fought desperately." The patrol suffered no casualties.[42]

Mysterious Dr. Beck's Guerrillas Raid Calhoun in Northeast Henry County

On Sunday evening, June 12 a mysterious guerrilla leader identified only as "Dr. Beck, a notorious character," lead 18 to 20 bushwhackers on a brutal raid of the village of Calhoun in northeast Henry County. Beck's men initially captured Lieutenant Thomas Sallee of the town's citizen guards as they began the raid, but Sallee broke away and ran to his house where he fought back, killing Beck himself. In all the excitement Mrs. Sallee accidentally wounded her husband in the foot while handing him a loaded firearm. Sallee, formerly a sergeant in a local company of the 60th EMM, limped off into nearby woods before the bushwhackers could close in on him. Three of his fellow citizen guards were also wounded in the gunfight in town, as were several of the Rebels. The guerrillas took lots of goods from a store owned by a northern sympathizer, and burned buildings mostly owned by northern men. They burned Sallee's boarding house, called "Calhoun House," a church, blacksmith shop, and various outbuildings. They seemed to single out property owned by Doctor Willis S. Holland, who had earlier been surgeon of the Union 60th EMM, as they torched two dwellings of his, his stable, and a church he had built. The raiders brought into town a prisoner named Johnson who they killed, and seriously wounded another prisoner they had, John Hastain of Henry County, and also mortally wounded another man who was merely traveling through the region and happened to be in Calhoun at this time. This seems to be the only guerrilla action conducted by this "Dr. Beck," or at least that survives in some form of record. His band may be that of the late John Rafter killed the previous September 4 during a raid on Quincy, northwest Hickory County, since Rafter's men operated mostly in east Henry County.[43]

Guerrillas Hunting Militiamen in Hickory and Pettis Counties

There were more guerrilla killings of northern sympathizers in this region during the early days of July 1864. About 30 to 40 guerrillas attacked First Sergeant David McGee and Corporal William W. T. Bernard, both of Company A of the 60th EMM two-and-a-half miles from Quincy, northwest Hickory County, on the morning of July 2. The pair put up a good fight, killing two of the Rebels and seriously wounding a third. McGee was slightly wounded and managed to escape, but the southerners killed Bernard and afterwards mutilated his body. An anonymous correspondent at Warsaw, Benton County, sent an article to one of the St. Louis newspapers telling about the incident. This person claimed these bushwhackers were from Benton, St. Clair, Henry, and Hickory Counties, and that their female relatives supported their activities by "conveying news, acting spy and feeding the men of the bush."[44] On the following day guerrillas killed a Union Captain McBride traveling back toward his St. Clair County home from Sedalia, according to a Sedalia correspondent to a St. Louis newspaper. This writer claimed that guerrillas had recently killed four other men of northern sympathy in west Pettis County, so McBride was probably killed there as well.[45]

Guerrillas Terrorize Leesville in East Henry County

Leesville in east central Henry County was a town primarily of northern sympathy, which led John Rafter and his guerrilla band to victimize the town and surrounding farms the previous year. Fearing a return of the bushwhackers, Leesville men organized a citizens guard with enough members to keep twelve men on duty at all times. On July 21 some of the citizen guard brought back from the Union garrison at the county seat of Clinton 21 rifle muskets, 19 cartridge boxes for wearing by individual shooters, and 3,000 rounds of ammunition. That same day less than two miles from town a hidden guerrilla attempted to shoot at some of the guard, but the hammer of his firearm snapped with a loud pop but the cartridge failed to fire. The report failed to detail what happened next, but it would appear one side or both beat a hasty retreat. Later on July 21 other residents saw some of the bushwhackers three miles from town. It seems that some members of Rafter's old band returned to harass Leesville again.[46]

On August 2 northern forces at or near Osceola, county seat of St. Clair County, captured Rebel recruiter, Private John M. Edwards, and later sent him along under guard to the St. Louis area military prisons. The Union prison officials at the Alton prison wrote of Edwards that he was an "unassigned recruiter," since they could not determine to which Confederate unit he belonged, but at least Edwards avoided the deadly label of guerrilla with its usual death penalty.[47]

Edwards may have been part of a band of Rebels stealing horses in Hickory County east of St. Clair County. On August 4 the Springfield Union district headquarters ordered Captain Jacob Cassairt of the 8th Cavalry MSM to take five of his men to Hickory County and put a stop to southerners taking horses there. The surviving records do not indicate what Cassairt found there, if anything, or if the horse stealers were local guerrillas or some merely passing through.[48]

August Actions in Bates County

This region was relatively quiet for the rest of August until the 21st when eight or nine bushwhackers raided near Potosi, Kansas and carried away four or five local men as prisoners as they rode back to the Missouri line. First Lieutenant Joseph H. Phillips and some of his troopers of the 15th Kansas Cavalry from the nearby Mound City garrison tracked the raiders through the night and caught up to them at daybreak near Papinsville, southeast Bates County. During the ensuing fire-fight the captives broke away to freedom, Phillips' patrol killed one guerrilla and wounded two or three others, all at no Union loss. The Kansans also captured five or six of the Rebels' horses, too. A guerrilla captured earlier admitted to his captors back at Mound City that this band had been camping along the Marais des Cygnes River in south Bates County.[49]

As August and the summer drew to a close on the contentious Osage River basin, this region grew strangely quiet, even though there were several weeks of good fighting weather left before winter cold returned. Much of the reason is that Confederate commanders in northwest Arkansas called the majority of Rebel recruiting bands and guerrillas back to them in preparation for Major General Sterling Price's upcoming Missouri invasion.

Summer 1864 in the Northern Ozark Hill Country

This summer also blossomed in scattered violence in the wooded hill country of the northern Ozarks, also called the Springfield Plateau. The rugged nature of these broken hills dissected by crooked, rocky ravines and creeks made travel difficult, but Union forces learned earlier in the war that Rebel regular and irregular forces would on occasion cross the Arkansas border to enter Missouri through this rugged terrain in order to advance unnoticed to threaten isolated Union garrisons and supply lines.

Rebels Scouting in Douglas County Area

Typical of the scattered nature of the fighting in this tree-covered region was Captain Jacob Cassairt's patrol of 8th Cavalry MSM through from his Forsyth, Taney County, base through Ozark and Douglas Counties between June 5 and 12. Cassairt's orders specified him to scout along the three principle north-south waterways of hilly Douglas County—Beaver Creek, Big Creek, and the North Fork of the White River. Near Mountain Home the patrol came across and captured guerrillas a couple at a time, two of them belonging to Confederate Colonel John T. Coffee's command. On the return trip during a heavy rainstorm the night of June 10/11 two of the captive guerrillas bolted for freedom and the troopers killed one while the second escaped. In the excitement one of the Federals accidentally shot and critically wounded another of the prisoners thinking the man was part of the escape, and the patrol left this man behind when they rode on in the morning. The patrol learned from the prisoners and residents that 40 bushwhackers had been in east Douglas County before the patrol's arrival but rode east toward Salem before only the day before the Federals arrived. They also learned that Confederate Brigadier General Shelby was in command of the Rebels of north Arkansas and planned a raid toward Rolla, and that Confederate Colonel Sidney D. Jackman with 300 men was then in the Sylamore Mountains in northwest Arkansas.

This information matched similar information Federal forces were receiving from other scouts and informants.[50]

Guerrilla Raid in Greene County

Even small numbers of guerrillas could bedevil Union forces, as a handful of bushwhackers proved in or near Greene County for several days in June. The Federals had a large, active garrison at Springfield, county seat of Greene County, so any southerners who operated in this immediate area were daring indeed. Some Rebels attacked a small group of unprotected, private freight wagons on the main road from Rolla to Springfield in about Greene County June 9 or 10. Union Captain Richard C. Chitwood took a patrol of 8th Cavalry MSM from the Springfield garrison in pursuit; killed two guerrillas; and recaptured 80 pounds of coffee, "quite a large amount of dry goods," and two horses. The weight and bulk of the stolen cargo may have slowed the bushwhackers' ability to outrun Chitwood's patrol and cost two of them their lives.[51] Sometime in June two unidentified Union soldiers paid with their lives for straggling from their unit along a road not far from the old Wilson's Creek battlefield of 10 August 1861 near present-day Republic in southwest Greene County. Guerrillas caught the pair separated far from their comrades, took them to the nearby woods, killed them, and took their shoes.[52] Two bushwhackers named Seely and Hanly escaped from the jail at Springfield the night of June 13/14. The Union district commander, Brigadier General John B. Sanborn, warned one of his subordinate commanders at Mt. Vernon, county seat of Lawrence County to the west, about the escape, so these two may have originated from that area. Sanborn specifically called Seely and Hanly "murderers," so perhaps it was they who had killed the two hapless soldiers for their shoes and were subsequently captured, but this is only conjecture.[53]

At the end of June unidentified guerrillas about 9 o'clock in the evening robbed blacksmith F. H. Cornogs at or near his home outside Ozark in central Christian County. A few days later the Union district headquarters quizzed the local commander at Ozark, Captain Jackson Ball of the 6th Provisional EMM, why he failed to pursue the robbers. Captain Ball vehemently replied that he only heard of the robbery at three that next morning, whereupon he led a pursuit of 20 militiamen who tracked the bushwhackers 20 miles and turned back only when they realized they were not gaining on the fast-moving Rebels. Captain Ball may also have been embarrassed about this incident since Cornogs' son Hiram just joined the local company of the 72nd EMM (Ball's former command) there in Ozark May 1. Ball was also justifiably frustrated that Rebels could rob a family of northern sympathy that close to him and get away without suffering loss.[54]

Band of Union Deserters Stealing Stock in Ozark County

On July 1 the Springfield headquarters of the District of Southwest Missouri ordered the Federal commander at Cassville, Barry County, to investigate a report they received that a band of eleven Union military deserters, including a Samuel Haskins, based in the White River hills was stealing horses from Missouri farms, trading them for cattle across the border in Arkansas and selling the cattle to farmers in Missouri. The census and military records associate Samuel C. Haskins with Ozark County, while this report states that these privateers were selling the cattle two counties to the west on Crane Creek in Stone County. This points to a criminal enterprise stretching across at least three counties and two states. This case is part of guerrilla warfare because an organized band of armed military deserters used their military skills and experience to prey upon a weak populace in a land temporarily without civil law, and, in effect became another military force in this area.[55]

Rebel Traveling Group Led by J. Frank Gregg Formerly of Quantrill's Command

A traveling band of about 25 Quantrill band members passed through this region in early July 1864 on their way back from the South to west-central Missouri. Union military reports indicated the leader was J. Frank Gregg, and the Federals chronicled this band's exploits as they rode north eventually to Lafayette County. The band chose this unlikely route so they could cross the wide obstacle of the Osage River at the well-known Duroc Ford in east-central Benton County. They told this to a local man forced to guide them partway who later escaped. Federals first found this band near Hartville, Wright County, July 9 when members of the newly organized 16th Missouri Cavalry (formerly 6th Provisional EMM) fought them there and killed one outright and mortally wounded four more of the guerrillas at no evident loss to the troopers. The cavalry also captured firearms, saddles, blankets, and other items, and continued to track the bushwhackers through northeast Webster County. These Federals turned back when another Union cavalry unit took up the Rebels' northbound trail across Laclede County.[56]

Union Veterans Fight Guerrillas in Douglas, Taney, and Wright Counties

During the third week in July some of the Yankee patrols of the new 15th and 16th Missouri Cavalry Regiments fought with bushwhackers in Douglas, Taney, and Wright Counties. About July 17, 18, or 19 Captain James H. Sallee's company somewhere in Douglas County fought an unidentified guerrilla band of about 30 men. Many of Sallee's men were veterans of over three years of fierce guerrilla warfare of this area, having served in home guards, then the 73rd EMM, and then the 7th Provisional EMM before serving in Company B of the 16th. This background was key to their killing 14, or about half of this Rebel band, and capturing a number of horses. There seem to be no other accounts of this victory by hardened local soldiers.[57] About the same time a few miles to the southwest, a patrol of 15th Missouri Cavalry led by Captain Phillip Rohrer killed four more bushwhackers along Cane Creek in central Taney County east of the county seat of Forsyth.[58] On July 22 elements of the 16th fought a skirmish with unidentified southerners somewhere in Wright County to the north, but no other details remain of this action.[59]

Guerrillas Active in Laclede County During August

Mrs. Lizzie Gilmore at Lebanon, county seat of Laclede County, wrote in a letter to cousins that guerrillas were active five miles from town on August 7. She heard they shot an unnamed older man in the face and chest, and wondered if the man's wounds would be fatal. She confided in her letter about the bushwhacker conflict in her area "both parties do all kinds of meanness that they can think of but little good." Since Mrs. Gilmore's husband was at that time with the Union army in Georgia, this seems a strong condemnation of the Union forces in the area as well as the southern partisans.[60]

Tracy Attempts Raid on Hartville

During the evening of August 11 Confederate Lieutenant Colonel Jesse H. Tracy led about 100 to 150 riders of Colonel Edward T. Fristoe's Arkansas cavalry regiment in what apparently was a raid on the garrison of the 16th Missouri Cavalry at Hartville, county seat of Wright County. Tracy's raiders approached Hartville from Texas County to the east, but the veterans of the 16th were alert and drove the Rebels south toward the Arkansas line with losses of one killed and three wounded and no Union casualties. Fristoe's regiment was composed of inexperienced recruits, so Tracy may have been giving part of the regiment some combat experience, perhaps with the hope that they could overwhelm the Hartville garrison and bring away some badly needed firearms. Tracy's raid showed the vulnerability of the isolated Yankee posts in this wooded, rolling countryside, but the outcome could have been much worse for the Yanks.[61]

Between August 15 and 24 elements of the Union 6th Missouri Cavalry and 1st and 2nd Arkansas Cavalry fought unidentified Rebels somewhere in southwest Missouri and northwest Arkansas, but no details remain. Perhaps these Federals fought with Tracy's riders after the Hartville raid.[62]

The guerrillas in Laclede County mentioned earlier in the month by Mrs. Gilmore in her letter were evidently still active somewhere in the Laclede County area between August 20 and 27. A Lebanon weekly newspaper reported that guerrillas about that time killed Laclede County man Isaac Whitson in the area. Whitson's military record shows he joined Captain D. A. W. Morehouse's Laclede County citizen guards company only a few days before on August 1, and his joining the guards may have prompted the bushwhackers to kill him.[63]

Union Militia Fights Confederate Regulars in Polk County

On August 28 Captain Samuel W. Headlee and his patrol of 15 troopers of the 16th Missouri Cavalry garrisoned at the village of Fair Grove in northeast Greene County fell upon a Confederate Captain Pace and seven Rebel recruiters riding northbound in Polk County. The Federals killed Pace and one southerner, wounded another, and captured one of the group, all at no northern loss. Captain Headlee was surprised that all eight of the Confederates were in the full uniform of Rebel regulars—a rarity in Missouri's guerrilla warfare. When the Yanks asked the sole prisoner about his mission, he lightly retorted that "they were going north to take part in the election" in early November. The prisoner's remark was only partly in jest, because Confederate Major General Price was timing his coming Missouri raid partly to disrupt northern election hopes, if his forces could disrupt the Union hold on Missouri enough. The southern hope was that the Democrat's peace candidate could win more support if the South seemed unbeatable. The Union report of this skirmish mentioned that Captain Pace was from St. Joseph. However, the Yanks also recovered letters Pace carried from Rebel soldiers of Colonel Robert Lawther's 10th Missouri Cavalry (CSA) intended for family and friends in Jefferson Township of north-central Cole County and perhaps other places.[64]

Thus ended a summer season of desultory fighting in the southwest quadrant of Missouri. Although this region was the scene of a steady tempo of guerrilla fighting all summer, the pace was less than that of other parts of the state and even of previous summers in this same area. Much of the coming and going of Confederate recruiters and bushwhackers here had been preparatory to Rebel Major General Sterling Price's long-expected invasion of Missouri that would begin late in September. However, this autumn incursion would take place in southeast Missouri and would only cross the southwest corner of the state as Price's army in defeat retreated through here on their way back to Arkansas.

Fourteen

June Through Mid-July 1864 in Northeast Missouri

The Federal reverses in the Red River Campaign in Louisiana and in Arkansas during the spring of 1864 ultimately led large numbers of Missourians in the Confederate army to ride north back to their home state in time for summer operations, particularly in areas of strong southern sympathy. Both Confederate recruiters and guerrillas returned to the northeast quadrant of the state in numbers this region had not seen since the ambitious campaigns of 1862. This new resurgence was partly to prepare for the long-awaited Missouri liberation by the state's former governor, Confederate Major General Sterling Price, now in charge of the Rebels in Arkansas, and whose home was in Chariton County in this part of Missouri. One of this region's most accomplished behind-Union-lines southern recruiters, Colonel Caleb Dorsey, returned to this part of the state in early June, and capable guerrilla chief Captain Clifton D. Holtzclaw was already here with his band. Both leaders, in their own way, were prepared to challenge Union occupation of this part of the Show-Me State. More were coming, too.

Detective Terman's Murder Spree in Chariton County During Early June 1864

Southerners needed little encouragement to oppose the occupation of northwest Missouri by Union troops this year, but an unprincipled Federal detective conducted his own crime spree in Chariton County during early June that served to further incite secessionist thought. Northern frustration at the inability to win a clear victory over the irregular Rebel forces in this state caused many Union soldiers and northern civilians to turn more and more to radical thought and action. An extreme example of such misdirected frustration was U.S. Detective J. W. Terman, alias "Harry Truman," who perverted his Federal authority to conduct a murder, arson, and robbery spree in Chariton County in early June, often riding drunk with his mistress in a carriage escorted always by a strong bodyguard of Federal troops. Ohio-born Terman had served as a teenager in a distinguished Texas military unit during the Mexican War, and as a "Free State" advocate in the "Bleeding Kansas" struggles of the 1850s had become an ardent opponent of the proslavery southerners. This adventurer turned his daring, experiences, and prejudices into support of the Union cause as an aggressive plain clothes detective of the "radical" stripe, and, as such, developed information about certain southern civilians in Chariton County who posed as loyal, innocent citizens while secretly supporting southern guerrillas. During Terman's subsequent trial, testimony revealed that his earlier undercover work for Major General Rosecrans infiltrating the Order of American Knights may have won Rosecrans' endorsement for Terman's crazy scheme to root out hidden bushwhacker supporters in Chariton County. Trial testimony later revealed that Rosecrans' Department of the Missouri gave Terman wide latitude and an imprecise mission, but with sufficient official backing that at the Union garrison of Macon City Lieutenant Colonel Daniel Draper of the 9th Cavalry MSM ordered Sergeant Thomas J. Wesley and 23 troopers to consider "Captain Harry Truman" as chief of scouts and detectives and do whatever he told them to do. At Terman's trial Sergeant Wesley testified that Draper specified that they were "placed under Capt. Truman—to obey him in every respect as we would one of the officers of our own regiment ... that we were going out with the prisoner as scouts, and probably we would have some rough work to do, and if we were ordered to kill a man to do it." Terman was also given some local citizen guards to do his bidding, and local authorities instructed all his men to wear civilian clothes for their mission with "Captain Truman." By late May 1864 so many Rebel guerrillas were infiltrating into all parts of Missouri that the Union authorities were becoming desperate to stem the tide. This was a recipe for abuse of power, which soon became obvious as Terman's murderous work began.[1]

All of Terman's depredations in this area in June 1864 may never be known, cloaked as they were with official backing, and conveniently forgotten by an embarrassed command overwhelmed by the influx of large numbers of irregular Rebels in this region. The trial transcript mentioned that his campaign lasted about three weeks, and Terman himself reported afterwards in his usual exaggerated style that it ran "through the counties of Howard, Boone, Randolph, and Chariton." It appears Terman used Bucklin, on the railroad in southeast Linn County, as a base and operated mainly in Chariton County. Although his trial specified the murder by hanging or shooting of eight separate Chariton County men, as well as nine counts of robbery, twelve counts of larceny-mostly stolen horses-and one count of arson, these were only in Chariton County. Local sources repeated some of the same eight names mentioned in Terman's trial, but also a number of other Chariton County men not listed in court, and noted that most of his victims were unarmed older men.

The guerrillas' own postwar chronicler, former Confederate Major John N. Edwards, in his 1877 book, *Noted Guerrillas,* listed the names of six Howard County men Terman had killed there, but there appear to be no names of men he killed in Randolph or Boone Counties. Taken as a whole, Terman's controversial June campaign may have killed between 18 and 25 southern men in Chariton and Howard Counties. It is likely that local authorities did not introduce more victim identities at the trial in July at St. Joseph because citizens were distrustful and fearful of the same Union command that sent such a lawless expedition among them in the first place. To their credit, military and civil officials in north Missouri expressed outrage and indignation at the atrocities that citizens and local military people reported to them of the "Captain Harry Truman" debacle beginning in the first days of June. District commander Brigadier General Clinton B. Fisk, Governor Willard Hall, and an assortment of local officials and Union military leaders passed along sordid details of the campaign as they heard of them, but the exploding nature of increasing guerrilla warfare across the state prevented stronger corrective action. J. W. Terman was convicted at trial and sentenced to prison, and Major General Rosecrans and some of his staff suffered rightful humiliation in the eyes of national leadership for sponsoring Terman's half-baked scheme in the first place.[2]

Raids and Fights of Holtzclaw's Band Between June and July 15

Captain Clifton D. Holtzclaw and his bushwhacker band provided a strong southern reaction to Detective Terman's depredations. A Fayette, Howard County, newspaper reported that residents encountered twenty bushwhackers from Linn County near Glasgow in west Howard County in the waning days of May. Holtzclaw's men were mostly Linn Countians, and they operated in Howard County much of the spring of 1864, so residents there probably knew some of them. Unidentified Union troops sent to fight this band found them at the bridge near Rocheport in southeast Howard County the evening of June 1 and the Federals wounded two guerrillas for one of their men wounded.[3]

Holtzclaw's Keytesville Raid of 3 June

At sundown on June 3 fourteen members of Holtzclaw's band raided Keytesville, county seat of Chariton County. The band first attempted to round up all the men known for their northern sympathy at their respective homes, but E. A. Holcomb and his brother resisted with firearms and seriously wounded one of the bushwhackers. Several of the guerrillas then laid siege to the Holcomb residence for a while and, after assuring Mr. Holcomb they would not kill him, he surrendered to avoid harm to his house or other prominent northern sympathizers the band already held and were using as shields around the Holcomb house. Some townspeople of southern sympathy also intervened to convince the guerrillas not to harm anyone. Holtzclaw's men took firearms, horses, and other objects they desired from stores and homes, and the Holcombs and other town leaders paid ransom to the raiders to ensure the further safety of property and lives. The Rebels then destroyed some tax records at the county clerk's office and left, but most of the county's records had already been taken to Brunswick in southwest Chariton County for safekeeping. During the Keytesville raid Captain Holtzclaw set a pattern he would repeat in future raids of haranguing citizens about his men returning to mete out punishment to residents who abuse southern sympathizers and threatening vengeance against any community leaders who harass the families of southern soldiers and guerrillas. Such pointed speeches became a trademark of Holtzclaw raids. The bushwhacker leader spoke from personal conviction on these points since the previous August Federals of the 9th Cavalry MSM sent to arrest Holtzclaw's dad in Howard County killed him with a pistol shot in the head, allegedly by accident.[4]

Guerrillas Murder Northerners in Revenge for Terman's Murders of Southerners

On June 12 six young, "roughly dressed" but well-mounted bushwhackers four miles west of Laclede, south Linn County, robbed two citizens of firearms and cash, and then rode south toward Chariton County. These were probably also Clifton Holtzclaw's men.[5] Atrocity usually followed atrocity in a circle of violence in Missouri during guerrilla warfare, and the murders by U.S. Detective J. W. Terman created like violence. Judge Lucius Salisbury, Jr. of Prairie Township, south-central Chariton County, fled the county and telegraphed Union district headquarters that on the night of 13/14 June guerrillas, perhaps of Holtzclaw's band, murdered four of the judge's near neighbors for their northern sympathy.[6] The vengeful guerrillas returned to their grisly work the night of 15/16 June and murdered four more men of known northern sympathy, as Judge Salisbury also reported by telegraph to the Union district office, naming two of the victims.[7]

Holtzclaw's Laclede Raid on 18 June

Captain Holtzclaw next took his band of 15 bushwhackers on an ambitious raid of the railroad town of Laclede in south Linn County at 5 in the afternoon of June 18. This raid was not as successful as the raid on Keytesville had been June 3. The guerrillas had prior knowledge of details of the town, as they rode first to the post office and took control of the firearms kept there for the town's defense. As in Keytesville, Holtzclaw had his men line up many of the men of Laclede and the captain gave a threatening speech to these 50 or 60 men about the inadvisability of resisting southern forces, the retribution his band would perform on anyone harming southern people as had been done recently in Chariton County, his loathing of abolitionists, and a revelation that he had friends in Laclede who informed him of all that took place there. During his speech Holtzclaw's men in small groups first attempted to round up hiding and fleeing townspeople. A discharged Union veteran, David M. Crowder, fired his revolver out an upstairs window and seriously wounded guerrilla James Nave, although guerrilla return fire killed Crowder. Local attorney and owner of the drug store, John H. Jones, panicked at the shooting and ran from the raiders. When Jones refused repeated orders to stop they shot him dead in the street. After this, the raiders concentrated on taking what they desired from stores, although they wasted time unskillfully bashing locked safes with axes and sledgehammers. The raid was cut short by the distant whistle of an approaching westbound train which sent the bushwhackers scurrying for their horses. The raiders then rode south out of town carrying as plunder a large amount of dry goods and about $1,200 in cash. Several guerrillas took an open express wagon for their wounded comrade Nave and a quantity of the loot and drove it out of Laclede on the road along the railroad track.

Union Pursuit of Holtzclaw's Band

Unbeknownst to Holtzclaw and his men, two townsmen had escaped when the raiders first rode into town, traveled the six to eight miles east to the town of Brookfield, and alerted the small Union garrison there led by Lieutenant David M. Lewis of the Linn County citizen guards. Lewis and his few men climbed on the locomotive of the westbound train and prepared to do battle with the raiders. The citizen guards did not see most of the raiders ride south toward Chariton County, but they soon caught up to the guerrillas in the appropriated express wagon bouncing along the road next to the track. Shooting from the speeding locomotive, Lewis' men killed one Rebel outright, mortally wounded Nave with another bullet, and seriously wounded a third bushwhacker in the wagon. Sadly, the guards' fire also badly wounded the express

Union troops used their control of the railroad for rapid pursuit of Clifton Holtzclaw's guerrillas after the Laclede raid (The Werner Company, *The Story of American Heroism*, 1896, p. 83).

driver the guerrillas had forced to drive the wagon. Amid the hail of bullets the two guerrillas still able to ride cut the wagon horses from the traces and rode them south to safety, abandoning their shot-up companions and a large collection of loot from the raid. Lieutenant Lewis had the train take his small command into Laclede where he quickly organized a pursuit from citizen guards there. Lieutenant Lewis and his new posse tracked the remainder of Holtzclaw's band into northeast Chariton County over the next day or two where he arrested some residents of southern sympathy who attempted to steer the Yankees from the true path Holtzclaw's raiders took. In all, Holtzclaw lost about one quarter of his band in and after the Laclede raid, and his battered command barely escaped the hornet's nest of angry northerners the raid stirred. Holtzclaw took the remnant of his band back to Howard County, his prewar home, for operations there over the next few weeks.[8]

Two Unidentified Guerrillas Race Through Brunswick

Two bushwhackers who may have been part of Holtzclaw's band created a stir in south Chariton County on June 22 and 23, a couple of days after the Laclede raid pursuit ended. The pair wore Federal uniforms and crossed the Missouri River from Saline County on the ferry into the town of Brunswick the evening of June 22. As the ferry touched the shore the pair forced a fellow passenger to trade his "very fine mare" for one of their horses, and then dashed through town with drawn revolvers. The galloping pair encountered two troopers of the 9th Cavalry MSM riding on one horse, and fired on them ten or twelve times, shooting the horse in the head and slightly wounding one of the soldiers before riding quickly out of town.[9] On the following day it was probably this same guerrilla pair that robbed a man on the road somewhere north of Brunswick.[10]

Two Small Actions in Howard County on 1 and 3 July

Six miles south of Fayette, Howard County, on July 1 a sergeant's detail of 15 troopers of 9th Cavalry MSM out gathering forage for their garrison's horses ran into Holtzclaw's band which had been spending the morning on the Henry Miller farm. After the brief meeting engagement the Federals claimed they killed two guerrillas and wounded another at the loss of one trooper killed and another wounded. The cavalry reported Holtzclaw now had 25 riders, which, if true, meant more men joined his band after they returned operations to Howard County.[11]

Late in the evening of July 3 four guerrillas probably of Holtzclaw's band captured and then mortally wounded a discharged soldier named Brashears from Linn County who had been visiting his Howard County relatives and was evidently on his way home. The keeper of the Howard County Poor Farm, three or four miles from Fayette, heard the shots and found Brashears lying with two head wounds and his hands tied behind his back. The keeper of the Poor Farm was attempting to transport Brashears to town for treatment when the wounded man expired. Locals conjectured that the four bushwhackers may have followed Brashears to Howard County from Linn County watching for a chance to catch him in a vulnerable moment.[12]

Holtzclaw's Band Raids Franklin and Rocheport on 4 or 5 July

Apparently it was also Holtzclaw's band that raided both villages of Franklin in south-central Howard County and Rocheport in west-central Boone County the same day—either July 4 or 5. New Franklin residents counted 13 or 14 raiders who liberally took from the two stores and tied a U.S. flag to one of their horse's tail and dragged it through the street. The raiders also denounced the Franklin postmaster for being an employee of Abraham Lincoln's. Besides the flag, they took only store goods and harmed no person. The same men rode the few miles east to rob Rocheport the same day. A few bushwhackers lined up a number of citizens in the street while other guerrillas robbed the stores—in the manner that Holtzclaw's men usually raided a town. Here, the raiders took what they wanted not only from stores but from residents and broke open some safes, too. Again, the Rebels harmed no person. After the raiders left, the merchants of Rocheport decided they had been robbed enough, and shipped their remaining goods to St. Louis on the eastbound steamer *T. L. McGill*. On July 6 nineteen different guerrillas raided Rocheport a second time, taking money and threatening men who had been militia members earlier in the war. Evidently, it was this second group of bushwhackers that also raided Franklin again on the evening of July 7. Residents there mentioned that this group was led by Bob Stapleton of a Howard County family. Residents recognized several of all the raiders as "idle young men of Howard and Chariton counties, who have taken to this mode of life recently." Perhaps Holtzclaw and Stapleton had a disagreement, or maybe the two groups preferred to operate independently.[13]

Holtzclaw's Band Abducts Prominent Northerners Then Loses Them 9 July

Captain Holtzclaw and his fifteen men found very tempting a well-publicized meeting Union district commander, Brigadier General Clinton B. Fisk, held with local citizen authorities at the Howard County seat of Fayette the evening of July 9. The purpose of the meeting was to raise a Howard County chapter for citizens' self defense against guerrillas, in accordance with Major General Rosecrans' June 28 General Orders Number 107, calling for counties to hold such meetings and organize themselves with Federal help. Three miles west of the meeting, Holtzclaw's bushwhackers set an ambush and captured one group of notable Howard County residents led by Colonel Clark H. Green of the 46th EMM as they rode horses and carriages back from the meeting toward Glasgow. The guerrillas quickly realized that the general was not in this group and placed guards about their prisoners to await the bigger prize. About an hour later,

Union Captain Henry S. Glaze's Company H, 9th Cavalry MSM, operated mostly in Howard and Boone Counties during the summer of 1864 (private collection, courtesy of the late Bob Younger and Mary Younger and Andy Turner).

General Fisk rode along the same road escorted by Captain Henry S. Glaze's company of 9th Cavalry MSM. Just before the general's detail approached the ambush site, a lady who lived nearby and had observed the earlier captures stepped forth and warned the Yankees about the bushwhackers ahead of them. Captain Glaze decided to ambush the ambushers and led his troopers in a wide arc that outflanked Holtzclaw and his men. In the shooting that followed, Holtzclaw's men released the captives in order to concentrate their aim on the cavalry and their own survival. Among the wounded of both sides was a young guerrilla teenager mortally wounded, and a Rebel bullet gave Captain Glaze a flesh wound in his arm. The bushwhacker guarding Colonel Green wounded the colonel badly in his arm before dashing off into the brush. The Union side was fortunate not to suffer more hurt in this fight. Although Holtzclaw failed to strike a mortal blow against his enemy, he once again proved he was a wily, imaginative opponent, eager to take the battle to his enemies. Within the next few days other equally daring guerrillas rode into this region and Holtzclaw began operating in concert with other bands in more mobile warfare across a wider area.[14]

Actions of Dorsey's Recruiters and Guerrilla Bands in "Little Dixie" Between June and July 15: Perkins, Bryson, Purcell, Tom Todd

Colonel Caleb Dorsey of Pike County was one of the most successful behind-Union-lines Confederate recruiters throughout the Civil War in northeast Missouri, taking southern men from there to the Rebel army in Arkansas during four years of the war.[15] Much of Dorsey's success inside Union-occupied Missouri derived from the stealth with which his command recruited and lived—avoiding contact with Union troops and relying on southern civilians for logistics needs. Dorsey, with a recruiting cadre of 112 to 125 trusted men traveled back to this region in late spring of 1864 from Arkansas across southwest Missouri operating with this same practiced stealth, as described in Chapter Seven. In late May or early June Dorsey brought his well-traveled command across the Missouri River into Boone County. Already in this region were some Rebel recruiters and scores of guerrillas who traveled this spring through great Union hazards across southeast Missouri to this quadrant of the state. A number of them gravitated to Colonel Dorsey's recruiting operation across several counties to the extent that in present day it is almost impossible to determine who traveled to northeast Missouri with Dorsey and who came on their own. Among Dorsey's cadre in northeast Missouri during 1864 were Colonel Caleb Perkins of Randolph County, Captain George W. Bryson of Boone County, Captain Young A. Purcell of Audrain County, Captain Tom Todd of Howard County, Captains Elliott D. Majors and Frank Davis of Monroe County, and Captain Miles Price of Montgomery County. Captain Clifton D. Holtzclaw operated with Dorsey's command, too, after Colonel Dorsey's command arrived in the region. These leaders were veterans of regular and irregular Confederate service, but not all kept to Colonel Dorsey's hidden tactics and discrete operational style. Dorsey's recruiting command extended loosely across Boone, Callaway, Audrain, Monroe, Howard, and Randolph Counties, which after the war was considered part of a region of such profound southern adherence that people nicknamed a large portion of northeast Missouri as "Little Dixie."[16]

Union Spy's 9 June Intelligence Report

One of the first indications the Union authorities had that such a large Rebel recruiting command was north of the Missouri River came from the report of a spy named William Jones. Jones on June 9 contacted four of Colonel Caleb Perkins' men in east Howard County looking for horses, and he discovered that this quartet was part of Perkins' own recruiting command of 65, then in the Perche Hills of west-central Boone County—a neighborhood of strong southern sympathy. Perkins of Randolph County led southern men from that county in the early months of the war in the Missouri State Guard, and he had recruited men from this region each year of the war.[17] These men evidently kept from Jones the information that the total Confederate recruiting party was twice what they stated. The four Confederates told the spy that they were "just in from Price's army," and had crossed the Missouri River into northeast Missouri on June 7. This spy also confirmed that Colonel Sidney D. Jackman, who had bedeviled the Union military in this same area the previous year, did not return this year, but was far away commanding his own military unit. The spy Jones also pinpointed the military mission that General Price had for the Missouri guerrillas this summer and fall, which was destroying railroads between St. Louis and St. Joseph at the proper time to prevent the Federals from concentrating their military force when Price would bring his army into Missouri. Whether Union authorities believed Jones' report or not, this astute spy handed the Union side valuable, accurate intelligence.[18]

Conflicting Intelligence Reports

However, the Federals received a bewildering variety of spy and other intelligence reports whose credibility ran the gamut from the ridiculous to the very useful. On June 10 a Union provost marshal at Fulton, Callaway County, passed along a report he received that there were 400 Rebels in that county, which was a vast exaggeration.[19] The Yanks' intelligence problem with the guerrilla war in Missouri had changed from a lack of information early in the war to 1864 when a flood of contradicting, often inaccurate reports and rumors frequently bewildered the decision makers. Adding credence to the spy Jones' report was a similar message to the Union authorities that northern sympathizer Clark H. Green of Glasgow, west Howard County, sent just a few days later on June 23, based on assertions he was hearing from southern sympathizers of the area. Clark repeated Jones' assertion that "the railroads in North Missouri are to be crippled, and, while Shelby is raiding, Price is to move secretly for Saint Louis" and added the ominous note that "the leaders are in the country and are getting encouragement from residents." Not only did Green's information match Jones, but what they outlined weeks later turned out to be much of the true plan for General Price's invasion of Missouri.[20]

Rebel Prisoners Escape From Mexico Jail

About June 13 or 14 an uncertain number of Rebel prisoners at Mexico, Audrain County, escaped from their Union jailers, although details are lacking. The northern troops commonly held captured guerrillas and Rebel recruiters in small town jails for short periods, and throughout the war in this area there was a spate of such escapes that embarrassed the Federals.[21]

Colonel Perkins' Publicity Stunt

Union authorities were perturbed to receive a late report June 21 that during the second week of the month Colonel Caleb Perkins appeared in the town of Middle

Grove, southwest Monroe County, in his full Confederate uniform—in the middle of Union-occupied Missouri! Perkins was shrewd enough to perform this stunt in a town of predominant southern sympathy, and it undoubtedly enhanced his recruiting mission. His performance also demonstrated the weak hold the Union forces had on "Little Dixie" even so late in the war. Obviously, Perkins' recruiting tactics differed a bit from Colonel Caleb Dorsey's stealthy approach.[22]

Bryson Captures Wagonload of EMM Firearms and Munitions

On June 17 one Rebel recruiter found a target too tempting to ignore and struck. Confederate Captain George W. Bryson, a Boone Countian and veteran of the Vicksburg Siege, was recruiting at the John Barnes home of north Boone County when he learned that a small detail of Union soldiers unloaded a shipment of firearms and ammunition from a railroad car at Centralia, not far away, and were taking the shipment in a horse-drawn wagon south toward Columbia on the main road. Bryson rapidly mounted his men, raced to an excellent ambush site, and shot up the Union detail as they rode along. The detail was Major Frank D. Evans of the local 61st EMM and five troopers of the 9th Cavalry MSM—all that Evans could get in Columbia on short notice—and a civilian driving a borrowed wagon. The Rebel shooting wounded two troopers and unhorsed a third man, sending one of the wounded and the unhorsed trooper escaping into the brush. Major Evans took what was left of his escort and attempted to escape toward Columbia, but the wagon horses were wounded and the Union soldiers were forced to abandon the wagon three miles from the ambush site and escape to town to get help. Evans was disgusted to discover there were no Union troops at Columbia when he arrived, and he was forced to abandon any thoughts of pursuit. Meanwhile, Captain Bryson and his men took possession of the Yankee shipment of 50 shotguns and several cases of ammunition that was intended to arm the newly formed Boone County General Orders Number 107 citizen guards unit, but instead would arm Bryson's Confederate recruits. Ironically, Captain Bryson decided he did not want all of the purloined shotguns so his men burned the wagon and fourteen of the firearms with it. The Jefferson City *State Times* newspaper complained sarcastically that "if it is deemed expedient to lose a cargo of guns, we know of no better method than to send them through Boone county with a weak guard." When the Federals sent a replacement shipment of the lost weapons and ammunition a few days later, they sent it this time to Jefferson City, and carried it to Columbia with a sizable escort.[23]

On the evening of June 19 two Rebels came to the house of the township constable, Wilhare Sorrell, in Prairie Township of southeast Randolph County and demanded supper. Sorrell told them his wife was sick and that he could not feed them, whereupon, the pair said they were going to take Sorrell's horses. As they walked toward the stable Sorrell fired upon the Rebels and they shot and wounded him in two or three

No. 345.

Double-barreled shotgun (Schuyler, Hartley, and Graham, *Illustrated Catalogue of Arms and Military Goods*, 1864, p. 127).

places and left. Although the two Rebels told Sorrell's neighbors that they had killed him, he survived.[24]

Bryson's Ill-Fated Mexico Raid

Captain Bryson and his men, buoyed by their successful hijacking of the weapons shipment north of Columbia on June 17, a few days later met with reverse while trying to raid Mexico, the county seat of Audrain County to the northeast. While Bryson was maneuvering his men in small groups to surround the town, unidentified northern troops discovered the threat and attacked before the Rebels were ready, seriously wounding Bryson. His upset men cancelled the attack and withdrew, taking their wounded captain to some known southern sympathizers not far away who oversaw the captain's medical needs and over the next several weeks nursed Bryson back to health.[25]

Purcell Leads Bryson's Band into Rougher Activities

Apparently, Captain Young A. Purcell took over command of Bryson's small company near Mexico. Purcell of Audrain County had been active in this area as a recruiter and guerrilla chieftain the previous two years, so Bryson's men were in capable hands. Purcell operated more as a guerrilla chieftain than a regular recruiter, as he enjoyed fighting and seemed to disdain the style of quiet, hidden recruiting that others were performing in the region. Further, Purcell was less inclined to make his men conform to the rules of war and respect the noncombat status of civilians. A Federal detective, T. J. Stauber, sent to the Missouri provost marshal general a detailed study of Purcell's band's depredations during June 23, 24, and 25 in Audrain County. Stauber chronicled how the Rebels ate with sympathetic citizens but stole what they needed from northern sympathizers—particularly the families of men away serving in the Union army. The detective described how the raiders singled out the family of a Sanders who left the area shortly before after receiving death threats. Stauber wrote that they "pilfered his house, broke up his furniture, took and destroyed the clothing of his children, and abused his wife." Purcell's men also stripped the farm of Captain Martin E. Swift of the 61st EMM of many items, and then Purcell "ordered several of his men to 'finish the work,'" whereupon these Rebels turned from loading the plunder on their mounts with revolvers in their hands. Unarmed Captain Swift then believed these men meant to kill him and ran for his life and escaped but with two bullet wounds. Purcell's terror tactics may have been intended to drive northern sympathizers away from southern neighborhoods to lessen the likelihood of citizens informing on him to the Federals. Detective Stauber indicated that Purcell's gang then rode for the noted Rebel sanctuary of the "Blackfoot Region" in the Perche Hills in west-central Boone County. He also wrote that Purcell's band belonged to the command of Colonel Caleb Dorsey, then headquartered near Goodwin's Mill in southeast Monroe County.[26]

Six Unidentified Guerrillas Abuse Woman Near Allen

During the morning of June 30 six unidentified bushwhackers near Allen, east-central Randolph County, crudely robbed Mrs. Armand Price at home while her husband was away in the Union military. According to regional newspaper accounts, the six demanded money and took offense when Mrs. Price denied she had any. The men held the lady, striking her, whipping her with branches, and tearing off a portion of her clothes. The robbers then found over $100 Mrs. Price had hidden either on her person or in the house. Possibly, she sought to lessen her ordeal by telling these miscreants where they could find the cash, as the accounts do not specify how the Rebels finally came by the money. Before they left, these "gentlemen of the brush" set fire to some of Mrs. Price's finer dresses and part of the woods near her home. The St. Joseph newspaper reported also on June 30 a band of about twenty bushwhackers briefly raided the nearby town of Allen, but took little and did little damage. Since Rebel recruiters and guerrillas had heretofore honored the sanctity of women's privacy with very few exceptions, this attack on Mrs. Armand Price and other area females, if accurately reported, marked a loathsome turning point in Missouri's guerrilla war. These six raiders' behavior seemed similar to that of Captain Young A. Purcell's men in the Audrain County area a few days before, so these may have been of his band.[27]

Unidentified Guerrilla Band Raids Allen and Renick

These six Rebels were part of a band that also on June 30 performed light raids on the railroad towns of Allen and Renick. The distant St. Joseph newspaper reported only on the Allen raid, said the raiders numbered "about twenty," and did not take much. The St. Louis newspaper benefited from having a correspondent on the spot in Allen. This correspondent named two rural Randolph County residents that the raiders robbed of between five and six hundred dollars in one instance and of $150 in "greenbacks" in the second occurrence. Next, the unidentified guerrillas rode into Allen, but only robbed "an old man of twenty dollars—all he had" and took a double-barreled shotgun from someone else. The writer testified that the four men robbed were all "unconditional Union men," and that the raiders avoided two stores in town owned by southern sympathizers. The bushwhackers gave a short speech to some of the residents warning death to men who joined the local General Orders Number 107 citizen guard unit. Guerrilla chieftain Captain Clifton D. Holtzclaw was known to give such speeches when he raided communities, but Holtzclaw and his band were proven to be over thirty miles to the southwest in central Howard County the next morning. Since the actions of this band seemed similar to those of Purcell's band in Audrain County just a few days before, these were probably Captain Bryson's former men then commanded by Purcell. After riding south of Allen, these raiders rode by the village of Renick purposely showing themselves, but "they did not take anything nor interrupt anyone."[28]

An unidentified quartet of guerrillas on the evening of July 6 shot and critically wounded Indiana-born, young farmer Frank Ross who lived in the far northeast corner of Howard County close to the Boone County line. The Fayette newspaper that reported this incident gave few details, but the bushwhackers must have considered Ross a threat.[29]

Perkins' Public Speech at Dripping Springs

Meanwhile, Confederate recruiters and guerrillas were also active in several parts of Boone County in late June 1864. As mentioned earlier, recruiter Colonel Caleb Perkins seems to have made his headquarters in the notoriously southern community of Perche Hills of west-central Boone County, near a place called Dripping Springs. Sometime in late June Perkins called in area civilians to hear a speech at Dripping Springs. This sudden spate of public speaking by southern recruiters and guerrilla leaders mirrored their optimism that the liberation of Missouri from Yankee tyranny was not far off. Colonel Perkins told the crowd that his men "had a right to be here; that he intended to stay"; that he expected to have between 200 and 300 men in this neighborhood in just a few days; and that the local southerners needed to make an effort to feed all of his men. Union Colonel John F. Williams, the commander of the 9th Cavalry MSM, on an expedition in this area heard about and reported Perkins' speech.

Ironically, Williams countered with speeches of his own as he traveled through the countryside, advising residents to work together in the citizens guard advocated by the Department of the Missouri's General Orders Number 107 to defend their homes and communities from this onslaught of Rebels. Colonel Williams' expedition of 9th Cavalry MSM chased six mounted southerners in the Perche Hills but only managed to kill one of their horses and captured a led horse those riders had recently stolen and a firearm they dropped. Near Hallsville in northeast Boone County Union troops probably of the 9th Cavalry MSM chased more Rebels but with little success. Colonel Williams' complained that "they ride the best horses in the country, and when pursued, take to the brush and soon disappear. We will have to use strategy as well as pluck to get them."[30]

Union Colonel John F. Williams commanded the 9th Cavalry Missouri State Militia (private collection, courtesy of the late Bob Younger and Mary Younger and Andy Turner).

Tom Todd's Small Band Raids Boone County Villages

Guerrilla chief Captain Tom Todd was active in west Boone County at this time with less than a dozen bushwhackers. Prewar Tom Todd was a Baptist minister of Boone and Howard Counties, and as a guerrilla leader he was known for his long, red beard.[31] With only nine men Todd robbed stores in Rocheport the afternoon of June 27, taking about $125 worth of boots and clothing. It may have been Tom Todd's irregulars who took three horses from a farm at the village of Providence, just a few miles from Rocheport, the evening of June 28. That same night raiders, probably also of Todd's band, robbed a store at the small village of Everett in west Boone County of about $200 worth of goods.[32]

Handcock's Guerrillas and Others in Callaway, Montgomery, and Warren Counties Between June and July 15

Guerrillas were also active further to the east early this summer in Callaway, Montgomery, and Warren Counties. Most of these rode up from Arkansas through southeast Missouri this spring, and their only identifiable leader at that time was William Handcock. There is little in the surviving record to tell about Handcock, but it appears that he was born about 1836 and lived before the war in Osage County. During 1863 Handcock worked closely with brothers Joel Franklin Ramsey and Barton J. Ramsey from Franklin County. Those of the radical Rebel stripe such as Handcock and the Ramseys were forced to operate as exiles away from their home counties along the south bank of the Missouri River because the large German-American populations of Osage, Gasconade, and Franklin Counties strongly controlled that area for the Union. This is apparently the reason these three operated as guerrillas in Montgomery and

Warren Counties on the north bank of the Missouri River. Handcock may have been among a group of southern horsemen who raced through Hermann, north Gasconade County, on May 14 in a successful, daring maneuver to force their way across the Missouri River and enter neighborhoods of southern sympathy along the north bank, as described in Chapter Six.[33]

Several groups of unidentified Confederate recruiters and guerrillas made the perilous journey north from Arkansas, through southeast Missouri, and back across the Missouri River mostly in May 1864 to northeast Missouri to carry on their war there. They created a stir when they first made the difficult river crossing in small groups and raided isolated farms and small villages to obtain subsistence as they passed. As these bands of riders made their way into the interior, quiet returned to this region as they took a few days to rest and refit. All remained quiet in Montgomery and Warren Counties until the middle of June when black residents informed a Union patrol that there was a Rebel band near Pinckney, in south-central Warren County, although they could offer no details. Since this group committed no offense to northerners, this may have been a Confederate recruiting cadre busy bringing in men of southern sympathy.[34]

Handcock's Band Raids Big Spring in Montgomery County on 7 July

Area guerrillas gathered in the Williamsburg and Reedsville area of east-central Callaway County and began raiding July 7, led by Bill Handcock. This group of about 38 riders raided communities of northern sympathy along south Montgomery and Callaway Counties on that day. They first entered a settlement called Big Spring about eight miles northwest of Rhineland in south Montgomery County where they shot one farmer to death working in his field, wounded another man, stole a number of horses and robbed Charles Neidergerte's store there of about $3,000 in goods and cash. Neidergerte remained in the store while the looters were at work for a while, but wisely took no action to stop them even though several tried to deliberately provoke him. Neidergerte finally slipped out and escaped when he overheard some of the Rebels arguing the pros and cons of killing him.

Handcock's Band Raids Rhineland

The riders next raided the village of Rhineland about five miles and across the Missouri River from the Union garrison at Hermann while some guerrillas watched the roads for the arrival of the militia. A storeowner and another village resident ran the long distance to the river and swam to safety even while the raiders fired a number of shots after them. Most of the bushwhackers' firearms were shotguns and revolvers, effective only at short range, which prevented the shooters from hitting the fleeing men. The guerrillas took advantage of the merchant's absence to load up a quantity of his goods onto some of their horses and destroyed part of the rest.

Pursuit of Handcock's Band

Meanwhile, the two Rhineland escapees warned Captain Will T. Hunter at Hermann, and he mounted 22 troopers of his garrison of 3rd Cavalry MSM. This small Union force was delayed for a time because the ferryboat had to build up steam before it could cross to the north bank of the Missouri River. Accounts differ as to what happened next, but it seems Handcock's bushwhackers expected the Yanks to pursue them from Hermann, and they ambushed Hunter's patrol just after it landed on Montgomery County soil and drove the outnumbered Federals back some distance to the east. When

Hunter's troopers regrouped, the raiders were already riding west toward the southwest corner of Callaway County after other adventures. As the guerrillas rode along they plundered homes before a second Union patrol of the 9th Cavalry MSM from Fulton rode into view. Not wanting to be trapped between this new threat and Captain Hunter's patrol in his rear, Bill Handcock dispersed his band to find their way in small groups probably to a designated rendezvous point.[35]

Union authorities ordered Captain Hunter to continue the pursuit of the scattered guerrillas with his patrol of 3rd Cavalry MSM, apparently even after the patrol of the 9th from Fulton headed back to base. Thus far, Hunter's men had done little to stop Handcock's raid or avenge the victims. As the patrol searched the countryside on their way back to Hermann three miles west of Rhineland they captured one-armed, South Carolinian Colonel James Brewer and his teenage son James, Jr. Fifty-one-year-old Brewer had military experience before the Civil War and was instrumental in helping recruit and train area southerners in the first months of the war in this region. One of the Rhineland residents recognized the elder Brewer as one of the Rebels who raided the village in May 1863 and took part in a killing then. Since it seems that both Brewers had also been riding with Handcock's raiders on this day, too, Captain Hunter had them shot to death by the road. Locals later buried father and son and placed rails around the graves, which an 1885 Montgomery County history stated were still visible when that history was written.[36]

Guerrilla Actions in Mississippi River Counties Between June and Middle July: Dorsey, Shaw, and Others

Guerrilla warfare during the spring of 1864 had been active in the northeast Missouri counties along the Mississippi River because many of the southern irregulars there found refuge among southern sympathizers in the Illinois communities along the eastern bank of the river. Union authorities were confounded by political considerations that kept them from eliminating these sanctuaries, so the guerrilla activities in west bank communities continued into the summer of 1864, too. Furthermore, skilled Confederate recruiter Colonel Caleb Dorsey brought recruiting cadre here early this summer that met with some success, particularly in the Pike County area.

Union Leaders Send in Toughs from 7th Kansas Cavalry

Local Union decision-makers overcame the lack of northern troops in some of these counties by bringing in Kansas toughs from the notorious 7th Kansas Cavalry in late May and the first few days of June, as explained in Chapter Eight. This Kansas regiment was in St. Louis for just a few days being re-equipped before returning to hotter war fronts, and Union officers found some kind of incentive to send some of these combat veterans by boat to some river towns afflicted by pesky bushwhackers. As explained earlier, in the last days of May some of these hard-bitten troopers had worked off a "kill list" of 52 notorious southern sympathizers in Pike County killing seven or eight of them before being hurried out of the county as people began asking questions. Northern Missouri district commander, Brigadier General Clinton B. Fisk, notified his superiors at the Department of the Missouri on June 3 that the Seventh Kansas scout returned to Palmyra [Marion County] to-day. They mustered out 2 guerrillas." Fisk's message implies that in addition to the Kansans' earlier special work in Pike County, some of these troopers managed to kill two more southerners in Marion County, too.[37]

Southerners Break Guerrillas from Louisiana Jail

The secessionist cause was still very much alive two counties south in Pike County. About the middle of June southern sympathizers somehow stole the key to the Louisiana jail and released several guerrillas being held there. As mentioned in Chapter Eight, these southerners had attempted and failed in late April to break their friends out of this jail, but their persistence finally succeeded. Colonel Dorsey's Confederate recruiting command quietly rode into northeast Missouri in early June and recruited southern men in Pike County. Perhaps some of the recruiting cadre had a part in helping these men escape.[38]

During the evening of June 22 five unidentified, armed men robbed John M. True of $1851 as he traveled the road near Bowling Green in central Pike County. True was bringing home the money from trading stock in St. Louis. This may have been a simple case of highway robbery, but perhaps southern sympathizers knew their neighbor was taking stock away to sell and informed local guerrillas to watch for him. The Louisiana weekly newspaper editor believed the true robbery was the work of guerrillas. The secessionist cause deep inside Union-occupied Missouri needed money to operate, and Rebels often took it at gunpoint.[39]

Pike County Dilemma Caused by De-activation of 49th EMM

An exchange of letters in late June between responsible Pike County northern sympathizer William Fuller of Louisiana, the county seat, and Brigadier General Fisk emphasizes another crisis in that county. Fuller indicated that black people in Prairieville, southeast Pike County, reported Rebel recruiter Major Webb Shaw "was organizing a rebel company to make a raid on this place some night."[40] Fuller stressed that Pike County's only active Union troops had recently been relieved and disbanded. It seemed that Major General Rosecrans had in middle June called numerous local Enrolled Missouri Militia units to active duty. In Pike County, the general's call went to Captain Hiram Baxter and 60 enlisted men of the 49th EMM Regiment on June 17 who obediently began active duty in Louisiana. In their desperate belief that bushwhackers and Rebel troops may soon overwhelm them, these militiamen responded to the emergency with excess and committed a number of atrocities against known southern sympathizers, much as the Kansas cavalrymen perpetrated here in the last days of May. Apparently, local newspapers failed to or refused to report these acts, but Brigadier General Fisk shortly knew of them. However, other prominent area leaders appealed to Governor Willard Hall that:

1. There was not enough of a Rebel threat that required the service of the 49th EMM,
2. Baxter's men "were producing all the troubles there were in the county," and
3. Asked the governor to remove these militiamen from their midst as a menace.

The governor, previously a militia general of this region himself, ordered the Pike County militiamen returned to inactive status immediately, which they promptly obeyed. Ironically, in his June 25 letter to General Fisk, Mr. Fuller in his plea for troops to replace Captain Baxter's company even offered another alternative: "If we cannot have our own militia, send us a company of Kansas men. They are a perfect terror to all rebels around." The general did not honor this request, but he did promise to find some way to provide security to northern sympathizers of the county. This Pike County dilemma seems to ask the question that as the guerrilla war in this region began moving toward a deciding point off in the not-too-distant future, just how desperate would the two sides become to prevail over each other?[41]

Middle Summer in Northeast Missouri: Rising Southern Hopes and Growing Northern Fear

The guerrilla war that had renewed itself this spring of 1864 in northeast Missouri as a buried seed sprouts and pushes its stalk resolutely through the soil to daylight had by late June and early July come to full bloom. By this time the several Rebel recruiting bands and bushwhacker gangs in much of northeast Missouri seemed more than available Union troops could handle.

Union Detective's Accurate 30 June Intelligence Report

The astute Federal detective T. J. Stauber on June 30 submitted another insightful intelligence report to General Rosecrans' headquarters, with rather accurate concepts about where the Confederate irregulars operated. The detective could not always tell whose band was whose nor could he distinguish between recruiters and guerrillas—a problem the Union military had throughout the war in Missouri—but his findings correlate well with what little documentation remains of these southerners' activities. Stauber identified their base areas as the Perche Hills of northwest Boone County; much of Pike County; the area around Mexico in Audrain County; and peninsula-shaped Calhoun County, Illinois along the east bank of the Mississippi River where a number of southern combatants operated in self-imposed exile. The detective wrote that these secretive Rebels used northeast Missouri creek beds and river basins for movement between base areas and sanctuary neighborhoods, thus avoiding the roads watched by Union patrols and informants. He identified the most important of these "lines of movement" as Cedar Creek between Boone and Callaway Counties; Auxvasse Creek of Callaway County; the Cuivre River in Audrain, Montgomery, and Lincoln Counties; and the Salt River between Randolph, Marion, Ralls, and Pike Counties.[42]

Missouri's Union chief, Major General Rosecrans, had hoped that the northern forces under his command in the Show-Me State, depleted over the calm winter by demands to send troops to other war arenas, were sufficient to stem the rising Rebel tide with careful management and spirited leadership. As the numbers of southern forces in northeast Missouri grew with the progress of summer 1864, his doubts about the adequacy of his force in that quadrant grew, too. On July 6 Rosecrans lamented in a plea for more troops to Union army chief of staff Major General Henry W. Halleck that "all my cavalry force is operating against the numerous bands of rebels,

General Henry W. Halleck was at this time chief of staff under General Grant (Underwood and Clough, *Battles and Leaders of the Civil War*, vol. 1, 1887, p. 276).

which have come up from Price's army, and are now plundering, murdering, and robbing." His plans to mobilize citizen volunteer groups under his June 28 General Orders Number 107 to help stem local Rebel presence was too little and too late. EMM Brigadier General Joseph Douglass at Columbia sadly informed Rosecrans that the counties present-day Missourians still call "Little Dixie" "are mostly under the control of the enemy; that they are not even able to hold township and county meetings, as contemplated in ... General Orders Number 107, and plead for immediate assistance." With the full expectation of Missouri's southern population and much of the northern population that Confederate Major General Sterling Price was bringing his army to invade the state, the rest of the summer of 1864 in the northeast quadrant looked exciting indeed.[43]

Fifteen

Mid-July Through August 1864 in Northeast Missouri

By mid-summer 1864 large numbers of southern irregulars and an outnumbered, defending Union military in northeast Missouri were locked in a desperate struggle for mastery of the region. Their determination was made more acute with many, persistent rumors that former Missouri governor, Major General Sterling Price, and his army of thousands of Confederates in neighboring Arkansas were planning to invade the state in the approaching weeks. The gravity of this situation led many on both sides to violate the customary rules of warfare and commit atrocities on both each other and civilians who got in the way.

At this time Confederate recruiter Colonel Caleb Dorsey of Pike County and his cadre operated quietly mostly in Pike, Lincoln, St. Charles, Montgomery, and Warren Counties in the east part of this region. Confederate recruiter Colonel Caleb Perkins of Randolph County and his cadre worked with more ballyhoo mostly in Boone, Howard, and Randolph Counties to the west. Both commands seemed to share recruiting opportunities in Monroe and Audrain Counties. All these counties had large number of residents of southern backgrounds sympathetic to the South's cause, so that in postwar years the region around these counties was aptly nicknamed "Little Dixie." Other Rebel recruiters operated with varying degrees of success in the region, but Colonels Dorsey and Perkins attracted the most recruits.

The guerrilla bands of northeast Missouri were a mixed lot, and their status is confusing since a number of them also helped with Confederate recruiting, and casualties forced them to change leaders on occasion. A common rule of thumb to distinguish guerrillas from recruiters is that guerrillas preferred offensive action against Union troops and their supporters, whereas recruiters fought the Yanks only when necessary, as their war was located somewhere else. Both kinds of southern irregulars were forced at times to seize subsistence, horses, clothing, and weapons from civilians, since there were no Confederate sources for such things close at hand. However, guerrillas were more prone to violence and destruction when they robbed stores and homes. In this manner they often made up for their small numbers with intimidation and terror tactics.

The principle bushwhacker bands of northeast Missouri at mid-summer 1864 included William Handcock in Warren and Montgomery Counties; Clifton D. Holtzclaw in Howard, Chariton, Linn, and Boone Counties; Young A. Purcell in Boone and Audrain Counties; and Tom Todd in Howard and Boone Counties. A violent new guerrilla band rode into northeast Missouri in mid-July all the way from west-central Missouri.

Bill Anderson's First Campaign in Northeast Missouri Between July 15 and 31

Captain William T. Anderson led his band of 22 riders dressed in Yankee uniforms out of the west-central region of the state, where they left nine dead northern men in Carroll County, as described in Chapter 18, into northeast Missouri during the night of July 12/13. The gang raided here for nineteen days between July 13 and July 31, before they rode back to the west. Anderson brought his band to this region for a couple of reasons. First, as member Hamp B. Watts wrote in his 1913 memoir, the large number of aggressive Federal troops and the difficulty of obtaining sustenance for men and horses in the largely depopulated west-central region compelled Captain Anderson to lead his men to an operations area without those problems. Watts was not a member until later, but he was quoting what Anderson and the other men told him.[1] Second, Anderson spent his younger years in Huntsville, county seat of Randolph County, before his family moved to what is now Lyon County, Kansas in the 1850s. When Bill raided Huntsville he recognized and seemed to enjoy talking to old acquaintances. Since living in Huntsville his father, one brother, and one sister died, and another sister was maimed, so the man later known as "Bloody Bill" may have had happy memories of the Huntsville area from when his family was still intact. Captain Anderson kept his men on the move raiding most of the nineteen days they spent in northeast Missouri. His band generally traveled in Yankee blue uniforms in the mode of the west-central bushwhackers. These were tactics adopted to both deceive and confuse the Yanks. Heretofore, northeast Missouri bushwhacker bands remained close to their favored sanctuary areas, for the most part, and dressed in civilian clothes.[2]

The first recorded acts of violence Anderson's band committed in northeast Missouri in Chariton County included killing the man they forced to guide them as they left Carroll County, seizing horses from farms they passed, and badly beating two citizen guardsmen in the Porches Prairie region of southwest Chariton County on July 13. On July 14 the band rode on east and robbed a stagecoach three or four miles east of Salisbury in southeast Chariton County near the west Randolph County border. Anderson's band noted nothing unusual about the coach passengers, and after taking their valuables they rode on. Three of the guerrillas must have uncovered the full identity of one of the passengers to be Captain Henry Snyder of the local 35th EMM from some paper in his wallet they took, because this trio shortly returned to the coach. These bushwhackers pulled Snyder aside, and, in front of the other shocked people, shot him several times until he died.[3]

Bill Anderson Raids His Hometown 15 July 1864

Before daybreak on July 15 this bushwhacker band raided the Randolph County seat of Huntsville, Bill Anderson's former hometown. Throughout this raid Bill remained in his saddle, calmly directing his busy men with waves of his hand and curt orders as they herded the men into one bunch on the main street and went about their looting. The local Huntsville newspaper later commented that "Anderson lived in this place when he was a boy and showed some favors to one or two of his old school mates whom he recognized." This newspaper also commented about the guerrillas' demeanor that "their almost total abstinence from liquor was a subject of remark by all." And their weaponry: "They were the best armed men we have seen during the war, some of their belts swinging as high as eight navy revolvers, while the most of them were provided with revolving rifles."

Guerrilla George Maddox demonstrates how witnesses at the Huntsville raid described the raiders as carrying numerous pistols (National Park Service collection at Wilson's Creek National Battlefield, historian Connie Langum).

The only killing took place when all the raiders seemed busy breaking open safes and looting stores in the gloomy pre-dawn light. Mr. George Damon, a hotel guest from a St. Louis firm who the raiders had threatened, ran from the group of prisoners to escape, despite warnings from other townsmen. Anderson himself and a couple of his men followed, shot Damon down, and repeatedly fired into his prostrate form until he was dead. A few bushwhackers while looting pistol-whipped slow or balky storekeepers and clerks, but no other serious injuries resulted. The town newspaper tallied up the cash stolen to be over $45,000 and listed among the stolen items: four horses, saddles and tack, drugs, dry goods, seven firearms, and seven watches. There were 22 bushwhackers in all, although some sources state there were 35. The guerrillas spent two hours in Huntsville and could have taken more time if they would have known there were no Union troops in Randolph County at the time. Captain Anderson's band left on the Renick road to the southeast. Six miles south of town the raiders badly injured a Joel Smith while pistol-whipping him, took one or two horses from his farm, and possibly robbed others nearby. Captain Edward K. Smith with a patrol of his company of 9th Cavalry MSM from their Sturgeon garrison in north-central Boone County rode northwest in pursuit. They collided with Anderson's band ten miles south of Huntsville and chased the band four miles in which they claim to have wounded one Rebel. Then the bushwhackers' superior mounts pulled away from the Federals' jaded horses, ending the chase.[4]

The existing record is confusing about the actions of the Anderson gang during the next three days, except they turned south and rode across Howard County to the southern end by July 18. Colonel George H. Hall at Sedalia, regimental commander of the 4th Cavalry MSM, wrote on July 18 about a report he received from his Captain Joseph Parke, stationed at Boonville across the Missouri River from Howard County: "Captain Parke reports from Boonville that a large number of rebels are reported in Howard County. It is said 150 are drilling every day between Fayette and Franklin, and that Franklin was robbed yesterday."

Colonel Hall's boss, Brigadier General Egbert B. Brown at Warrensburg, mangled Captain Parke's message about Rebels "drilling daily" into Rebels "killing daily" when he wrote "Captain Parke ... reports 150 guerrillas in Howard County, killing daily, and that Franklin was robbed yesterday." First, it is unlikely that Rebels in Howard County were "killing daily," because various guerrilla bands had intimidated most of the rural northern sympathizers in that very southern county by July 1864 into either leaving the county altogether or moving into the larger towns of Fayette, Glasgow, or Roanoke whose small Union garrisons offered a modicum of protection. Colonel Hall's description about 150 Rebels "drilling daily" more closely matches the activity of Confederate Colonel Caleb Perkins' many recruits in hidden camps in the nearby Perche Hills and throughout parts of Howard County by this time, as mentioned in the previous chapter. Bushwhackers did not drill. That was one of the attractions for adventurous young southern men to join the guerrillas instead of the regular military. Young Hamp Watts of Howard County, one of the few chroniclers of Anderson's band, perhaps along with other local southern men joined Anderson's band in Howard County in July, and possibly did that now. Perhaps they had earlier joined the Confederate regulars under Colonel Perkins and grew disillusioned with all that drilling. Second, perhaps Anderson's band raided Franklin in south-central Howard County on July 17. No detailed documentation of this raid survives, so the raiders may have also been Holtzclaw's band, Tom Todd's band, or even recruits of Colonel Perkins command—all of whom were in the area at this time.[5]

Bill Anderson Raids Rocheport 18 July

Anderson's band entered the war-ravaged Missouri River village of Rocheport the morning of July 18, but did little damage. In fact, as the Columbia newspaper reported, the guerrillas remarked to some residents that "they were robbers and thieves, but didn't think they could take much from Rocheport as from appearance the place had been pretty well cleaned out before their arrival." Then some of the bushwhackers astounded locals by telling them that they already had plenty of money anyway, and showed off wallets and purses "crammed with greenbacks taken at Huntsville" on July 15. The chatty raiders also told townspeople that their aim in riding to Rocheport was to find boats there to cross to the south side of the river, but the Federals were controlling even the small craft to prevent just such a use. One of Anderson's lookouts alerted the band to the approaching southbound steamer *War Eagle,* built in Cincinnati in 1858. Anderson's band delighted in the sport of shooting at passing river steamers during the summer of 1863 while operating in Lafayette County, and the raiders lined up to prepare just such a reception for the side-wheeler *War Eagle*. Anderson's men could not know that in addition to regular packet trade along the Missouri River this vessel was also carrying Union Brigadier James Totten and his bodyguard of 15 soldiers on a tour of river towns in his capacity as inspector general for the Department of the Missouri. Therefore, when the guerrillas let loose a volley at the 223-foot-long *War Eagle,* Totten's escort fired one right back at them, toppling one probably wounded Rebel from his horse. In all, the guerrillas fired about thirty bullets at the steamer, inflicting no real damage, although a shot passed through a passenger's coat. Two miles downstream *War Eagle* stopped to warn the northbound 1857-vintage, Virginia-built *Minnehaha* and the 1858-vintage Cincinnati-built *Iatan* about the trigger-happy guerrillas at Rocheport. General Totten was delighted to see that these two side-wheelers were carrying Lieutenant Colonel Dennis J. Hynes and several companies of his 17th Illinois Cavalry on their way upriver to help strengthen the Federal presence in several garrisons. The general ordered the cavalry to mount up, deploy on the north shore, ride around to the rear of Rocheport, then sweep through the village and surprise the bushwhackers. They complied, but discovered the Rebels must have detected their presence and left.[6]

Anderson and his men were young and daring, but they were security-conscious and did not consider all of the Federals to be fools. Captain Anderson's self-preservation tactic seemed to be to leave a neighborhood immediately after a raid or skirmish. Just after the Rocheport raid this band probably rode back north to southeast Randolph County. Sometime on July 18 the Union Glasgow commander reported 22 guerrillas "passed within seven miles east" of town, and perhaps these were Anderson's gang.[7]

Bill Anderson Raids Railroad Towns of Renick and Allen

Bill Anderson's band somehow acquired a mission change and added to their numbers between their July 18 Rocheport raid and their next raid July 23 on Renick and Allen in Randolph County. Anderson's goal after leaving Carroll County July 14 seems to have been to visit his old hometown of Huntsville in Randolph County and then possibly to cross the Missouri River at Rocheport and raid in the counties on the south bank. As described earlier, there were no boats for the bushwhackers to use in south Howard County to cross this major river obstacle, and they received stiff answering fire from the riverboat they attacked. Then, from July 23 until Anderson led his band back to northwest Missouri July 31, his men aggressively attacked railroad infrastructure in northeast Missouri, a target in which they had not demonstrated interest previously. One possible explanation for this change is that Captain Anderson perhaps conferred with Confederate Colonel Caleb Perkins and his recruiting cadre known to be in the Howard and Boone County area at this time and they may have encouraged Anderson's guerrillas to attack the railroads. As will be shown in Chapter Eighteen, at this time Confederate Colonel John Calhoun Thornton's southern insurgency in the Platte County area to the west was being chased eastward by overwhelming Union cavalry forces. Perhaps Colonel Perkins and his cadre asked Anderson to assist their beleaguered comrades by preventing the Union military from using the railroads to send reinforcements to that fight. Lastly, Anderson added to his numbers between July 18 and 23 because his flashy, hard-riding band was literally riding circles around the Federals and getting observable results.

Captain Anderson's band, now grown to about 40 riders, raided Renick, southeast Randolph County, on the morning of July 23. First the bushwhackers pulled down the telegraph wires, then robbed the stores, the railroad agents, and some homes in town. They also set fire to the railroad depot. Next, the guerrillas rode the seven miles north to raid the railroad town of Allen, and two local young men of the neighborhood joined the gang as they left. Nobody on either side was hurt in Renick that day.

At Allen were 35 or 40 soldiers of the 17th Illinois Cavalry led by Second Lieutenant Ebenezer Knapp and some members of 46th EMM that had ridden there from Glasgow to pick up a shipment of firearms, probably for citizen guards. These troops were inside the railroad depot eating about noon on July 23 when Anderson's gang rode into town shooting. The guerrillas immediately captured about half of the cavalry horses tied to the rail near the depot. Seeing the danger, the Union soldiers made a barricade of salt barrels and bales of hay and commenced shooting at the attacking Rebels. As the soldiers fired from behind their makeshift barricade, the guerrillas sought cover and besieged the place, deliberately killing nine of the horses still tied to the rail to put the cavalry afoot. Some of the bushwhackers mentioned to residents their plan to shoot into the train when it arrived, so some Allen ladies walked south along the track and stopped the northbound train about three miles from town to prevent more damage and bloodshed. As if to verify the warning, the train crew could hear shooting from the direction of Allen, so they backed the train south to Sturgeon and put aboard some soldiers there as a train guard. Meanwhile, Anderson's raiders could not take the depot by force, so they robbed the stores, took stagecoach horses, and withdrew from town toward the west with some wounded and perhaps some dead, leaving behind the bodies of their two new recruits from Renick, killed by Union firing in the initial assault. Despite all the shooting, the only Union casualty in Allen was one soldier wounded in the leg.[8]

Second Lieutenant Knapp gathered enough horses to mount his men along with ten civilian volunteers and set out west to pursue Anderson's band with this force of 39 men. On the following day about three miles from Huntsville the hunter became the hunted as Anderson's band launched a successful ambush on Knapp's expedition in thick woods, killing one each of the 17th Illinois Cavalry and the 46th EMM, wounding one Yankee, and capturing a number of their horses. Knapp's men managed to kill one Rebel whose body was left on the scene and possibly wounded a few more. After Anderson's men moved on, Lieutenant Knapp's battered command returned to the killing ground to discover that the guerrillas had mutilated the dead Yanks by taking scalps and mutilating their faces. On one of the dead the Rebels left a note:

"You come to hunt bushwhackers. Now you are skelpt. Clenyent skelpt you. Wm. Anderson." The name on the note undoubtedly referred to Archibald "Little Archie" Clements of west Johnson County, who was notorious in Anderson's band for taking delight in killing captive enemies with his knife and mutilating the dead dating back to autumn of the previous year.[9]

Archibald "Little Archie" Clements was one of Bill Anderson's inner circle of about a dozen, and one of the most bloodthirsty (John N. Edwards, *Noted Guerrillas*, 1877, p. 238; courtesy of the late Bob Younger and Mary Younger and Andy Turner).

There can be no doubt that a few in Anderson's band repeatedly murdered helpless civilian and military captives and mutilated the dead. The strong hatred antagonists in this "give-no-quarter" guerrilla war had for each other led both sides to such despicable practices, but a few like Clements in Anderson's band routinely engaged in such savagery. New band member Hamp Watts in his memoirs admitted Anderson's band did contain a few with "predatory instincts and natures" who were "used because the time, opportunities and conditions gave them power." Confederate authorities in the Trans-Mississippi West did not endorse such gruesomeness, and it was counterproductive to their cause. However, the fear that such practices engendered in Union troops discouraged many from even facing Anderson's men in battle, particularly among the EMM and the new citizen guards. This psychological effect served as a combat-enhancing force multiplier for this gang to the extent that many northern troops, especially militia, dreaded facing Anderson's band.[10]

Bill Anderson Raids Railroad Towns of Shelbina and Lakenan

Just after the Huntsville fight with Lieutenant Knapp's men Anderson took his now 36 riders on another railroad raid through Monroe and southeast Shelby County between July 25 and 28. His band rode into Middle Grove in southwest Monroe County the evening of July 25, and from this move area Union commanders mistakenly anticipated these bushwhackers were going to raid the county seat at Paris. The Union military sent troops to Paris, but, the old saying goes, these Yankees "came up with an empty sack" because the guerrillas had a different goal in mind. That became apparent when Anderson's band bypassed Paris and on July 26 raided the railroad towns of Shelbina and Lakenan in southeast Shelby County burning depots, railroad rolling stock, water towers, an empty blockhouse, and the 150-foot-long Salt River Bridge on the Hannibal and St. Joseph Railroad. Also at Shelbina Anderson's men lined up the town men, as they had at Huntsville July 15, and robbed them and the stores and a few houses, but then quickly rode east to Lakenan. At Lakenan the band suffered their only casualty of this raid when one guerrilla shot another to death over a watch they had taken at Shelbina. Anderson forced the farmer at whose farm this occurred to bury the dead bushwhacker. The Union 38th EMM (nicknamed "the Railroad Regiment") was assigned the task of protecting vital railroad infrastructure and manning the empty blockhouse, but nobody anticipated such a threat and much of the regiment was not on active duty. In fact, Union leaders were so shocked that Rebels had wreaked this amount of destruction that their first reports said that 500 southerners had done it. When Union soldiers arrived at the scene they pressured one southern sympathizer to confess he had fed the bushwhackers, and from his tally of how many hungry mouths he served they learned that only 36 raiders committed all the damage. The Federals repaired the bridge in only a few days and made known local southern sympathizers join in with the work crews.[11] Anderson's band rode west from Monroe County into the village of Milton in east-central Randolph County the morning of July 28, ending their railroad-busting expedition through Monroe and Shelby Counties. Since there was no Union threat nearby, the band remained in Milton a few hours and left in the afternoon.[12]

Each of the several little railroad towns Bill Anderson's band raided in northeast Missouri this year showed more than normal "wear and tear" afterwards (Charles C. Coffin, *Redeeming the Republic*, 1889, p. 214).

Bill Anderson attempted to attack Huntsville again July 30. Since his previous raid there July 15 the town had assembled its own garrison of citizen guards led by Lieutenant Colonel Alexander F. Denny of the 46th EMM. Anderson learned this and deployed his men in ambush positions while he developed a subterfuge to entice the amateurish citizen guard out to the countryside to their doom. With just a couple of guerrillas Anderson rode to the home of Denny's elderly father, Judge David Denny. Anderson hanged the judge three times from his gatepost, while sending a servant the two miles to town to notify Lieutenant Colonel Denny and hopefully cause him to rush to the rescue right into the prepared ambush. Friends in town figured this ploy was a trap and physically restrained the very upset militia officer from rash actions. Anderson left the judge for dead and joined his men in their ambush positions, but after a while realized that the citizen guards would not take the bait and moved off. Meanwhile, the prostrate Judge Denny regained consciousness and eventually recovered from his hanging ordeal.[13]

Bill Anderson with a Bodyguard Rides West Leaving Brother Jim Leading the Band

Bill Anderson, left, and his younger brother, Jim (private collection, courtesy of Charles Orear).

On July 31 Bill divided his band, keeping with him eleven dependable men who had ridden with him since the summer of 1863, and placing the remainder, including the newer men, under the leadership of his younger brother Jim. Jim Anderson and the larger portion of the band would continue to operate in that part of northeast Missouri, while Bill and his eleven hand-picked "reliables" rode for an expected junction with the guerrilla band of Charles "Fletch" Taylor over three counties to the west in Clay County. The 1886 Caldwell County history asserts that Taylor sent a rider for Bill Anderson proposing that their combined bands could raid into Iowa. However, a Confederate staff officer sent by General Sterling Price in Arkansas called a number of the west-central Missouri guerrilla chiefs together for a protracted council of war in Lafayette County to begin August 4, and possibly Anderson was riding to attend that meeting with his eleven bodyguards. Bill Anderson would have brought larger numbers of his band if he was going to join Taylor's band to raid into Iowa. Whatever the reason, Anderson's sudden departure ended his first protracted campaign in northeast Missouri, but he would return.[14]

Holtzclaw and Bill Jackson in Howard and Chariton Counties Between Mid-July and Mid-August

On the same day that Bill Anderson's band first raided Huntsville, July 15, Captain Clifton D. Holtzclaw's band began raiding miles to the northwest along the border between Sullivan, Grundy, and Linn Counties. A number of Holtzclaw's men originated from Linn County, and so were familiar with this area, but Grundy and Sullivan Counties had not witnessed much war violence since 1861 and 1862. Holtzclaw's band specifically targeted Lindley in the east edge of Grundy County since it was known as a center of the notorious "Grundy County Militia"—actually, some companies of the 30th EMM—that had raided southern homesteads in the counties around during the previous two years. The reputation of the rapacious "Grundy County Militia" was that no southern hen house or smoke house in this region was safe while they were around.

Holtzclaw's Lindley Raid of 15 July 1864

Holtzclaw and 26 bushwhackers rode quietly into the town of Lindley at six in the morning of July 15. Some of the raiders wore Federal uniforms which fooled residents who would otherwise have given alarm. As was this band's custom, they first gathered and guarded all the men, and then spent the next three hours in a methodical search of businesses and homes for loot. As the townspeople watched the proficiency of the robbers, they realized that the raiders had good advance intelligence about where to find what they wanted. In one instance guerrillas commanded a lady at her front door to go back into her home and bring out to them two Union overcoats that she had packed away some time earlier. Some of the raiders concentrated on opening storage trunks in private residences and broke them open if the owner failed to promptly bring a key. Other guerrillas went after cash, revolvers, clothing, and the like from the stores. Several of the Rebels "clothed themselves in new suits from head to foot" at one store as a newspaper correspondent later wrote. Captain Holtzclaw did not lecture the townspeople at Lindley as he had at other towns, but his men seemed to attack more the property of "radical" northern sympathizers and tended to spare of the property of "conservative" northern sympathizers, as Holtzclaw and his men mentioned during the raid. The difference between these terms was that the "radicals" were determined to restore the Union at any cost and especially through force and the death of most Confederate soldiers, while the "conservatives" were willing to accept restoring the Union by welcoming the errant Rebel military and citizens "back into the fold" with few preconditions. Perhaps the guerrillas treated Lindley differently than towns in previous raids because they perceived this was primarily a northern town with few if any southern sympathizers. Early in the raid Captain Holtzclaw himself robbed a Reverend Anderson of his watch and wallet and forced the cleric to accompany him on a tour of the town to identify the best horses that the guerrillas could take. Holtzclaw informed the preacher on this horseback tour of town about the rationale for these raids and failed to note in one instance that the minister coyly showed him a horse stable that actually belonged to an avowed "conservative" northerner. Holtzclaw explained to the pastor that southerners were going to "take possession of the polls and have things their own way" in the November election. The guerrilla leader did assert that southerners would retake the state that fall "by fair means or foul," probably referring to the long-awaited invasion of Missouri by Confederate General Price's army from Arkansas. Holtzclaw also boldly claimed to Reverend Anderson that guerrillas intended to raid all north Missouri towns this fall and use the money and valuables they took to support the Confederacy. Before they left, the guerrillas attempted to differentiate between the "radical" and the "conservative" northerners of Lindley and in several cases returned to "conservatives" items they had earlier seized from their homes and businesses. About nine that morning the raiders left with their loot and ten stolen horses heading to the south, having harmed no person of the town.

Holtzclaw's band soon turned east into the northwest corner of Linn County and stopped to have lunch at a farm, but Captain Ezekiel L. Winters of the citizen guards from Lindley and about 40 volunteers—many who were former members of the 30th EMM or "Grundy County Militia"—chased them away to the south before the farmer could even cook the food. The guerrillas were forced to fight delaying actions while continually heading south across west Linn County as Winters' posse tenaciously pursued. Some of these skirmishes were uneven, as each of Holtzclaw's men carried their own arsenal of two to four revolvers and one or two shotguns apiece while the citizen guards carried only their private firearms and limited amounts of ammunition. In one ambush four of the posse received wounds and in another guerrilla fire killed one and mortally wounded another. Captain Winters suspected a trap at one location and sent his force around both flanks, which flushed Holtzclaw's band from another ambush site and sent them scampering quickly out of the way. When the bushwhackers finally reached Chariton County they had supper with a farm family. The farmer later related that Holtzclaw himself seemed to be slightly wounded. He also said his family fed 21 guerrillas in the house and afterwards band members took food to four more comrades lying in the barn who were evidently wounded. The band did not linger long in Chariton County, as a reliable source reported Holtzclaw and 25 men were seen near Glasgow, west Howard County, the morning of July 19.

Three of the Holtzclaw guerrillas noted during the Lindley raid for their aggressiveness and daring were Joseph Gooch and Howard Bragg of Linn County and Jim Jackson, a Texan who evidently admired the Missouri guerrillas from afar and traveled to the Show-Me State to join them. The reputations of these three were destined to grow in the weeks ahead. However, notoriety also has its dark side. After the war a Lindley resident won a suit in civil court against Gooch and Bragg for the $1,800 Holtzclaw's band took from him in this raid.

The Lindley raid also resulted in a spate of northern depredations against southerners in this area. Captain E. L. Webb and some of his citizen guards of neighboring Sullivan County assisted the Grundy County men in the pursuit, and afterward arrested two men they encountered in the countryside. Webb later claimed his men were taking this suspicious duo to Milan, the Sullivan County seat, for questioning when his men shot and killed the pair claiming they were trying to escape. Unidentified Union troops guarding railroad facilities arrested another suspicious southerner and turned him over to Captain Webb and his citizen guards at Milan. Evidently, some of citizen guards later took this man out of the jail and lynched him. Their July depredations must have encouraged Captain Webb's men to continue killing men into August, too. While First Lieutenant James Sterling's patrol from this company was searching south

Sullivan County for bushwhackers reported there sometime that month, a member of the patrol murdered William Calhoun while the man was guiding the patrol across his property. Four or five years later a local jury indicted James Head for the Calhoun killing, but Head died of complications from a broken leg before the trial could proceed.[15]

Bill Jackson's Band Joins Holtzclaw

Captain Holtzclaw limited his activities mostly to Howard and Chariton Counties and building up the health and strength of his band between July 19 and 28 to the point that he had 75 riders by July 28. During this period he took into his command the bushwhacker band of Bill S. Jackson of Arrow Rock, southeast Saline County. Bill was the son of Missouri's 1861 pro-southern governor, Claiborne Fox Jackson, who took his office into exile when the Federals occupied the state and who died in Arkansas the previous December. Captain Bill Jackson and his band operated for a time in Howard County the previous autumn, so they were not strangers there. However, it must have been confusing to some that among Holtzclaw's subordinate leaders at this time were Bill Jackson, the former governor's son from Saline County, and Jim Jackson from Texas, since the two Jacksons were not related.

Holtzclaw's Butler House Fight of 27 July

Perhaps the larger size of his band contributed to Holtzclaw stepping back into the limelight between July 27 and 30. The brushy forks of the Chariton River south of Keytesville, Chariton County, was a popular guerrilla hideout, and by this time of the war Union troops watched this area for guerrilla activity. The new Keytesville commander, Captain Joseph Stanley of the local 35th EMM, tracked Holtzclaw's band there on July 27, but failed to find the bushwhackers and backed off, fearing an ambush in the thickets. On July 28 Stanley sent First Lieutenant Louis Benecke and 43 men of this regiment back there where near Union Church at Nathaniel Butler's house the militia rode onto Holtzclaw's band eating breakfast. As Captain Stanley later wrote of Benecke's patrol's reactions finding their enemies eating a meal "they were charged upon at once and supplied with Federal pepper." In their initial shock the bushwhackers scrambled to their mounts and escaped the scene, but they quickly reformed and counterattacked the outnumbered militiamen not once but several times. The southerners probably seemed surprised that Lieutenant Benecke's men held to their position, and they paid a price for their underestimation of the Union patrol's grit. When Holtzclaw's bloodied band finally left the scene the militia reported they had killed four guerrillas and wounded about twelve more, including "severely" wounding Bill Jackson. They also counted one dead southern horse and gathered from the battlefield one live horse, a number of revolvers and shotguns, hats, blankets, and other items. Union losses were limited to one horse badly wounded and one man slightly wounded.

Captain Stanley's reports and other records revealed what may have caused the guerrillas' mistaken confidence that Lieutenant Benecke's militia would not put up much of a fight. Stanley wrote in his report that Holtzclaw and other Confederate recruiters in this area made serious inroads in local militia ranks this summer by recruiting large numbers of these militiamen into Rebel ranks. The Confederacy had sent into north Missouri a hefty contingent of experienced recruiters with the strong recruiting incentive that General Price and his army in Arkansas was coming soon, and Captain Stanley had difficulty sifting through the ranks of the 35th EMM to piece together enough reliable men to man even one patrol in any strength. A number of these militiamen blatantly stated that they would not fight against men bearing the Confederate flag. After the July 28 fight at Butler's house six or seven militiamen who had been lately riding with Holtzclaw left his band and sheepishly returned to the 35th EMM.[16]

Holtzclaw's Letter Exchange with Captain Stanley

Beginning the day after the Butler house fight, Captain Stanley and Captain Holtzclaw exchanged correspondence, even though as enemies. Holtzclaw initiated the letter-writing to Stanley with anger after hearing that northerners near Bee Branch in northeast Chariton County murdered unidentified southerners, and threatened to kill two northern sympathizers for each southern one that the militia killed. Incidentally, the Brunswick newspaper reported a few days before that unidentified guerrillas on July 22 in that area murdered northerners Lawrence D. Long, Jesse Mason, and John Willard, so it seems unknown northerners may have taken revenge among Bee Branch residents in a typical Missouri Civil War "circle of violence" revenge killing. Holtzclaw and Stanley exchanged their personal pledges to treat the others' men fairly in battle and as prisoners. Holtzclaw's stated aim was to protect southern noncombatants, while Stanley, feeling vulnerable amid a sea of Confederate recruiters and guerrillas, was probably seeking assurances that he and his men would live through this experience. Since Captain Stanley wrote to Captain Holtzclaw without superiors' approval, he had to account for this correspondence later, but seemed to suffer no ill effects. This was another proof of the old military adage that "it is easier to obtain forgiveness than permission, especially if the plan succeeds."[17]

Sterling Price's Son Edwin Conducts Interviews with Guerrilla Leaders

The same day that Captain Holtzclaw sent his first letter to Captain Stanley he granted a most unusual interview somewhere near Keytesville, central Chariton County. Former Confederate Brigadier General Edwin W. "Stump" Price of Chariton County sought out Holtzclaw to interview the guerrilla leader about his military mission and official status in northeast Missouri. Edwin Price was a paroled former prisoner of the Yankees, and the eldest son of Confederate Major General Sterling Price. Union Major General Rosecrans and Brigadier General Fisk actually sent Price to interview the leading Confederate irregular commanders of this region and ascertain their mission and connection to the Confederate command structure, whether or not Price confided this to Holtzclaw. Earlier in the war, the captured Brigadier General Edwin Price convinced his captors that he was disillusioned with the Confederate cause and took an oath of allegiance to the Union to prove it. Based on this, Price's Union captors granted him full pardon and he represented himself in public thereafter as a northern supporter. Edwin's change of heart greatly embarrassed his distinguished father to the Confederate high command and engendered rumors and suspicion about Sterling Price's own allegiance. In the interview, Captain Holtzclaw also told Edwin Price that his own primary mission was to recruit, and if the Union military left him alone he would do that and leave. Holtzclaw added, however, that while he was recruiting he also felt it was his duty for the protection of southern people in his region to target "radical" northerners who victimized them and who promoted the enlistment of black men into the Union army.

After Price's interview with the guerrilla leader he gave a rousing speech to Holtzclaw's men on the following day. Price mentioned having recruited Holtzclaw into the southern Missouri State Guard during 1861, which drew cheers from the men. Price recognized many of his former neighbors and friends in the group and acknowledged that many were former Confederate soldiers. Price attributed the overzealousness of such local Union militia companies as the one at Brookfield, Linn County, and Captain Joseph Stanley's company of the 35th EMM at Keytesville for having compelled these men into guerrilla service. So he asserted that guerrilla warfare in this region was the fault of the local Union troops, to which his audience readily agreed. Edwin Price lingered in the Chariton and Howard County area over the next two weeks seeking out hidden Confederate leaders who would agree to his interviews. Confederate Colonel Caleb Perkins told Price much the same as Holtzclaw—that he was in this region to recruit on written authority of General Sterling Price, and if not bothered by Union troops he would perform that duty to the best of his ability and then leave. He said his instructions were to continue recruiting in this region until either the corn ripens or Price's army comes to him. If the southern army failed to invade Missouri by the ripening of the corn crop, his duty was to take his recruits to Price's army wherever they were located. Colonel Perkins added that while recruiting he felt it was his duty to stop northern depredations such as those committed in early June by the U. S. detective Harry Truman. Perkins said that he was against bushwhacking and murder, but admitted that some of his men had committed such acts. He implied that this was unfortunate, but even this activity still fell under the authority of General Sterling Price. He took exception to the actions of Bill Anderson and his band, and others, and threat-

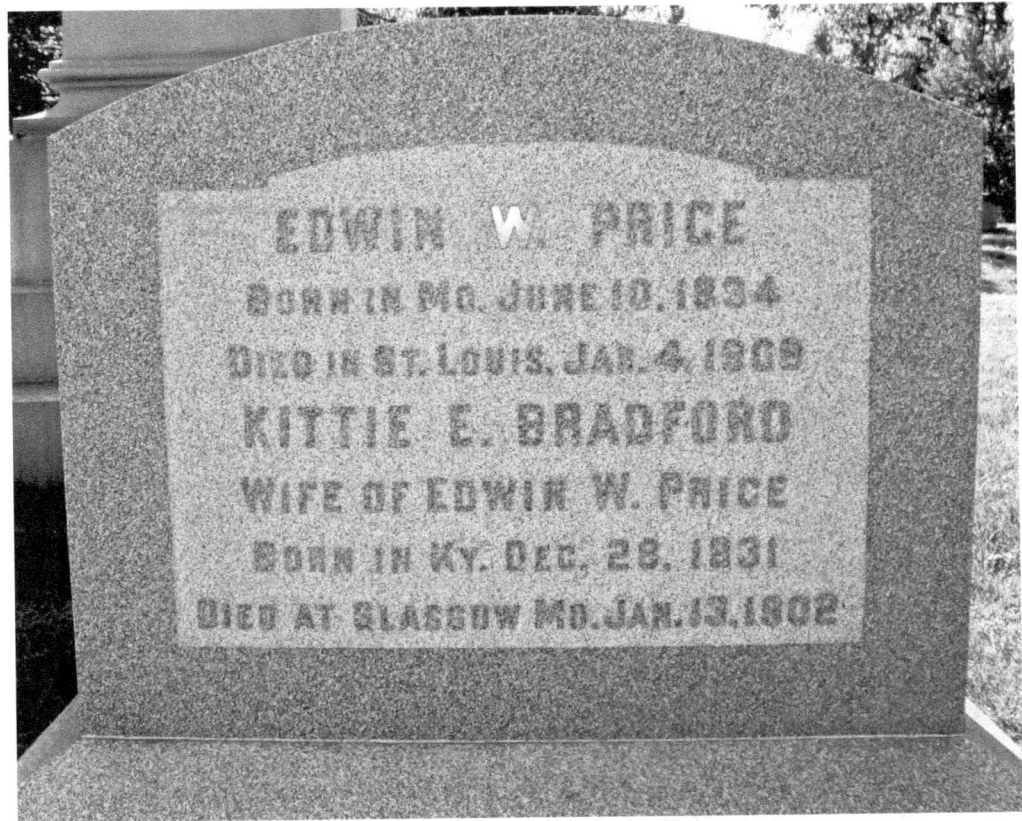

The grave of Edwin "Stump" Price beside that of his more famous father, Sterling Price, in Bellefontaine Cemetery in north St. Louis (author's photograph).

ened to drive them from "his military recruiting district" if they did not cease their depredations upon southern people there. Edwin Price also interviewed Confederate Captain Miles Price—evidently, not related to Edwin—in the area around Rocheport. Captain Price from near Pendleton in west Warren County, served in the southern cause from the start of the war, was captured as a recruiter in Boone County in April 1863, escaped from Gratiot Street Prison in St. Louis in July 1863, and now was back in this region recruiting again, probably as part of Colonel Perkins' command. Oddly, little seems to remain about Edwin Price's interview with Captain Price except the mention that the captain was "a very polite man." Former General Edwin Price reported back to Union General Fisk about the second week of August with the findings of his interviews.

The testimony of these leaders that they were under the written orders of Major General Sterling Price, Edwin's father, implied to some northern leaders that General Price was responsible for the excesses of their men, especially the atrocities of some of the guerrillas. Oddly, later in the war Confederate authorities—not Union ones—brought charges against General Sterling Price for employing ruthless Missouri bushwhackers while taking no measures to correct their behavior.[18]

Holtzclaw's band fought in only minor actions in Howard County during the first several days of August. On August 3 Major Reeves Leonard of the 9th Cavalry MSM led a detachment of his cavalry and the 1st Iowa Cavalry into a small skirmish with an unidentified guerrilla band near Fayette, central Howard County, "and pursued them until dusk, a distance of fifteen miles, capturing horses, arms, clothing, and etc." There was no mention of casualties. Union authorities had recently sent the veteran 1st Iowa Cavalry back to north Missouri from Arkansas in answer to Major General Rosecrans' anxious pleas for more troops.[19]

The Missouri River town of Glasgow in west Howard County was a sanctuary of sorts for area northern sympathizers since Major Lucius C. Matlack and some troopers of his 17th Illinois Cavalry were stationed there, and the town was further protected by its own company of General Orders Number 107 citizen guards. However, a noted northern sympathizer, Benjamin W. Lewis, who corresponded regularly with Brigadier General Fisk, the district commander, wrote on August 11 that Matlack was inefficient and his troopers were poorly disciplined boys new to guerrilla warfare, were short of horses, and they were badly armed. At that time Matlack's Illinois troopers lacked pistols and their only firearms were muskets, which were difficult to reload on horseback and had a slow rate of fire compared to the guerrillas' multiple revolvers. Lewis further complained that the 65 or 70 citizen guards were poorly organized although enthusiastic. To prove the vulnerability of Glasgow, Lewis recited how Captain Holtzclaw himself stopped by farmer John Earickson's house only two miles from town the evening of August 9 and took a fine horse from the man, made him hand over $100, and then coolly engaged Earickson in conversation for about an hour about a variety of local Civil War topics. Mr. Lewis also complained to General Fisk that forty guerrillas, who may have been Holtzclaw's, took breakfast at another man's house four miles northeast of town the morning of August 11. Obviously, Captain Holtzclaw harbored no fear of the Glasgow garrison, but up to this time he was not known to raid any town with a garrison defending themselves on ground of their choosing.[20]

After this time Holtzclaw and his men began to operate more in concert with other area bushwhacker bands and take their brand of war away from their sanctuary areas of Howard and Chariton Counties.

Late July and August Increase in Guerrilla Activity in Howard, Boone, and Audrain Counties; and Union Reinforcements

Between the middle of July and mid–September 1864 a variety of Rebel guerrilla bands and recruiting groups challenged the Union military in the south-central counties of northeast Missouri. As word spread of the approaching invasion of Missouri by Sterling Price's Confederate army in Arkansas, more and more of the southern irregulars ventured out into the open. Some of these groups learned to work together to confront Union forces.

A southern recruiter known only as Captain Holloway brought his 27 men into the village of Roanoke in the north tip of Howard County the evening of July 19 and delivered a bold speech. Holloway, a local man, demanded the residents' firearms that he stated he intended to use against the Glasgow garrison when he joined forces with the recruiting command of Colonel Caleb Perkins. [21]

Union EMM General Douglass Besieged at Columbia

On July 20 two unidentified guerrillas stopped the northbound stagecoach near Hallsville in north Boone County, and removed at the point of a gun Private James Palmer of the 2nd Missouri Cavalry ("Merrill's Horse") traveling in civilian clothes on furlough. The pair then sent the coach on its way while the bushwhackers kept Palmer with them. Nothing was heard from the missing trooper until on July 24 locals discovered his bullet-riddled body hidden under a pile of logs not far from where he was removed from the stagecoach.[22] The Union command in the Boone County area reached a turning point on the next day, July 21. Militia general Brigadier General Joseph B. Douglass at Columbia sent a courier to the Union garrison at Sturgeon informing the commander there that Douglass discovered that a large body of guerrillas were hovering around the roads on all sides of Columbia waiting to capture him if he were to leave town. The besieged general added that he was "in fortifications" and if the Rebels entered town after him Douglass could hold them off for long enough for help to come rescue him. The district commander, Brigadier General Fisk at his St. Joseph headquarters, immediately ordered the Sturgeon garrison to "raise the siege at Columbia and bring him [General Douglass] out" and gave the assurance that "force will very soon be furnished you for the relief of all."[23] After General Douglass was rescued

Brigadier General Joseph B. Douglass, an Enrolled Missouri Militia officer of northeast Missouri, repeatedly found himself in danger during 1864 (private collection, courtesy of John F. Bradbury).

This photograph of part of the business section of Columbia, Boone County, was taken during 1864 (Walter B. Stevens, *Centennial History of Missouri*, vol. 2, p. 213).

and taken to Sturgeon, Fisk admitted on July 24 to a subordinate officer that "there are indications of serious trouble in Howard, Randolph, and Boone [Counties]."

Union Reinforcements: Bartlett's Battalion of 3rd Cavalry MSM

The help that Fisk mentioned was Major Solon A. C. Bartlett and a battalion of his 3rd Cavalry MSM sent across the Missouri River from Jefferson City to Boone County in the hopes that these additional troops could chase the guerrillas away. Major Bartlett seemed unsure that his men could prevail as he telegraphed Major General Rosecrans July 24 that "Boone County is infested with rebels to the number of 200 or 300." The only positive news Bartlett could muster in his early report upon entering the Boone County hotbed of active guerrilla war July 22 was that his men chased two Rebels in west Boone County and killed one—a "Captain Angel." The dead man was actually Doctor John M. Angell of northwest Boone County, a Kentucky man who evidently divided his time the previous three years to practicing medicine as well as helping to recruit and train for the southern cause near his home. The troopers left Angell's body in the road where he fell, but soon after Rebels nearby buried the physician with military honors including the firing of a volley aver his grave.[24]

Standoff in Audrain County: Purcell Vs Gannett

Meanwhile, a standoff was taking place in Audrain County northeast of Boone County between bushwhackers perhaps of Captain Young Purcell's band and Union First Lieutenant Isaac Gannett, the assistant provost marshal at Mexico. Gannett, born in Massachusetts and living in Chicago before the war, was detailed into this position away from his regiment, the Kansas 7th Cavalry, possibly to recover from a wound. The 7th was known throughout the Missouri border region as a notorious jayhawker unit for the horrendous atrocities men of the unit committed earlier in the war, so Lieutenant Gannett probably came into his job in the provost marshal's office with experience dealing with tough men and tough situations. During the night of July 22/23 bushwhackers abducted twenty-something F. J. Davis from the household of his father, the Reverend D. B. Davis, eleven miles west of Mexico. Earlier in the war the younger Davis had been a member of the local 61st EMM, which may be why the guerrillas grabbed him. First Lieutenant Gannett then angrily arrested four or five well-known local southern men and held them as hostages for Davis' safe return. The effect of Gannett's challenge was lost since the Rebels had already killed their hostage, which locals over in north Boone County reported when they found Davis' lifeless body hanging in a tree. The Chicago lieutenant next ordered his uncomfortable hostages to raise money themselves to recompense the Davis family for the loss of their man. Not to be outmaneuvered, the guerrillas on the evening of July 24 abducted several more northern sympathizers near Mexico and sent word to the assistant provost marshal to release his hostages or they would kill 25 more northern men. The determined Yankee lieutenant answered this challenge by arresting 25 more southerners. Eventually, Gannett relented at least in his threat to kill the southerners he held when the Rebels sent word that they would kill ten northern men for every southerner he executed. However, the lieutenant kept some of the hostages as his prisoners for a time as a guarantee against more guerrilla threats, and this version of a "Mexican standoff" eventually ended.[25]

Between July 27 and 28, Major Bartlett led his newly arrived battalion of 3rd Cavalry MSM across parts of Boone and Howard County where these Federals encountered "seven small squads of guerrillas," killing five at no apparent Union loss. Bartlett seemed more confident after this experience, as he reported that some of the bushwhackers his force encountered were "terror-stricken." Meanwhile, Brigadier General Douglass moved his location to Mexico for safety, but directed Major Bartlett to leave his logistics wagons and his sick troopers at Columbia, so his combat forces could better chase the guerrillas. It seems Union troops were attempting to regain the offensive against the hundreds of Rebels in this area.[26]

Mystery Guerrillas Shoot at Riverboats

About July 29 unidentified guerrillas in southwest Howard County fired on the Cincinnati-built, side-wheeler *Sioux City* on her north-bound passage. The captain reported no damage or casualties when the vessel stopped at Glasgow the morning of July 30.[27] Both Holtzclaw's and Bill Anderson's bands were busy elsewhere at this time, and could not have fired on the *Sioux City*, but there were numerous other small bands of bushwhackers across the region. Famous William C. Quantrill was at that time hiding in self-imposed exile near Boonsboro in that same part of Howard County with his teenage wife and five to eight guerrillas as bodyguards, after George Todd and Bill Anderson deposed him from leadership in his former band in late spring. Quantrill and his men scrupulously avoided offensive action during their three-month stay at this hidden camp, since they were too small in numbers to effectively fight any Union troops, and they did not want to attract attention to themselves.[28] Therefore, the boat shooters were probably guerrillas south of the Missouri River.

Jim Anderson Raids a Church on 31 July

On July 31 as Bill Anderson and a small part of his band rode west out of northeast Missouri, as previously described, his brother Jim and the remainder of the group went raiding in northwest Randolph County and southwest Macon County. Jim Anderson's band surrounded a church in session on that Sunday in northwest Randolph County and took as prisoners 32 men and older boys from the congregation. Anderson and his men took these worried abductees along with them to the Hebron Church in south Macon County, where the bushwhackers questioned the prisoners about their loyalties. All but eight of the abducted church-goers stated that they would serve the South. The guerrillas stripped, beat, and shaved the heads of these eight men, and then made two of them kneel and pray. All the victims thought that the Rebels were going to kill the pair, but they only wanted to intimidate, and soon after released all eight to return home as best they could. Union authorities were confused since they could not distinguish between the two Anderson brothers and these activities by Jim Anderson's riders as well as Bill Anderson's smaller group riding west both took place July 31.[29]

Early August Guerrilla Raids in South Boone County

An unidentified band of about fifteen bushwhackers was active during the first days of August in south Boone County. On August 2 they inquired at the village of Stonesport where two certain black men could be found and a resident gave them directions to the nearby village of Buffington where the two men worked as haulers. The guerrillas rode directly to where the men were working and without a word or explanation shot them both dead. These two black men were runaway slaves then employed as freedman by native Pennsylvanian Mr. Buffington, and the subject of an earlier law suit by the former slave owner against Buffington which was suspended for the duration of the war by district commander Brigadier General Fisk. One of the two had earlier joined the Union army but had been discharged. These guerrillas then robbed houses in the village, destroyed personal belongings, and fired into Buffington's own house. Buffington's daughter rode to Jefferson City to summon help, but a pursuit could not be assembled until August 5 probably due to the great guerrilla presence all over the region.[30]

It was evidently the same bushwhacker band that robbed the nearby village of Providence August 3. They robbed the stores mostly of "ready-made" clothing and cash, and searched the homes of men who had been members of the local militia. In some instances where they found Union uniforms in those dwellings the guerrillas tore them to shreds in contempt. These Rebels robbed nearby farms during the next several nights for horses, firearms, and cash.[31]

Early August Guerrilla Council of War in Monroe County About 4–7 August

Evidence that a Confederate central authority directed some activities of the various independent guerrilla bands appeared in two locations in Missouri simultaneously between about August 4 and August 7. On those dates Confederate officers under Major General Sterling Price's orders conducted joint war councils with Rebel recruiting and bushwhacker leaders near Middle Grove, southwest Monroe County, as others were conducting similar sessions in northwest Lafayette County, miles to the west, at the same time. The central theme of these meetings was how those various Rebel irregular units could assist the coming invasion of Missouri by Price's Confederate army then in Arkansas. John N. Edwards, who postwar was the sympathetic chronicler for the Missouri guerrillas, mentioned the Lafayette County meeting in his 1877 *Noted Guerrillas,* and even named the staff officer sent to conduct it. At that time, Major John N. Edwards was Brigadier General Joseph Shelby's adjutant and probably had access to this information. No documentation survives to specify who conducted the Middle

Grove meeting, and it is possible that Colonel Caleb Perkins himself instigated and led that meeting without aid from Price's staff. Further, no record survives to tell what transpired at Middle Grove, but subsequent actions offer clues. Apparently, General Sterling Price wanted guerrillas to continue harassing and attacking the Union military, since those attacks continued through August and September in northeast Missouri at an unprecedented rate. Earlier rumors indicated Confederate authorities wanted guerrillas to attack the Union military's use of railroads here, and such attacks took place between July and October. Amazingly, the Union's previously weak Missouri intelligence apparatus heard August 3 about the Middle Grove war council, but failed to take the information seriously. The Yanks' information was that Colonel Caleb Perkins, a second unidentified colonel from Boone County, and Major Elliott D. Majors of Monroe County represented the recruiting commands. The mystery colonel from Boone County could have been either Lieutenant Colonel Quinton L. Peacher of east-central Boone County or David B. Cunningham of south Boone County, since both recruited in this region at least by September. The Federals also heard that Frank Davis of Monroe County and Bill Anderson were guerrilla chiefs attending. Perhaps it was Bill Anderson's brother Jim who attended the Monroe County meeting since Bill apparently attended the Lafayette County meeting at this time.[32]

Jim Anderson Battles Near Huntsville 7 August and Other Actions

If Jim Anderson attended the Middle Grove war council he was certainly back in the Huntsville, Randolph County, area by August 7, for he fought a desperate battle with Union forces there that day. Lieutenant Colonel Alexander F. Denny led a combined force of his own citizen guards, local 46th EMM, and a sergeant's detail of 9th Cavalry MSM that found Jim Anderson with only ten men at ten that morning in the Bagby farm five miles south of town and immediately charged the outnumbered bushwhackers. In the short fight the Union forces killed one Rebel outright and wounded another in the neck before Anderson and the remaining guerrillas dispersed into the brush. There were no Union losses. Denny's patrol found on the dead bushwhacker's body almost $400 in gold, silver, and greenbacks as well as letters from residents of Dallas, Texas. They also recovered from the battle scene two horses, at least five revolvers, other firearms, and several guerrilla hats decorated with feathers. Bill Anderson left his brother with as many as 30 men on July 31, so perhaps these ten guerrillas had been Jim's bodyguard to the war council at Middle Grove before the Bagby farm fight.[33]

Unidentified guerrillas made three attacks on the North Missouri Railroad in Audrain and Randolph Counties August 8 and 9, possibly after being encouraged to do so as a result of the recent war council at nearby Middle Grove. On the morning of August 8 Rebels tore up six miles of track southeast of Mexico in Audrain County. That night guerrillas fired on a freight train near Renick, southeast Randolph County, but nobody was hurt. At six the following morning unknown parties fired about 100 bullets at another train near Renick, but hit no person.[34]

By this time of the summer guerrillas and new Rebel recruits committed so many robberies to acquire what they needed that many went unrecorded, unless someone died. During the evening of August 9 guerrilla Bill Campbell and four other bushwhackers stopped a Mr. Wagner on the road nine miles north of Mexico, then afterwards shot the man twice, killing Wagner. The next morning at about ten o'clock Campbell and another bushwhacker named Nichols boldly rode through Mexico with revolvers in their hands greeting citizens they knew, and then stopped on a hill outside town in plain view. Some residents exchanged shots with the daring pair, but they calmly rode off into the brush after having made their appearance. Obviously, these two bushwhackers wanted to prove their daring.[35]

Accurate Union Spy's Report Covering 15 to 24 August

Between about August 15 and 24 a Union spy named George Williams, operating with the knowledge of the Huntsville Union commander, infiltrated various Rebel camps in Randolph and Chariton Counties. In Chariton County Williams found at least two companies of Rebel recruits camped together waiting to receive firearms. The spy knew that their commander, Captain Joseph Price, traveled to St. Louis about this time to purchase firearms where he was arrested, perhaps on information the spy provided. Williams also spoke to members of a band of 25 new guerrillas mostly from around Roanoke. In southwest Randolph County he met and talked with bushwhackers from the bands of Holtzclaw, Jim Anderson, Tom Todd, Pitney, and also more recruits from Colonel Caleb Perkins' command. A number of these Rebels told the spy that "they were going to make that county [Randolph] hotter than hell," and they seemed confident they could hold Randolph County against whatever the Union military threw at them. Williams discovered some of the guerrillas planned to attack a passenger train on the North Missouri Railroad, so he mailed a letter of warning to the Union garrison at Huntsville. The spy determined later that the Huntsville postmaster opened the letter and tipped the guerrillas to William's true identity. Williams reported to Major John McDermott who commanded the 250 troopers of 1st Iowa Cavalry that had entered this area August 9. He told McDermott the current location of the various bands of Rebels, but the major seemed to distrust the spy's information and let the opportunity slip from his grasp. George Williams then resumed his spying role on August 21 by joining for a while four bushwhackers of Jim Jackson's band in north Randolph County. These guerrillas explained to the disguised spy that all the Rebels in this region were under Colonel Caleb Perkins' direct command except for Bill Anderson's band, which remained independent. They also said they expected General Joseph Shelby to bring his cavalry brigade raiding to the Missouri River within two weeks.[36]

August 15 and 16 Battle of Dripping Springs in Northwest Boone County

On August 15 and 16 Holtzclaw's and Tom Todd's bands engaged in battle with Union troops in northwest Boone County. Captain William Hebard and a small detachment of his men of the 17th Illinois Cavalry rode across Howard County from their Glasgow garrison and camped for the night at Dripping Springs, northwest Boone County. Captain Holtzclaw and his band of up to 100 attacked the Illinois cavalry from a cornfield next to the springs at eleven that night, mortally wounding one of the cavalry pickets and severely wounding another. Hebard and his men knew the bushwhackers remained in place around them and spent the rest of the night fortifying their position as best they could. At first light on August 16 the guerrillas renewed the attack and held the Illinois troopers in siege at the springs for five hours with frequent gunfire. The Illinois cavalry suffered no more serious casualties, but killed and wounded some of their attackers. Union troops at Columbia, ten miles to the southeast, and elsewhere heard about the ongoing fight, and reinforcements from detachments of the 3rd Cavalry MSM, 9th Cavalry MSM, and the local 61st EMM converged on Dripping Springs and attacked Holtzclaw's men for about 45 minutes until the bushwhackers withdrew. In this part of the fighting the Union forces killed at least four guerrillas, whose bodies were left upon the field, and wounded perhaps seven or eight more, at a loss of nine Union soldiers slightly wounded. The northern force also captured 12 to 15 horses and a number of pistols and other firearms left on the battlefield. While all of the Union troops were riding to Columbia after the fight, Captain Tom Todd and his small guerrilla band ambushed the column about four miles from town, wounding one man and several horses. The northern troops returned a brisk fire upon this new enemy and Todd's men promptly fled into the woods and dispersed with unknown losses. Local sources later confirmed that 16 guerrillas were definitely wounded both at Dripping Springs and the road ambush. Nearby residents had to bury the four dead southerners at Dripping Springs.[37]

Wounded Bill Anderson Turns Leadership Over to His Brother Again After 14 August

There were other guerrilla developments in the region during the fighting in Boone County and shortly after. Bill Anderson and his command now of between 65 and 100 riders was surprised August 14 in an attack by a combined force of local militia in southeast Carroll County resulting in a few guerrillas killed and several wounded including Bill himself in the leg, as narrated in Chapter Nineteen. The badly wounded were taken in by southern families across Chariton County and nursed back to health. Postwar bushwhacker chronicler John Edwards wrote in 1877 that Bill's brother Jim in Chariton County took temporary command while his older brother convalesced. Jim Anderson evidently kept the band in the Chariton County area for a few days until a number of the wounded recovered enough to ride. Edwards then noted that Jim led the battered band southeast to the sanctuary of Howard County where friends helped the group "get back on its feet."[38] Meanwhile, Captain Joseph Parke and a large patrol of his 4th Cavalry MSM from their Boonville garrison rode around Howard County on August 16 and 17 skirmishing with several small guerrilla bands. Captain Parke reported that he chased several bushwhacker groups but was only able to wound one man, capture three horses, and a few shotguns and revolvers.[39]

Jim Anderson, Holtzclaw, and Perhaps Bill Stewart Between 19 and 22 August

Major John McDermott led his several companies of the 1st Iowa Cavalry in Randolph County and heard and reported August 19 at Huntsville that Confederate Colonel Caleb Perkins had commanded his forces including those guerrillas commanded by Holtzclaw and Bill Anderson to concentrate near Mount Zion Church in northeast Boone County. McDermott told his superiors that he was leading his cavalry in that direction.[40]

Some of Major McDermott's information was faulty, as Captain Holtzclaw and Jim Anderson each had their bands in southeast Howard County August 20, as did two Federal patrols from two separate regiments. Captain William Hebard and his patrol of ninety-one troopers of 17th Illinois Cavalry a short distance from Rocheport encountered about 150 bushwhackers who gave the correct Union recognition sign but then fired on the Illinois troopers. It appears these guerrillas were of the bands of Captain Holtzclaw, Jim Anderson, and possibly Bill Stewart. Stewart hailed from near Cornelia in south-central Johnson County and during 1862 was in a local guerrilla band there before joining Quantrill that summer. He led his own small bushwhacker band in the Johnson County area during July 1864 and had only brought his men into northeast Missouri a few days before this. The bushwhackers may have deliberately provoked the Illinois troopers because of their reputation as being poorly trained, armed, and led, but to their surprise the men of the 17th stood up to the guerrilla fire and returned steady shooting of their own, suffering only one man severely wounded. This led the guerrillas to back off and disperse with unknown but probably slight losses. Captain Hebard later crowed about this fight "on Saturday, the 20th near Rocheport, I met and attacked a force under the notorious bushwhacker William Anderson, defeating him gallantly and driving him clear out of sight." Actually, Holtzclaw seemed to be the overall guerrilla leader in this fight, and it was Jim Anderson and his 28 riders in this action and not Bill. Hebard and the 17th Illinois Cavalry had been working with Major Reeves Leonard and 120 of his troopers of the 9th Cavalry MSM who were not far away at the time of this fight, and the assurance of having those comrades nearby may have bolstered the spirit of these Illinois troopers. The combined guerrilla force rendezvoused at their campground shortly after the short fight and set an ambush for Major Leonard and his 120 men who shortly rode into this area. Leonard and his Missourians had either the good fortune or skill to avoid the ambush and instead charged the large body of southerners at the camp who scattered again throughout the landscape with no mention of losses to either side. While a frustrated Major Leonard and his troopers searched through the woods and brush of southeast Howard County, Jim Anderson and his 28 riders raided the often-raided town of Rocheport not far way. Shortly after they rode out of town Holtzclaw and his men rode in and poked around the ruined village a bit on their own before they left, too. A Columbia newspaper article about these actions addressed what these guerrillas encountered in poor Rocheport: "The business interest of Rocheport is almost broken up, owing to the repeated incursions of the guerrillas. A great many citizens have left the place." In his report Major Leonard also made a poignant remark about operating inside such a southern area as Howard County: "No one in that county will inform me of the rebel movements, but I cannot move without their knowing all about me."[41]

On the following day, August 21, Major Reeves Leonard and his force of 9th Cavalry MSM encountered what must have been some of Jim Anderson's men to the west near Franklin and killed two of them. A St. Louis newspaper commented that bushwhackers robbed a Franklin store about this time, so this must have been Anderson's work, too. Former Confederate Major John N. Edwards in 1877 provided the details of the fight that resulted in the loss of the two Anderson men. Edwards stressed that Bill disbanded his band in Howard until September 2 so the several wounded from the August 14 fight in Carroll County, including himself, could fully recover. Edwards complained that "his brother Jim— inferior in every fighting respect to William— operating a little along the main thoroughfares." What evidently happened was that five

Major Reeves Leonard commanded the Union Fayette garrison during 1864 (private collection, courtesy of the late Bob Younger and Mary Younger and Andy Turner).

of the Anderson men negligently sat down to dinner at the home of southern sympathizers without the vital step of setting out one or two pickets to keep watch. It must have been Major Leonard's troopers who were astonished to trap these careless bushwhackers inside the confines of a house by the road without security. The sixty Yankees turned the yard into a shooting gallery as four of the panicked guerrillas ran from the house, killing two outright while the other two escaped, although badly wounded. Edwards related that the fifth man coolly remained in the house, hid his bushwhacker weapons and accessories, and disguised himself successfully to the Federals as one of the family. Edwards implied that if Bill Anderson would have been in charge he would not have permitted such carelessness among the men. Anderson member and local resident Hamp Watts in his 1913 memoir described the same incident, but pointed out that at least one of the family members was later banished from the state for her part in helping these bushwhackers.[42]

After the fight near Rocheport Holtzclaw took his band back to the Glasgow neighborhood across the county, as on the night of August 21/22 his band attacked the pickets of the 17th Illinois Cavalry outside of town. The Illinois pickets held their posts and returned fire, discouraging any further guerrilla action. The Glasgow Union commander, Major Matlack, knew Holtzclaw was responsible because one of his men found on the ground one of the letters Captain Stanley at Keytesville, Chariton County, sent to Holtzclaw in their exchange of notes there a month before, as described earlier in this chapter.[43]

Bill Stephens in Macon and Adair Counties 21 and 22 August

At this same time Rebel recruiter Captain Bill Stephens was active in Macon and Adair Counties almost three counties to the north. Stephens of Randolph County had been active in the southern cause in his home county during 1861, enlisted in the Confederate army in 1862, returned to Missouri to recruit during early 1863, was captured in St. Louis that summer, and a month later escaped from the Gratiot Street Prison in that city.[44] He may have been operating as a recruiter earlier in the summer perhaps under command of Colonel Perkins, but he was certainly on his own now leading guerrillas. A Hannibal newspaper article gave highlights of Stephens' band's raid in Macon and Adair Counties during August 21 and 22, and which seems to be the only source for the Rebels' raid here. According to this local newspaper, on August 21 Stephens and his band robbed some families of Macon County south of the railroad, creating a panic that sent some citizens rushing to the Union garrison at Macon City for protection. Meanwhile, Stephens took his men north of the railroad in Macon County, unknowingly passing within three miles of a body of ninety unidentified Union militiamen, who may have been guarding railroad infrastructure. On August 22 these bushwhackers raided briefly in south Adair County, unaware that the militia they passed hours earlier were now catching up to them. Ten of these Union soldiers under an unnamed lieutenant were in advance of the rest of the mounted column and came across the guerrilla camp the evening of August 22. The lieutenant and his few men boldly rushed Stephen's campsite, killing one Rebel and scattering the rest in all directions. This Union vanguard also captured several horses and a number of firearms, hats, blankets, and coats that Stephens' men left in their haste to get away. These northern troops chased the guerrillas in the night for about ten miles until further pursuit became dangerous to the pursuers.[45]

During all the action in Howard County August 20, 21, and 22, Major John McDermott with his force of 1st Iowa Cavalry chased guerrillas probably of Tom Todd's or

Young Purcell's band throughout Boone County. Whomever his men chased dispersed just east of Rocheport perhaps after Major Leonard's and Captain Hebard's Union forces fought guerrilla forces near there a day or so earlier. McDermott took his Iowans back to their base at Bucklin, southeast Linn County, perhaps by rail, arriving August 23. McDermott still maintained that his men had been chasing Bill Anderson's band those several days in Boone County. The Union spy George Williams reported that on August 23 Bill Anderson with sixty men tore down telegraph line a mile or two from Huntsville, Randolph County, within sight of about 100 soldiers of the Huntsville garrison. Hearing all this would have amused Anderson, recovering from his August 14 leg wound somewhere in Howard County. It seems that just his name alone was worth a band of sixty bushwhackers.[46]

Low Water Level of Missouri River Enhances Guerrilla Mobility on 23 and 24 August

An informant told the Union military at Columbia that he observed a group of "rebels" using two flat boats during several hours of August 23 to cross their horses and themselves from Cole County to the north bank of the Missouri River northwest of Claysville at the southern tip of Boone County. It appears this unidentified body of guerrillas was just entering northeast Missouri after riding north from Arkansas. The river crossers may have been the same guerrillas who raided the nearby village of Providence about that same day, but no record remains to provide details. Their crossing was undoubtedly made easier by the drought-induced, low water level, reported that same day upriver at Kansas City. The falling river level would lessen the obstacle of crossing the Missouri River for guerrillas for the rest of this fighting season, enabling them to confound the Union military by crossing back and forth with more ease through the Union's district boundaries.[47]

The low water level of the Missouri River was also a concern for the protection of river traffic, since the steamers had to avoid the shallows and had less opportunity to distance themselves from bushwhackers shooting from the banks. On August 24 guerrillas of either Holtzclaw's or Anderson's band delivered heavy fire into the slow-moving, northbound side-wheeler *Omaha* twelve miles south of Glasgow, and one of the 100-or-so bullets badly wounded a man aboard. Men on the *Omaha* fired back, and reported seeing two of the Rebels fall. The Indiana-built, 1856-vintage vessel was one of the older river haulers, and at Glasgow the captain refused to venture further upriver. He either wanted another vessel to accompany his or a Union military escort aboard, as he was concerned about how vulnerable the *Omaha* would be at wood stops. The district commander could not spare the troops, but directed the larger *Fanny Ogden* to steam to Glasgow and accompany the *Omaha* to her Leavenworth, Kansas destination. He also ordered Major Matlack at Glasgow to send 100 men to the ambush site and deal with the bushwhackers, who were undoubtedly gone when his men got there.[48]

Rise of Jim Jackson's Murderous Career as a Guerrilla Leader on 23 and 24 August

A guerrilla band that was an offshoot from Holtzclaw's killed northern men in south Chariton County August 23 and 24. A letter writer in Keytesville identified the leader only as "Jackson," but since Holtzclaw's lieutenant Bill Jackson was then operating in Saline County, this leader was probably Jim Jackson, the Texan. This Jackson's band used the sanctuary of the "forks of the Chariton River" as a base, and attracted some local southern men as new members of the band. On August 23 these bushwhackers shot a black man to death at Martin C. Hurt's "tobacco factory." On the following day near Hamner's Mill in Prairie Township of south-central Chariton County they abducted William Carter from his family because he was a private in Captain Joseph Stanley's local company of the 35th EMM. The young man's hysterical mother recognized some of the members of the band as neighbors and one was even a cousin, and they promised the woman that they would not hurt Bill Carter as they took him away. However, at a nearby farm one of the band killed young Carter by literally blowing the man's head apart with a shotgun blast at close range, despite the promise. These acts of violence seemed to mark the initiation of Jim Carter as a guerrilla chief, and set a pattern he followed hereafter for wanton murder of black men and the savage killing of men who had served in Union units.[49]

Frank Davis in Monroe County on 24 August

There was also action in nearby Monroe County on August 24. A Union patrol probably of the 3rd Cavalry MSM rode from Sturgeon in north Boone County to Middle Grove, southwest Monroe County, that day hoping to catch the local guerrilla leader Frank Davis there. Instead, they captured Confederate Colonel Caleb Perkins' younger brother William who was well-armed although hiding under a bed. The younger Perkins allegedly attempted to escape that night from captivity at Sturgeon and the guard mortally wounded the man.[50] Captain William E. Fowkes' company of 60th EMM from Paris, Monroe County, found Frank Davis' guerrilla band that same day near Madison in the west part of the county, but their discovery was not entirely satisfying. Davis' guerrillas' outnumbered the Paris militia, who organized a defensive position and held off the large numbers of Rebels until the Sturgeon commander could send reinforcements to help them. The militia humbly claimed to have killed one southerner and wounded a second, and their losses seem to have been slight.[51]

Bill Anderson Takes Back His Band from His Brother on 25 or 26 August

Bill Anderson ended his convalescence and took back command of his band by August 25 or 26, united with Clifton Holtzclaw's band, and determined to commit grave damage to the Union forces riding about the area. Taking eleven days or so to recover from a bullet wound in the leg may seem inadequate in present day, but to a fit, young man in his mid-twenties with Anderson's determination and temperament it must have seemed to last an eternity. Besides, Bill may have been dissatisfied with his younger brother's handling of the men in Bill's absence, since two or three died in that period—some of them by negligence. Certainly Bill had to be upset that several Union columns were riding around the region fighting occasionally with guerrillas who could not seem to inflict any real damage on them. Bill set out to change that.

Bill Anderson began by riding around west and south Boone County August 27 occasionally skirmishing with Major Reeves Leonard's large force of 9th Cavalry MSM. Perhaps the fierce guerrilla chief was trying to entice Leonard to enter Howard County again where the terrain favored the guerrillas and the populace seemed more supportive and less inclined to inform against the Rebels. After the war, John N. Edwards—the guerrilla's supportive chronicler—exaggerated this one day event in Boone County transforming three practically bloodless skirmishes into a major battle against Reeves Leonard, but Edwards may have misinterpreted what participants told him about it. Major Leonard put his own slant on the day's action: "I had three lively skirmishes with Anderson's band yesterday, south and west of Columbia, thoroughly routing and scattering them." Some Union commanders misinterpreted the bushwhacker tendency to disperse and scatter as a sign of defeat, when, to the guerrillas, it was merely another "tried-and-true" tactic in their "bag of tricks." From the bushwhacker point of view, dispersing and scattering to meet at a pre-determined rendezvous point later was merely a method to break contact with the enemy, perhaps to find a better place to continue offensive action elsewhere. Three armed bushwhackers possibly of Anderson's or Holtzclaw's band on this day robbed the mail coach on its way to Rocheport, tearing open the letters for money inside and reading the letters for information that might prove useful. This mail robbery was to have grave consequences.[52]

Anderson, Holtzclaw, and Stewart at Rawlins' Lane Fight of 28 August near Rocheport

The following day, August 28, marks one of Bill Anderson's more stellar triumphs, the Captain Parke defeat near Rocheport, locally known as the fight in Rawlins' Lane. Anderson's and Holtzclaw's combined band had retired from south Boone County to south Howard County hoping to draw an unwary Yankee unit after them when opportunity rode their way. Captain Joseph Parke and his portion of the 4th Cavalry MSM at Boonville were part of the Union's District of Central Missouri and unfamiliar with actions north of the Missouri River in the District of North Missouri. Parke knew vaguely there was guerrilla action in south Howard County, so he took what he considered a large patrol of 44 of his troopers across the Missouri River to investigate the robbery of the Rocheport mail coach the day before. His patrol passed through Franklin heading east and the captain ignored warnings from citizens about large number of guerrillas ahead. Hearing about Parke's approach, Anderson sent for Bill Stewart and his small band of ten nearby to join the larger group in anticipation of the approaching fight—about 100 gunmen in all. About four miles west of Rocheport guerrillas decoyed Parke's command with two apparently retreating riders who drew the Yanks into denser vegetation. Suddenly, about 75 guerrillas split the patrol with the captain and seven or eight troopers isolated in a narrow lane in the front and the largest portion of his combat patrol leaderless on the other side of all the bushwhackers. Anderson next launched Archie Clements with a dozen men to feint toward Captain Parke and the smaller portion of the Yanks to keep them busy while he concentrated most of his force on a group of 24 to 28 who took refuge at a log house in the river bottom. Clement initially obeyed the order by faking an attack. However, Captain Parke and his few men unexpectedly abandoned his imperiled command and retreated north toward Fayette. Clements promptly forgot his orders and pursued those galloping Yanks almost all the way to town, for which Anderson severely reprimanded Clements afterwards. Meanwhile, some guerrillas made bloody work of eight troopers they overran when they initially split Parke's column, scalping, castrating, skinning, hanging, and in general mutilating dead and severely wounded troopers. The larger body of the 4th Cavalry MSM troopers heard the shooting and shouting out in the woods, but did not know what it meant. The majority of the bushwhackers kept this group pinned down at the log house, but the guerrillas with their short range pistols and shotguns could not break the desperate defense of the troopers shooting through chinks between the logs during several rushes. These Feds kept the Rebels at bay until dark and then retraced their steps to Franklin and returned to Boonville, glad to be alive. Meanwhile, Captain Parke and his few men were happy to encounter Major Reeves Leonard and his command of the 9th Cavalry MSM who accompanied them back to the battle site where they found the mutilated bodies of seven of their dead comrades and took them

When the guerrillas attacked Captain Joseph Parke and his large patrol of 4th Cavalry MSM, the captain and a few retreated to nearby Fayette and abandoned the rest to their fate (The Werner Company, *The Story of American Heroism*, 1896, p. 336).

back to Boonville. The abuse of the corpses clearly told the Union troops that this was the handiwork of Anderson's band. The guerrillas retired with their victory and many captured Union horses as Major Leonard and his troopers of the 9th approached the battle area.

The total accounting of the battle was eight dead Federals and two wounded, including another dead trooper whose remains locals found and buried several days after the fight, and six troopers who returned to Boonville by one method or another a day or two afterwards. Another casualty of this fight was Captain Joseph Parke himself. His district commander, Major General Alfred Pleasonton, abhorred the way Parke rode away from the battlefield and deserted his men in the clutches of their enemy and wrote two days later "I recommend that Captain Parke be dismissed from the service for this affair." One month to the day after the fight Parke resigned his commission and left the 4th Cavalry MSM. No source seemed to record Rebel losses, but it appears at least two guerrillas died and several were wounded. As the overall southern leader Anderson had clearly demonstrated his prowess as a guerrilla field commander with great skill over a veteran foe. As he moved his jubilant command away from Major Reeves Leonard's relief force, he immediately dispersed his 100 or so men, sending them in small groups to sanctuary neighborhoods around Howard, Chariton, and Boone Counties.[53]

Bill Anderson's Surprising Vacation at Rocheport in Late August

On August 30 Bill Anderson himself with about 28 of his men took over the war-torn village of Rocheport and held a drunken guerrilla carnival there for a couple of days as if on a vacation from the war for a while. The guerrilla chief had established a reputation with the Federals for riding hard immediately after a fight and putting a great distance ahead of any pursuit, so Union forces did not expect him to linger next to his August 28 battleground as he did this time. No Union garrisons were close by, either, except the garrison of the 4th Cavalry MSM at Boonville, and those men were not inclined to return to Howard County for a few days. Besides, the frustrated Union forces in this region had their hands full fighting bushwhackers at every turn, and could not answer each alarm. Rocheport itself seemed less of a threat now to the Rebels since nearly all the northern sympathizers left after so many raids, and the remaining residents were less likely to inform on the guerrillas to the Federals. Some of the war weary citizens welcomed a celebration for a change, too. This oasis in the middle of a bitter war seemed to suit Anderson, and he even called Rocheport "my capital."

Anderson acquired his own navy during this sojourn at Rocheport. The steam tug *Buffington* docked around the bend from the town for the night on August 30, and the guerrillas learned of it and captured the vessel. The captain and the clerk did not immediately acquiesce to the guerrillas' demands, so the bushwhackers killed the captain and badly wounded the clerk. The *Buffington* belonged to the state penitentiary at Jefferson City, was manned by inmates of the place, and were on a trip upriver to obtain a load of oats to take back to the prison when taken. Anderson forced the convict crew to take some of his men across the river to Cooper County where they stole horses, committed other mayhem, and then returned to Rocheport aboard the waiting vessel, as described in Chapter 20. Later, Anderson released the *Buffington* unharmed. Without even an investigation, on September 1 Union authorities assessed all the residents of Rocheport to pay $10,000 to the family of the *Buffington's* murdered captain, based on the mistaken assumption that the town residents were all southern sympathizers and voluntarily helped Anderson's gang.[54]

Holtzclaw's Defeat at Forks of the Chariton River About 30 or 31 August

The rest of Anderson's and Holtzclaw's bands were scattered across the area, and part of Holtzclaw's group encountered trouble about the same time Bill Anderson and some of his men frolicked at Rocheport. At Glasgow about the last of August twenty-five men of the Chariton County citizen guards under Lieutenant John A. Vance invited a Federal detective named Murphy to accompany them back to the forks of the Chariton River to find some "real guerrillas." As promised, Vance's men flushed from that great thicket Holtzclaw's subordinate Joseph Gooch and some of the band, killing four and capturing three horses and two revolvers, although Gooch himself escaped. Lieutenant Vance awarded Detective Murphy an impressive pair of Mexican spurs worn by one of the dead Rebels. Perhaps the bushwhacker with the Mexican spurs was one of several Texans, like Jim Jackson, who traveled north to Missouri that spring to join Captain Holtzclaw's exciting band. The source of this story is a sketchy St. Louis newspaper article which apparently lacks corroboration from any other resource, but contains enough verifiable detail that it may be true.[55]

Union EMM General Douglas' Bad News on 31 August

The Union militia general, Joseph B. Douglass, still at Mexico, on the last day of August had no positive news in a report he sent to district commander Brigadier General Fisk. The usually well-informed Douglass told Fisk the shocking news that in Boone County alone there were then three camps of Rebels under Confederate Colonel Perkins, guerrilla chief Tom Todd, and others—one of 200 men, another of 160, and a third of unknown size. Some of these men were telling people that they belonged to the command of Brigadier General Joseph Shelby. Douglass then gave his honest assessment that with the various Union forces available to him he could not hope to drive this many southerners away.

As if that was not enough bad news, Douglass felt compelled to say of the 17th Illinois Cavalry in his area that "all reports from them are that they are almost worthless," "few of them are mounted, and when they are out their principle business is to pillage and plunder the citizens." The distraught militia general illustrated the point by detailing the depredations that a detail of them performed as escort to a telegraph repair crew between Glasgow in northwest Howard County and Allen in central Randolph County a few days before. Evidently, the men of this detail stole so much from homes along the way that a local citizen guard commander heard of it and ordered the Illinois troopers stopped and searched. General Douglass wrote that the searchers reported to him that they recovered from these soldiers "blankets, bed quilts, a large lot of ladies clothing, including silk and lawn dresses, and all kinds underclothing, gentlemen's wear, overcoats, dress coats, vests, and etc." Considering that the 17th Illinois Cavalry had only been in the war zone for a few weeks, such behavior coupled with their lack of training and firepower indicated that these troopers would be of dubious value in a fight.[56]

Thus, as August 1864 drew to a close, the advent of September boded ill will for the northern cause in this central part of northeast Missouri, especially with the threat of an impending invasion of Missouri by the Confederate army in Arkansas looming.

Scattered Rebel Actions Along the East Edge of Northeast Missouri from Mid-July Through August 1864: Handcock, Ramsey, Dorsey

There were a few guerrilla actions in Callaway, Montgomery, and Warren Counties during late July and August 1864, mostly involving the band led by William Handcock and Frank Ramsey based in Montgomery County. Although he gave little outward sign he was about, Confederate Colonel Caleb Dorsey quietly recruited during this period in Montgomery and Warren Counties, and other counties, but Union authorities heard little about his activities.

Handcock's and Ramsey's guerrilla band occasionally ventured out of Montgomery County in their forays, but their expedition to the northwest corner of Callaway County on July 25 proved deadly to the band. The bushwhackers were incensed that Doctor James M. Martin of that neighborhood persisted in flying the U.S. flag from his rooftop, and they paid the New York–born doctor-farmer a visit just after noon that day to express their disapproval. There appears to be no surviving record of what happened to Martin or his flag when the guerrillas rode into his farmyard, but the Fulton newspaper recorded that unidentified people murdered "a free negro" named Peter Brown about that day in north Callaway County, perhaps as part of this incident. Also on July 25 Union authorities in the area heard about Handcock and Ramsey's venture and sent out First Lieutenant Abraham Kempinsky with a patrol from his 67th EMM. Kempinsky and his men were veteran guerrilla hunters, having killed notorious Joe Cole in Montgomery County the previous December. On their way to find Handcock and Ramsey the militia patrol evidently encountered and captured local bushwhacker and prison escapee John L. Wright, for his subsequent prison ledger entry says he was recaptured that day in Callaway County. Lieutenant Kempinsky's patrol certainly found Handcock and Ramsey's bushwhackers somewhere in the area the morning of July 26 for they killed Handcock, wounded Ramsey, and captured a horse and revolver. After his recovery, Frank Ramsey led this bushwhacker band hereafter.[57]

Captain Will T. Hunter of 3rd Cavalry MSM at Hermann heard on the morning of August 1 that bushwhackers were committing depredations across the Missouri River somewhere in Montgomery County. Captain Hunter was not specific about what he heard, but this was probably the work of James Ramsey and his band. Hunter led a patrol to investigate but found no guerrillas. He did find small boats at nearby Portland, southeast Callaway County, that Rebels had used to cross the Missouri River recently and he destroyed them. Some citizens of Portland were organizing a citizen guard unit according to the provisions of Department of The Missouri General Orders Number 107, but Hunter was suspicious about the loyalty of the townspeople. He confirmed his doubts within the next day or two when he sent there "a party in disguise" pretending to be guerrillas. This group of men brought back word that the Portland people treated them well as fellow southerners, one senior lady bemoaned the recent death of guerrilla leader John Handcock who she said was a friend of hers, and one citizen even offered to assist them in attacking Captain Hunter and his troopers! Hunter wrote angrily in his report that "I have never met with a more bitter set of rebels that the citizens of Portland," and he strongly advised Union authorities not to issue arms to the new Portland citizen guard unit.[58]

On August 6 in the railroad town of Warrenton, central Warren County, officials arrested a married couple for having suspicious items in their luggage. C. C. Wells and his wife Ollie L. Wells had in their bags money, jewelry, and other items identified as having been stolen by bushwhackers from northern sympathizers in Howard, Randolph, and Chariton Counties, according to the Columbia newspaper. They were both arrested as bushwhackers for "operating with a gang supposed to be Anderson's men." Perhaps the couple believed they had enough stolen loot to start life anew and were fleeing the war zone.[59]

James Ramsey's Ill-Fated Raid in Callaway County During Mid-August

James Ramsey led his guerrilla band of between 25 and 40 raiding farms in east Callaway County about the middle of August. On August 22 these bushwhackers raided the river town of Portland, robbing stores and residents and charging citizens a "tax" of $25 each. The Kansas City newspaper heard that this band hanged a man in Portland, but neither the Fulton newspaper account nor that of the Union assistant provost marshal at Fulton mentioned such an act, and they both were closer to the scene. After Ramsey's band left town, they rode to the Williamsburg area of northeast Callaway County where they robbed farmers of money and horses—taking $5,000 from one wealthy landowner. They halted a Doctor Wilkerson on the road, and the Fulton newspaper said they "demanded his horse, but he begged them out of it." Meanwhile, the small Union garrison at the county seat of Fulton heard of these depredations and on August 23 evidently sent part of Captain Thomas L. Campbell's company of 9th Cavalry MSM who located the guerrillas and attacked, killing Ramsey. The remainder of the band escaped and, evidently undeterred, that evening robbed the untended home of a man away being baptized.[60]

Colonel Dorsey's Quiet Recruiting Makes Too Much Noise 24–30 July

Meanwhile, to the east in St. Charles and Lincoln Counties rumors of bushwhacker violence in the region as well as Confederate Colonel Dorsey's quiet recruiting created northern unease. During the week of July 24–30 Union authorities activated one company of the 27th EMM at O'Fallon in St. Charles County and sent them along the roads by night to investigate a report that lots of Rebels were gathering at Troy in Lincoln County to the northwest. Many of the German-Americans of the 27th acquired a reputation of depredations against civilians earlier in the war, and the many drunk members of this company on the march to Troy seemed intent on proving this was still true. These bullying militiamen broke into homes, shot at houses, pressed horses and firearms, cursed and cajoled citizens, badly beat a fellow northern sympathizer for refusing to accompany them, passed insults to ladies they met, and generally brought discredit to the cause they represented.[61] A St. Louis newspaper proclaimed that a guerrilla was identified and captured in east-central St. Charles County August 10, giving locals reason to wonder how many more were about.[62]

Bushwhackers were far more aggressive in Pike, Ralls, Marion, and east Monroe Counties to the north in these same weeks. Captain Young A. Purcell's band was active in Monroe, Ralls, and Pike Counties, as well as Audrain County using intimidation and occasionally murder to further the southern cause.

Perhaps it was one of Purcell's guerrillas who fired at but missed James Brashears sitting on his porch near Spencer's Creek in south Ralls County near the Pike County line the afternoon of July 17. Brashears was a sergeant in a local company of the 53rd EMM, which may have been the reason the bushwhacker fired on him.[63]

On July 22, Union Colonel J. T. K. Hayward, commander of the 38th EMM, complained to district commander Brigadier General Fisk that guerrillas were hunting EMM members at their homes in the northwest part of Marion County with the express intent to kill them as they found them. Not surprisingly, a number of northern sympathizers in that neighborhood sought refuge in Hannibal where the colonel had his headquarters. The colonel also reported that ten of the more stalwart militiamen in Warner Township in southwest Marion County armed themselves and "are ready to take [to] the brush and fight the devil with fire." General Fisk sent a reply to Hayward the next day telling the colonel to "order out such militia and direct such movements as the emergency in Northeast Missouri may require." In other words, the situation had deteriorated so badly that all local commanders needed to activate whatever militia they had and prepare to defend themselves and their communities with little hope for outside help.[64]

In late July unidentified bushwhackers took outspoken northern sympathizer Thomas Spalding from his home near Elizabethtown in northeast Monroe County and shot him to death. About the same time they attempted to kill an unnamed northern sympathizer in the same neighborhood, but the sniper's bullet passed through the man's hat and not his head.[65]

EMM Murders of Flannagan and Mallory on 28 July

Part of the 69th EMM at LaGrange, east Lewis County, received a report from some citizens that west Marion County farmers William C. Flannagan and Edward Mallory were harboring and feeding guerrillas. Therefore, Second Lieutenant William Kishbaum and a heavy patrol of forty militiamen of Company D of this regiment on July 28 rode to the named men's farms in two different neighborhoods of Marion County, arrested them, then took them back northeast toward LaGrange. When Fishbaum's large patrol reached the Tucker Mill neighborhood in south Lewis County, the militiamen shot them both to death, and left their bodies near the road. Several days later rural families near the mill discovered the murdered farmers' bodies that had been partly devoured by hogs. Both Flannagan and Mallory were Virginia-born southern men held in high repute in the Marion County area, and each left widows and several children. There were threats and counter-threats between area men of differing loyalties over this outrage, and the act was long remembered locally.[66]

Just a few days later about July 30 to August 2 Captain John D. Meredith led a number of members of his company of the 53rd EMM around Marion County chasing bushwhackers. Meredith had some success disguising some of his men as Rebels and fooled some of the real ones. Colonel Hayward at Hannibal reported August 3 that Captain Meredith's militiamen chased some groups of guerrillas into Ralls and Monroe Counties, and wrote that the 53rd men "mustered out of service" a number of southern irregulars, but provided no specifics.[67]

Guerrilla Siege of Johnston House in Ralls County and Other August Actions

It appears the bushwhackers Captain Meredith's men chased into Ralls County still had plenty of fight. On the night of 3/4 August unidentified guerrillas surrounded the home of Robert Johnston near Sydney in northeast Ralls County and demanded entrance. Robert's son was Major Albert V. E. Johnston who had served the Union cause in the 2nd Provisional EMM Regiment during 1863 and was now away helping to train the raw recruits of the newly assembled 39th Missouri Infantry Regiment as one of the regimental staff officers. Perhaps these southerners knew this, and that may have been the reason they stopped there. The Johnston family locked themselves into the dwelling and refused the Rebel demands, whereupon the guerrillas peppered the place with numerous bullets, grazing one of the girls. Only when the bushwhackers loudly prepared to torch the house did Robert Johnston reluctantly allow them to enter. These intruders did no more harm to the family, but seized two firearms, a horse, sundry other articles and departed. That same night the gang robbed a nearby store of goods worth about $100 and about $45 in cash.[68]

Colonel Hayward at Hannibal reported a few days later that on August 6 sixteen recruiters and recruits robbed farmsteads near West Ely in south-central Marion County, perhaps to demonstrate that the Union militia could not drive them away. The colonel was able to identify the leaders of this band as Major Henry Snider, Captain "Kinkard" or Kincaid, Captain L. M. or Matthew Frost, and probably Captain Harry Horatio Hughes, all from this part of northeast Missouri. Hayward campaigned against these officers in 1862 when they were part of Confederate Colonel Joseph C. Porter's recruiting command in this same area, so they were familiar to him. These recruiting officers may have been part of Colonel Caleb Dorsey's recruiting command known to be operating in this region, although if they were, they were not keeping a low profile as Dorsey preferred.[69]

About the third week of August Captain Albert Lancaster's command of 53rd EMM from New London in Ralls County somewhere in the county apprehended teenager Legran G. Utterback of southwest Ralls County, who confessed to being a guerrilla in Captain Young A. Purcell's band. Utterback also implicated several Ralls County residents who had been giving aid lately to Purcell's group.[70]

There was also irregular Rebel activity in Knox, Clark, Scotland, and Schuyler Counties in the far northern corner of northeast Missouri between middle July and the end of August 1864. Part of this area witnessed Union depredations by unidentified northerners in Schuyler County in early 1863 and furloughed Union soldiers in part of this same region during the spring of 1864, but actual guerrilla violence had been noticeably absent in these counties since 1862. Union Colonel Samuel M. Wirt, commander of the 50th EMM, at Edina wrote on July 25 and 27 to Major General Rosecrans after Wirt's earlier correspondence to Brigadier Generals Fisk and Douglass produced no reply. Wirt and notable northern sympathizers wanted authority to activate some of the EMM in Edina, Knox County seat, due to one report that eighty guerrillas were camped in the northeast corner of the county near Colony and a reputable report from someone who counted 31 armed bushwhackers to the east in Lewis County. Colonel Wirt was particularly alarmed that on July 25 two armed men six miles from Edina inquired about the location of a local legislator's residence, and when he heard that bushwhackers raided Shelbina in Shelby County 35 miles to the south on July 26. Reasoning that Rebels were all around Knox County, Colonel Wirt and other civil authorities on their own authority activated 85 mounted men of the 50th EMM and ordered them to seize firearms from county residents of southern sympathy. Those actions probably seemed tame to the non-responding Generals Fisk and Douglass, since literally hundreds of Rebel bushwhackers were threatening to overwhelm Union forces in other parts of northeast Missouri by this date.[71]

Just a few miles to the northeast another incident played out on a stage covering the corners of three counties. First Lieutenant George W. McWilliams led a detachment of 69th EMM from Deer Ridge in the northwest corner of Lewis County looking for guerrillas in the southwest corner of Clark County. Samuel Dillard ran from his house with George Standerford as McWilliams' patrol approached. The militia shot at the fleeing men, killing Dillard, while the younger Standerford escaped. It appears Dillard was running to his rifle later found in the field where he died. Standerford, of north-central Knox County, had enrolled in the 50th EMM at Edina just that spring, perhaps to allay suspicions that he was a southerner, because his military record card states "no service rendered."[72]

Mike McCully's Schuyler County Raid in Mid-August

Mike McCully of southwest Schuyler County near Greentop had been a strong southern advocate since early in the war when he served in Bill Dunn's guerrilla group there during 1862. His older brother, John McCully, had been killed leading area men against northerners in this region in 1861. At age 46 in 1864 Mike was known in his extended family for his temper, especially against Yankees, but with nine children, this Tennessee-born, middle-aged farmer seemed an unlikely bushwhacker. However, about the middle of August Mike McCully with two other men rode south through Schuyler County forcibly taking one horse and one firearm as they went. No record survives to tell if this trio was leaving to join Confederate forces further south or simply leaving, but after the war McCully moved most of his family to Arkansas. Shortly after McCully and his companions left, local militia of Schuyler and Putnam Counties traveled through Schuyler County burning barns and corncribs of southerners to discourage them from assisting guerrillas in the future.[73]

As the tempestuous summer of 1864 drew to a close in northeast Missouri at the end of August, hardly a county in it had been spared guerrilla violence. With the autumn would come the liberating or invading southern army from Arkansas led by Confederate Major General Sterling Price, carrying with it the southern hope that the unexpected show of force here could change the course of the war. Specifically, southerners hoped a Yankee defeat in Missouri would affect the national election in early November, draw Union forces away from other war fronts, and perhaps even win for southern Missourians a state free of northern occupation for the first time in over three years.

Sixteen

Before the Insurgency Ignited: June Through Early July 1864 in Northwest Missouri North of the Missouri River

By June 1864 the Confederacy had hundreds of guerrillas and recruiters operational in the northwest quadrant of Missouri. Most of these were veterans bushwhackers of Missouri's brand of "no quarter" guerrilla warfare and knew they faced only death if they should fall alive into the hands of the Union military. Many of these irregular fighters returned to this embattled part of the state this year with the intent to take it away from the Yankees, hopefully timed with Major General Sterling Price's planned liberation of Missouri with his Rebel army from Arkansas. Union troops in northwest Missouri heard the persistent rumors of the invasion by the Rebel army from the south and already faced scores of experienced killer bushwhackers in the countryside. Both sides could sense that the summer of 1864 was stacking up to produce some of the most desperate guerrilla warfare of the entire conflict.

The Growing Threat to the Union Military in Platte County Takes Form

Ironically, a severe Rebel threat to the Union's hold on Missouri came about in the summer of 1864 from one of the Union's own innovations. In autumn 1863 the northern military reluctantly formed the 81st and 82nd Enrolled Missouri Militia Regiments with returned Confederate soldiers and other known southerners in the strongly pro-southern area of Platte, Buchanan, and Clinton Counties as a last resort to deal with persistent Jayhawker raids that came across the Missouri River from Kansas with regularity. Only to protect their lives and property from these raiders did hundreds of southern men agree to join these new Yankee units, that the critics derisively dubbed the "Paw Paw Militia." The EMM program developed in a hurry two years before was primarily a "grassroots" home guards that remained at home unless needed in the immediate area, and these about 80 regiments across the state attracted much scorn since they were basically untrained, poorly armed, and indifferently led—but at least these amateur, bumbling paramilitary units were basically loyal to the Union. The 81st and 82nd EMM Regiments, on the other hand, were knowingly and admittedly composed mostly of southern men defending their homes from raids made ironically by northerners from Kansas. The whole EMM program was a stopgap to provide what in essence was a private state army to defend against incursions into the state by Jayhawkers, southern guerrillas, and Confederate recruiters. However, the "Paw Paw Militia" was an unknown quantity facing fellow southerners in the form of bushwhackers and Confederate recruiters. The numerous, loud critics of the "Paw Paws" cried out that these troops were not only unreliable against Confederate regulars and irregulars, but that they would break their oaths, join such Rebel groups, and then turn their Federal muskets on fellow Union troops if the opportunity arose.[1]

The opportunity came to Platte County during the winter of 1863/1864 in the form of Confederate Colonel John H. Winston and Lieutenant Colonel John Calhoun "Coon" Thornton, who returned to their home county and secretly began recruiting for the Rebel army. The "Paw Paw Militia" soon knew Winston and Thornton were quietly bringing in recruits, and the very presence of the 81st and 82nd EMM in this area passively shielded this activity, since these were the militia supposed to ferret out and stop just such an activity or at least report it. The problem was that the southern men of the "Paw Paws" were loyal to their oath as far as protecting their communities from Kansas Jayhawker raids, but were also steadfast against opposing the Confederate cause many of them had wholeheartedly served earlier in the war. Therefore, the "Paw Paws" initially ignored the activities of Winston and Thornton and also refused to report them to their superiors. Northern sympathizers in Platte County leaked word of Colonel Winston's activities to Platte Countian Captain William J. Fitzgerald of the 16th Kansas Cavalry, who bypassed the "Paw Paws" and guided his own raid March 22, 1864, which captured Winston at home, as described in Chapter 10.

This still left Lieutenant Colonel J. C. Thornton actively recruiting in a strong southern community made even more southern by the frequent Jayhawker raids of the last few years. By early June 1864 he had several companies secretly organizing and drilling across several townships of the Platte County area, which information the local "Paw Paw Militia" refused to report to their chain of command. Those same Union superiors were by summer of 1864 so inured by the constant criticism of the 81st and 82nd EMM that they failed to interpret danger signs in the form of growing numbers of guerrilla violent acts in the Platte County area committed by these burgeoning southern recruit companies steadily growing in numbers in the countryside. Many of these violent acts were those of the recruits intimidating locals to prevent them from informing authorities, and also raiding nearby stores to obtain needed items. There were also guerrilla bands in the area fighting for the cause.

June and Early July Actions in the Platte County Area: Unheeded Warnings

Overton and Fielding Raid New Market

On June 1 Confederate Captain Holmes Overton, Lieutenant John G. Oldham with about 30 local guerrillas led by George Fielding skirmished with 16 local militiamen of 87th EMM near Arnoldsville in south Buchanan County at sunrise and about noon raided New Market in north-central Platte County. Evidently, this was the bushwhacker band that had been targeting militiamen and other northerners for assassination in the Platte and Buchanan County area for weeks. The occasion for the sunrise fight took place because this detail of the 87th EMM was taking a guerrilla prisoner to headquarters for questioning and had stopped at a home for breakfast when the Rebels attacked. The militiamen lost four men killed and a few southerners were wounded.

The militia found proof that some of these same bushwhackers were involved in the killing during May of Captain Hamilton S. Wilson and Private John Christian of their regiment in separate incidents in Buchanan County, as mentioned in Chapter 10. Overton's band initially captured two or three of the 87th men, but they managed to escape shortly, and brought back the names of several of the Buchanan County men among the guerrillas that they recognized. When Fielding and this same band raided New Market about noon, the local company of "Paw Paw Militia" of the 82nd EMM meekly surrendered their firearms to the raiders, who broke apart the unwieldy muskets and then robbed one store of $3,000 in goods and cash. The robbers also took several horses, and when they left several of the "Paw Paws" joined the band and rode off with them. This seems one of the first mentions that some of the many southerners in the ranks of the "Paw Paws" began to join the Rebel forces in this area, but there would soon be many, many more.[2]

A skirmish June 3 at Goose Creek in central Platte County proved that not all of the 82nd EMM men were disloyal to their uniform. On that day a patrol of the 82nd skirmished with what was probably the same guerrilla band involved in the June 1 violence. The militiamen exchanged shots with the pickets for the band of about 75 bushwhackers and both sides retreated with no casualties. However, one of the Union horses threw its militiaman rider and a number of the Rebels fired at him without effect before his comrades could rescue the hapless man.[3]

Murder of Trooper Bailey Near Weston

About this same time near Weston in west Platte County three guerrillas killed a local man, Thomas Bailey, who was a member of the 16th Kansas Cavalry. At the time Private Bailey was on furlough to visit his family in Platte County. A number of northern men of this area joined Kansas units throughout the war thinking this would give them better survivability than joining local Missouri militia outfits. A sideline to Bailey's demise is that for days afterward Kansas cavalry patrols searched the neighborhood off and on to find his body, and finally made the grim discovery about two weeks later.[4]

Union Officers "Cry Wolf"

Union Captain W. T. Woods of the 82nd EMM at Weston on June 10 passed along to Brigadier General Clinton B. Fisk, the district commander, the word he received that Quantrill and as many as 1,000 of his bushwhackers were then camped on the Goose Neck Bend of the Platte River in northeast Platte County. Woods added that few of these guerrillas had shoulder weapons, but they all carried from one to four .36 caliber "navy" revolvers. The district headquarters sent Captain Fitzgerald and a patrol of his 16th Kansas Cavalry to that vicinity that reported back that this was not the case, whereupon an officer in the district office at St. Joseph sarcastically replied to Captain Woods that:

> We are glad to learn that there was no cause for all this alarm, and that 4,000 navy revolvers were not being used against us. You will ascertain who the two reliable parties were who gave you this important information and direct them to report forthwith to these headquarters under arrest. We have been looking for something reliable for several days.

Sometimes even improbable rumors contain some truth and deserve deeper study. Of course, Union authorities did not know that Quantrill's own lieutenants, George Todd and Bill Anderson, deposed him about two weeks before and he was no longer

Sixteen—Before the Insurgency: Northwest Missouri North of the River

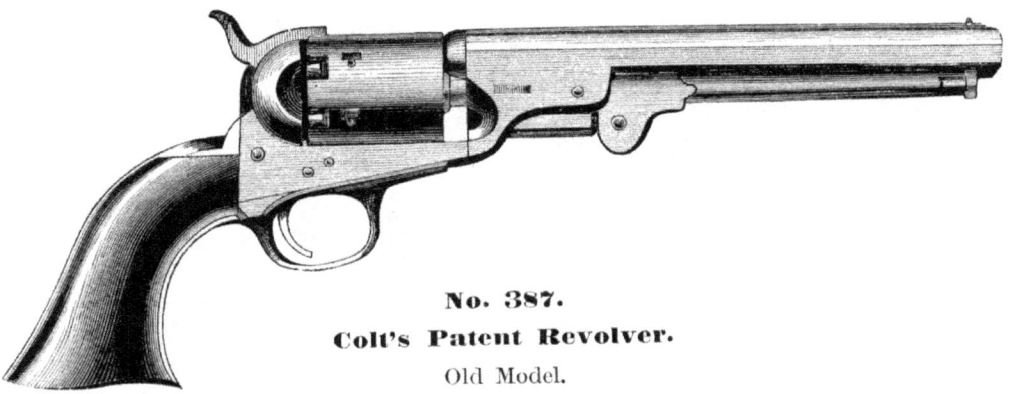

No. 387.
Colt's Patent Revolver.
Old Model.

The guerrillas' favorite sidearm was the Model 1851, six-shot, caliber .36, Colt's Navy Revolver, and they often carried several of them (Schuyler, Hartley, and Graham, *Illustrated Catalogue of Arms and Military Goods,* 1864, p. 137).

in command. However, those who did command Quantrill's former band sometime in June did send an undetermined number of veteran bushwhackers to serve as security and a defensive reaction force to protect Lieutenant Colonel Thornton's fledgling new command in the Platte County area. The danger to the northern cause in this area now seemed to be that the St. Joseph headquarters had received so many exaggerated warnings from a variety of sources "crying wolf" that the Union command hardened itself against nearly all such reports whether they contained truth or not. This attitude was not serving the northern cause well and promised disaster in the near future.[5]

The Ridgely Raid of 11 June

The well-publicized Ridgely fight in northeast Platte County June 11 led Union officials to clear intelligence that revealed Confederate Colonel Thornton's entire operation, numbers, and timetable, although the skeptical northern leadership differed both about its veracity and what countermeasures to take. That intelligence also dramatically demonstrated the growing danger to loyal Union troops in Platte County which area Union leaders also largely discounted. The several written versions of this fight differ widely, but it seems that the same guerrillas from the Arnoldsville and New Market fights of June 1 rode to Ridgely June 11 specifically to assassinate Platte Countian Captain William Fitzgerald of the 16th Kansas Cavalry because Fitzgerald's aggressive patrolling in the area was taking a toll of the Rebels and threatened to expose Colonel Thornton's highly successful recruiting, as guerrilla and participant Jim Cummins wrote in his 1903 memoirs about his part in this fight. Confederate Captain Holmes Overton, Lieutenant John G. Oldham, and guerrilla subordinate George Fielding led about 20 mounted bushwhackers in Union uniforms into the main street of Ridgely at eleven in the morning where real Union militia under Captain Benjamin F. Poe from Plattsburg, Clinton County, thought they were comrades in arms and rendered a salute. The disguised Rebel force returned the salute and calmly waited in the saddle in the middle of the street for the prearranged signal to strike while Captain Overton dismounted and presented fake credentials to Union Captain Fitzgerald on the sidewalk. At this very moment, one of the real militiamen recognized two brothers from Buchanan County known to be bushwhackers and shouted a warning. Pandemonium ensued as both sides attempted to shoot each other at close quarters and some of the Rebel horses bolted in panic. On the southern side, Captain Overton was instantly killed and Fielding was grievously wounded but managed to ride out of town before he collapsed by the road. The other guerrillas realized they had in an instant lost the advantage of surprise and after a few shots rode quickly out of town in all directions, several of them with wounds. One of the Union soldiers was killed and two were wounded on the Ridgely street, but none of the bushwhacker bullets hit Captain Fitzgerald, whose death seemed to be the aim of this raid. Soon afterwards, a passerby noticed the suffering Fielding groaning and bleeding profusely by the road a short distance from town and the highly agitated Union troops fetched him back where Fitzgerald and others elicited much information from him before they summarily executed the man. George Fielding revealed Lieutenant Colonel John Thornton's entire recruiting operation with timetable and the fact that he already had 300 men. The badly wounded prisoner also revealed that Overton, Oldham, himself, and the others were indeed assassinating a number of strong northern sympathizers in the area and revealed names of men they had already killed and some, including some present at his interrogation, they still intended to kill. Further, the dying Fielding told his questioners that Thornton personally approved the kill list and ordered the bushwhackers to take direct action to eliminate those men. Fitzgerald also found on Fielding's person the furlough paper belonging to Private Thomas Bailey of Fitzgerald's own company killed by the bushwhackers two or three days before near Weston, as described earlier. In his brief account of this action to superiors Captain Fitzgerald touched on the intelligence gains but also emphasized the peril faced by real Union troops in the Platte County area: "We are in a bad fix here. Can't get away without assistance. We have no ammunition, and can't get it. Send men to relieve us, if possible. I can't go away; we are preparing to defend ourselves the best we can."

District commander General Fisk wrote to General Rosecrans about this "desperate little fight" and stressed the intelligence gained from George Fielding's confession. He wrote in bitterness about Fielding's revelation that eleven of the raiders were turncoats and "were on the muster-rolls of a militia company in this county, and they carried a Federal musket all winter." Fisk also revealed to his boss that he would probably soon reluctantly accept General Curtis' offer to send in Kansas troops to help him restore order in the Platte County area. Incredibly, Union Major John M. Clark of the 82nd EMM "Paw Paw Militia" wrote to Brigadier General Fisk discounting Captain Fitzgerald's hard-won intelligence by dismissing the Ridgely fight as a mere "private feud" and a product of "personal vengeance." The hidden nature of guerrilla war in this region seemed to have baffled the northern leaders to the point that they could not agree on any remedy. Lieutenant Colonel Thornton, meanwhile, was startled to hear that the dying Fielding revealed his entire operation to Captain Fitzgerald, who had already proven to be a dangerous man to Thornton's scheme. Therefore, the Rebel commander must have ordered all his recruiters, recruits, and guerrillas to "stand down" and keep a lower profile for the next three or four weeks until the Federals were lulled back into their previous complacency about the true threat that his Platte County insurrection posed to the Union military. The Platte County area was suddenly much more serene over the next three weeks as Thornton quietly worked to prepare a future nasty surprise for the Yankees.[6]

Raid on Farley and Attack on the Fort Leavenworth Woodcutters

The week of June 12 through 18 was noticeably less violent in the Platte County area. Unidentified southerners on June 12 committed a bloodless raid upon the village of Farley in southwest Platte County, taking what they wanted.[7] The following day only a short distance to the northwest twenty bushwhackers described as "in their shirt sleeves and citizens clothes, armed with revolvers" only a mile from the ferry landing opposite the Union Fort Leavenworth attacked three teams of wood-cutters sent out from the fort, killing one of them, and taking six horses." Union Major General Samuel R. Curtis, head of the Kansas department, felt this attack was too close to his responsibilities to ignore and corresponded with Major General Rosecrans of the Missouri Department and General Fisk about why northern troops on the Missouri side seemed unable to prevent or react to the attack on the wood-cutters.

The Kansas Patrol That the Rebels Allowed to Pass

Partly to investigate what was happening in Platte County Major Robert H. Hunt of the 15th Kansas Cavalry at Fort Leavenworth led a patrol of 30 of his troopers and those of the 16th Kansas Cavalry between June 13 and 17 across Platte County and back again. They rescued Captain Fitzgerald at Ridgely and searched around Weston in vain for the body of the murdered Private Bailey of his company of the 16th Kansas Cavalry.

Thirty of the hated Kansas troopers would have been tempting bait to the burgeoning southern forces then in Platte County, but evidently Lieutenant Colonel Thornton permitted them to come and go unmolested in order to continue to hide the true size of his force from the confused Union leadership. Major Hunt's very vulnerable patrol found little to report, and he sarcastically wrote that they "talked with the people; glad to see us. They are all Union people, every one," but he mentioned in his report one farmer deep in the interior of Platte County "who seemed to be alarmed that we had ventured out so far with so small a force. He added that there were at least 500 guerrillas within 10 miles." The Kansans did discover a recently used, empty southern camp eight miles north of Parkville at the southern tip of Platte County, and saw elusive Rebel lookouts throughout their patrol. In some places local militia escorted the Kansans through the countryside, but although relations between the two forces seemed friendly, they were also strained. Major Hunt concluded that Platte County was inhabited mostly by southern sympathizers who were disarmingly pleasant to his command, but he reported to his superiors that there were about 300 Rebels there under the overall command of Lieutenant Colonel John C. Thornton of the Confederate army. This tidbit Hunt probably repeated from Captain Fitzgerald.[8]

More Warnings of Coming Insurrection

The week of June 19 through 25 was also quiet in the Platte County area. Probable Rebel recruits robbed isolated farms in west and northwest Platte County June 20 and 21 to obtained needed items. That these men threatened no violence to their victims tended to identify them as recruits rather than bushwhackers.[9] On the morning of June 21 troopers of the 16th Kansas Cavalry near Weston finally found the remains of their dead comrade, Private Thomas M. Bailey, about two weeks after bushwhackers killed the man, as described earlier. On June 23 a detail of six 82nd EMM was taking to Platte City two former members who had deserted to Thornton's Rebels. Near Bee Creek north of town the detail was overwhelmed by twenty guerrillas who took their prisoners away from them without firing a shot. The leader of the bushwhackers told the sergeant of the detail that they wished no harm to the local militia and, strangely, even offered to help if the militia ever got into a fight with "Radical" Union troops.[10]

One of the St. Joseph newspapers printed about June 23 a report learned from passengers on the railroad cars in north Platte County of a strong rumor circulating in Weston and other parts of the county that the Rebels there were preparing for a raid on unnamed towns and villages there. The newspaper article closed by stating "it is our opinion, from all the facts in our possession, that is it well enough for these people to be on the watch, for at any moment may a force attack them." The uprising foreshadowed in this report was still over two weeks away, but the rumors were a fair warning of what was to come.[11]

The week of June 26 through July 2 reflected a continuation of this strange quiet period probably imposed by Thornton on his rapidly growing command to lull the Federals. Some local northern men of influence recognized the threat of Lieutenant Colonel Thornton's hidden operation preparing in and around Platte County, although many of those in power seemed to regard their warnings as baseless. On July 1 the *St. Joseph Herald* issued another strong alert about the untrustworthiness and duplicity of the "Paw Paw Militia" of the area under the headline "Words of Warning." The article reprised a short history of the "Paw Paws" and mentioned that they failed to report the recruiting of Confederate Colonel John Winston under their very noses in Platte County for about five months until General Curtis and Captain Fitzgerald of the Kansas Department learned of it and took action to capture Winston. The article stated that 18 to 20 strongly loyal Union military men had in recent weeks been assassinated in Platte, Clay, and south Buchanan Counties, and families of northern sympathy had been driven out of Clay and Platte Counties. The St. Joseph paper also reported that unidentified guerrillas rode through New Market in north-central Platte County June 28 and bragged that their side then had 2,000 men "preparing for a raid in Northwest Missouri which will extend into the State of Iowa." These riders also offered a bounty of "a dollar a head" for Union troops in the area, although that was probably just braggadocio.[12] A Department of the Missouri staff officer at Kansas City on July 1 appraised General Rosecrans that one of General Curtis' aides in the Department of Kansas sent a telegram of warning to Colonel James H. Ford, the commander of the 2nd Colorado Cavalry, just south of the Missouri River from Platte County. The telegram read in part: "We have reliable information that Colonel Thornton is in Platte City at the head of 600 guerrillas, having been joined by three companies of militia [Paw Paw]. Three other companies are said to be reported to join him before morning. There are indications that they will attack Weston."

It would appear that a substantial portion of Missouri's controversial "Paw Paw Militia" switched sides and voluntarily tumbled into the arms of the Confederate forces. This is startling news and apparently it was correct, but also notable is the fact that this telegram was sent around the chain of command of the apparently complacent Department of the Missouri to one of their field commanders directly from an aide to the commander of the Kansas Department. The aide, and perhaps others, felt the information in the telegram was vital enough to violate strong precepts of military protocol.[13] Also on July 1 newspaperman and on-the-spot chronicler of Platte County's daily life throughout the war, William Paxton, noted that the Australian circus was performing at Weston, and matter-of-factly mentioned that bushwhackers were on the same day in camp four miles from town. Perhaps some of them quietly came to Weston and were spectators in the circus audience, too.[14] Actually, southern forces did not raid Weston in spite of their overwhelming numbers at this time or on any of the next several days probably because Thornton was not ready to launch his assault on Union-occupied northwest Missouri just yet.

On the Eve of the Insurgency: The Bradley House Fight of 3 July

The tempo of war in Platte County accelerated during the week of July 3 through 9 until by Thursday July 7 Colonel Thornton unleashed the first of his attacks that he hoped would trigger a massive insurgency across north Missouri. The relative quiet of the previous few weeks was disturbed at four in the afternoon on Sunday July 3 when Union Lieutenant Colonel Daniel M. Draper led 50 troopers of his 9th Cavalry MSM in an attack upon 18 guerrillas or Confederate recruits at a Mrs. Bradley's house by the Platte River 2.5 miles north of the county seat of Platte City. Draper's patrol heard perhaps from an informant that there was a band of Rebels at the Bradley house, so they rode there expecting trouble. They found six armed men in the house who waited until the Federals were at the back door before they opened fire hoping to escape as the Yankees dove for cover. These troopers were veterans and wise to such tricks, and they killed five running southerners and badly wounded the sixth who barely managed to escape. Twelve more Rebels then attacked the patrol out of the nearby woods which resulted in a two-hour gunfight before both sides broke contact. Total losses were one Union trooper seriously wounded and another badly wounded while Confederate losses were six killed outright and several others wounded. The southerners were all armed with short-range revolvers which accounts for the lop-sided casualty results. At one point in the fight Thomas Fielding, brother of George Fielding executed after the Ridgely fight of June 11, appeared to offer to surrender and wounded the two Federals as they approached him before the other Yanks cut him down with a fusillade of shots, according to participants of the 9th Cavalry MSM. A local version of this

Lieutenant Colonel Daniel M. Draper led his troops of the 9th Cavalry MSM in the Bradley House fight of 3 July against 18 unidentified Rebels near Platte City (private collection, courtesy of the late Bob Younger and Mary Younger and Andy Turner).

part of the fight has Fielding sacrificing himself so a wounded comrade could scamper away, and perhaps to wreak revenge on Federals for the recent death of his brother.[15]

The July 3 fight at the Bradley house seemed to cause southern forces in the area to come out of hiding and make assertive appearances around Platte County. On Tuesday July 5 bushwhackers stopped the mail carrier between Weston and Platte City and searched through the contents of his bag. They released the man but warned him that they would kill him next time they found him carrying the mail.[16] Two days later, Thursday July 7, Lieutenant Colonel Thornton unleashed the force of bushwhackers sent to him from south of the Missouri River to raid the village of Parkville in the south tip of the county, as the opening act of his insurgency.

June Through Early July 1864 in Buchanan County and Farther North

Buchanan County was also touched by the increasing violence mostly associated with the growing Confederate presence to the south in Platte County during the early summer of 1864. The location of Brigadier General Clinton B. Fisk's headquarters of the northern district of Missouri in St. Joseph did not seem to deter guerrilla actions in the area.

The St. Joseph Jail Break of 5 June and Its Deadly Aftermath

The summer began on an exasperating note for the Union military here June 5 when eleven desperate guerrilla prisoners and common criminals escaped from the jail at St. Joseph and headed in different directions to elude their pursuers. These prisoners, including some who faced death sentences for bushwhacking, bribed one of the guards, and at seven o'clock on that Sunday morning overwhelmed the rest of the militia guard force and left the building equipped with the guards' muskets and cartridge belts. Being so equipped allowed these men to pass themselves as militia to passersby as they walked along. On their way out of town they forced three men on the road to hand over their revolvers. For the next several days citizen guards and militia of several counties searched the countryside for the fugitives. By June 6 these forces managed to kill two of the escapers and they wounded and recaptured a third. That evening four of the newly freed Rebels passed themselves again as militia looking for bushwhackers stopped at a rural farm and were given supper. By June 7 the citizens guards and militia caught three more of the evaders, evidently at Kidder, northwest Caldwell County. Two more surrendered in Andrew County to the north, and elements of the 9th Cavalry MSM, stationed in St. Joseph, caught two more who still had the captured muskets and cartridge boxes when they were taken.[17] Near Breckenridge in northwest Caldwell County on June 9 Captain Merrill Givens of the 33rd EMM was accidentally killed and one of his men seriously wounded by elements of the Livingston County militia when the two groups mistook each other for the escapees. Some members of the 33rd EMM rode that same night to the home of one of the known evaders not far from the scene of the mistaken shooting and murdered a relative and burned a barn belonging to the family. Evidently, two or three of the jail escapers who had earlier committed crimes in Caldwell and Livingston Counties managed to make good their escape.[18]

Public Execution of A. J. Lanier at Savannah on 10 June

Union authorities had returned Confederate soldier A. J. Lanier of Andrew County publicly executed June 10 near the wagon depot in his hometown of Savannah in a highly publicized killing intended to be a warning to guerrillas. Lanier had returned to his home county after serving as an artilleryman in the Confederate army and was arrested in late May 1863. A Union military tribunal tried and convicted Lanier, and gave him a death sentence for (1) his alleged part in the 1861 arson of a mill at Rochester in east Andrew County, (2) his oath violation, and (3) for his acting as a guerrilla. The Union military kept the condemned man in confinement at the Gratiot Street Prison in St. Louis until a day before his execution and then sent Lanier by railroad across the state back to his hometown to a public execution by musketry. As mentioned in Chapter Twelve, Lanier and his prison comrades tried and almost succeeded June 9 in digging their way out of the Gratiot Street facility just hours before Lanier was to be sent to the train, but the guards coming to take the condemned prisoner caught them all in the act. Lanier steadfastly denied that it was he who set fire to the mill back in 1861 even after his conviction, and many citizens of the Andrew County area were sympathetic to his plight. The prisoner was an orphan known for impetuous acts in the Savannah area before the war, but the heavy-handed example Federal authorities made of him executing him in his Confederate butternut trousers still filthy from his attempt to dig his way to freedom hours before in St. Louis, his bravery facing execution, and signs of his religious faith in his last hours elicited much sympathy

One of the charges against A. J. Lanier was that he deliberately burned down the mill at Rochester in 1861 (Underwood and Clough, eds., *Battles and Leaders of the Civil War*, vol. 2, p. 341).

for A. J. Lanier and caused locals to remember his execution for many years after the war. His was one of the most publicized, best-remembered executions of the war in Missouri, and the sympathy it evoked was the opposite effect desired by the Union leadership.[19]

Threatening Notes at Rock House Prairie on 16 June

On June 16 ten armed, mounted guerrillas near Rock House Prairie of east-central Buchanan County left threatening notes at the homes of several northern sympathizers. One such note read: "Order No. 1. You are hereby notified to leave the country within three days. You are for Lincoln, and we don't intend you shall remain here." These threatening notes were also intentional irony, for northern extremists the previous summer in this same area left very similar notes at the homes of southern sympathizers which led to many moving out of the region. Obviously, these unidentified bushwhackers were responding in kind a year later.[20]

Unidentified Night Raiders Near Sparta

Five or six unidentified night riders visited four rural homes around Sparta in central Buchanan County the night of 23/24 June, but took mostly firearms and some money. At a fifth home a Mr. Moore flourished a revolver and the angry raiders fired pistol bullets through the front door, unintentionally sending slugs thudding into a wall near a sleeping little girl. The St. Joseph newspaper article describing this night of raids mentioned that the night riders told their victims they were "from Kansas" and threatened them not to tell the Union military authorities for three days on the peril that they would return and kill the occupants and burn the homes. This threat meant that the robbers intended to remain in the area for a while, whereas Kansas Jayhawker raiders almost always slipped back over the Missouri River to safety on the Kansas shore by daylight. Also, there had not been Jayhawker raiding in this area for some weeks. Perhaps these clues indicated that the raiders were actually southern Missouri bushwhackers and not Kansans at all.[21]

Threats Against the 87th EMM

Many members of the Union 87th EMM in Buchanan County were dedicated, northern sympathizers, and Second Lieutenant Thomas D. Ridge of Captain John R. Snyder's Company E was among that number. At the end of June Ridge and a few fellow 87th men passed themselves as guerrillas to a Walter Bevins near Taos, south-central Buchanan County in order to elicit information from the man about guerrilla activities in the area. The excitement of the rising southern cause in northern Missouri evidently caused Bevins to confide more to his supposed bushwhacker guests than should be prudent. The man told these "southern men" that local bushwhackers had intended to attack Captain Snyder's company of 87th EMM, unaware that the men to whom he was speaking were members of that unit. He then told them that the guerrillas cancelled that plan when they heard Snyder's company disbanded. The host also confided that there were 2,000 Confederates ready to rise up in north Missouri, and the local Confederates were waiting for the "Paw Paw Militia" of the 81st and 82nd EMM to acquire firearms in about ten days after which they would all "make a grand raid." Bevins was confident that in about three weeks southerners in Missouri would rise up and throw off the yoke of the Federals. Second Lieutenant Ridge wrote a letter to the *St. Joseph Weekly Herald* from Arnoldsville on June 28 revealing all this information, which the paper printed on its front page July 7.[22]

The Schoolhouse Flag Tussle in Gentry County on 3 July

That same issue of the *Herald* printed another article demonstrating the growing high spirits of some southern sympathizers near Gentryville in south-central Gentry County on July 3. A number of these southern citizens gathered at the Liberty School near town to display their displeasure at two U.S. flags flying over the building.

One woman seized a flag and sat on it, whereupon the young man who put the flag on the building threatened her with a revolver to her head. A second woman snatched the flag out from under the first one and gave it back to the armed man to defuse the situation. A number of southern sympathizers present at this schoolhouse melee commented loudly that guerrillas would soon see that the offending U.S. flag would fly over them no more. The newspaper editor attributed this outbreak of southern defiance to "men professing to be in correspondence with guerrillas."[23]

Charles Fletcher "Fletch" Taylor led a group of former Quantrill members with Clay County backgrounds to their home area in spring 1864 first to settle old scores there (John N. Edwards, *Noted Guerrillas*, 1877, p. 238; courtesy of the late Bob Younger and Mary Younger and Andy Turner).

Clay and Clinton Counties Between June and early July: Taylor and Shepherd with a Teenage Recruit Named Jesse James

Clay County Guerrillas Return for Revenge

During the summer of 1863 bushwhacker leader Ferdinando Scott brought his small Clay County guerrilla band south of the Missouri River to Quantrill, and in late May 1864 a number of these same men returned to their home area to settle old scores. Scott died fighting in Jackson County in 1863, but scrappy Charles Fletcher "Fletch" Taylor seems to have been in charge of this group of about fifteen bushwhackers that came from Quantrill's former command to Clay County in late May 1864, dressed in Union uniforms. "Fletch" Taylor was born in May 1842 in Zanesville, Ohio, but prewar was living in the Independence area where his English-born father had established a high school. During 1863, young Taylor earned a reputation in the Quantrill band as a daring bushwhacker eager to complete the most death-defying missions, and as a killer. Taylor had a knack for getting into trouble in Texas during the winter of 1863–1864, but Quantrill still named him as one of his lieutenants. Twenty-two-year-old "Fletch" Taylor proved during 1864 to be a very determined, capable leader of men on his own, and a true survivor.[24] Some of the men who came with Taylor were such Clay Countians as Frank James, Peyton Long, Jim Cummins, Doc Rupe, and Allen Parmer, while Taylor himself, Archie Clements, and James Bissett were originally from south of the Missouri River. Frank James brought his 16-year-old, younger brother Jesse into the guerrilla service about this time. Although young, the teenager had suffered abuse at the hands of the local Union militia, was familiar with firearms, and seemed

Allen Parmer (sometimes written as "Palmer") was a Clay Countian who served under Quantrill, Fletch Taylor, George Todd, and went to Kentucky with Quantrill in December 1864 (John N. Edwards, *Noted Guerrillas*, 1877, p. 178; courtesy of the late Bob Younger and Mary Younger and Andy Turner).

promising to be a proficient bushwhacker if he could survive until his seventeenth birthday in September.[25] Between June 1 and June 6 these Quantrill men executed several vulnerable, local men who were either informants to the Union military or Yankee soldiers who had caused them grief. The guerrillas' blue uniforms may have helped four of them to trick, capture, and murder Private Brantley Y. Bond of the 6th Cavalry MSM at his home near Claysville in northeast Clay County where he was evidently on furlough. Bond was a veteran of the tough Lone Jack battle of August 1862, and lore says that he had helped hang the James' step-father, Reuben Samuel, almost to death. Shortly afterwards these bushwhackers called Sergeant Alvis Dagley of the 89th EMM out of a field and then shot him to death as he crossed the fence. Dagley was staying with another family near Claysville in Washington Township probably for his own safety, was a veteran of the local 48th EMM, and had also been in the 4th Provisional EMM. A patrol of the 4th Provisional EMM had executed a Clay County guerrilla named Park Donovan the previous September when his stolen horse could not jump a fence and left him lying injured in the road; and bushwhacker Jim Cummins wrote in his memoir that the bushwhackers murdered these men for killing the helpless Donovan and denying his last request to pray before they finished him. There are vague references that Taylor's guerrillas also murdered a Moses Barnes or Baines in either Clay County or nearby in Platte County after he fed them a meal thinking they were Union cavalrymen. One northern sympathizer at Osborn in northeast Clay County reported to General Fisk at St. Joseph that on June 6 these bushwhackers killed six Union soldiers in that neighborhood and stole two horses, although perhaps some of his claims may have been exaggerations heightened by hysteria. Two other Union militiamen fled the Claysville area

George Shepherd was another Clay Countian who served under several guerrilla chiefs, but later in 1864 became a chief himself (John N. Edwards, *Noted Guerrillas*, 1877, p. 373; courtesy of the late Bob Younger and Mary Younger and Andy Turner).

north into western Caldwell County just in case their names were on the guerrillas' kill list.[26]

A local record says on June 15 another Quantrill guerrilla, George Shepherd with six comrades boldly rode through Missouri City in south Clay County, "but did no damage." Perhaps the seven riders merely wanted to prove they were brave enough to show themselves in public. Shepherd and some of his men would return to the Clay County area later.[27]

The week of June 19 through June 25 proved to be a violent one in the Clay and Clinton County area. Sometime this week in northern Clay County Second Lieutenant Carey H. Gordon and ten troopers of the 9th Cavalry MSM rode onto a camp of about twelve guerrillas who fired at them first. Gordon's patrol fired two volleys into the bushwhackers and then charged the camp causing the Rebels to scatter into the brush. The Federals reported no losses to themselves, two Rebels wounded, and they captured four horses.[28] Five or six unidentified guerrillas raided a German-American settlement in northeast Clinton County, some miles north of Clay County, the evening of June 21 taking mostly cash. They evidently used an informant very familiar with their victims, as the raiders seemed to know not only who had money, but in some cases how much they had.[29]

The Mysterious "Doctor Davis" Leading Guerrillas

This raid is similar to one that bushwhacker Jim Cummins described in his 1903 memoir in which a man he identified only as "Davis" convinced three Clay County guerrillas—Cummins, Doc Rupe, and a King—to accompany him to the Cameron vicinity of northeast Clinton County sometime during the war to stop a Yankee lieutenant colonel from recruiting for the 6th Cavalry MSM and steal the recruits' horses. Cummins described their adventures raiding rural homes looking for the horses to take. There are other references to a Davis or "Doctor Davis" who led southern men in the nearby Livingston, Daviess, and Grundy County area in 1862 who is poorly identified; and Cummins' comrade Davis may be the same man.[30] The Liberty newspaper mentioned that unidentified guerrillas raided the village of Greenville in the northeast corner of Clay County about the night of 22/23 June, but gave no other details.[31] On June 23 a delegation of Clay County residents traveled to St. Joseph to plead with General Fisk to remove a company of militia from Gentry County—probably Company A of 31st EMM—from their midst. A St. Joseph newspaper quoted the committee to say those militiamen were intimidating southern sympathizers in rural neighborhoods to the extent that about 300 civilians were forced "to flee into the brush to save their lives."[32] About June 23 or 24 unidentified Union troops in north Clay County killed a Smith who lived in Fishing River Township of the southeast part of the county. The northern troops evidently killed the man for being a bushwhacker, and left his body lying in the road.[33]

Militia Kills Coffman and Taylor Vows Revenge

As the week drew to a close about June 24 or 25 two local guerrillas, David Coffman of southeast Clinton County and the ubiquitous Davis, stole horses and money from farms in Coffman's neighborhood. Coffman was riding a horse he took from Jefferson Pryor, father of Benjamin F. Pryor of the 13th Missouri Cavalry Regiment. Benjamin Pryor was in the area and with a few friends joined a patrol of Clinton County militia, or 89th EMM, and shortly rode onto the two bushwhackers. As Davis and Coffman jumped their horses over lane fences to escape Davis got away. However, Pryor's horse Coffman was riding failed to jump one fence, the animal dumped the guerrilla in a lane, and the Union soldiers shot him dead. Guerrilla leader Charles "Fletch" Taylor of Quantrill's band was upset hearing about the death of fellow guerrilla Coffman, because he revealed later a local citizen committee made a treaty of nonviolence with Taylor who felt Coffman's death violated the agreement. This committee may have been the same one that a few days before pleaded with General Fisk at St. Joseph to remove the Gentry County militia from Clay County, so perhaps guerrilla Taylor had set the departure of those militiamen as a condition for his truce with the Clay Countians. Whatever the circumstance, Taylor and his men claimed vengeance for the death of David Coffman shortly thereafter.[34] Fletcher Taylor's band of about fifteen guerrillas and others escalated the level of violence in Clay and Clinton Counties over the following week. Either Taylor accelerated the violence tempo to cover the activities of Confederate Colonel John C. Thornton's recruiting command to the west in Platte County, to avenge the June 24 or 25 Union killing of fellow guerrilla Coffman, or both.

Attack on the Bigelow Brothers

During the night of June 25/26 Taylor threw his entire command of about 15 into the task of killing Yankee schoolteachers Salmon G. and John G. Bigelow at Salmon's home in northeast Clay County. Earlier in the war Salmon was captain in the local 48th EMM, and lately was a private in the 89th EMM. The Ohio-born Bigelow brothers were known in northeast Clay County for their strong northern sympathy, but Taylor's men accused the two Bigelows of depredations against local southerners. The Bigelow brothers did not accept their fate lightly and fought desperately but in vain against the bushwhackers who besieged them and finally killed the pair in an all-out assault on the house. During the intense shooting young Jesse James accidentally shot off a portion of his own finger with a revolver. Postwar guerrilla chronicler John N. Edwards gave the Bigelows compliments he customarily withheld from Yankees:

> The brothers—unsupported and outnumbered—fought to the death. The house sheltered them much, and they were otherwise cool, dangerous, athletic men.... Taylor ordered a charge. Bursting down doors and breaking away all obstructions, the guerrillas ended the combat with one furious rush. Frank James killed Captain Bigelow at the head of a flight of steps, and Jesse James, wounded as he was, followed [John Bigelow] into a lumber room and shot him there, defending himself desperately with a piece of a bedstead.

Taylor's men suffered at least two men wounded and two horses killed. In his 1903 memoir guerrilla Jim Cummins mentioned carrying for the rest of his life the haunting memory of the sight after the battle of Salmon Bigelow's twelve-year-old daughter Elizabeth weeping over the loss of her father:

> I was an eyewitness to the killing of these men, and, with some others, remember a little twelve-year-old daughter following us and bewailing the death of her papa and asking and praying what would become of us for the killing or her poor father. This little girl, with her grief and tears, often comes most vividly to my mind, and when reading a few months ago of the suicide of my old comrade, Jim Younger, the little grief-stricken face came up before me.

Charles Taylor addressed a letter of explanation for killing the Bigelows to the Union commander at nearby Liberty soon after:

> Sir—in accordance with promises I made to Mr. Gosney, one of the peace committee, in relation to leaving Clay county, if the Radicals would also leave (which, I believe, was the understanding), I got my men together and proceeded toward Clinton county, and had got

there when I heard about Coffman being killed. I immediately returned to avenge his death, and I did by killing the two Bigelows. I then started for Platte [County] with some of my men, intending to stay out of these counties according to promises; but hearing of one of my own men being killed, I have come again to avenge his death—and I will do it ... and I am going to stay here until the Radicals all leave this county.[35]

On the next day, June 26, Taylor's men killed Clinton Countian, New Hampshire–born Bishop A. Bailey seven miles north of Liberty in north Clay County as the middle-aged shoemaker was returning home after business in the town. Bailey's family reported him missing the same day, and locals discovered his body with a bullet wound in the head a couple of days later. At least two of the Bailey men served in uniform on the Union side, which probably caused the bushwhackers to murder the man.[36] The St. Joseph newspaper reported that also on June 26 a witness saw forty guerrillas at one of the Biggerstaff homes in either central or northwest Clinton County, but provided no other details.[37] A Union atrocity took place in north Clinton County along the railroad during the night of June 27/28. A returned Confederate veteran, Private Absalom Harpold of near Kingston in central Caldwell County and lately from Company D of the Confederate 3rd Missouri Infantry, visited his large family for about a week and then decided he would secretly hide in a freight car on the railroad and make his way west to California until the war was over. The veteran of three years southern service had discussed with his family surrendering himself to local authorities, but decided against it. Harpold's plan went awry near Cameron, northeast Clinton County, when soldiers probably of the local 33rd EMM found him hiding in a freight car and seized him. These militiamen may have assumed Harpold was a bushwhacker and hanged the 43-year-old father of nine children to a beam of a nearby building until he was dead.[38]

Tiffin's Militia and Taylor's Guerrillas Hunt Each Other

On June 29 or 30 Captain Clayton Tiffin's Ray County militia company from Richmond rode into Clay County after hearing about guerrillas there and discovered what they had heard was true. The Ray County men fought Taylor's bushwhackers in three separate skirmishes, but found them to be wily opponents who fired and melted back into the brush. Near Centerville Captain Tiffin's men discovered guerrillas at a farm where they were making the farmer cook breakfast for them, and chased them off before they could eat it. Near Haynesville in the northeast corner Second Lieutenant Isaac McKown and a Rebel shot into each other at close range killing the southerner and severely wounding McKown with a hip wound. Tiffin was forced to order his men to scatter in the brush in guerrilla style when he realized that Taylor's men were hunting them rather than the other way around. Tiffin concluded that "we have quite a rough time of getting the bushwhackers out of this county." His commander back in Ray County, Captain D. P. Whitmer, hearing from Tiffin, reported to district command "Captain Tiffin tells me that Clay County is full of guerrillas, mostly citizens, and many of whom were armed as militia last winter, and I am well satisfied it is even so; and further, that it will not do to rely on any but true and reliable Union men to fight these devils...." It appeared that Union leadership was discovering that the "Paw Paw Militia" was more of a liability than an asset and was starting to join the guerrilla side in large numbers.[39]

Taylor's Band Ambushes Kemper's Patrol on 4 July

"Fletch" Taylor struck once more July 4 against Union militia in Clay County before he took his men west to assist Confederate Lieutenant Colonel Thornton's command to the west in Platte County. The Union commander of Liberty, Captain William B. Kemper, and 45 troopers of his Company C of the 9th Cavalry MSM tracked Taylor's now 25-or-so men to the rugged headwaters landscape of the Fishing River near Centerville in central Clay County. On the morning of Independence Day Kemper and some of his men paused to water their horses at a creek that ran along a bluff. At that moment Taylor's men atop the bluff fired a volley into the blue troopers killing two and seriously wounding the captain and another man—all at no loss to the bushwhackers.[40]

Ray, Caldwell, Daviess, and Carroll Counties Between June and early July

The normally peaceful interior counties of Ray, Caldwell, Daviess, and Carroll Counties witnessed increased violence throughout the early summer of 1864 because of the great influx of guerrillas throughout north Missouri. The previously idle Union militiamen in these counties were hard pressed to reply to the new threats resulting in some measure of chaos.

Confusion Hunting St. Joseph Jail Escapees

Between June 8 and 11 Union militia and volunteer citizen posses in Daviess and Caldwell Counties reacted and over-reacted to a handful of guerrilla escapees from the St. Joseph jail on June 5, as described earlier in this chapter. A former Union infantry captain at Hamilton in north Caldwell County reported June 9 that "there is a gang of some 40 or 50 bushwhackers about 10 miles north of here, and have killed 1 of our men last night." Since no other source reported any such numbers of bushwhackers in this region at this time, the captain and his volunteer civilians must have encountered another civilian posse from another town in the dark.[41] Of course, as stated earlier in the chapter, two of these citizens' posses collided near Breckenridge in southeast Daviess County at daybreak on June 26 resulting in the death of a militia captain and the wounding of another posse member. On June 11 Lieutenant W. T. Filson's patrol of 33rd EMM a few miles east of Kingston in central Caldwell County captured two men who gave false names and were probably part of the escaped party of prisoners from St. Joseph. The militiamen correctly identified the duo as a Dr. M. C. McCamey of southeast Linn County and a Biggs or Briggs. While Dr. McCamey was telling the patrol he was well acquainted with Union Brigadier General Odon Guitar, who would vouch for him, the other man attempted to break away and the militiamen shot him dead. Lieutenant Filson took the doctor

Union Brigadier General Odon Guitar was well known in north Missouri to the point that a captured southerner told his captors that General Guitar would vouch for him (private collection, courtesy of the late Bob Younger and Mary Younger and Andy Turner).

north to Hamilton on the railroad and notified Union authorities in Linn County, two counties to the east, to come take charge of him. Lieutenant William Lewis of the Linn County citizen guards came with some of his men by railroad the following day. They must have known Dr. McCamey as a Rebel because shortly after taking charge of him shot the doctor to death, and he was buried beside Biggs or Briggs. Evidently, both men were truly escapees from the St. Joseph jail break and these local militiamen decided not to return them to prison.[42]

On June 25 a citizens' posse near Hamilton killed two of three guerrillas and the third quickly surrendered and begged for his life. When his captors asked their prisoner to name his accomplices, he at first refused, but quickly agreed to comply when the posse began to hang him from a tree limb. The prisoner cooperated fully with the posse by naming his accomplices and also a number of sympathetic residents of the area who had provided food and shelter for the bushwhackers. The posse kept the cooperative guerrilla in chains so he could testify against those local people he named. It was apparent that the Union militia and citizen's posses of Caldwell County viewed guerrilla warfare as a life and death matter and acted accordingly.[43]

More of Quantrill's Former Guerrillas Move North of the Missouri River

In late June and the first days of July some of Quantrill's former bushwhackers crossed the Missouri River into the south edge of Ray County. During the night of June 28/29 two teenage guerrillas crossed to the north side of the river and raided the river port of Camden, taking goods from a store. Residents knew the pair as a Stevenson, who had lately been carrying the mail between Lexington and Independence, and a youth named Thornton.[44] Unidentified bushwhackers robbed two stagecoaches in south Ray County across the Missouri River from Lexington on July 2. First, they took $2,300 in cash and four horses and destroyed the mail from one coach, then, near the same place that evening took $1,200 in greenbacks and ten gold watches from another one.[45] By the first days of July the Union area commands began to hear that an undetermined number of Quantrill's west-central Missouri guerrillas was moving north in Lafayette County and then crossing the Missouri River to assemble in the Fishing River area of southwest Ray County in large numbers. On July 5 First Lieutenant William Kessinger of the 1st Cavalry MSM, temporarily in command at Lexington, reported to his regimental commander at Warrensburg, Colonel James McFerran, that "the bushwhackers are all near the river, and no scout reached their places of rendezvous of late, and the body of them seem to be below here."[46] On July 7 the *St. Joseph Weekly Herald* printed: "From gentlemen just from Kansas City and Lexington we learn the most of the guerrillas on the south side of the [Missouri River] have crossed over. A large camp is at Fishing River, and is under command of Quantrill. [George] Todd is also near at hand. These guerrillas are now gathering in force for the purpose of raiding in Northwest Missouri."[47] The newspaper could not know that Quantrill's lieutenants had deposed him over a month before, that he was at that time in exile in southwest Howard County with a small bodyguard, and that George Todd and Bill Anderson with most of their men were still in their familiar territory in Jackson and Lafayette Counties south of the river. However, Confederate Colonel John C. Thornton's burgeoning recruiting command in the Platte County area had been requesting assistance from regional bushwhackers to provide a screening force to protect the numerous inexperienced and poorly armed recruits during operations they were just about to unleash there. A large number of guerrillas responded to this appeal and perhaps a number of them were those reported encamped in the Fishing River area of southwest Ray County in the early days of July 1864.

Gordon's Guerrillas Raid Carroll County in Early July

Carroll County to the east had been relatively peaceful this spring and early summer, but that changed in the first days of July. Carroll County would be the scene of horrible guerrilla atrocities later that summer, and bushwhacker leader Silas "Cy" M. Gordon of Platte County and his small band committed some depredations there in early July. Captain Gordon was active throughout the war first in his own Platte County in 1861, then in regular Confederate service in 1862 and 1863, then in autumn 1863 he led bushwhackers in southwest Missouri, and in spring 1864 returned briefly to Platte County where he led a small band of guerrillas. Perhaps these were the same irregulars he led in Carroll County. Three unidentified "knights of the bush" on the morning of July 5 robbed the home of discharged Union veteran George Schmitt of the 3rd Cavalry MSM in the west part of Carroll County, taking clothing and about $150 in cash. Then, against the entreaties of Schmitt's wife and sister, the three robbers took the former Union cavalryman about 100 yards away from the house and shot him to death. Although local residents could not identify these guerrillas, the raiding of a nearby village two days later seems to indicate these men were of "Cy" Gordon's band.[48] Early on the morning of July 7 Captain Gordon and his band of about 15 bushwhackers raided the river port of Miles Point in southwest Carroll County. They took cash and goods from three stores, several dwellings, and some residents before they mounted to leave. At that moment Captain Lyon S. Francis and his company of local members of the 65th EMM that had been activated only the day before rode up and fired on the departing raiders, causing them to flee precipitously. Although the militia shooting seemed to miss the targets, in their haste to escape the bullets five of the guerrillas rode into a nearby slough where their horses got mired, and the riders abandoned the animals and much of their plunder to escape on foot. Afterwards, a militiaman accidentally discharged his firearm killing one man and wounding another.[49] Later in July there were be considerable more killing in Carroll County.

Therefore, throughout June and into early July 1864 Confederate irregular forces prepared a great uprising north of the Missouri River while various busy guerrilla bands and sub-bands distracted the attention of the area Union military from the preparations centered in and around Platte County just north of Kansas City. Confederate recruiter Lieutenant Colonel John C. "Coon" Thornton had by this time gathered around him hundreds of new recruits, scores of turncoat Union "Paw Paw Militia," and a force of an undetermined number of veteran bushwhackers to act as a security force or mobile screen. Thornton's variegated force would unleash their insurgency deep in the heart of Union-occupied Missouri beginning July 7.

Seventeen

Before the Insurgency Ignited: June Through Early July 1864 in Northwest Missouri South of the Missouri River

The southern guerrillas of the northwest quadrant of the state that operated south of the Missouri River were also affected by the large-scale conspiracy Confederate Lieutenant Colonel John C. "Coon" Thornton prepared to start in early July, although to a lesser degree than those closer to him north of the river. Those various bushwhacker outfits south of that water body were well aware and delighted with the persistent rumors that the Rebel army in Arkansas led by the former Missouri governor, Sterling Price, would invade Missouri and wrench it away from the Union occupation, but nobody in June and early July seemed to know when that would occur. Many of these irregular fighters hoped their struggles and small-unit actions could somehow benefit the Confederacy in their part of the state, although they were probably uncertain how they could help. The bands of George Todd and Bill Anderson, operating at the western end of this region were well aware of Lieutenant Colonel Thornton's efforts on the other side of the river since they sent some of their men to assist him. All guerrilla groups across this band of west-central Missouri viewed summer as their most advantageous season to inflict the most damage on the Yankee military here, and the large number of guerrilla actions here in June and early July certainly proved that to be the case.

June Through Early July Actions of Todd, Anderson, Wilhite, and Others in Jackson, Cass, Johnson, and Lafayette Counties

South of the Missouri River the bushwhackers formerly under Quantrill's leadership basically split into two independent bands following George Todd in mainly Jackson and Cass Counties and Bill Anderson in Lafayette County since they were already fully familiar with these areas. Further, some splinter groups of from ten to twenty followed this or that veteran guerrilla into Johnson County or sanctuary neighborhoods across the region, until the 200 or 300 bushwhackers that used to answer to Quantrill were widely spread across the landscape operating in and out of these sub-units.

The active components on the Union side in these four counties were the 2nd Colorado Cavalry along the Kansas border with various Kansas regiments west of that line answerable to the Department of Kansas; the 1st and 7th Cavalry MSM operating in

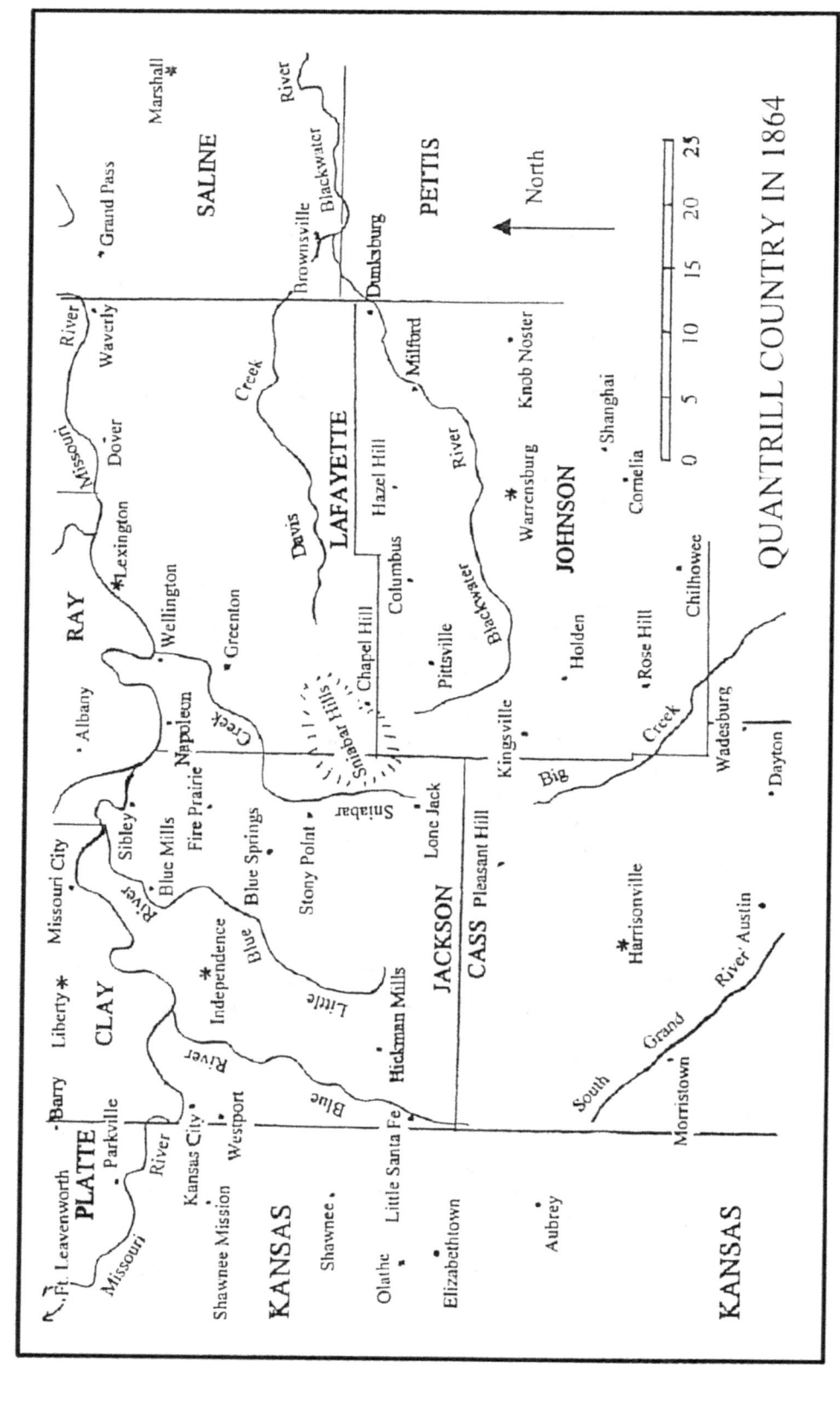

Lafayette and Johnson Counties; the 4th Cavalry MSM east of that; and a hodgepodge of small remnants of old EMM outfits and the new General Order Number 107 citizen guards units here and there in some towns.[1] On June 7 the state EMM apparatus activated only Company A of the old 77th EMM Regiment in Jackson County perhaps to guide and assist the Colorado troopers who were not as knowledgeable about the local terrain.[2] The Union leaders would probably have desired to activate some of the other EMM units, like the 71st in Lafayette County and the 40th in Johnson County, but over two years intense bushwhacker combat had thinned their ranks by decimation or intimidation and there were hardly enough left in service to call up. Besides, many of those same men were welcome additions to some of the new citizen guard outfits. All of these troops east of the Kansas border and south of the Missouri River were part of the District of Central Missouri commanded by one-armed, New York-born Brigadier General Egbert B. Brown from his Warrensburg headquarters in Johnson County. General Brown had been preparing for this guerrilla onslaught since the winter with new tactics mostly seasoned with common sense, but this summer his district was in for the most desperate combat his veterans could imagine. General Brown's leadership skills would be severely challenged by this crisis.

Probable Anderson Guerrillas Shoot Up Riverboat *Prairie Rose* on 4 June

The first four days of June witnessed an increasing pace of guerrilla activity across this part of west-central Missouri. In Lafayette County unidentified guerrillas on June 4 fired on the Pennsylvania-built stern-wheeler *Prairie Rose* near Waverly, northeast Lafayette County, as she steamed upriver bound for Fort Leavenworth with a government cargo. The bushwhackers fired mostly revolvers at the 1854-vintage steamer, shielding themselves on the south bank behind several women and children to dissuade the boat crew from shooting back. The bullets hurt nobody and had little effect because Captain William Eads had earlier strengthened the pilot house and other vital parts of the *Prairie Rose* with extra boards, as required by Union orders. Later, two pro-southern members of the vessel's crew were arrested as saboteurs for attempting to handicap their boat and refusing orders to defend her. Bill Anderson's men favored sniping at passing riverboats, and they were known to base in northeast Lafayette County, so the guerrillas that fired on the *Prairie Rose* June 4 were probably of his band. However, Anderson himself and eleven of his closest comrades were not involved because that morning they rode fast heading southeast across Saline County on their way to raid in Cooper County, as described later in this chapter.[3]

Todd's Guerrillas Murder Former Union Captain Axline Near Hickman Mills

Meanwhile, in Jackson County to the west Captain Jacob Axline, formerly of the 2nd Battalion MSM and who created an impressive record for himself during the Battle of Independence on August 11, 1862, was waylaid and killed by bushwhackers probably of George Todd's band the evening of June 3 while on his way home to Hickman Mills in the west part of the county. Axline's murder created a flurry of editorial invective in the Kansas City newspaper and in a letter to General Rosecrans blaming district chief Brigadier General Brown for allowing southerners to return to the depopulated Jackson County and asking Rosecrans to replace Brown with someone bolder and more resolute. General Rosecrans actually had his Inspector General James Totten investigate Brown's leadership of the Central District and considered replacing him, but Totten found no pressing cause for firing the man, and Rosecrans decided to back General Brown for a while longer.[4]

Todd's Men Rob Stagecoach and Cut Telegraph Near Little Blue

On the morning of June 4 Todd and about forty guerrillas in the brush along the Little Blue River stopped the eastbound stagecoach carrying mail from Kansas City and took the mailbag and two of the horses, and about thirty bushwhackers cut the telegraph line between Lexington and Independence in two places. By 1864, taking mailbags and reading the contents was common practice for bushwhackers in parts of Missouri because of the useful information they learned from the official and private correspondence, and they relished cutting the Union army's telegraph line because of the nuisance value it caused. Brigadier General Brown lost more favor with his boss Rosecrans by proposing to stop the mail thefts and telegraph line sabotage by issuing a policy of immediately shooting the first guerrilla caught in the area of the mail or telegraph offense and repeating the process until the guerrillas leave the mails and telegraph lines alone. After some thought, department headquarters replied three days later forbidding Brown's suggestion because such executions "throw too much responsibility into the hands of irresponsible parties" and "become the source of great demoralization to our own troops."[5]

The Pros and Cons of Union Foot Patrols in Early June

The first full week of June, between June 5 and June 11, witnessed lots of action mostly in Lafayette and Johnson Counties. On the morning of June 5 near Wellington in northwest Lafayette County at least four guerrillas fired on the side-wheeler *Sunshine,* the 1860-vintage, Pennsylvania-built victim of several other earlier war actions in Missouri. Nobody was hit, but this was the second steamer fired upon in two days in Lafayette County.[6]

A few miles to the south near Greenton this same day Sergeant Matthew Shackelford's foot patrol of twenty troopers of the 1st Cavalry MSM surprised and shot up a group of eight bushwhackers at a rural house. At no apparent loss to themselves, these Yanks killed one Rebel outright, mortally wounded two more, killed two horses, and captured three other horses, marking Sergeant Shackelford's June 5 patrol as an unqualified success. Foot patrols were a Union innovation of 1864 in this district, having the advantage of secrecy and surprise most times and the dangerous disadvantage of lack of mobility, especially considering the bushwhackers had outstanding mobility and much better intelligence sources. Foot patrols worked better against small bodies of Rebels, but were vulnerable after late May this year when large numbers of guerrillas returned from the South. The example of a foot patrol "gone wrong" would happen a week hence with disastrous consequences for the Union.[7]

Other Union patrols, on foot and mounted, in this region found signs that many bushwhackers in groups were active but evidently not looking for combat. Perhaps these southern men and their mounts were still recovering from the long trek back to this area from the South, as a patrol in northwest Johnson County found two horses "running at large in woods, appeared to be pretty well rode down."[8]

In east-central Johnson County former members of the Union 40th EMM at the village of Knob Noster who were now citizen guards reported to the nearest Union post ten miles west at Warrensburg late in the morning of June 5 that the night before a resident hiding in the brush saw ninety guerrillas mostly dressed in Union uniforms riding by about five miles to the northeast, and the local men feared the Rebels were preparing to raid the village. A lieutenant of the 1st Cavalry MSM rode out from Warrensburg with forty troopers that same afternoon and spent the night in Knob Noster, but he concluded that the man the night before must have actually seen a true Union patrol and rightly or wrongly dismissed the whole business as a false alarm.[9] Another example of one of the many Union patrols actively looking for guerrillas was that of Lieutenant Daniel Shumate and 20 troopers of the 1st Cavalry MSM who conducted a foot patrol north and northeast of Warrensburg to the Blackwater River and back between June 5 and 9. About ten miles from town the evening of June 5 Shumate's patrol fired on twelve bushwhackers leading five horses bearing heavy packs, but evidently hit nothing. At sunrise of June 7 the Yankee patrol fired on a man accompanied by two women who all escaped leaving behind a Federal overcoat and blanket. That evening eighteen guerrillas fired on Shumate's patrol without hitting anyone, and then retreated to the brush. Evidently, there were plenty of bushwhackers in this region in small groups, but they mostly seemed to be avoiding contact with the searching Federal patrols. It seems another disadvantage of foot patrols is that the Federals had only seconds to hit their targets, because they lacked the horses to carry them close to the target for another try later.[10]

A sergeant's mounted patrol of 7th Cavalry MSM from Warrensburg spent June 6 through June 10 scouring the countryside around Post Oak Creek in south-central Johnson County and encountered one or two bushwhackers at a time, but only managed to wound one Rebel during the entire patrol. There were a number of veteran guerrillas from this neighborhood such as John Brinker, Francis Marion "Gooly" Robinson, Bill Stewart, and others, who fought against Yankees here during 1861 and 1862, and evidently returned to their old neighborhood at this time to look in on their families. Some of these guerrillas returned during July 1863 and killed several old enemies. Hearing these men were back was probably the reason this Federal patrol spent so much time in this area.[11]

Bill Anderson Slaughters Corporal Parman's Foot Patrol Near Kingsville

Actions that took place the week of June 12 through 18 were on the whole disastrous for the Union in west-central Missouri. Corporal Joseph V. Parman with 14 other enlisted men of Company M, 1st Cavalry MSM from the Holden garrison on a foot patrol searched the brush along the north side of the new Pacific Railroad to just beyond Kingsville on June 11 without seeing much sign of guerrillas. The corporal's patrol spent that night by the home of a Mrs. Longacre near the new Pacific Railroad about three miles northwest of Kingsville. In the morning the corporal led his patrol a short distance away from Longacre's toward the brush when Bill Anderson and about 40 guerrillas disguised as Federal cavalrymen attacked them from the rear and flank and shot up the patrol. Corporal Parman at first attempted to hold the bushwhackers at bay by forming a skirmish line with his troopers, but Anderson's men rode among them quickly killing five and the rest broke into a run for the nearest brush. Only Corporal Parman and two of his troopers managed to get to the bushes, hide, and escape. Some of the remainder of Company M quickly rode out from Holden, verified the corporal's report of the fight from the location and condition of the twelve bodies on the ground. Some of the dead men had apparently been attempting to surrender since they were shot between the eyes. Nearly all were stripped of their uniforms and other equipment useful to the guerrillas, and the Rebels scalped one of the dead. Although Anderson and his band could have simply happened upon Parman's patrol, there remains the strong possibility that a southern sympathizer in that neighborhood saw this patrol the previous day and sent word to the guerrillas. A few miles to the north before the fight Anderson's band robbed a stagecoach, taking the horses and about $250 from one businessman, and rifling the mail which the guerrillas left strewn over the ground. The stagecoach driver later said he counted 36 bushwhackers when they stopped his coach. Anderson wrote his own version of this fight July 7 and sent it to the Lexington newspaper addressed to Colonel James McFerran, commander of the 1st Cavalry MSM, but his intent seemed to be to boast and intimidate rather than provide news:

> Colonel McFerran, I have seen your official report ... you have been wrongfully informed ... I had the honor, sir, of being in command.... To enlighten you on the subject and to warn you against making future exaggerations I will say to you in the future to let me know in time, and when I fight your men I will make the proper report. As to the skirmish I had with your men in Johnson [County], I started to Kingsville with fifty men to take the place, but before I arrived there I discovered a scout, fourteen or fifteen of your men, on the prairie some half a mile distant to my left. I immediately gave chase. They fled. There were not over eight of my men ever got near them. They did not surrender or I would not have killed them, for I understood that Company M were Southern men; they sent me that word. I ordered them to halt and surrender. I was astonished to see them refuse after sending me such word. One of their lieutenants even planned the assassination of General Brown and the taking of his headquarters but I refused to commit so foul a deed. But they refused to surrender and I had them to kill. I regret to kill such good Southern men, but they are fit for no service but yours, for they were very cowardly. Myself and two men killed nine of them when there were no other men in sight of us. They are such poor shots it is strange you don't have them practice more. Send them out and I will train them for you.... Farewell, friend.

Elements of Company M, 1st Cavalry MSM tracked Anderson's band to the Sni Hills of southwest Lafayette County over the next day or two and skirmished with them once or twice in what appeared to be a vain effort to exact a measure of revenge, but with little effect. The death of twelve combatants at one time on either side was nothing new in Missouri's guerrilla war, but that such veterans would die in such a one-sided action attracted lots of notice. The tragedy of Corporal Parman's patrol represented the worst consequence of foot patrols in this district.[12]

Several Small Actions Across West-Central Missouri from June 12 to 14

For the next couple of days there were several small actions in this region which were less harmful to the Federal side. On June 12 and 13 patrols of the 2nd Colorado Cavalry from the garrison at Harrisonville fought small actions against unidentified guerrillas in Cass County resulting in one Federal wounded in a June 12 skirmish south of town and two dead bushwhackers on June 13 somewhere near town.[13] Evidently, George Todd's guerrillas were still active in Jackson County also on June 13. That day bushwhackers robbed the Kansas City to Lexington mail coach at Fire Prairie Creek in the northeast corner of the county, and the incident irked the Kansas City daily newspaper to the extent that it added in the note of the robbery that "we got no paper mail here yesterday morning."[14] That same day bushwhackers attacked eight troopers of the 2nd Colorado Cavalry escorting a wagon full of supplies along the road between Westport and Hickman Mills not far from the Kansas border, according to the Kansas City newspaper. A Lawrence, Kansas newspaper erroneously reported that 17 Union soldiers escorting this wagon were killed, which elicited a second article about the incident from the Kansas paper to clarify the misinformation. The guerrillas captured and burned the wagon and took away the mules, while the troopers took to the brush to escape. One of them had to travel a distance to throw off his Rebel pursuers but reported back to his unit some hours later in one piece but with a tale to tell.[15] That night just outside Lexington at Judge John F. Ryland's home, one of his sons discovered four guerrillas attempting to steal their horses and chased them away with gunfire, although the raiders managed to take away one of the horses. These guerrillas evidently were part of Jeff Wilhite's small band that operated in the area this summer.[16] On the next day somewhere near Holden in west Johnson County a patrol of the 1st Cavalry MSM wounded a guerrilla in a skirmish.[17] Also on June 14 the mail coach escort from Lexington got into a skirmish along the road near the Hambright family home in the northeast corner of Jackson County not far from Sibley. The escort consisted of a sergeant and twenty troopers of the 1st Cavalry MSM and they fought with an estimated sixty bushwhackers probably of Todd's band. The terse Union army report of the action only stated that the Federals had two horses wounded but that they "dismounted 3 of the rebels," probably meaning that they shot and killed or wounded three of the guerrillas' horses. After ensuring the mail coach arrived safely in Kansas City and on their way back to the Lexington garrison, the sergeant and his men restrung a portion of the telegraph line that bushwhackers had earlier pulled down.[18]

Anderson's Band Defeats Sergeant Shackleford's Detail in South Lafayette County

The 1st Cavalry MSM suffered a second defeat in two days on June 14 against Bill Anderson's rampaging bushwhackers, this time in south-central Lafayette County. The same Sergeant Matthew Shackleford who led the successful June 5 foot patrol as described earlier met disaster this day on his way back to his Warrensburg garrison with 35 mounted troopers and two wagons filled with rations. Near the William Whitsell home in south-central Lafayette County about twelve miles south of Lexington Bill Anderson with 48 guerrillas attacked the Federals in the open. Sergeant Shackleford saw that the nearest brush was too far away to reach so dismounted his men and drove back three bushwhacker attacks. At that point as the sergeant attempted to move the wagons he realized that the Rebels would pick off the exposed drivers and overwhelm the entire detail. Reluctantly, Shackleford had the Federals run for the brush on foot leaving the wagons, cargo, the mules, and most of their mounts to the enemy. Nine troopers died and Anderson's men killed most of the mules and burned the wagons and cargo, but the remainder of the Yanks managed to escape. Guerrilla losses were slight, and postwar participants evidently told John Edwards that the Yankees for certain wounded at least one of their men. Bill Anderson's second field victory in two days coming just a few days after a successful raid to Cooper County and back made the guerrilla leader and his men seem almost invincible. In his July 7 letter to the Lexington newspaper Anderson commented on the Whitsell farm fight against Sergeant Shackelford's men. He singled out the detail's commander back in Warrensburg, Captain Milton Burris, and chided Burris for bragging that he would "give me a thrashing." Further, Anderson addressed Colonel McFerran about:

> Forty-eight of your men coming from Lexington with three wagons had the audacity to fire on my pickets, and very impudently asked me to come out of the brush and fight them. I obeyed reluctantly. They dismounted and formed on a hill. I formed under their fire under the hill and charged. They fled and I pursued. You know the rest. If you do not, I can inform you; we killed ten on the ground and wounded as many more. Had all my men done their duty we would have killed thirty of them.

Bill Anderson and his men, except for those north of the Missouri River in Clay County, remained in the Lafayette County area but were less active over the next several days.[19]

Joint Union Missouri-Kansas Cavalry Expedition in Jackson County

The rest of the week between June 14 and June 18 saw less bushwhacker activity in this region but considerably more Union activity. Federal patrols found evidence that 25 to 30 guerrillas in north Johnson County were moving about in small groups, but the Yanks could not catch them.[20] Colonel James H. Ford of the 2nd Colorado Cavalry obtained the improbable information that there were 500 Rebels in east Jackson and west Lafayette Counties, evidently concentrating to strike. Ford's superior, Brigadier General Egbert B. Brown, doubted the numbers but immediately contacted the Kansas Department commander, Major General Samuel R. Curtis, who made some of his troops available to assist Ford and thereby help defend Kansas border communities from the threat of another raid like the disastrous Lawrence raid of August 21 the year before. Therefore, Colonel Ford with 150 of his troopers worked in concert with similar numbers of Department of Kansas soldiers of the 5th, 11th and 15th Kansas Cavalry under Colonel Thomas Moonlight, a Kansas cavalry brigade commander, between June 16 and 18 on a giant double envelopment from the border northeast to the Sni Hills of southwest Lafayette County. These Colorado and Kansas cavalrymen used mounted and foot patrols across large parts of Jackson and Cass Counties to drive the bushwhackers ahead of them. Little documentation remains to detail the Kansas portion of this expedition, but the Colorado troopers flushed several small camps and small bodies probably of George Todd's guerrillas from the thickets of Jackson County using a combination of some troops moving through the brushy bottoms while others rode along the open ridgelines attempting to intercept fleeing bushmen. One foot patrol of Coloradoans shot into a party of six or eight Rebels near Raytown and thought they killed two or three of them. Another foot patrol shot into a group of ten to twelve bushwhackers and wounded one or two. Colonels Ford and Moonlight hoped they had cleared Cass and Jackson Counties of guerrillas when they met near Sibley in northeast Jackson County on June 18, just before the Kansans returned to their side of the border. The Union expedition seemed to suffer no casualties, but the wily Rebels lost only a few men and had a few campsites compromised. A Kansas City newspaper article crowed about thirteen dead guerrillas, but this was probably an exaggeration, as Colonel Ford avoided giving a body count in his report. In spite of all the concerted effort, when the Union cavalry returned to garrison the guerrillas were free to return to their numerous remaining hideouts and campsites.[21]

Union Colonel James H. Ford, commander of 2nd Colorado Cavalry Regiment (National Park Service collection at Wilson's Creek National Battlefield, historian Connie Langum).

Jeff Wilhite's Raid on the Ryland Farm Near Lexington on 17 June

Guerrilla sub-chief Jefferson Wilhite seemed intent on consummating unfinished business just outside Lexington before the week finished. About six in the evening of June 17 Wilhite and five bushwhackers attempted to raid Judge Ryland's farm where they had been unsuccessful stealing horses a few nights before. The judge and one of his older sons repelled the raiders with gunfire, killing two of the Rebels' horses and wounding two others, and Wilhite's men scampered off in frustration. Ironically, the Rylands discovered that one of the horses they killed was the one the same bushmen stole from them on June 13.[22]

Flurry of Union Patrols During Week of 19–25 June

The week of June 19 through 25 was calmer in Jackson and Cass Counties, because of the Colorado and Kansas cavalry expedition through there immediately before, but was active in Johnson and Lafayette Counties. Brigadier General Brown, smarting from the Federal defeats on June 12 and 14, sent to his boss, Major General Rosecrans, a summary of all Union actions in his district between June 10 and 20 which shows a very large amount of Union patrolling for Monday, June 20. Perhaps Brown ordered the extra patrols to get his soldiers' minds and his boss' mind off of the recent defeats and rebuild confidence:

- On that date First Sergeant C. B. Vaughan led a patrol of 2nd Colorado Cavalry from Harrisonville throughout Cass County and killed two guerrillas and wounded two others at no Union loss.[23]
- In Johnson County to the east on that day Colonel James McFerran, commander of the 1st Cavalry MSM, led a patrol of his own men from the Warrensburg garrison into the countryside near town where they killed one bushwhacker and wounded two others evidently for no Federal casualties.[24]
- Also on June 20 First Lieutenant William Kessinger led a patrol of 23 troopers of the 1st Cavalry MSM west and south of Lexington that killed three Rebels and wounded another five at the loss of one horse killed or wounded and two revolvers lost.[25]
- Sergeant H. J. Coy of the 2nd Colorado Cavalry and his patrol operating generally east of their Kansas City station in Jackson County on that date killed two bushwhackers and wounded six more, killed or wounded four Rebels' horses, and captured an astounding 55 firearms all at the loss of one trooper wounded. A St. Louis newspaper reporter at Lexington reported that Sergeant Coy's men encountered and fought sixty guerrillas on June 20. For these Colorado troopers to capture that many firearms, they may have discovered and attacked a bushwhacker hideout where the Rebels scattered quickly leaving so much hardware behind or they found a hidden weapons cache.[26]

General Brown's patrol table mentions several other Federal scouts on June 20 which did not indicate either Union or Rebel losses and perhaps these others did not involve shots fired . The St. Louis newspaper correspondent at Lexington also reported that on June 24 Captain Milton Burris of the 1st Cavalry MSM leading a patrol killed three guerrillas and seriously wounded two more somewhere in the area. The correspondent also mentioned that the 1st Cavalry MSM had established a temporary base thirteen miles south of Lexington along the main Lexington to Warrensburg road in an area bushwhackers were known to frequent.[27]

Guerrillas Attack *West Wind* with Rifles Near Wellington on 24 June

On Friday, 24 June the side-wheeler *West Wind* near Wellington and opposite Camden while slowly steaming upriver encountered a guerrilla hailing her from the south bank of the Missouri River waving a handkerchief and a revolver. When the 1859-vintage, Pennsylvania-built steamer failed to respond, the hailer gave an order to fire and out from hiding stepped about forty guerrillas dressed in Union uniforms who began peppering the slowly moving vessel with bullets. The crew and passengers ducked for cover as the determined guerrillas fired about 200 to 300 shots of which about one hundred struck the *West Wind,* and the crew and passengers flattened out on the deck when some of the bullets came through the protective bulwarks. Crew members later said that some of the Rebels were evidently firing Enfield rifles, as a number of these large slugs pierced the three-boards-deep protective planking and went caroming through the boat. One bullet embedded itself into the mattress on top of which the night watchman was sleeping and one slug sent wood splinters into another crewman's hand, but that was the only casualty on board. The *West Wind* had difficulty maneuvering away from the shooters since the river level was so low and she was steaming against the current, but the only damage besides the crewman with the wounded hand were the numerous bullet holes. The guerrillas, who may have been Bill Anderson's band known for shooting at passing steamers, evidently realized that pistol bullets were not strong enough to harm the riverboats and obtained the more potent rifle muskets in order to perform more damage. Such firearms were usually scorned by the fast-riding bushwhackers because of their slow rate of fire and the difficulty of reloading while on horseback, so perhaps these shooters cached these near the river for just such an operation. Since many of the guerrillas were returnees from regular Confederate service a number of them were proficient with these weapons.[28]

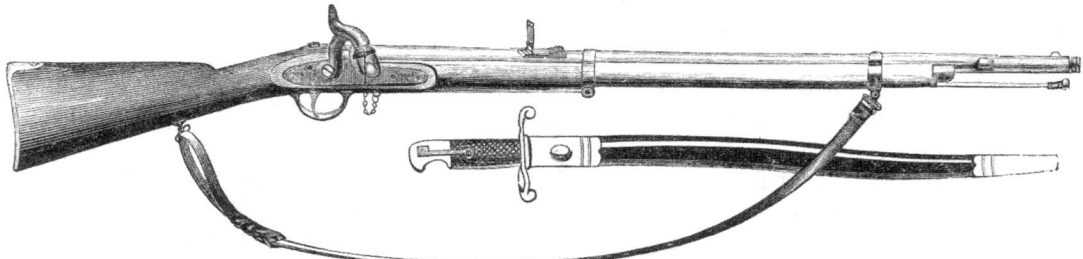

The English-made Enfield rifle-musket was a reliable firearm, and both sides of the American Civil War imported them in large numbers (Schuyler, Hartley, and Graham, *Illustrated Catalogue of Arms and Military Goods*, 1864, p. 128).

Large Numbers of Guerrillas Moving Near Knob Noster on 24 June

Two other events took place on June 24 in the region. First, Sergeant B. F. Poe of the citizen guards at Knob Noster in east central Johnson County notified Union Colonel James McFerran at Warrensburg ten miles to the west that there were about "one hundred bushwhackers 2 miles north of here in timber" and asked the obvious question "what shall I do?" Colonel McFerran probably recalled that the Knob Noster citizen guards on June 5 reported similar numbers of guerrillas near town which a patrol of McFerran's 1st Cavalry MSM could not substantiate. Perhaps this flavored the colonel's sharply worded reply to the sergeant when he asked Poe to "ascertain the name of the farmer from whom you get your information" and "did he count them? Give full particulars as to time, distance, direction, and etc." Perhaps this was the end of the matter, but it was also possible that a body of guerrillas was traveling through the countryside past Knob Noster to avoid the large Union garrison and district headquarters at nearby Warrensburg.[29]

President Lincoln Questions General Brown's Ability

Also on June 24 President Lincoln telegraphed the Department of the Missouri commander, Major General Rosecrans, personally that "complaint is made to me that General Brown does not do his best to suppress bushwhackers. Please ascertain and write to me at once." Rosecrans and his headquarters staff had exchanged heated messages recently with Brigadier General Brown regarding differences of opinions about tactics fighting the resilient, veteran bushwhackers in the tempestuous District of Central Missouri, and Lincoln's harsh inquiry would not improve Rosecrans' opinion of the one-armed Brown. Still, Rosecrans must have reasoned that Brown was doing his best commanding combat troops in an impossible situation. Rather than relieve the general immediately Rosecrans chose to send his inspector general, Brigadier General James Totten—experienced in Missouri operations since 1861—to see for himself. Totten sent an interim reply two days later on June 26 from Brown's headquarters at Warrensburg that "his troops appear to be very active, and, in my opinion, are doing good service." The general's reply to the president does not appear in the official reports, but perhaps Rosecrans based his reply on his inspector general's personal findings. The strained relationship between Rosecrans and his subordinate Brown staggered along without giving the commander of the Department of the Missouri much comfort for about

Union Major General William S. Rosecrans (Charles C. Coffin, *The Boys of '61*, p. 33).

another month when Rosecrans finally replaced Brown with another general. Rosecrans' handling of this issue did little to improve Lincoln's confidence in Rosecrans himself, which was badly shaken with "Old Rosy's" defeat by Confederate General Bragg at the Battle of Chickamauga the previous September. Now, with the Missouri situation heating up, high Union authorities were beginning to wonder if giving the general a second chance in this former "backwater of the war" was such a good idea.[30]

There were fewer guerrilla war incidents between June 26 and July 7 in Jackson, Cass, Lafayette, and Johnson Counties, and these were not severe compared to those of two weeks before. On Sunday June 26 General Brown obtained the evidently false information that most of the guerrillas in Jackson and Lafayette Counties were concentrating in the Sni Hills and he sent much of his cavalry there with few Rebels to find. That same day Brown was forced to postpone the planned execution of captured bushwhacker Marion D. Erwin, because guerrilla chief Bill Anderson sent a message that he was holding Duck, the Wellington postmaster, and two other northern sympathizers as hostages for Erwin's release. As was the custom in Missouri for such cases, General Brown ordered his men to seize six prominent southern sympathizers of the Wellington area and hold them in shackles for the safe return of Anderson's three hostages. Whether Anderson released his hostages is not clear in the record, but Brown released guerrilla Erwin despite his conviction by a tribunal. Union authorities in northeast Missouri would in spring 1865 recapture and execute Erwin there anyway.[31]

Union Chase of 30 to 40 Guerrillas Across Johnson County on 27–28 June

Johnson County witnessed more excitement Monday and Tuesday, June 27 and 28 when Union forces there chased a band of between 30 and 40 unidentified bushwhackers around the county. On Monday morning the guerrillas fought with citizen guards at or near the village of Dunksburg in the northeast edge of the county, killing a Bell and a G. McGuire in an ambush. Union Captain Squire Ballew with 50 troopers of 7th Cavalry MSM from the Warrensburg garrison found the guerrillas' tracks near Dunksburg and followed them about 18 miles south to Big Muddy Creek in southeast Johnson County where they found and fought the Rebel band about three o'clock that afternoon. One of the Union troopers shot a southerner dead and was himself killed in a short fight. As the guerrillas fled from their pursuers they came across two Cooper brothers in their lane in the southeast corner of Johnson County and shot both men to death as they passed, perhaps suspecting they were more citizen guards. The Rebels changed direction near the Cooper home and rode back towards the northwest casting off coats, extra horse equipment, letters, photographs, and the like, perhaps to save weight on their tired horses. Captain Ballew's patrol lost the trail of the southerners near the West Fork of Post Oak Creek a few miles southwest of Warrensburg in south-central Johnson County. Later in the afternoon of June 28 a few miles north near Blackwater River residents reported "small bodies of bushwhackers that had been robbing." Perhaps the guerrillas that the cavalry had been chasing across the county were taking food and maybe horses to replace their worn ones.

Captain Ballew later learned that a few days before this action the guerrilla band forced a local man named Peak to guide them around the village of Knob Noster with its alert citizen guard force and then released him on their way north to reconnoiter and later attack the Dunksburg citizen guards unit. The captain was furious that Peak did not report what he knew to Union authorities after the Rebels released him. That as many as forty guerrillas passed near Knob Noster sometime prior to this June 27 and 28 action could add credence to that questionable report from Knob Noster on June 24 that someone saw a large band of bushwhackers in that area, as described earlier in this chapter.[32]

There were fewer guerrilla actions between June 30 and July 7 compared to earlier fighting and most of these involved bushwhacker challenges to Union control of transportation modes. On June 30 two guerrillas near Lone Jack in southeast Jackson County robbed the coach carrying the mail between Lexington and Pleasant Hill.[33] During the night of July 1 and 2 guerrillas carried away the flatboat that served as a ferry across a creek on the road from Lexington to Dover in northeast Lafayette County, probably to use for crossing the Missouri River in the near future. An informant report to the Union military later in the war indicated that Bill Anderson's band was in that neighborhood about July 2, so it appears they took the boat. The Union commander at Lexington, First Lieutenant William Kessinger of the 1st Cavalry MSM, on July 5 wrote "there has been nothing of especial interest since my last report, except some firing into boats at Waverly."

Anderson Celebrates Independence Day Shooting Riverboats

Anderson's band was responsible for shooting into the vessels at Waverly on Independence Day. Anderson with about fifteen riders first attempted to ride directly on board the 1863-vintage, Paducah-built, side-wheeler *Live Oak* docked at the Waverly landing, but the watch officer was quick to sever the cable and shove the vessel away from the frustrated bushwhackers, as some of them fell into the water with the falling gangplank. Anderson and company then peppered the vessel with between 150 and 200 bullets, wounding the watch officer in a hand and killing a horse on board before the *Live Oak* could escape out of pistol range. A crewman and a passenger were left ashore by the vessel's sudden departure and the bushwhackers questioned them before releasing the pair. The guerrillas' questioning revealed somehow that they were aware two gentlemen from Kansas were aboard and they had wanted to capture them, but nobody seemed to know how Anderson and his men knew about that. Several of the guerrillas had their photographs made at a studio in Waverly and a few hours later fired on the new, Pennsylvania-built, side-wheeler *Post Boy* when she steamed past the town. First Lieutenant Kessinger also reported that on Independence Day unidentified Rebels "took a skiff at Wellington, and pressed a wagon and hauled it to near Sibley." He also wrote that "the bushwhackers are all near the river," and, indeed, a summary of their actions at this time seem to bear him out.[34] What the Federals did not realize, but the guerrillas must have known was that Rebels in the Platte County area were about to unleash a powerful insurgency just a few miles away north of the Missouri River, as detailed in Chapter 18. Evidently, a number of the southern irregulars in Lafayette County and northeast Jackson County were preparing to cross to the north side of the river using the stolen boats to assist their comrades.

General Brown's Confusion Worsens

District of Central Missouri commander Brigadier General Brown at Warrensburg was confused by the often contradictory intelligence reports his troops and informants sent him. He reported to St. Louis headquarters July 5 that some guerrillas were "moving south, in some cases reporting that they were going to join Shelby, and some of the same parties returned within the past two days." He also wrote that "several bands of guerrillas have reappeared on the line of Jackson and Lafayette Counties, and that a party of 100 was at Waverly yesterday morning commanded by Quantrill, and that others are coming in from the north side of the river, apparently concentrating for a raid." Brown did not know that Quantrill was in exile in Howard County and that Bill Anderson commanded those bushwhackers near Waverly. The general drew his own conclusions and wrote "look out for a move toward Cooper County." On July 6, the day after Brown's report, the Kansas City newspaper printed a letter from a correspondent in Warrensburg where the general had his headquarters which stated that "it is understood here [Warrensburg] that a petition has been sent by citizens of Kansas City to General Rosecrans for the removal of General Brown ... on the ground, among others, that he has permitted the rebels of Jackson County, expelled by General Ewing, to return to their homes." This lack of support was bad for General Brown's self confidence in the face of new guerrilla operations, and probably further harmed General Rosecrans' faith in him, too.[35]

Todd's Band Defeats Captain Wagoner's Patrol Near the Little Blue on 6 July

Captain George Todd's guerrilla band of 63 riders enjoyed a battle victory in the "Captain Wagoner fight" on July 6 to match the two Bill Anderson won in June in this region. About three miles south of Blue Springs near the county poor house and the G. N. Grinter farm, in Blue Township of central Jackson County, Todd's men that morning captured a stagecoach on the Independence-to-Pleasant Hill Road and held the passengers for several hours in the Grinter house. Colonel James Ford of the 2nd Colorado Cavalry and a cavalry escort were taking Inspector General James Totten on an inspection trip of Union posts in the area, and Todd may have learned this and thought they would travel this route. Totten's and Ford's party instead took another road, but a second group of Yankees rode into the bushwhacker trap about two that afternoon. Captain Seymour W. Wagoner with 26 troopers of Company C, 2nd Colorado Cavalry from the Raytown garrison foolishly rode along on patrol showing careless disregard for their flank and rear security. Todd himself and one other guerrilla acted as the "bait" by leaping on their horses at the Grinter house and riding off as if the Federals had surprised them. Wagoner and his men gave chase right into one of Todd's favorite ambush sites nearby located in a deep road cut two miles south of the Little Blue River where many of these same bushwhackers had defeated Union troops several times earlier in the war. In the road cut southerners under Todd's lieutenant Dick Yeager or Yager shot up the patrol killing the captain and seven of his men, but three guerrilla memoirs expressed admiration that Wagoner and his

Union Captain Seymour W. Wagoner of the 2nd Colorado Cavalry and seven of his men died in George Todd's ambush near the Little Blue on 6 July 1864 (National Park Service collection at Wilson's Creek National Battlefield, historian Connie Langum).

French-made Lefaucheux pin-fire revolvers were issued to a few Union units west of the Mississippi River (United States Department of War, *Atlas to Accompany the Official Records of the Union and Confederate Armies*, 1891–1895, drawings of revolvers on p. 393).

men fought back bravely against the overwhelming volume of fire in the killing zone. Todd's men had only brief encounters with the Colorado troopers heretofore, and they were curious as to how they would fight. The cavalry survivors retreated bearing a badly wounded man and leaving behind their dead and three sound horses. A Kansas City newspaper account states that some guerrillas "brutally treated" the bodies of the dead Yanks. The Rebels suffered three men wounded, one seriously, and five of their horses died in the shooting. In his 1914 memoir guerrilla John McCorkle wrote how the guerrillas experimented with the ungainly "French Dragoon" revolvers the Federals left on the battleground, which they found "very heavy at the muzzle" and complicated to use. Even bushwhacker marksmen found the pistols fired low, which may account for the light casualties among the Rebels and the heavy toll on their horses in this engagement. Normally, battlefield acquisition was vital to these guerrillas, but they left these clumsy revolvers on the ground in disgust. Todd used the captured coach to bear away his casualties, leaving the frustrated passengers to walk from the scene. Wagoner's patrol underestimated the lethality of the bushwhackers, but the Coloradoans would look to prove themselves anew after "the Captain Wagoner fight." A foot patrol of the 2nd Colorado Cavalry about six that evening a few miles east of this fight badly wounded two Rebels who escaped. The troopers reported that one of the guerrillas wore a Confederate officer's uniform, but they could not identify the man.[36]

Bill Anderson's Manifesto of 7 July

On the following day, July 7, Captain Bill Anderson or one of his men at his behest somewhere in Lafayette County penned his bushwhacker manifesto and sent it to the Lexington press to print. He addressed his lengthy diatribe thus:

> To the editors of the two papers in Lexington, to the citizens and the community at large, General [Egbert B.] Brown, and Colonel [James] McFerran [commander of the 1st Cavalry MSM] and his petty hirelings, such as Captain [Milton] Burris [also of the 1st Cavalry MSM], the friend of Anderson:

The longest of his four letters Anderson addressed to the newspaper editors. It contains Anderson's explanation as to why he chose guerrilla war, his disdain for renegades and robbers, bragging about his expertise at conducting successful guerrilla warfare, and dire warnings to area men not to join the new General Orders Number 107 citizen guard units:

> Mr. Editors:
> In reading both your papers I see you urge the policy of the citizens taking up arms to defend their persons and property. You are only asking them to sign their death warrants. Do you not know, sirs, that you have some of Missouri's proudest, best, and noblest sons to cope with? Sirs, ask the people of Missouri, who are acquainted with me, if Anderson ever robbed them or mistreated them in any manner. All those that speak the truth will say never. Then what protection do they want? It is from thieves, not such men as I profess to have under my command. My command can give them protection than all the Federals in the State against such enemies. There are thieves and robbers in the community, but they do not belong to any organized band; they do not fight for principles; they are for self-interest; they are just as afraid of me as they are of Federals. I will help the citizens rid the country of them. They are not friends of mine. I have used all that language can do to stop their thefts; I will see now what I can do by force. But listen to me fellow-citizens; do not obey this last order. Do not take up arms if you value your lives and property. It is not in my power to save your lives if you do. If you proclaim to be in arms against the guerrillas I will kill you. I will hunt you down like wolves and murder you. You cannot escape. It will

not be Federals after you. Your arms will be no protection to you. Twenty-five of my men can whip all that can get together. It will not be militia such as McFerran's, but regulars that have been in the field for three years, that are armed with from two to four pistols and Sharps rifles. I commenced at the first of this war to fight for my country, not to steal from it. I have chosen guerrilla warfare to revenge myself for wrongs that I could not honorably avenge otherwise. I lived in Kansas when this war commenced. Because I would not fight the people of Missouri, my native State, the Yankees sought my life, but failed to get me. Revenged themselves by murdering my father, destroying all my property, and have since that time murdered one of my sisters and kept the other two in jail twelve months. But I have fully glutted my vengeance. I have killed many. I am a guerrilla. I have never belonged to the Confederate Army, nor do my men. A good many of them are from Kansas. I have tried to war with the Federals honorably, but for retaliation I have done things, and am fearful will have to do that I would shrink from if possible to avoid. I have tried to teach the people of Missouri that I am their friend, but if you think that I am wrong, then it is your duty to fight. Take up arms against me and you are Federals. Your doctrine is an absurdity and I will kill you for being fools. Beware, men, before you make this fearful leap. I feel for you. You are in a critical situation. But remember there is a Southern army, headed by the best men in the nation. Many of their homes are in Missouri, and they will have the State or die in the attempt. You that sacrifice your principles for fear of losing your property will, I fear, forfeit your right to a citizenship in Missouri. Young men, leave your mothers and fight for your principles. Let the Federals know that Missouri's sons will not be trampled on. I have no time to say anything more to you. Be careful how you act, for my eyes are upon you."

Anderson's second letter addressed to Colonel James McFerran gave his version of the fights of June 12 against Corporal Parman's ill-fated foot patrol in west Johnson County and of June 14 against Sergeant Shackelford and his woebegone detail in south-central Lafayette County. The bushwhacker leader indicated he read McFerran's own official report of these two actions; he wanted to correct the record about what really happened; and his remarks are contained with the narratives of those fights earlier in this chapter.

Captain Anderson's third and shortest letter was addressed to the aggressive Union Captain Milton Burris, commander of Company I, 1st Cavalry MSM, and commandant at the very exposed Prairie Mound Church garrison of his company thirteen miles south of Lexington. Most of the troopers Anderson's band killed on their June 14 battle victory over Sergeant Shackelford's detail in that area were members of Company I, and Captain Burris must have made threats against Anderson's band for revenge. Anderson in his letter to Colonel McFerran stated "I understood that Burris was anxious to give me a thrashing." In his July 7 letters Anderson now made these warrior taunts directly to the captain: "To Burris: Burris, I love you; come and see me. Goodby, boy; don't get discouraged. I glory in your spunk, but damn your judgment."

Anderson addressed his fourth letter to the Central District commander Brigadier General Egbert B. Brown regarding Brown holding as prisoners a guerrilla Marion D. Erwin and Annie Fickel, a local teenage girl. The Union army held Miss Fickel for her part in an attempted escape plot of one of Andy Blunt's bushwhackers from the Lexington jail February 22 that resulted in the death of a Yankee soldier, as narrated in Chapter Four. Captain Anderson's last letter reads:

General Brown:

I have not the honor of being acquainted with you, but from what I have heard of you I would take you to be a man of too much honor as to stoop so low as to incarcerate women for the deeds of men, but I see that you have done so in some cases. I do not like the idea of warring with women and children, but if you do not release all the women you have arrested in La Fayette County, I will hold the Union ladies in the country as hostages for them. I will tie them by the neck in the brush and starve them until they are released, if you do not release them. The ladies of Warrensburg must have Miss Fickle [sic] released. I hold them responsible for her speedy and safe return. General, do not think that I am jesting with you. I will have to resort to abusing your ladies if you do not quit imprisoning ours. As to the prisoner Ervin you have in Lexington, I have never seen nor heard of him until I learned that such a man was sentenced to be shot. I suppose that he is a Southern man or such a sentence would not be passed. I hold the citizens of Lexington responsible for his life. The troops in Lexington are no protection to the town, only in the square. If he is killed, I will kill twenty times his number in Lexington. I am perfectly able to do so at any time.

Yours, respectfully, W. Anderson, Commanding Kansas First Guerrillas."

Annie Fickel's military tribunal sentence of imprisonment was published in the Kansas City newspaper on July 7, the same day as Anderson's letters, and his hearing that she was to be sent to prison may have triggered his letter-writing campaign. General Brown sent Anderson's letters along to his boss, General Rosecrans, with the remark "as a curiosity and specimen of a guerrilla chief's correspondence." One of Bill Anderson's obvious goals of his letter cannonade was to intimidate, and, Anderson was a master of intimidation. He did not reveal in these missives that the core group of his most trusted band members with him would four days later set out to the east on an ambitious raid in a new operations area.[37]

Anderson, Shumate, and Others in Central Missouri in June and Early July 1864

Guerrilla war came brutally to the central Missouri counties of Saline, Pettis, Cooper, Moniteau, Morgan, Cole, and Miller during the early summer of 1864. There were raids here by some of Quantrill's former men and Bill Anderson's band, both from outside of this area. There were also actions involving local bands such as Wiley Shumate's of Miller and Cole Counties, and unidentified men in other places.

Bill Anderson's Cooper County Raid of 4–5 June

In only two days between June 4 and 5 Captain Bill Anderson with only eleven of his most-trusted men conducted a lightning raid across four counties. These twelve riders swiftly rode southeast from their base in northeast Lafayette County early the morning of June 4, across south Saline County along the Blackwater River, into central Cooper County to their target about noon that day, then returned to Lafayette County on a more southerly route across north Pettis County. The closest that the veteran 4th Cavalry MSM got to Anderson's raiders was one hour behind them over the entire route. Since the arrival of Anderson's band back in west-central Missouri in late May they had operated mostly in central and northeast Johnson County and in Lafayette County under pressure of the experienced Yankee 1st and 7th Cavalry MSM there. This sudden, long distance raid seemed to represent breaking away from former operations away from familiar sanctuary areas and experimenting with a more mobile form of guerrilla fighting that would soon be a standard tactic of Anderson's operations.

The details of this raid reveal not only bushwhacker innovation but also brutality. The raid seemed to have its origins in the unsuccessful robbing that two bushwhackers conducted in central Cooper County in middle May, as reported in Chapter Nine.

It seems that Tom Cranmer, who had Johnson County roots, and John Thomas Warren from Clay County tried without success to rob wealthy farmer William H. Mayo not far from Bell Aire and Pilot Grove in central Cooper County on May 14. This pair may have had other escapades in Cooper County and perhaps later told Bill Anderson that central Cooper County was ripe for plunder, as Anderson seemed to use Cranmer and Warren as his guides on this expedition. Cooper Countian Nathaniel Leonard was then startled late in the morning of June 4 to see twelve riders in Union uniforms complete with sky-blue greatcoats armed with a few carbines and multiple revolvers ride up to his Ravenswood plantation house. Leonard was familiar with the appearance of northern troops since his son Charles was commander of Company H of the local 52nd EMM and the 4th Cavalry MSM was garrisoned in the region, but something about the appearance and manner of these cavalrymen aroused his suspicion. Leonard and other men of the farm quickly took up defensive positions inside the house and held off the raiders for a time, but quickly surrendered when Anderson had his men kindle three fires against the exterior of the elegant Ravenswood mansion. Up to this time Leonard had only a hand wound, but his resistance to the raiders seemed to mark his household for retribution except for the intercession of pro-southern neighbor Mrs. Corum who convinced Anderson and his men to spare the lives of these northern neighbors of hers and not burn the elegant house. The locals put out the fires while the bushwhackers used the time to seize three of the Leonard horses and take "clothing, jewelry, and etc." from inside Ravenswood. Anderson then compelled Nathaniel's son Leverett to guide the band to certain wealthy farms of central Cooper County. The raiders next robbed the neighbors, the James S. Hutchinson family, and non-chivalrously choked middle-aged Martha Hutchinson to get her to confess where she had hidden her valuables. At another home, the guerrillas took all the clothing in the house, regardless of gender. At the wealthy home of William H. Mayo the bushwhackers learned by questioning the slaves that Mr. Mayo had ridden to the Pilot Grove post office to get his mail and they decided to go there, too, after they looted his home of what they wanted and released Leverett Leonard to return home safely. At the post office, the raiders lined up the men and methodically robbed them, according to an eyewitness account. When Mr. Mayo objected to the loss of his gold watch and chain Bill Anderson fired a revolver close to his feet causing Mayo to panic and start running. Anderson rode after the man and killed Mayo with a pistol shot to the head. Another guerrilla on foot chased and wounded Thomas Brownfield who had been hiding, but Brownfield ran when he heard the shooting. Brownfield saved himself by pointing his own pistol at his pursuer who went back to get reinforcements, giving the local man time to hide in nearby brush. The bushwhackers then rode quickly to the west to escape Cooper County before a pursuit materialized, and thus barely saved having to battle a passing patrol of 4th Cavalry MSM led by Captain William D. Blair that had crossed their trail of robbery and was looking for them. At four that afternoon Anderson's group raided the village of Longwood in northeast Pettis County, lingering there to also eat and rest their horses. Both Anderson's raiders and the pursuing Federal patrol camped that night along the border between Pettis and Saline Counties, but on the morning of June 5, Anderson wisely changed his course to the northwest and passed Brownsville nine miles to the north. The following Union patrol lost time trying to find the Rebels' tracks for a while and then around the border between Saline and Lafayette Counties determined the Rebels dispersed into small groups of two to four men each, probably to meet at a predetermined rendezvous place. In their wake, Cooper County witnesses and officials exaggerated the raiders' numbers mostly as 20 riders, but the

52nd EMM commander reported the figure as high as "100 to 200." Meanwhile, Captain Blair, the ground commander, and his regimental commander, Colonel George H. Hall, accurately determined there were only twelve guerrillas, their leader was Anderson, several of the band members were from Johnson County, and that two of these were Cranmer and a Warren. On June 6 a Union patrol of the 1st Cavalry MSM in west Lafayette County recovered stolen goods marked that it had been shipped to "W. H. Mayo." Taken as a whole, this fast-paced raid helped Anderson and his men perfect how to conduct mobile guerrilla warfare over long distances and succeed as long as they chose their fights carefully and relied almost entirely on speed and the use of the offensive when they did fight. They could see also just how this form of long distance, rapid-fire raiding made them less vulnerable than before and greatly demoralized the populace who realistically felt intimidated against such deadly, determined foes who could appear at their doorstep without warning.[38]

New Frankfort Raid of 7 June

During the evening of June 7 about twenty unidentified bushwhackers raided the small German-American village of New Frankfort near the Missouri River in northeast Saline County. Captain Albert Brackman's Company E of the 9th Cavalry MSM, then garrisoning the railroad town of Macon City in Macon County two counties to the northeast, contained many men from New Frankfort. Captain Brackman requested that a number of his men be allowed to return home "to see after their families." He added that "the bushwhackers committed all sorts of depredations and infamies; killed one of my discharged soldiers." Writing about the raid, the Columbia newspaper of June 24 stated only that the guerrillas "sacked it and killed two or three of its citizens." The 1911 Carroll County history mentioned that the guerrillas burned down nine houses and a church during their foray there and killed one citizen. This raid made obvious the fact that large Saline County was only lightly protected by Union troops, since widespread guerrilla and Confederate recruiter activity elsewhere made great demands on the available cavalry.[39]

The shortage of Yanks in Saline County was obvious when Captain Wilson L. Parker's superiors ordered his patrol of the 4th Cavalry MSM to ride sixty miles from Sedalia in Pettis County to intercept guerrilla activities near the village of Miami on the Missouri River in the north-central edge of Saline County the second week of June. Parker's men detected trails and tracks through the rugged, wooded Pinnacles of the Missouri River southwest of Miami for two days before his troopers saw two suspicious men run from a rural house occupied by a Mrs. Haney, her two teenage daughters, and a Miss Williams. After the troopers discovered in the house secret mail from Rebel soldiers in Arkansas "and a quantity of merchandise, supposed to have been stolen" perhaps from the New Frankfort raid, the pro-southern ladies became indignant. They "said they had fed bushwhackers and would again, and gloried in bushwhackers." About 100 yards from the house the Federals discovered the hidden but empty camp of the two guerrillas they had seen running from the house and seized there two horses and a U.S. mail bag. Before Captain Parker's patrol returned to Sedalia by June 15 they saw in this neighborhood and exchanged fire with a number of solitary guerrillas, but the two horses and the four Rebel ladies were the only captures they made.[40]

During the night of 17/18 June ten bushwhackers near Arrow Rock in southeast Saline County robbed the home of E. Keaton evidently because these guerrillas knew Keaton was a member of the local citizens guard company. Perhaps they even knew

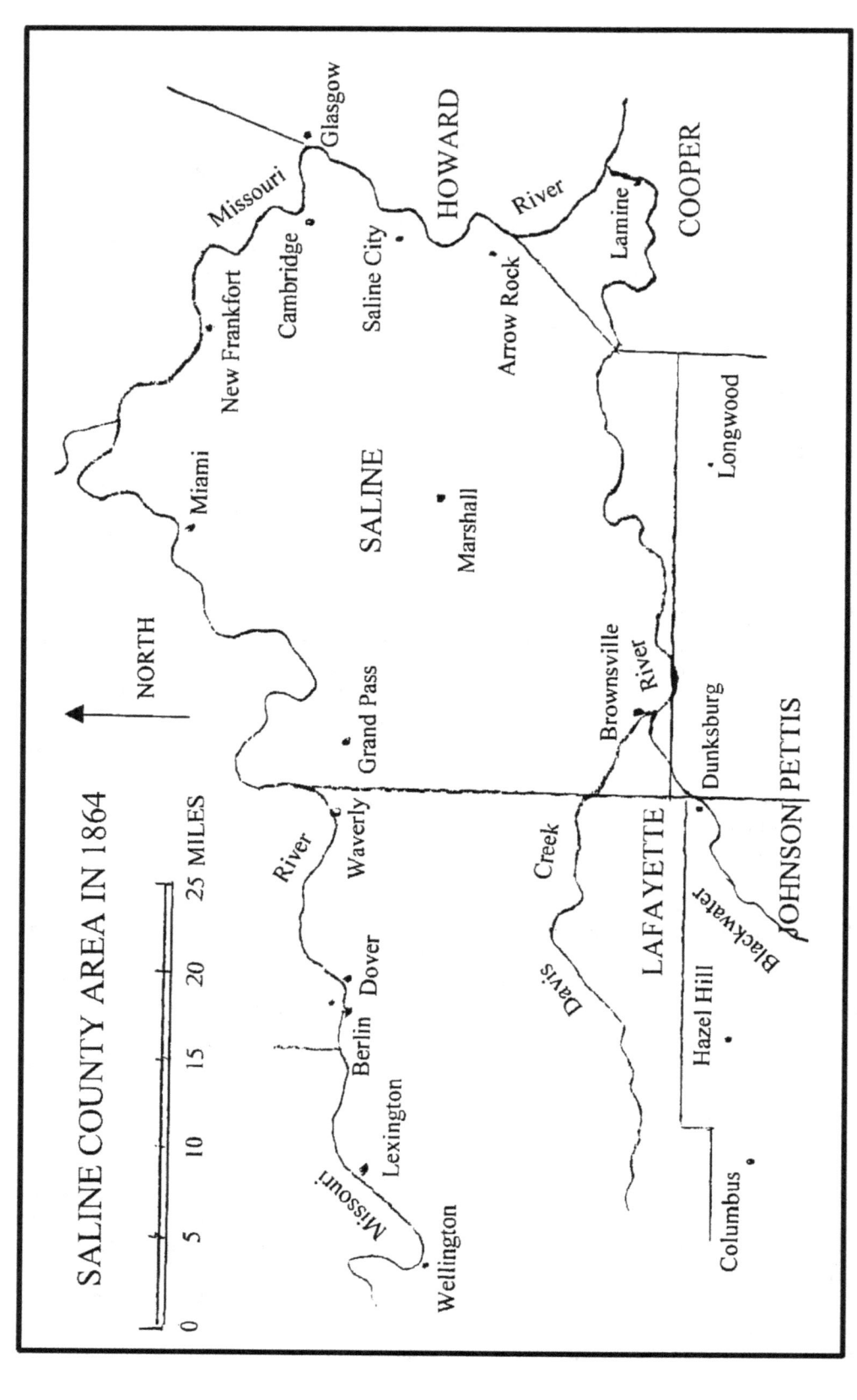

the guardsman had been standing guard to protect Arrow Rock earlier that evening. Keaton drew out his pistol and wounded one of the house robbers in the neck, whereupon the guardsman was able to escape to the nearby home of an elderly northern sympathizer. Later, the two men returned to Keaton's robbed house and found on Keaton's floor a neckerchief containing a bullet hole and a quantity of blood that must have belonged to the wounded guerrilla.[41]

4th Cavalry MSM Victory Over Carroll County Rebels in North Saline County

A poorly documented story in a local Carrollton newspaper claims that elements of the 4th Cavalry MSM returned to the Miami area of north Saline County sometime in late June and won the type of victory that had eluded Captain Wilson Parker's patrol when they were there a few days before. The article claimed that Major Douglas Dale with his troopers overwhelmed a small Confederate recruit company of less than thirty Carroll County southern men three miles from the village, killing six, capturing 18, arresting four women, and recovering goods stolen from a store in the earlier New Frankfort raid, all at no Union loss. The four ladies were sewing the cloth stolen at New Frankfort into clothing for the recruits when arrested. The account further states that the cavalrymen captured two horses and a saddlebag that contained the roll of the Carroll County men, and even named two of the Rebels. Records of the 4th Cavalry MSM state that Second Lieutenant Columbus Dale—not Major Douglas Dale of this regiment—took Company E from its Sedalia garrison between June 23 and 28 for patrolling in Pettis and Saline County, mentions a skirmish in Pettis County on June 26, but has nothing to say about such a victory as described in the Carrollton newspaper. It seems the "fog of war" either invented a Union victory in north Saline County in late June 1864, or obscured one.[42]

Guerrillas made two appearances June 23 in the mostly southern village of Miami, according to a newspaper article just a few miles to the east in Brunswick, Chariton County, across the Missouri River. Miami's isolation in the north tip of Saline County so far from other towns seemed to make it popular with guerrillas. Many of its residents supported the southern cause, and for this southern combatants usually respected the citizens and their property. Four guerrillas passed through the town that morning and created no problems. However, two bushwhackers that evening robbed two stores and four residents taking "what they wanted" and burned down the Baptist church before leaving. The Brunswick newspaper article could only explain this uncharacteristic Rebel treatment of Miami by reminding the readers that the residents "were entirely unarmed" and, therefore, unable to resist such lawlessness.[43]

In South Saline County Captain Parke's Patrol Fights Guerrillas in Thicket

On the morning of June 26 Captain Joseph Parke—the same officer who would later be humiliated fighting against Bill Anderson near Rocheport in northeast Missouri on August 28, as described in Chapter Fifteen—dismounted his patrol of 25 men of the 4th Cavalry MSM as they followed horse tracks into a large thicket just north of the Blackwater River near the Sedalia to Marshall road in south-central Saline County. Inside the thicket Parke and his troopers confronted seven men wearing parts of U.S. uniforms, but were confused at first because the unidentified men wore the Union military district's red recognition badge in their hats. Headquarters had devised the colored badge system to distinguish real Union troops from guerrillas wearing U.S.

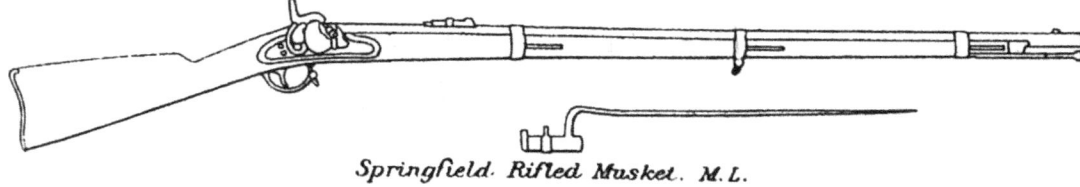

U.S. Springfield rifled musket model 1863, shown with socket bayonet (United States Department of War, *Atlas to Accompany the Official Records of the Union and Confederate Armies*, 1891–1895, drawings of shoulder arms, p. 393).

uniforms. The seven unidentified men quickly proved their identity as guerrillas by opening fire and running away, so the true Yanks began shooting and chasing the fleeing figures. The Rebels ran for their lives through the thick brush throwing away their three-pound revolvers to speed their flight, and four of them escaped. Captain Parke's patrol killed three and wounded two more at the light cost of one Federal trooper with a flesh wound in his arm. They captured six horses, one mule, one U.S. Springfield rifle, one musket, and one revolver. The troopers were frustrated they could not find more of the Rebels' discarded handguns in the thick vegetation after the fight, but taken in its entirety, they were pleased with the results of the fight.[44]

Wiley Shumate Resumes Guerrilla War in Miller and Cole Counties

Guerrilla war returned to Miller and Cole Counties at the center of Missouri in June of 1864, after a year of relative peace here during 1863. During 1862, the unidentified bushwhacker leader here, known only under the assumed title of "General Crabtree," recruited for the South in this area and frequently attacked northern sympathizers. Local militiamen mortally wounded Crabtree here about September 1862; the guerrilla leader died of his wounds; and comrades secretly buried his body in a hidden grave. One of Crabtree's former subordinates, Wiley H. Shumate of north Cole County, left Crabtree during August 1862 to serve a few months in the Confederate Pindall's Battalion of Sharpshooters in Arkansas, but returned home in 1863 and for a time followed peaceful pursuits. The return in spring of 1864 of a few other area Rebel soldiers and the talk of General Sterling Price invading Missouri to eject the Union troops evidently persuaded Shumate with some of his southern friends to return to the warpath. Ironically, Union authorities who never heard about Crabtree's demise back in autumn of 1862, assumed that Crabtree was still in charge and directing Shumate's actions.[45]

Local Judge Clyde Lee Jenkins wrote what seems to be the first, known record of Wiley Shumate's local guerrilla war in his 1971 Miller County history. Jenkins told of area bushwhackers' unsuccessful efforts June 26 to persuade Miller County treasurer William Matthews at his home near Saline Creek northeast of Tuscumbia to surrender the county funds to them. Matthews steadfastly refused to divulge his hiding place for the county money, even though Shumate and about ten to twelve men ransacked the house and confiscated most of the contents, including Matthews' personal $990 in cash that they discovered. After the outlaws left, Matthews later dug up Miller County's $7,971 from under his door step and surrendered it to proper authorities at the Tuscumbia courthouse.[46]

Judge Jenkins wrote that the day after Shumate's band raided Treasurer Matthews' home, they raided the Miller County seat at the small Osage River town of Tuscumbia on June 27. At first, Shumate scattered his men in twos and threes to quietly scout the town to determine how much Yankee opposition awaited them there. They probably knew Miller County had organized a Provisional Enrolled Missouri Militia or citizens guard company in accordance with General Rosecrans' General Orders Number 107; but they saw little evidence of it in Tuscumbia and quickly seized the whole place, possibly without firing a shot. A few of the guerrillas lined up all the fifty or so townsmen at gunpoint along the steep bank of the Osage River while the other raiders ransacked the courthouse, stores, and homes taking whatever they wished and that they could carry away on horseback. Shumate and his men captured local Sergeant John Bear of the citizens guard and placed him on a horse with his hands tied, commenting that "you are the first bear we have captured for some time, and will treat you no worse than the other wild critters in the woods." Meanwhile, the townsmen lined along the riverbank helplessly watched as the bushwhackers broke all the town's muskets and shotguns against the hull of a river steamer moored at the town pier and pitched the handguns into the deep Osage River waters. Just at that moment one of Shumate's men watching the north road toward Jefferson City came galloping into town reporting that a column of about sixty cavalry was approaching from that direction. Whatever punishment Wiley Shumate and his men had in mind for the worried inhabitants of Tuscumbia was forgotten as they quickly made the line of townsmen swear an oath to the Confederacy and then raced out of town with Sergeant Bear as their captive. The guerrillas wisely hid from the Yankee column and later paroled and released Sergeant Bear unharmed. Considering Crabtree's old band and Shumate were not shy about killing and mayhem, Tuscumbia was fortunate not to suffer more grievous harm.[47]

Public Execution of Guerrilla John Wilcox in Jefferson City
12 August

In a vain attempt to quell Shumate's band from more depredations, the Union District of Central Missouri published Special Orders Number 141 on July 1 asserting that they would execute prisoner John P. Wilcox, captured in Cole County March 31, if Shumate's band committed any further atrocities. Wilcox was wounded when the Union patrol of 4th Cavalry MSM captured him; they treated his wound; and they held Wilcox in confinement in a Jefferson City hospital until it healed. However, a late May military tribunal convicted Wilcox as a guerrilla and he faced execution when his condition improved. About June 21 Wilcox attempted to cheat the Federals out of his execution by escaping from the hospital, but he was recaptured. Now he was a pawn in the game of psychological warfare the Union military was playing with Shumate. As narrated in Chapter Twenty, Wiley Shumate disregarded the Federal ploy and continued bushwhacker operations, and the District of Central Missouri publicly executed Wilcox at Jefferson City on August 12.[48]

Thus, by early July the numerous guerrillas and Confederate recruiting commands throughout northwest Missouri were challenging the limited number of Union military forces there and seemingly softening them by almost constant warfare to prepare for the long-awaited advent into the state of Confederate Major General Sterling Price and his army to liberate Missouri from "the yoke of northern tyranny." Just in early July a portion of those recruits and bushwhackers would unleash an insurrection in the middle of Federally occupied Missouri to prepare for Price's coming.

EIGHTEEN

The Premature Insurgency That Failed During July 1864 in Northwest Missouri North of the Missouri River

Confederate recruiter Lieutenant Colonel John Calhoun "Coon" Thornton, based in Platte County of northwest Missouri, ignited a large insurgency there beginning July 7, 1864. This able commander drew together for the attempt not only his hundreds of new recruits, but also scores of turncoat Union "Paw Paw Militia" of the 81st and 82nd EMM and even veteran guerrillas borrowed from nearby bands. Lieutenant Colonel Thornton had been quietly recruiting local southern men into his command for months. For a while, Confederate Colonel John H. Winston of south Platte County was Thornton's commander in the field, but Federal troops discovered Winston's activities and location and captured him in March, as described in Chapter Ten. Meanwhile, Winston's subordinate, Thornton, escaped detection and worked hard to bring in literally hundreds of recruits for the southern army. The apparent object of Thornton's uprising in early July 1864 was to seize and hold a portion of northwest Missouri until Confederate Major General Sterling Price and his army in Arkansas could ride north and join forces with Thornton's men in the liberation of Missouri from its Union occupation. Lieutenant Colonel Thornton's isolation so far removed from other regular Confederate forces prevented him from fully coordinating his northwest Missouri uprising with them, and he seemed to have a murky grasp on what help he might expect from Arkansas and when it would come.

The Insurgency Ignites in Platte County at Parkville on 7 July

Southern forces centered in the Platte County area began offensive operations against northern forces there on July 7 with a raid on Parkville in the south tip of the county. Heretofore, all the southern irregulars working under Lieutenant Colonel Thornton in this area hid their activities from Union troops and avoided contact with them. On this July 7 veteran Quantrill bushwhacker Captain Charles "Fletch" Taylor led between 56 and 80 guerrillas in Union uniforms into Parkville about sunrise and immediately besieged the small garrison of Company E, of the 82nd EMM inside the stone building by the Missouri River that served as their armory. Locals later discovered that Taylor backed his raid with a similar number of warriors waiting along a woods north of town in case his men encountered unexpected resistance, but Taylor did not call for this reserve. Taylor's sudden arrival caught the local militia scattered throughout town, and the siege of ten of the militiamen at the stone warehouse did not last long. The bushwhackers fired back at the resisting northerners from a building across the street, and shoved two local women of northern sympathy into the window casements and fired around them so as to discourage the Union troops from returning the fire. At least one woman assisted the northern side of the fight, as Mrs. George B. Mitchell joined her husband shooting at the guerrillas from the stone warehouse until he was seriously wounded and she suffered her own serious wound in her breast. After the war bushwhacker participants told their interviewer, John N. Edwards, that they tried to avoid shooting this lady, but that Oliver Shepherd fired into one of the armory windows at the same instant that she popped into view to shoot and therefore his bullet hit the woman

Oliver Shepherd took part in the raid on Parkville on 7 July (John N. Edwards, *Noted Guerrillas*, p. 373; courtesy of the late Bob Younger and Mary Younger and Andy Turner).

by accident. After the Mitchells received their wounds, "Fletch" Taylor and some of his men battered down the door of the warehouse and threatened to burn the building. The besieged militiamen, led by a wounded First Lieutenant George W. Noland of Company E, 82nd EMM surrendered upon condition that they would be fairly treated as prisoners of war. Meanwhile, other members of the raiding force gathered the remaining loyal members of the local militia and "Fletch" Taylor paroled them, too. Two guerrillas confronted Private Isaac Brink of the 16th Kansas Cavalry who was home on furlough, and after he unbuckled his revolver holster and handed it over they shot him to death. Brink's was the only fatality during the raid, although several Rebels were wounded and three or four locals were wounded including Mrs. Mitchell. With the cease of gunfire, the raiders pillaged stores and homes, taking cash, valuables, and clothing—including women's clothing, presumably for their own family members. Although the bushwhackers limited themselves only to what they could carry away on horseback, they took an amazing amount of goods, and even stripped one woman's house of nearly all her belongings. The southerners were careful not to victimize the property of fellow southerners, however. A number of the local militiamen, including Company E commander Captain Thomas J. Wilson and several other residents of northern sympathy escaped the town and made their way across the river to Kansas for safety. Parkville residents including the paroled militia were shocked to see a number of their former militia comrades of the neighborhood among the ranks of the raiders, and were perturbed to hear some of the raiders when meeting other militia members known to hold southern sympathy to recognize their names and comment "Oh, you are all right," and not even require these militiamen to take parole. Obviously, the guerrillas had many friends among the residents of Parkville and were well versed in who they regarded as enemy and who they did not. Taylor or some of his men commented with confidence that "they had the country and would hold it." Since these were the same words Lieutenant Confederate Colonel Thornton used to describe his mission in the Platte County area, Thornton may have given Taylor's raid his blessing. When Taylor's guerrilla force left in the direction of Platte City, many of the more southern-leaning militiamen left with them. As Union officials of the region heard the details of the Parkville raid they concluded they could no longer trust the Platte County militia and turned to Major General Samuel R. Curtis and his troops of the Department of Kansas for help in putting down what they feared was growing into a full-blown uprising. Curtis himself set the tone for much of what later followed by writing July 9 about the Rebels in Platte County "immediate vengeance should follow the path they trod. Double the same taken from the sympathizers in the vicinity."[1]

There were other signs during the rest of that week that the southern irregular forces in Platte County were conducting other offensive operations. A Platte County chronicler recorded that also on July 7 unidentified guerrillas burned the house of a William Schaback and wounded the owner in the arm about six miles from Weston in west-central Platte County. The 1860 Platte County census shows a 30-year-old Prussian-born laborer named Peter Shaback living in the town of Weston. This man and a John Schnabeck, who was three years older than Peter, enlisted at the end of 1861 in the same company of the Union 18th Missouri Infantry and served in that regiment until mustered out three years later in December 1864. Perhaps one of these Schnabecks was on furlough near Weston in early July 1864 when attacked and wounded by bushwhackers.[2] About a day or two later Union Lieutenant Colonel Robert T. Van Horn, lately of the 25th Missouri Infantry Regiment and at this time mayor of Kansas City as well as editor of that city's daily newspaper, was quoted in one of the St. Louis daily newspapers as saying that the guerrillas who had been lately hovering near Kansas City had all crossed to the north side of the Missouri River into Platte County. The brief mention of this in the news did not specify how Van Horn acquired such information, it seems unlikely that George Todd would have moved his entire band there, but it seems highly possible that Todd may have sent reinforcements to Platte County to assist "Fletch" Taylor with his new aggressive operation there.[3] On Saturday, July 9 elements of the Union military reported that a witness spotted Captain Taylor's band estimated as high as 150 riders in the Goose Neck Bend area of the Platte River in central Platte County.[4]

Thornton's Platte City Raid

On Sunday, July 10 Confederate forces raided the county seat of Platte City with hardly a bullet fired. Lieutenant Colonel John Calhoun "Coon" Thornton chose this action as his own personal entry into offensive action, and flawlessly executed the raid. In a move contrary to normal guerrilla tactics, Thornton announced the presence of his large force while they were two miles from Platte City about eight that morning, which worked to warn the few available militia still loyal to their uniform to clear out along with some of the small numbers of civilians of northern sympathy. One of these fugitives was Major John M. Clark of the 82nd EMM, who later claimed he left town at this time to look after a sick child, but in truth, many of the "Paw Paw Militia" no longer obeyed officers who were truly loyal to the Union, and Clark apparently left for his own safety. Therefore, when a very confident Lieutenant Colonel Thornton and force of about 400 Confederate recruits entered town about one in the afternoon, they did so as conquering heroes to a receptive crowd of nearly all sympathetic southerners. Most members of several companies of 82nd EMM or "Paw Paw Militia" garrisoned in Platte City and villages in the area used the time since hearing Thornton was approaching to pull out of hiding Confederate gray uniforms and happily donned them for the joyous reception, causing a newspaper correspondent at Leavenworth to later remark that "the Paw-paws have at last shown their hand." Lieutenant Colonel Thornton's officers diligently worked to conscript the turncoat "Paw Paw Militia" into their own ranks, pressing horses to provide enough mounts for these "new" troops. Although hundreds of the "Paw Paw Militia" had been secretly flocking to Thornton's banner in the preceding weeks, the Platte City raid of July 10 marked the first time any number did so publicly, and this brazen act would later cost many of them their lives. One of the Rebels tore down the U.S. flag, tied it to the tail of his horse, and dragged it through the street while another ran up the flag of the Confederacy. Someone killed and dressed some beef cattle and Thornton's men invited their admirers to help themselves to the meat, and a sumptuous feast was prepared and enjoyed, leading a pro-Union St. Joseph newspaper to wryly remark later that "the fatted calf was brought out." The colonel gave a tough speech claiming what he believed that "I have the troops to whip any force they [the Federals] can bring against me," and that he had been assigned "to this portion of Missouri and we will hold it." He stated that he was "opposed to murdering and burning," but if the Federals took those actions he would "use a heavy hand." Union officials in the region heard that Thornton instructed his troops "to spare no Federals upon any terms" in this speech, and that he said General Price's army was scattered throughout the state awaiting the signal to rise up and attack the Union military. Such remarks reinforced the old 1862 rule of "no quarter" and tended to discard ideas of granting parole and clemency. About two that afternoon some men broke into Lawson Holmes' dry goods store, presumably because Holmes was a northern sympathizer, and crowds of men and some women carried off armloads of the looted inventory.

The guerrillas working with Colonel Thornton's command did not play a prominent role in the Platte City raid, and some sources indicate they remained on the sidelines, perhaps at Thornton's direction. Captain Fletcher "Fletch" Taylor, from Independence and a former Quantrill man, returned to Thornton's side with his estimated 150 guerrillas sometime this afternoon after raiding that morning a few miles to the north in south-central Buchanan County. Part of Taylor's foray there took place south of the village of Taos where his band captured and killed three unidentified Union soldiers in a thicket. In that same neighborhood Taylor's men besieged in his home Northern Methodist Reverend Charles Morris, outspoken as a northern sympathizer and reputed to inform on his southern neighbors. Morris with two companions resisted the overwhelming odds with gunfire until the bushwhackers torched the house and then gunned down the middle-aged farmer/preacher when the smoke and flames forced Reverend Morris out into the yard. Guerrilla chronicler John N. Edwards quoted Taylor describing a heated discussion he had with Lieutenant Colonel Thornton in Platte City. Edwards wrote that Taylor considered Thornton's idea of holding that corner of northwest Missouri until General Price's army could come a "strange notion," and that his plan was "untenable." Taylor claimed he told Thornton that he had too few men for a regular army, too many men to function effectively as a guerrilla force, and that he "was 500 miles from a base line." Taylor strongly felt Thornton should take his recruiting command away to the South before disaster struck, although Edward's version about such advice may have been hindsight speaking, considering how badly John "Coon" Thornton's uprising concluded a few days later. Perhaps Taylor did have a strong disagreement over strategy with Thornton, since both Taylor and Thrailkill took their bands away from his command for independent operations a few days later.

The day after the Platte City raid, on July 11 Captain John Thrailkill brought his band of between 50 and 75 bushwhackers to join the celebration. Thrailkill of Holt County had been captured by Union forces in this area a year before recruiting for the Confederacy, was convicted by a Yankee military tribunal and sentenced to a long prison term, but escaped from the military prison at Alton, Illinois as recently as June 28. Even though new to guerrilla war, the captain was learning quickly, but conducted his operations honorably and seemed to abhor the widely recognized "no quarter" rule for guerrilla warfare in Missouri.[5]

The Union Counterattack at Camden Point

Union reaction to Thornton's Platte City raid of July 10 so soon after Taylor's Parkville raid on July 7 was sudden and decisive, as if making up for months of ignoring the shaky loyalty of the "Paw Paw Militia" and the dangerous Confederate recruiting almost under Yankee noses.

Generals Rosecrans, Curtis, Brown, and Fisk worked fast to field a force by river steamer and road to Platte County by early July 13 in order to battle this Rebel force quickly, perhaps thinking Thornton would logically take his command back into hiding after his recent success. This task force totaling about 400 to 450 men consisted of:

- Colonel James H. Ford and two companies or about 150 troopers of his 2nd Colorado Cavalry from the Kansas City area south of the Missouri River, and about 30 more men with the 2nd Colorado Artillery Battery,
- Lieutenant Colonel Daniel M. Draper and three companies or about 200 of his cavalrymen of the 9th Cavalry MSM from the St. Joseph garrison and surrounding region,
- Colonel Charles R. "Doc" Jennison and one company or 40 troopers of the 15th Kansas Cavalry and one company or about 30 cavalrymen of the 16th Kansas Cavalry from Ft. Leavenworth on the Kansas side of the Missouri River. Jennison was also the commander at Fort Leavenworth.

Several members of the 16th Kansas had Platte County area roots, served earlier in the war in the local 39th EMM there before seeking asylum in Kansas from southern death threats, and were effective scouts in this area. Colonel Ford was named overall commander of this sudden force, and his troopers took the lead after the entire force assembled at the Missouri River town of Weston in west-central Platte County. Patrols from this massive force on July 13 quickly fixed Lieutenant Colonel Thornton's force location at the village of Camden Point in north-central Platte County where Thornton moved his hundreds after leaving Platte City on July 12. Ford's large task force quickly moved out directly toward Camden Point. At this inopportune time Captain "Fletch" Taylor with his guerrillas and scores of the new Rebel recruits left Thornton in disagreement with his refusal to use "hit and run" tactics, riding east to Clay County to commence independent operations. Apparently, Taylor did not know how close the Federal task force was to Thornton's command, nor did he foresee that his argument with Thornton would be proven correct so soon.[6]

Lieutenant Colonel Thornton's force was not prepared for a fight at Camden Point the afternoon of July 13. They were enjoying a celebration picnic with many of the area civilians just north of town when southern pickets on the other side of town skir-

The initial Union attack at Camden Point galloped down a narrow country lane (Underwood and Clough, eds., *Battles and Leaders of the Civil War*, vol. 2, 1887, p. 668).

mished with Colorado troopers of the advance guard, and the alarm quickly spread. Without Fletcher Taylor's large guerrilla force to provide security and fight back, the situation looked grim indeed, when guerrilla chieftain Captain John Thrailkill became the man of the hour. As a regular cavalry captain during General Marmaduke's raid on southeast Missouri in April 1863 Thrailkill earned mention in dispatches for skillfully leading a rear guard action to hold off a Yankee pursuit then, and he did it again this day. While Lieutenant Colonel Thornton and most of his remaining men beat a hasty retreat away from the picnic scene, Captain Thrailkill threw together a mounted rear guard of about 150 guerrillas, recruits, and former "Paw Paw Militia" that were still on the scene. The advance guard of the 2nd Colorado Cavalry rode quickly down a lane to battle, but the country road limited their line to only four troopers across upon which Thrailkill's thrown-together battle line concentrated their fire. Several on each side fell, but the unexpected resistance slowed the Union juggernaut for a few minutes enabling Thornton and the others to make good their escape. After the Federals regrouped and came again Thrailkill's line broke and the rest of the fight was Union cavalry hunting down fleeing individual Rebels. The total losses from the day's fighting were for the Federals four dead and several wounded, and for the Rebels 18 killed and several wounded. The Union troopers of the various units were considerably worked up for this battle by the great haste and excitement as well as and hearing about Thornton exhorting his men not to spare the lives of Federals, so some of the 18 killed southerners were actually wounded men that Union troopers killed at close range as they found them. Union troopers particularly singled out for such treatment Rebels in new-looking gray uniforms they assumed to be traitor "Paw Paw Militia."

Union Depredations in Platte County After Camden Point

As Colonel Ford and the other officers of this Union task force planned for their next move in the afterglow of their victory, a number of their soldiers, incensed by the picnic and festivities locals lavished on Thornton and his Rebels, engaged in a punitive orgy of looting and arson in the Camden Point area. Soon smoke columns from many burning buildings filled the evening sky. Some of the goods burned were Thornton's carefully husbanded supplies and munitions which was lawful for the victors to destroy, but some soldiers continued their arson into July 14 until fully two-thirds of the town was destroyed, and at least one local man was murdered. In the remains of one of the burned hemp warehouses Union troopers gawked at a number of ruined Rebel rifle-muskets and the charred remains of three Confederates who may have been hiding there when the building was burned. Some local sources attributed much of the mayhem to members of the 15th Kansas Cavalry company, but other units indulged in the vengeance, too. More was to come.[7]

On July 14 and 15 Jennison's Kansans and Ford's Coloradoans took their brand of destruction nine miles south to Platte City, which had surrendered so freely to Thornton on July 10 and then feted him and his men. These Federals methodically torched and looted buildings they associated with southerners including public buildings and two churches, and homes of known southern sympathizers. In all, they burned down between eleven and thirteen structures there.

Beginning right after the Camden Point fight, the entire Union force began to capture small isolated groups of Thornton's Rebel force in their travels, and eventually held scores if not hundreds of these southern men in captivity, many of the "Paw Paw Militia" facing trial and execution for treason.[8]

Other Guerrilla Actions North of the Missouri River Between July 7 and 14 Including Anderson's Carroll County Raid of July 12

While guerrilla violence and Thornton's long-awaited uprising took place in Platte County between July 7 and 14, other counties of northwest Missouri north of the Missouri River also experienced isolated incidents—of course, at a much smaller scale. On July 8 First Lieutenant John D. Page's patrol of the local 51st EMM near Richmond in Ray County rode onto an unidentified bushwhacker group of unspecified size and immediately charged them. The southerners fired upon the attacking horsemen killing Page outright, wounding First Sergeant Robert Goode and two other men and killing five of the militia horses. Despite the return fire and his own three bullet wounds, First Sergeant Goode rallied the patrol and inflicted unknown casualties upon the Rebels, scattered them, and captured several of their horses. The militiamen found letters and Confederate money on the captured mounts indicating at least several of the guerrillas had in recent weeks traveled to Missouri from the Confederate army in Arkansas. A few days after this fight and the funeral for the lieutenant, the state EMM apparatus gave First Sergeant Goode a direct commission to second lieutenant for the leadership skills he displayed under fire.[9] During July 12 about 36 bushwhackers were busy in Buchanan County scouting perhaps for Lieutenant Colonel Thornton's forces to the south in Platte County, and seizing horses. They robbed one farmer of northern sympathy of some of his property including horses, and briefly captured and held a Buchanan County deputy sheriff.[10]

Also on July 12 Bill Anderson's band of about 22 guerrillas left its base in the northeast corner of Lafayette County riding east to a new area of operations. The band seems to have been inactive since Bill's letter writing spate on July 7, as described in Chapter Seventeen, but they showed great energy today. They were heading to northeast Missouri to operate for a few weeks, but had to cross the Missouri River and traverse part of Carroll County first. Anderson did not plan ahead by bringing his own boat, so the band rode along the south bank in northwest Saline County until they found a small skiff they could use to cross. Unfortunately, the boat was on the other side and one of Anderson's men drowned swimming over to fetch it back. The rest of the crossing was uneventful but slow using one skiff to ferry guerrillas and horses to the Carroll County side a few at a time. Thus, the band gradually arrived by mid-afternoon July 12 in the southeast corner of Carroll County, a neighborhood known for its northern sympathy. Over the next four hours Captain Anderson conducted the first of his several murder sprees across Carroll County this year. On this date Union officials in the county were holding meetings to raise volunteer citizen guardsmen in response to General Rosecrans' recently published General Orders Number 107, and Anderson's men in their own Yankee uniforms deceived and then murdered several local men on their way to one of the meetings, and others working at their farms. An older man stood up to Anderson and talked back to him causing guerrilla Archie Clements to cut the senior's throat from ear to ear for his impertinence. One young man conducting business at a local mill was actually southern

Bill Anderson's guerrilla band rode through Carroll County several times during 1864, and each time murdered unsuspecting northern sympathizers they encountered (Charles C. Coffin, *The Boys of '61*, 1896, p. 213).

in sympathy, but pretended to support the northern side when Anderson's raiders accosted him. When he realized the true identity of these riders in blue he could not convince the bushwhackers he had been lying and they hanged him anyway. In all, that afternoon Anderson's men killed nine men, many of whom were current or former Union soldiers. They also took firearms, horses, food, and other items from unhappy farm folk on their way. That night the band crossed the Grand River into Chariton County at Rocky Ford, forcing a local man to guide them whom they evidently later killed. At least for a few weeks west-central Missouri was rid of Anderson's killers, but they would be back, and in the meantime northeast Missouri had to learn how to cope with them, as discussed in Chapter Fifteen.[11]

The Violence Moves East to Clay and Ray Counties After Camden Point

Union Colonel James H. Ford of the 2nd Colorado Cavalry on July 15 took his expeditionary force east from Platte County into Clay Count to locate and continue the fight with Confederate Lieutenant Colonel John Thornton's mixed Rebel force. The mystery for the Yanks consisted in finding Thornton's force, badly scattered after the Union victory at Camden Pont and guerrilla "Fletch" Taylor's earlier departure both on July 13. As a result, Thornton's, Thrailkill's, and Taylor's southerners were dispersed across northern Clay County and Clinton County, and some reports said Rebels were in DeKalb County further to the north. At first, the residents of St. Joseph feared their town was the Rebels' next target, and strengthened their defense posture. Northern leaders, recalling how large-scale Rebel recruiting drives in this part of the state raced for Arkansas earlier in the war, had General Egbert Brown position some of his district's 7th Cavalry MSM in a screen along the south bank of the Missouri River centered around Sibley, northeast Jackson County, looking to prevent Thornton's men from crossing the river in just such a move to the south. Brown deployed other troops on the new, Pennsylvania-built side-wheeler *Post Boy* patrolling the river looking to catch Rebels trying to cross, too. Department chief Major General Rosecrans directed Colonel Ford to hound Thornton's uprising literally to death and issued a broadside scolding "citizens of Northwest Missouri" for permitting Thornton to remain in their midst for all those months and demanding they now "help to exterminate these common enemies of mankind." All said, between July 14 and 16 the Federals tried their best to close the box around Thornton's hundreds of men—but, where were they?[12]

In truth, after Camden Point and between July 14 and 17 the southern insurgency was trying to concentrate and organize its battered force to take the offensive again, mostly in northeast Clay County. Obviously, Lieutenant Colonel Thornton's boast that with his force he could hold the region against whatever the Union military threw at them was now recognized to be overconfidence, and it seems mostly the bushwhackers attached to Thornton's force held it together now. Captains Fletcher Taylor and John Thrailkill basically split up the more willing combatants of Thornton's force to be bushwhackers henceforth with the former Quantrill guerrillas and hard-bitten admirers under Taylor. Those desiring to be guerrillas but less prone to death and mayhem and favoring Thrailkill's more regular cavalry approach joined his newer band with Joe Macy as his second-in-command. The remainder that still wanted to fight but not as guerrillas remained with Lieutenant Colonel Thornton to replenish a few more days until Union ardor was distracted so they could perhaps ride south to Arkansas. It was no longer viable to hold onto the belief that Major General Sterling Price's army in Arkansas would soon come to help them liberate Missouri, or to even rescue them from the fierce Federal force that slammed into them at Camden Point and continued to hunt for them. Thornton would continue to use Taylor's and Thrailkill's bushwhackers as his security force for a few days until Union pressure lessened and he could again act on his own. A great many, perhaps hundreds, of former Thornton men—particularly the "Paw Paw Militia" facing a probable death sentence for treason if caught—in groups of varying sizes began to desert Thornton and the southern cause and desperately began to infiltrate from northwest Missouri in all directions.[13]

Meanwhile, various elements of Colonel Ford's aggressive Union force continued the violence they directed against southern residents and property in Platte County now in Clay County. Even Colonel Ford expressed his low opinion of the citizens' loyalty of this region as he wrote General Rosecrans July 15:

> I would respectfully suggest that the citizens of those counties should not be armed [referring to Rosecrans' General Orders Number 107]. Nine out of ten are disloyal and have aided Thornton in recruiting his forces. They take loyalty like gin and sugar and pass it off just as easy. I have killed no citizens; none but those that were in arms fighting us; but any amount of the citizens need killing. Nine out of ten of the citizens are assisting Thornton, giving him all the information and keeping everything from me.[14]

Ford's advanced guard on July 14 seemed to share the colonel's attitude and committed atrocities when they entered Liberty. They killed one man driving a wagon load of flour to Liberty from Parkville, shot and killed another Clay County man on the road south of Liberty, and killed a third man at his home allegedly because he had whipped a black girl. These three men were well-known locally as southern men, and Liberty area people were incensed at these senseless killings and the looting some of the northern troops committed.

Contradictory local lore indicates a portion of Captain John S. Thomason's Clay County Company I, 82nd EMM "Paw Paw Militia"—evidently not one of the eight companies of that regiment that joined Thornton—with some civilian volunteers, decided to strike back at these offensive Yankees in their midst, but the two primary versions differ in most parts of what happened next. The 1885 Clay County history gave the skirmish date as July 12 and said that four or five local former members of the 6th Cavalry MSM, "or men on furlough" fired on some of Thomason's "Paw Paw Militia" who were in a house. The 82nd EMM men returned the fire, charged out of the house at the mystery Yanks, and chased them off, killing one northerner and wounding a second. This version made no mention of Colonel Ford's expedition. A 1954 Liberty newspaper article quoted two local citizens, Ernest L. Capps and Professor C. G. Wolfskill of the local William Jewell College, who studied the violence near town that July and probably came closer to the truth. This article described the northern atrocities of "Jennison's raiders" or Kansas Jayhawkers on July 14 with names of victims and specific locations, correctly identified them as part of Colonel's Ford's force that came to Liberty, but stated Colonel Jennison's troops were solely of the 16th Kansas Cavalry and omitted any mention of the 15th Kansas Cavalry being part of this Union force. Capps' and Wolfskill's research allowed them to name at least eight of about twenty "returned Confederate veterans" who banded together in horror at the Yankee depredations and set up an ambush in order "to gain revenge for what happened the previous day." The names of four of those men in the revenge posse seem to match members of Captain John S. Thomason's local Company I, 82nd EMM, which was enrolled in September 1863 purposely with men of southern sympathy to defend Clay County partly against Kansas jayhawking raids, although the 1954 article made no mention of the connection with Captain Thomason's company. A St. Joseph newspaper wrote later in July that Company I "marched into Liberty stacked their arms and disbanded" in protest when they first heard about Colonel Ford's expedition charging into the region, as if to prove the mixed allegiance of this "Paw Paw Militia" company. Capps and Wolfskill identified the leader of this impromptu posse as local farmer Abraham Estes who learned that the Kansas raiders were ordered to leave their local quarters at the Liberty U.S. arsenal and ride back west to Fort Leavenworth. Estes and his gang executed their ambush at a bend in that road about 4.5 miles west of Liberty and "killed and wounded an unknown number." In the Union return fire and counterattack Estes died and another southerner was wounded in the leg, but escaped. Capps and Wolfskill told the Liberty newspaper that the Kansas troops confiscated a local farm wagon to haul their dead and wounded on to Fort Leavenworth, and that other Union troops investigated the ambush and interviewed locals, but failed to identify the southerners who attacked the Kansas soldiers. Capps and Wolfskill bemoaned the failure of *The Official Record of the Union and Confederate Armies* to make any mention of this skirmish—which they claimed took place July 15—but the itinerary of Company C, 16th Kansas Cavalry, referring to their part in the expedition in Missouri between July 12 and 18, stated that they were "engaged in a skirmish near Camden Point and one near Liberty, Missouri," but gave no other specifics. There is no mention of any such action near Liberty in reports of Colonel Ford's expedition, and neither the Kansas 15th or 16th Cavalry Regiments' records had much to say about it, either. Colonel Ford reported that General Curtis withdrew the Kansas troops from the expedition the evening of July 17, so Abraham Estes' ambush of some of them evidently took place July 17 or 18.[15]

The Fredericksburg Fight of 17 July

The aggressiveness of the Union expedition in this area did not diminish the danger posed by the remaining hundreds of Rebel combatants under Lieutenant Colonel Thornton and Captains Taylor and Thrailkill, which they aptly demonstrated on July 17. The Yanks sent out two mounted patrols that day east from Liberty in an attempt to locate the Rebels, and Captain Thomas Moses' patrol of 47 men painfully accomplished that mission. Less than a mile from the village of Fredericksburg on the western edge of Ray County Moses' patrol—consisting of troopers of Companies A, C, D, and M 2nd Colorado Cavalry and accompanied by Captain Lyman D. Rouell—rode onto riders approaching them wearing U.S. uniforms. Captain Rouell had been cashiered from the 2nd Colorado May 30, but chose to accompany Colonel Ford's expedition as a volunteer, and Captain Moses sent Rouell ahead to identify the blue uniformed riders. The mounted men replied to Rouell's coded challenge with the correct password, but still fired a pistol shot toward the captain. The now agitated Captain Rouell yelled to the mystery riders that they were making a mistake to which one of them yelled "God damn you! We will show you who is mistaken!" and charged the Federals, shooting as they came. Moses and Rouell quickly saw that there were at least two or three times their number coming at them and the Union patrol fired into the Rebel advance, temporarily stopping it. At this juncture Moses was still not sure they were shooting at fellow Union troops and called out to them to identify themselves, to which one of the attackers shouted in reply that they were "Bushwhackers, God damn you!" This removed all doubt, and Captain Moses quickly realized his patrol stood no

Eighteen—Premature Insurgency in Northwest Missouri North of the River

The Fredericksburg fight of 17 July was a desperate slugfest fought in the brush and woods near town (Mottelay and Campbell-Copeland, eds., *The Soldier in Our Civil War*, vol. 2, 1885, p. 244).

chance of survival only twenty yards from a large, aggressive enemy still advancing and "yelling like devils." Moses immediately ordered his men to disperse into the brush and save themselves, which they quickly did, while the two Colorado captains gamely stood their ground firing their revolvers at close range into the faces of the guerrillas to give their men time to escape. Captains Moses and Rouell, nicked by minor wounds and with bullets whizzing past them, then attempted to fight through to rejoin their men, but were cut off by Rebel flanking movements. The two officers continued to shoot back, spurning repeated calls to surrender, until they, too, had to run into the brush to save their own lives. There were so many guerrillas in blue uniforms that they evidently became confused and failed to identify and kill the fleeing Union officers riding past them and through the heavy vegetation. The two evading captains eventually made their way back to Liberty, collecting scattered members of their patrol as they went, and passing themselves as bushwhackers when approached by southerners. Afterwards, the surviving Coloradoans estimated the Rebel attacking force may have contained between 200 and 300 and was led by guerrilla leaders "Fletch" Taylor and John Thrailkill, and perhaps Lieutenant Colonel Thornton, too. They numbered their own losses as six killed, four wounded, and two missing, and were disgusted to report that their Starr carbines failed them on the battlefield and they owed their lives to their pistols only. Captain Moses reported that he fired all the 18 revolver bullets he carried, and counted five bullet holes in his hat and uniform, and that his horse was hit four times but still carried him from danger. One bullet grazed his forehead and another severed his saber belt. Captain Rouell's clothing was similarly holed and his horse also wounded, and he had minor grazing wounds. Local residents later told the Coloradoans that the guerrilla force buried sixteen men and hauled away 21 wounded men in wagons. Indeed, several of the escaped troopers told of guerrillas they killed in order to make good their escape from the area. John N. Edwards, the guerrilla chronicler, wrote based on interviews soon after the war that it was mainly Captain "Fletch" Taylor's guerrillas who were the Rebel advance that day who fought the battle, but did not provide casualty figures. Edwards listed the southern spoils of battle to be 33 horses, 28 "dragoon revolvers," and 40 Starr carbines, which he mentioned was one of an array of breechloaders with which the Yankees were experimenting. The southern force won a victory against Captain Moses' patrol July 17, but suffered losses, and had to continue toward the east and northeast to stay away from Colonel Ford's pursuit. This Rebel movement toward the east pleased Union General Fisk, who desired Ford's expedition to drive the Rebels into the reach of the 17th Illinois Cavalry and 1st Iowa Cavalry who awaited them two counties east.[16]

Guerrillas Raid Fredericksburg, Elkhorn, and Albany

As the large Rebel force rode into Ray County, the majority entered unfamiliar territory where they were unsure who was friend or foe, and did not tend to linger. After the fight outside of town on July 17 some of the guerrillas robbed the store at little Fredericksburg as they rode through and then robbed a store at nearby Elkhorn, too.[17] At Elkhorn, Captain Thrailkill heard that northerners had recruited a new company for the Yankee 44th Missouri Infantry a few miles south at Albany, and took his band south to deal with this threat. At Albany Thrailkill learned the Union recruiting company had left earlier to reinforce the garrison at the county seat at Richmond, and this side trip caused his gang to bring up the rear of the Rebel force when they rejoined the others on July 18.[18] Meanwhile, Union Captain David P. Whitmer of the local 51st EMM, commanding at Richmond, heard alarming reports from his scouts on the afternoon of July 17 that Lieutenant Colonel Thornton, with 300 to 400 riders, was only ten miles from town and sent a plea for help to other Union forces in the region since he had only thirty men in town to hold the place. This accounts for the absence in Albany of the company there when Thrailkill's band rode into that town. Bill Anderson's guerrillas would fight near Albany over three months later with dire results.[19]

Thornton's Force Changes Course to Bypass Richmond

The amalgamated Rebel force radically changed course on July 18 and veered north bypassing Richmond—in effect ruining Union General Fisk's plan for the Confederates to come to grief against troops he had notified to expect them to the east. Perhaps the guerrillas learned of Captain Whitmer's call for help from two members of the 51st EMM Taylor's men caught that day about seven miles from Richmond. The prisoners were Second Lieutenant Jesse C. Tunnage and Private John F. Shoemake, whom the bushwhackers killed and mutilated along with a Colorado trooper they captured the day before at the Fredericksburg fight. Union troops later found the three bodies on the road.[20] Meanwhile, in the south part of Ray County this same day an unidentified body of southerners attempted to cross the Missouri River opposite Lexington, but were deterred by Union troops on the south bank placed there earlier to prevent just such an occurrence. Colonel Ford reported the movement of this "large party" to General Fisk and sent a steamboat loaded with one section of artillery and Major Henry Suess and some of his troopers of the 7th Cavalry MSM just to ensure that this body of Rebels did not cross. Perhaps these Rebels were some of Thornton's recruits and turncoat "Paw Paw Militia" attempting to escape their fate north of the river.[21] A few miles to the north Captain "Fletch" Taylor's bushwhackers committed more mayhem as they approached the town of Knoxville in north-central Ray County. They stopped the stagecoach, destroyed the mail, and took the horses; then captured and killed another local member of the 51st EMM, Private Perry J. Wilson.[22]

Thornton's Force Raids Knoxville

The village of Knoxville had warning that the Rebels were coming on July 18 and about one hundred pro-northern residents assembled to attempt to face the challenge, although only about half of them had firearms. Most of them next followed good advice sent from the 51st EMM's Captain Clayton Tiffin to disperse and hide in the brush. However, a few remained in town to see what would happen until guerrillas in blue uniforms appeared just outside of town. First Lieutenant William Stone of the local 51st EMM company rode out to investigate and called to the blue-clad riders to identify themselves, since Missouri guerrilla warfare had evolved by 1864 into a deadly guessing game of combatants hiding identities and assuming false ones to gain advantage. These mounted men replied that they were "Illinois 100-days men," who were stop-gap, poorly trained Illinois units that had recently been rushed into Missouri to bolster Federal strength in the current emergency. Obviously, these guerrillas had been reading some of the intercepted Union military dispatches and newspapers commenting on the new type of Illinois cavalry units, but Stone and the others were wisely skeptical and quickly left town. As the guerrillas rode into Knoxville they shot and killed a slave man who was running away from them, then rifled through two stores in town, robbed a few citizens, and rode on having spent about an hour there. A local account stated after the war that this was Captain Thrailkill's guerrilla band, but it was probably instead "Fletch" Taylor's who had been in the vanguard on July 18, or perhaps both of the bands.[23]

The Pursuing Union Vanguard Stops Short

For the previous several hours a Union mounted pursuit column of about 250 Union troops from Liberty led by Major Jesse L. Pritchard composed of his own 2nd Colorado Cavalry and local militiamen had been tracking the large southern force across Ray County on July 18. The Union military version of this incident stated that when Pritchard discovered the guerrilla body dispersed after leaving Knoxville, he immediately turned his command around and returned to Liberty because the horses and men were exhausted from the long pursuit. A local story has it that the major halted his large body of cavalry a couple of miles short of Knoxville to rest the horses and riders at the very time the bushwhackers were in town looting the place. After the Rebels left Knoxville, for unknown reasons, Pritchard took his command back to Liberty without even striking a blow at the nearby Rebels, much to the disgust of the militia riding with the expedition. This local tale of this incident, however, exaggerated the strength of Pritchard's force to about 400 riders, but this was almost double their true numbers. Pritchard's more aggressive commander, Colonel James Ford, was temporarily distracted on July 18, since he traveled to Kansas City to exchange secure telegrams with General Rosecrans. Ford was concerned that few Union troops were south of the Missouri River to keep track of George Todd's guerrilla band of up to 200 who were then moving about in Ford's normal assigned operating area. Rosecrans ordered the colonel to continue his operations north of the river a few days more and that he would find other troops to confront Todd's gang. Major General Rosecrans obviously decided that " a bird in the hand was better than two in the bush" by ensuring that Ford punished Lieutenant Colonel Thornton's force thoroughly before looking for other foes, but the Colorado colonel allowed his concentration of Thornton's Rebels to waver for a few days. As a result of Major Pritchard's prevarication and Colonel Ford's distraction, however, the Union pursuit of Thornton, Taylor, and Thrailkill faltered on July 18 and 19. The large Rebel command took advantage of the temporary absence of their pursuers to return to offensive tactics as they rode out of Ray County toward the northeast.[24]

Thornton's, Taylor's, and Thrailkill's Rebels Raid Through Carroll, Livingston, Caldwell, and Clinton Counties

Thornton's Strategy and the Union Strategy for Beating Him

Lieutenant Colonel John C. Thornton's Rebel force of between 300 and 400 found many supporters in Clay County, but Ford's pursuit pushed them east into Ray County and rushed them through that county so fast that they did not stop long enough to seek friends. On July 18 without a close pursuit, Thornton's forces rode out of the northeast corner of Ray County into the junction of Carroll, Livingston, and Caldwell Counties and resumed the offensive with the twin guerrilla commands of Captain "Fletch" Taylor and Captain John Thrailkill acting as spearheads. Although the previous pursuit of Colonel Ford and his 2nd Colorado Cavalry and part of the 9th Cavalry MSM was far behind them, the Union command activated all available Enrolled Missouri Militia across this whole region, and a cloud of these part-time soldiers would pester the large Rebel force wherever they went. Given the large-scale Federal reaction to Thornton's uprising in this region and the continued Union pursuit that was still coming, this large Rebel force had only a few options. Thornton's original plan was to hold out in this part of northwest Missouri until some part of the regular Confederate force south in Arkansas could come join them or, at worst, come escort them south to safety. Thornton and his men evidently did not yet realize that the Rebel army in Arkansas would not be ready to come to Missouri for two more months, so Thornton's force was totally on its own. He could employ the twin guerrilla commands of "Fletch" Taylor and John Thrailkill as shock troops and carry on behind-enemy-lines offensive war moving around this region in hit-and-run tactics for some time. As long as such tactics kept Thornton's main force away from Union punitive actions, the daring-do of continually embarrassing the Yanks would continue to draw new recruits to Thornton's banner and make his command stronger. The actions of other Confederate recruiting commands and other guerrilla bands around this part of Missouri may keep the Federals busy, stretched thin, and prevent them from massing too much force against Thornton's command. This premise relied on those southerners maintaining a steady warfare to keep the northerners busy—an uncertain gamble. As a last resort, if the Yankee cavalry closed in with overwhelming numbers, the Rebels could borrow a page from the bushwhacker's book and simply disperse to rendezvous later at some pre-designated place. As long as they scattered in predominantly southern neighborhoods, local sympathizers could succor and hide them.

Thornton's offensive from July 7 through July 18 attracted enough Yankee attention that they tightened control around this part of northwest Missouri. The Federals had troops along the Missouri River on the south and west and their continued control and use of the Hannibal and St. Joseph Railroad across Livingston, Caldwell, Clinton, and Buchanan Counties meant they kept Thornton's force from moving too far north, for the most part. Basically, this meant that Thornton and his men could only operate in those portions of eight northwest Missouri counties between the Missouri River and the Hannibal and St. Joseph Railroad, and that is exactly what they continued to do.

Thrailkill's Defeat of Union Militia at Black Oak

By the morning of July 19 Thornton's guerrillas were at the Black Oak neighborhood in the southeast corner of Caldwell County near the corner of Ray, Carroll,

Livingston and Caldwell Counties and began probing to the north to see what Union troops were ahead. Captain Charles Fletcher Taylor's bushwhackers found and killed two militiamen of the 33rd EMM at their homes. Nearby and east of them Captain John Thrailkill's guerrilla band rode onto about thirty men of Company E, 33rd EMM gathering for duty, and fooled them with their blue uniforms and by cleverly called out hurrahs for notorious jayhawking Senator James Lane of Kansas, and captured most of them. Some of the startled militiamen escaped, but Thrailkill's band captured and paroled 26 men of this company and three or four other militiamen with them. "Fletch" Taylor and his men shortly rode up and demanded Thrailkill turn the prisoners over to them, but Captain Thrailkill knew Taylor's bushwhackers would murder the paroled prisoners and refused, placing some of his men around the captives as guards to protect them. Thrailkill's refusal infuriated Taylor and his men who were aware that the 33rd EMM was known for atrocities against southern men in the Caldwell County area earlier in the war, but they were forced to accept the situation. This incident clearly contrasted the difference between Taylor's "cutthroat" style of warfare that often involved murdering disarmed Yankee prisoners, mutilating dead enemies, robbing and looting with Thrailkill's "regular army" or "civilized" method of conducting irregular war that avoided harming noncombatants or captives.[25]

Thornton's Brief Excursion Into Carroll County and Tough Choices

Also on July 19 Lieutenant Colonel Thornton briefly took his large command east to the northwest corner of Carroll County, weighing what he should do next and making a major decision. His force remained near the village of Mandeville a few miles northwest of Carrollton only a few hours, but this marks a turning point, as this was the easternmost point of Thornton's campaigning this summer in Missouri. Thornton told his men he was entertaining the thought of leading them quickly south through Carroll County to infiltrate through the Yankee cordon guarding the Missouri River, which he had hoped would be more lightly guarded this far to the east. He announced that the Federals were expecting such a move and that it would be foolhardy to try to cross the river now. Lieutenant Colonel Thornton was also exploring the idea of taking the command east to Howard County and possibly connecting with the Confederate recruiting command of Colonel Caleb Perkins, then very active in Howard, Boone, and Randolph Counties as described in Chapter Fifteen. This Thornton also rejected probably because he would have to lead his command across the rest of Carroll County and all of Chariton County where his men did not know the ground or the people. It is uncertain if the commander mentioned this latter option to his men that night.

Thornton Advances Northwest into Caldwell County

Apparently, Thornton decided to lead his command back into their more familiar battleground of northwest Missouri and continue to battle the Union troops there in mobile warfare. The Rebels broke camp and moved back across the Caldwell County line that same night of July 19/20, and from that time onward conducted their operations west of this point. Thornton evidently also decided to allow his guerrillas more latitude to rampage far ahead of the main body from this time forward, based on actions that transpired beginning July 20. Over the next several days Thornton's command operated sometimes in three widely separated, fast-moving parts, creating great confusion in the surviving records as to just which part was where.

Brief Guerrilla Incursion into Livingston County

No known combat action took place in Carroll County on July 19 or 20, but just hearing the Rebels were there created pandemonium at the Union St. Joseph district headquarters and at Carrollton and Chillicothe, county seats of Carroll and Livingston Counties, respectively. Evidently, Thornton sent either Taylor's or Thrailkill's irregulars northeast along Muddy Creek in the corner of Livingston County toward Utica, burning homes of northern sympathizers and taking what they needed, perhaps to create a feint to conceal his actual intention to ride fast to the west. General Fisk reported to department headquarters that "Thornton and his Confederate fiends are now in Livingston County, about 400 strong. They are leaving a track of blood and ashes." In Carrollton and Chillicothe northern sympathizers feared their town was Thornton's next target and activated every man who could carry a firearm. This had a bad eventual effect for Lieutenant Colonel Thornton's command in that the Union militia, discharged veterans, and other volunteers arrayed themselves to fight his rampaging force. It is doubtful the Livingston County northerners would have responded in those numbers if the Rebels had not entered Carroll and Livingston Counties July 19 and 20.[26]

Thornton's Force Raids Kingston and Mirable

Starting July 20 Thornton's force moved with new direction and clarity as they rode straight west and raided first the undefended Caldwell County seat at Kingston at three that afternoon. There the raiders took thousands in greenbacks from the county treasurer's office and other safes in one hour's time, but Captain Thrailkill dissuaded some of the men from burning the courthouse and from robbing homes or damaging property. The Rebel force rode on to the southwest and raided the undefended village of Mirabile about eleven that night taking money and goods from stores and robbing some residents. The raiders also learned that local militia had the day before captured and then killed two of Thrailkill's men near Mirabile who had earlier deserted the band and were riding back to their homes in Platte County. The indignant guerrillas rounded up a dozen townsmen threatening to kill them in revenge. A local tale says that only when one of the prisoners showed Thrailkill the Masonic sign for distress did he intervene and force the very reluctant raiders to free the townsmen. The hard feeling about the two killed guerrillas did motivate their comrades to commit more robbery in Mirabile than they had in Kingston, and they remained in town following that purpose for about three hours before riding on west. The raiders rode three miles west of town, dismounted, and slept until daybreak of July 21 before crossing the Clinton County line.[27]

Taylor Raids in Clinton County

Fletcher Taylor's bushwhackers must have taken a more northerly route into Clinton County, since a clear record remains that they killed a militiaman that day in Shoal Township of the northeast corner. The Caldwell County history told the story about the blue-uniformed guerrillas riding past John H. Christopher's house in that area, causing him to rush out and ask their identity. One of the bushwhackers replied they were "militia, out after bushwhackers," to which Christopher excitedly replied "that's right; clean them out; don't leave one to tell the tale. I am a militiaman, too." Indeed, there is a record that Christopher was then a member of the local 89th EMM. Taylor's men took the surprised militiaman away from the house, then shot him to death and rode their horses over his corpse. Although the Union military records are confused about where Thornton's, Taylor's, and Thrailkill's men were riding during these days, there was one report that a witness saw hundreds of Rebels riding in that corner of Clinton County that day, so that had to be Taylor's guerrillas. The location for Lieutenant Colonel Thornton and the main body of his force this day is unknown and they could have been riding with Taylor's bushwhackers, although one Union report stated Thornton and 500 Rebels were still located at Mandeville in northwest Carroll County, where they were the evening before. Evidence a day later placed Thornton and at least some of his main body in south Ray County, so they must have ridden there about this time.[28]

Thrailkill's Plattsburg Raid of 21 July

The main focus of attention for July 21 was on the Clinton County seat of Plattsburg and Thrailkill's successful raid on the town that day. The Enrolled Missouri Militia garrison there had some warning. Sixty guerrillas that may not have been associated with Thornton's raiders rode within eight miles of the town the day before, and on July 21 a witness reported seeing hundreds of Rebel riders passing by the village of Bedford six miles to the east heading straight for Plattsburg. At nine that morning there was no doubt as Captain Thrailkill and his band of about 200 openly appeared and demanded the surrender under a flag of truce. Thrailkill's note signed by him as "Major, Commanding Confederate Forces" said: "I hereby demand an immediate surrender of the town. We are not bushwhackers, but Confederate soldiers. Your men will be treated as prisoners of war." The Union commander, Captain Benjamin F. Poe of the 89th EMM, sent a rebuff to "Maj. John Thrailkill" saying "Sir: We are not here for the purpose of surrendering, but to defend the flag of our country." During a brief skirmish that took place during the exchange of these messages Union Captain John W. Turney of the 89th EMM was shot from his saddle and killed, and another militiaman wounded, but Captain Poe had most of his men and some civilian volunteers blockade themselves in the courthouse. Thrailkill's men remained a healthy distance from the bristling garrison at the courthouse, but helped themselves to ammunition and other items from stores in Plattsburg. As Captain Thrailkill heard reports about an approaching Union column, he cut short the siege of Captain Poe and his men and rode off toward the southeast in the direction of Haynesville before this new Yankee force got closer. After riding a few miles Thrailkill changed course and led his men to the west toward familiar ground in northeast Platte County.[29]

Thrailkill and Taylor Continue the Fight
While Thornton and a Remnant Depart

Major Cox's Strange Guerrilla Hunter Unit

The approaching Union force that propelled Thrailkill's band away from Plattsburg was a strange amalgamation of various EMM units and civilian volunteers from Daviess, Livingston, and Caldwell Counties led by Major Samuel P. Cox of Daviess County. Earlier in the war Cox was a major in the 1st Cavalry MSM and had lately been active in the General Orders Number 107 citizen guards of Daviess County when General Fisk gave him a special task. Fox' new job was to pull together as much Enrolled Missouri Militia as would respond to him and lead them as sort of a "hunter-killer" force "to pitch into the rebels" anywhere in the region. Actually, Fisk was desperate to field troops against Thornton's growing little southern army, and he even admitted on

July 21 that Cox's crazy command was "not sufficient in number or morale to cope with the increasing force of fiends," but they were what he had left. Much of the reason that Thornton's Rebel irregulars were able to ride across Caldwell County and raid Kingston and Mirable almost without opposition on July 21 is that most of the local militia was responding to Cox's summons to join his command organizing at Breckenridge in the northeast corner of the county. Major Cox and his patchwork task force of about 400 men rode through Kingston and Mirable hours behind the guerrillas and what they observed in the Rebels' wake hardened their resolve. As they pushed their mounts after the southerners small groups of militiamen attached themselves to Cox's command, until one postwar source said that by the time they got to Plattsburg there were about 640 of them, at least from the 33rd, 65th 89th and perhaps other EMM regiments and several area county citizen guards units. Even the militiamen Thrailkill paroled near Black Oak July 19 had joined, violating their parole. Later, when Colonel James Ford of the 2nd Colorado Cavalry saw them, he commented that Cox's force was "poorly armed"—mostly with muzzle-loading, single-shot rifle muskets common to the EMM regiments—and they were not as well mounted as Thornton's men. A lot of the men were Union veterans of one type or another; and many of them were well-meaning neophytes; but, they were determined to rid this region of the Rebels.[30]

Cox Battles Thrailkill at Union Mills 22 July

Cox's amalgamated unit spent the night at Plattsburg, then rode on to the southwest July 22 to Gosneyville, present-day Paradise, near where they found the tracks where Thrailkill's raiders changed course heading toward the northwest which they followed to Union Mills in the northeast corner of Platte County. About three miles from that village about two o'clock that afternoon the advance of the militia force saw a local woman fire a pistol in the air to warn the Rebels, but also warned them, too. Close to this they found the guerrillas in thick brush and gamely attacked. Due to the thick undergrowth only about a quarter of the Yankee troops could shoot at the Rebel muzzle flashes at a time, and after firing the militiamen had to withdraw to reload their single-shot rifle muskets. Early in the fight Cox's men were such a polyglot mixture of clothing, uniforms, and firearms that the guerrillas were unsure who they were fighting.

The fight near Union Mills on 22 July was fought in thick brush (Underwood and Clough, eds., *Battles and Leaders of the Civil War*, vol. 1, p. 644).

One southerner called out to them to identify themselves, asking if they were Federals, to which one of the militia captains yelled back "Yes, we are Federals, and if you will all come out of the brush we will whip hell out of you!" The EMM troops were established for defense and not for offensive warfare, and the realization that so many of them would aggressively track and attack a large, better-mounted, better-armed, veteran group of guerrillas in difficult terrain must have been difficult to accept at first. This brush fight surged back and forth for some minutes until the militia moved forward again to find the Rebels had dispersed and left the battlefield to them. Cox's Yanks thought Thrailkill's band outnumbered them two to one, but actually he had about 200 against about 640 northerners. There remains no record of Rebel losses, except the Yanks found two of Thrailkill's dead and captured another man. Some Union sources and area newspapers thought seven of the southerners in all were killed at this fight. Cox's command suffered one man killed, two or three severely wounded, several others slightly wounded, and one bullet hit the major's horse, too.[31]

Thornton and Part of His Command Head South from Ray County

About the time of Thrailkill's Union Mills fight Lieutenant Colonel John C. Thornton and a portion of his main body managed to escape the Federal cordon around his home region and depart the area. Thornton's location and that of his main body was not well recorded at this time except in some disjointed Union military reports. Witnesses reported to the Federals that the Rebel leader and eighty Rebels were around noon July 22 within three miles of the river in south Ray County not far from Lexington. Colonel Ford of the 2nd Colorado reported later that he had "reliable information" that about eighty southerners successfully crossed to the south bank of the Missouri River that night, so it appears that Thornton and at least that many of his hundreds left their home region, evidently to remain for a while in the company of guerrilla George Todd's capable band in the Lafayette County area on the south side of the Missouri River. The low water level of the river at this time undoubtedly aided the Thornton men in their crossing. In effect, this ended his northwest Missouri uprising or insurgency, even though hundreds of Thornton's men were still scattered about the region in small groups. Of course, Thrailkill and "Fletch" Taylor still commanded guerrilla bands that each contained scores of irregulars including a number of former Thornton recruits, and these now independent groups would continue their warfare. Others roamed the area in smaller groups trying to carry on their war as best they could, and a large number of others scattered in yet smaller groups were desperately trying to infiltrate Yankee lines to escape northwest Missouri to save themselves from prison and possible execution. General Fisk quoted one prisoner as telling him that two of Lieutenant Colonel Thornton's greatest disappointments of the previous few days were the overwhelming uprising of the pro-northern citizens of northwest Missouri against him and the failure of Confederate General Shelby to ride to them as Thornton was led to believe would happen. On July 22, the same day as the fight near Union Mills, northern forces near Kidder in the northwest corner of Caldwell County captured four men who had deserted Thornton's force. In their own defense, some of them said they had been forced to join the southerners and they were quick to assert they had left the southern unit because their experience with it had disgusted them. The St. Joseph newspaper also published the statement of one of the former "Paw Paw Militia" who with four others deserted Thornton at Carroll County July 19, when the southern command found the Missouri River too well guarded to cross to safety. This man was quick to name names and give incriminating details.[32]

Union Reinforcements Enter the Hunt as Cox's Unit Rests

By this time in the campaign the Federals were throwing as many troops as they could gather into squelching the northwest Missouri uprising. Although Cox's large militia task force was worn from their pursuit and the Union Mills fight and went home to rest and refit, Colonel Ford's 2nd Colorado Cavalry renewed its activities in Platte, Clay, Clinton, and Buchanan Counties over the next few days.[33] General Fisk held part of the 9th Cavalry MSM close to his St. Joseph headquarters as a reserve, but he sent in portions of the 17th Illinois Cavalry and the 1st Iowa Cavalry from northeast Missouri, as well as part of the 6th Cavalry MSM and companies of the 30th EMM from Livingston, Grundy, and Mercer Counties to root out Thornton's uprising once and for all.[34] Some of these units were not able to arrive in the affected part of northwest Missouri until after Thornton left and the remaining parts of his once large force went into hiding to wait out the Yankee campaign in sanctuary areas, but the Federals did not know that. During the excitement of this campaign a Union staff officer confused the earlier report of Thornton's July 19 and 20 presence at Mandeville in northwest Carroll County and re-issued that old spot report as a new threat on July 22. As a result, militiamen of the 30th EMM from counties to the north rattled around Carroll County for a few days looking in vain for any Rebels to kill. In their frustration and zeal some of them turned to plundering citizens and their homes, evidently murdered middle-aged farmer and northern sympathizer David Gilbert and his son-in-law working in the field a few miles from DeWitt, and generally "insulted and abused" not only the residents but even members of Carroll County's own 65th EMM while looking for hundreds of Rebels who were not even there. A company of the 30th EMM from Grundy County while attached to the 4th Provisional EMM the previous November and December had engaged in heavy foraging and petty thievery while riding through Carroll County, and perhaps some of those same militiamen thought they would repeat their fun this time. General Fisk may have known of these proclivities of the 30th EMM, as when he assigned them this mission he specifically gave their colonel a warning against such behavior. Overall, though, General Fisk felt he had thrown enough suitable troops at the northwest insurgency that he would soon hear good results, and he crowed to General Rosecrans' headquarters that "volunteers are rolling into Saint Joseph and Chillicothe by the hundred." The St. Louis department headquarters caught Fisk's enthusiasm and telegraphed back to him that "troops and militia are moving in on Mr. Thornton in such numbers and on every road that he must be met with by somebody."[35]

The Pace of the Insurgency Slows Noticeably

The pace of active guerrilla operations slowed noticeably soon after Thrailkill's 22 July fight with Cox's militiamen near Union Mills and Thornton's July 23 escape across the Missouri River. It seems many southerners were pondering what to do and where to go next in light of the large numbers of Yankee troops hunting for them throughout this region. Most of the remaining southern combatants north of the Missouri River sought refuge in known sanctuary areas to wait until the flood of Union troops wearied of riding around the countryside looking for them and returned to their garrisons—a tried and true guerrilla tactic. On July 24 Major J. Nelson Smith with a squadron of the 2nd Colorado Cavalry was tracking a guerrilla band from northeast Platte County southeast into northern Clay County when he stopped the column for a rest break in the late afternoon and sent foragers on ahead. The detail rode onto nearby pickets the Rebels had placed to protect their main body and in a rapid exchange of shots killed one of the Rebels. Major Smith and the rest of the squadron heard the shooting, galloped to the site, and pursued the remainder of the fleeing pickets and routed the main guerrilla body, killing two more at no Union loss before the rest of the southerners dispersed into the woods and brush in the gloom of dusk. Smith could not identify which guerrilla band he fought, but it could have been either Thrailkill's or Taylor's since they both had a few days earlier made friends and found good hiding places in north Clay County.[36] Union Brigadier General Fisk acknowledged the true state of affairs July 24 when he wrote to his superiors at St. Louis that "Thornton's Confederates, pressed on all sides, are scattering in small squads.... Colonel Ford informs me of the general break-up of the rascals. We shall have to hunt them from their hiding-places."[37]

General Price Reacts to News of Thornton's Uprising

Ironically, on July 22 in distant Camden, Arkansas Missouri's Major General Sterling Price was writing to Missouri's governor-in-exile at Marshall, Texas, Thomas C. Reynolds, his impressions that supported his plan to invade Missouri and liberate the state from its Federal occupiers. In response to Governor Reynolds' urging, Price concurred "that such an expedition practicable ... desirable and important." Price elaborated:

> You will see from the [news]paper I enclose you that our forces are in possession of Platte County, and that our cause is in the ascendant in many parts of the State. It is significant that a company of State troops, sent to defend Platte City, went over in a body, with their arms, to the Confederates. My opinion is that the people of Missouri are ready for a general uprising, and that the time was never more propitious for an advance of our forces into Missouri. Our friends should be encouraged and supported promptly. Delay will be dangerous. Unsustained, they may be overpowered by superior numbers.

In similar vein Price wrote to his superior, General E. Kirby Smith on July 23:

> The accumulating testimony of the state of affairs in Missouri derived from private individuals, private

General Price's statue at Keytesville, Chariton County (Eugene M. Violette, *A History of Missouri*, 1918, p. 390).

letters, and the public prints, show that the Federals have but few reliable forces in the State, their garrisons being manned almost entirely with their State militia, in whose loyalty they have but little confidence.... I am also assured that the Confederate flag floats over nearly all the principal towns of North Missouri.[38]

Apparently, General Price deluded himself with a combination of misleading newspaper articles and testimonies into believing what he desired most to believe—namely that Missouri was ripe for his invasion in that the Union defenders were weak and unreliable and that a large number of the populace would welcome his conquering army with open arms.

Guerrilla Actions During July in Northwest Missouri North of the Missouri River Separate from Thornton's Operations

Guerrillas Raiding in Buchanan County

Not all Rebel forces north of the Missouri River rode with Thornton in his mobile operations those days in July. The St. Joseph newspaper of July 19 reported that about 100 southerners camped 24 miles south of the city a day or two before, according to some local men these Rebels held as prisoners in their camp for a while. The article further stated that these local men knew these southerners conscripted against their will three unnamed men from Taos in south-central Buchanan County and killed two northern sympathizers—one a youth. The article writer did not know the names of the slain. In response to the newspaper article a patrol of the local 87th EMM rode to Taos, but there seems to be no record about what they discovered there.[39] At ten in the morning of July 18 it was probably these same guerrillas who raided the village of DeKalb not far away in southwest Buchanan County. The raiders took firearms, horses, and wearing apparel from residents and when last seen were riding to the east.[40]

Guerrillas Raiding in Platte County

There were also small bands of guerrillas active in Platte County during this time. Major General Curtis, the Kansas Union commander, reported that bands of between twenty and fifty bushwhackers were "prowling about" Weston in the west and Ridgely in the northeast about July 17. These men told residents that they wanted vengeance on the large number of Union troops in the area and that they considered Centreville—modern-day Kearney—in central Clay County, as the rendezvous point for their operations. There is an anecdote printed in the 1885 Platte County history perhaps of this time that may relate to this. It says guerrilla chief James A. Rupe of north Platte County led his local band against Captain William J. Fitzgerald's Yankees formerly of the local 39th EMM and at this time members of the 16th Kansas Cavalry. The story related that Rupe's bushwhackers at a place called Slash Valley in north Platte County killed three of the northerners, wounded Fitzgerald and another man, and the Yanks retreated back to Ridgely. There is no other source to corroborate this account, but the county history names the Union dead and wounded, and military service records in either the 39th EMM or 16th Kansas Cavalry archives in either state verify that the troopers named were actual members of those units.[41]

Violence in Andrew County on 21 July

An isolated incident took place in west Andrew County on July 21. Captain William R. Trapp's local company of one-year citizen guards sent an unnamed lieutenant and a few men five miles west of the county seat of Savannah to near Hackberry Ridge to demand a resident surrender his firearms. The citizen was identified in the St. Joseph newspaper article about this incident only as a Mr. Frogg, but military records shows an A. R. Frogg served in the 81st EMM or "Paw Paw Militia" at Savannah earlier. Perhaps this Frogg kept his musket instead of surrendering the weapon when the "Paw Paw Militia" program came under suspicion of disloyalty earlier this month. Mr. Frogg objected to the lieutenant's demand and instead fired on the citizen guardsmen, giving the lieutenant "two dangerous wounds." The newspaper article does not specify what became of Frogg except to say the outraged squad burned his dwelling to the ground.[42]

More Guerrillas Raiding in Buchanan County

The St. Joseph newspaper also reported two acts of guerrilla violence on Sunday, July 24. That morning several bushwhackers raided the village of Bloomington in southwest Buchanan County. The southerners took goods from a store there and left. Later that day perhaps the same guerrillas on Rock House Prairie not far away near Woodward's country store exchanged shots with an unidentified Union militia squad—perhaps the 87th EMM. No other details seem to have survived of this fight.[43]

Developments in Gentry County

Gentry County miles away to the north did not witness much Civil War violence during 1864, but on July 25 local militia discovered an abandoned Rebel camp near the village of Havana in the southeast corner of the county. The militia arrested an unidentified southerner who had been in the camp, and to save himself the man gave the militia a list of local southern sympathizers who had been aiding and feeding the Rebels there.[44]

Federals Search Ray and Clay County in Vain

About July 26 Colonel Edwin C. Catherwood and his 6th Cavalry MSM troopers and the veteran portion of the 1st Iowa Cavalry combed the Fishing River and Crooked River country of Clay and Ray Counties without discovering hardly a trace of Lieutenant Colonel "Coon" Thornton's Rebels there. Actually, large numbers of Thornton's former command including both the guerrilla bands of Thrailkill and Taylor and others were "laying low" in that very country with local southern people feeding them and watching the Yanks for them. The guerrillas were temporarily inactive waiting for a time when the Federals would grow weary of searching. Meanwhile, about this time "Fletch" Taylor sent a rider east to summon his fellow guerrilla leader Bill Anderson from the Randolph and Howard County area to a council of war planned in this region for early August and possibly so their two bands could raid together.[45]

The Circle of Violence Flames in Buchanan County

A local newspaper reported that on July 27 unidentified riders dressed in Union uniforms entered a farm field only six miles from St. Joseph and shot down two of a number of men harvesting in the field, and then rode off. The men working in the field were volunteers harvesting the crop of a man away in Union military service when this attack took place. Both of the men who were shot were members of a local militia unit—perhaps the 87th EMM—and evidently were not killed but seriously wounded. Colonel R. C. Bradshaw, commander of the 87th EMM, soon after the attack led a company of his regiment after the assailants, but was unable to find the shooters.[46]

This July 27 shooting in the field was one of the sparks that ignited a spate of northern revenge killing in the Buchanan County area similar but smaller than a savage campaign discharged Union soldiers and others conducted in this region the year before. District commander General Fisk exerted every caution to prevent an 1864 recurrence of a terror drive that killed or chased away many of the southern sympathizers from Andrew County in 1863, because such vigilante killings only incited southerners to more atrocities and prolonged the war.[47] However, the large-scale southern conspiracy out of Platte County this month forced Fisk to rely in large part on ill-trained, ill-led, and poorly disciplined local militia and citizen posses to counteract the hundreds of "Paw Paw Militia" turncoats, guerrillas, and frustrated Rebel recruits that still remained in northwest Missouri in late July. The first public notice that northerners were murdering southern sympathizers in this region came from a July 27 article from one of the St. Joseph newspapers which stated that a patrol of the new 88th EMM led by Major Spell Castle in south Buchanan County about the day before found seven corpses. Another St. Joseph newspaper story identified the slain as southern sympathizers mostly of Crawford Township in south-central Buchanan County not far from the north boundary of Platte County, and said other militia had taken these men from their homes and killed them. One of the dead was the father of Confederate Captain John Chesnut, who had served the southern cause in this area since 1861, was a Confederate staff officer during 1864, and was in the region at this very time conveying directions to the west-central guerrilla bands regarding preparing for Major General Sterling Price's long-awaited invasion of Missouri.[48] On July 30 near Agency Ford in the center of Buchanan County unidentified militia arrested Jacob Roland and a Meadows from the area, then shot and killed both as they allegedly attempted to escape.[49] On August 2 also near Agency Ford family members looking for elderly Ambrose McDaniel found his body lying under a tree, shot to death by unknown assassins. On that same day four miles from St. Joseph unknown men shot from ambush and mortally wounded Jeremiah Smith who was on his way from the city back to his farm in the south-central part of Buchanan County. Since both men were well-known locally for their southern sympathy, the local Union militia was suspect in their demise, too.[50]

Union Troops Find and Attack Rebels in Clay County

On the morning of July 28 Colonel Catherwood's 6th Cavalry MSM located and attacked about 100 of Lieutenant Colonel Thornton's force near Haynesville and Fishing River in northeast Clay County, and killed several of them in a fire fight. This was the largest body of Thornton's force the Federals had been able to find in one bunch in four days, but the Yanks did not know who commanded this group. Catherwood himself concluded in a message to General Fisk "Thornton had undoubtedly left. From all I can learn they are all leaving." The guerrillas' postwar chronicler, Confederate Major John N. Edwards, described an incident involving "Fletch" Taylor's guerrilla band that may have been the Rebels Catherwood's men fought. Taylor and his men were in a well-hidden campsite along Clear Creek on the north side of Fishing River near the prosperous farm of David T. Duncan and "some little distance away from the more frequented lines of travel." Some of the Clay Countians in Taylor's band attended a worship service, perhaps on Wednesday, July 27, in a rural church on Clear Creek, partly as a way to thank the church members for helping them and partly to talk with local girls at the service. Edwards suggested that some of the locals informed on the guerrillas to Captain John W. Younger and his citizen guard company at Liberty, and Younger and some of his men evidently guided Catherwood's cavalry to the Duncan farm resulting in the skirmish. Edwards indicated Taylor's men were overconfident about the secrecy of their camp and the Union troops came blasting away into the midst of the sleeping guerrillas, killing a few men and horses, and wounding several bushwhackers as they hurriedly dispersed.[51]

The Federals Scale Back Their Hunt

During the last days of July Union district commander General Fisk believed the forces he had begged and borrowed from other regions, districts, and departments had helped to break the back of Confederate Lieutenant Colonel Thornton's northwest Missouri uprising and felt compelled to return many of them. As Fisk wrote July 29 "the Thornton conspiracy is fast flickering out. We are drag-netting every brush patch and killing a good many of the rascals." He finally released Colonel James Ford and his 2nd Colorado Cavalry from their operations north of the Missouri River after many pleadings by Colonel Ford to return to their normal assigned area south of the river to duel with George Todd's able band of former Quantrill bushwhackers who had been raiding freely while the Coloradoans had been away. Fisk sent Colonel John H. Shanklin and his 30th EMM back to their home counties after their few days of fruitless searching in the Carroll County area. The district commander had already released a few days before Major Samuel Cox and his amazing mixed group of Livingston, Caldwell, Daviess, and Clinton County militia and citizen guards, as mentioned earlier. Higher Union commanders like Fisk could only use part-time militia like Shanklin's and Cox's men for a few days during extreme crises, and then had to release these men to defend their home communities and return to their civilian jobs in order to feed their families. Such forces with all their limitations were stop-gap emergency forces, at best, but a general could only keep them a few days at a time or they would not respond well at the next crisis or state authority may even deny their use to him. Major General Samuel R. Curtis, commanding the Kansas Department, had back on July 17 and 18 already withdrawn his Kansas troops back from Clay County to Fort Leavenworth on Kansas soil, but he felt free to employ small, select numbers of his troops, such as Captain William Fitzgerald's company of 16th Kansas Cavalry, to scout in Platte County across from Fort Leavenworth to watch for Rebel threats from there. Any Kansas troops had to be careful in Platte County, though, as General Fisk confided to the Kansas Department staff on July 29 that he had about 500 men, "a portion of them clad in citizens' dress" roaming that county trying to stamp out the remaining embers of the uprising. However, the Union command of northwest Missouri north of the Missouri River still had parts of the 6th and 9th Cavalry MSM regiments, parts of the new 17th Illinois Cavalry, other militia units, and troops on one or two riverboats patrolling the Missouri River on the job searching for those parts of the uprising or insurgency that still remained in place or had not slipped away.[52]

Death to the Union Turncoats!

At this time General Fisk and his superiors reached a decision about how to treat the turncoat EMM that the Union troops were capturing and who were surrendering now that the insurgency had clearly failed in its full intent. The man Clifton B. Fisk keenly and personally felt the betrayal of those turncoat "Paw Paw Militia" that kept their federally supplied weapons and accouterments but traded their blue uniforms for gray ones and trampled on their sworn duty as Union soldiers. Throughout the war in Missouri Fisk's rhetoric in message traffic was often picturesque against the Rebels, but during this insurrection it reached a level of personal savagery. In his reports Fisk repeatedly called Thornton's Rebels "fiends" and wrote such dire threats as "we can exterminate the whole clan" on July 21. On July 26 Fisk asked his superior headquarters at St. Louis: "What shall I do with young men who desert Thornton and surrender with the oft-told tale of deception, sorrow, repentance, and etc.?" Two days later Fisk referred to numbers of the turncoat "Paw Paw Militia" who "petitioned me from the brush to permit them to 'return and live,'" and he wrote that he deferred "proper disposition of their cases" and he again pleaded with Department of the Missouri headquarters: "Please advise me in this delicate duty. What can I do with them?" Fisk meant, of course, was it his prerogative to execute those men who had forsaken their duty and deserted to the enemy perfunctorily? Also on July 28, while he awaited his boss' answer Fisk pitifully even asked of the neighboring Department of Kansas staff that same question while communicating on another matter. There does not seem to have been a reply from this office, which is fitting for a military office not in Fisk's chain of command. Department assistant adjutant-general Oliver D. Greene at St. Louis finally replied to General Fisk's delicate question July 29 with only an opinion, but one that was carefully thought out and worded:

> General Fisk: Your dispatch asking for instructions as to the manner of disposing of such of the Paw Paws as went over to Thornton and are now coming in and giving themselves up is received. My opinion of the matter is that as many of them as are captured in arms, and resisting, should not be brought in as prisoners. This not from a spirit of revenge or blood thirstiness, but as mercy to them, for under no conceivable circumstances can they escape the penalty of their unpardonable crimes. In the history of the world there is not an instance of a soldier's deserting to the enemy being pardoned if caught. Of course if any lay down their arms and surrender without being so compelled by the force of arms, it would be murder to slay them. They must be held for action in due course of law.

In essence, those "Paw Paw Militia" who joined Lieutenant Colonel Thornton and later voluntarily surrendered to the Union military would face a military tribunal to determine if they would be executed or face a less severe punishment on a case-by-case basis—that is, "due course of law" for various shades of treason based on witnesses and testimony. Of course, captured guerrillas would face only execution, which was the Union military's order in Missouri since spring of 1862. Any of Thornton's command who had not been "Paw Paws" and could prove they were legitimate Confederate soldiers or recruits could escape the death sentence and face internment in a military prison as prisoners of war.[53]

Guerrillas Become Active in Clay, Ray, and Platte Counties

Also during July 29, 30, and 31 guerrilla activity increased considerably across Clay, Ray, and Platte Counties after several days of relative quiet. Maybe the guerrilla bands detected that some of the Union troops were leaving the area. Perhaps Taylor's,

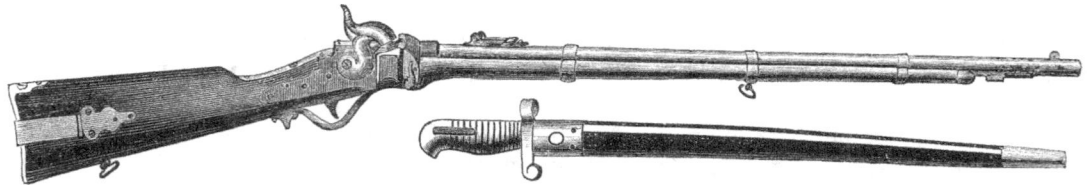

Many members of Captain Thrailkill's guerrilla band carried Sharps rifles (Schuyler, Hartley, and Graham, *Illustrated Catalogue of Arms and Military Goods*, 1864, p. 128).

Thrailkill's, and other bands were deliberately trying to draw Union attention away from an important guerrilla council of war across the Missouri River in north Lafayette County planned for early August. Part of the reason may have been that those guerrilla men of action simply grew tired of hiding and clamored to return to the offensive. On July 29 Colonel Ford of the 2nd Colorado Cavalry back in Kansas City reported "large numbers of bushwhackers in and around Parkville and Barry" in the south tip of Platte County. He advised the district command to continue patrolling the Missouri River near there, as if he thought these guerrillas may be trying to cross south into Jackson County.[54] Major John Tunison of the recently arrived 138th Illinois Cavalry Regiment at Weston in west Platte County that same day commented to General Fisk's headquarters that he believed there were "not more than 250 armed rebels in Platte County," "divided into squads" and "reorganizing" after the collapse of Thorton's command.[55] About July 30 or 31 elements of the Union 6th Cavalry MSM killed four bushwhackers in the Fishing River bottom not far from Albany in southwest Ray County, and discovered and burned several hidden guerrilla campsites in the thick brush along the river. Evidently, these guerrillas were part of "Fletch" Taylor's band, although Union leaders somehow believed they were part of either a Zeigler's, George Shepherd's, or Thrailkill's band.[56] On July 29, 30, and 31 Thrailkill's band of about ninety armed with revolvers and Sharps rifles raided homes and stores belonging to northern sympathizers at the intersection of Platte, Clinton, and Clay Counties, according to local residents. They took store goods, money, bedding, and horses in the villages of Ridgely, Smithville, Gosneyville, and Carpenter's Store—present day Trimble. They cut and took one farmer's hay for their horses and at homes of Union militiamen away on duty cursed the women, took all the adult clothes, tore up the children's clothes, and generally harassed the family members, although they harmed nobody. One militiaman home to visit his sick wife barely escaped from seven of Thrailkill's guerrillas who later told his wife that they had intended to kill the man. Obviously, Thrailkill's men conducted this operation to harass and intimidate northern sympathizers and perhaps attract Union attention to his operation and away from some other area.[57] On July 31 unidentified guerrillas robbed several northern sympathizers near Farley, and local northern troops heard there were as many as 100 bushwhackers in the area.[58]

The month of July 1864 thus marked the end of the greatest internal threat to the Union occupation of this portion of Missouri during the war with the collapse of the "Paw Paw Militia" insurgency. Lieutenant Colonel John Calhoun "Coon" Thornton proved himself a master of stealthily recruiting hundreds of southern men into Confederate service many miles behind Yankee lines. However, his campaign failed largely because he underestimated the Federal reaction to his uprising and overestimated his own force's ability to hold a portion of northwest Missouri. Thornton's information that General Shelby with his Rebel cavalry would ride north from Arkansas to rescue his command was naive and untrue, leaving Thornton to face combined Union might with his two supporting guerrilla bands as his most capable offensive weapon. The most resilient and self-sustaining portion of Thornton's command were these two guerrilla commands of former Quantrillian Charles Fletch "Fletch" Taylor and former Confederate Captain John Thrailkill, and they not only survived Thornton's uprising, but emerged from the ruins of the uprising with acceptable casualties and reputations intact. In fact, Taylor's and Thrailkill's guerrilla bands in late July 1864 were quite ready to face new Union challenges, while Lieutenant Colonel Thornton and his recruits were content just to leave Missouri without being killed or captured.

August would bring new guerrilla operations north of the Missouri River with Bill

Anderson and his bushwhacker band returning to renew mobile operations. Additional guerrilla bands led by Billy Chiles and Cyrus Gordon would begin their own actions mostly in the Platte and Buchanan County areas. Union troops in the area would continue to capture and kill remnants of Thornton's dissipated command and perform occasional atrocities against southern sympathizers.

Nineteen

Renewed Guerrilla Operations During August 1864 in Northwest Missouri North of the Missouri River

Lieutenant Colonel Thornton's departure from his chosen recruiting and operating area of northwest Missouri north of the Missouri River in late July 1864 freed his two supporting guerrilla bands under "Fletch" Taylor and John Thrailkill to cease their efforts to protect Thornton's fledgling command and begin their own independent operations. During August several other guerrilla bands operated in this same region, most notably the effective but vindictive Bill Anderson, but also "Cy" Gordon and Billy Chiles, providing new threats to the tenuous Federal hold on this corner of Missouri. In effect, the surge of new guerrilla groups into this part of northwest Missouri in August 1864 thwarted hopes of Union commanders here that the defeat of Thornton's hundreds of new Confederate troops in late July would serve to suppress the Rebel movement here.

Early August Raid of Bill Anderson's Band Through Carroll, Ray, and Clay Counties

The vengeful guerrilla chief Bill Anderson with ten of his men passed westbound through Carroll County August 1 and 2. This was only about a week after the last of the Yankee militia from counties to the north ceased their depredations in Carroll County while searching for Rebels that were not even there, and rode back home. Fellow guerrilla chieftain "Fletch" Taylor had summoned Anderson from his operations in Howard and Randolph Counties to join him for a war council with other chiefs scheduled August 4 and 5 south of the Missouri River. Local lore says that Taylor was hoping Bill Anderson and his men would also join Taylor's men in a raid north to the Iowa border. Anderson responded to Taylor's summons with alacrity, but only brought ten of his most trusted men, leaving most of his band, including his newest members, under the leadership of his brother Jim back in the Randolph County area, as described in Chapter Fifteen. Bill Anderson seemed to feel a particular hatred against the northern men of Carroll County for some reason, as his men murdered several of them every time his band passed through this year. His eastbound trip through this county July 12 resulted in the violent deaths of nine northern sympathizers, as described in Chapter Eighteen. The northern men of Carroll County quickly developed a mutual hatred for Anderson and his men from their sudden, murderous jaunts through this place, but they also developed a potent fear of these deadly bushwhackers who appeared among them with little or no warning.

It happened just that way this time, too. Anderson and his ten riders hurried across Chariton County July 31 with hardly a Yankee notice and crossed the Grand River to enter Hurricane Township of northeast Carroll County Monday morning, August 1. There was so much guerrilla activity during this part of the summer of 1864 that the passage of eleven murderous bushwhackers committing atrocities as they rode was lost in the flurry of Union army reports and Missouri newspaper accounts of many other actions across the region at this time. However, the 1881 Carroll County history recorded step-by-step and victim-by-victim Anderson's terrible progress westbound across the northern part of the county and into Ray County. Soon after the guerrilla band crossed the river into Carroll County they abducted Kentucky-born William A. Darr as a forced guide to lead them through this unfamiliar ground. As they rode along Anderson lectured Darr about the guerrilla chieftain's low opinion of many supposed southern sympathizers of Missouri who cooperated with the Yankees and failed to lift a hand to oppose them. Anderson's tirade to his involuntary guide about "lukewarm southerners" may provide a clue about why the guerrilla chief singled Carroll County out for special murderous punishment. William Darr's carefully measured conversation with Anderson may partly account for the guerrillas' release of the man when his usefulness to them ended—a fate different from many of their forced guides the bushwhackers perceived as northerners. The guerrillas also picked up former 65th EMM militiaman Isaac W. Dugan on the road, who fell into the trap of believing for a while the blue-clad riders were Union troops, a deadly joke Anderson's men played on the unwary. The guerrillas did not kill the ex-militiaman on the spot because they enjoyed the sport of kicking and hitting Dugan's unmanageable horse as they rode along just to watch their new captive struggle trying to keep the animal in control.

Anderson's Fight at Mitchell's in Carroll County 1 August

The guerrillas and their involuntary guests stopped at Mary

Local citizen guards tracked Bill Anderson's band to the Mitchell house (The Werner Company, *The Story of American Heroism*, 1896, p. 250).

Mitchell's house and Mrs. Mitchell and three other ladies present were forced to cook a meal while the Rebels made Isaac Dugan feed the horses. Anderson's transit across the county earlier in July and the militia depredations in the county just a few days before served to keep the local citizen guards alert and local guard leader John W. Hudson found the band's tracks and stealthily approached the Mitchell place with a posse of a dozen. Anderson failed to post lookouts this time, contrary to custom, and Hudson's citizen guards crept close enough to shoot through the windows and doors just after the bushwhackers finished their meal, splintering furniture and crockery as the ladies panicked and the perturbed bushwhackers returned the fire. Anderson's men prided themselves on carrying multiple loaded revolvers with additional loaded pistol cylinders in their pockets giving them a tremendous volume of fire. In contrast, the citizen guards had to make do with muskets and shotguns with a slow rate of fire. Once Anderson and his men realized the fire imbalance, they became the hunters instead of the hunted, and Hudson and his men were fortunate to escape with some slight wounds, with one exception. Posse member John Kirker's horse fell with him, and guerrilla John Maupin shot the man, then scalped and decapitated his victim with a sheath knife, and finally propped up the ghastly remains perhaps as a taunt to area northern sympathizers. Captive Isaac Dugan attempted to escape from the guerrillas in the confusion, but a posse member shot him to death thinking poor Dugan was one of the Rebels. One of the bushwhackers and two of the women and an infant also received minor wounds. Caroline Mitchell tried to run away at the height of the gun battle, but when she ignored repeated guerrilla orders to halt Anderson shot her in the back himself. Caroline Mitchell fell to the ground with a painful but non-lethal wound. When chided by the other guerrillas about shooting a woman, Anderson replied "Well, it has got to come to that before long anyhow."

Anderson led his men and guide William Darr off right away, in case the gunfire attracted more unwelcome company. The Rebels robbed three houses, burned two of them, and soon after gave Darr his freedom as they took a Mr. Latham as their next guide. The band then left the roads and rode cross-country to the village of San Francisco in north-central Carroll County where they freed Latham, and took four more men as prisoners and guides. Anderson may have partly taken the four local men as hostages to keep any pursuers at bay, which almost became a reality. Local Union troops of the 65th EMM were in pursuit and closing in to the point they actually saw the guerrillas in the distance a time or two, but the onset of darkness foiled the militia plan to catch up to Anderson's band.[1]

Anderson's band with prisoners rode on west at daylight August 2, crossing the line into Ray County. Near the village of Russellville in northeast Ray County the guerrillas' Yankee uniforms deceived Mr. Russell and one of his grown sons, and Anderson's men shot them to death in the roadway. The 1881 Carroll County history stated that the younger Russell was a Federal officer home on leave. As the bushwhackers rode on west they happened upon young Ralph Oliphant riding his mule, and they also led him to believe they were Union soldiers. Oliphant innocently told the blue-clad riders them that he was "a union man," and Anderson asked him if he could kill a bushwhacker. When he asserted that he could, Bill Anderson shocked Oliphant by telling him "Well, damn you, you'll never have a better chance, for we're all bushwhackers." The gang stripped off the poor farm laborer's clothes, badly beat him with switches, then made a noose out of his mule's reins and tried to get the animal to drag its poor master to death down the road. After repeated tries, the guerrillas could only get the animal to run a few steps at a time before stopping, so they tired of the sport and rode on, leaving a battered but still alive Ralph Oliphant lying in the dirt. Somewhere north of Richmond

Woot Hill rode with Bill Anderson's band across Carroll and Ray Counties. Hill's guerrilla shirt is evident in this etching made from his wartime photograph (John N. Edwards, *Noted Guerrillas*, 1877, p. 324; courtesy of the late Bob Younger and Mary Younger and Andy Turner).

in central Ray County Anderson released unharmed the four forced guides his band abducted near San Francisco the previous afternoon.[2]

The Carroll County militia and citizen guards followed Anderson's small band well inside Ray County, but turned the pursuit over to Ray County locals evidently of the 51st EMM to continue the chase. Such local troops were not always eager to catch up to such proficient killers as Anderson's men, but unidentified Ray and/or Clay County troops tracked Anderson's band all day and at evening of August 2 attacked the bushwhackers, killing three or four of their horses. It seems Bill Anderson had a rule in his band if any man failed to keep up he had to watch out for himself. John Edwards, the guerrillas' chronicler, said that after the militia killed the horses of Archie Clements, Woot Hill, Jesse Hamlet and Hiram Guess their comrades left them behind and they had to walk through the night. In his memoir, Harrison Trow wrote that Hamlet fashioned a makeshift raft, crossed the Missouri River on it, and walked to a hideout of the George Todd band in Lafayette County with his tale of woe.[3]

"Paw Paws," Billy Chiles, and Others During Early August 1864 North of the Missouri River

Small actions during the first week of August north of the Missouri River showed a continued strong guerrilla presence in parts of this region and a variety of northern troops desperately trying to contain them. On Tuesday, August 2 unidentified Union troops near Atchison, Kansas across the Missouri River from the junction of Platte and Buchanan Counties captured twenty "Paw Paw Militia" from Company D of the 82nd EMM. These turncoat EMM from Platte County were attempting to escape from Missouri when apprehended.[4] Normally quiet Harrison County up north by the Iowa border witnessed hidden

Hidden snipers fired upon a northerner along a road about dark 2 August in normally quiet Harrison County, but their shots missed him (Wilbur F. Gordy, *American Leaders and Heroes*, 1903, p. 113).

snipers shooting at a northern sympathizer riding along the road about dark August 2 in the west-central part of the county. Nobody was hurt, but this was a rare display of gunplay that far north.[5] Unidentified Union guards chased off southern arsonists who attempted to set fire to the railroad bridge over the Platte River east of St. Joseph in Buchanan County about this same time.[6]

On Wednesday, August 3 young William H. "Billy" Chiles with about 30 guerrillas raided in the Rock House Prairie neighborhood of east-central Buchanan County taking horses and other items from isolated farms. Union mounted troops sent to the area failed to find these guerrillas. Billy was one of the sons of Christopher and Rachel Chiles of the northeast corner of Jackson County, and at times earlier in the war served with Quantrill in west-central Missouri along with his brothers Kit and Dick Chiles. Actually, the St. Joseph newspaper wrote that this was the work of Billy's brother Dick Chiles, but reports of Billy's activities in this region later this month clarified that this was indeed his small guerrilla band.[7]

Also on August 3 Federal district commander Brigadier General Fisk replied to a

Brigadier General Clinton B. Fisk defended his troops to the Union department chief (Major John Lawrence, "Brevet Major-General Clinton B. Fisk," *The Ladies' Repository*, 26 [April 1866] no. 4, pp. 196–7).

rebuke from his boss Major General Rosecrans regarding several reports of atrocities by his troops in this region with this heartfelt defense of his soldiers:

> I expected there would be some depredations committed in spite of all I could do, but I assure you that when they are all summed up they were not numerous or of magnitude. When loyal men leave their own wasting harvests, march 100 miles with their barefooted farm horses, to seize arms and beat back a band of cut-throats, and find a class of villains, old rebels, sympathizers, and bushwhacker-feeders quietly at home securing their crops and in no fear, it makes them feel like stirring up the snakes a little. The only wonder is that I have been able to control them as well as I have.

Fisk avoided further censure for this excuse of his men's excesses by promising to investigate the reported incidents.[8]

Large Remnant of Thornton's Insurgents Remain Hiding in Clay and Ray Counties

Most of the Union effort at counter-guerrilla operations north of the Missouri River centered on the large numbers of irregular Rebels that remained in Platte, Clay, and Ray Counties in early August.

General Fisk used a combination of Kansas and Illinois cavalry and detectives in Platte County while the 6th Cavalry Regiment MSM and the 150 veteran troopers of the 1st Iowa Cavalry searched the recesses of Clay and Ray Counties in an attempt to ferret out nearly 300 guerrillas hiding there.

Also operating throughout this area were local militia and citizen guards on the northern side who displayed growing competence fighting guerrillas.

The searching Yankee soldiers also came across scattered groups of the several guerrilla bands mostly idle in Clay, Ray, and Platte Counties while their leaders took part in the Confederate war council of Wednesday and Thursday, August 3 and 4 across the Missouri River. On Tuesday, August 2 unidentified Federals near Missouri City in southeast Clay County crowded a reported 200 guerrillas to the river and most of them crossed to northeast Jackson County on the south bank.[9] Also on August 2 fugitive "Paw Paw Militia" Captain L. A. Ford and a number of his men of Company C, 82nd EMM from the Weston area of west Platte County surrendered at Parkville, south Platte County, to unidentified Union troops who took them to the post jail at Fort Leavenworth.[10]

On August 3 Lieutenant William N. Perkins' patrol of 6th Cavalry MSM fought somewhere in Clay County with "Fletch" Taylor's band, and reported killing one man and five of their horses at the cost of one Federal slightly wounded.[11] Also on this Wednesday guerrillas reportedly of Thrailkill's band attacked Captain George W. McCullough and his patrol of 25 Clinton County militia near Gosneyville in northwest Clay County and chased them over three miles. Both sides suffered only minor wounds.[12] John Edwards wrote about this time that unidentified Federals surprised five of "Fletch" Taylor's men at a Mrs. Anderson's house near Missouri City. The Yanks chased the small guerrilla party about six miles, killing one.[13]

Billy Chiles Near Plattsburg on 5 August

A local newspaper reported that on Friday, August 5 witnesses saw Billy Chiles with about ten to fifteen southern horsemen riding not far from the town of Plattsburg in central Clinton County. Evidently, one of the bystanders heard these riders say they were heading south to cross the Missouri River between Kansas City and Lexington, but that turned out not to be true.[14]

More of Thornton's Remnant Slip Across the Missouri River to the South Bank

Colonel Ford of the 2nd Colorado Cavalry passed along a report from his men that about sixty of Taylor's and Thrailkill's men crossed to the south bank of the Missouri River from near Missouri City on August 5, but that as many as 240 guerrillas were in hidden camps along the Fishing River in south Clay and Ray Counties. Ford also mentioned that a few bushwhackers had been crossing to the south bank near Sibley nightly, perhaps aided by the low water level of the river this summer.[15]

Also on that Friday Colonel A. J. Barr of the 51st EMM at Richmond, county seat of Ray County, reported to Union officials the cryptic comments that "we are in great excitement here, killing some rebel every day. It is almost impossible to control the men."[16]

That night in west Platte County opposite the town of Leavenworth Captain Francis LeClair's patrol of 20 troopers of the 17th Illinois Cavalry chased a body of mounted guerrillas for some distance killing one and capturing a horse. Over the next two days Captain Samuel H. B. McReynolds of the same regiment in Platte County with a large patrol engaged guerrillas in two more running fights killing one Rebel, mortally wounding another, and capturing five horses. McReynolds also heard during his patrol that guerrilla leader Thrailkill was concentrating his band near Smithville in northwest Clay County perhaps with the goal of raiding Platte City to the west. Of course, this Federal officer did not know at that same time Thrailkill was still south of the Missouri River in Lafayette County after completion of the guerrilla council of war.[17]

General Fisk must have sent elements of the "Gentry County Militia" two counties to the south to operate in Platte County, since Major David Cranor and parts of that unit chased guerrillas in north Platte County on Saturday, August 6, killing one.[18]

At the completion of the tempestuous week of July 31 through August 6 Colonel Edwin C. Catherwood of the 6th Cavalry MSM at Liberty in Clay County astoundingly reported that his men that week had killed fifty guerrillas, and that he was then holding several prisoners including Rebels who voluntarily came to town and surrendered themselves. Catherwood's claim of killing so many bushwhackers is not supported by corroborating reports, but Platte, Clay, and Ray Counties were so volatile at this time that even newspaper reporters stayed away and newspapers were content to print reports from the Union military or other second-hand accounts of what was transpiring there. Even guerrilla postwar memoirs are mostly silent about this period.[19]

Quiet Week of August 7–13 North of the Missouri River

Unexpected developments caused the week of August 7 through 13 north of the Missouri River to be less violent than the previous week. Major David Cranor and his riders of the "Gentry County Militia" searched Platte County the entire week for hidden Rebels, killing two more, wounding one, and capturing several horses. Evidently, some of the guerrillas who operated here before left or hid well.[20] On Monday, August 8 General Fisk informed the Kansas department commander, Major General Samuel R. Curtis, that Fisk had just deployed a patrol from St. Joseph across the Missouri River into Kansas after some more "Paw Paw Militia" who were attempting to escape from Missouri. Curtis replied with alacrity for Fisk to "go ahead and take any bushwhacker that attempts to come to my side of the river," mainly because an Indian outbreak in west Kansas at that time demanded more of his attention and available troops. So, on the following day the Missouri patrol near Atchison, Kansas apprehended and brought back six more "Paw Paw Militia" of Company D, 82nd EMM to face Federal justice for their part in the July insurgency.[21] Much of the reason Union troops seemed more aggressive than the guerrillas during early August in Platte, Clay, and Ray Counties was that a number of the chieftains had been in a council of war with representatives of Confederate Major General Sterling Price's southern army in Lafayette County south of the Missouri River for at least two days in early August. These band leaders probably suspended most offensive action until their return, and two of the leaders, "Fletch" Taylor and John Thrailkill, lingered a few extra days with their comrades in George Todd's band before re-crossing the river to return to their men. As detailed in Chapter 20, Taylor and Thrailkill while on their return trip the evening of Monday, August 8 rode into a citizen guard ambush on the south side of the Missouri River resulting in critical wounds to Taylor and a serious wound to Thrailkill's neck. While they sought medical help, Taylor at least may have sent word back to his guerrillas on the north side of the river that Bill Anderson was to take command until Taylor recovered enough to lead again. It took Anderson a couple of days to organize this unexpected new command of his own men and Taylor's men before he could re-commence full offensive operations again. Meanwhile, Charles Fletcher Taylor remained south of the river with friends seeing to his medical needs; Captain John Thrailkill managed to return to the north side of the river where southerners transported him to a sanctuary area for his neck wound to heal—probably in Platte County. This confusion in the guerrilla command is the main reason much of the week of August 7 through 13 was relatively peaceful in this area.[22] "Fletch" Taylor had purposely invited Anderson to come to him so their united bands could raid north into Iowa, and since Jim Cummins of Taylor's band mentioned this in his memoirs, Taylor must have told at least some of his men about this Iowa raiding plan, too. Now, with Taylor critically wounded, this plan was forgotten.[23] Meanwhile, Colonel Catherwood was still commanding his own 6th Cavalry MSM and parts of the 9th Cavalry MSM in aggressive cavalry and foot patrols in the Clay County area. So many of his available horses were worn down from all the patrolling that he employed about 100 of his troopers in foot patrols with some success. He bragged to his superiors August 8 that *"we kill a few almost every day."*[24] On August 9 and 10 Bill Anderson had to pull together between 100 and 150 bushwhackers of his, Taylor's, and Thrailkill's bands from separate, scattered, well-hidden camps mostly in Clay County and ready them for another mounted expedition under the very noses of Catherwood's searching troopers.

Guerrillas Murder Columbus Whitlock Fetching a Doctor for His Sick Mother

On Wednesday, 10 August unidentified bushwhackers abducted local man Columbus Whitlock traveling on a road in northwest Clay County and took him to Wilkinson's Creek near Smithville where they took some of Whitlock's clothing and murdered the unarmed man. Whitlock was on his way to bring a doctor for his sick mother and reportedly had three small children at home, but he had been a private in the local 48th EMM before his discharge a year before—and that was probably reason enough for the guerrillas to kill him. The poor man's captors may not have believed the man's personal crisis as he explained and perhaps pleaded with them. His death was widely printed in newspapers around Missouri because of the humanitarian plight of the man at the time he was murdered. Such wanton killings and their publicity were gradually wearing down sympathy for guerrillas in many parts of the state. The guerrilla band to which the men who killed Whitlock belonged was never clearly identified.[25]

Billy Chiles Again in Southeast Buchanan County

Meanwhile, to the west in the southeast corner of Buchanan County Union Captain John R. Snyder of the 25th EMM leading a patrol of 20 militiamen or citizen guards on Wednesday, 10 August surprised Billy Chiles' camp killing two bushwhackers and wounding a third while the remainder scattered into the brush.[26]

Anderson Heads East to Initiate Mobile Warfare Again

Back in Clay County also on August 10 a patrol of Colonel Catherwood's 6th Cavalry MSM skirmished somewhere in the county with some of Taylor's men killing one and wounding about four more.[27] These guerrillas may have been moving from their hideouts in response to Bill Anderson's call to rendezvous. In this same area a number of Taylor's and Thrailkill's men felt the need to steal horses, weapons, ammunition, and money to prepare for traveling, as the Liberty newspaper of August 12 reported bushwhackers suddenly began taking such things. Evidently, under the patrolling onslaught by Colonel Catherwood's searching troopers most of the bushwhackers kept a "low profile" over the last several days, and the Liberty newspaper noted the change in behavior, but failed to grasp the meaning of it.[28] Local newspapers knew that Bill Anderson was now in a position of greater responsibility, as they reported to their readers. The *St. Joseph Weekly Herald* of August 11 printed several paragraphs about the despicable nature of Bill Anderson's style of guerrilla warfare citing burning buildings in his railroad raid on Shelbina and Lakenan in northeast Missouri during July and his men's torture of prisoners and mutilation of dead enemy from his August 1 and 2 expedition through Carroll and Ray Counties. This article employed such words as "heartless," "cold-blooded," "barbarous," "devil incarnate," "fiendishness," "diabolism," "outrages," and concluded that "the barbarous deeds of unlettered savages, fired with a spirit of revenge for wrongs and injuries done them, may be searched in vain to find a parallel for this." The Liberty weekly paper on August 12 spared their readers such hyperbole about Anderson, stating simply that the bushwhackers then in the Clay County area "are said to be under the command of that infamous desperado Billy Anderson." Of course, the press of Liberty was less sheltered from southern anger than that of St. Joseph with its larger Union garrison and being the seat of the Union District of North Missouri.[29]

The numbers of men of Anderson's own and Taylor's guerrilla bands who assembled under Anderson's leadership August 10 and 11 varies in surviving accounts from 60 to just over 100, out of between 200 to 275 guerrillas purported to be in this region at the end of July. Union military action had thinned their ranks over the previous several days leaving a number dead or recovering from wounds in the care of friends; many had earlier crossed to the south side of the Missouri River to escape Colonel Catherwood's dragnet; guerrilla couriers may have missed a few who failed to hear of the rendezvous; and some like Captain Thrailkill's men chose not to respond from their dislike of Bill Anderson's hard personality and extreme style of warfare.

Anderson's Ambush of Captain Colley's Group Near Fredericksburg on 12 August

As Bill Anderson set out from Clay County heading east on August 12 his new command did not have long to wait for action. In east Clay County his riders came across and captured Privates Smith Hutchings and John Hutchings of the 48th EMM who were riding from home to re-join their unit. Perhaps the bushwhackers kept the Hutchings alive to serve as guides into Ray County. Meanwhile, the militia mostly of the 51st EMM in Ray County took to the field to locate and fight Anderson's band. Captain Patten Colley of Company E, 51st EMM took about 20 of his militiamen to the Elkhorn neighborhood of west-central Ray County. Captain Colley's advance pickets reported they saw guerrillas and Colley and all of his little force rode to do battle. Anderson's men had seen Colley's pickets, also, and prepared a nearby ambush about four miles south of Fredericksburg. The captain and his men rode into Anderson's ambush and fought gamely but were overwhelmed. After the captain and four militiamen were killed the remainder dispersed into the brush and saved themselves from slaughter. A few Rebels were killed or wounded, and Major John Grimes of the 51st EMM said he had information that four guerrillas died in this action. The bushwhackers guarding the Hutchings men knifed them to death before the fight commenced and mutilated their bodies, as was the custom in this band.[30]

After the fight near Fredericksburg Anderson and his band passed to the north of Richmond still heading east, and stopped for the night in that vicinity. On the morning of August 13 Anderson's band passed south of Knoxville where they intercepted two couriers of the 51st EMM carrying orders from Richmond to their comrades

A vulnerable northern courier passing through dangerous country (Edwin Forbes, *Life Studies of the Great Army*, 1876, "The newspaper correspondent").

at Knoxville. The bushwhackers shot, knifed, and scalped the couriers and then rode their horses over their bodies. Not far away Anderson's men stopped local farmer James M. Maupin driving his wagon and they shot him to death on the spot. They may have discovered Maupin was also a militiaman of the 51st EMM not on active duty at that time. Anderson stopped his command at or near Russellville, northeast Ray County, for the night. Union authorities lost track of Anderson and his men for about a day at this point, thinking the guerrillas were heading north to raid in Caldwell County. Local militia trailing Anderson's band a couple of hours behind probably knew they were still on track following the dead bodies left in the band's wake.[31]

The details of Anderson's accomplishments from Russellville late on August 13 east into Carroll County early on August 14 veer into the realm of folklore because only poor documentation survives of this part of Anderson's expedition. A St. Louis newspaper quoted a Caldwell County newspaper as reporting that in the Russellville neighborhood the bushwhackers "killed eight men, and shot and wounded two women and a babe; although whether the report is reliable is more than we can say." The numbers of the dead men and the mention of wounding a woman or two and an infant are reminiscent of this band's experiences in nearby Carroll County during their last two raids through there. Add to that, no more reliable source endorses such events or names any of the victims. In contrast, Major John Grimes of the 51st EMM reported that after the guerrillas killed the two couriers of his regiment and murdered the off-duty member of the unit driving a wagon, the bushwhackers killed "one citizen, burnt one house, stole a number of horses, and committed a number of other depredations."[32] A St. Louis paper quoted an earlier edition of the *Bethany Union* with another such article that is short in corroborative detail. The article said an unnamed German-American of Carroll County later told the story in Bethany, Harrison County, that while about forty guerrillas were passing he saw some approach his home and left for the brush before they arrived. The refugee then said from hiding he shot and killed three of the raiders and then ran for his life, after which the others burned his home to the ground. The newly homeless man said that Union troops following the guerrillas fought with them the following day and both sides suffered four deaths.

Conceivably, this former Carroll Countian was describing Anderson's passing through west Carroll County the morning of August 13 and the great fight the bushwhackers had with the local Ray and Carroll County militia in southeast Carroll County on August 14. Though skimpy in verifiable details, this cryptic tale may actually be true.[33]

Local EMM Groups Defeat Anderson at Wakenda Creek on 14 August

In east Ray County on the morning of August 13 the guerrillas veered sharply to the southeast so they entered Carroll County at its southwest corner near the river town of Miles Point. The band rode parallel to the Missouri River and at the port of Hill's Landing they murdered Private James Warren of the 7th Cavalry MSM from Carrollton waiting for a passing steamer to take him back to duty at the end of his furlough. The band camped that night not far from Hill's Landing. Anderson sent scouts to determine the security of Carrollton a few miles to the north, and they concluded the Union garrison at the county seat town was alert and on watch. If Bill Anderson had any thoughts of raiding Carrollton this news dissuaded him, and on Sunday morning, August 14 he led his band eastward, killing one older man and robbing several houses. At noon the band took a rest in the brush beside Wakenda Creek in southeast Carroll County at a place known as either Simpson's or McElree's Ford and about a mile from the Sambo Slough. Afterward, the guerrillas called this place "Flat Rock Ford." The writer of the 1881 Carroll County history wrote his theory that Anderson deliberately slowed the pace of his raid in south Carroll County in order to allow the local militia to catch up to him, and perhaps he did. Bill Anderson realized from captured dispatches that elements of the 51st EMM from Ray County were pursuing him, and the guerrillas knew such militiamen were not as well equipped, armed, trained, led, or mounted as the regulars of the Missouri State Militia, as they had proved with Captain Patten Colley and his Company E men near Fredericksburg August 12. Evidently, Anderson's main goal was to inflict punishment on the Union military, and usually any EMM unit foolhardy enough to attack Anderson's men was "easy pickings" to them. Anderson knew that at least on August 12 and 13 Captain Clayton Tiffin and his Company A, and First Lieutenant James Baker and his Company G, 51st EMM -about 100 men—had been following his band. What the guerrillas did not know was that the Ray County force continued to trail the guerrillas long past the Carroll County border and that Captain D. A. Calvert and over 100 men of the Carroll County EMM joined in the hunt with the Ray County men, so that the Union pursuit of the Rebels now numbered about 250 men in all. Anderson also underestimated the militia desire to fight him, as his guerrillas' killings and mutilation of dead comrades in Ray and Carroll Counties on several trips through had thoroughly motivated the militia past their fear to a compelling desire to strike back. Anderson's guerrillas were about to face a rare reverse because Anderson and his men underestimated the militiamen's resolve.

The combined militia force detected the guerrillas at Simpson's Ford on Wakenda Creek were not moving and immediately Captain Tiffin with about fifty militiamen charged in on horseback. Anderson's pickets fired warning shots and the guerrillas mounted and prepared to fight in a hurry. The Rebels were holding a man named Fox as prisoner, and as the Union attack began the bushwhackers guarding him killed Fox. This was probably Kentucky-born, 24-year-old farmer George Fox who lived in this area. Tiffin's charge passed completely through the guerrillas, knocking a number of them out of their saddles, but at such close range the bushwhackers' revolver fire hit a number of Tiffin's men, too. The Rebels attacked next, and the militiamen backed into the brush and desperately fired back at the guerrilla horsemen and stopped their advance. The fight continued in close range in the brush and trees for about thirty minutes with the Ray and Carroll County men advancing and retiring, shooting and loading the whole time. Tiffin's initial charge and the militiamen's dogged determination not to retreat greatly surprised the guerrillas, who seldom encountered EMM who would remain fighting after the first shots. Bill Anderson and a number of his "reliables" were wounded, too, so the bushwhackers retreated this time and left the field of battle to the militiamen. The victorious but bloody militiamen pressed on east after their battered foe, but did not pursue beyond the Grand River and the Chariton County line. Two days later a company of veterans of the 1st Iowa Cavalry and some Livingston County militia rode on into Chariton County after Anderson's guerrillas, but the trail was cold by then.

The total number of militia killed was between ten and fifteen, as several succumbed to wounds and died days later at home in Ray and Carroll Counties, and more than that number were wounded by the guerrillas' accurate shooting. The toll for the bushwhackers was surprisingly high—a rarity for men Anderson commanded. Five or six Rebels died, including a wounded man captured and executed on the spot and three lifeless bodies the guerrillas carried away with them strapped to horses. What was unexpected about the guerrilla losses was the great number and severity of the wounded. Bill Anderson himself lost his horse and hat, which the militia claimed as trophies, and took a bullet in his leg that caused him to be inactive for several days. Sixteen-year-old Jesse James was critically wounded in the chest, and other wounded included his older brother Frank, Arch Clements, Hiram Guess, and several other accomplished bushwhackers. A rough estimate would place the total Rebel killed and wounded between 15 and 25, or one out of every four or five combatants on the southern side. This fight effectively stopped Anderson's raiding for several days, and the guerrillas struggled to carry off their many wounded on horseback and move them several miles out of unfriendly Carroll County east to cross the Grand River at Rocky Ford into Chariton County with its large southern population where southern families tended them. The rest of the band, including those slightly wounded, connected in Chariton County with the rest of Anderson's band Bill left in that area July 31, still under the command of his brother Jim, as described in Chapter Fifteen.

The August 14 fight at Simpson's Ford of Wakenda Creek was one of the few "stand-up" fights that Anderson lost. Bill Anderson suffered this defeat mainly because he underestimated the ability of the local militia to become angry enough at the excesses of his men that they would overcome their great fear of his killers and mix into them as equals. He counted once too often on his enemies' fear as a force multiplier for his men. The Simpson's Ford or Wakenda Creek action would not noticeably change the way Bill Anderson conducted his war afterward, but from that point on Anderson and his men faced the hard reality that victories would have to be won by paying a higher price. This August 14 fight was also noteworthy in that the bushwhackers' superior rate of fire and accuracy with firearms failed to carry the battle in their favor, mainly because the militia outnumbered them and refused to back off. Unit for unit, the militia and citizens guard outfits varied as Napoleon said "from the sublime to the ridiculous," but properly motivated and led, many of them were proving their worth in battle.[34]

Chiles, Gordon, Thrailkill, and Others North of the Missouri River Between Middle and Late August 1864

While Bill Anderson's new band was raiding east between August 12 and 14, other guerrillas groups were active in other parts of northwest Missouri north of the Missouri

River. These were an assortment of bushwhackers usually working independent of each other. Regional newspapers reported an unusual raid by unidentified men across the Missouri River into Atchison County in the far northwest corner of the state about mid-August. The *St. Joseph Tribune* first broke this story in a vague report mentioning armed men who crossed the river in skiffs and battled with Atchison County's home guards, but gave few details since the paper's sources were not on the scene. Some Atchison Countians in letters had predicted such cross-river attacks, and neighboring Holt County endured a Kansas jayhawking raid a few months before in January, as described in Chapter Four. A clue that the St. Joseph paper provided about the raiders in its closing remark said this action "is an extension of the rebel-Indian outbreak in the West." At this time plains Indians were attacking isolated communities and wagon trains as close as central and west Kansas and Nebraska, so the Union command there was activating the few available troops to squelch this Indian outbreak. Official records indicate that some of these troops included Kansas militiamen from communities just across the river from Atchison County, Missouri. Perhaps some of those Kansans on their way to deal with the Indian outbreak took the time to cross the river and strike a blow at despised pro-slavery Missourians before they left. Oddly, the newspaper mentioned that the raiders came from Nebraska, yet the military official records indicate that the Department of Kansas director, Major General Samuel R. Curtis, was in Nebraska City less than ten miles upriver from Atchison County on August 15. He may have been on the scene responding to this raid by that date.[35]

81st EMM Attack Billy Chiles' Band at Ridgely in Mid-August

Also about the middle of August Captain Milton M. Claggett's company of 81st EMM at Ridgely, northeast Platte County, remained loyal to the Union cause and proved it by attacking Billy Chiles' guerrilla band in that area and capturing 25 of their horses. Some of the militiamen steadied their aim by resting their firearms on a rail fence and wounded Chiles himself in the shoulder and a grazing shot across his upper lip. By the time they took down the fence so they could pursue into the field the wounded Chiles had escaped, but he sent word to Claggett's company that he would have vengeance on them.[36]

Another Large Group of Thornton's Remnants Cross South of Missouri River

Two counties away to the southeast in south Ray County a Richmond newspaper claimed that near Richfield in southeast Clay County about 200 guerrillas crossed to the south side of the Missouri River on Monday, August 15. Considering all the guerrillas and Confederate recruits that had been making this crossing since Thornton's uprising floundered in late July, it is amazing that so many were still passing this way out of this region.[37]

Militiamen Murder Whiteneck in Caldwell County on 16 August

Throughout the war some militiamen in Caldwell County singled out men of southern sympathy in their communities and assassinated them as their contribution to defeating secession—a practice called "night riding." During the evening of August 16 they targeted a Henry D. Whiteneck two miles south of Mirable in southwest Caldwell County. They fooled Whiteneck into coming with them to his own doom by sending to him one of their members with a boyish face and a story that 25 lost Iowa soldiers were waiting nearby for him to guide them to the county seat at Kingston. Soldiers from other states usually did not have personal scores to settle and were not known to commit atrocities like Missouri Yanks, so this was a convincing ploy. The local militiamen shot Whiteneck to death only one hundred yards from his house, so at least his wife and children heard the shots and had a chance to claim the body and not wait days to discover his fate.[38]

"Cy" Gordon Returns to Platte County

Between August 16 and the end of the month Billy Chiles and former Confederate Captain Silas "Cy" Gordon separately continued their guerrilla war to torment the Union troops in the Platte County area. On the evening of August 16 three miles east of the town of Leavenworth, Kansas, in west-central Platte County five bushwhackers from one of those bands woke up either William or James Wallace and at the point of revolvers forced the Irish-born farmer to his stable where they made him bridle and saddle two of his horses. They left with Wallace's horses and saddles, and did no further harm, although the guerrillas also took several horses from Wallace's neighbor. Soon Captain John H. Burts and part of his company of the 39th EMM rode in response to the horse thefts and near the Vennaman farm skirmished briefly with the bushwhackers, wounding one of them.[39]

The militiamen's prisoner would not know if they would take him to jail or kill him a few yards down the road (Charles C. Coffin, *My Days and Nights on the Battlefield*, 1887, p. 205).

Former Confederate Captain and Platt Countian Silas "Cy" M. Gordon made a dramatic return to Platte County on August 18 and 19. On August 18 a patrol of the 17th Illinois Cavalry acted on a tip and surrounded a house in which Gordon and four of his men were sleeping. Gordon and his men jumped onto their horses, but the Federals chased them so closely that to escape the guerrillas had to abandon their mounts and hide in a sugar cane field. The Illinois troopers captured the saddled Rebel horses and back at the house found the bushwhacker chief's coat, hat, and boots. This reverse did not seem to deter "Cy" Gordon from visiting the county seat of Platte City the next day with six of his men. With his bodyguard handy, Gordon talked to acquaintances freely in the street, made a brief speech, then took boots, bridle, saddle, and other items without paying and left town.[40]

Cy's mother, Lecretia Gordon, lived just two miles from Platte City until her death in February 1864. During 1861 Silas had been a prominent southern recruiter and had also proven himself as a daring guerrilla fighter who confounded Union troops repeatedly in the county. This forceful, unconventional leader only left the area late in 1861 in order to prevent a Fort Leavenworth officer from fulfilling his promise to burn Weston to the ground if Gordon did not leave. This Platte Countian then became a captain in the Confederate First Missouri Cavalry Regiment in which later guerrilla chief John Thrailkill was also a captain. Gordon served in this unit until he evidently deserted during February 1863 in order to fight the remainder of the war as a guerrilla leader.[41] Gordon made a brief appearance in the Platte County area during April 1864, as described in Chapter Ten, and in Carroll County in early July, as described in Chapter Sixteen.

It is possible that Cy Gordon deliberately avoided the Platte County insurgency in both the buildup phase and the execution phase throughout the earlier months of 1864 with the thinking that he was too well known to Union authorities, and just the publicity from his presence could have ruined the project. Northern sympathizers in the area now wondered if Gordon's flashy return to Platte County so soon after the defeat of Thornton's uprising was to bring renewed hope to the southern cause here, or provide a diversion so more of Thornton's survivors could escape from the region.

Gordon's form of guerrilla war was certainly flashy. Major Hiram Hillard's command of 17th Illinois Cavalry from their Weston garrison on August 20 chased Gordon—now with eight men—about five miles, during which the wily Cy Gordon doubled back on his own track three times to fool the Yanks. Hillard complained to superiors that Gordon was rapidly picking up new men, and that the guerrilla chief was so persuasive that Hillard could no longer trust the local Union militiamen except the German-Americans. The following day Hillard's men unsuccessfully chased Gordon's band again—this time Gordon was leading nine men—between the Union garrison town of Weston and Platte City. It seems the bushwhackers were deliberately trying to wear down the Federals' horses, which were inferior to their own. A harried Major Hillard begged to use the services of Captain William Fitzgerald and his company of 16th Kansas Cavalry which was stationed across the Missouri River, since those were Platte County area men with extensive anti-guerrilla experience. Hillard's district commander, Brigadier General Clinton B. Fisk, denied his request, probably to keep peace between the respective Missouri and Kansas Union commands, and prevent atrocities Fitzgerald's men were known to commit.[42] On the next day, August 22, near Farley in southwest Platte County Major Hilliard's men proved they were not afraid of Gordon's band by engaging them in a running fight for several miles and even charged a guerrilla battle line whenever the bushwhackers would stop and form one. One Federal was badly hurt falling off his horse and cavalry fire killed two Rebels.[43] This same day northern sympathizer George S. Park at Parkville in the south tip of the county sent a report to General Fisk that revealed Gordon was actually attempting to revive the battered southern cause in Platte County. Park also warned that there were still several well-armed, dedicated guerrillas scattered around the county.[44]

Thornton and Thrailkill Return to Take 150 More Rebels South of the Missouri River

Incredibly, back in southeast Clay County during the night of August 23/24 between 150 and 300 guerrillas or Confederate recruits crossed to the south side of the Missouri River at the same unguarded spot south of Richfield where 200 allegedly crossed on August 15. An exasperated Union Colonel Edwin C. Catherwood confirmed the numbers through multiple witnesses, although Union Major Henry Suess of the 7th Cavalry MSM at Lexington on the south bank reported that only 150 horsemen crossed. Suess also reported that these combatants were personally led by Lieutenant Colonel Thornton and Captain John Thrailkill. If true, this means that Thornton returned to the north side to bring these men over and that Thrailkill ended his convalescence in Platte County to make this trip and remove what remained of his former band. It is also possible that many of these departing southerners had also been in hiding recovering from wounds suffered in earlier fighting. Catherwood reported the Rebels converged simultaneously on the crossing site from different hiding places at great speed to confound Union pursuit. He disgustingly referred to these night-riding Rebels as they "went in a trot in the night," and complained that his troopers only managed to shoot down a few of them as they raced by. The southerners had skiffs hidden in the willows of an island in the middle of the river, and spent three or four hours successfully ferrying their men across riding in the skiffs while leading their swimming horses behind them. The Rebels benefited from the low water level of the river, an unguarded crossing site, and skillful advance planning to effect the crossings of so many riders from an area teeming with Union troops.[45]

Chiles and Gordon Remain Active in Buchanan and Platte Counties

Starting about August 25 Chiles and his band were taking horses from farms near Arnoldsville in southeast Buchanan County. It was probably the same group on August 28 at Martin's Mill near DeKalb in southwest Buchanan County that robbed homes of northern sympathizers. Those six bushwhackers took money, but did no other harm to the residents or their property. During this same time a large patrol of 17th Illinois Cavalry exchanged shots with unidentified guerrillas in this same area and chased Cy Gordon with five men near Platte City in central Platte County. This further evidence of Chiles' and Gordon's tenacity testifies that they intended to continue combat operations in the Platte and south Buchanan County area for some time to come, even though many other Rebels were leaving this area to go south of the Missouri River.[46]

Northerner Assassinates Dr. Walker in Platte County

A blatant example of Missouri's hideous wartime circle of violence took place on Sunday, August 28 near Platte City in central Platte County. Eight assassins rode to Doctor Joseph Walker's wealthy estate that day determined to kill the prominent southern sympathizer. When at first they could not find the man, they split into pairs and searched the grounds until one pair encountered Dr. Walker riding back from treating a patient. The killers forced him to dismount and fired numerous bullets into Walker's body, then rode away not realizing he was still alive. The doctor's family came to his side after hearing the distant shots and before he died named one of his killers as John Morris, who had lived in the neighborhood. Dr. Walker, who for many years had served as a surgeon in the U.S. Army, had earlier in the war been convicted of strong southern statements in public including one as a member of the Platte County Defensive Association that threatened death to any Northern Methodist preacher in the area who continued to preach, specifically naming the Reverend Charles Morris. A military tribunal banished Walker to Chicago for such disloyal statements, but the doctor later paid bond and obtained permission to return home to Platte County. When Thornton's southern insurgency broke out in early July, some guerrillas evidently of "Fletch" Taylor's band on July 10 murdered Reverend Morris near Agency Ford in central

Buchanan County for defying the association's gag order, as described in Chapter Eighteen. Local authorities apprehended John Morris, based on Dr. Walker's dying statement that he was one of his killers, and he was tried for the murder. However, at Morris' trial he contended the assassins forced him to guide them to his former neighborhood against his will, and he was exonerated of the crime. William M. Paxton, the Platte County historian who lived through the war years here, wrote in 1897 that "John Morris was no relative of Rev. Charles Morris," but that a son of the murdered Reverend Morris traveled from New Orleans to Leavenworth where he assembled a team of hardened characters who carried out the Walker assassination. In his Platte County history Paxton kept his written comments about the Morris and Walker murders to a minimum, but did concede that "the tragedy produced consternation in the county."[47]

Summary of August 1864 Guerrilla Actions North of the Missouri River

So, August in this region was a bitter month for the southern guerrillas here. This followed close behind the disintegration of Lieutenant Colonel John Calhoun Thornton's uprising in late July 1864. The Confederate council of war in early August across the river in Lafayette County encouraged southern hopes by issuing clear goals for the bushwhackers, but the serious wounding of guerrilla chieftains "Fletch" Taylor and John Thrailkill on August 8 while returning from the council left their bands in temporary confusion. Bill Anderson with a few of his most-trusted men returned to this region following a brutal, murderous raid through Carroll and Ray Counties on August 1 and 2, and he took command of most of "Fletch" Taylor's men in their chief's absence. Anderson led this combined bushwhacker group east on August 12 in another of his fast-paced, long-distance raids, but in southeast Carroll County on August 14 Ray and Carroll County militia bested his band during a rest break, killing and wounding several. Even Anderson himself took a bullet in the leg that forced him off the bushwhacker trail for about two weeks of convalescence. On August 23 and 24 Thornton and the recovered John Thrailkill briefly returned to Ray and Clay Counties and led perhaps 200 or more of their men from hiding across the Missouri River, signifying that they were giving up this region. Throughout August to the west in Platte and Buchanan Counties small guerrilla bands led by Captain Silas "Cy" Gordon and Billy Chiles made demonstrations to bolster flagging southern spirit.

Southerners Maintain Hope for Autumn 1864 and the Advent of Price's Army

That being said, the overall southern hope remained strong and looked forward to the advent of autumn and with it a Confederate army to wrest Missouri from Union control. Even Missouri newspapers controlled by northern editors warned all residents of the strong probability that Union reverses in Louisiana and Arkansas would release Rebel forces to invade the Show-Me State in the fall when the ripened corn crop would provide feed for southern horses and men.[48] Therefore, the fall of 1864 promised to provide a climax to three years of guerrilla war.

Twenty

Supporting the Insurgency: Mid-July Through August 1864 in Northwest Missouri South of the Missouri River

The two major bushwhacker bands in west-central Missouri at the beginning of July were those led by George Todd and Bill Anderson. On July 12 Anderson led his men across the Missouri River raiding in Carroll County, as described in Chapter Eighteen before riding to new adventures in northeast Missouri. George Todd's band, under Quantrill's leadership before Todd and Anderson deposed him earlier in the summer, took a supporting role of Lieutenant Colonel Thornton's Confederate conspiracy as it ignited and continued just over the Missouri River from Todd's hideouts in Jackson and Lafayette Counties. Meanwhile, smaller guerrilla bands operated in limited fashion toward the center of the state challenging Union presence in their home areas in their own distinctive styles.

Isolated Actions Across West-Central Missouri During Middle July 1864

"Fletch" Taylor and John Thrailkill Busy North of the Missouri River Providing Security for Thornton's New Rebel Recruits

Guerrilla violence gradually slackened throughout June and into the first week of July in George Todd's operating area of Jackson and Lafayette County, as described in Chapter Seventeen.

A number of Todd's bushwhackers who hailed from north of the Missouri River were under the leadership there of Charles Fletcher "Fletch" Taylor providing security for Lieutenant Colonel Thornton's budding uprising as it ignited July 7 in Platte County and soon after spread to the surrounding area. Confederate Captain John Thrailkill was also the head of a guerrilla band north of the river working for Thornton. It appears that Todd and his remaining men limited their activities south of the Missouri River to support Thornton's uprising north of the river with reinforcements if needed and later to provide sanctuary to Thornton's hundreds of recruits as well as Taylor's and Thrailkill's guerrillas when overwhelming Federal force squelched the insurrection. In essence, Todd and his 150 to 200 guerrillas kept the "back door" open when Thornton's, Taylor's, and Thrailkill's men eventually needed to escape across the Missouri River to where Todd's men could help hide and protect them. It appears

Bill Anderson's band made sport of shooting at Missouri River steamers (Eugene M. Violette, *A History of Missouri*, 1918, p. 184).

Todd deliberately limited his active guerrilla operations to handle this mission supporting Confederate forces in this region.

Bill Anderson with his band operated independently during late June and early July, which is how Anderson usually conducted his guerrilla war. Evidently, it was Anderson's band that attacked the steamer *West Wind* on the Missouri River near Wellington June 24, as described in Chapter Seventeen. Anderson and his men were known for sniping at passing riverboats from the riverbank and seemed to regard it as great sport. By the beginning of July Anderson moved his band from the northwest corner of Lafayette County across the county to the northeast corner near the villages of Dover and Waverly. His band on July 2 took small boats to use later to cross the Missouri River and they attacked riverboats from the Waverly pier July 4. As detailed in Chapter Seventeen, while in that vicinity Anderson sent letters dated July 7 describing his attitude about guerrilla war to Union officials and the Lexington newspaper. By July 12 Anderson used the stolen boats to cross his closest comrades into Carroll County which they raided as they rode along taking their brand of guerrilla war to northeast Missouri for a few weeks. Possibly, Anderson took a hiatus from west-central Missouri because he disagreed with George Todd's mission of supporting the Confederate uprising in Platte County, but this is only conjecture.

Warren Welch Targets 77th EMM Near Independence

Some guerrilla actions took place during this time, as bushwhackers reacted to opportunities that arose. In his postwar memoirs Todd member Warren Welch wrote how he first obtained the guerrilla leader's permission to conduct a limited raid on the local 77th EMM under a Captain James D. Meador near Independence in Jackson County so that Welch may have a chance to recover his horse the militia had taken from him before. Welch with three companions sometime in late June or early July watched a road leading from Independence for a few days until they saw sixteen militiamen with three wagons leave town to gather forage from farms in the area. Welch decoyed the militiamen leading to a running fight, and, although the guerrillas did manage to kill one of the militia horses, they were not able to reclaim Welch's horse.[1]

Sometime during early July twelve guerrillas of either Bill Anderson's or Jeff Wilhite's band ate breakfast at the Houx farm in Washington Township of south-central Lafayette County. One of the Houx children stood watch for Federals on a nearby hilltop, but after the meal one of the bushwhackers beat the Houx' slave Jackson with poles and boards for earlier refusing to watch. Sometime after this, Jackson escaped from the Houx family, reported what happened there that day, and was the chief witness against Fanny Houx for feeding the bushwhackers during her tribunal. Fanny was convicted and sentenced to military prison for "aiding and abetting guerrillas." Before the war Jackson would not have been permitted to testify against a white person under Missouri civil law, but martial law allowed it.[2]

Wilson's and Brownlee's Guerrillas Target Citizen Guards Near California

On July 9 toward the center of the state on the Boonville Road six miles west of California in west Moniteau County unidentified guerrillas attacked a Union forage-gathering detail of about fifteen local citizen guards, killing John Hunt of the area and severely wounding Sloan B. Lamb of northeast Cooper County. Local guerrillas under Bob Wilson of Morgan County and Charles Brownlee of Cooper County conducted an active guerrilla campaign beginning later in July across all three of these counties, so perhaps this was their work. Large numbers of northern sympathizers across Cooper and Moniteau Counties—particularly German-Americans—were forming citizen guards companies in response to Union Major General Rosecrans' General Orders Number 107, and it was in guerrillas' best interest to discourage them.[3]

Most actions during the week of July 10 through 16 throughout west-central Missouri were the work of small guerrilla bands operating independently. During this week Bill Anderson removed his band from the region, as described earlier, and George Todd's band seemed to avoid conflict in their hideouts across Jackson and Lafayette Counties in order to better support Thornton's uprising north of the Missouri River.

Wilhite's and Austin's Band in Warder Church Fight 10 July Near Wellington

On Sunday, July 10 Jeff Wilhite's and Green Austin's small local band that had been operating in the Lafayette County area came to ruin at a fight two miles from Wellington in a desperate skirmish called the "Warder's Church Fight." It began that Sunday morning when a slave woman at Wellington told a large passing patrol of 7th Cavalry MSM led by Captain Murline C. Henslee that two guerrillas had been in town that morning, and then rode off to attend a Hardshell Baptist service along Sni-A-Bar Creek two miles south of town at Warder's Church, named after the Joseph Warder family that lived nearby. Captain Henslee with his 50 troopers scouted the church from a distance, taking note that it stood on a bluff protecting it from approach on one side and that steep-banked Sni-A-Bar Creek inhibited approach from another side, except for a small wooden bridge in plain view of the front of the building. Therefore, Captain Henslee sent a sergeant and six mounted troopers pounding across the bridge and past the church to a blocking position on the hilltop to the rear. The Baptist service had packed the building, but the guerrillas fired without effect from the open windows at the sergeant's detail as the seven cavalrymen thundered past. Once the advance guard blocked the primary escape route, Captain Henslee brought the remainder of his men at a gallop across the same bridge as the church-goers streamed from the building in panic. Jeff Wilhite, Greene Austin, and six or seven men attempted to flee shielded by

Twenty—*Supporting the Insurgency in Northwest Missouri South of the River*

The Union control of the little bridge across the steep-banked Sni-A-Bar Creek blocked the guerrillas' retreat from Warder's Church (Underwood and Clough, eds., *Battles and Leaders of the Civil War*, vol. 3, 1887, p. 643).

sympathetic worshippers, but Captain Henslee ordered the crowd to "squat," and his troopers began to fire at the standing or running guerrillas as the civilians dropped to the ground in obedience to the order. The fifty troopers shot down and killed or mortally wounded five of the band including Jefferson Wilhite, Greene Austin, and local men who were part of the group. One guerrilla escaped by waiting to come out of the church until the fight had passed by and then rode away in another direction. Another bushwhacker on foot escaped when one of the Yankee horses stumbled and threw its rider to the ground, and the quick-thinking bushwhacker fled on the Federal mount. The Union troopers suffered minor wounds and only lost the one horse. Captain Henslee emphatically asserted in his report that his men's shooting harmed none of the noncombatants during the action. However, there was one broken heart, as the Federals understood later that one of Austin's and Wilhite's band was to be married to a local girl in the church at the conclusion of that worship service, and, of course, their intrusion spoiled the plan. This small band grew careless, and paid dearly for poor security at Warder's Church.[4]

On Monday and Tuesday, July 11 and 12 Union troops in Johnson County chased small bodies of guerrillas, but failed to inflict much damage on them. Someone spotted ten to twelve bushwhackers three miles southeast of Knob Noster in east Johnson County on July 11. Knob Noster's own citizen guard pursued these Rebels, but they scattered into the brush, probably to meet later at a predetermined rendezvous point.[5] On the following day, elements of the 7th Cavalry MSM near Columbus in north-central Johnson County spotted six or seven bushwhackers and attempted pursuit, but these troopers had been scouting in Lafayette County for three days and their tired horses were not up to the chase.[6]

J. Frank Gregg's Traveling Band Raids in Morgan and Cooper Counties on Way North

A band of about twenty to thirty of Quantrill's former guerrillas led by J. Frank Gregg coming late back into Missouri from wintering in the South or having left the Confederate army rode into central Missouri on Tuesday evening, July 12 on their way north. This band's exploits while they traveled through southwest Missouri earlier in July are detailed in Chapter Thirteen. Evidently, these bushwhackers crossed the substantial obstacle of the Osage River at or near Duroc Ford in east Benton County. However, once past the river Gregg's band did not ride north or northwest directly toward their comrades in Jackson and Lafayette Counties, but they veered to the northeast. During Tuesday night, July 12/13, Gregg's band attempted to raid Versailles, county seat of Morgan County, but were repelled in the darkness by the new citizen guard unit of the town. Versailles had earlier in the war endured raids by renegade Union soldiers as well as bushwhackers, so their citizen guard force was keen on the town's defense. A local Union commander wrote that several of Gregg's guerrillas hailed from Morgan County, so the attempt on Versailles may have been for their benefit.[7] At nine in the morning of Wednesday, July 13 three miles north of Tipton in south-central Cooper County Gregg's band held up the stagecoach coming from Boonville. The raiders took valuables from the mail, two horses, robbed the passengers, and even took hats, boots, and pants from some of them.[8] J. Frank Gregg's band continued north to near Pilot Grove in central Cooper County where they robbed one man of $89 and then hanged him in a tree. The hanged man's slave cut the victim down as soon as the robbers left and saved his life. The band robbed other farmers nearby, taking a horse from one of them. One of the bushwhackers told a passer-by that they were members of Shelby's brigade. Indeed, guerrilla J. Frank Gregg may be the same First Lieutenant J. F. Gregg on the roll of Company B, 12th Missouri Cavalry in Shelby's brigade, and several of Quantrill's men performed some service in Shelby's brigade at times during the war. It is possible that Gregg and his men were carrying messages or escorting staff officers from the Confederate army to southern recruiting commands in west-central Missouri. Gregg's band rode on north into Saline County next.[9]

On Thursday morning, July 14 five bushwhackers robbed the stagecoach only three miles west of Independence in northwest Jackson County. The guerrillas took not only the mail, the stage horses, and the passengers' valuables, but forced some of the passengers to swap clothes with them. Under normal circumstances Union troops stationed in Independence would have reacted quickly to such an incident, but the lieutenant in command did not consider he could spare troopers to pursue the stage robbers. By this date, Colonel Ford, the commander of the 2nd Colorado Cavalry, had taken the greater part of his regiment north of the Missouri River with him to defeat Thornton's insurgency there, as described in Chapter Eighteen. He left just a handful of his troopers to watch over Jackson and Cass Counties until the remainder of the regiment could return. The few Coloradoans left behind were forced out of necessity to pick their fights very carefully fearing the guerrillas could mass and overwhelm them.[10]

Gregg's Traveling Band Travels Through Saline County

Meanwhile, witnesses near Arrow Rock in southeast Saline County saw twelve guerrillas riding toward the northwest also on Thursday, July 14. This was probably J. Frank Gregg's traveling band of bushwhackers moving steadily north through Saline County. Guerrilla Warren Welch revealed in his memoir that he was a member of

Gregg's fast-moving band that intimidated Captain George W. Bingham's local citizen guards company somewhere in north-central Saline County probably about Friday, July 15. Welch wrote that Bingham temporarily took his company north of the Missouri River by boat probably to southeast Carroll County to avoid Gregg's band, and brought them back after the bushwhackers had passed on west. Gregg again went out of his way by riding to Miami in north Saline County, but that neighborhood was well-known for its southern sympathy, so Gregg probably selected the out-of-the-way village as a safe stop for his tired travelers. Warren Welch wrote that as Gregg's band passed on west through northwest Saline County about Saturday, July 16 they attacked an unidentified Union squad on the prairie, killing four of them. They passed into northeast Lafayette County near Waverly and through Dover, then crossed Tabo Creek in central Lafayette County to complete their long journey.[11]

Bill Stewart and Two Others Raid Boonville

On Friday three bushwhackers went on a crime spree in the western part of Boonville, county seat of Cooper County. Two of them, Bill Stewart of Johnson County and Al Carter from northeast Missouri crossed on the ferry boat from Howard County across the Missouri River by pressuring the ferry operator with drawn revolvers and their assurance that they were carrying important dispatches from Confederate Colonel Caleb Perkins. Colonel Perkins was then commanding a successful southern recruiting command over several counties of northeast Missouri as described in Chapters Fourteen and Fifteen, and it is possible that he entrusted dispatches to Stewart and Carter. Once the ferry arrived at the Boonville landing, Stewart and Carter galloped through the streets brandishing two revolvers each until they were joined by local guerrilla Robert Sloan, who had earlier agreed to guide the pair through the area. Boonville had no active duty military garrison at this time, which is probably the reason the two

A Civil War era ferry landing (Underwood and Clough, eds., *Battles and Leaders of the Civil War*, vol. 1, 1887, p. 488).

bushwhackers behaved as they did in town. The three stole horses and robbed some citizens and encountered elderly farmer John H. Boller driving his buggy to town. Bill Stewart approached Boller, demanded his money, and reached for Boller's watch. The old farmer resisted when Bill Stewart attempted to rob him, so he mortally wounded the old man by emptying the loads of one revolver into him. Local citizen guards then responded to the assaults and robberies and chased the trio some distance, critically wounding Sloan with a head wound and capturing him.[12]

A local guerrilla returned to his home area on Saturday, July 16. A Union cavalry captain determined that "Dave Root" with three or four comrades had frequented his home area around Tabo Creek and "Mount Heber" Church in central Lafayette County. Evidently, this bushwhacker was actually Dave Poole, known for colorful exploits particularly in the area around his home near Tabo Creek and Mount Hebron Church and present-day Mayview in Washington Township. He may have just ridden into Lafayette County with J. Frank Gregg's traveling guerrilla band, or he may have grown restless after days of inactivity in George Todd's band in the region.[13]

Federals Strike Stewart's Band on Clear Creek in Johnson County 16 July

Bill Stewart was another bushwhacker returning to his home area also on Saturday, the Cornelia or Shanghai neighborhood south of Warrensburg in south-central Johnson County. Stewart and Al Carter must have ridden across Pettis County and directly there after their crime spree in Boonville on July 15, because Union Captain James M. Turley's patrol of 25 troopers of the 7th Cavalry MSM fought with Stewart's band near Cornelia at Clear Fork Creek on Saturday evening, July 16, killing five of the guerrillas. These bushwhackers took a great chance operating in this neighborhood, since nearby Warrensburg was the home of the Union District of Central Missouri and several companies of the veteran 7th Cavalry MSM garrisoned there. Captain Turley wrote that Stewart's next-in-command was Kentucky-born farmer Lindsay Hutchinson of near Holden in west Johnson County who, like Stewart, operated as a guerrilla in Johnson County earlier in the war and had returned several times to bring violence to his neighbors of northern sympathy. Sometime during the war unknown parties burned the village of Cornelia, so perhaps that took place at this time. A month later Stewart and his small band of guerrillas operated in southeast Howard County miles to the northeast, and fought alongside Bill Anderson's guerrilla band to defeat Captain Joseph Parke's command of 4th Cavalry MSM near Rocheport August 28, as described in Chapter Fifteen.[14]

Increased Guerrilla Offensive Operations the Week of July 17–23

The week of July 17 through 23 saw George Todd's large guerrilla band leave their hidden campgrounds in Jackson and Lafayette Counties for a mobile raid to the east and back. Meanwhile, most of the 2nd Colorado Cavalry remained north of the Missouri River for about two more weeks until July 29 trying to hunt down remnants of Confederate Lieutenant John C. Thornton's uprising there. The absence of large numbers of the "Mountain Boomers" from the Union District of Central Missouri limited Yankee ability to learn bushwhackers' locations and react timely to guerrilla actions there. Meanwhile, guerrilla warfare at the center of the state increased this week with

Wiley Shumate's guerrillas active again in the Miller and Cole County area. Furthermore, more offensive actions occurred in Cooper, Moniteau, and Morgan Counties. By week's end Lieutenant Colonel Thornton and some of his troops ended their insurgency north of the Missouri River under the weight of the large Federal counter-guerrilla effort there and crossed the Missouri River to probably seek sanctuary with Todd's band in north Lafayette County.

Todd's Band Raids Across Lafayette and Saline Counties

By Monday July 18 George Todd led his band of 117 riders on an extended raid across Lafayette and Saline Counties that lasted until they returned to their Lafayette and Jackson County sanctuary areas July 21 and 22. Todd's decision to go ahead with his bold raid was probably influenced by the continued absence of most of the Union 2nd Colorado Cavalry and by the need to distract Yankee attention away from Thornton's faltering uprising north of the Missouri River.

Gregg's Band Raids Near Pleasant Hill

Based on guerrilla Warren Welch's memoirs, it appears Todd sent J. Frank Gregg's newly arrived bushwhacker band south toward Pleasant Hill in northeast Cass County probably as a demonstration to draw Union attention away from Todd's raid toward Saline County to the southeast. Gregg specifically wrote that on the way to Pleasant Hill the guerrillas visited with and ate a meal with the Pacific Railroad construction crew in west Jackson County only nine miles southwest of the small Union garrison at Independence, which the Federals mention happening on July 18. This is partly corroborated by a July 21 statement by Captain George West of the 2nd Colorado Cavalry then at Liberty, Clay County fighting Thornton's uprising, but who had earlier been the military commander at Independence near the railroad construction project. Captain West wrote in detail about problems he encountered because area guerrillas cultivated friendships with the railroad work crews by sharing meals and liquor in return for which the construction workers refused to report passing bushwhackers to the Union military authorities. Warren Welch recorded in his memoir that an unidentified Union unit attacked them while they were eating with the railroad workmen, but that they counter-attacked and drove the Yanks away. Welch remembered with delight how the railroad boarding house landlord voluntarily gave the guerrillas 75 pounds of the Pacific Railroad's cooked beef and bread, which the bushwhackers were thrilled to take with them.[15] As a result of these actions by J. Frank Gregg's men, on July 18 area Federals were aware that George Todd's band of 100 to 150 was moving somewhere, and wrongfully concluded that Gregg's antics in Jackson County meant that Todd was maneuvering to attack the small, weak garrison of Coloradoans at Independence. Warren Welch's memoir surprisingly placed Welch both in this July 18 foray or demonstration toward Pleasant Hill and in the Arrow Rock raid, too, even though Todd and company set out that same night. Welch's information matches corroborating evidence for both activities. Evidently, Welch and perhaps the rest of J. Frank Gregg's small band made the effort to ride hard and rendezvous with the raiding party somewhere along the way to Arrow Rock. Ironically, on July 18 Major General Rosecrans' office at St. Louis informed Brigadier General Brown at Warrensburg that "the general says he has secret information that the rebels are meditating a raid on Jefferson City." Rosecrans' informant at least knew that Todd and company were going to raid to the southeast—except the secret source had Todd's band traveling twice as far as they actually rode.[16]

Todd with 117 Riders Sets Out on a Deep Raid to the Center of the State

Whether J. Frank Gregg's actions in Jackson County were part of George Todd's plan or not, Todd's raiding band of 117 guerrillas certainly benefited from the wrong assumptions that diverted Union attention from Todd's actual raid. Todd and his large band rode cross-country past small hamlets like Mount Hope and Chapel Hill the night of July 18/19 and thus rode out of the western part of Lafayette County so often scouted by Union patrols and watched by informants. On the morning of July 19 Todd's raiding party passed nine miles south of the Union garrison at Lexington, which sent a large patrol that could not locate the body of guerrillas. Meanwhile, Union troops stationed in Jackson County searched in vain for Todd's large band between Independence and Pleasant Hill, where Union leaders thought their men could find the Rebels, and each town in the region tightened their security just in case Todd was on his way to raid them. Belatedly, on July 20 an informant told a Federal captain at Holden that well-known Confederate recruiter Colonel Jeremiah V. Cockrell of Johnson County and a Greer with about 100 scattered recruits were camped near Chapel Hill, but patrols found nothing. The Union district headquarters at Warrensburg was closer to the truth when that same day they sent a warning to the Union commander at Glasgow in Howard County that George Todd with 150 riders was going into Saline County, but with all the conflicting intelligence reports Yankees in the field did not give much attention to this one. Also on July 20 District of Central Missouri commander Brigadier General Egbert B. Brown realized that his boss, Major General Rosecrans, was losing faith in his abilities to stop the bushwhackers in his district, so he sent a long, glowing report crowing about various small victories his forces had accomplished over the previous several days. Considering what was to happen later that same day, Brown's boss would have thought better of him if he had never sent that report.[17]

Todd's Large Group Raids Arrow Rock and Dick Yager Is Badly Wounded

Why did George Todd select the town of Arrow Rock in southeast Saline County to raid? Todd with 117 guerrillas had to cross the breadth of Lafayette and Saline Counties to get there, and afterwards take them back again. The Arrow Rock area was divided in loyalty and, seemingly had little to offer Todd as a goal for a raid. However, J. Frank Gregg's traveling band went by the place July 14, and probably gave information to Todd about how many and what kind of Union troops garrisoned the town, and also provided Warren Welch as a guide. Todd may have selected Arrow Rock as a target because it was so far away and the Federals would not expect a raid there. Bill Anderson and his band performed such operations several times already, and that may have encouraged George Todd that he could perform long-distance raids, too. Perhaps George Todd needed to execute something fantastic to take some pressure off of Thornton's uprising north of the Missouri River which was careening into Caldwell County at this time, as indicated in Chapter 18.

Todd's 117 men hit Arrow Rock at dusk on July 20 from two directions at once. Todd with half of the command rode into town from one direction and Dick Yager took half of the group and blocked the Union soldiers' retreat to the Missouri River on the east side. A company of ninety citizen guardsmen grabbed their firearms and ammunition and quickly left the two-story frame building near the center of town that served as their barracks and escaped into the gloom of approaching night. Second Lieutenant D. C. Woodruff commanded about 25 troopers of the 1st Cavalry MSM in a brick building nearby and they resisted guerrilla assaults for three quarters of an hour before they, too, beat a hasty foot retreat, leaving all their horses behind that the raiders took. One trooper was slightly wounded in this fire fight, but the raiders suffered three or four men seriously wounded, including Dick Yager, and several others had minor wounds. A lady of the town suffered a broken ankle from a stray bullet. There were no deaths at Arrow Rock. The Rebels torched the building that had housed the citizen guards, and some sources thought this fire was also meant to dislodge the defending 1st Cavalry MSM troopers nearby. After all the northern troops left, the bushwhackers concentrated on raiding stores and breaking open safes to take anything they could carry. They removed about $20,000 in cash and goods and 40 horses, including the cavalry mounts. Todd split the band into two parts for the way back and took his part directly west for Lafayette County starting about eleven that evening. Todd saw that a wagon was provided for Yager with his critical head wound and sent him guided by Warren Welch and the other half of the force north to the Cambridge neighborhood of northeast Saline County. Welch knew some southern refugees from Jackson County were living there and deposited Yager and possibly the other seriously wounded guerrillas with those southern families to nurse as best they could, as was the bushwhacker custom. Warren Welch also wrote that the group with which he rode skirmished briefly three or four miles north of Arrow Rock with unidentified Union troops from Marshall, killed a couple of them, and shots fired in the dark killed horses on each side, but no other source confirms this. Beyond that, all the able-bodied raiders returned to their sanctuary areas in the Sni-A-Bar Hills of east Jackson and southwest Lafayette County over the next few days.

Rosecrans Replaces Brown with New Man Pleasanton as Head of Central District

There were several different effects of Todd's Arrow Rock raid. This raid brought consternation to the Federals on a lesser scale than the Yankee inability to prevent or stop Quantrill's terrible Lawrence, Kansas raid almost a year before, but it was troubling, just the same. It was obvious to everyone that a large enough guerrilla force could still raid just about any town it wished. Union commanders had already concluded they could not both defend the towns and defeat the guerrillas, had set up the citizen guards mostly to fill that need, but the press and public did not always accept that logic. This raid was a great victory for Todd and the southern cause in the region, although the severe wounding of the versatile Dick Yager or Yeager was a real blow. One area newspaper joked about previous claims that Federals had finally killed the capable Yager with the headline "Dick Yeager Killed Again," hinting that reports of the man's demise were premature—which they were. Department of the Missouri chief Rosecrans was understandably disappointed in his troops' inability to inflict punishment on a large body of bushwhackers in the open. This failure finally convinced Rosecrans that his District of Central Missouri commander, Brigadier General Egbert B. Brown, was not the man for that job. Rosecrans replaced Brown with Major General Alfred Pleasanton on July 23. As described in Chapter Five, Pleasanton was a cavalry expert, and in April the War Department sent him to Rosecrans to use his expertise at mounted warfare to help hold Missouri for the Union. Pleasanton had commanded the cavalry of the Army of the Potomac back east during 1863, and made substantial improvements, but his tendency to take credit for the work of others and bullheadedness made enemies and General Ulysses Grant replaced him. Just as Rosecrans and other generals sent to the "backwater war" in Missouri had a second chance to redeem tarnished careers, now Pleasonton had a chance to prove his worth. But, Rosecrans himself was well known among his peers as a "thinking general" or a man of ideas, and on July 25 directing from a distance one of his subordinate troop commanders perhaps he was considering tactics after the embarrassing Arrow Rock raid that led him to write "night marches, unexpected routes, and concealing movements in the woods are the means of striking terror into the hearts of the bushwhackers."[18]

Shumate's Band Raids the Long House in Miller County

On July 18, the same day that Todd's force set out on the Arrow Rock raid, a smaller raiding party of bushwhackers attacked one of their enemies in Miller County, miles to the southeast. Evidently, it was seven of Wiley Shumate's Miller and Cole County bushwhacker band that rode to Union Captain William Long's house and set fire to it when the captain refused their demands that he come out. Captain Long was company commander of Company K of the 47th EMM since the program was begun in the summer of 1862, but moderate state officials had him ejected from the program for being "too hard on rebels" earlier in this summer of 1864. Much of the guerrilla war in the Miller County area was personal as shown in a number of "circle of violence" episodes there, and those seven bushwhackers that set fire to Long's house were probably reacting to some earlier violence the captain had committed against their side. Captain Long wounded one of his attackers, but when he jumped from the flames his tormentors shot him to death. Long's distraught father assembled a posse of citizen guards that pursued the Rebels but failed to catch the assassins.[19]

Union General Rosecrans replaced Brigadier General Brown with Major General Alfred Pleasonton as chief of the District of Central Missouri on 23 July 1864 (National Park Service collection at Wilson's Creek National Battlefield, historian Connie Langum).

Wilson Band Raids in Cooper and Morgan Counties

Another small guerrilla band conducted their first attack this season on the evening of July 19. This was the band of mostly Morgan County bushwhackers led by veteran guerrilla Bob Wilson of that county including a few members of the former Charles Brownlee band of Cooper and Moniteau Counties. It seems Brownlee remained in the regular Confederate army, but some of his former band members returned and joined the Smith band.

Over the next several weeks this band of about a dozen men made life uncomfortable for northern sympathizers in Morgan, Cooper, and Moniteau Counties. For unknown reasons that evening three members evidently of this amalgamated group burned a corncrib and other outbuildings on the wealthy Elisha Warfield farm in south-central Cooper County.[20] On the following night of July 20/21 bushwhackers of this band captured and executed three northern men who had testified against their comrade Patrick Mullins in his tribunal that led to his execution at Tipton on April 23 as described in Chapter Nine. The three murdered men were Peter Hays, John Farmer and Peter Thixton of Moreau Township of east-central Morgan County. Thixton and Farmer served in two different companies of the local 43rd EMM. The Union military report of the triple murder stated that these men were all killed "about nine miles south of Tipton" indicating perhaps that the bushwhackers seized these men at home and took them to that location.

On Thursday morning July 21 the same guerrilla band robbed two men near California.[21] On Friday night, July 22/23, members of this same band fired on the Tipton to Boonville stagecoach about five miles south of Boonville, probably because the driver refused their demand to stop. The assailants fired two loads of buckshot at the driver, but instead hit a passenger named Siceloff riding on the seat with the driver. The hapless passenger was a student returning to his studies at a college in Fayette. The coach hurried the rest of the way to Boonville to obtain medical aid for the badly wounded young man.

A newspaper correspondent at Boonville theorized that guerrillas in that region were deliberately attacking Union means of communication by destroying telegraph lines nearby and attempting to take the Federal mail pouch from the coach.[22] Based on this steady series of attacks, robberies, and murders these bushwhackers committed during the last five days of this week, they obviously intended to continue to challenge Union control of this three-county area.

George Todd Evidently Assisted Thornton's First Group of Survivors Move South

During Saturday night July 23/24, as described in Chapter Eighteen, portions of Confederate Lieutenant Colonel John C. Thornton's recruits from north of the Missouri River crossed to the south side of that river to find sanctuary in the Lafayette County area from the large collection of Union military pressing against them in Platte, Clay, and Ray Counties. Evidently, guerrilla chieftain George Todd assisted these refugees to find hideouts in order to remain in safety there and avoid attracting unwanted Yankee attention to their presence. There is little direct evidence of Todd's cooperation with Thornton's men, but it was in his best interest to exert influence on that many southern combatants in the middle of his operating area.[23]

Continued High Tempo of Guerrilla Operations South of the Missouri River During the Week of July 24 Through 30

Over the next several days starting with July 23 the 7th Cavalry MSM and part of the 2nd Colorado Cavalry increased their patrol activity in Lafayette, Cass, Jackson, and Johnson Counties in response to reports perhaps from informants that several small bodies of Rebels were active in this area. Either these southern riders were Todd's guerrillas leading Union attention away from Thornton's men in hiding, or they were small groups of Thornton's men seeking their own hideouts, or both. It is also possible that the leaders of these two Federals regiments were attempting to court favor with their new district commander, Major General Alfred Pleasanton, who on July 23 replaced their sacked former commander, Brigadier General Brown. The old saying that "a new broom sweeps clean," could be appropriate to officers of these two regiments wanting to appear part of the solution instead of part of the problem to their new district chief.[24]

Wilson's Band Raids East in Moniteau County and then West in Cooper County

Meanwhile, the small bushwhacker band in Cooper, Moniteau, and Morgan Counties continued their rampage. On Monday, 25 July two of them robbed some people near the Pacific Railroad stop at Clark's Station—present day Clarksburg—between California and Tipton.[25] On Thursday, July 28 this same band robbed northern sympathizers across a wide swath of Cooper County. They began in the northeast corner where they robbed Union veteran H. Tally of $400 cash and his revolver, and then robbed Captain H. Meyers of $100. They next robbed some residents near Pilot Grove in the west-central part of the county. No details of these depredations seem to remain except the bushwhackers made one unfortunate man remove and hand over his trousers with only his shirt to cover his modesty. Lastly, the same band forced their way into the home of wealthy, Virginia-born Judge John A. Trigg in the northwest corner of the county just as Trigg returned home from nearby Arrow Rock. The raiders took a "good" horse, three watches, and loaded ten horses with clothing from the household, all estimated to be worth $500. The guerrillas explained that they wanted cash most of all, but they reluctantly accepted the judge's explanation that because of the war he kept all his money in St. Louis. As the bushwhackers left the premises one of them mockingly asked the jurist "if he was as good a Union man as ever."[26]

On Tuesday, July 26 General Pleasanton ordered a change that involved the northwest corner of Cooper County. In order to protect the strategic La Mine bridge over the Osage River on the Pacific Railroad there, this new Union commander of the District of Central Missouri ordered a topographical engineer to select a site there for a blockhouse or small fort. It was obvious that the Union military could not control all of Missouri, but they would fortify and man strategic bridges of the vital railroads to protect them from guerrillas and behind-Union-lines Confederate raiders. This tactic of keeping control of lines of communication involved truly static defense—the very antipathy of the mobile cavalry defense that the Union used to hold on to the rest of Missouri. However, like the fortifications and cannons that guarded vital river ports along the Mississippi River on Missouri's east boundary, retaining control of such strategic sites was vital to retaining control of the state.[27]

Federals Chase Guerrillas in Southwest Johnson County

Union troopers of the 7th Cavalry MSM encountered a guerrilla band of about twenty twice in Johnson County on July 27 and 28. First, on Wednesday, July 27 a corporal and four privates hunting for a stray horse on Blackwater River in a few miles north of their Holden garrison rode into twenty bushwhackers they later claimed were led by Dick Yager. Of course, as described earlier, Yager was still critically wounded and convalescing in northeast Saline County at this time, so the troopers were mistaken about that. In spite of being outnumbered four-to-one, the small Yankee detail put up a real fight, killing two Rebels and seriously wounding their leader, although no Federals were hit. Captain Melville U. Foster, the commander at Holden, may have discovered the southerners' whereabouts from an informant, because he went hunting for this band in southwest Johnson County on Thursday with a force of forty. Foster detailed a sergeant with half of the patrol to sweep down Panther Creek driving the guerrillas to his half of the force waiting at a well-known ford on Big Creek. The sergeant "drove them easily" according to Foster's report, but the fleeing Rebels missed the ambush Foster had waiting. The whole Federal patrol then pursued the bushwhackers and at Louisa Pemberton's farm near the village of Rose Hill caught up to them. As before, the Yanks shot up the southerners—killing two, wounding four, and capturing three horses—without suffering hardly a scratch themselves. These two lopsided victories may be a testament to the fighting abilities of the veteran troopers of the 7th Cavalry MSM, but they could also indicate that these guerrillas were not veterans. Perhaps these twenty bushwhackers were part of Thornton's refugees from north of the Missouri River, untrained in the type of intense guerrilla war conducted in this area.[28]

Angry Confrontation Between Missouri and Kansas Troops at Harrisonville 28 July

Also on Thursday, July 28, trouble of a different sort came a few miles to the southwest in Harrisonville, county seat of Cass County. Captain Orren A. Curtis's Company F of 15th Kansas Cavalry disregarded the warning of Captain Alex Robinson's Cass County EMM company guard to halt and rode arrogantly into town. These two units were both part of the Union war effort, but the border troubles dating back to the 1850s here left these two units more as antagonists than allies. There was little tenderness between Kansans and Missourians. Robinson's guard followed the insolent Kansans and pointed his firearm at them, leading the cavalry to point theirs in his direction. Both the picket and the Kansans threatened to fire on each other, but after both sides faced each other over gun barrels, cooler heads prevailed and Captain Curtis' company reluctantly left town toward the southwest. Soon after in that direction it was undoubtedly the Kansas cavalry that burned eight to ten houses to the ground that the controversial General Orders Number Eleven ordered evacuated the previous year, and on the following day they torched several other vacant houses west of Harrisonville. To the Kansas cavalry empty houses offered shelter to guerrillas, so by torching them they removed such temptations, but this also gave notice to the Cass Countians that the Kansans would not tolerate Rebels.[29]

That night, July 28/29, and the following two nights the Union military in Jackson and Lafayette Counties noted that George Todd and between 150 and 200 bushwhackers moved east toward Lafayette County from north and east Jackson County. Union authorities mistakenly mentioned in these reports that Quantrill and Confederate recruiter Colonel Jeremiah Vardaman Cockrell were partly in command of these moving irregulars. They did not know that Quantrill was then in exile in Howard County, and no corroborating source placed Colonel Cockrell in the area at this time. However, Cockrell conducted his southern recruiting in such a stealthy form that those Federal officers may have been correct about his being there after all. The Union authorities naturally calculated that Todd and his large guerrilla band were moving out on another raid, but that was not correct this time. Since an important council of war was scheduled in north Lafayette County between Confederate staff officers and guerrilla chieftains in early August, perhaps this bushwhacker movement was in preparation for that council.[30]

Area Federals learned on Friday, 29 July of a guerrilla camp near Jane Renick's farm in Jackson Township of northwest Johnson County near Offutt's Knob. Therefore, on Saturday Lieutenant Elisha Horn led a large patrol of 93 troopers of the 7th Cavalry MSM from Warrensburg to this location near Chapel Hill to search out and attack these Rebels at daybreak. Sweeping the headwaters of Honey Creek north of Columbus Horn's men discovered the recently vacated guerrilla camp two miles from Widow Renick's place. The Federal moved their search north around Chapel Hill and found fifteen to twenty bushwhackers about 1.5 miles south of town and attacked them. At no Union loss Horn's force killed one Rebel, wounded another, and captured two horses. They also recovered from the fleeing southerners three double-barrel shotguns, one single-barrel shotgun, "and 1 common rifle"; all of which they destroyed. Again, the lopsided nature of this Union victory and the absence of captured revolvers tends to indicate these southerners were not well-versed in guerrilla warfare, and may have been refugee combatants from Thornton's uprising north of the Missouri River.[31]

Unidentified Guerrillas Shoot at *Sioux City* in Northwest Cooper County

Speaking of the Missouri River, unknown bushwhackers fired on the westbound steamer *Sioux City* about July 29 ten miles northwest of Boonville somewhere about northwest Cooper County, as reported in Chapter Fifteen. The source of the report was the Union commander at Glasgow, west Howard County, who mentioned the attack in a report after the vessel stopped there a day or two later, but gave no specifics. The *Sioux City*, built in Cincinnati in 1857, frequently plied the Missouri River as a transport for the Union military during the war, and was no stranger to the threat of attack. The brief mention of this in the Union military records does not state from which side of the river the shooters fired, but the two prime suspect bands north of the river were not near this location about this date. Bill Anderson's men—who made great sport of firing on the Union-controlled steamers—were raiding railroads far away in Monroe County at this time; and Clifton D. Holtzclaw's band was then still in south Chariton County, as described in Chapter Fifteen. The deposed bushwhacker leader Captain William Quantrill and a small bodyguard were then camped in a remote part of the south Howard County countryside, but they were deliberately not drawing attention to themselves, and it seems unlikely they would have risked making local Union troops curious by shooting at passing riverboats. A more likely candidate was the Morgan County guerrilla band then led by Bob Wilson which was then operating with skill and speed in Cooper County, and raided Judge Trigg's home in this same neighborhood the day before on July 28, as previously described. There is no other record that this Cooper, Moniteau, and Morgan County unit fired on steamboats, but they were in the area about this time.[32]

An Important War Council and Different Guerrilla Bands Operate South of the Missouri River During the Week of July 31 Through August 6

The week of July 31 through August 6 south of the Missouri River was notable for the landmark council of war Confederate staff officers held with some of the region's guerrilla chieftains mainly on August 3 and 4 in north Lafayette County. The bushwhacker groups of this area were mostly inactive during this week in support of and providing security for this strategic conference, so there is a noticeable dearth of guerrilla action in Jackson, Lafayette, Cass, and Johnson Counties for much of this week. During this relative lull period the Federals attempted to keep in touch with their enemy with the usual pattern of mounted patrols, although these accomplished little. Therefore, the arena of most guerrilla fighting for a few days switched further east to small bands operating in Saline, Pettis, Cooper, and Moniteau Counties.

Two troopers of the 7th Cavalry MSM stationed at Warrensburg took advantage of this strange lull period to write home August 5 about what they observed in the Johnson County area over the previous several days:

> The Union People down here Are not doing Much at farming as They have to Lay Out to Keep from being killed by the Secesh [secessionists] We hear of Union Men Being killed through the country nearly every Day Feed is very scarce down here And our Horses Looks very bad.... There is plenty of Men not in the servis in this Part of the country but the Most of Them are conservative secesh.

Some of the bushwhackers operating in this area were evidently driving out or killing isolated rural farmers of northern sympathy in order to prevent the Federals from discovering guerrilla movement and camps in the countryside from informants. This was a return to a similar practice here during 1862, and many of these killings are unrecorded.[33]

On Monday, August 1 Sergeant Coy and a patrol of undermined size of the 2nd Colorado Cavalry somewhere in Jackson County south of Independence found two guerrilla camps in a swamp. Sergeant Coy somehow determined that one camp housed 25 bushwhackers and the second was home to 40. Before the Rebels fled, the Coloradoans killed one of them and wounded another at no Union loss. Union authorities had only permitted the main part of the 2nd Colorado Cavalry to return to base in Jackson County from north of the Missouri River over the weekend, and the reunited regiment was obviously quick to get back to the guerrilla hunting business in their normally assigned area.[34]

Bill Jackson and Woodson's Band Operates in Saline County

Miles to the east in Saline County the county's own guerrillas began active operations about Sunday, July 31, and they lost little time asserting themselves. Mostly this was the combined band of Bill S. Jackson of Arrow Rock and Tom Woodson of Heath's Creek Township of northeast Pettis County. Bill Jackson, son of the late governor of Missouri, Claiborne Fox Jackson, had been active as a guerrilla chief since 1862, but operated mostly north of the Missouri River in Howard County. Earlier this summer Jackson and his band operated with Clifton D. Holtzclaw in Howard and Chariton Counties north of the Missouri River, as described in Chapter Fifteen. When Jackson learned at the end of July that the new Union district chief, Major General Pleasanton, stripped the active-duty 1st Cavalry MSM troops from Saline County to concentrate against George Todd's band further west, he left Holtzclaw to return home with subordinates Bill Durrett and John Will Piper and several of his men to operate in the vacuum left by the departed 1st Cavalry MSM troopers. Tom Woodson operated as a guerrilla chief first in early 1862 in north Pettis County. Little is recorded about his wartime career, so perhaps he was part of the regular Confederate army in the interim. When Woodson brought his small band into the mix with Jackson they had about 25 riders altogether, and young southern men of the Arrow Rock area eagerly joined them.[35]

Jackson's and Woodson's Band Raid Arrow Rock

The first indication to Union authorities of problems in Saline County took place suddenly about Sunday, July 31 or Monday, August 1 when the citizen guard company of Arrow Rock disappeared from their barracks leaving behind forty rifle-muskets. Only a few days earlier on July 20 this company had the presence of mind to escape with these firearms and ammunition in the face of George Todd's 117 raiders. Now, the prospect of facing the onslaught of another body of bushwhackers so soon after Todd's convinced the guardsmen to flee, leaving behind their rifles. When Todd's men raided the town a few days before these guardsmen had a chance to learn that guerrillas in 1864 came well armed, and could easily outgun citizen guards armed with slow, muzzle-loading, single shot rifles. Add to that the real danger that the local guerrillas who just arrived back in the area knew the guardsmen's identities and would probably seek them out at home totally unnerved the local guard company. The Union commander at Boonville to the east discovered the disappearance of the Arrow Rock citizen guards and reported it to his commander on August 2. Also on that Tuesday, about 25 of Jackson and Woodson's bushwhackers raided the town of Arrow Rock, taking what they wanted from local merchants, and exchanging shots with Captain George Bingham of Company H of the local 71st EMM, may have been in town to secure the abandoned citizen guard weapons.[36]

Major Henry Suess of the 7th Cavalry MSM aboard the steamer *Fanny Ogden* sent a telegram the following day from Glasgow to report that small bands of guerrillas were reported not only at Arrow Rock but also at Miami and Cambridge in north Saline County. It seems various bushwhacker bands converged on Saline County rapidly because of the recent absence of the active-duty 1st Cavalry.[37] During the night of August 3 and 4 sixteen of Jackson and Woodson's guerrillas including Bill Durrett other known local men searched the home outside Arrow Rock of Dr. Glen O. Hardeman, formerly of the local 71st EMM. The raiders left threats with Hardeman's wife about the doctor's fate if they found him, then seized clothing, bedding, a knife, and some bullets and left.[38]

Mystery Guerrillas Raid in the Miami Area of North Saline County

There seems to be no surviving evidence that identifies the guerrillas at Miami and Cambridge in north Saline County August 2, as reported by Major Suess at Glasgow. Suess reported from Glasgow that "they fired at some militia opposite Miami," and perhaps those militia were citizen guards of the area. Suess also reported that a witness reported seeing a group of bushwhackers riding west near Plains City in north-central Saline County. Perhaps George Todd sent some of his guerrillas riding around north Saline County to detract Union attention from the Confederate council of war scheduled to begin in north Lafayette County later that week, but that is conjecture.[39]

Wilson's Band Robs Store Near Tipton on 3 August

On Wednesday, August 3, Bob Wilson's local guerrillas raided John C. G. Goodwin's country store about five miles north of Tipton in east-central Cooper County. The 25 bushwhackers waited until the stagecoach passed before they raided the mercantile, and the Boonville newspaper commented that this was the second time they robbed the place.[40]

Confederate Council of War on 4 and 5 August

A Confederate strategic council of war convened August 4 and 5 between Rebel staff officer Captain John Chesnut of Platte County and perhaps other officers and various guerrilla chieftains in northwest Lafayette County to coordinate bushwhacker operations in support of Major General Sterling Price's long-awaited invasion of Missouri, scheduled to take place in a few weeks during September. This unprecedented meeting was held simultaneously with another one at the same time near Middle Grove, southwest Monroe County, as described in Chapter Fifteen. Not all the chiefs of scattered small bands of guerrillas received notification in time to attend, but at least in the Lafayette County meeting Lieutenant Colonel John Calhoun "Coon" Thornton, George Todd, John Thrailkill, Charles Fletcher "Fletch" Taylor, and Bill Anderson represented the bushwhacker side. Captain Chesnut was disappointed that Captain William Quantrill could not attend, but, then, General Price and his staff had no way of knowing that Bill Anderson and George Todd deposed Quantrill in late May or early June, and that the former Kansas schoolteacher moved to south Howard County with a small dedicated bodyguard to camp out in self-imposed exile. Guerrilla chronicler John N. Edwards recorded that Captain Chesnut expressed Sterling Price's plan proposing the major bands operate north of the Missouri to draw the Union military away from south Missouri where Price planned to enter the state with his regular troops. This seemed acceptable to those present, and "Fletch" Taylor proposed a fast-moving raid to the Iowa border where the Federals did not expect bushwhacker operations. The other attendees expressed admiration for Taylor's venture, but he could not know that within a few days Union troops would severely wound him, and none of those present would ever carry out his south Iowa raid. After the council ended some of the attendees remained in George Todd's camp a few extra days refreshing old acquaintances, relating stories of their adventures, and exchanging ideas. Oddly, local Union troops knew about the council of war, probably from informants, but they could not pinpoint the location—along Sni-A-Bar Creek five miles west of Greenton—in time to intrude upon it.[41]

Back in Arrow Rock the morning of Friday, August 5, the wife of Dr. Hardeman endured another surprise visit by the local bushwhackers. This time it was Tom Woodson and four others ostensibly hunting for runaway slaves. In her letter to her husband Mrs. Hardeman named six local youths she heard had joined the guerrillas.[42]

Bill Jackson Raids Marshall in Saline County on 5 August

Also on Friday Bill Jackson with ten or twelve bushwhackers raided the Saline County seat of Marshall, since the Union leadership had removed the detachment of the 1st Cavalry MSM that had their garrison there. Jackson's men shot several black men in town and just outside town, and three of those died of their wounds. One of the guerrillas burned the courthouse to the ground and the raiders burned a house or office belonging to Judge John A. Trigg. This is the same judge whose home in northwest Cooper County unidentified guerrillas robbed July 28, as already described. The raiders remained in Marshall several hours and plundered some before they left.[43]

Jackson Raids New Frankfort on 6 August

Bill Jackson must have believed he should act fast before the Federals returned, because on Saturday, August 6, he led his band to raid the mostly German-American village of New Frankfort in the northeast corner of Saline County. Jackson and his men were particularly brutal in New Frankfort, because the town was home to the families of a number of men away in the Union military. The bushwhackers killed a Union soldier named Eisner who was either discharged or home on furlough, burned eleven homes of soldiers' families, and threatened and abused several soldiers' wives. The arsonists allowed some of the wives and children five minutes to remove treasured items before they torched their dwellings, but gave no such consideration to others. In some instances a few of the bushwhackers kicked and beat some of the soldiers' wives, and tore their clothing, before burning their home. In addition to torching the eleven homes, Jackson's men also destroyed the post office, schoolhouse, and a church. When they left, the raiders threatened to return and burn the rest of the buildings of the village if the soldiers' families did not leave within the next few days. During this raid Jackson seemed to emulate the atrocities of Bill Anderson's band.[44]

The Union reaction to the Marshall and New Frankfort raids August 5 and 6 was a combination of panic and exaggeration and an immediate infusion of troops. Union officials were shocked at the Saline County outbreak since there were plenty of guerrillas other places in the region to fight, and they were disappointed that the well-intentioned but poorly prepared and poorly armed citizen guards were insufficient to keep Saline County pacified. Two prominent northern sympathizers in Boonville, north Cooper County, to the east sent word to department chief General Rosecrans August 6 that they had "reliable information that the rebel force in Saline County numbers over 400 men," although they added with bravado that "we do not fear small bands of rebels." General Rosecrans' headquarters expanded the 400 number into a mythical plan of George Todd's for a bushwhacker takeover of Saline County in order to provide an entry point for Confederate Brigadier General Joseph Shelby's cavalry brigade to rush north and cross the Missouri River there. On the practical side Lieutenant Colonel Bazel F. Lazear led several companies of the 1st Cavalry MSM back to Saline County from Lafayette County on August 6 to handle the crisis. Lazear and his column rode into Saline County ready to employ extreme tactics to restore Federal control and he reported back to district headquarters at Warrensburg about finding "terrible panic in the county" and "wild rumors." The lieutenant colonel soon passed along the more cool-headed appraisal that "from the best information I can get I do not believe there are 100 guerrillas in this county," and perhaps there were less than fifty![45]

Adding fuel to the Union rumor about Shelby's cavalry coming to central Missouri, a citizen guard posse on Friday, August 5, captured three apparent Shelby brigade deserters near the village of High Point in west Moniteau County, although a fourth man got away. The prisoners stated that they had recently deserted from Shelby's unit, and were visiting friends in the area. Of this trio, Lafayette Hall of north Moniteau County had a record of service under Shelby, but Thomas Blalock of Cooper County evidently changed sides, since a man by that name served in Cooper County's Union 52nd EMM at Boonville the previous year. Union authorities passed Hall along to the Alton Military Prison as a captured Confederate soldier, but a later military tribunal sentenced Blalock to the state penitentiary in Jefferson City.[46]

Hutchinson's Guerrilla Band Raids in West Johnson County

Toward the Kansas border in west Johnson County, Federal cavalry patrols seldom found guerrillas. Captain William P. Baker's patrol of the 7th Cavalry MSM riding along Big Creek or Crawford's Fork along the Cass County line on Friday, August 5 chased a small bushwhacker group, killing one and capturing a horse. Subsequent actions in this area indicated that this band was led by Lindsey Hutchinson of the Holden neighborhood, who rode with fellow-Johnson Countian Bill Stewart's small band earlier this summer, as narrated earlier in this chapter. Hutchinson seemed to be operating with a few guerrillas of his own now.[47] Unless there were unreported skirmishes at this time, this lone report of a dead guerrilla seems to indicate that George Todd was controlling Rebels in the region to stay out of sight for the time being.

The West Counties Have Light Action While the East Counties Continue in a Heavier Tempo South of the Missouri River During the Week of August 7–13

The week of August 7 through 13 continued with only occasional actions in Jackson, Cass, Johnson and Lafayette Counties as George Todd continued planning future operations as a result of the momentous guerrilla council of war in northwest Lafayette County the previous week. He seemed to orchestrate the influx of refugee Rebels from Thornton's failed uprising north of the Missouri River to find sanctuaries, "lay low," and avoid contact with Federal patrols until the uprising leaders decided what course of action to take next. As in the previous week, the tempo of violence continued with hardly any sign of decreasing east of the border region as the bands led by Bob Wilson, Tom Woodson, Bill Jackson, and others fought to limit the Union influence in the counties of the center of the state.

Woodson's Band in Northwest Cooper County and Jackson's Band in North Saline County

As stated earlier, Union Lieutenant Colonel Bazel F. Lazear with several companies of the First Cavalry MSM rode back into Saline County on Saturday, August 6 with orders to "operate against bushwhackers and their abettors." Lieutenant Colonel Lazear surveyed the damage made to the town during the recent raid, then led his troopers around the county in an attempt to confront the guerrillas and prevent them from performing further harm to northern sympathizers in the area. Tactically, Lazear's force spent the next several days swatting at small bodies of guerrillas with some limited success. On Sunday, August 7, some of the First Cavalry MSM at Lamine in northwest Cooper County rode onto Tom Woodson's guerrillas visiting homes to recruit new members and killed one and wounded another before the remainder escaped. The dead guerrilla was teenager William Hall from near Tipton. Woodson's men shot a black man in the neighborhood just before the troopers arrived. On Monday, August 8, some of the Union cavalry came across Bill Jackson's band of about fifteen eating lunch near Saline City in east Saline County killing two and wounding and capturing Jackson's lieutenant, Dick Durrett. Durrett was shot in the ankle and could not run away. The next morning Lazear had his men prop up the wounded Rebel lieutenant against a fence and executed him by firing squad. Durrett's final words were "tell the boys to keep on fighting."[48]

Lieutenant Colonel Lazear and his men faced a more insidious enemy in Saline

County than the bushwhackers in the form of a recalcitrant, strongly pro-southern population, and Lazear set out a program to conquer this enemy in order to undermine the guerrilla movement in the area. Lazear had good backing for what he set out to do in Saline County. The new district commander, Major General Alfred Pleasonton, quickly adopted the "radical" philosophy of tactics against the rebellion in his district, and rejected the "moderate" stance that his predecessor, Brigadier General Egbert B. Brown, seemed to use. In fact, Pleasonton seemed to regard his own replacement of the less effective Brown as a repudiation of moderation and a call for the more radical, violent solution to the southern rebellion. Pleasonton was aware that one of the most dedicated adherents to the moderate stance was Lazear's boss and commander of the 1st Cavalry MSM, Colonel James McFerran, so Pleasonton had Colonel McFerran assigned to court martial duty in Jefferson City for the foreseeable future, which made Lieutenant Colonel Lazear the acting commander of the 1st. Further, General Pleasonton also made Lazear military commander of the sub-district including Saline County, leaving no doubt that Lazear had backing to conduct anti-guerrilla war there as he saw fit.[49]

Lazear Arrests Southern Ladies in Saline County

Lieutenant Colonel Lazear's tactics in response to his orders to "operate against bushwhackers and their abettors" were extreme in his actions against the "abettors." While on their way toward the county seat of Marshall, one of Lazear's advance scouts arrested a Mr. Gaines who told them he spent time in the Alton Military Prison earlier in the war. The troopers took Gaines with them, shot and wounded the man when he attempted escape, and brought him to Marshall to account for his actions and get treatment for his wound. After talking to residents in different parts of Saline County Lazear wrote "this is certainly the most rebellious county I have been in," and his subsequent actions reflected this opinion. As Lazear stated in a report to headquarters a few day later, "this county needs rough handling." The lieutenant colonel confronted southern sympathizer Marshall Piper of the Arrow Rock area and demanded Piper report to him the following day. On Sunday, August 7 when Piper rode into Arrow Rock as ordered, Lazear had the man immediately shot for violating his oath taken earlier in the war specifically by harboring and feeding bushwhackers, failing to report it to authorities, and refusing to discuss what he knew with him! The lieutenant colonel was very concerned that many residents of the area had been encouraging and assisting the local bushwhackers. Particularly, young women in their teens and twenties loudly espoused the southern cause, encouraging a number of teenage boys and young men to join Bill Jackson's and Tom Woodson's bushwhacker bands. What was so galling to Lazear and his men was these women's rudeness to his troops and confident air that they could openly support the southern cause with impunity. Therefore, Lieutenant Colonel Lazear arrested several young ladies of Marshall, Arrow Rock, and Saline City and impounded them under guard for several days under the threat to send them out of the county. To forestall the guerrillas' threats against northern sympathizers of the community Lazear arrested several prominent men of southern families as hostages, too.[50]

There were several, isolated guerrilla actions to the west closer to the Kansas border on Monday, 8 August. Lieutenant James L. Combs' forage detail of 7th Cavalry MSM on Norris Creek in south-central Johnson County near the Henry County line skirmished with a small bushwhacker band. The Rebels' shooting wounded one of the detail's horses. These guerrillas seemed to be under the leadership of local man

Lindsey Hutchinson who had ridden with fellow Johnson Countian Bill Stewart earlier this summer.[51] Also that Monday unidentified guerrillas robbed the eastbound stagecoach between Independence and Lexington only five miles from Lexington. About a week later the Union district headquarters at Warrensburg ordered an officer to collect for the damages from southern sympathizers who lived near the holdup site, the assumption being that some of these southerners knew of the presence of the bushwhackers and could have reported them to Union authorities.[52]

Wounding of "Fletch" Taylor and Thrailkill Near Wayne City 8 August

About ten o'clock that same Monday evening a small skirmish occurred near the river village of Wayne City four miles from Independence in north-central Jackson County that was to have important consequences for the guerrilla community of west-central Missouri. Citizen guards of that neighborhood stretched a chain across the road in the Rush Bottom neighborhood near town and four bushwhackers rode into it in the dark. This prompted the citizen guards hidden nearby to shoot at the mounted figures inflicting dangerous wounds to two of them and serious but less deadly wounds to the other two. Guerrilla chieftains Charles "Fletch" Taylor and John Thrailkill with bodyguards Henry Porter and Allen Parmer remained in George Todd's bushwhacker camps for several days after the important council of war of the previous week, and they were riding to a site selected for crossing the Missouri River to return to their waiting bands when they entered the "killing zone" of the guardsmen's ambush. Taylor took the worst of the shots and in his own words "one pistol was shot from my side, another from my hand, my horse was mortally wounded, and my left arm shattered just below the elbow. My horse went fifty feet and fell.... With the assistance of Allen Palmer [Allen H. Parmer] I mounted behind Thrailkill just as he received a ball in the back of his neck." The other two received a shoulder wound and a leg wound, and the bleeding quartet somehow made

This late war or postwar picture of Taylor reflects the loss of his left arm (National Park Service collection at Wilson's Creek National Battlefield, historian Connie Langum).

their way east a few miles to the Wellington neighborhood of northwest Lafayette County. There some of George Todd's guerrillas abducted two local doctors who amputated "Fletch" Taylor's left arm, saving his life, and treated the others' wounds, too. Taylor's grievous wounds stopped any talk of his leading a long-range guerrilla raid into south Iowa as described earlier, and his convalescence necessitated Bill Anderson to take command of his band for several weeks. Thrailkill's shorter convalescence forced his band to remain mostly idle for several days, as described in Chapter Nineteen. All four men showed remarkable presence of mind under fire, survivability, and courage in a situation that would have killed lesser men.[53]

Guerrilla Assault on Knight House Near Kansas City

Sometime that night of August 8 and 9 four unidentified men stopped by the William Knight family home 1.5 miles from Kansas City and initially asked directions to some neighbors. Knight hesitated to answer the men's questions, and they next demanded to know where he kept his horses. Mr. Knight refused to answer further questions whereupon the strangers set fire to his house while the homeowner ran to get a firearm. The Knight daughters put out the flames which infuriated the four men who rekindled the house two or three more times, causing the excited young women to extinguish the fires each time the men set them. This infuriated the four raiders who threatened to shoot the girls if they did not go back into the house. When the Knight daughters refused, the men fired 15 to 20 shots at them. One bullet took off a girl's finger, and another bullet grazed her sister's back. By this time Mr. Knight had obtained his own firearm perhaps from a hiding place and shot and wounded one of the intruders who all promptly left. The Knights and the local authorities did not know if the four men in the night were guerrillas, Kansas jayhawkers, or just lawless outlaws.[54]

A glimpse at the mid–1850s appearance of fledgling Kansas City (Walter B. Stevens, *Centennial History of Missouri*, vol. 2, 1921, p. 551).

Miles to the east the following night in Cooper County fourteen miles south of Boonville fifteen guerrillas cut the telegraph line and carried away about a mile of it to the woods where they destroyed the wire. These were probably the bushwhackers of Bob Wilson's band of that area who had been active there over the previous days.[55]

Wilcox's 12 August Jefferson City Execution Motivates Shumate to Strike Back

There was a public guerrilla execution in the state capital of Jefferson City on Friday, August 12, because Wiley Shumate's bushwhacker band continued active guerrilla warfare in Cole and Miller Counties during June and July, as described in Chapter Seventeen. Union officials had earlier threatened to execute band member and oath violator John P. Wilcox, captured in April, if Shumate did not cease operations. This threat failed to have the desired effect and northern officials were doubly perturbed that Wilcox escaped from the prison hospital in Jefferson City June 21 and Union troops recaptured him only after an embarrassing and extensive manhunt. Therefore, Union troops conducted the pre-announced public execution that Friday in front of a large crowd. Tragically, the muskets of the twelve shooters misfired on the first attempt, and another firing party had to finish the grisly job. This act convinced Wilcox's chief, Shumate, to intensify his guerrilla war against the Yanks in more dramatic fashion than ever over the coming weeks.[56]

Also on Friday, August 12, miles to the west a corporal's forage-gathering detail of eleven troopers of 7th Cavalry MSM near Holden in west-central Johnson County engaged Lindsay Hutchinson's bushwhacker band of eight in a "lively skirmish." The cavalry suffered no casualties, but it is not known if the guerrillas had anyone hurt. The Federals captured five Rebel firearms when the shooting ended.[57]

Just a few miles to the north on Saturday, August 13, unidentified guerrillas robbed the Warrensburg to Lexington stagecoach at "the Mounds" near present-day Mayview in central Lafayette County. As in the case of the stage robbery August 8 the Union military district headquarters sent an officer to the neighborhood of the robbery to collect damages from southern sympathizers. A Union military report of August 29 stated that notorious guerrilla Dave Poole from the neighborhood near present-day Mayview "boasted that he would neither allow the stage nor telegraph to remain in operation on the Lexington and Warrensburg route," so this must have been his work.[58]

Union Patrol Discovers and Kills Convalescing Dick Yager in Northeast Saline County

Also on Saturday Captain William Meredith's patrol of the 1st Cavalry MSM somewhere near New Frankfort, Cambridge, and present-day Gilliam in northeastern Saline County found and killed the badly wounded Dick Yager. Yager was convalescing from the head wound he suffered during the July 20 Arrow Rock raid, and the Yankees did not discover the identity of the bushwhacker they killed until several days later. Unknown persons were tending Yager in an outdoor camp hidden in the brush near where the Ike Flannery family was living as refugees from Jackson County when Meredith's patrol noticed and followed a trail that led to the camp. The patrol captured seven horses and five more horses that George Todd's men left just after the Arrow Rock raid. This may have indicated that guerrillas had been in the area recently to see how Yager was recovering. The troopers also arrested a member of the large Gilliam family of the neighborhood for tending the wounded guerrilla, but Miss Jennie Flannery later gave herself up as the person caring for the bushwhacker in order to free the innocent Mr. Gilliam.[59]

Lazear Releases Captive Saline County Ladies Upon Their Oath

Shortly after Miss Flannery's surrender Lieutenant Colonel Lazear sent several of the jailed young Saline County ladies, including her, by wagon to the Union district headquarters at Warrensburg to await disposition of their cases. Lazear had already released the men held since they had sworn oaths not to oppose the U.S. Government and given bond. These southern women did not have to wait long, since by this time they were cowed by their jail experience—as Lazear hoped they would be—and all but one took the oath and obtained release at Warrensburg. Union officials sent the one young lady who refused to prison where she recanted of her stand, finally took the oath, and was allowed to return home. By these and other forceful steps Lieutenant Colonel Lazear impressed upon the southern citizens in Saline County that they had to at least respect Federal might.[60]

An 1860s image of Charles Yeager's (or Yager's) younger sister Louisa in a mourning dress—likely upon the occasion of his death, 13 August 1864 (private collection, courtesy of Charles Orear).

Few Actions Across West-Central Missouri South of the Missouri River During the Week of August 14–20

The week of August 14 through 20 was surprisingly light in number or intensity of skirmishes across west-central Missouri. Little took place in Jackson or Cass Counties, although some guerrilla acts occurred in Lafayette and Johnson Counties. Lindsay Hutchinson's band continued to make trouble in south Johnson County, and Bob Wilson's band committed some depredations in the Morgan County area, but Saline County was quiet for a change most of this week.

Guerrillas Attack Civilian Wood Cutters Near Lexington

At some time this week about eight to ten unidentified bushwhackers attacked and robbed several local residents cutting timber along the Missouri River bank a short distance west of Lexington in north-central Lafayette County. The mounted raiders knocked a few of the citizens down, robbed some of them, and shot Daniel Williamson of Lexington to death. It is difficult to determine what the guerrillas wanted from these woodcutters, unless perhaps these noncombatants had accidentally come too close to the bushwhackers' hideout, and the Rebels wanted to intimidate the people so they would leave.[61]

Hutchinson's Band Active in West Johnson County Area During 15–17 August

There was a spate of guerrilla action in the Johnson County area starting on Monday, 15 August. On that day it was probably Hutchinson's small guerrilla band that cut the telegraph line about one mile east of Big Creek near along the main road between Pleasant Hill and Holden at about the Cass and Johnson County line. The bushwhackers then carried away 60 yards of the wire to make it harder for the repairmen to mend the break.[62] Also on August 15 part of a patrol of 4th Cavalry MSM from their Chapel Hill station in northwest Johnson County followed a trail on foot half a mile into the brush. The six troopers suddenly came face to face with six guerrillas and started shooting while the southerners started running. The cavalrymen reported that they wounded two of the bushwhackers and captured four horses at no loss to themselves. The patrol's local commander, Major George W. Kelly, reported that he learned of several small groups of guerrillas in that area.[63] Second Lieutenant Daniel V. Marr with a patrol of thirty troopers of the 7th Cavalry MSM looking for Hutchinson's guerrilla band in south-central Johnson County and north-central Henry County found three of them on Tuesday, August 16. The trio was staying in some huts along Honey Creek and the troopers saw the bushwhackers run out as they approached. The cavalrymen did not have time to shoot before the Rebels disappeared into the brush, and failed to find them during a search afterward.[64] On Wednesday, August 17 fifteen guerrillas robbed and burned the eastbound stagecoach and cut the telegraph line again at the Big Creek bridge near present-day Strasburg in east-central Cass County near the site where the same men evidently cut the telegraph line August 15. These actions seemed to be deliberate provocations by small bands of guerrillas, perhaps intended to distract Union attention away from the presence of Confederate Lieutenant Colonel John "Coon" Thornton and hundreds of his former uprising members then hiding in the Lafayette County area to the north.[65]

Private War in Morgan County Between Wilson's Guerrillas and Northerners

A war erupted inside of a war in northeast Morgan County during this week of August, and may have passed without written record had not a Union officer mentioned it to an area newspaper the following month. The informant was Lieutenant William Argo of the 7th Cavalry MSM, who in his capacity as provost marshal conducted interviews among northern sympathizers in that neighborhood to discover what happened. What attracted Lieutenant Argo to northeast Morgan County was the guerrilla arson of the home of the widow of the late Lieutenant Charles Newkirk of the local 43rd EMM on Wednesday, August 17 and the revenge burning of the home of bushwhacker John Beanland on Saturday, August 20. The lieutenant concluded that the Bob Wilson band was led by John Beanland; that the guerrillas camped in woods somewhere in the headwaters of the Moreau River in east Morgan County; and that southern families such as Bob Wilson's and that of Patrick Mullins who the Federals executed in April

1864 assisted these bushwhackers. Argo maintained that the guerrillas robbed "nearly every Union family within twelve miles" of the Wilsons and Mullins of amounts "varying from $1,700 down." Band members may have also burned homes of other northerners. Argo further stated that gang members stole prize horses from at least two farms in the region and robbed travelers along the roads of north Morgan County, even in the outskirts of the county seat of Versailles on August 6. The lieutenant was not sure, but it appeared that the band included two black men who committed holdups at gunpoint on the roads of the area, although these two may have been lawless renegades and not associated with the bushwhackers. Other sources fail to corroborate some of Lieutenant Argo's findings which include innuendo and rumor common to Union provost marshal investigations, and he maintained that guerrilla John Beanland's name was "Greenland." In general, though, Lieutenant Argo's information offers a rare glimpse into one neighborhood's local civil war within a war. This outbreak could also account for Bob Wilson's band's inactivity for a while.[66]

There were two skirmishes in north Lafayette County on Friday, August 19 and Saturday August 20 involving details or patrols of the 1st Cavalry MSM. On August 19 a detail of this regiment led by First Lieutenant Benton Miller on their way back to Saline County from Lexington ran onto nine guerrillas near Lexington. There is no record of Union losses but the Union military account states that Miller's detail mortally wounded one bushwhacker, wounded a second less seriously, and captured four horses.[67] On the following day near Dover in northeast Lafayette County Lieutenant Colonel Lazear himself led a detachment of the 1st Cavalry MSM that rode onto about 40 to 60 guerrillas in the evening twice, killing three Rebels and capturing four horses. Lazear's men recovered a small Rebel flag that was dropped on the ground. West-central Missouri guerrillas did not commonly display Confederate flags, so perhaps these southerners were some of Lieutenant Colonel Thornton's refugees from north of the Missouri River, since Thornton recruited as a component of the Confederate service.[68]

Tricking and Executing Citizen Flanagan in Saline County

During the evening of August 20 Union soldiers, perhaps of the 1st Cavalry MSM, masqueraded as bushwhackers to wagon maker Charles Flanagan a few miles east of Marshall to see if he would report them to northern authorities, as his earlier oath required. The poor wagon maker gave them one pair of wool socks, he recommended a good hiding place, and when the fake guerrillas commented on the oath he took requiring him to report them, Flanagan assured them he would not do that. When he failed to show at Marshall the following day, Federals arrested and jailed him at the county seat. Union forces there executed Flanagan on August 24, as part of Lieutenant Colonel Lazear's "rough handling" campaign in Saline County.[69]

Increased Violence Across West-Central Missouri South of the Missouri River During the Week of August 21–27

In contrast to the previous week, the Union's District of Central Missouri exploded into violent guerrilla action during the week of August 21–27. As another part of the contrast with the previous week, actions during this fourth week of August took place more in the west along the Kansas border counties of Jackson, Cass, Lafayette, and Johnson while the counties to the east were noticeably quiet. Lieutenant Colonel Lazear's "rough handling" campaign in the Saline County area since August 6 was mostly the cause for the peace here. Apparently, the increased tempo of fighting to the west was the result of demonstrations by the George Todd band to draw Yankee attention away from Lieutenant Colonel Thornton's refugees in Jackson and Lafayette Counties then starting on their long trek south to join the rest of the southern army in north Arkansas.

Sabbath day on August 21 was a day of peace in more ways than one, since apparently no guerrilla violence took place in the entire district. This made the large number of bushwhacker actions the rest of the week even more glaring in contrast. It was almost like the guerrillas enjoyed their Sunday to steel themselves for serious work coming on the following days.

Welch's Small Patrol Reconnoiters Cooper and Moniteau Counties for Todd

About this time George Todd assembled a patrol of his own to explore unfamiliar Cooper and Moniteau Counties for a raid he would conduct in the closing days of August. Todd's Arrow Rock raid of July 20 in that direction had been successful—except for the serious wounding of the versatile Dick Yager. Perhaps, now he wanted another lightning raid just like it. In his postwar memoir Warren Welch described how Todd tasked him to lead this reconnaissance patrol to identify local bushwhackers and southern sympathizers in those two counties that could assist Todd's band when they rode through that region a few days later. Todd offered Welch the pick of the band to take along, but Welch limited his scout team to ten men. Warren Welch's small patrol all wore Union uniforms pretending to be part of the First Cavalry MSM so as to avoid undue attention. They relied on stealth to cross first Lafayette County and Saline County and traveled by night until they reached Cooper County. Welch and his men kept their role to reconnaissance and avoided contact with Union troops, for the surviving record mentions no commotion along their route. Welch wrote about the conversation his team had with two Union soldiers near Boonville, in which the guerrillas' disguise as Federals worked, and the bushwhackers allowed the two clueless soldiers to go on their way. Welch wrote that the return trip was dramatic, as unidentified Union troops pursued them probably across Saline and Lafayette Counties and the guerrillas dared not stop to eat or sleep for four days.[70]

The Union military took the offensive during actions on Tuesday, August 22, as they had in a few skirmishes the preceding week. One patrol of the 1st Cavalry MSM led by Lieutenant Colonel Lazear himself on Davis Creek in central Lafayette County blasted three bushwhackers from their saddles, perhaps with carbine fire, and captured their horses. A pleased Major General Pleasonton, the district commander, presumed that the three guerrillas were "supposed to be mortally wounded."

Federals Try to Eradicate Guerrilla Dave Poole in His Own Neighborhood

Actually, Lazear's force of the 1st Cavalry MSM split into four parts to search the thickets and woods of Davis, Cottonwood, and Tabo Creeks across central Lafayette County in a broad sweep for bushwhackers. The different columns on several occasions saw small parties of Rebels fleeing on horseback, but had difficulty hitting them with long distance fire and also failed to run them down because of the guerrillas' superior horses. Another column on Tabo Creek hit and severely wounded one southerner and captured six horses. General Pleasonton was hoping the Tabo Creek action would stop the bragging of local bushwhacker Francis Marion "Dave" Poole whose family home was on the Tabo. Lazear borrowed some of his Saline County tactics by ordering the arrest of Poole's friends along Tabo Creek, since he failed to capture Poole.[71]

Union Arrest of Several Southern Families in West Johnson County for Aiding Guerrillas

Captain Melville U. Foster's Company G of the 7th Cavalry MSM from their garrison at Holden borrowed one of Lazear's tactics on August 22 and 24 by arresting several families of known southern sympathy from the neighborhood where guerrillas robbed the stagecoach and twice cut the telegraph line in west-central Johnson County during the previous few days. The Federals first took the families to Holden and then escorted them to their district headquarters at Warrensburg for safekeeping when credible sources reported large numbers of Rebels near Holden. Those families were the Benjamin Durritt and Francis Cowarden families of the Holden area and the Stoner family from Jackson County. The Stoners probably settled in this neighborhood after being ejected from their home county by the notorious General Orders Number Eleven the preceding autumn. These families were now for all practical purposes hostages against future depredations by bushwhackers in the Holden area.[72]

Continuing Prison Adventures of Annie Fickel of Lafayette County

Also on Tuesday, August 22, a military tribunal in St. Louis increased an earlier tribunal sentence of Annie Fickel of Greenton, west-central Lafayette County, to several more years in prison. Miss Fickel had been originally sentenced to three years imprisonment in early July 1864 at Warrensburg for her part in the attempted 22 February 1864 breakout of a guerrilla from the Lexington jail. Her sentence may have been lighter, except a Union soldier died in the escape attempt in which she was a conspirator, as described in Chapter Four. To serve her sentence, Federals sent Miss Fickel eventually to Myrtle Street Prison in St. Louis to cook for the prisoners, where, unfortunately for her, several fellow prisoners conspired to help break out the very attractive Miss Fickel, as described in Chapter Twelve. These male prisoners evidently felt jailing this particular woman was a crime against humanity. Therefore, the latest Federal tribunal on August 22 ruled that 24-year-old Annie Fickel was even in prison continuing to resist and challenge United States authority and changed her sentence from three to ten years to be served at the state penitentiary in Jefferson City. Word of Miss Fickel's latest misfortune undoubtedly caused sadness and consternation among southerners of Lafayette County. As described in Chapter Twelve, President Lincoln would the following year intervene in this case and order Miss Fickel freed based on the amount of time she already served.[73]

Resolving Critical Percussion Cap Shortage in Todd's Band

Perhaps George Todd's large guerrilla force in this area was constricted from carrying out offensive tactics because of a logistics shortage, as indicated in a bushwhacker memoir written after the war. In his postwar memoir Todd member John McCorkle wrote that he and two comrades on August 23 encountered Federal troops while attempting to reach his uncle John Wigginton's house and obtain there and return to base with a large supply of revolver percussion caps that cousin Mollie Wigginton had traveled to Illinois to purchase for the bushwhackers. McCorkle specified that Miss Wigginton brought back 35,000 of the caps in a false bottom of her trunk. The members of the Federal patrol that chased McCorkle and his comrades away returned to the house and shot to death elderly John Wigginton for aiding guerrillas, but did not find the percussion caps which the bushwhackers later returned and took. Perhaps Todd and his men gave much of their own supply of revolver caps to Lieutenant Colonel Thornton's refugee Confederates just prior to their departure, leaving an inadequate supply for Todd's men to use for offensive operations during those few days in August. A shortage of this same item stymied William Quantrill's operations here for three or four weeks during May 1862, forcing Quantrill and his lieutenant George Todd travel to Illinois under disguise in order to purchase the caps. Possibly, this same shortage was responsible for the noticeable absence of offensive bushwhacker actions during August 1864. McCorkle did not specify where in Lafayette County Mr. Wigginton lived during August 1864, but possibly these three guerrillas rode into a part of Lieutenant Colonel Lazear's four-pronged search and kill operation that persisted in this county between August 22 and August 30.[74]

The shooter of most Civil War–period firearms had to fit a small, round percussion cap on the nipple behind the bullet and powder charge that set off the gunpowder and actually fired the bullet down the barrel (Schuyler, Hartley, and Graham, *Illustrated Catalogue of Arms and Military Goods,* 1864, p. 137 [close-up of cylinder and percussion cap nipples of Model 1851 Colt's Revolver]).

Probable Movement South of Thornton's Survivors Group Through Johnson County

Also on Tuesday, August 23, the same Captain Foster that arrested the southern families and brought them to his Holden garrison in west-central Johnson County the day before, sent a startling report. He wrote "Quantrill and Yeager, with about 200 men, are in the vicinity of Walnut Creek, twelve miles west of this place, and that they will attack us to-night to release a lot of prisoners we have." Of course, Quantrill and Dick Yager were in no position to attack anybody in this region, as narrated earlier, but Foster may have been correct that 200 Rebels were at Walnut Creek in the southwest corner of Johnson County near Rose Hill. Possibly, this large body of southerners contained some of Lieutenant Colonel Thornton's men from north of the Missouri River who sought refuge a few weeks before with George Todd's guerrilla band in Lafayette County. If this is true, these Confederates were possibly setting out on their long trek to join other regular Confederate forces miles to the south in Arkansas.[75]

Poole's 23 August Revenge Raid on German Area of Southeast Lafayette County

Also on August 23 guerrilla Dave Poole with as many as 40 comrades raided the German-American community in Freedom Township of southeast Lafayette County near present-day Concordia—probably in revenge for the recent Union attack on Poole's neighborhood on Tabo Creek. Poole raided this Teutonic enclave several times during the war, and it seemed to be his favorite target, probably because it was just a few miles from his Tabo Creek home and because many of the men were members of the Union 71st EMM. Poole and his men rode up to C. Heinrich Ehlers, a captain in the 71st, at his hemp rope factory and mortally wounded the man. The bushwhackers also killed a thirteen-year-old boy at home and Friedrich Ehlers and William Kuecker. John McCorkle confided in his postwar memoir that he joined Poole on this raid, and that they fooled the locals by wearing Union uniforms and carrying a captured Union flag. In previous raids the locals saw the guerrillas approaching and retreated into a formidable stockade for safety, but the blue uniforms and U.S. flag fooled the residents this time. Later that day fourteen-year-old John Kammeyer, who was herding the family cows near Fuchs Bridge over Davis Creek, met a guerrilla resplendent with two shiny revolvers and riding a beautiful horse. The mounted man asked the boy if any robbing and shooting had occurred in the neighborhood recently, to which the youth replied "that there had been a great deal of it." The guerrilla then asked the teenager if he heard of Dave Poole, to which Kammeyer replied

that Poole "was one of the bad bushwhackers." The Rebel then told John that "you can go home and tell your folks that you have just talked to Dave Poole," and rode off without harming Kammeyer or his cows. Poole's publicity-seeking raises the possibility that Todd sent him on that raid to deliberately draw Yankee attention away from the large body of Rebels riding in southwestern Johnson County at that time. This was about the time Poole bragged that he could prevent stage and telegraph traffic from flowing between Warrensburg and Lexington, so possibly Poole gave Kammeyer that message to pass along to the Federals at this same encounter. Lieutenant Colonel Bazel F. Lazear ordered Poole's family arrested and held as hostages to cool that guerrilla's ardor.[76]

Modern historians of the Concordia area German-American community are puzzled to know why Dave Poole repeatedly targeted their ancestors throughout the war (John N. Edwards, *Noted Guerrillas*, 1877, p. 180; courtesy of the late Bob Younger and Mary Younger and Andy Turner).

Continued Travails of Probable Thornton Survivor Group in Cass County

On the night of Wednesday, August 24–25 Kansas troops stationed along the border near Paola, west of Missouri's Cass County, learned that "a force of about 300 bushwhackers started from the neighborhood of Morristown last night to attack some point south, supposed to be Mound City." No such attack materialized, and probably these were the same Rebels Captain Foster at Holden reported on Tuesday. This Kansas report indicates they passed near Morristown along the South Grand River in west-central Cass County, which is roughly twenty miles west of their location from a day before, assuming this was the same body of southern horsemen. Evidently, this was a group of Thornton's refugees from the uprising north of the Missouri River trying to ride south for Arkansas, because, in spite of this alarming report, this large group attempted no offensive action against Union troops in this area and seemed to be avoiding contact with the bluecoats. This was confirmed by a large patrol of 7th Cavalry

William E. Chester, several years after the war (courtesy of a private collection).

MSM from Warrensburg and Holden scouting along Big Creek and the Johnson and Cass County border beginning August 25. This patrol found the two-day-old trail of about 140 Rebels said to be led by a Captain or Major Palmer, according to what residents told the patrol's chief scout, who passed himself as a guerrilla to obtain this information. The scout, William E. Chester of Knob Noster, also learned that part of this southern body was unarmed but equipped with good horses and provisions, and the riders told locals that "they were aiming to get south." It appears that the earlier group of 300 mounted Rebels was in reality this band of 140 originally from north of the Missouri River, and they were slowly working through southern sympathizers in this region to obtain food and forage, preparatory to launching the long run to Arkansas.[77]

George Todd separated his large guerrilla band into segments and launched an offensive in Jackson, Lafayette, Cass, and Johnson Counties starting Thursday, August 25. A corporal's foot patrol of fourteen troopers of the 2nd Colorado Cavalry at six that morning eight miles east of Pleasant Hill in the northeast corner of Cass County fought 60 guerrillas killing two, wounding several, and injuring several of the bushwhackers' horses for no Union loss. When the Rebels dismounted and came at the Coloradoans from the front and both flanks, the corporal wisely pulled his men back to Pleasant Hill. The guerrillas then broke contact, or this fight may have ended differently. Shortly after this engagement a large patrol of the 7th Cavalry MSM from nearby Holden and Warrensburg moved into this area looking in vain for the sixty guerrillas.[78] A sergeant's patrol from the 4th Cavalry MSM out of their garrison at Chapel Hill had a skirmish with guerrillas that Thursday somewhere in southwest Lafayette County or northwest Johnson County, but no other details survive.[79] Also on Thursday a foot patrol of 1st Cavalry MSM discovered a cavalry horse that Todd's band captured at Arrow Rock July 20 in the brush near Dave Poole's home on Tabo Creek in central Lafayette County. They watched the horse for a time from hiding then shot and killed a guerrilla named Rutherford when he came to feed and water the animal.[80] On Friday, August 26 Captain or Major Palmer's 140 Rebel riders rode south between Pleasant Hill and Harrisonville, leaving behind them the various Union patrols trying to find them.[81] Also on Friday the large patrol of 7th Cavalry MSM searching Walnut Creek in the southwest corner of Johnson County south of Rose Hill chased three guerrillas, probably of Hutchinson's band, out of the brush and may have wounded one of them before they escaped. On Saturday, August 27 this Federal patrol discovered that Palmer and his 140 riders left that area 36 hours before and were too far to the south for them to pursue.[82] That same morning miles to the north near Fire Prairie Creek in northeast Jackson County a sergeant's foot patrol of 2nd Colorado Cavalry fired on three bushwhackers fleeing. Later in the day near Bone Hill the same patrol saw eight guerrillas too far away to waste a shot. These Coloradoans found several bushwhacker campsites that had seen use lately and the tracks and trails used recently by many Rebel horses. The Federals later discovered that George Todd activated his men to ride around throughout the Jackson and Lafayette County area to help cover the tracks of about 150 of Thornton's refugees who crossed to the south side of the Missouri River Wednesday evening August 24 and divert the attention of the many searching Union patrols.[83]

Continued Violence Across West-Central and Central Missouri South of the Missouri River During the Partial Week of August 28–31

The last four days of August 1864 saw widespread guerrilla violence in west-central Missouri south of the Missouri River both in the western counties of Jackson, Johnson, Cass, and Lafayette as well as the counties to the east near the center of the state. George Todd continued his band's active skirmishing and visible movement for a couple more days to draw attention away from parts of Lieutenant Colonel John C. "Coon" Thornton's refugee groups that were finally departing the Lafayette County area and starting out on their long trek south to Arkansas. This activity also served to cover Todd's sudden departure from this area Monday and Tuesday to ride to and raid in Cooper and Moniteau Counties miles to the east for a few days. In Miller County at the heart of Missouri on Tuesday Wiley Shumate's bushwhackers returned to active operations after a break of several weeks with a dramatic attack on local citizen guards. This return to war probably resulted from the Federals' public execution in Jefferson City of fellow band member John Wilcox on August 12, as described earlier. Bob Wilson's Morgan County guerrilla band was still quiet and not actively riding in Morgan, Cooper, and Moniteau Counties probably because they were striving with increasing citizen guardsmen pressure near the homes of their families in Morgan County, as earlier narrated.

More of Thornton's Survivors Move South While Todd's Band Increases Action

George Todd's segmented guerrilla band continued its small unit actions against Union patrols on Sunday 28 August and Monday 29 August. A sergeant's foot patrol of the 2nd Colorado Cavalry near Bone Hill in northeast Jackson County on 29 August learned that George Todd himself with 24 of his riders were there the day before on Sunday. Todd had a conference with other Rebels there, perhaps more of Thornton's refugees from the other side of the Missouri River. Indeed, the Colorado foot patrol saw plenty of tracks in that neighborhood and estimated that 150 riders had been there recently.[84] Also on Sunday a patrol of the 7th Cavalry MSM from Captain Melville Foster's Holden garrison southwest of town encountered a band of about 120 riders who fired into the Federals. The outnumbered patrol wisely retreated, but noted first that a number of the Rebels were unarmed and "many of them appeared to be recruits," so this group was probably another batch of Thornton's refugees on their way south. Indeed, the Union commander at Pleasant Hill, a few miles to the west, reported that his patrols discovered "several trails, all leading south."[85] Another patrol on August 28 of a sergeant and six troopers of the 4th Cavalry MSM from their Chapel Hill garrison somewhere near the intersection of Jackson, Lafayette, and Johnson Counties skirmished with four Rebels and "captured some of their equipment." The patrol reported no casualties on either side from this encounter.[86] That same Sunday two patrols of the 7th Cavalry MSM from Holden and Warrensburg sweeping through creek bottoms in east Cass County and west Johnson County near Crisp's Mill, six miles from Rose Hill, encountered two groups of Rebels of between seven to ten riders. The Federals chased the southerners, wounding one or two and capturing a few horses. That evening one of those same Union patrols rode into 15 guerrillas about six miles south of Chapel Hill and chased them three miles, capturing one horse. These same two patrols of 7th Cavalry MSM skirmished with small groups of bushwhackers in this same "Basin Knob country" between Rose Hill and Chapel Hill on Monday, August 29 and wounded two Rebels and captured several horses and firearms.[87] It appears that a second and perhaps a third group of Thornton's refugees moved through west Johnson County and Cass County on August 28 and 29, and that some Union patrols encountered parts of them. Possibly, Todd's and other guerrillas conducted limited operations in the area to draw Federal attention away from these travelers, and may have even escorted them for part of their journey. Union sources reported another large group of Rebels concentrated on Sni-A-Bar Creek in northeast Jackson County on 30 August and rode off to the southwest, but Federal troops could not locate them. This was probably another traveling group of Thornton's refugees heading for Arkansas.[88]

Todd's Band Rides East to Raid Cooper and Moniteau Counties

It appears that George Todd set these actions in motion before he left late Sunday, August 28 or Monday with about forty of his men and Dave Poole and his thirty guerrillas on a long distance raid to Cooper and Moniteau Counties at the center of the state. According to Warren Welch's memoir, Todd greeted Welch's weary reconnaissance patrol as it returned from that area Sunday, August 28. Welch reported on the results of his patrol including the mention that he lost one man to enemy action August 24 probably on the way back. After his report, Welch's exhausted patrol members spurned food to sleep for some hours, and then quickly ate and accompanied Todd on the raid. George Todd left about half of his band in the Jackson and Lafayette County area during this operation, perhaps to ensure that the refugees from north of the Missouri River got off to a good start in his absence.[89]

Shumate Avenges Wilcox Against Starling's Patrol on Curtman Island 30 August

On Tuesday, August 30 miles to the southeast in Miller County Wiley Shumate's local guerrilla band exacted vengeance for the Yankee's August 12 Jefferson City execution of band member John Wilcox. Union Lieutenant John P. Starling's patrol of local citizen guards from Mount Pleasant in northwest Miller County rode about twenty miles to the northeast corner of the county looking for Shumate's bushwhackers in the area where the band was known to gather. The fifteen to twenty guardsmen searched for a while along creek bottoms and thickets in this rough hilly country and then broke for lunch on Curtman's Island in the Osage River near the mouth of Big Tavern Creek. Shumate's men had been watching the progress of the neophyte citizen guards, who had only been on active duty for a week, and struck when they observed the guardsmen stack their shoulder arms and began eating their lunch without posting proper guards. Shumate captured the entire patrol and released some men, but not members of the local Union League they accused of depredations against southerners in the area. Some of the League men served earlier in the war in the local 42nd EMM. The bushwhackers executed these seven remaining men including the lieutenant and rode away to the north. The surviving members of the patrol traveled the several hours to their Mount Pleasant area homes where they told of their misfortune. Miller Countians collected six of the bodies and took them home for burial, but missed the remains of one guardsman. This mortally wounded man crawled away after the Rebels left and died among some boulders on a nearby hillside, where locals found his remains days or weeks later. Later on this same Tuesday Shumate's band raided a store in Brazito in central Cole County, where they killed the father-in-law of the owner and one of the employees, then took some of the goods. Shumate's guerrilla band thus firmly asserted that they were re-commencing hostilities in this area.[90]

Locals Shoot Up Two of Todd's Foragers in Cooper County

Also on Tuesday, George Todd's raiding party of 40 of his own band and Dave Poole's command of 30 bushwhackers reached central Cooper County near present day Bunceton in Kelly Township at the end of their long ride from Lafayette County. They sent several men out to gather food and forage and Union citizen guards shot up one group, mortally wounding Riley Crawford of Poole's band and wounding Bill Greenwood in the leg. Crawford was a favorite of the guerrillas, as he was only 16, had a good attitude, and endured all trials and tribulations alongside his older comrades. After Federals of Colonel William Penick's hated 5th Cavalry MSM (old) murdered Riley's dad Jeptha Crawford in January 1863, his distraught mother took him to Quantrill and specifically asked that he make a guerrilla out of the boy so he could avenge his father's killing. Watching the boy slowly die from a wound in his bowels gave the guerrillas a strong desire to retaliate against those guilty of shooting the youth.[91]

Bill Anderson's Men Cross Missouri River to Raid in Northeast Cooper County

A few miles to the north on Tuesday evening, August 30 in Rocheport, Bill Anderson and a portion of his bushwhacker band captured the steam tug *Buffington*, as related in Chapter Fifteen. Anderson permitted a few of his more adventurous men to force the vessel's crew to take them across the Missouri River and wait a few hours on the south bank while they raided for horses in Cooper County, as described in the St. Louis *Daily Missouri Democrat*. Another issue of that same newspaper described how these killers employed torture and murder to take what they wanted during their several hour spree in northeast Cooper County. Ironically, this took place while George Todd and about half of his band were also raiding in Cooper County, but they were not known to torture unarmed civilians as were some of Bill Anderson's men. Evidently, these few raiders did manage to steal a few horses, but also took time for mayhem. This took place seven or eight miles southeast of Boonville along the Petit Saline Creek where the bushwhackers pulled out Christian Krohn's toenails with plyers, then cut off his fingers, before they hanged him almost to death to get him to talk—all in front of his little family. When Krohn did not or could not reveal a hiding place, the robbers shot him to death and set fire to his house. Krohn's stricken widow, holding their ten-month-old baby, told her husband's murderers what she thought of them, which shamed one or two of them into putting out the fire before they left. Sometime in the early hours of August 31 Anderson's men made it back to the *Buffington* with their booty and returned aboard the steam tug that took them back across the Missouri River to Rocheport.[92]

Todd's Band Raids Pilot Grove on 31 August

Back in central Cooper County on Wednesday August 31, Todd's and Poole's bushwhackers put into action a plan they devised to avenge the shooting of their two comrades the day before. Cooper County had a large southern population, but Warren Welch's advance scouts probably told the leaders that Pilot Grove in west-central Cooper County was an enclave of German-Americans with strong Yankee sympathy. The band rode in and surrounded the village while a revival was underway at the Mount Vernon Methodist Church. The bushwhackers happily took horses tied outside the church and helped themselves to the lunch prepared for the church attendees, while the leaders talked with Thomas Cooper and Robert Magruder, known locally for their southern sympathy, perhaps to discover who were the prominent Yankee supporters of the community. The guerrillas then abducted Otho Zeller and Peter Mitzell and took them with them. Both Zeller and Mitzell were German-American farmers in their middle fifties known to have large families and to have moved to Cooper County from eastern states just a few years before the war. Soon after this the raiders killed the pair and left their bodies at Lone Elm Prairie in the center of the county. A few days later locals recalled that Cooper and Magruder talked to the murderous bushwhackers and they would face a retribution of their own in a few weeks.[93]

Todd may have directed citizens to give false reports about his band to Union officials while he was on this raid; because about noon on August 31 obliging witnesses gave local Yankee officials two separate fake reports stating that Todd with 200 riders were either between Dover and Waverly in northeast Lafayette County or in southeast Saline County this day. No other guerrilla bands could muster that many riders in those locations at this time except George Todd.[94]

Todd's Band Probably Besieges Tavern Near Prairie Home in East Cooper County

One of the detailed stories of this period of the war in Cooper County may have taken place this night between Todd's guerrillas and local citizen guards. After killing Zeller and Mitzell, Todd's raiders spent the night of August 31 and September 1 in east-central Cooper County in the area of Lone Elm Prairie and Prairie Home, because they intended to raid in Moniteau County to the east the following day. The folklore of this time of the war states that a few Union citizen guards were spending the night at Dr. Hyram A. Tompkins' inn a short distance west of Prairie Home when guerrillas rode up to the place. During the fire fight that followed all the citizen guards managed to escape into the night except for their leader, a "Captain Boswell," who died of gunshots. The 1860 and 1870 census reports shows three different Boswell men who lived in east Cooper County at this time, but did not live there as of 1870. However, the surviving record fails to state which of these men died at Tompkins' inn that night.[95]

This sudden increase in guerrilla violence ushered in the month of September 1864. Those bushwhacker leaders who attended one of the two councils of war designed and held for them by Confederate staff officers in Lafayette and Monroe Counties knew that later in September Major General Sterling "Old Pap" Price would be bringing his army back into Missouri after a two-and-a-half year absence. These guerrilla chiefs relished their roles to assist their liberators, and struck out at the Yankees with new ferocity.

Afterword

Throughout the long winter of 1863 and 1864, guerrillas left a few members in several parts of Missouri to both bolster the hopes of southern Missourians and also to watch over convalescing comrades recovering from wounds. In southeast Missouri such partisan leaders as Confederate Colonels Thomas R. Freeman and Timothy Reeves, and bushwhacker chiefs such as Frank Smith, Sam Hildebrand, Nathan and John Bolin, and Vernon Campbell, and several others offered continuous defiance against a determined but reduced Union troop presence in occasional combat. Leaders of the few remaining guerrillas in northeast Missouri included Clifton Holtzclaw and John Drury Pulliam, but they kept a low profile and avoided contact with Union soldiers. In northwest Missouri most of the left-behind partisans consisted of Andy Blunt's small group from Quantrill's band and several returned Confederate cavalry troopers from Brigadier General Jo Shelby's command, although many of the Shelby cavalrymen returned to their units in Arkansas once they felt assured their families were safe. Union Major General William S. Rosecrans replaced Schofield as the Federal commander in Missouri, and after Provisional Governor Hamilton Gamble died on January 31, Willard Hall took over the governor's job, and both General Rosecrans and Governor Hall tried to bring new solutions to fight Missouri's guerrilla war in 1864.

Some developments in the spring of 1864 deceived General Rosecrans and his subordinate leaders into believing they could handle whatever the Confederacy threw at them with the number of troops they had. Rosecrans inherited the impressive 2nd Colorado Cavalry Regiment that arrived in Quantrill country of west-central Missouri this winter full of pioneer bravado, but limited by troublesome firearms. Spring came late this year, so some guerrilla groups returning to Missouri from wintering in the South delayed their trip a few days or weeks from April to May until the grass was high enough for their horses to eat, and perhaps raising false hopes with overconfident Union leaders. Also, persistent Union patrolling by veteran troops did manage to defeat some of the stay-behind guerrillas this winter and early spring. For example, Yankee cavalry in Quantrill country of Jackson and Lafayette Counties over time killed a number of guerrillas who remained to keep southern hopes alive and watch over comrades convalescing from wounds with southern friends. On March 7 a patrol even killed their chief, Andy Blunt, whom Quantrill placed in command until his return. After this, a number of Blunt's surviving men retreated two counties south to Henry and Benton Counties to improve their survival rate. Further, Union troops in southeast Missouri's "Bootheel" captured the aggressive guerrilla chief John Bolin on February 2, although a mob in Cape Girardeau a few nights later lynched him. General Rosecrans had a reputation for original thought and useful innovations, and he encouraged Brigadier General Edwin B. Brown of the central district to develop new ways to confront the guerrilla problem.

One of their ideas was to put the troopers on foot patrols to catch careless guerrillas in the countryside. Foot patrols had initial success in the winter when only small numbers of guerrillas remained. Unfortunately, foot patrols could become dangerous when footsore Yankees faced overwhelming numbers of mounted guerrillas without the horses to enable them to flee. One of Rosecrans innovations that had lasting value was his creation of a vast system of local citizen guards to defend themselves and especially the towns, freeing other Union soldiers to get into the countryside and engage in mobile warfare against the guerrillas. Rosecrans had no trouble selling the citizen guards system as a means to ease transition from martial law back to civil law in Missouri, too. Minor Union successes, a new commander with new ideas, and an illusion created by a late spring combined to encourage the Union command that they could handle things in Missouri when the rest of the guerrillas returned.

Meanwhile, some developments gave Missouri southerners hope that they could achieve victories in 1864 that would eject the Yankee troops from their state. Former Missouri governor, Major General Sterling Price, took command of the Confederate troops in Arkansas and began planning to take his army to Missouri later in the year. Also, Federal reverses in Louisiana and Arkansas this spring compelled Yankees in Arkansas to abandon isolated posts and concentrate their forces, which allowed hundreds of Confederate recruiters and bushwhackers to ride mostly unopposed through northeast Arkansas and southeast Missouri to their home areas. The Union side in Missouri in the spring of 1864 had fewer troops than before since the peaceful winter convinced Federal leaders to send troops from Missouri to meet needs in other war theaters. General Rosecrans hoped his new citizen guards program would help fill the gaps. So, scores of irregular fighters infiltrated all the way to northeast Missouri and a number of guerrillas also crossed the Mississippi River back to northeast Missouri from where they had been hiding with southern sympathizers in Illinois all winter. The Union District of North Missouri commander, Brigadier General Clinton B. Fisk, wondered if he could muster enough full-time soldiers, militia, and citizen guards to counter the threat with all the groups of traveling Rebels riding into his district. Missouri Confederate troops left their units with and without permission to return home and conduct irregular war to finally drive the Yankees away. As a result, numerous local guerrilla bands popped up in numbers not seen since 1862, so many by summer that in some places bushwhackers operated with little interference from Union troops.

Also this spring, other groups of traveling Rebels—namely, William Quantrill's, Confederate Colonel Caleb Dorsey's recruiting team, Bill Anderson's, and several southwest Missouri bushwhacker bands—rode back through Missouri's mostly depopulated southwest quadrant, evading most of the Union patrols. As guerrilla sub-chiefs Bill Anderson and George Todd arrived in west-central Missouri by late May 1864 they confronted and forcefully deposed William Quantrill as their chief because of his periods of inactivity the previous summer and differences that came to the forefront in Texas during the winter. Quantrill did not resist, but moved to exile in Howard County with a small bodyguard of devoted followers where he remained until autumn, although neither Union nor Confederate commands heard of this development. Throughout the spring some southern recruiters and bushwhackers increased the tempo of combat, encouraged by the strong rumors that General Price was preparing to lead an army to throw the Yankee soldiers out of the state later this year. The Rebel recruiting team of Colonel John Winston and Lieutenant Colonel John C. Thornton quietly gathered scores of southern men in the Platte County area north of the Missouri River since the winter. Even after Union troops captured Colonel Winston at his Platte County home on March 21, Thornton confidently continued to bring men into his recruiting command, even a large number of local Union militia.

The bushwhackers made their own innovations in irregular fighting this summer. Bill Anderson and George Todd initiated a mobile form of warfare, in which they left sanctuary areas more often and conducted roaming combat across great distances, enabling them to use mobility and surprise with more effect. Anderson's and Todd's men wore Union uniforms while traveling, fooling passersby and Union troops alike, and they changed to their decorated "guerrilla shirts" and plumed hats whenever they rested in southern neighborhoods. Bushwhacker bands operated in a number of localities at the same time, as southerners increased their efforts in a determined push to overwhelm the Yanks and take an active part in their best chance to help the southern cause succeed in Missouri. This is how by summer 1864 numerous guerrilla bands operated in parts of the state that had not seen this activity for two years, and while northern commanders sent the few available troopers to deal with the higher priority threats, some bushwhackers were free to raid towns and rural stores and steal horses with impunity. In desperation some Union commanders stooped to such extreme means as in Pike County sending in troopers from a passing Kansas cavalry regiment to kill known southern sympathizers off a kill list in order to sway the balance of power back to the northern side.

As northern troops of various kinds experienced exasperation at not being able to bring the elusive Rebel recruiters and guerrillas to decisive combat, some of them turned their frustration into atrocities against southern civilians and captive combatants, which tended to reinforce enemies' belief in their cause and created more hostility against the Federal cause. An extreme case of this criminality took place in late spring when Federal Detective Terman, alias Harry Truman, convinced the Union command in St. Louis that with an escort of Federal troops he could single out and eliminate enough prominent southern sympathizers hiding behind the façade of their age and respectability in their communities to make other southern sympathizers reconsider their support of the Confederacy. The Union command granted Terman the requisite permits, resulting in the murder of two to three dozen prominent, influential older men in Chariton and Howard Counties in late May and early June. An unforeseen result was the "circle of violence" in which one violent act motivates the aggrieved side to reciprocate, and over the next few weeks guerrillas killed a like number of northern sympathizers in this same area, and the cycle continued as Union militia and guardsmen killed even more known or suspected southern men. Similarly, large numbers of furloughed Union infantrymen returned home for long visits in northeast Missouri this summer as a reward for re-enlisting, and a number of them committed violence against southern sympathizers in a misconceived form of community cleansing before they returned to distant war theaters.

Likewise, guerrilla enthusiasm turned to depredations against northerners. Bill Anderson's men in particular increased their killing of defenseless civilians and mutilation of enemy dead. For a while, such bushwhacker savagery was a combat multiplier for the guerrillas in that Union militia and citizen guardsmen were understandably reluctant to face Anderson's ruthless killers in combat. However, after seeing and hearing about comrades and neighbors become victims to such excesses, more and more Yanks turned their fear into loathing and a burning desire to mete out justice. Union District of North Missouri commander Fisk on several occasions this summer and fall and out of desperation to find more troops channeled this desire to selected, cool-headed, battle-experienced staff officers who assembled amalgamated groups of a polyglot of militia and guardsmen into temporary combat forces with sufficient numbers in north Missouri that not only tracked but attacked bushwhacker bands. Two such *ad hoc* groups were able to meet and defeat veteran guerrillas in open combat this summer, particularly against John Thrailkill's band at Union Mills on July 22 and against Bill Anderson August 13 at Wakenda Creek. In both examples, these hurriedly assembled combat groups took casualties but persevered under withering guerrilla fire and drove bushwhackers from the battlefield with losses of their own, having the added advantage that bushwhackers underestimated the resolve of the usually fearful militia and guardsmen.

A seminal feature of this summer's guerrilla fighting revolved around the insurgency staged by Confederate recruiter Lieutenant Colonel John C. Thornton during July that evolved into maneuver combat through at least eight counties of northwest Missouri north of the Missouri River. Thornton's command's persistence over six months accumulated hundreds of recruits, including large numbers of already controversial Union "Paw Paw" militia of the 81st and 82nd Enrolled Missouri Militia—many of whom were deliberately enrolled in 1863 despite their known southern sympathy to counter pesky Kansas jayhawking raids. Union authorities downplayed the import of many of the warnings that such a hidden Rebel recruiting force was at work just north of Kansas City, attributing such reports to hysteria by uninformed pessimists. Thornton's insurrection failed under his mistaken notion that if he led his recruits into combat action against Union troops in this area, Confederate Major General Sterling Price's troops would ride north from Arkansas to assist his force. Nearby guerrilla bands—especially Quantrill's former band commanded by George Todd and a Clay County guerrilla band loaned Thornton guerrilla sub-bands commanded by Confederate Captain John Thrailkill and former Quantrill lieutenant Charles Fletcher "Fletch" Taylor. Those bushwhacker groups served as a security screen to protect the neophyte, mostly unarmed, untrained recruit force from slaughter by Union troops. Union authorities were shocked when Thornton's men on July 7 raided Parkville in southern Platte County, and then raided the county seat of Platte City July 10. The Union command hastily assembled a substantial cavalry task force which attacked Thornton's command while it was celebrating their recent victories at Camden Point in north-central Platte County July 13, killing 15 of his men at little northern loss. Thornton quickly realized that (1) his command could not long defend itself against overwhelming Yankee cavalry if they remained in place, and (2) help from the Rebel army in Arkansas would not come to his aid in time to save his command. Therefore, Lieutenant Colonel Thornton led his mixed force on mobile warfare through eight counties north of the Missouri River, strongly shielded by Taylor's and Thrailkill's guerrilla bands, in a vain attempt to force some kind of development that would help him. General Price had already determined to invade Missouri in September, two months away, so his army could subsist off the field crops ready for harvest at that time. Using aggressive guerrillas as his main combat power, Thornton maintained his mobile warfare until about July 23, when he realized that to persist would result in the probable slaughter of his recruits, and he sent most of them into hiding in Clay and Ray Counties while he took one group from his command across the Missouri River and sent it south to join Rebel forces in Arkansas. Over the next several days Thornton moved the remaining troops of his command in manageable groups at night south of the Missouri River where George Todd's large guerrilla band presumably helped hide and shield them until they were organized to ride for Arkansas. Surprisingly, these various groups of Thornton's surviving recruits, led by veteran Confederate officers and NCO's, avoided disaster by evading Union patrols and successfully reached the southern army in Arkansas. Aiding in their success was the scarcity of Union troops immediately south of the Missouri River since their commanders moved most of them north of the river to attack him, plus increased guerrilla actions underway during July and August across parts of southwest Missouri which diverted Union troops from detecting these furtive southbound groups. Meanwhile, some of Thornton's command broke away in desperate attempts to escape across the prairie into the territories to the west and northwest, but Union troops captured many of these refugees, and subjected the turncoat EMM among them to tribunal and execution for deserting to the enemy during war.

Confederate General Price from Arkansas sent some staff officers traveling behind Union lines to Missouri where they conducted councils of war with Rebel recruiters and guerrilla leaders in early August to clarify what Price expected them to do when his army would later enter the state. These staff officers conducted two simultaneous councils of war in Lafayette County and also in Monroe County in early August evidently directing those guerrilla bands to attack railroad infrastructure to slow Union reinforcements moving against Price's army when it entered the state in the fall.

A Glimpse into the Future of Missouri's Guerrilla War in Autumn 1864 and Beyond

Guerrilla war continued from the summer of 1864 unabated into the fall of 1864 as if to welcome the long-awaited advent of Confederate Major General Sterling Price and his army of about 12,000 that crossed the boundary from Arkansas into Missouri at Ripley County on September 19. The story of Price's great raid as a whole belongs to a history of regular troops of the Confederacy and not guerrillas. However, General Price appealed to the numerous guerrillas in Missouri as fellow southern soldiers and welcomed a number of them into the ranks of his regular units. Indeed, many guerrillas had served earlier in the war in some of those units, and actually fought part of the war as regulars and part as guerrillas. Further, many recruiters General Price sent back into Union-occupied Missouri to recruit throughout the war instead formed or joined bushwhacker bands in their home area because they thought they could achieve more as guerrillas than as regular soldiers, and some men simply found guerrilla fighting more exciting than regular soldiering. Missouri's hopes for southern victory drooped with the defeat of Price's army in western Missouri in October 1864, and the retreat of his beaten force back to Arkansas.

Surprisingly, large numbers of guerrillas believed their own war continued regardless of the victory or defeat of General Price's army, and regardless of their own losses including some of their most talented leaders. Most of the remaining bushwhackers rode to winter in Texas, as they had before, leaving a substantial remainder in northwest, northeast, and southeast Missouri to oversee comrades convalescing from wounds with friendly households, but also to hold the place for the return of the others in the spring of 1865. Unlike previous winters, a number of these left-behind guerrillas continued in active operations against Union troops, which surprised the Union command. Part of that surprise came from how bitter the weather was this winter, as the winter of 1864 and 1865 was particularly snowy and cold—to the extent that creeks and rivers remained ice covered for longer periods of time, and the Mississippi River remained closed to vessels for much of the winter. Some of these aggressive bands included those led by the secretive Jim Ryder and J. Frank Gregg in northwest Missouri; in northeast Missouri Jim Anderson, the Hines brothers, and the murderous Jim Jackson; and in southeast Missouri Sam Hildebrand, Nathan Bolin, and Confederate Colonels Tim Reeves and Thomas R. Freeman. Winter guerrilla fighting was limited by weather considerations and bushwhackers' reliance upon the continued support of southerners in the countryside who shared shelter and subsistence despite a dim outlook for the future of the southern cause. Yankee patrols would occasionally kill one or two bushwhackers, and on rare occasions more than that, and likewise Union forces suffered loss, too.

Therefore, by spring 1865 the stay-behind guerrillas were reduced in numbers, and the cold weather that lingered meant that the bushwhackers returning to Missouri delayed their arrival until April with larger numbers coming back in May. Needs of the Union army to send troops to fight Indians on the plains reduced troop strength in Missouri to much lower numbers than even the spring of 1864. This, along with the end of hostilities on all other battle theaters of the war meant that the Union command needed to contend with how to bring an end to Missouri's guerrilla war, which by bushwhacker aggressiveness evident in May 1865 gave every indication that it would continue well into the summer. The Federals faced the choice of ending the war by exterminating the several hundred remaining guerrillas, which was impossible, or finding a peaceful solution that would please both sides—which seemed inconceivable, too. Wise counsel made the second option viable and peace so long delayed came with surprising rapidity once the wisdom of the terms were evident. Even then, guerrilla fighting continued on well into June, with occasional revenge killings beyond that.

Notes

ONE

1. Broadfoot Publishing Company, *The Supplement to the Official Records-Series 2-Record of Events-Itineraries of Military Units*, Wilmington, North Carolina: Broadfoot Publishing Company, 1995–1998, vol. 74, 2nd Wisconsin Cavalry, 747–8 (hereinafter cited as Broadfoot, *Supplement to the "O.R."* with appropriate volume and page numbers).

2. U. S. Department of War, *The War of the Rebellion: A Compilation of the Official Record of the Union and Confederate Armies*. Washington, D. C.: Government Printing Office, 1880–1901, vol. 34, part 2, 57 (hereinafter cited as *O.R.* The series designation is omitted in most references in this work, since they are from series 1, except where stated otherwise).

3. Joseph H. Crute, Jr., *Units of the Confederate States Army*, Midlothian, Virginia: Derwent Books, 1987, 206; Stewart Sifakis, *Compendium of the Confederate Armies. Kentucky, Maryland, Missouri, The Confederate Units and the Indian Units*, New York: Facts on File, 1995, 105 (hereinafter cited as "Sifakis, *Compendium of the Confederate Armies*, Missouri volume").

4. *O.R.*, vol. 34, part 2, 130; Joanne Chiles Eakin, *Missouri Prisoners of War From Gratiot Street Prison, Alton, Illinois, Including Citizens, Confederates, Bushwhackers, and Guerrillas*, Independence, Missouri: published by author, 1995, Samuel M. Anderson entry (hereafter cited as "Eakin, *Missouri Prisoners of War*" with at least the surname of the prisoner. Eakin's work does not have page numbers).

5. *O.R.*, vol. 34, part 2, 244. (This author's earlier volumes in the *Guerrilla Warfare in Civil War Missouri* Series have information about Colonel Coleman in 1862 and 1863, and the 1863 volume has more about Colonel Freeman.)

6. *O.R.*, vol. 34, part 2, 280–1, 325; "Bushwhackers in Phelps County," *Daily Missouri Democrat*, St. Louis, 15 February 1864; United States Government, *1860 Missouri Census*, household of 47-year-old stone mason R. W. Wade, born in Virginia with children born in Texas, Hawkins Township, south Phelps County.

7. "Missouri Items," *Daily Missouri Democrat*, St. Louis, 11 February 1864, from the *Lebanon Union*, Lebanon, Laclede County, 6 February 1864; Seyffert, Wilhelm and Augustus, Notebook of Activities, Company E, 13th Cavalry Missouri State Militia stationed Waynesville, October 1862 through September 1864, Western Historical Manuscripts Collection, University of Missouri Library, Columbia, Missouri, call number 2888, volume 2.

8. Broadfoot, *Supplement to the O.R.*, part 2, vol. 35, 5th Cavalry MSM, 139; State of Missouri, Secretary of State's Office, Missouri State Archives, military service record of Private F. L. Kelton of Company A, 5th Cavalry MSM.

9. *O.R.*, vol. 34, part 1, 116, part 2, 281.

10. *O.R.*, vol. 34, part 1, 113–5; United States Government, *1860 Missouri Census*, households of 23-year-old Haman Judd and 50-year-old Mark M. Judd, Cipin Township, Howell County.

11. *O.R.*, vol. 34, part 1, 138, part 2, 313, 323, 337–8; Frederick H. Dyer, *A Compendium of the War of the Rebellion*, New York: Thomas Yoseloff, 1959, vol. 2, 809 (hereinafter cited as "Dyer, *Compendium*"); "Banditti in Southwest Missouri," *Daily Missouri Democrat*, St. Louis, 20 February 1864; "Another Mail Robbery," *Missouri Statesman*, Columbia, Boone County, 26 February 1864.

12. "Wagons Robbed," *St. Joseph Weekly Herald*, Buchanan County, 3 March 1864, quoting earlier *Lebanon Union*, Laclede County.

13. *O.R.*, vol. 34, part 2, 326; United States Government, *1860 Missouri Census*, household of 47-year-old Jesse McCarty, Franklin Township, south-central Dent County.

14. *O. R.*, vol. 34, part 2, 397.

15. *O.R.*, vol. 34, part 1, 146; Dyer, *Compendium*, vol. 2, 809.

16. *O.R.*, vol. 34, part 2, 363.

17. Michael Fellman, *Inside War: The Guerrilla Conflict in Missouri During the American Civil War*, New York: Oxford University Press, 1989, 26, 274 (hereinafter cited as "Fellman, *Inside War*").

18. *O.R.*, vol. 34, part 2, 438.

19. *O.R.*, vol. 34, part 1, 116.

20. "A Horrible Affair," *Kansas City Daily Journal*, Jackson County, 12 January 1864; *O.R.*, vol. 34, part 2, 74; State of Missouri, Secretary of State's Office, Missouri State Archives, military service record of Private Daniel Crites of Company G, 56th Enrolled Missouri Militia, who also served during 1863 in the 8th Provisional EMM. (Author's note: The town of Dallas after the war changed its name to Marble Hill.)

21. Dyer, *Compendium*, vol. 2, 809; *O.R.*, vol. 34, part 2, 177 (troop disposition report for this area).

22. *O.R.*, vol. 34, part 1, 124, part 2, 243–4, 248; "From Cape Girardeau," *Daily Missouri Democrat*, St. Louis, 8 February 1864; Dyer, *Compendium*, vol. 2, 809; Larry Wood, *Other Noted Guerrillas of the Civil War in Missouri*, Joplin, Missouri: Hickory Press, 2007, 215.

23. *O.R.*, vol. 34, part 2, 253–4; "From Cape

Girardeau," *Daily Missouri Democrat*, St. Louis, 8 February 1864; Dyer, *Compendium*, vol. 2, 809; "The Guerrilla, Bolin, Hung by Soldiers," *Kansas City Daily Journal*, Jackson County, 13 February 1864; Wood, *Other Noted Guerrillas of the Civil War in Missouri*, 215–7.

24. *O.R.*, vol. 34, part 2, 34; Broadfoot, *Supplement to the O.R.*, part 2, vol. 34, 2nd Cavalry MSM, 671.

25. Broadfoot, *Supplement to the O.R.*, part 2, vol. 34, 2nd Cavalry MSM, 671; "Sam Hildebrand Certainly Dead," *Kansas City Daily Journal*, Jackson County, 15 January 1864.

26. *O.R.*, vol. 34, part 1, 144–5; Broadfoot, *Supplement to the O.R.*, part 2, vol. 34, 2nd Cavalry MSM, 671; Dyer, *Compendium*, vol. 2, 809.

27. Broadfoot, *Supplement to the O.R.*, vol. 34, 2nd Cavalry MSM, 671.

28. James E. Bell, *History of Early Reynolds County, Missouri*, Paducah, Kentucky: Turner Publishing Company, 1986, 67 (for background about Reeves); Kirby Ross, editor, *Autobiography of Samuel S. Hildebrand: The Renowned Missouri Bushwhacker*, Fayetteville, Arkansas: University of Arkansas Press, 2005, 184, 187–8 (for information about Leeper) (hereinafter cited as "Ross, *Autobiography of Samuel S. Hildebrand*).

29. *O.R.*, vol. 34, part 2, 57, 74; (This Tucker does not appear to be Captain William T. Tucker, known for aggressive guerrilla raids in south-central Missouri not far to the west in 1863, but appears to be another known to operate in Wayne County as per *O.R.*, vol. 22, part 2, 676.).

30. *O.R.*, vol. 34, part 2, 181–2; Jerry Ponder, *The Civil War in Ripley County, Missouri*, Doniphan, Missouri: *The Prospect-News*, 1992, 10 (Ponder did not document his sources; so this work will regard his writings as folklore unless corroborated from other sources.); United States Government, *1860 Missouri Census*, household of Joseph Thannisch showing 17-year-old G. B. Thannisch, Current River Township, south-central Ripley County.

31. *O.R.*, vol. 34, part 2, 160; Dyer, *Compendium*, vol. 2, 809.

32. *O.R.*, vol. 34, part 2, 213; Ponder, *The Civil War in Ripley County, Missouri*, 10.

33. *O.R.*, vol. 34, part 2, 254.

34. *O.R.*, vol. 34, part 1, 153.

35. Bruce Nichols, *Guerrilla Warfare in Civil War Missouri, Volume II*, Jefferson, North Carolina: McFarland and Company, 2007 (relates activities like this during 1863 with some Union countermeasures against them).

36. Eakins, *Missouri Prisoners of War*, Miss Lizzie Hardin entry and Mary (Lizzie) Harens entry.

37. Eakins, *Missouri Prisoners of War*, xiv.

38. *O.R.*, series 2, vol. 6, 662–3.

39. *O.R.* series 2, vol. 6, 967–70.

40. Eakins, *Missouri Prisoners of War*, viii.

41. *O.R.*, series 2, vol. 6, 662.

42. *O.R.*, series 2, vol. 6, 980–3.

43. Eakins, *Missouri Prisoners of War*, viii.

44. *O.R.*, series 2, vol. 6, 983, 992.

45. Eakins, *Missouri Prisoners of War*, Everett and Ridgeway entries.

46. Griffin Frost, *Camp and Prison Journal*, Quincy, Illinois: *Quincy Herald* Book and Job Office, 1867; reprinted Iowa City, Iowa: Camp Pope Bookshop, 1994, 103–4 (hereinafter cited as "Frost, *Camp and Prison Journal*").

47. Frost, *Camp and Prison Journal*, 106.

48. *O.R.*, series 2, vol., 6, 858; Dyer, *Compendium*, vol. 3, 1188 (short history of 10th Kansas Infantry Regiment); Broadfoot, *Supplement to the O.R.*, part 2, vol. 21, 10th Kansas Cav, 595, 617.

49. Fellman, *Inside War*, 107, 286; Nichols, *Guerrilla Warfare in Civil War Missouri, Volume II, 1863*, 190 (for circumstances of Captain Thrailkill's capture); Wood, *Other Noted Guerrillas of the Civil War in Missouri*, 168–70; James W. Farley and John W. Farley, *Missouri Rebels Remembered Si Gordon and John Thrailkill*, Independence, Missouri: Two Trails Publishing, 2005, 92.

50. Frost, *Camp and Prison Journal*, 111–12; Bruce Nichols, *Guerrilla Warfare in Civil War Missouri, Volume I, 1862*, Jefferson, 126–7; "Escape of Thirty-Five Prisoners of War at Alton—Col. Magoffin Among Them," *Daily Missouri Democrat*, St. Louis, 28 July 1862.

51. Eakin, *Missouri Prisoners of War*, Crews, Nemier, Rudder, and two Schultz entries.

Two

1. *O.R.*, vol. 34, part 1, 101–2; Dyer, *Compendium*, vol. 2, 809; State of Kansas, *Report of the Adjutant General of the State of Kansas*, 1861–65, vol. 1, Topeka, Kansas: Kansas State Printing Company, 1896, 191 (hereinafter cited as "State of Kansas, *Report of Adjutant General*").

2. *O.R.*, vol. 34, part 2, 299–301; Nichols, *Guerrilla Warfare in Civil War Missouri, Volume II, 1863*, 89.

3. *O.R.*, vol. 34, part 2, 510; United States Government, 1860 *Missouri Census*, Washington, D. C., Government Printing Office, Martha Freeman household, Shoal Creek Township, northwest Newton County; United States Government, *1860 Kansas Census*, Washington, D. C., Government Printing Office, household of William W. Hill, physician, Humboldt Post Office, Allen County.

4. Wiley Britton, *Memoirs of the Rebellion on the Border*, 1863, Chicago: Cushing, Thomas, and Company, 1882, reprinted Florissant, Missouri: Inland Printer Limited, 1986, 453–4; Dyer, *Compendium*, vol. 2, 809.

5. *O.R.*, vol. 34, part 2, 80–1; Broadfoot, *Supplement to the O.R.*, vol. 21, 5th Kansas Cavalry, 272, 274.

6. *O.R.*, vol. 34, part 2, 411–13, and troop disposition report on 202–05.

7. "Recovered," *Howard County Advertiser*, Fayette, 5 February 1864.

8. "Outlaws Punished," *Daily Missouri Democrat*, St. Louis, 9 March 1864; Carolyn Bartels, *The Forgotten Men: Missouri State Guard*, Shawnee Mission, Kansas: Two Trails Publishing Company, 1995, 311 (showing Lafayette Roberts' military record during 1861); Eakin, *Missouri Prisoners of War*, Deardorf entry; State of Missouri, Secretary of State's Office, Missouri State Archives, military service record of Private Reuben S. Deardorff of Company D, 26th Enrolled Missouri Militia; United States Government, 1860 *Missouri Census*, household of John J. Roberts showing 18-year-old "Layfetteh" Roberts, Linn Township, south-central Cedar County;

also David Dearduff household showing 19-year-old farm laborer, Indiana-born Thomas Dearduff.

9. Patrick Brophy, editor, *Found No Bushwhackers: The 1864 Diary of Sgt. James P. Mallery*, Nevada, Missouri: Vernon County Historical Society, 1988, 18 (hereinafter cited as "Brophy, *Found No Bushwhackers*").

THREE

1. "Danger in North Missouri," *Daily Missouri Democrat*, St. Louis, 30 January 1864; State of Missouri, Secretary of State's Office, Missouri State Archives contains the military service records of three Wainscott men from Polk County who served throughout the war in Confederate service.

2. "Theft and Shooting," *Daily Missouri Democrat*, St. Louis, 10 February 1864; "Outrages in Linn County," *Howard County Advertiser*, Fayette, 19 February 1864, quoting earlier *Macon Gazette*, Macon City, Macon County; (No headline), *Missouri Statesman*, Columbia, Boone County, 13 May 1864; United States Government, *1860 Missouri Census*, household of 74-year-old Seth Botts, Sr., born North Carolina, and household of 47-year-old Seth Botts, Jr., born Tennessee, both in Township 58, Range 22, Linn County; household of John L. Anderson, showing 15-year-old laborer Garret Anderson born Ohio in Township 60, Range 21, Linn County; household of William Sidener in Clay Township, Monroe County; State of Missouri, Secretary of State's Office, Missouri State Archives contains the military service records of Private Garrett Anderson in 23rd Missouri Infantry Regiment (USA), discharged on surgeon's certificate after being POW; Bugler Phillip Faust in the 7th Missouri Cavalry Regiment (USA), discharged for disability; Corporal William Sidener in Company F, 62nd Enrolled Missouri Militia (EMM); Private Tarry Harris in the 2nd Provisional EMM Regiment.

3. Dyer, *Compendium*, vol. 2, 809.

4. (No headline), *Missouri Statesman*, Columbia, Boone County, 18 March 1864 (gives depositions of subjects of military tribunal in Macon City); United States Government, 1860 *Missouri Census*, shows no such name as Dabney Santon or anything similar; Nichols, *Guerrilla Warfare in Civil War Missouri, Volume II, 1863*, 233 (for some information about Captain Ingram or Ingraham in this area during September 1863).

5. Larry Wood, *Other Noted Guerrillas of the Civil War in Missouri*, 133–4; Nichols, *Guerrilla Warfare in Civil War Missouri, Volume II, 1863*, 240; Birdsall and Dean, *The History of Linn County, Missouri*, Kansas City: Birdsall and Dean, 1882, 352; Bartels, *The Forgotten Men*, 169; Richard C. Peterson, James E. McGhee, Kip A. Lindbert, Keith I. Daleen, *Sterling Price's Lieutenants: A Guide to the Officers and Organizations of the Missouri State Guard, 1861–1865*, Shawnee Mission, Kansas: Two Trails Publishing, 1995, 118 (hereinafter cited as "Peterson, et al., *Price's Lieutenants*").

6. (No headline), *Missouri Statesman*, Columbia, Boone County, 19 February 1864; "From Pike County," *Missouri Statesman*, Columbia, Boone County, 26 February 1864.

7. "Portrait of the Guerrilla Cobb," *Liberty Tribune*, Clay County, 29 August 1862, quoting earlier *Fulton Telegraph*, Callaway County; National Historical Company, *History of St. Charles, Montgomery, and Warren Counties, Missouri*, St. Louis: Paul V. Cochrane, 1885, 620; Joseph A. Mudd, *With Porter in North Missouri: A Chapter in the History of the War Between the States*, Washington, D. C.: The National Publishing Company, 1909, 202 (hereafter cited as "Mudd, *With Porter in North Missouri*"); Herschel Schooley, *Centennial History of Audrain County*, Mexico, Missouri: Mcintyre Publishing Company, 1937, 78.

8. *O.R.*, vol. 34, part 2, 553–4; United States Government, 1860 *Missouri Census*, household of John Board, Stringfield's Post Office, northeast Callaway County, household of Caleb Berry, Williamsburg Township, east Callaway County.

9. National Historical Company, *History of St. Charles, Montgomery, and Warren Counties, Missouri*, 620; Mudd, *With Porter in North Missouri*, 206.

10. "From Price's Army," *Liberty Tribune*, Clay County, 5 August 1864, from the earlier *Missouri Statesman*, Columbia, Boone County.

FOUR

1. "Worth Remembering," *St. Joseph Weekly Herald*, Buchanan County, 25 February 1864; William M. Paxton, *Annals of Platte County*, Kansas City, Missouri: Hudson-Kimberly Publishing Company, 1897, 356, 358.

2. "Rushville, Mo., Jan. 12th 1864," *St. Joseph Weekly Herald*, Buchanan County, 21 January 1864.

3. Nichols, *Guerrilla Warfare in Civil War Missouri, Volume II, 1863*, 111; "Nebraska City Correspondence," *Daily Missouri Democrat*, St. Louis, 8 April 1863.

4. State of Missouri, *Report of the Committee of the House of Representatives of the Twenty-Second General Assembly of the State of Missouri Appointed to Investigate the Conduct and Management of the Militia*, Jefferson City, Missouri: W. A. Curry, public printer, 1864, 376 (hereinafter cited as "State of Missouri, *Report of Committee of Twenty-Second General Assembly to Investigate the Conduct and Management of the Militia*"); Joanne Chiles Eakin, *A Civil War Guerrilla Goes on Trial: The Case of G. Byron Jones in 1864*, Shawnee Mission, Kansas: Two Trails Publishing, 1997, 9; "A Notorious Guerrilla Caught," *St. Joseph Weekly Herald*, Buchanan County, 4 February 1864.

5. Nichols, *Guerrilla Warfare in Civil War Missouri; Volume II, 1863*, 311–3.

6. Hildegarde Rose Herklotz, "Jayhawkers in Missouri, 1856–1863," *Missouri Historical Review*, 18, no. 1 (October 1923), 99; United States Government, 1860 *Missouri Census*, household of C. A. Perry, age 42, occupation: trader, Weston Township, western Platte County.

7. "Robbery in Holt County," *St. Joseph Weekly Herald*, Buchanan County, 4 February 1864; "A Man Killed and Robbed by Marauders," *Daily Missouri Democrat*, St. Louis, 5 February 1864.

8. "Robbery," *St. Joseph Weekly Herald*, Buchanan County, 25 February 1864, quoting *Grand River News*, Albany, Gentry County, 7 February 1864; United States Government, *1860 Missouri Census*, household of George B. Finley, Atlantus Grocery, northwest Gentry County.

9. (No headline), *Kansas City Daily Journal*, Jackson County, 27 February 1864; "Murder in Holt," *St. Joseph Weekly Herald*, Buchanan County, 3 March 1864; "Murder in Holt," *Missouri Statesman*, Columbia, Boone County, 11 March 1864; United States Government, *1860 Missouri Census*, household of 45-year-old Kentucky-born Lewis Garnet with wife and five children (age 9 and older born in Kentucky, age 8 and younger born in Missouri); State of Missouri, Secretary of State's Office, Missouri State Archives, military service record of Kentucky-born Private Lewis Garnett shows Missouri State Guard service during 1861, service at Elkhorn Tavern in 3rd Missouri Battalion Cavalry in Captain Burns' Company B, and discharge in March 1863 for "overage."

10. Missouri Historical Company, *History of Carroll County, Missouri*, St. Louis: Missouri Historical Company, 1881, 338; S. K. Turner and S. A. Clark, *Twentieth Century History of Carroll County, Missouri*, Indianapolis, B. F. Bowen and Company, 1911, 278.

11. "Another Raid from Kansas," *Howard County Advertiser*, Fayette, 5 February 1864, quoting *Liberty Tribune*, Clay County, 22 January 1864; Herklotz, "Jayhawkers in Missouri, 1856–1863," *Missouri Historical Review*, 99; *O.R.*, vol. 34, part 2, 386; National Historical Company, *History of Clay and Platte Counties, Missouri*, St. Louis: National Historical Company, 1885, 246; Historical Publishing Company, *History of Clay County, Missouri*, Topeka, Kansas: Historical Publishing Company, 1920, 135; State of Missouri, *Report of Committee of Twenty-Second General Assembly to Investigate the Conduct and Management of the Militia*, 389–90.

12. Missouri Historical Company, *History of Carroll County, Missouri*, 338; United States Government, *1860 Missouri Census*, household of 23-year-old Illinois-born Daniel Glover, Morris Township, Carroll County; State of Missouri, Secretary of State's Office, Missouri State Archives, military service record of Private Daniel T. Glover shows him enlisted at Macon County in 1862 in Company G, 2nd Missouri Cavalry Regiment with service until 1865.

13. "Wyandot Alarmed," *Daily Missouri Democrat*, St. Louis, 5 February 1864, quoting *Kansas City Daily Journal*, Jackson County, 27 January 1864.

14. "Fatal Affair," *Liberty Tribune*, Clay County, 19 February 1864, repeated in *Missouri Statesman*, Columbia, Boone County, 11 March 1864; State of Missouri, Secretary of State's Office, Missouri State Archives, military service record of Sergeant James H. Hampton of Company K, 82nd EMM, on active duty between 2 November 1863 and 22 March 1864; United States Government, *1860 Missouri Census*, household of North Carolina-born James Harris in Washington Township, Clay County, showing 20-year-old Harrison Harris and three younger teenage brothers.

15. Joanne Chiles Eakin and Donald R. Hale, *Branded As Rebels*, Independence, Missouri: Wee Print, 1993, 139; United States Government, *1860 Missouri Census*, household of Pennsylvania-born 68-year-old Christopher Faber showing large real and personal property assets; household of Missouri-born 42-year-old John Dawson as the "keeper of Sweet Springs" "renter of farm" with no real property assets only $500 in personal assets along with "ten unoccupied and comfortable dwellings at the Sweet Springs"; both in Salt Pond Township, southwest Saline County.

16. "A Dead Body Found," *Howard County Advertiser*, Fayette, 18 March 1864; "Missouri Items," *Daily Missouri Democrat*, St. Louis, 23 March 1864; United States Government, *1860 Missouri Census*, household of Kentucky-born, 51-year-old, "judge circuit court" George W. Miller in Boonville Township, north-central Cooper County; household of Kentucky-born, 55-year-old, farmer William Miller, Pilot Grove Township, central Cooper County.

17. John N. Edwards, *Noted Guerrillas*, or *the Warfare of the Border*, St. Louis: H. W. Brand and Company, 1877, reprinted Dayton, Ohio: Morningside Books, 1976, 64, 360.

18. Joanne Chiles Eakin, *Warren Welch Remembers: A Civil War Guerrilla From Jackson County, Missouri*, Shawnee Mission, Kansas: Two Trails Genealogy, 1997, 16 (hereinafter cited as "Eakin, *Warren Welch Remembers*").

19. *O.R.*, vol. 34, part 3, 51.

20. Nichols, *Guerrilla Warfare in Civil War Missouri, 1862*, 98–9.

21. Albert Castel, *William Clarke Quantrill: His Life and Times*, New York: Frederick Fell, Incorporated, 1962, 95 (hereinafter cited as "Castel, *Quantrill*"); William E. Gregg manuscript, "A Little Dab of History Without Embellishment," Western Historical Manuscripts Collection, University of Missouri Library, Columbia, Missouri, collection number C375, folder 1, 27 (hereinafter cited as "Gregg manuscript"); John P. Burch, *Charles W. Quantrell: A True History of His Guerrilla Warfare on the Missouri and Kansas Border During the Civil War of 1861 to 1865*, Vega, Texas: published by author, 1923, 92–3, 101–2 (hereinafter cited as "Burch, *Quantrell*").

22. Castel, *Quantrill*, 101.

23. Nichols, *Guerrilla Warfare in Civil War Missouri, Volume II, 1863*, 183, 198.

24. *O.R.*, vol. 34, part 1, 85; part 2, no, 245, 376–7. (Author's note: The author also consulted with Missouri Civil War historian Terry E. Justice by telephone and email in early 2008 regarding Justice's study of Shelby Brigade period documents from the National Archives and Records Administration. These records from the April 1864 Camden Arkansas campaign assert many of Shelby's men were armed with Sharps breechloaders.)

25. Eakin, *Warren Welch Remembers*, 4; Nichols, *Guerrilla Warfare in Civil War Missouri, Volume II, 1863*, 282, 284, 288.

26. State of Missouri, Secretary of State's Office, Missouri State Archives, military service record of Second Lieutenant W. W. Welsh, Company C, 2nd Missouri Cavalry Regiment (CSA), showing notation "Deserter from Aug. 10, 1863."

27. State of Missouri, Secretary of State's Office, Missouri State Archives, military service record of Private Jacob Weddington, Company A, 2nd Missouri Cavalry Regiment (CSA), showing present during January and February 1864; Nichols, *Guerrilla Warfare in Civil War Missouri, Volume II, 1863*, 319.

28. "Danger in North Missouri," *Daily Missouri Democrat*, St. Louis, 30 January 1864.

29. Nichols, *Guerrilla Warfare in Civil War Missouri, Volume II, 1863,* 306, 319–20.
30. Vivian Kirkpatrick McLarty, editor, "The Civil War Letters of Colonel Bazel F. Lazear," *Missouri Historical Review* 44, no. 4 (July 1950): 399.
31. Ibid., 398.
32. *O.R.*, vol. 34, part 1, 85; part 2, 130; (No headline), *Kansas City Daily Journal,* Jackson County, 20 January 1864; Eakin, *Warren Welch Remembers,* 4–5.
33. *O.R.*, vol. 34, part 2, 130, 150–1, 161, 214, 375; "More Outrageous Proceedings," *Missouri Statesman,* Columbia, Boone County, 29 January 1864; Margaret Mendenhall Frazier, editor, *Missouri Ordeal, 1862–1864: Diaries of Willard Hall Mendenhall,* Newhall, California: Carl Boyer III, 1985, 174; United States Government, *1860 Missouri Census,* households of Shother Renick and James F. Musselman in Clay Township, northwest Lafayette County.
34. *O.R.*, vol. 34, part 2, 214.
35. Ibid.
36. *O.R.*, vol. 34, part 2, 255.
37. Eakin, *Warren Welch Remembers,* 5.
38. Ibid.
39. *O.R.*, vol. 34, part 1, 128; part 2, 314; Dyer, *Compendium,* vol. 2, 809; Broadfoot, *Supplement to the O.R.*, part 2, vol. 21, 5th Kansas Cavalry, 274–5.
40. Frazier, *Missouri Ordeal, 1862–1864: Diaries of Willard Hall Mendenhall,* 179; United States Government, *1860 Missouri Census,* two households of James Whites in Clay Township, northwest Lafayette County (Mendenhall's diary mentions that one of the victims of the Jayhawkers was a "Mr. Jas White.").
41. *O.R.*, vol. 34, part 2, 376–7.
42. *O.R.*, vol. 34, part 1, 151; Broadfoot, *Supplement to the O.R*, part 2, vol. 35, 4th Cavalry MSM, 56; Wiley Britton, *The Civil War on the Border,* volume 2 of 2, 363.
43. *O.R.*, vol. 34, part 1, 862; "Conspiracy to Murder in Order to Release a Prisoner," *Lexington Weekly Union,* Lafayette County, 27 February 1864; Dyer, *Compendium,* vol. 2, 809; Frazier, *Missouri Ordeal, 1862–1864: Diaries of Willard Hall Mendenhall,* 180–1; Edwards, *Noted Guerrillas, or the Warfare of the Border,* 360–4; William Young, *Young's History of Lafayette County, MO,* Indianapolis: B. F. Brown and Company, 1910, 135–6; State of Missouri, Secretary of State's Office, Missouri State Archives, military service records of John Kincaid of Company L, and Privates William Sabins and John R. Burns of Company I, all of 5th Provisional EMM.
44. *O.R.*, vol. 34, part I, 862; (No headline), *Kansas City Daily Journal,* Jackson County, 2 March 1864; "Two Returning Soldiers Murdered," (and a second article without headline), *Kansas City Daily Journal,* Jackson County, 3 March 1864, from earlier *Lexington Weekly Union,* Lafayette County; (No headline), *Daily Missouri Democrat,* St. Louis, 9 March 1864, quoting *Kansas City Daily Journal,* Jackson County, 2 March 1864; Frazier, *Missouri Ordeal, 1862–1864: Diaries of Willard Hall Mendenhall,* 181; Edwards, *Noted Guerrillas, or the Warfare of the Border,* 365; Young, *Young's History of Lafayette County, MO,* 134; United States Government, *1860 Missouri Census,* household of 66-year-old Tennessee-born farmer A. G. Young in Lexington Township, Lafayette County; State of Kansas, *Report of the Adjutant General of the State of Kansas, 1861–65,* vol. 1, 171 (entries for both Sanders and Mockbee in Company B, 6th Kansas Cavalry Regiment, showing Mockbee's discharge for disability and notation by Sanders "Killed Feb. 22 '63 [sic] while on furlough, by guerrillas").
45. Dyer, *Compendium,* vol. 2, 809.
46. *O.R.*, vol. 34, part 1, 151; Britton, *The Civil War on the Border,* volume 2 of 2, 263.
47. *O.R.*, vol. 34, part 2, 459–60.

FIVE

1. *O.R.*, vol. 34, part 2, 188; Patricia Faust, editor, *Historical Times Illustrated Encyclopedia of the Civil War,* New York: Harper and Row, 1986, 661; Mark M. Boatner, III, *The Civil War Dictionary, Revised Edition,* New York: David McKay Company, Incorporated, 1988, 726–7.
2. *O.R.*, vol. 34, part 2, 188; Faust, *Historical Times Illustrated Encyclopedia of the Civil War,* 642–3; Boatner, *The Civil War Dictionary, Revised Edition,* 708; Ezra J. Warner, *Generals in Blue: Lives of the Union Commanders,* Baton Rouge: Louisiana State University, 1964, 410–1; Richard S. Brownlee, *Gray Ghosts of the Confederacy: Guerrilla Warfare in the West, 1861–1865,* Baton Rouge: Louisiana State University Press, 1958, 181 (hereinafter cited as "Brownlee, *Gray Ghosts of the Confederacy*"); "The Command in Missouri," *Missouri Statesman,* Columbia, Boone County, 29 January 1864, from the earlier *Chicago Post;* "General Rosecrans Assigned to the Department of the Missouri," *Missouri Statesman,* Columbia, Boone County, 29 January 1864, from the earlier *Cincinnati* or *Philadelphia Bulletin;* James A. Hamilton, "The Enrolled Missouri Militia: Its Creation and Controversial History," *Missouri Historical Review* 69, no. 4 (July 1975), 419.
3. *O.R.*, vol. 22, part 2, 570–1 (details the transfer of three counties of the District of the Border to the District of Central Missouri on 23 September 1863, and foreshadows the eventual breakup of the controversial District of the Border); vol. 34, part 2, 49, 79–80, 684–5, 731; Richard S. Brownlee, *Gray Ghosts of the Confederacy,* 181–2; Castel, *William Clarke Quantrill: His Life and Times,* 168–9.
4. "Death of Gov. Gamble," *St. Joseph Weekly Herald,* Buchanan County, 4 February 1864; William E. Parrish, *The Civil War in Missouri: Essays from the Missouri Historical Review, 1906–2006,* Columbia, Missouri: The State Historical Society of Missouri, essay by Marguerite Potter, "Hamilton R. Gamble, Missouri's War Governor," 100; Leslie Anders, *The Twenty-First Missouri: From Home Guard to Union Regiment,* Westport, Connecticut: Greenwood Press, 1975, 164.
5. Anders, *The Twenty-First Missouri: From Home Guard to Union Regiment,* 164; Nichols, *Guerrilla Warfare in Civil War Missouri, Volume II, 1863,* 188–9; Perry S. Rader, *The Civil Government of the United States and the State of Missouri and the History of Missouri,* Columbia, Missouri: E. W. Stephens, Publishers, 1898, 352–3.
6. Faust, *Historical Times Illustrated Encyclopedia of the Civil War,* 602; Albert Castel, *General Sterling Price and the Civil War in the West,* Baton Rouge: Louisiana State University Press, 1968, 171–2; Ezra J. Warner, *Generals in Gray: Lives of the Confederate*

Commanders, Baton Rouge: Louisiana State University Press, 1959, 246–7.

7. *O.R.*, vol. 34, part 3, 154; Faust, *Historical Times Illustrated Encyclopedia of the Civil War*, 587; Boatner, *The Civil War Dictionary, Revised Edition*, 655–6; Warner, *Generals in Blue: Lives of the Union Commanders*, 373–4.

8. Nichols, *Guerrilla Warfare in Civil War Missouri, Volume I, 1862*, 65, 171–2; Nichols, *Guerrilla Warfare in Civil War Missouri, Volume 11, 1863*, 47, 130.

9. *O.R.*, vol. 34, part 2, 311.

10. *O.R.*, vol. 34, part 3, 348–50; Paxton, *Annals of Platte County*, 359.

11. *O.R.*, vol. 34, part 2, 429, 487–8.

12. *O.R.*, vol. 34, part 2, 567.

13. *O.R.*, vol. 34, part 2, 506, 618–9, 648.

14. *O.R.*, vol. 34, part 2, 775–7.

15. *O.R.*, vol. 34, part 4, 581–2; James A. Hamilton, "The Enrolled Missouri Militia: Its Creation and Controversial History," *Missouri Historical Review* 69: 419–20; William Fannin, "Defenders of the Border: Missouri's Union Military Organizations in the Civil War," *Pioneer Times*, 6 (July 1982) 3, 200–1.

16. Warner, *Generals in Blue: Lives of the Union Commanders*, 47–8.

17. *O.R.*, vol. 34, part 2, 291–2; (State of Missouri, *Report of Committee of Twenty-Second General Assembly to Investigate the Conduct and Management of the Militia* is a direct product of this investigation by the Missouri General Assembly this winter.)

18. *O.R.*, vol. 34, part 2, 321–2.

19. *O.R.*, vol. 34, part 2, 327–8.

20. Ibid.

21. Ibid.

22. *O.R.*, vol. 34, part 2, 327.

23. Ibid.

24. "From California, MO.," *Daily Missouri Democrat*, St. Louis, 31 January 1862.

25. *O.R.*, vol. 34, part 2, 817–8.

26. *O.R.*, vol. 22, part 2, 224.

27. *O.R.*, vol. 41, part 4, 562.

28. *O.R.*, vol. 34, part 2, 556.

29. *O.R.*, vol. 34, part 3, 30.

30. *O.R.*, vol. 34, part 3, 383.

31. *O.R.*, vol. 41, part 1, 308–9.

32. Castel, *General Sterling Price and the Civil War in the West*, 196.

33. Castel, *General Sterling Price and the Civil War in the West*, 199.

Six

1. "Another Murder," *Charleston Courier*, Mississippi County, 4 March 1864; "Murdered By Guerrillas," *Kansas City Daily Journal*, Jackson County, 15 March 1864, quoting earlier *Daily Missouri Republican*, St. Louis; Edison Shrum, *The History of Scott County, Missouri Up to the Year 1880*, Sikeston, Missouri: Scott County Historical Society, 1984, 112.

2. Shrum, *The History of Scott County, Missouri Up to the Year 1880*, 112.

3. Ross, *Autobiography of Samuel S. Hildebrand*, 97–101, 215n–217n.

4. *O.R.*, vol. 34, part 1, 868; Dyer, *Compendium*, vol. 2, 809.

5. *O.R.*, vol. 34, part 1, 872–5; Dyer, *Compendium*, vol. 2, 809; Broadfoot, *Supplement to the O.R.*, part 2, vol. 34, 1st Missouri Cavalry, 468.

6. *O.R.*, vol. 34, part 1, 872–4; Dyer, *Compendium*, vol. 2, 809; Broadfoot, *Supplement to the O.R.*, part 2, vol. 34, 1st Missouri Light Artillery, 127.

7. Shrum, *The History of Scott County, Missouri Up to the Year 1880*, 112–13; *O.R.*, vol. 34, part 1, 892; Dyer, *Compendium*, vol. 2, 809; "A Week's Scout," *Charleston Courier*, Mississippi County, 22 April 1864; "Effective Scouting in Southeast Missouri," *Kansas City Daily Journal*, Jackson County, 6 May 1864, from the earlier *St. Louis Union*.

8. *O.R.*, vol. 34, part 1, 911; part 3, 482–3; "Guerrillas in Southeast Missouri," *Missouri Statesman*, Columbia, Boone County, 13 May 1864 (this article is a copy of Colonel Rogers' summary of the action given in *O.R.*, vol. 3, 482–3); Dyer, *Compendium*, vol. 2, 809; James E. McGhee and James R. Mayo, *Stoddard Grays: Confederate Soldiers of Stoddard County, Missouri 1861–1865*, Shawnee Mission, Kansas: Two Trails Publishing, 1995, 40, 49; State of Missouri, Secretary of State's Office website, Missouri State Archives, military service records of Private Harrison Whitson of Company K, 5th Missouri Cavalry, CSA, from St. Luke, Stoddard County; and Private Hollas Saddler of Company I, 6th Missouri Infantry and 2nd Missouri Infantry of Cape Girardeau County.

9. *O.R.*, vol. 34, part 3, 690; part 4, 112, 144; "From Cape Girardeau," *Daily Missouri Democrat*, St. Louis, 6 June 1864.

10. *O.R.*, vol. 34, part 2, 638; Shrum, *The History of Scott County, Missouri Up to the Year 1880*, 112; Frederick Way, *Way's Packet Directory, 1848–1994*, Athens, Ohio: Ohio University Press, 1994, 65. (Author's note: The abuse of women and children mentioned by Colonel Rogers in 19th century parlance may have been no more than cursing and shoving. Union commanders in Missouri tended to portray southern guerrillas as savage and uncouth and embellish reports with such exaggerations. Also, Shrum's 1984 county history does not cite his reference for naming the vessel as the *C. E. Hillman*, but Way's authoritative, short history of this named vessel during the war seems not to place her any farther west than Nashville, Tennessee. It is still possible Shrum correctly named the boat, but the scant evidence seems to indicate otherwise.).

11. *O.R.*, vol. 34, part 2, 668–9; Ross, *Autobiography of Samuel S. Hildebrand*, 97–101.

12. *O.R.*, vol. 34, part 3, 42; United States Government, *1860 Missouri Census*, household of Housan Kenner in Beauvais Township of east-central Ste. Genevieve County; Peterson, et al., *Price's Lieutenants*, 75; Bartels, *The Forgotten Men*, 33, 369; Eakins, *Missouri Prisoners of War*, Valle entry.

13. *O.R.*, vol. 34, part 1, 875–6; part 4, 127–8; "From Pilot Knob," *Daily Missouri Democrat*, St. Louis, 11 April 1864; Ross, *Autobiography of Samuel S. Hildebrand*, 216–7.

14. Ross, *Autobiography of Samuel S. Hildebrand*, 102–7, 217n–218n; United States Government, *1860 Missouri Census*, lists F. E. Abrret household in Potosi and Breton Townships of east-central Washington County; United States Department of War, Adjutant General's Office, *Official Army Register of the Volunteer Force of the United States Army for the Years 1861–'65*, Washington, D. C. vol. 6 of 8, 206

(hereinafter cited as "United States Department of War, *Official Army Register*," with appropriate volume and page number); Dyer, *Compendium*, vol. 3, 1032 (for short history of 17th Illinois Cavalry); *O.R.*, vol. 34, part 4, 50.

15. Broadfoot, *Supplement* to *the O.R.*, part 2, vol. 34, 3rd Cavalry MSM, 747.

16. *O.R.*, vol. 34, part 2, 604.

17. *O.R.*, vol. 22, part 2, 765 (showing both Woodson and Herder at Pilot Knob in December 1863); State of Missouri, *Annual Report of the Adjutant General of Missouri for the Year 1865*, Jefferson City, Missouri: Emory S. Foster, Public Printer, 1866, 461 (showing officers of 3rd Cavalry MSM and mentioning Woodson's dismissal); Nichols, *Guerrilla Warfare in Civil War Missouri*, vol. II, 1863, 146–9, 242–5 (showing Freeman operating in this area in 1863), 256–7 (showing Crandall operating in this area in 1863); Donald R. Hale, *Branded As Rebels, Volume Two*, Independence, Missouri: Blue & Grey Book Shoppe, 2003, 30 (Dick Boze); Nichols, *Guerrilla Warfare in Civil War Missouri, 1862*, 124, 165 (for information about Charles Barnes' operations in this region in 1862; Charles Barnes, who operated primarily in Shannon, Dent, and Crawford Counties is not to be mistaken for guerrilla leader Reuben Barnes, who operated farther to the east).

18. *O.R.*, vol. 34, part I, 642–3; Hale, *Branded As Rebels, Volume Two*, 98 (George Evans).

19. "Pilot Knob," *Daily Missouri Democrat*, St. Louis, 12 May 1864.

20. *O.R.*, vol. 34, part I, 921, 238; Dyer, *Compendium*, vol. 2, 809, 810; Broadfoot, *Supplement* to *the O.R.*, part 2, vol. 35, 3rd Missouri Cavalry (Union), 182; William C. Winter, *The Civil War in St. Louis: A Guided Tour*, St. Louis: Missouri Historical Society Press, 1994, 142 (Confederate Colonel Solomon G. Kitchen).

21. *O.R.*, vol. 34, part 4, 50; Ross, *Autobiography of Samuel S. Hildebrand*, 105–7.

22. *O.R.*, vol. 34, part 4, 50, 127; "From Cape Girardeau," *Daily Missouri Democrat*, St. Louis, 6 June 1864.

23. *O.R.*, vol. 34, part 1, 644–7; Dyer, *Compendium*, vol. 2, 809.

24. D. Dennis Burns, "William Wilson, A Missouri Guerrilla," manuscript, collection number 995, vol. 3, document 98, Western Historical Manuscripts Collection, University of Missouri Library, Columbia, Missouri, p. 3 of 14 (hereinafter cited as "Burns, 'William Wilson, A Missouri Guerrilla,' manuscript"); John F. Bradbury, Jr., "'Bushwhacker' Bill Wilson: Incidents on the Rolla-Salem Road," *Newsletter of the Phelps County Historical Society*, 5 (April 1992), 3–7, 11; George Clinton Arthur, *The Bushwhacker: A Story of Missouri's Most Famous Desperado*, Boston: Christopher Publishing, 1938. (Author's note: Oddly, the usually inclusive *O.R.* contains no mention about Bill Wilson during April and May 1864, but it does not say much about operational details in south-central Missouri in this timeframe, either.)

25. "Missouri Items," *Daily Missouri Democrat*, St. Louis, 28 March 1864, quoting earlier *Rolla Express*, Phelps County; United States Government, *1860 Missouri Census*, reveals four different Davis households in Rolla Township that includes that part of Phelps County north of Rolla that contains Spring Creek.

26. Burns, "William Wilson, A Missouri Guerrilla," manuscript, 5–6.

27. Bradbury, "Bushwhacker' Bill Wilson: Incidents on the Rolla-Salem Road," *Newsletter of the Phelps County Historical Society*, 4–5.

28. Bradbury, "'Bushwhacker' Bill Wilson: Incidents on the Rolla-Salem Road," *Newsletter of the Phelps County Historical Society*, 5; "From Rolla, Missouri," *Daily Missouri Democrat*, St. Louis, 30 April, 1864.

29. Bradbury, "'Bushwhacker' Bill Wilson: Incidents on the Rolla-Salem Road," *Newsletter of the Phelps County Historical Society*, 6; United States Government, *1860 Missouri Census*, household of Sarah Bond on page 50 of Massey Township, west-central Phelps County; household of L. Lewis on page 39 of Massey Township; household of John Lewis on page 284 of Spring Creek Township, southeast Pulaski County; and household of James Mathews on page 283 of Spring Creek Township.

30. Faust, *Historical Times Illustrated Encyclopedia of the Civil War*, 106–7, 619–20; Boatner, *The Civil War Dictionary*, 688.

31. *O.R.*, vol. 34, part 3, 548, 718–9; Mark K. Christ, *Rugged and Sublime: The Civil War in Arkansas*, Fayetteville, Arkansas: The University of Arkansas Press, 1994, 114–123, 126.

32. *O.R.*, vol. 34, part 3, 627, part 4, 164–5; United States Government, *1860 Missouri Census*, lists in Green Township of central Phelps County, 20-year-old Missouri-born laborer A. J. Kitchen.

33. *O.R.*, vol. 34, part 4, 113.

34. *O.R.*, vol. 34, part 1, 922 (The *O.R.* in this reference clearly states the Union unit involved in this action was the "Fifteenth Missouri State Militia," a unit that never existed. This author holds that the unit was actually the 1st Infantry MSM, which at the time of this action was scattered in small detachments along the length of both the Pacific Railroad and the "southwest branch of the Pacific Railroad" in this region, as cited in unit histories below. Cuba was located on the "southwest branch" of the Pacific Railroad during the war.); Dyer, *Compendium*, vol. 2, 810; vol. 3, 1321–2 (for short history of 1st Infantry MSM); State of Missouri, *Annual Report of the Adjutant General of Missouri for the Year 1865*, 438–9 (for short history of 1st Infantry MSM).

35. Emma Comfort Dunn, "Civil War Era—The Diary of John W. Goddard," *Ozarks Mountaineer* (July-August 1982), 22–3; John W. Goddard diary, which he kept between April and October 1864, while living in northeast Crawford County, in private collection of his descendant, Dottie Braunsdorf of St. Louis County. State of Missouri, Secretary of State's Office, Missouri State Archives, military service record of Private John Goddard of Company K, 63rd Enrolled Missouri Militia, who enrolled in this unit 5 October 1864 at Rolla. (Author's note: Therefore, Goddard may have been interested enough in the war after his diary recording of what he heard about what transpired in his neighborhood May 13 and 14 to join the northern war effort later that year.).

36. *O.R.*, vol. 34, part 4, 12–3; "St. Charles Correspondence," *Missouri Statesman*, Columbia, Boone County, 20 May 1864; "Raid on Herman [sic]," *Missouri Statesman*, 27 May 1864; "Bushwhackers at

Hermann," *Howard County Advertiser*, Fayette, 20 May 1864; Goodspeed Publishing Company, *History of Franklin, Jefferson, Washington, Crawford, and Gasconade Counties, Missouri*, Goodspeed Publishing Company, 1888, 652; Nichols, *Guerrilla Warfare in Civil War Missouri*, 1862, 165 (for event 19 November, 1862 in which Hermann residents sheltered runaway slaves from slave catchers).

37. *O.R.*, vol. 34, part 4, 296–7; Dyer, *Compendium*, vol. 3, 1188 (Contains short history of 10th Kansas Infantry Regiment, which states only that this regiment was guarding prisons in St. Louis at this time. It is possible, however, that one or more companies were sent to guard railroad facilities along the "southwest branch of the Pacific Railroad" during May 1864. As a result of this Rebel band's violent ride across Franklin County Union authorities sent a detachment of 7th Kansas Cavalry there with orders to hunt down guerrillas, according to *O.R.*, vol. 34, part 3, 655 and part 4, 33–4, 112. These cavalrymen arrived as ordered 25 May, but there seems to be no record about what they encountered, and they were recalled back from Franklin County about May 29.) United States Government, 1860 *Missouri Census*, household of E. Gibler, 38-year-old Prussian-born merchant, Boon Township, southwest Franklin County.

38. *O.R.*, vol. 34, part 3, 655; part 4, 33–4.

39. *O.R.*, vol. 34, part 3, 592.

40. *O.R.*, vol. 34, part 1, 953–4; Dyer, *Compendium*, vol. 2,810; John F. Bradbury, Jr., "Hunting Bushwhackers for a Living: The Second Wisconsin Cavalry in the District of Rolla, 1863–1864," *Newsletter of the Phelps County Historical Society*, 10 (October 1994), 1, 3–15; "From Rolla," *Daily Missouri Democrat*, St. Louis, 1 June 1864; "Guerrillas Near Rolla," *Daily Missouri Republican*, St. Louis, 1 June 1864; "Soldiers Murdered by Guerrillas," *Missouri Statesman*, Columbia, Boone County, 10 June 1864, from earlier *Daily Missouri Republican*; Daughters of Union Veterans, *Missouri: Our Civil War Heritage, Volume 3*, St. Louis: Daughters of Union Veterans, Julia Dent Grant, Tent # 16, 1994, 217–19; Broadfoot, *Supplement to the O.R.*, part 2, vol. 74, 2nd Wisconsin Cavalry, 737; "Guerrillas Blockaded in a Cave," *Liberty Tribune*, Clay County, 10 June 1864, from the earlier *St. Louis Union*.

41. Frost, *Camp and Prison Journal*, 121.

42. Ibid., 122; Eakin, *Missouri Prisoners of War*, Cushman and Withers entries.

43. *O.R.*, series 2, vol. 6, 1113.

44. Ibid.,1123.

45. Frost, *Camp and Prison Journal*, 122; Eakin, *Missouri Prisoners of War*, Mosby [sic] and White entries; *O.R.*, series 2, vol. 7, 43 (This inspection report of Alton Military Prison written April 13 mentions that four prisoners escaped earlier in the month, so two others than Captain Moseley and Mr. White may have escaped with them.).

46. Internet exchange December 27–29, 2006, between the author, Ross Brooks, and Hugh Simmons about the arrest and imprisonment of Thaddeus A. Ripley, in "The Missouri in the Civil War Message Board," http://history-sites.com/mb/cw/mocwmb/; Eakin, *Missouri Prisoners of War*, Ripley entry; Frost, *Camp and Prison Journal*, 135–6.

47. *O.R.*, series 2, vol. 7, 35.

48. Ibid., 43–44.

49. Ibid., 81–8.

50. Eakin, *Missouri Prisoners of War*, Jamison entry; Burns, "William Wilson, A Missouri Guerrilla," manuscript, 8–9.

51. "Large and Important Seizure of Arms and Munitions of War at the Levee," *Missouri Statesman*, Columbia, Boone County, 13 May 1864, from the earlier *Missouri Daily Republican*, St. Louis.

52. Eakin, *Missouri Prisoners of War*, McDaniel entry.

53. "Sentence of Dr. Wright," *St. Joseph Weekly Herald*, Buchanan County, 29 April 1864; Nichols, *Guerrilla Warfare in Civil War Missouri. Volume II*, 1863, 40.

54. Eakin, *Missouri Prisoners of War*, Fornshill entry.

Seven

1. "Letter From Southwest Missouri," *Missouri Statesman*, Columbia, Boone County, 29 April 1864.

2. "From Springfield, MO," *Daily Missouri Democrat*, St. Louis, 30 April 1864; "Three Men Murdered By Bushwhackers," *Daily Missouri Republican*, St. Louis, 23 April 1864; "Murder of a Former Resident of This county," *Boonville Monitor*, Cooper County, 11 June 1864 (the Boonville newspaper printed an obituary for Thomas W. Allison, who had formerly lived in the area); United States Government, *1860 Missouri Census*, household of Thomas W. Allison, Green Township, northwest Lawrence County.

3. *O.R.*, vol. 34, part 3, 829; Ward L. Schrantz, *Jasper County, Missouri in the Civil War*, Carthage, Missouri: The Carthage Press, 1923, 177–8.

4. "Forty-Five," *Daily Missouri Democrat*, St. Louis, 9 March 1864.

5. *O.R.*, vol. 34, part 2, 486.

6. *O.R.*, vol. 34, part 2, 531–2; Ann Davis Neipman, "General Orders No. 11 and Border Warfare During the Civil War," *Missouri Historical Review* 66, no. 2 (January 1972), 201.

7. *O.R.*, vol. 34, part 2, 652; United States Government, 1860 *Missouri Census*, household of Martha Long in Lone Oak Township, south-central Bates County, is closer to the origin of this report at Rockville than the household of P.B. Long in Spruce Township, east-central Bates County (only two Longs listed in this county).

8. *O.R.*, vol. 34, part 1, 856–8; part 3, 22; "Bushwhackers Killed," *Kansas City Daily Journal*, Jackson County, 12 April 1864, from the earlier *St. Louis Union* (this article, with the same headline, was repeated in the Kansas City newspaper on 16 April 1864); Dyer, *Compendium*, vol. 2, 809; Britton, *The Civil War on the Border*, vol. 2, 364–6; Broadfoot, *Supplement to the O.R.* part 2, vol. 34, 1st Cavalry MSM, 490.

9. Brophy, "*Found No Bushwhackers*," 22; Nichols, *Guerrilla Warfare in Civil War Missouri, Volume II, 1863*, 166 (referencing Pony Hill in 1863 in this area); Internet query 8 July 2008 by Lynna Summers, "'Pony' Hill, bushwhacker" in "Missouri in the Civil War Message Board," http://history-sites.com/mb/cw/mocwmbl, in which Mrs. Summers identified "Pony" Hill as her husband's great-grandfather and his actual name as James Napoleon "Pony" Hill; United States Census, *1860 Missouri Census*, lists in

Little Osage Township of north Vernon County, the household of 25-year-old farmer James N. Hill having no real estate value and only $440 worth of personal property. His household also consisted of 22-year-old Missouri-born female E. J. Hill and 9-month-old James N. Hill.

10. Brophy, *"Found No Bushwhackers,"* 22.

11. *O.R.*, vol. 34, part 3, 119–20.

12. *O.R.*, vol. 34, part 3, 186; Burch, *Quantrell,* 229.

13. "Missouri Items," *Missouri Statesman,* Columbia, Boone County, 8 April 1864, quoting earlier *Springfield Journal* (which also identifies the dead Fulbright only as a son of E. R. Fulbright who formerly lived in Greene County and moved "to Dixie" earlier in the war); Peterson, et al., *Price's Lieutenants,* 199–201 (mentioning James McSpadden as a Missouri State Guard officer during 1861, and that his unit in which he was recruited from counties in the Springfield area); Broadfoot, *Supplement to the O.R.* part 2, vol. 38, 3rd Battalion Missouri Cavalry (CSA), 180–1 (showing Captain James Walker McSpadden and Second Lieutenant Lewis Brashears serving in the same battalion); State of Missouri, Secretary of State's Office, Missouri State Archives, military service records of Private William F. Fulbright and Second Lieutenant Lewis Brashears as both serving specifically in Company C of 3rd Battalion Missouri Cavalry under Captain McSpadden; U.S. Government, 1860 *Missouri Census,* lists in Clay Township the households of Lewis Brashears, Elijah Hunt, and Eliza Dodson, and lists in Campbell Township the household of E. R. Fulbright.

14. *O.R.*, vol. 34, part 1, 906.

15. *O.R.*, vol. 34, part 3, 593.

16. *O.R.*, vol. 34, part 4, 164, 168.

17. William Elsey Connelley, *Quantrill and the Border Wars,* Cedar Rapids, Iowa: Torch Press, 1910, reprinted Ottawa, Kansas: Kansas Heritage Press, 1992, 449; Castel, *Quantrill,* 168.

18. Nichols, *Guerrilla Warfare in Civil War Missouri, Volume II, 1863,* 96–8; Donald L. Gilmore, *Civil War on the Missouri-Kansas Border,* Gretna, Louisiana: Pelican Publishing Company, 2006, 267.

19. O.S. Barton, compiler, *Three Years With Quantrill: A True Story Told by His Scout John McCorkle,* Armstrong, Missouri: *Armstrong Herald* Print, 1914, reprinted Norman, Oklahoma: University of Oklahoma Press, 1992, 146 (hereinafter cited as "Barton, *Three Years with Quantrill");* Castel, *Quantrill,* 168.

20. Edwards, *Noted Guerrillas, or the Warfare of the Border,* 227; Barton, *Three Years with Quantrill,* 145–6.

21. Barton, *Three Years with Quantrill,* 145–6; Edwards, *Noted Guerrillas, or the Warfare of the Border,* 227.

22. "Inhuman Barbarity," *Missouri Statesman,* Columbia, Boone County, 6 May 1864, quoting earlier *Springfield Journal;* United States Government, *1860 Missouri Census,* household number 1515 of Jones Weems, age 67, born North Carolina with wife Bethania, age 65, born North Carolina, and household number 1510, G. W. Weems, age 41, born Tennessee, with wife and several teenage and younger children including 15-year-old Kendrick Weems and 13-year-old Martin Weems, both born Missouri; all in Benton Township, south-central Newton County; State of Missouri, Secretary of State's Office, Missouri State Archives, military service records of Privates Kindrick Weems and Martin A. Weems in Company I, 76th Enrolled Missouri Militia, who served in 1864 and 1864, especially Kindrick who enrolled in this unit 30 April 1864, just days after the attack on his father and grandfather.

23. *O.R.*, vol. 34, part 3, 260–1.

24. *O.R.*, vol. 34, part 3, 311.

25. *O.R.*, vol. 34, part 3, 499; Brophy, *Found No Bushwhackers,* 26; Castel, *Quantrill,* 168; Edwards, *Noted Guerrillas, or Warfare of the Border,* 216.

26. Castel, *Quantrill,* 168; Barton, *Three Years with Quantrill,* 147–8; Edwards, *Noted Guerrillas, or the Warfare of the Border,* 228–9.

27. *O.R.*, vol. 34, part 3, 829, 835 (Confederate reports showing Colonel Jackman was in Arkansas with his troops at this time); Nichols, *Guerrilla Warfare in Civil War Missouri, Volume II, 1863* (chapters 2, 6, 10, and 15 detail Jackman's accomplishments in Missouri during 1863).

28. Eakins, *Missouri Prisoners of War,* Dorsey entry.

29. *O.R.*, vol. 34, part 3, 283 (this author could not discover details about the "Parker" mentioned).

30. *O.R.*, vol. 34, part 3, 288, 328.

31. "The Rumored Raid on Boonville," *Missouri Statesman,* Columbia, Boone County, 13 May 1864, quoting *Boonville Advertiser* of 7 May 1864.

32. *O.R.*, vol. 34, part 3, 419, 445.

33. *O.R.*, vol. 34, part 3, 690–1.

34. "Jackman About," *Missouri Statesman,* Columbia, Boone County, 29 April 1864, quoting the *Randolph Citizen,* Huntsville, Randolph County, of 22 April 1864.

35. *O.R.*, vol. 34, part 4, 147.

36. Nichols, *Guerrilla Warfare in Civil War Missouri, Volume II, 1863,* 90.

37. *O.R.*, vol. 34, part 3, 328, 593; Schrantz, *Jasper County, Missouri in the Civil War,* 168–70 (Author's note: Captain Stemmons and his men were also members of the 76th Enrolled Missouri Militia, from which they were officially detailed into the 7th Provisional EMM.).

38. *O.R.*, vol. 34, part 3, 420 (The actual number of Marchbanks' men in this instance was probably closer to 50, since he operated during 1863 with about that many).

39. Bartels, *The Forgotten Men: Missouri State Guard,* 229–30; Brown and Company, *History of Vernon County, Missouri,* St. Louis: Brown and Company, 1887, 280, 320, 334–5; J. B. Johnson, *History of Vernon County, Missouri,* Chicago: C. F. Cooper and Company, 1911, 298, 305–7; Nichols, *Guerrilla Warfare in Civil War Missouri, Volume I, 1862,* 32, 56, 82, 184, 210; Nichols, *Guerrilla Warfare in Civil War Missouri, Volume II, 1863,* 95–9, 156, 159–60, 214, 225, 281–2, 287–8, 290–2, 324–5; Leo E. Huff, "Guerrillas, Jayhawkers and Bushwhackers in Northern Arkansas During the Civil War," *Arkansas Historical Quarterly* 24, No. 2 (Summer 1965), 141–2 (showing Marchbanks in Shelby's command in north Arkansas in early spring 1864).

40. Brophy, *Found No Bushwhackers,* 26.

41. *O.R.*, vol. 34, part 3, 499, 500, 524–5, 537; "Bushwhackers—Stage Robbed," *Daily Missouri Republican,* St. Louis, 10 May 1864, printing article written by their correspondent in Lexington, Lafayette County, on 7 May 1864.

42. *O.R.*, vol. 34, part 4, 167.

43. Goodspeed Publishing Company, *History of Newton/Lawrence/Barry and McDonald Counties, Missouri*, Chicago: The Goodspeed Publishing Company, 1888, 322; State of Missouri, *Annual Report of the Adjutant General of Missouri for the Year 1865*, 608 (for full name and military unit of Lieutenant Wear; (Author's note: Lieutenant Wear and his men were also members of the 76th Enrolled Missouri Militia from which they were officially detailed into the 7th Provisional EMM.).

44. *O.R.* vol. 34, part 3, 593.

45. (No headline), *Kansas City Daily Journal*, Jackson County, 26 May 1864, citing the *Fort Scott Monitor*, Bourbon County, Kansas, of 21 May 1864.

46. Johnson, *History of Vernon County, Missouri*, 300; *O.R.*, vol. 34, part 1, 935–7; Dyer, *Compendium*, vol. 2, 810; Brophy, *Found No Bushwhackers*, 27.

47. *O.R.*, vol. 34, part 1, 935–7, part 3, 629, 643; Johnson, *History of Vernon County, Missouri*, 300–1; Brophy, *Found No Bushwhackers*, 27; "Guerrillas Near Fort Scott," *Kansas City Daily Journal*, Jackson County, 19 May 1864; Broadfoot, *Supplement to the O.R.*, part 2, vol. 21, 15th Kansas Cavalry, 472, 478.

48. Britton, *The Civil War on the Border*, vol. 2, 354.

49. *O.R.*, vol. 34, part 3, 641.

50. *O.R.*, vol. 34, part 1, 940–1; part 3, 679, 692; Schrantz, *Jasper County, Missouri in the Civil War*, 171–2, 175–6; Dyer, *Compendium*, vol. 2, 810; Britton, *The Civil War on the Border*, vol. 2, 354; Brownlee, *Gray Ghosts of the Confederacy*, 186; (Author's note: Captain Rohrer and his men were also members of the 26th EMM, from which they were officially detailed into the 7th Provisional EMM. Captain Richey and his men were members of the 76th EMM from which they also were officially detailed into the 7th Provisional EMM.).

51. *O.R.*, vol. 34, part 1, 941–2; Dyer, *Compendium*, vol. 2, 810; Britton, *The Civil War on the Border*, vol. 2, 354–9; Brownlee, *Gray Ghosts of the Confederacy*, 186–7; (Author's note: First Lieutenant Elder, Sergeant Cavender, and their men were also members of the 76th EMM, from which they were officially detailed into the 7th Provisional EMM.).

52. *O.R.*, vol. 34, part 4, 11–2, 13.

53. *O.R.*, vol. 34, part 1, 945.

54. Western Historical Company, *History of Greene County, Missouri*, St. Louis: Western Historical Company, 1883, 472–3; Jonathan Fairbanks and Clyde Edwin Tuck, *Past and Present of Greene County, Missouri*, Indianapolis: A. W. Bowen and Company, 1915, 376. *O.R.*, vol. 34, part 4, 21–2, 167.

55. Schrantz, *Jasper County, Missouri in the Civil War*, 172–4; (Author's note: Captain Stemmons and his men were also members of the 76th EMM, from which they were officially detailed into the 7th Provisional EMM.).

56. "Guerrilla Operations," *Missouri Statesman*, Columbia, Boone County, 10 June 1864; *O.R.*, vol. 34, part 1, 954–5, part 4, 144, 247; Schrantz, *Jasper County, Missouri in the Civil War*, 176; Britton, *The Civil War on the Border*, vol. 2, 359–60; Dyer, *Compendium*, vol. 2, 810.

57. *O.R.*, vol. 34, part 1, 957–8; Dyer, *Compendium*, vol. 2, 810.

Eight

1. *O.R.*, vol. 34, part 2, 778; Nichols, *Guerrilla Warfare in Civil War Missouri, Volume II, 1863*, 156, 200–1, 209 (for Union support to escaping slaves during 1863 in Missouri).

2. *O.R.*, vol. 34, part 2, 639; "Robbers at Work—A Man Killed," *Missouri Statesman*, Columbia, Boone County, 25 March 1864, quoting earlier *Randolph Citizen*, Randolph County; "Killed," *Howard County Advertiser*, Fayette, Howard County, 18 March 1864; (Author's note: This event was also reported in the *California Weekly News*, Moniteau County, 9 April 1864, and in the *Palmyra Spectator*, Marion County.).

3. "Missouri Items," *Missouri Statesman*, Columbia, Boone County, 8 April 1864, quoting earlier *Randolph Citizen*, Randolph County; State of Missouri, Secretary of State's Office, Missouri State Archives, military service record of Private John T. Lewis in Company F, 61st EMM from 9 October 1862 at Columbia or Sturgeon, Company A, 1st Provisional EMM and Company G and Company L, 9th Cavalry MSM, mustering out 18 May 1865 at St. Louis. This source also has brief military service record of Private Solomon Lewis in Company D, 1st Provisional EMM beginning 28 May 1863 at Renick with notation that he deserted at Renick 5 June 1863.

4. "Missouri Items," *Missouri Statesman*, Columbia, Boone County, 8 April 1864, quoting the earlier *Randolph Citizen*, Randolph County of 1 April 1864; United States Government, *1860 Missouri Census*, reveals several Grotjohn households all in the Keytesville area of Chariton County, and the P.Y. Irvin household in Miami Township, north Saline County, which contains William A. Irvin, age 20, Melvin R. Irvin, age 17, and Alfred L. Irvin, age 15 in 1860. Both the elder Irvins were born in Virginia, which the younger members were born in Missouri; State of Missouri, Secretary of State's Office, Missouri State Archives, military service records of Private William A. Irvin of Saline County captured at Milford (northeast Johnson County) 19 December 1861, sent to Alton Military Prison, but no record for Melvin, Alfred, or Green Irvin or similar name.

5. *O.R.*, vol. 34, part 2, 471, 787; part 3, 509; (Author's note: Switzler was also the editor of Columbia's *Missouri Statesman* newspaper.).

6. "Colonel A. F. Denny," *Missouri Statesman*, Columbia, Boone County, 12 April 1864, quoting earlier *Randolph Citizen*, Randolph County; (Author's note: It is not clear if this was a guerrilla act directed against the captain, an awkward attempt to rob the house, or the act of a madman. The newspaper article also pondered the actual nature of the intruder's foolhardy persistence.).

7. *O.R.*, vol. 34, part 1, 882; part 3, 96–7, 157, 232, 250, 576–7; "Jackman About," *Missouri Statesman*, Columbia, Boone County, 29 April 1864, quoting *Randolph Citizen*, of 22 April 1864; State of Missouri, Secretary of State's Office, Missouri State Archives, military service record for Private John Smith who enlisted in 9th Cavalry MSM in early 1862, and was discharged 4 April 1863 per Special Orders Number 62; (Author's note: There were a couple of notable Missouri Confederates named Frost, but they were definitely not in northeast

Missouri at this time, and the Federals should have probably known that.).

8. "Horses Stolen," *Howard County Advertiser*, Fayette, 20 May 1864; United States Government, 1860 *Missouri Census*, household of 24-year-old Missouri-born Thomas Ward with wife and young child in Richmond Township, central Howard County.

9. "Murdered by Bushwhackers," *Daily Missouri Republican*, St. Louis, 1 June 1864, quoting *Central City and Brunswicker*, Brunswick, Chariton County, 26 May 1864; "Murdered by Bushwhackers," *Howard County Advertiser*, Fayette, 3 June 1864; "Bushwhacking in Chariton—Six Union Men Killed," *Daily Missouri Republican*, St. Louis, 10 January 1865; United States Government, 1860 *Missouri Census*, lists in Clark Township, northeast central Chariton County, the household of Virginia-born 36-year-old blacksmith Charles M. W. Phillips of modest personal and real property and his wife and four children born in Missouri and Iowa; and in Yellow Creek Township, just west of Clark Township, household of 39-year-old Kentucky-born female Melvina Wilkie of modest personal and real property contains three of military age: 19-year-old L. R. Wilkie and 17-year-old M. W. Wilkie, both born in Kentucky, and 43-year-old Scotland-born farmer William Wilkie.

10. (No headline), *Missouri Statesman*, Columbia, Boone County, 27 May 1864; United States Government, 1860 *Missouri Census* fails to identify any Randolph County household by the name of "Conrad"; State of Missouri, Secretary of State's Office, Missouri State Archives, military service record for Private George W. Conrad, enrolled 1 April 1863 into Company D, 1st Provisional EMM at Huntsville [county seat of Randolph County], and served on active duty through 29 November 1863 (this may be the Conrad militiaman referred to by the guerrillas). (Author's note: Missouri Civil War era newspapers commonly used the title "Esquire" when referring to someone of accomplishment and worthy of public respect, such as an attorney or well-to-do farmer, so "Esquire" may not be Mr. Conrad's first name.)

11. "Wanting a Horse," *Missouri Statesman*, Columbia, Boone County, 27 May 1864; United States Government, *1860 Missouri Census*, lists in Jackson Township of central Monroe County 53-year-old Kentucky born B. F. Minor, having moderate amounts of real and personal property.

12. Nichols, *Guerrilla Warfare in Civil War Missouri* 1862, 15, 17, 64, 178 (for some of Colonel Dorsey's 1862 activities behind Union lines in Missouri); Nichols, *Guerrilla Warfare in Civil War Missouri, Volume II, 1863*, 159–60, 237–8, 323 (for some of Colonel Dorsey's 1863 activities behind Union lines in Missouri); *O.R.*, vol. 34, part 4, 147 (in this report the Union military mistakenly thought Colonel Dorsey's recruiting command was under the command of Colonel Sidney D. Jackman, who was then in north Arkansas leading his own troops).

13. *O.R.*, vol. 34, part 4, 91–2; "Guerrillas in Missouri," *Missouri Statesman*, Columbia, Boone County, 17 June 1864, from the earlier *Macon Gazette*, Macon, Macon County.

14. "Negro Shot," *Howard County Advertiser*, Fayette, 3 June 1864, quoting earlier *Missouri Statesman*, Columbia, Boone County; (slaves were emancipated in Missouri effective 1 January 1865).

15. Nichols, *Guerrilla Warfare in Civil War Missouri, Volume II, 1863*, 69, 136, 238 (for Ramsey's and Briscoe's adventures during 1863 and Joe Cole's death).

16. *O.R.*, vol. 34, part 2, 554.

17. *O.R.*, vol. 34, part 3, 539.

18. Ibid., 596, 642; "Bushwhackers About," *Missouri Statesman*, Columbia, Boone County, 27 May 1864, quoting earlier *Fulton Telegraph*, Callaway County; "Bushwhackers About," *Howard County Advertiser*, Fayette, 3 June 1864, also quoting the same article in *Fulton Telegraph;* United States Government, *1860 Missouri Census*, listing households of James Craig in High Hill Township, southeast Montgomery County; John Tatum in Prairie Township, northeast Montgomery County; and David W. Baker in Danville Township, west-central Montgomery County.

19. Nichols, *Guerrilla Warfare in Civil War Missouri, Volume II, 1863*, 69–71, 237–8 (for details of Pike County guerrilla warfare during spring and fall 1863).

20. *O.R.*, vol. 34, part 3, 278.

21. "Robbed," *Missouri Statesman*, Columbia, Boone County, 20 May 1864; U.S. Government, *1860 Missouri Census*, lists four different Griffith households in Buffalo Township in north Pike County and one in Cuivre River Township in central Pike County; (Author's note: The newspaper article claims the robbed man was "W. A. Griffith," but those initials fail to match those in the census.).

22. "Bushwhackers in Pike County," *Daily Missouri Democrat*, St. Louis, 23 May 1864; "Thieves in Pike County," *Howard County Advertiser*, Fayette, 3 June 1864, from the earlier *St. Louis Union; O.R.*, vol. 34, part 4, 96 (this seems to be merely a comment about the seventy raiders taken from the Howard County newspaper); United States Government, *1860 Missouri Census*, lists in Spencer Township, west Pike County, the household of 52-year-old Virginia-born farmer William Kindrick that included several sons in twenties and teens.

23. *O.R.*, vol. 34, part 4, 90, 92, 96.

24. "Trouble in Pike County," *Daily Missouri Democrat*, St. Louis, 6 June 1864 (The *Democrat* at times took an editorial stance less favorable to the radicals and more conciliatory to moderates and southerners. This article was evidently written with information supplied by those southerners who took refuge in St. Louis, seemed sympathetic to their plight, and avoided incurring the wrath of the Union leadership by bemoaning the loss of revenue from "the troubles in Pike" rather than criticizing that leadership directly for the use of known jayhawkers to murder southerners and chase others away.); Broadfoot, *Supplement to the O.R.*, part 2, vol. 21, 7th Kansas Cavalry (gives no clue as to the "special" operations some of the troopers undertook in Pike County, but indicates that elements of some companies were in late May 1864 stationed in St. Louis before proceeding to Memphis June 4); *O.R.*, vol. 34, part 4, 112 (contains a 29 May cryptic note from the department headquarters to commander of St. Louis and southeast Missouri district that he "call in the detachment of the Seventh Kansas Cavalry under the command of Captain [William S.] Moor-

house, with orders to report to the headquarters of the regiment, unless you have such information as would seem to imperatively demand its presence where it now is." Captain Moorhouse was commander of Company B of the 7th Kansas.).

25. "What 'Our Dear Erring Brethren' Are Doing in Lewis County," *Daily Missouri Democrat*, St. Louis, 16 March 1864, from the earlier *National American*, LaGrange, Lewis County; State of Missouri, Secretary of State's Office, Missouri State Archives, military service record for Private William Winsell who enrolled 21 August 1862 in Captain Lewis' Company, 69th EMM at LaGrange, Lewis County, and performed 114 days active duty there, with the remark that Winsell "Enlisted M.S. [Missouri State?] Service," thus leaving EMM service to do that.

26. "Missouri Items," *Daily Missouri Democrat*, St. Louis, 29 March 1864 (Mr. Ingersoll does not appear in the 1860 Missouri census under this spelling or any similar spelling.).

27. "Marauders Caught," *Daily Missouri Democrat*, St. Louis, 5 April 1864; United States Government, 1860 *Missouri Census*, lists 57-year-old Kentucky-born carpenter James McCalister household of Monticello, Dickerson Township, central Lewis County, with several sons in twenties working as carpenters and one a blacksmith.

28. *O.R.*, vol. 34, part 1, 892; part 3, 216, 311; (No headline), *Daily Missouri Democrat*, St. Louis, 26 April 1864, from the earlier *Paris Mercury*, Monroe County; "Shot," *Missouri Statesman*, Columbia, Boone County, 6 May 1864; Dyer, *Compendium*, vol. 2, 809; State of Missouri, Secretary of State's Office, Missouri State Archives, military service records for Captain James M. Foreman, Company D, 70th EMM; Private Benedict G. Durbin, who at age 44 enrolled in Company H, 70th EMM at Salt River Bridge 12 August 1862; United States Government, 1860 *Missouri Census*, lists in Washington Township, north-central Monroe County, the household of B. J. Durbin, age 40, born Kentucky, farmer, modest real and personal worth, with wife born Kentucky and seven children from age 1 to 17, all born in Missouri; (Author's note: Author cannot confirm, but has read and noted that *Palmyra Spectator*, Marion County, 3 June 1864, reported death of B. J. Durbin "wounded at the affair in Shelbina sometime since.").

29. "Capture of Murderers and Robbers," *St. Joseph Weekly Herald*, Buchanan County, 12 May 1864; Daughters of Union Veterans of the Civil War, 1861–1865; *Missouri: Our Civil War Heritage*, 213–4.

30. *O.R.*, vol. 34, part 3, 710–1; "Lawlessness in Northeast Mo.," *Howard County Advertiser*, Fayette, 27 May 1864; United States Government, 1860 *Missouri Census*, lists in Sweet Home Township, northeast Clark County, these three individuals who appear to be those whose Athens stores were listed as burned in the Fayette newspaper: George Gray, age 55, born Kentucky, merchant; Alfred Bedall, age 24, born Missouri, grocery; David Kennedy, age 53, born Virginia, farmer. Also, in St. Francisville is Robert McKee, age 48, born Maryland, merchant, with large real and personal property assets. In Alexandria Township is the pro-Union letter writer, William Bishop, age 42, born Virginia, speculator with large real and personal property assets, wife born Indiana, three small children born Missouri.

31. *O.R.*, vol. 34, part 2, 742; "War in Putnam County," *Daily Missouri Democrat*, St. Louis, 5 April 1864; Leslie Anders, *The Eighteenth Missouri*, Indianapolis, Indiana: Bobbs-Merrill Company, 1968, 190–3 Birdsall and Dean, *The History of Linn County, Missouri*, 353; Goodspeed Publishing Company, *History of Adair, Sullivan, Putnam, and Schuyler Counties, Missouri*, Chicago: The Goodspeed Publishing Company, 1882, 499–501.

32. Goodspeed Publishing Company, *History of Lewis, Clark, Knox, and Scotland Counties, Missouri*, Chicago: The Goodspeed Publishing Company, 1887, 707–8; Leslie Anders, *The Twenty-First Missouri: From Home Guard to Union Regiment*, 168–9; United States Government, 1860 *Missouri Census*, lists in Benton Township, north-central Knox County the household of 54-year-old Kentucky-born merchant Thomas A. McMurry, and that of 47-year-old Kentucky-born farmer Rice McFadden.

NINE

1. *O.R.*, vol. 34, part 2, 484.
2. *O.R.*, vol. 34, part 2, 579–80.
3. Frazier, *Missouri Ordeal, 1862–1864: Diaries of Willard Hall Mendenhall*, 183; "Bushwhackers At Work," *Kansas City Daily Journal*, Jackson County, 9 March 1864, from the earlier *Lexington Union*; United States Government, 1860 *Missouri Census*, lists in Lexington Township, household of John Catron.
4. *O.R.*, vol. 34, part 2, 532, 604–5; Edwards, *Noted Guerrillas or the Warfare of the Border*, 363; "Bushwhacker Blunt Killed," *Kansas City Daily Journal*, Jackson County, 12 March 1864.
5. Eakin, *Warren Welch Remembers*, 16; "Bushwhacker Blunt Killed," *Kansas City Daily Journal*, Jackson County, 12 March 1864; *O.R.*, vol. 34, part 2, 804; part 3, 51; Brownlee, *Gray Ghosts of the Confederacy*, 183; United States Government, 1860 *Missouri Census*, lists in Sni-A-Bar Township of southwest Lafayette County the households of two Welch families including that of 40-year-old Kentucky-born farmer Sam F. Welch and 16-year-old Kentucky-born Warren Welch.
6. *O.R.*, vol. 34, part 2, 604–5; Frazier, *Missouri Ordeal, 1862–1864: Diaries of Willard Hall Mendenhall*, 186; Rose Mary Lankford, *The Encyclopedia of Quantrill's Guerrillas*, Evening Shade, Arkansas: published by author, 1999, 283, 365; United States Government, 1860 *Missouri Census*, lists in Washington Prairie Township, west-central Pettis County, the household of the Reverend Moses B. Arnold; and in Davis Township, east-central Lafayette County, the household of Minister F. R. Gray.
7. *O.R.*, vol. 34, part 2, 604–5.
8. Frazier, *Missouri Ordeal, 1862–1864: Diaries of Willard Hall Mendenhall*, 186.
9. *O.R.*, vol., 34, part 3, 22.
10. *O.R.*, vol., 34, part 1, 861–2; "Bushwhacker Killed," *Missouri Statesman*, Columbia, Boone County, 15 April 1864, quoting the earlier *Lexington Union*, Lafayette County; Broadfoot, *Supplement to the O.R.*, part 2, vol. 34, 1st Cavalry MSM, 490; Dyer, *Compendium*, vol. 2, 809.
11. *O.R.*, vol. 34, part 3, 524.
12. *O.R.*, vol. 34, part 1, 649.
13. *O.R.*, vol. 34, part 1, 649–50, 651–2; Wiley

Britton, *The Civil War on the Border*, New York: G. P. Putnam's Sons, two volumes, 1890–1891, vol. 2, 363–4; Dyer, *Compendium*, vol. 2, 809; Broadfoot, *Supplement to the O.R.*, part 2, vol. 34, 1st *Cavalry MSM*, 490,508 (Author's note: The clerk of the 1st, writing about this effort, recorded only that they "wounded Colonel James."); Bartels, *The Forgotten Men: Missouri State Guard*, 169 (for Jeans' military record of 1861); James E. McGhee, *Guide to Missouri Confederate Units, 1861–1865*, Fayetteville, Arkansas; University of Arkansas Press, 2008, 97–9 (for some of Jeans' military record in the Jackson County regiment); United States Government, *1850 Missouri Census*, lists the Jeans household living in Kaw Township of northwest Jackson County with member 23-year-old, Kentucky-born Beal G. Jeans.

14. *O.R.*, vol. 34, part 3, 93–5.

15. "Information Wanted," *Kansas City Daily Journal*, Jackson County, 25 May 1864 and later editions; United States Government, *1860 Kansas Census*, lists in Palmyra Township of south Douglas County in Baldwin City on the Santa Fe Trail south of Lawrence, in the household of J.A. Hollyman, wagon maker, the family of 38-year-old Ohio-born miller O. Denison and several children born in Indiana; (Author's note: This author could not determine if the Denison family ever discovered the fate of their missing husband and father.)

16. Albert Castel, *William Clarke Quantrill: His Life and Times*, 169.

17. (No headline), *Kansas City Weekly Journal of Commerce*, Jackson County, 16 April 1864; *O.R.*, vol. 34, part 3, 93–5 (containing a patrol report by Second Lieutenant Gooding of this period in this area, but lacking the specific episode mentioned in the newspaper).

18. *O.R.*, vol. 34, part 3, 120.

19. *O.R.*, vol. 34, part 3, 239.

20. *O.R.*, vol., 34, part 3, 259–60, 284; Frazier, *Missouri Ordeal, 1862–1864: Diaries of Willard Hall Mendenhall*, 190; United States Government, *1860 Missouri Census*, lists several Atkinson households in Washington Township, south-central Lafayette County; and in Lexington Township of north-central Lafayette County, the household of 28-year-old Missouri-born farmer N.C. Ewing, his 25-year-old Missouri-born wife, Catherine, and their two small children, 2-year-old Anna and 6-month-old Joel; State of Missouri, Secretary of State's Office, Missouri State Archives, shows military service record for Private James W. Atkinson in Company D, 71st EMM, performing 40 days active duty at Lexington in late 1862, but this may not be the same Atkinson who served briefly in the citizen guard in spring 1864.

21. *O.R.*, vol. 34, part 1, 903; Edwards, *Noted Guerrillas or the Warfare of the Border*, 227–8, 229–30; Barton, *Three Years with Quantrill*, 147 (Author's note: Since guerrilla John McCorkle survived the war and dictated this memoir, Edwards may have obtained McCorkle's experience in this fight from him.); Dyer, *Compendium*, vol. 3, 1004–6 (short histories of the 2nd and 3rd Colorado Infantry and the 2nd Colorado Cavalry); Castel, *William Clarke Quantrill: His Life and Times*, 168–9; Edward E. Leslie, *The Devil Knows How to Ride: The True Story of William Clarke Quantrill and His Confederate Raiders*, New York: Random House, 1996, 299.

22. *O.R.* vol. 34, part 3, 22, 326–7; "The Late Scout," *Liberty Tribune*, Clay County, 6 May 1864, from the earlier *Kansas City Daily Journal*, Jackson County.

23. *O.R.*, vol. 34, part 1, 902–4; part 3, 326, 365; "Bushwhacking," *Kansas City Daily Journal*, Jackson County, 3 May 1864, from the *Warrensburg Tribune*; "Another Interesting Letter from Our Warrensburg Correspondent," *Kansas City Daily Journal*, Jackson County, 5 May 1864; Britton, *The Civil War on the Border*, vol. 2, 366–8; Edwards, *Noted Guerrillas or the Warfare of the Border*, 228–9; Dyer, *Compendium*, vol. 2, 809; Barton, *Three Years with Quantrill*, 147 ; Paul R. Petersen, *Quantrill in Texas: The Forgotten Campaign*, Nashville, Tennessee: Cumberland House, 2007, 189.

24. *O.R.*, vol. 34, part 3, 421, 499.

25. *O.R.*, vol. 34, part 3, 538; "Bushwhackers," *Missouri Statesman*, Columbia, Boone County, 13 May 1864, from the *Lexington Weekly Union*, Lafayette County, 7 May 1864; State of Missouri, Secretary of State's Office, Missouri State Archives, reveals no military service record for a Private John Foster or Rafter of Captain Eli Hughes' Company K, 6th Cavalry MSM, as the two above sources indicate.

26. Frazier, *Missouri Ordeal, 1862–1864: Diaries of Willard Hall Mendenhall*, 193; United States Government, *1860 Missouri Census*, lists in Lexington Township the household of 37-year-old Missouri-born merchant C. B. Kavanaugh and his wife and five young children all born in Missouri, and in Grand Pass Township of northwest Saline County the household of R. P. Kavenaugh; Missouri Historical Company, *History of Saline County, Missouri*, St. Louis: Missouri Historical Company, 1881, 321 (This 1881 county history and the 1910 one referenced below maintain that the Kavanaugh killed by Union soldiers was the R. P. Kavenaugh who lived in Grand Pass Township of northeast Saline County.); William Barclay Napton, *Past and Present of Saline County, Missouri*, Chicago: B. F. Brown and Company, 1910, 198.

27. *O.R.*, vol. 34, part 3, 462.

28. *O.R.*, vol. 34, part 3, 499.

29. *O.R.*, vol. 34, part 3, 501, 524; (headline not obtained), *Daily Missouri Democrat*, St. Louis, 13 May 1864.

30. *O.R.*, vol. 34, part 3, 525.

31. "An Interesting Letter from Warrensburg—The Progress of the Pacific Railroad, Etc." *Kansas City Daily Journal*, Jackson County, 26 April 1864.

32. *O.R.*, vol. 34, part 3, 612.

33. (No headline), *Kansas City Daily Journal*, Jackson County, 26 May 1864, from *St. Joseph Tribune*, Buchanan County, of 24 May 1864 (The Kansas City editor quoted the St. Joseph newspaper article, but added a note that he heard of no such incident and doubted the veracity of the story.).

34. *O.R.*, vol. 34, part 3, 622; "Bushwhackers Killed," *Kansas City Daily Journal*, Jackson County, 25 May 1864, from the earlier *Lexington Weekly Union*, Lafayette County; "Probably Death of Quantrel [sic], The Guerrilla," *St. Joseph Weekly Herald*, Buchanan County, 26 May 1864; "Probably Death of Quantrill," *Howard County Advertiser*, Fayette, 27 May 1864.

35. *O.R.*, vol. 34, part 3, 624–5; United States

Government, 1860 *Missouri Census*, lists in Sni-A-Bar Township, northeast Jackson County, the household of 45-year-old Virginia-born farmer Richard Hopkins and 20-year-old Virginia-born sawyer William F. Hopkins.

36. *O.R.*, vol. 34, part 3, 709; United States Government, 1860 *Missouri Census*, lists in Pleasant Hill Township, northeast Cass County, in the Joseph Watkins household, 18-year-old Kentucky-born blacksmith Benjamin Watkins.

37. "Execution of One of Quantrill's Men," *Daily Missouri Democrat*, St. Louis, 25 May 1864; "Confession of Willard F. Hadley," *Liberty Tribune*, Clay County, 17 June 1864; Nadine Hodges and Mrs. Howard W. Woodruff, *Genealogical Notes from the "Liberty Tribune"* 1858–1868, Liberty, Clay County: published by authors, 1975, vol. 2 of 2, 75 (summarizes 17 June 1864 article about Hadley in *Liberty Tribune*); "Confession of Willard Francis Hadley," *Missouri Statesman*, Columbia, Boone County, 1 July 1864, from earlier *Missouri State Times*, Jefferson City, Cole County; United States Government, 1860 *Missouri Census*, lists in Lee Township, west-central Platte County, in farmer John Davis's household 21-year-old Indiana-born laborer William Hadley (Author's Note: Census-takers usually had difficulty locating young, active, single men, so details about Hadley in this census were probably provided to the census-taker as guesswork by Mr. Davis or someone else nearby.); State of Missouri, Secretary of State's Office, Missouri State Archives, military service record of W. F. Hadley states only that he was a member of Company I, 1st Missouri Cavalry (CSA); McGhee, *Guide to Missouri Confederate Units, 1861–1865*, 48 (explains that Company I, 1st Missouri Cavalry (CSA) was commanded by Captain Silas Gordon); Paxton, *Annals of Platte County, Missouri*, 323; Michael Fellman, *Inside War: The Guerrilla Conflict in Missouri During the American Civil War*, 291; Internet query 16 June 2008 by Casey Reed, "William Francis Hadley, Missouri Guerrilla" in "Missouri in the Civil War Message Board," http://history-sites.com/mb/cw/mocwmb/, with subsequent discussion by others through 21 June 2008.

38. "Three of Tod's [sic] Men Killed," *Kansas City Daily Journal*, Jackson County, 25 May 1864, repeated also word for word in the *Daily Missouri Republican*, St. Louis, 1 June 1864.

39. *O.R.*, vol. 34, part 1, 943; part 3, 719–20; "Bushwhackers at Independence, Mo.," *Kansas City Daily Journal*, Jackson County, 25 May 1864; "From Independence," *Daily Missouri Democrat*, St. Louis, 2 June 1864; Brownlee, *Gray Ghosts of the Confederacy*, 188; Mrs. Ellen Williams, *Three Years and a Half in the Army; or, History of the Second Colorados*, New York: Fowler and Wells Company, 1885, 45–6 (Mrs. Williams commented that the Starr carbine "when properly adjusted, but of uncertain fire, a very important defect, when the life of a brave man was depending"); United States Government, National Archives and Records Administration, article by Michael P. Musick, "War in an Age of Wonders, Part 2, Civil War Arms and Equipment," in agency periodical *Prologue* 27, no. 4 (winter 1995) citing a Civil War period report which "names eleven officers of the First and Second Regiments, Colorado Cavalry, in the second quarter of 1864, who say: 'These officers agree that [Starr carbines] carry well, get out of order very easily, the locks break often, prefer large Cal., and that they are not sure fire, and are poorly made'"; Internet discussion involving the author and others regarding the firearms problems of the 2nd Colorado Cavalry in "Civil War Arms and Equipment Message Board" between 4 and 7 July 2008, http://history-sites.com/mb/cw/cwaemb/, citing the above two sources.

40. *O.R.*, vol. 34, part 1, 945–6; part 4, 21–2, 51; "From Warrensburg," *Daily Missouri Democrat*, St. Louis, 31 May 1864; Britton, *The Civil War on the Border*, vol. 2 of 2, 368–9; Brownlee, *Gray Ghosts of the Confederacy*, 188; Kansas City Historical Company, *The History of Johnson County, Missouri*, Kansas City: Kansas City Historical Company, 1881, 875 (with a brief word about Judge King, where he lived, and his death); State of Missouri, Secretary of State's Office, Missouri State Archives, military service record for First Lieutenant John Taggart in Company M, 40th EMM at Warrensburg, Johnson County, with many days of active duty during 1863 and 1864; "Mail Robbed," *Kansas City Daily Journal*, Jackson County, 27 May 1864.

41. *O.R.*, vol. 34, part 4, 51, 52, 65, 66, 114; State of Missouri, *Annual Report of the Adjutant General of Missouri for the Year 1865*, 441 (for officer roster of 1st Cavalry MSM showing Captain Moore's service into 1865).

42. *O.R.*, vol. 34, part 4, 52–3; Brownlee, *Gray Ghosts of the Confederacy*, 188–9.

43. *O.R.*, vol. 34, part 4, 51, 68–9.

44. Dyer, *Compendium*, vol. 2, 810.

45. *O.R.*, vol. 34, part 1, 954; part 4, 52, 198–9; Dyer, *Compendium*, vol. 2, 810; "Guerrillas in Missouri," *Missouri Statesman*, Columbia, Boone County, 17 June 1864, from earlier *Warrensburg Tribune*; United States Government, 1860 *Missouri Census*, shows in Post Oak Township of south-central Johnson County the households of Dennis Hackler, Noah Tesson, and Mrs. Cecil (mentioned as suffering loss in the fire in the above *O.R.* page 199 reference).

46. Dyer, *Compendium*, vol. 2, 810; Broadfoot, *Supplement to the O.R.*, part 2, 7th Cavalry MSM, 468.

47. "Mount Hope Burned," *Kansas City Daily Journal*, Jackson County, 1 June 1864, from the earlier *Lexington Weekly Union*, Lafayette County; "Mt. Hope Burned," *Missouri Statesman*, Columbia, Boone County, 10 July 1864, also referring to the earlier *Lexington Weekly Union*.

48. Gregg manuscript, 86–7; Castel, *William Clarke Quantrill: His Life and Times*, 157–8, 161–4; Leslie, *The Devil Knows How to Ride*, 288–9; Paul R. Petersen, *Quantrill of Missouri: The Making of a Guerrilla Warrior*, Nashville, Tennessee: Cumberland House, 2003, 346; Gilmore, *Civil War on the Missouri: Kansas Border*, 265–6; Brownlee, *Gray Ghosts of the Confederacy*, 140; Evault Boswell, *Quantrill's Raiders in Texas*, Austin, Texas: Eakin Press, 2003, 100–3, 112–3, 115.

49. Nichols, *Guerrilla Warfare in Civil War Missouri, Volume II, 1863*, 176–7.

50. Nichols, *Guerrilla Warfare in Civil War Missouri, Volume II, 1863*, 219–28.

51. Nichols, *Guerrilla Warfare in Civil War Missouri, Volume II, 1863*, 286; Connelley, *Quantrill and the Border Wars*, 434.

52. Connelley, *Quantrill and the Border Wars*, 449–50 (particularly citing postwar letters from guerrilla Charles Fletcher Taylor and researcher W. W. Scott who interviewed witnesses Ike and Bob Hall and Donny Pence); Castel, *William Clarke Quantrill: His Life and Times*, 169–72 (particularly citing Bill Gregg manuscript and manuscript of witness Frank Smith); Leslie, *The Devil Knows How to Ride*, 300–1 (citing Connelley's findings); Gilmore, *Civil War on the Missouri-Kansas Border*, 266–8 and 350n (particularly citing Gregg's manuscript and Connelley's findings); Petersen, *Quantrill in Texas: The Forgotten Campaign*, 192 (Petersen's Texas book contains a list of those who eventually joined Quantrill in Howard County, listing as sources *Blue and Grey Chronicle* 7, no. 5 [June 2004], 3); *Confederate Veteran*, 1913; and Edwards, *Noted Guerrillas or the Warfare of the Border*, 307. He also cited as source *Boone's Lick Heritage* 6, no. 1 [March 1998] for writing that Quantrill employed the services of former Confederate lieutenant Warren Welch, already in west-central Missouri as stated earlier in this work, to guide his entourage at least part of the way to exile in Howard County. Welch omitted mention of this [and many other details] from the memoirs he wrote some time before his 1915 death.).

53. Broadfoot, *Supplement to the O.R.*, part 2, vol. 35, 7th Cavalry MSM, 453–4; Nichols, *Guerrilla Warfare in Civil War Missouri, Volume II, 1863*, 196–7 (for narrative of the 28 July 1863 raid on New Frankfort).

54. *O.R.*, vol. 34, part 3, 286–7; Broadfoot, *Supplement to the O.R.*, part 2, vol. 35, 7th Cavalry MSM, 468; (Author's note: The capture of Colonel Winston March 22 is described later in this same Chapter Nine of this work.).

55. Eakin and Hale, *Branded As Rebels*, 467 (Eakin and Hale gave as their source for this event the 1881 Saline County history without page number, but this author could not find the mention in that reference) ; United States Government, *1860 Missouri Census*, household of farmer Gustavus and Amelia Hendrick both born Germany and both age 34 with four children born New York in Jefferson Township, northeast Saline County, and household of 30-year-old Virginia-born farmer Robert Hendrick, his 25-year-old, Missouri-born wife Virginia and three small children born Missouri in Miami Township, north-central Saline County.

56. "Two More of Quantrill's Men Executed," *Daily Missouri Democrat*, St. Louis, 28 May 1864; "Horse Thieves Shot," *Missouri Statesman*, Columbia, Boone County, 3 June 1864.

57. "Murder," *Boonville Monitor*, Cooper County, 12 March 1864; "A Dead Body Found," *Howard County Advertiser*, Fayette, 18 March 1864; "Missouri News," *Daily Missouri Democrat*, St. Louis, 23 March 1864; James F. Thoma, *This Cruel Unnatural War: The American Civil War in Cooper County, Missouri*, Kingsport, Tennessee: published by author, 2003, 87.

58. United Daughters of the Confederacy, Missouri Division. *Reminiscences of the Women of Missouri During the Sixties*, Jefferson City, Missouri: Hugh Stephens Printing Company, 1913, 97–9; Petersen, et al., *Price's Lieutenants*, 176; Goodspeed Publishing Company, *History of Cole, Moniteau, Morgan, Benton, Miller, Maries, and Osage Counties, Missouri*, 359–60; James E. Ford, *A History of Moniteau County, Missouri*, California, Missouri: Marvin H. Crawford, 1936, 36; United States Government, *1860 Missouri Census*, lists in town of Tipton, west Moniteau County, in household of Waid Howard apparently three young men boarders including 22-year-old Pennsylvania-born Charles Brownlee; Nichols, *Guerrilla Warfare in Civil War Missouri, Volume II, 1863*, 182–3, 185–6, 202–3, 226 (for the adventures of Brownlee's band during 1863).

59. "Robbery," *Boonville Monitor*, Cooper County, 19 March 1864; Thoma, *This Cruel Unnatural War*, 87.

60. "Bushwhackers Captured," *Boonville Monitor*, Cooper County, 23 April 1864; Thoma, *This Cruel Unnatural War*, 89; Broadfoot, Supplement to the *O.R.*, part 2, vol. 35, 4th Cavalry MSM, 97.

61. *O.R.*, vol. 34, part 3, 259; "Capture of a Notorious Bushwhackers and Robber," *Boonville Monitor*, Cooper County, 16 April 1864; "Missouri Items," *Daily Missouri Democrat*, St. Louis, 19 April 1864; "Three Hundred and Eighty-Three Cans Rebel Powder Captured," *Kansas City Daily Journal*, Jackson County, 23 April 1864, from the earlier *St. Louis Union;* Thoma, *This Cruel Unnatural War*, 90; Ford, *A History of Moniteau County, Missouri*, 46 (Ford quotes the *California Weekly Times*, Moniteau County, 30 April 1864, telling about Mullins' execution with the note that he was raised about six miles from Tipton); United States Government, *1860 Missouri Census*, lists in Moreau Township, east-central Morgan County, in the household of farm manager Samira Mullins, 14-year-old Missouri-born William P. Mullins and 71-year-old Virginia-born Nancy Wilson.

62. Thoma, *This Cruel Unnatural War*, 92; United States Government, *1860 Missouri Census*, lists household of 42-year-old farmer Dryden Starke and 18-year-old John Starke, both born in Virginia; State of Missouri, Secretary of State's Office, Missouri State Archives, military service record for Corporal John D. Starke, who enlisted at age 22 at Otterville, 25 August 1864 and served until mustered out in 1865.

63. Thoma, *This Cruel Unnatural War*, 92; United States Government, *1860 Missouri Census*, lists in Palestine Township, west-central Cooper County, 45-year-old Virginia-born farmer W. H. Mayo with real property worth $36,000 and personal property worth $35,000, and large family mostly born in Kentucky.

64. Thoma, *This Cruel Unnatural War*, 92; *O.R.*, vol. 34, part 3, 690–1; "Rumor," *Howard County Advertiser*, Fayette, 27 May 1864; "Rumor," *Missouri Statesman*, Columbia, Boone County, 3 June 1864.

65. *O.R.*, vol. 34, part 4, 147.

66. Thoma, *This Cruel Unnatural War*, 92; "Robbery," *Boonville Monitor*, Cooper County, 28 May 1864; "Robbery," *Howard County Advertiser*, Fayette, 3 June 1864; United States Government, *1860 Missouri Census*, lists in Moniteau Township, northeast Cooper County, at Pisgah, the household of 64-year-old Virginia-born physician David P. Mahan and his wife next door to Calvin George's store; (Author's note: Since George had a large family, perhaps he took his wife and children out of the war zone and left Dr. Mahan to mind the store in his absence or sold the store to the physician.).

67. Thoma, *This Cruel Unnatural War*, 93; "Shooting of Mr. Nichols," *Boonville Weekly Monitor*, Cooper County, 28 May 1864; "A Worthy Citizen Killed," *Howard County Advertiser*, Fayette, 3 June 1864; United States Government, *1860 Missouri Census*, lists in Palestine Township, west-central Cooper County, the household of wealthy farmer James M. Nichols, age 51, born in Rhode Island.

68. State of Missouri, Secretary of State's Office, Missouri State Archives, military service record of Private Wiley Shumate, Company A, Pindall's Sharpshooter Battalion, who enlisted 29 August 1862 and deserted at Fort Smith, Arkansas, 10 January 1863; United States Government, *1860 Missouri Census*, lists in Jefferson City, Cole County, the household of 40-year-old Kentucky-born Methodist Evangelical minister Nathan Shumate, his wife, Harriett, and three children. The son Wiley is not listed; Internet discourse with Wiley Shumate descendant Glenn Hunt, googy@flash.net, between 27 September 2004 and February 2008.

69. "Bushwhacking Near the Osage," *Daily Missouri Democrat*, St. Louis, 18 April 1863; United States Government, *1860 Missouri Census*, lists a 30-year-old New York-born John Wilcox as an inmate of the State Penitentiary in Jefferson City, Cole County, but in Equality Township of central Miller County near Tuscumbia two young John Wilcox farmers, aged 27 and 18, with Virginia listed as birthplace.

70. "To Be Executed," *Daily Missouri Democrat*, St. Louis, 25 May 1864.

71. Eakin, *Missouri Prisoners of War*, Bond entries; United States Government, *1860 Missouri Census*, lists 14 different Bond families in various parts of Miller County, including at least three with a "Sarah" household member.

72. "Bushwhacking Near the Osage," *Daily Missouri Democrat*, St. Louis, 18 April 1864; (Author's note: This article contains only general remarks as to location of the incidents, and provides no names for the terror-stricken boy or the beheaded farmer. No other source corroborates any part of these incidents. It appears that the newspaper correspondent did not leave the safety of Jefferson City and was hoodwinked by Union soldiers telling tall tales to a gullible audience, but that is only conjecture.); United States Government, *1860 Missouri Census*, lists no such name as Kuntz in either Cole or Miller County or surrounding counties.

TEN

1. "Jayhawkers," *Kansas City Daily Journal*, Jackson County, 13 March 1864, quoting an earlier issue of *Atchison County Journal*; "Jayhawkers," *St. Joseph Weekly Herald*, Buchanan County, 17 March 1864, quoting word for word the *Kansas City* article.

2. "Arrival of Prisoners," *Missouri Statesman*, Columbia, Boone County, 25 March 1864, quoting *St. Joseph News* of 15 March 1864; State of Missouri, Secretary of State's Office, Missouri State Archives, shows no online record for a John Holley in the 4th Cavalry MSM, but a military service record for Private William Colton of Oregon, south Holt County, in Company A, 58th EMM; State of Kansas, *Report of the Adjutant General of the State of Kansas 1861-1865*, 480, listing Corporal Michael Eastman of White Cloud (village in northeast corner of Kansas next to Missouri River and near Nebraska border) as a member of Company D, 14th Kansas Cavalry Regiment; United States Government, *1860 Missouri Census*, lists in Oregon, south Holt County, household of 35-year-old Iowa-born, teamster William Colton and his small family; and in Jackson, Andrew County the household of 43-year-old Pennsylvania-born farmer James Duncan.

3. "Arrest and Imprisonment of Jayhawkers," *Kansas City Daily Journal*, Jackson County, 26 March 1864, quoting earlier *St. Joseph News*, Buchanan County; State of Missouri, Secretary of State's Office, Missouri State Archives, military service record of Private Andrew Farmer of Company E, 25th Missouri Infantry Regiment, discharged 8 June 1863; United States Government, *1860 Missouri Census*, lists household of Andrew Farmer in Dallas Township, in southeast tip of Holt County; household of Robert Wilson in Oregon Township of southwest Holt County; and household of Robert Wilson in Benton Township in center Holt County.

4. "Terrible Tragedy," *Daily Missouri Democrat*, St. Louis, 27 April 1864, quoting *Chillicothe Constitution*, Livingston County, of 21 April; (No headline), *Missouri Statesman*, Columbia, Boone County, 29 April 1864 (Author's note: There is no indication in either newspaper article of the eventual fate of the accused George Burton, nor anything in the local record to tell what became of him after the shooting.); United States Government, *1860 Missouri Census*, lists several Burton households in this area in both Livingston and Carroll Counties, but none with a son of military age by the name of "George Burton"; State of Missouri, Secretary of State's Office, Missouri State Archives, shows military service records for both Corporal Daniel P. Mayberry and Private Aaron Rankins of Company I, 65th EMM showing active service between 30 April 1863 and 31 October 1864, but no mention of wounds.

5. *O.R.*, vol. 34, part 3, 510, 526, 527, 577; "More Depredations," *Missouri Statesman*, Columbia, Boone County, 10 June 1864; Edwards, *Noted Guerrillas or the Warfare of the Border*, 232-3 (Edwards claimed these men conducted the Camden raid against orders not to conduct operations for a time while their leaders reconnoitered the situation in west-central Missouri, having recently arrived back in the area from Texas. This matches other accounts. Edwards added his usual false report of several Union militiamen killed and wounded at Camden, when in reality it was a robbery by several mostly inebriated guerrillas that resulted in no Union casualties.).

6. Jim Cummins, *Jim Cummins' Book, Written by Himself*, Denver: Reed Publishing Company, 1903, 1903, 55-6.

7. *O.R.*, vol. 34, part 4, 36-7, 133-4; State of Missouri, Secretary of State's Office, Missouri State Archives, military service record of Major Abraham Allen, of the 3rd (old) Cavalry MSM and then captain of the 6th Cavalry MSM where General Orders Number 112, 13 June 1863, called for his dismissal.

8. *O.R.*, vol. 34, part 4, 147; (No headline), *Kansas City Daily Journal*, Jackson County, 4 June 1864, from the earlier *Liberty Tribune*, Liberty, Clay County; (No headline), *Kansas City Daily Journal*, Jackson County, 5 June 1864.

9. "Missouri Items," *Daily Missouri Democrat*, St. Louis, 4 April 1864; *O.R.*, vol. 34, part 4, 133–4.

10. "Incendiarism and Theft in Buchanan County," *Missouri Statesman*, Columbia, Boone County, 6 May 1864, quoting *St. Joseph News*, Buchanan County, of 27 April 1864; "Destruction of Property—Incendiaries About," *St. Joseph Weekly Herald*, 29 April 1864.

11. *O.R.*, vol. 34, part 3, 384.

12. *O.R.*, vol. 34, part 4, 54; "From St. Joseph, MO." *Daily Missouri Democrat*, St. Louis, 19 May 1864; "The Murder of Christian" and "Terrible Murders By Hands of Guerrillas in North-West Missouri," *St. Joseph Weekly Herald*, Buchanan County, 26 May 1864; State of Missouri, Secretary of State's Office, Missouri State Archives, military service record of Private John Christian, age 30, who enrolled in Company E, 87th EMM at St. Joseph 30 April 1864 with note written across bottom of record "Murdered by guerrillas, May 27, 1864" (The date given is a few days later than the actual date of his death since he disappeared about May 16 and his body found May 18.).

13. *O.R.*, vol. 34, part 4, 54; "Capt. Wilson's Dead Body Found" and "Terrible Murders by Hands of Guerrillas," *St. Joseph Weekly Herald*, Buchanan County, 26 May 1864; "The Murders in North Missouri," *St. Joseph Weekly Herald*, Buchanan County, 2 June 1864; United States Government, 1860 *Missouri Census*, in James Wilson household of near DeKalb, Bloomington Township, southwest Buchanan County 21-year-old Missouri-born farmhand Hamilton Wilson; State of Missouri, *Annual Report of the Adjutant General of Missouri For the Year 1865*,622 (lists Captain Hamilton S. Wilson as commander of Company C, 87th EMM with remark "Killed by bushwhackers May 16, 1864"—although the captain was actually murdered May 18).

14. *O.R.*, vol. 34, part 4, 54; "Terrible Murders By Hands of Guerrillas in North-West Missouri," *St. Joseph Weekly Herald*, Buchanan County, 26 May 1864; "The Murder of Capt. McDonald," *Daily Missouri Republican*, St. Louis, 1 June 1864, quoting the earlier *Savannah Plain Dealer*, Andrew County; "The Murders In North Missouri," *St. Joseph Weekly Herald*, 2 June 1864; United States Government *1860 Missouri Census*, lists the James McDonald household in Camden Township, central DeKalb County; (Author's note: The author could find no record of a Captain James McDonald even as a militia officer in Missouri State records.).

15. *O.R.*, vol. 34, part 4,54; "The Murders in North Missouri," *St. Joseph Weekly Herald*, Buchanan County, 2 June 1864.

16. *O.R.*, vol. 34, part 3, 710; "More Murders" and "Another Man Murdered," *St. Joseph Weekly Herald*, Buchanan County, 26 May 1864; State of Missouri, Secretary of State's Office, Missouri State Archives, military service record of First Sergeant Harvey Bradford, Company E, 81st EMM.

17. *O.R.*, vol. 34, part 4,54; "Missouri Items," *Daily Missouri Democrat*, St. Louis, 2 June 1864; "The Murders in North Missouri," *St. Joseph Weekly Herald*, Buchanan County, 2 June 1864.

18. *O.R.*, vol. 34, part 4, 115; "From St. Joseph, Mo." *Daily Missouri Democrat*, St. Louis, 31 May 1864; "Important Discovery of Concealed Powder," *St. Joseph Weekly Herald*, Buchanan County, 2 June 1864; "Important Discovery of Concealed Powder," *Daily Missouri Democrat*, St. Louis, 2 June 1864; State of Missouri, Secretary of State's Office, Missouri State Archives, military service records of Private James Dysart, Company D, 81st EMM and Private Lewis Gaines, Company M, 82nd EMM; United States Government, *1860 Missouri Census*, household of William Sallee in Washington Township, just east of city of St. Joseph.

19. *O.R.*, vol. 34, part 2, 587–8.

20. Paxton, *Annals of Platte County*, 360.

21. *O.R.*, vol. 34, part 2, 659–60, 695, 707; "Missouri Items," *Daily Missouri Democrat*, St. Louis, 28 March 1864; "Capture of a Confederate Colonel," *Missouri Statesman*, Columbia, Boone County, 1 April 1864, quoting earlier *St. Joseph News*; Paxton, *Annals of Platte County*, 360; Harry Soltysiak, "Anarchy in Missouri," *Civil War Times Illustrated* 24, no. 8 (December 1985), 31; United States Government, *1860 Missouri Census*, lists in Platte County the household of John H. Winston in Pettis Township; United States Government, *1850 Missouri Census*, lists in Liberty Township, central Clay County, the household of Elizabeth Thornton including 16-year-old John Thornton.

22. Paxton, *Annals of Platte County*, 361; Farley and Farley, *Missouri Rebels Remembered Si Gordon & John Thrailkill*, 74.

23. Paxton, *Annals of Platte County*, 361; State of Missouri, Secretary of State's Office, Missouri State Archives, military service record for Franklin Luthy in both the 39th EMM and in Luthy's Platte County VMM.

24. *O.R.*, vol. 34, part 4, 12, 23, 90; "Seizure of Arms in Platte County," *Kansas City Daily Journal*, Jackson County, 25 May 1864, from earlier *Leavenworth Bulletin*.

25. "Troubles in Platte County," *Kansas City Daily Journal*, Jackson County, 26 May 1864, from *St. Joseph Weekly Herald*, Buchanan County, 24 May 1864; United States Government, 1860 *Missouri Census*, lists in Savannah, county seat of Andrew County, 34-year-old Ohio-born lawyer William Heren.

26. "Robbery in Platte County," *Daily Missouri Republican*, St. Louis, 1 June 1864.

27. "More Depredations," *Missouri Statesman*, Columbia, Boone County, 10 June 1864, quoting earlier *St. Joseph Weekly Herald*, Buchanan County; Paxton, *Annals of Platte County*, 362.

28. "Two Bushwhackers Caught," *Kansas City Daily Journal*, Jackson County, 1 June 1864, from the *Leavenworth Conservative* of 31 May 1864; Way, *Way's Packet Directory, 1848–1994*, 362 (Author's Note: The suspicious pair gave their names as T. C. Anderson and George Warren both from Platte County, but a search of 1860 Census entries shows no such names in any household of those surnames.).

29. "Robbers Near Weston," *St. Joseph Weekly Herald*, Buchanan County, 2 June 1864.

ELEVEN

1. *O.R.*, vol. 34, part 4, 197, 669–70; "From Cape Girardeau," *Daily Missouri Democrat*, St. Louis, 6 June 1864; McGhee, *Guide to Missouri Confederate Units, 1861–1865*, 107.

2. *O.R.*, vol. 34, part 4, 218; "From Cape Girardeau," *Daily Missouri Democrat*, St. Louis, 6 June 1864; Broadfoot, *Supplement to the O.R.*, part 2, vol. 34, 1st Missouri Cavalry, 453; State of Missouri, Secretary of State's Office, Missouri State Archives. These events seem to match military service record of 21-year-old Kentucky-born Private John Wright of Dunklin County, who served in southern Missouri State Guard (MSG) during 1861, later served in Company K, 5th Missouri Infantry at Corinth, Iuka, and Port Gibson, and at Port Gibson he was wounded, captured, and paroled, after which he deserted (perhaps to return home and serve his cause as a guerrilla); United States Government, *1860 Missouri Census*, household of Virginia-born farmer D. L. Guthrie containing 19-year-old Missouri-born son John W. Guthrie, in Miami Township of north-central Saline County (Missouri Civil War historian James E. McGhee asserts Guthrie hailed from Saline County, far from the "Bootheel" where he served so well.).

3. *O.R.*, vol. 34, part 1, 986–7; part 4, 218, 261; Dyer, *Compendium*, vol. 2, 810; Edison Shrum, *The History of Scott County, Missouri Up to the Year 1880*, 113.

4. *O.R.*, vol. 34, part 4, 197; "From Cape Girardeau," *Daily Missouri Democrat*, St. Louis, 6 June 1864.

5. *O.R.*, vol. 34, part 4, 218; "From Cape Girardeau," *Daily Missouri Democrat*, St. Louis, 6 June 1864; Ross, *Autobiography of Samuel S. Hildebrand*, 62, 76–7, 201n, 204–5n (Kirby Ross could find no record of the period in which Hicks was killed to confirm any kind of military service, and neither can this author, so unknown how Hildebrand believed him to be a Union captain unless Hicks had earlier been acting on his own when the guerrilla believed Hicks to be tracking his family. Ross found a 21 October 1865 Stoddard County Circuit Court determination that stated that Hildebrand and a Bud Hinkle shot Nathaniel Hicks to death on 10 January 1864[!] and a grand jury filed first degree murder charges against the pair. Hildebrand performed a number of complex, hazardous expeditions in southeast Missouri this summer, so his postwar confusion about the timeframe of his killing of Hicks is understandable; although the circuit court's confusion about the date of Hicks' killing only 16 months after the event is harder to accept. Ross also confirmed that Nathaniel Hicks' 1860 census entry [farmer, age 46, born in Tennessee] places him close enough to the stated location of the killing.); Robert H. Forister, *History of Stoddard County*, Bloomfield, Missouri: Stoddard County Historical Society, 1971, 24.

6. *O.R.*, vol. 34, part 4, 392.

7. *O.R.*, vol. 34, part 4, 325, 326; State of Missouri, Secretary of State's Office, Missouri State Archives, the Union account of this series of incidents stated the discharged cavalryman of the 2nd Cavalry MSM who was killed was named "Hazel." Although there seems to be no military service record for a soldier by that surname, there is one for a Private Stephen G. Herrald of Co. C, 2nd Cavalry MSM, from northeast Missouri who was discharged 20 March 1864 at Cape Girardeau in order to re-enlist as a veteran soldier; United States Government, *1860 Missouri Census* and 1860 *Arkansas Census*, fail to indicate among the many Suttons listed in this region any one of them listed as a physician.

8. *O.R.*, vol. 34, part 4, 443.

9. *O.R.*, vol. 34, part 4, 667, 682–3; McGhee, *Guide to Missouri Confederate Units, 1861–1865*, 77, 167; Nichols, *Guerrilla Warfare in Civil War Missouri, 1862*, 52, 166–7; Nichols, *Guerrilla Warfare in Civil War Missouri, Volume II, 1863*, 74; United States Government, *1860 Missouri Census*, household in New Madrid, New Madrid County, of Ohio-born, 36-year-old levy contractor Henry E. Clark, his Ohio-born wife and two small Missouri-born children.

10. Broadfoot, *Supplement to the O.R.*, part 2, 1st Missouri Cavalry (USA), 453.

11. *O.R.*, vol. 34, part 4, 583, 588; vol. 41, part 1, 43–5; part 2, 24, 36; "From Southeast Missouri," *Daily Missouri Democrat*, St. Louis, 14 July 1864; "Guerrilla Hunting in the Southeast," *Daily Missouri Democrat*, St. Louis, 16 July 1864 (both newspaper articles merely quoted Burris' reports that are also recorded in the *O.R.*); Nichols, *Guerrilla Warfare in Civil War Missouri, 1862*, 155, 158, 161, 200–1, 207 (for Burris' ineffectual expeditions against Quantrill's guerrillas in west-central Missouri during 1862); Way, *Way's Packet Directory, 1848–1994*, 176, 219; Dyer, *Compendium*, vol. 2, 810.

12. *O.R.*, vol. 41, part 1, 71.

13. *O.R.*, vol. 41, part 2, 24, 36, 205, 214, 238–40, 308.

14. *O.R.*, vol. 41, part 1, 77–8; part 2, 308.

15. *O.R.*, vol. 41, part 1, 79–81; Broadfoot, *Supplement to the O.R.*, part 2, 6th Missouri Cavalry, 183; Dyer, *Compendium*, vol. 2, 811; "Fight At Osceola," *Missouri Statesman*, Columbia, Boone County, 12 August 1864 (quoting Burris' report); Ross, *Autobiography of Samuel S. Hildebrand*, 116–19, 220–223n (the notes of which contrast Hildebrand's exaggerated claims of guerrillas inflicting casualties upon the Federal raiders with Burris' better documented claims that the truth was just the opposite).

16. *O.R.*, vol. 34, part 4, 524 (The remark that "the leaders are in the country" probably referred to Confederate recruiters of high rank already gathering recruits in several places of rural Missouri and the secret conspirators of the southern Knights of the Golden Circle.).

17. *O.R.*, vol. 41, part 2, 1020, 1023; Albert Castel, *General Sterling Price and the Civil War in the West*, 199–200.

18. *O.R.*, vol. 41, part 2, 1027–8.

19. *O.R.*, vol. 41, part 2, 1040–1, 1060–2, 1085–6; Castel, *General Sterling Price and the Civil War in the West*, 200.

20. "From New Madrid," *Kansas City Daily Journal*, Jackson County, 2 September 1864; United States Government, *1860 Missouri Census*, lists several Hayes and Cook households in New Madrid County; State of Missouri, Secretary of State's Office, Missouri State Archives, contain military service records for Privates A. D. Cook and Thomas Hayes of Captain James H. Howard's Company G, and Private Henry Hayes of Captain John L. Rainsburg's Company H, all of whom were on active duty in New Madrid County at this time; (Author's note: Although the newspaper reporter in New Madrid may have altered details in both stores to appeal to an audience of northern sympathy, the very pres-

ence of people and place name details and other particulars tends to indicate that some similar events actually happened.).

21. *O.R.*, vol. 41, part 2, 822, 838, 855; Ross, *Autobiography of Samuel S. Hildebrand*, 122–27 (Hildebrand described a raid he made in southeast Missouri during late August with four men, but he describes no such action as this attack on the forage train. Of course, compared to his other adventures Hildebrand may have thought sniping at some hay wagons was too minor an event to mention.).

22. *O.R.*, vol. 41, part 2, 956; part 3, 8, 28.

23. *O.R.*, vol. 41, part 4, 471.

24. *O.R.*, vol. 41, part 4, 565–6.

25. *O.R.*, vol. 41, part 1, 65; part 2, 148.

26. Fellman, *Inside War: The Guerrilla Conflict in Missouri During the American Civil War*, 168, 293n; Dyer, *Compendium*, vol. 3, 1317 (thumbnail histories of batteries of 2nd Missouri Light Artillery Regiment).

27. *O.R.*, vol. 41, part 2, 359.

28. Ivan N. McKee, *Lost Family—Lost Cause*, Freeman, South Dakota: Pine Hill Press, 1978, 54–61; Ross, *Autobiography of Samuel S. Hildebrand*, 224n; United States Government, *1860 Missouri Census*, lists in Jefferson Township of southeast Wayne County, the households of Missouri-born Blair and North Carolina–born Thomas McGee.

29. *O.R.*, vol. 41, part 2, 794; United States Government, *1860 Missouri Census*, lists the household of 27-year-old Missouri-born farmer Mancil Holder and his small family in the Poplar Bluff area of central Butler County.

30. McGhee, *Guide to Missouri Confederate Units, 1861–1865*, 168.

31. *O.R.*, vol. 34, part I, 994; "Guerrillas in Missouri," *Missouri Statesman*, Columbia, Boone County, 17 June 1864, from the earlier *St. Louis Union;* Dyer, *Compendium*, vol. 2, 810.

32. *O.R.*, vol. 34, part 4, 518.

33. Burns, "William Wilson, A Missouri Guerrilla," manuscript, 1–14; Bradbury, "Bushwhacker' Bill Wilson: Incidents on the Rolla-Salem Road," *Newsletter of the Phelps County Historical Society*, 1–12; Arthur, *The Bushwhacker: A Story of Missouri's Most Famous Desperado*, 1–122.

34. *O.R.*, vol. 41, part 2, 476; vol. 48, part 1, 258; State of Missouri, Secretary of State's Office, Missouri State Archives, military service record of Private Richard Watson of Captain Dawson's command in McDonald-St. Louis Battery (CSA) showing enlistment in Springfield 28 January 1862 after 1861 service with Colonel Thomas Roe Freeman's regiment in Missouri State Guard and lists numerous battles from Salem on 3 December 1861 through Vicksburg in 1863. This record states Watson was born in Dent County and listed his residence there at his enlistment; United States Government, *1860 Missouri Census*, lists in Township 37, Range 12 near Humboldt Post Office (north Pulaski County) the small family of 25-year-old Illinois-born farmer Richard Watson with 17-year-old Missouri-born wife Elizabeth and four-year-old Missouri-born son Thomas.

35. *O.R.*, vol. 34, part 4, 164–5; vol. 41, part 1, 734; part 2, 938–9, part 3, 588, 817; Eakin, *Missouri Prisoners of War*, entry for Captain W. H. Lenox of Crabtree's command; State of Missouri, Secretary of State's Officer, Missouri State Archives, military service record for Private William M. Lennox of Company D, Moore's 10th Missouri Infantry Regiment, showing enlistment 1 May 1862 and desertion 20 September 1862 at Pocahontas, Arkansas (and the identical records for Private David Lennox and Private John Lennox, but Captain John W. Lennox enlisted in the same company and regiment 1 August 1862, evidently served honorably, and was killed accidentally on the Missouri border 23 September 1863); United States Government, *1860 Missouri Census*, lists in Massey Township, northeast Phelps County, near St. James, shows household of 54-year-old wealthy Kentucky-born farmer Hamilton Lenox with older sons William (23, worker in marble yard), T. M. (22), J. W. M. (17).

36. *O.R.*, vol. 34, part 1, 115; Eakin, *Missouri Prisoners of War*, contains an incomplete record for a Private William T. Coats stating only that he was released sometime during the war from the Alton Military Prison on oath (which may or may not be the William Coats of Texas County); Broadfoot, *Supplement to the O.R.*, part 2, vol. 38, 270, record of events for Colonel William O. Coleman's regiment in lists of officers shows as officers of Company B, "[William] Coats, Capt."; "T. A. Yates, 1st Lt"; State of Missouri, Secretary of State's Office, Missouri State Archives, has record that Private W. M. Coats of Company C, Coleman's Regiment attended the 6th Annual Reunion of Missouri United Confederate Veterans at Houston, Missouri, according to UCV records on page 67 at Missouri Historical Society; United States Government, *1860 Missouri Census*, lists in Morris Township with Houston as post office, household of 30-year-old Tennessee-born farmer William Coates of modest real and personal property, 32-year-old Kentucky-born wife Rebecca, and four Missouri-born children ages 1 to 7 years; Email exchange between the author and Lloyd Ellis, eaglevalley@gotrain.org, of Cabool, Missouri, March and April 2008, regarding Mr. Ellis' great grandfather, Captain William Burdet Coats, and Mr. Ellis' extensive research into family history and war history of his ancestor.

37. *D.R.*, vol. 41, part 1, 42–3; Dyer, *Compendium*, vol. 2, 810.

38. "From Dillon, Missouri," *Daily Missouri Democrat*, St. Louis, 29 July 1864; "Murder in Texas County," *Daily Missouri Republican*, St. Louis, 29 July 1864; (No headline) *Missouri Statesman*, Columbia, Boone County, 5 August 1864; United States Government, *1860 Missouri Census*, lists in Boon Township of north Texas County the household of 38-year-old Missouri-born farmer Uri Phillips, who the census taker showed had only $300 in personal property but $5455 in real property; also lists in Liberty Township of southwest Phelps County the household of 38-year-old Ohio-born farmer A. Overlease of modest means and his Ohio-born wife and four small Ohio-born children (Henry Greiser does not appear in the 1860 census of this area under this or any similar spelling.); State of Missouri, Secretary of State's Office, Missouri State Archives, has military service record for Private Abraham Overleese who enlisted 1 August 1862 at age 42 at Rolla in Company G, 9th Missouri Cavalry Regiment, a few weeks later was mustered in at Benton Barracks, St. Louis, was later transferred to

Company L, 3rd Missouri Cavalry Regiment, and was mustered out of the 3rd in Little Rock, Arkansas during 1865.

39. *O.R.*, vol. 41, part 1, 74–75; part 2, 288; Eakin, *Missouri Prisoners of War*, entry for James W. Roberts.

40. *O.R.*, vol. 41, 476; United States Government, *1860 Missouri Census*, showing the location of Mill # 1 approximately near page 1062 of the census-taker's book of Piney Township in north-central Texas County since that page showed the household of R. W. Rodgers as the miller and on the same page men employed as sawyers, raftsmen, and teamsters for the mill. This page and Lynch Township census-taker's pages 1018 and 1019 show several of the residents Captain Muller suspected as having supported guerrillas as named in his report.

41. Dyer, *Compendium*, vol. 2, 811.

42. *O.R.*, vol. 41, part 2, 606.

43. Fellman, *Inside War: The Guerrilla Conflict in Missouri During the American Civil War*, 107, 286n.

44. *O.R.*, vol. 41, part 2, 960–1.

45. Ai Edgar Asbury, *My Experiences in the War, 1861–1865*, Kansas City: Berkowitz and Company, 1894, 27–8.

46. *O.R.*, vol. 41, part 2, 960–1.

47. *O.R.*, vol. 41, part 1, 734; part 2, 938–9; part 3, 106–7; "Guerrilla Murder and Robbery Near Rolla," *Daily Missouri Democrat*, St. Louis, 31 August 1864; "Further and Full Particulars of the Raid on Union Farm," *Daily Missouri Democrat*, 5 September 1864; Dunn, "Civil War Era—The Diary of John W. Goddard," *Ozarks Mountaineer*, 22–3.

48. *O.R.*, vol. 34, part 4, 443; A Union military troop disposition report filed June 30 reported the Pilot Knob garrison at that time housed parts of the 6th Missouri Cavalry, 135th Illinois Infantry, 3rd Cavalry MSM, Tyler's own 1st Infantry MSM, and the local 68th EMM nearby; *O.R.*, vol. 34, part 4, 624.

49. George F. Wilson, Maryhelen Wilson, and Lois Stanley, *Death Records From Missouri Newspapers, January 1861–December 1865*, Decorah, Iowa: Anundson Publishing Company, 1983, 173, 187; "Two Men Shot," *Perryville Union*, Perry County, 24 June 1864; United States Government, *1860 Missouri Census*, lists several Winsett households and three Francis Tucker households in various parts of Perry County.

50. Ross, *Autobiography of Samuel S. Hildebrand*, 108–9, 218–9n; State of Missouri, Secretary of State's Office, Missouri State Archives, military service records of Captain Ross Jelkyl, First Sergeant George Hart, and Privates John Zimmer and Louis Voges—all of Company B, 68th EMM, and from St. Francois and Madison Counties (none of these records addresses the killings of 27 June 1864); *O.R.*, vol. 34, part 4, 583; "Infernal Atrocity," *Missouri Statesman*, Columbia, Boone County, 15 July 1864, quoting earlier *St. Louis Union*; (Author's note: This article wrote the name of the murdered militiaman as "George Hartle," but the description of the torture, the location, and the timeframe match Hildebrand's description. A mystery of this expedition by Hildebrand was the accompaniment of a Confederate Captain Bowman, who Hildebrand wrote had a personal interest in revenge against George Hart "who, on a scout with some militia, had killed Captain Bowman's brother in order to get a very fine horse that he rode." This tends to explain why the guerrillas tortured Hart as well as killing the man. However, a correct identification among the several Captain Bowmans who served Missouri's southern cause is not clear in existing records.).

51. Ross, *Autobiography of Samuel S. Hildebrand*, 109; "Robbed By Guerrillas," *Daily Missouri Democrat*, St. Louis, 6 July 1864.

52. *O.R.*, vol. 41, part 2, 24.

53. Ross, *Autobiography of Samuel S. Hildebrand*, 110–1.

54. *O.R.*, vol. 41, part 2, 25.

55. Bollinger County Bicentennial Committee, *Bollinger County: 1851–1976*, Marceline, Missouri: Walsworth Publishing Company, 1977, 100; Geraldine Sanders Smith, *Civil War Times in Madison County, Missouri and Surrounding Counties*, St. Louis: published by author, 1999, 156.

56. Wilson, Wilson, and Stanley, *Death Records From Missouri Newspapers, January 1861–December 1865*, 76, 128; "Murder! Murder!" *Perryville Union*, Perry County, 8 July 1864; State of Missouri, Secretary of State's Office, Missouri State Archives, military service records for Private Jefferson Hartle of Company B, 79th EMM who served 18 days active duty in Bollinger County in April and May 1863, and 5th Corporal Bennet Murray who served between 8 August and 1 October 1861 in Company B. Fremont Rangers Home Guards at Cape Girardeau, Mo., and then mustered into Missouri State Militia (no record of this service in MSM found), with the notation "never was paid"; United States Government, *1860 Missouri Census*, lists both Bennett Murray and Jefferson Hartle households in Union Township, northwest Bollinger County; *O.R.*, vol. 41, part 2, 74.

57. "Death of a Noted Guerrilla," *Missouri Statesman*, Columbia, Boone County, 22 July 1864; Frost, *Camp and Prison Journal*, 147; Eakins, *Missouri Prisoners of War*, entry for Private Alfred Yates of Company D, Colonel Colton Greene's 3rd Missouri Cavalry Regiment (in all likelihood, the Union POW ledger obtained Yates' military unit from Yates himself, in Yates' vain attempt to be recognized and treated as a prisoner of war and not executed as a guerrilla. These ledger accounts contain many errors of all kinds and many known POWs are entirely missing from these records.); McGhee, *Guide to Missouri Confederate Units, 1861–1865*, 64 (shows that Company C—not D—of Colonel Greene's 3rd Missouri Cavalry contained Washington County men, perhaps indicating that Yates served the southern cause as both a regular soldier and as a bushwhacker); United States Government, *1860 Missouri Census*, in Union Township of east-central Washington County near the mining community of Lead Mines is the household of 67-year-old Kentucky-born farmer Charles Yates, his South Carolina–born wife Joyicy, with 25-year-old miner Missouri-born son Alfred.

58. Ross, *Autobiography of Samuel S. Hildebrand*, 112–121, 219–223n; "An Eccentric Bushwhacker," *Daily Missouri Republican*, St. Louis, 30 August 1864; "The Guerrillas in the Southwest [sic]," *Missouri Statesman*, Columbia, Boone County, 29 July 1864; *O.R.*, vol. 41, part 1, 87; part 2, 241, 267.

59. *O.R.*, vol. 41, part 1, 87; Dyer, *Compendium*,

vol. 2, 811; "The Guerrillas in the Southwest [sic]," *Missouri Statesman*, Columbia, Boone County, 29 July 1864; Ross, *Autobiography of Samuel S. Hildebrand*, 229–30.

60. "The Guerrillas in the Southwest [sic]," *Missouri Statesman*, Columbia, Boone County, 29 July 1864.

61. "Bushwhacking in Missouri: From Perry County, MO," *Daily Missouri Democrat*, St. Louis, 29 July 1864.

62. *O.R.*, vol. 41, part 2, 492; Ross, *Autobiography of Samuel S. Hildebrand*, 119–21, 223n.

63. "Bushwhacker Shot," *Daily Missouri Republican*, St. Louis, 14 August 1864; *O.R.*, vol. 41, part 2, 666.

64. "Local News: A Military Execution," *Daily Missouri Republican*, St. Louis, 28 December 1864; Goodspeed Publishing Company, *History of Franklin, Jefferson, Washington, Crawford, and Gasconade Counties, Missouri*, 424.

65. "Murder in Jefferson County," *Daily Missouri Democrat*, St. Louis, 26 August 1864; "Murder in Jefferson County," *Missouri Statesman*, Columbia, Boone County, 2 September 1864 from the *Daily Missouri Democrat* article of 26 August 1864; Goodspeed Publishing Company, *History of Franklin, Jefferson, Washington, Crawford, and Gasconade Counties, Missouri*, 423–4; State of Missouri, Secretary of State's Office, Missouri State Archives, shows several Private Hursts in Company E, 6th Missouri Cavalry, but none shows any evidence of discipline for the Pitzer murder; United States Government, *1860 Missouri Census*, lists 53-year-old Missouri-born farmer Durguid Pitzer in Merrimac Township of northwest Jefferson County.

66. Goodspeed Publishing Company, *History of Franklin, Jefferson, Washington, Crawford, and Gasconade Counties, Missouri*, 423–4; United States Government, *1860 Missouri Census*, household of 44-year-old Missouri-born farmer Thomas Wall in Big River Township of west-central Jefferson County; household of 41-year-old Indiana-born farmer Ire Drake of Plattin Township, southeast Jefferson County; five Gamel men of military age listed in Big River Township of west-central Jefferson County and Joachim Township of east-central Jefferson County; State of Missouri, Secretary of State's Office, Missouri State Archives, lists no military service records on either side for these names except 26-year-old miner James Gamel, who served in DeSoto for 22 days active duty in September and October 1864 in Union Company B, 80th EMM.

67. State of Missouri, *Report of the Adjutant General of the State of Missouri for the Year* 1865, 343 (shows Captain R. H. Montgomery of Company E, 6th Missouri Cavalry Regiment resigning as of 20 September 1864).

68. *O.R.*, vol. 41, part 3, 28–9.

69. Ross, *Autobiography of Samuel S. Hildebrand*, 122–7, 224–227n.

70. "Affairs in the Southeast," *Daily Missouri Democrat*, St. Louis, 1 September 1864; McGhee, *Guide to Missouri Confederate Units, 1861–1865*, 144–5 (about Berryman in Clardy's Battalion); Ross, *Autobiography of Samuel S. Hildebrand* (see index for a number of entries about Berryman, Highley, and Grady associated with Hildebrand); State of Missouri, Secretary of State's Office, Missouri State Archives, military service record of First Lieutenant Christian Helber (also spelled "Hilber") in both the 68th EMM and Company F, 47th Missouri Infantry; State of Missouri, *Report of the Adjutant General of the State of Missouri for the Year* 1865, 284–5 (for details about the formation of the 4th Missouri Infantry and Lieutenant Helber in it); Dyer, *Compendium*, vol. 3, 1338 (for details about the formation of the 47th Missouri Infantry).

71. *O.R.*, vol. 41, part 3, 29; Ross, *Autobiography of Samuel S. Hildebrand*, 212n (for background information about David Reed); United States Government, 1860 *Missouri Census*, lists in Cowan Township, east Wayne County, household of 36-year-old Indiana-born blacksmith David Reed; (Author's note: The "depredations" these guerrillas committed may have been the raid on the wagons carrying food near Bessville as mentioned earlier.).

72. *O.R.*, vol. 34, part 4, 196; State of Missouri, Secretary of State's Office, Missouri State Archives, military service record of Private Samuel King in Company L, 11th Missouri Cavalry Regiment, the mention of his desertion 24 April 1864, and his death at Sullivan 1 June 1864.

73. *O.R.*, vol. 34, part 4, 244; Dyer, *Compendium*, vol. 3, 1183 (short history of the 7th Kansas Cavalry).

74. *O.R.*, vol. 41, part 2, 148; "Bushwhackers in Crawford County," *Daily Missouri Democrat*, St. Louis, 21 July 1864; "Bushwhackers in Washington County," *Daily Missouri Democrat*, St. Louis, 3 August 1864; United States Government, 1860 *Missouri Census*, lists in Johnson Township of northwest Washington County on page 451 the household of 44-year-old New Hampshire–born, lumberman Samuel Grant, and on page 452 the household of Missouri-born farmer Felix W. Summers; State of Missouri, Secretary of State's Office, Missouri State Archives, military service record for Private Valentine P. Summers in Company H, 11th Missouri Cavalry, who enlisted at Rolla 14 July 1863 and was mustered in at St. Louis 28 July 1863 and deserted that same day; (Author's note: It may or may not be a coincidence that Summers deserted from the same regiment as Samuel King, and that they were both in the same neighborhood about a month apart.)

75. "The Guerrilla War: Marauding in Washington County," *Daily Missouri Democrat*, St. Louis, 16 July 1864, from the earlier *Washington County News* (This newspaper account made no attempt to number the Rebel raiders.); State of Missouri, *Report of the Adjutant General of the State of Missouri for the Year* 1865, 283–5 (for military background of Amos Maupin); (Author's note: The newspaper article claimed the victimized family was named "Rue," although no such name appears in this area in the 1860 census, but several Rulo households were in this part of Washington County.).

76. *O.R.*, vol. 41, part 1, 186; part 2, 421, 476; (Author's note: The author could find no other details of this raid on Vienna except these military reports that stated the town was robbed. So much was happening around the state at this time that none of the area newspapers covered this event.

77. *O.R.*, vol. 41, part 2, 596; Nichols, *Guerrilla Warfare in Civil War Missouri*, Volume I, 1863, 244 (containing some information about Colonel Hull in Missouri during 1863); McGhee, *Guide to Missouri*

Confederate Units, 1861–1865, 185 (containing some information on Hull as a regular Confederate officer); Peterson, et al., *Price's Lieutenants*, 87–8 (containing information about Hull's contributions to the southern Missouri State Guard early in the war); State of Missouri, Secretary of State's Office, Missouri State Archives, military service record for Lieutenant Colonel Edward or Edmund B. Hull in various commands throughout the war.

78. "Bushwhackers in Washington County," *Daily Missouri Democrat*, St. Louis, 12 August 1864; "A Bushwhacker Brought In," *Daily Missouri Republican*, St. Louis, 14 August 1864; "Another Rebel Mail Captured," *Missouri Statesman*, Columbia, Boone County, 26 August 1864.

79. Emma Comfort Dunn, "The Diary of John Goddard," *Ozarks Mountaineer*, 22–3; State of Missouri, Secretary of State's Office, Missouri State Archives, military service record of Private John Goddard who enrolled 5 October 1864 in Company K, 63rd EMM at Rolla at age 26, then served 68 days active duty mostly in the Sullivan, south-central Franklin County, garrison from that date until 2 December 1864; the author exchanged correspondence during November 1992 with Dottie Braunsdorf, 5451 Valleyside Lane, St. Louis, 63128 regarding her ancestor John Goddard's diary entries about his Civil War observations and participation in his neighborhood.

80. *O.R.*, vol. 41, part 1, 272; part 2, 855, 861; part 3, 28–9; "From Pilot Knob," *Daily Missouri Democrat*, St. Louis, 26 August 1864; "To All Whom It May Concern," *Daily Missouri Republican*, St. Louis, 30 August 1864; Dyer, *Compendium*, vol. 2, 811; McGhee, *Guide to Missouri Confederate Units, 1861–1865*, 88, 91 (showing Captain Evans' unit affiliation and actions in this area); (Author's note: Several of the above sources named Captain Evans' partner as a "Captain Harris," perhaps confusing the name with the local 32nd EMM officer, Captain Andrew J. Harris. The author presumed that these reports meant the name to be local Washington and Reynolds County Confederate recruiter "Captain Seth C. Farris," who actually recruited southern men in this area in 1863 and 1865.); Goodspeed Publishing Company, *History of Franklin, Jefferson, Washington, Crawford, and Gasconade Counties, Missouri*, 507 (showing Seth C. Farris as an active southern leader in Washington County during the war).

TWELVE

1. Eakin, *Missouri Prisoners of War*, three entries for Major John F. Rucker regarding this arrest and imprisonment through the end of the war; State of Missouri, Secretary of State's Office, Missouri State Archives, military service record for Major John F. Rucker of Sturgeon, Missouri; United States Government, *1860 Missouri Census*, in census of village of Sturgeon, Bourbon Township, north Boone County, in John Curtain household is 21-year-old Virginia-born laborer John F. Rucker.

2. *O.R.*, series 1, vol. 53, 999–1000.

3. *O.R.*, series 2, vol. 7, 228–366, 626–660; Castel, *General Sterling Price and the Civil War in the West*, 191–6; Louis S. Gerteis, "'An Outrage on Humanity': Martial Law and Military Prisons in St. Louis During the Civil War," *Missouri Historical Review*, 96 (July 2002) 4, 315–21; Louis S. Gerteis, *Civil War St. Louis*, Lawrence, Kansas: University of Kansas Press, 2002, 196–200; George E. Rule, "Tucker's War: Missouri and the Northwest Conspiracy," paper copyright 2002 by G. E. Rule on his website "The Civil War in St. Louis," http://www.civilwarstlouis.com/History2/tuckerswar.htm., 12 of 27 pages; "A Startling Rebel Plot of Great Magnitude," *Kansas City Daily Journal*, Jackson County, 30 July 1864, from the earlier *Chicago Tribune*; United States Government, *1860 Missouri Census*, lists in St. Louis city's ninth ward the household of 36-year-old Maryland-born superintendent of Gas Light Company Charles E. Dunn.

4. *O.R.*, series I, vol. 41, part 2, 147; "Guerrilla Raid Near St. Louis," *Daily Missouri Democrat*, St. Louis, 14 July 1964; Broadfoot, *Supplement to the O.R.*, part 2, vol. 35, 5th Cavalry MSM, 150.

5. "Robbery of Rinkle's Six-Mile House," *Daily Missouri Democrat*, St. Louis, 28 July 1864.

6. *O.R.*, series I, vol. 41, part 2, 879.

7. *O.R.*, series 1, vol. 41, part 2, 717.

8. "Spy Hung," *Kansas City Journal*, Jackson County, 27 August 1864; Frost, *Camp and Prison Journal*, 160–1.

9. "An Attempt to Burn a Steamboat," *Daily Missouri Democrat*, St. Louis, 14 July 1864; Way, *Way's Packet Directory, 1848–1994*, 223; Nichols, *Guerrilla Warfare in Civil War Missouri, Volume II, 1863*, 271 (regarding the September 1863 loss of the other steamer *Imperial*).

10. *O.R.*, series 1, vol. 41, part 2, 209; "Extensive Steamboat Conflagration at the Levee," *Daily Missouri Democrat*, St. Louis, 16 July 1864; Way, *Way's Packet Directory, 1848–1994*, 142, 188, 312, 350, 437–8, 483; Nichols, *Guerrilla Warfare in Civil War Missouri, 1862*, 13 (mentions steamboat *Sunshine* during 1862); Nichols, *Guerrilla Warfare in Civil War Missouri, Volume II, 1863*, 154, 272–3, 318 (mentions steamboat *City of Alton* twice during 1863 and steamboat *Sunshine* during 1861).

11. *O.R.*, series 1, vol. 41, part 2, 199, 209.

12. *O.R.*, series 2, vol. 7, 201; (See the related section in Chapter 1 regarding Surgeon Clark's comments about structural problems at the Gratiot Street Military Prison.).

13. Frost, *Camp and Prison Journal*, 135–6. (Author's Note: Sources differ as to whether the orphan A. J. Lanier should be called "Joseph" or "James.")

14. *O.R.*, series 2, vol. 7, 224–5; State of Kansas, *Report of Adjutant General*, 220; United States Government, *Official Army Register*, vol. 7, 10th Kansas Cavalry, 351.

15. *O.R.*, series 2, vol. 7, 398–9; Frost, *Camp and Prison Journal*, 139–41; Absalom Grimes, *Absalom Grimes: Confederate Mail Runner*, New Haven, Connecticut: Yale University Press, 1926, 216; "Attempt of Prisoners at Gratiot to Escape," *Daily Missouri Democrat*, St. Louis, 20 June 1864; Eakin, *Missouri Prisoners of War*, John C. Carlin, Joseph A. Colclazier, William M. Douglas, and Alfred Yates entries; State of Missouri, Secretary of State's Office, Missouri State Archives, military service records for Major Absalom Grimes, Lieutenant Jasper C. Hill, and Captain W. H. Sebring; United States Government, *1860 Missouri Census*, lists in Round Grove Township, northwest Marion County, in or near village of Emerson, the household of trader A. C. Bailey

including 18-year-old Illinois-born farm laborer John Carlin; Nichols, *Guerrilla Warfare in Civil War Missouri, Volume II, 1863*, 30 (tribunal conviction of guerrilla John Abshire during autumn 1864 for January 1863 killing of a Wayne County man), 271 (for capture of Colonel John C. Carlin and Lieutenant William H. Sebring with two others attempting escape from Gratiot Street Prison on 25 December 1863).

16. Eakin, *Missouri Prisoners of War*, Robert S. Lavelle, T. M. Meador, Edward Philips, and John Thrailkill entries; "Prisoners Escaped from Alton," *Daily Missouri Democrat*, 2 July 1864; Nichols, *Guerrilla Warfare in Civil War Missouri, Volume II, 1863*, 189–90 (regarding Union troops capturing Captain Thrailkill in Clinton County 19 July 1863).

17. *O.R.*, series 2, vol. 7, 398, 455–6.

18. *O.R.*, series 2, vol. 7, 470–1.

19. Eakin, *Missouri Prisoners of War*, W. R. P. Henderson entry; "Alton Prison Report," *Daily Missouri Democrat*, St. Louis, 28 July 1864.

20. Eakin, *Missouri Prisoners of War*, Wm. P. Wilson entry; McGhee, *Guide to Missouri Confederate Units, 1861–1865*, 84–5.

21. *O.R.*, series 2, vol. 7, 533–4, 535–7.

22. "Daring Attempt to Escape from Myrtle St. Prison," *Daily Missouri Democrat*, St. Louis, 15 August 1864; "Miss Anna Fickle," *Kansas City Daily Journal*, Jackson County, 7 July 1864; Eakin, *Missouri Prisoners of War*, Anna Fickle entry; Joanne Chiles Eakin, *Civil War Military Prisoners Sent to Missouri State Penitentiary*, Independence, Missouri: published by Mrs. Eakin, 1995, 4; United States Government, *1860 Missouri Census*, lists in Clay Township of northwest Lafayette County, the household of 50-year-old Virginia-born farmer Henry H. Fickel including his 21-year-old Missouri-born daughter, Anne E. Fickel (This author uses the census and other local records for the spelling of Miss Fickel's surname.).

23. *O.R.*, series 2, vol. 7, 661, 699–700, 772.

24. Frost, *Camp and Prison Journal*, 165–6.

Thirteen

1. *O.R.*, vol. 34, part 1, 966–7; Britton, *The Civil War on the Border*, vol. 2, 200–1; Dyer, *Compendium*, vol. 2, 810; State of Missouri, Secretary of State's Office, Missouri State Archives, military service record for First Lieutenant John R. Goode in Company K, 11th Missouri Infantry Regiment (CSA), who joined that unit at age 29; United States Government, *1860 Missouri Census*, lists in the household of Harmon Middleton in Marion Township, north-central Newton County, 26-year-old Missouri-born John R. Good.

2. *O.R.*, vol. 34, part 4, 227, 246–8, 313, 327; McGhee, *Guide to Missouri Confederate Units, 1861–1865*, 136–8 (details about Major Pickler's Confederate service).

3. *O.R.*, vol. 34, part 4, 344–5, 395–6; Schrantz, *Jasper County, Missouri in the Civil War*, 178–9; Eakin and Hale, *Branded As Rebels*, 293–4 (for identification of Edward McCullough); (Author's note: The mysterious Colonel Palmer and his recruiting command evidently continued north to west-central Missouri where Union forces reported them heading back south again with recruits about August 26, according to *O.R.*, vol. 41, part 1, 271–2, 292–3; and part 2, 913. Brigadier General Shelby's headquarters on May 27, 1864, according to *O.R.*, vol. 34, part 4, 633, ordered Major Jesse F. Pickler's battalion, including by name Captains David V. Rusk of Jasper County and Lafayette Roberts of Cedar County to recruit men in their home counties for the Confederacy, but little information remains to prove if they actually brought into their guerrilla bands more than just a few recruits, and a number of their men were killed fighting with Federals this summer.).

4. *O.R.*, vol. 34, part 4, 344.

5. (No headline), *Kansas City Daily Journal*, Jackson County, 11 June 1864.

6. *O.R.*, vol. 34, part 4, 363; Boatner, *The Civil War Dictionary*, 719; Ezra J. Warner, *Generals in Blue: Lives of the Northern Commanders*, 418–9.

7. *O.R.*, vol. 34, part 4, 456.

8. Schrantz, *Jasper County, Missouri During the Civil War*, 180–6; United States Government, *1860 Missouri Census*, lists in Marion Township near Carthage the small household of 23-year-old Tennessee-born farmer A. S. Humbard.

9. Schrantz, *Jasper County, Missouri During the Civil War*, 186–8; Eakin and Hale, *Branded as Rebels*, 393; United States Government, *1860 Missouri Census*, lists in Carthage the household of 66-year-old Virginia-born hotel keeper John Shirley, including his 12-year-old Missouri-born, daughter, Myra, and her 11-year-old brother, Edwin.

10. Schrantz, *Jasper County, Missouri During the Civil War*, 194–6; United States Government, *1860 Missouri Census*, lists in Center Creek Township, near Sherwood the household of 36-year-old Virginia-born farmer Andrew M. Rader and 16-year-old Missouri-born son William.

11. *O.R.*, vol. 41, part 2, 249; State of Missouri, *Report of the Adjutant General for the State of Missouri for the Year 1865*, 392 (for the conversion of the 6th and 7th Provisional EMM into the 15th and 16th Missouri Cavalry Regiments).

12. *O.R.*, vol. 41, part I, 75–7; Schrantz, *Jasper County, Missouri in the Civil War*, 188–192; Dyer, *Compendium*, vol. 2, 811.

13. Schrantz, *Jasper County, Missouri in the Civil War*, 197–200.

14. *O.R.*, vol. 41, part I, 188; "Missouri Items," *Daily Missouri Democrat*, St. Louis, 12 August 1864, from *Springfield Journal*, Greene County, 8 August 1864; Dyer, *Compendium*, vol. 2, 725.

15. *O.R.*, vol. 41, part 1, 193, 195; Schrantz, *Jasper County, Missouri in the Civil War*, 193–4; Dyer, *Compendium*, vol. 2, 811.

16. *O.R.*, vol. 41, part 1, 192–3; Dyer, *Compendium*, vol. 2, 811.

17. Broadfoot, *Supplement to the O.R.*, part 2, vol. 35, 8th Cavalry MSM, 539, 571; Dyer, *Compendium*, vol. 2, 811.

18. *O.R.*, vol. 41, part 1, 193, 196–7; Broadfoot, *Supplement to the O.R.*, part 2, vol. 35, 8th Cavalry MSM, 572; Dyer, *Compendium*, vol. 2, 811.

19. *O.R.*, vol. 41, part 1, 198; Broadfoot, *Supplement to the O.R.*, part 2, vol. 35, 8th Cavalry MSM, 542.

20. Broadfoot, *Supplement to the O.R.*, part 2, vol. 35, 8th Cavalry MSM, 572; Dyer, *Compendium*, vol. 2, 811.

21. *O.R.*, vol. 41, part 1, 198.

22. *O.R.*, vol. 34, part 1, 1000; "Bushwhackers

Routed," *Kansas City Journal,* Jackson County, 16 June 1864 (word for word copy with errors of Colonel Blair's report); "Fight With Bushwhackers," *Daily Missouri Democrat,* St. Louis, 17 June 1864 (word for word copy of Kansas City issue with a different headline).

23. Patrick Brophy, editor, *"Found No Bushwhackers"; The 1864 Diary of Sgt. James P. Mallery,* 31; Nichols, *Guerrilla Warfare in Civil War Missouri, Volume I, 1862,* 77–9, 111 (relating to Montevallo being strong in southern sympathy during 1862).

24. *O.R. vol.* 34, part 1, 1000; "Bushwhackers Routed," *Kansas City Daily Journal,* Jackson County, 16 June 1864; "Fight With Bushwhackers," *St. Louis Democrat,* St. Louis, 17 June 1864; Dyer, *Compendium,* vol. 2, 810 (Dyer called this an "affair at Montevallo" rather than a skirmish, and gave the date for it as June 12).

25. *O.R.,* vol. 34, part 4, 368, 396.

26. McGhee, *Guide to Missouri Confederate Units, 1861–1865,* 136; Eakin and Hale, *Branded as Rebels,* 372; *O.R.,* vol. 34, part 4, 633; Peterson, et al., *Price's Lieutenants,* 258; United States Government, *1860 Missouri Census,* lists in Linn Township of south-central Cedar County near White Hare the household of Tennessee-born farmer John J. Roberts and his Tennessee-born 18-year-old farm laborer son "Layfette."

27. *O.R.,* vol. 34, part 1, 1006, 1009–10; "Raid on Melville," *Missouri Statesman,* Columbia, Boone County, 1 July 1864, from the earlier *Springfield Journal,* Greene County; Broadfoot, *Supplement to the O.R.,* part 2, vol. 35, 15th Missouri Infantry, 806; Dyer, *Compendium,* vol. 2, 810.

28. *O.R.,* vol. 34, part 1, 1015–6; part 4, 456; Schrantz, *Jasper County, Missouri During the Civil War,* 178–80; Dyer, *Compendium,* vol. 2, 801.

29. *O.R.,* vol. 34, part 4, 526; "Murder of Captain Rogers," *Kansas City Daily Journal,* Jackson County, 25 June 1864, from the earlier *Leavenworth Conservative;* State of Kansas, *Report of the Adjutant General of the State of Kansas, 1861–65,* 198.

30. *O.R.,* vol. 34, part 1, 1038–9; Dyer, *Compendium,* vol. 2, 810.

31. *O.R.,* vol. 41, part 2, 63; Broadfoot, *Supplement to the O.R.,* part 2, vol. 21, 15th Kansas Cavalry, 479; State of Kansas, *Report of the Adjutant General of the State of Kansas, 1861–65,* 526–7 (noted for Sergeant William J. Wallace of Topeka that he was "Killed by guerrillas, July 4, '64, Cow Creek, Kan." and for Private Jesse H. Beeson of Olathe that he was discharged for disability).

32. *O.R.,* vol. 41, part 2, 63, 64.

33. *O.R.,* vol. 41, part 2, 165.

34. *O.R.,* vol. 41, part 2, 145, 165; "Guerrilla Demonstration Near Fort Lincoln," *Kansas City Daily Journal,* Jackson County, 20 July 1864, from earlier *Leavenworth Conservative;* Brophy, *"Found No Bushwhackers": The 1864 Diary of Sgt. James P. Mallery,* 34.

35. *O.R.,* vol. 41, part 2, 256.

36. *O.R.,* vol. 41, part 1, 13; part 2, 270, 361; McGhee, *Guide to Missouri Confederate Units, 1861–1865,* 138.

37. Brophy, *"Found No Bushwhackers": The 1864 Diary of Sgt. James P. Mallery,* 35; Brown and Company, *History of Vernon County, Missouri,* 341–2; Nichols, *Guerrilla Warfare in Civil War Missouri,* *Volume II, 1863,* 99, 278 (chronicling part of Mayfield women's Rebel activities during 1863).

38. *O.R.,* vol. 41, part 2, 491–2; "Bushwhackers at Cow Creek," *Kansas City Daily Journal,* Jackson County, 5 August 1864.

39. *O.R.,* vol. 41, part 2, 611.

40. *O.R.,* vol. 41, part 2, 924; Bartels, *The Forgotten Men,* 229–30 (giving military service record for Captain Robert Marchbanks during 1861 and 1862); United States Government, *1860 Missouri Census,* lists in Henry Township, northwest corner of Vernon County, household of Tennessee-born farmer N. R. Marchbanks, Tennessee-born 25-year-old farmer William Marchbanks, and Tennessee-born 23-year-old farmer Robert Marchbanks.

41. *O.R.,* vol. 34, part 4, 342–3; Nichols, *Guerrilla Warfare in Civil War Missouri, Volume II, 1863,* 16–7, 92 (showing actions involving parts of the 60th EMM in St. Clair County during 1863).

42. *O.R.,* vol. 34, part 1, 990–2 (regarding problems the 2nd Colorado Cavalry encountered with misfiring of their Starr carbines, see endnote #39 in Chapter 9); Dyer, *Compendium,* vol. 2, 810,

43. *O.R.,* vol. 34, part 1, 1001; "Bushwhackers in Calhoun, Mo.," *Daily Missouri Democrat,* St. Louis, 17 June 1864; Dyer, *Compendium,* vol. 2, 810; State of Missouri, Secretary of State's Office, Missouri State Archives, military service records of Surgeon Willis S. Holland of the staff of 60th EMM, and Sergeant Thomas Sallee of Company A, 60th EMM; (Author's note: The author and online researcher John Russell, MD, of Cape Girardeau, Missouri, studied several Beck males of this region in census and other records looking for the elusive "Dr. Beck," but found none whose occupation could warrant being called "doctor" alive before June 12 or dead after that date.).

44. "From Warsaw—Bushwhacking," *Daily Missouri Democrat,* St. Louis, 12 July 1864; State of Missouri, Secretary of State's Office, Missouri State Archives, military service records of First Sergeant David McGee and Corporal William W. T. Bernard; both of Company A, 60th EMM showing they each served 279 days active duty during late 1862 and early 1863 in Warsaw, and were both called to active duty in 1864, but provided no specifics about such duty in 1864.

45. "The Guerrilla Outrages," *Daily Missouri Democrat,* St. Louis, 12 July 1864; United States Government, *1860 Missouri Census,* shows as the only McBride in St. Clair County at that time 34-year-old Ohio-born schoolteacher Phillip McBride living in the household of farmer Calvin Parks in Monegaw Township, northwest-central St. Clair County; State of Missouri, Secretary of State's Office, Missouri State Archives, lists no military service for such a name as Phillip McBride.

46. *O.R.,* vol. 41, part 2, 389.

47. Eakin, *Missouri Prisoners of War,* John M. Edwards entry.

48. *O.R.,* vol. 41, part 2, 560.

49. *O.R.,* vol. 41, part 2, 808; "Guerrilla Fight," *Kansas City Daily Journal,* Jackson County, 3 September 1864.

50. *O.R.,* vol. 34, part 1, 970–1; Dyer, *Compendium,* vol. 2, 810.

51. *O.R.,* vol. 34, part 4, 312–3.

52. Western Historical Company, *History of*

Greene County, Missouri, 472; Jonathan Fairbanks and Clyde Edwin Tuck, *Past and Present of Greene County*, 375; (Author's note: The Fairbanks and Tuck history mentioned that the two soldiers were infantrymen who were part of a detail escorting a wagon train to Springfield from Cassville, county seat of Barry County. As of the end of June the only Union troops listed as garrisoning Cassville were six companies of the 2nd Arkansas Cavalry, according to *O.R.*, vol. 34, part 4, 625, so perhaps the two killed men were actually cavalrymen of that unit.).

53. *O.R.*, vol. 34, part 4, 396; United States Government, *1860 Missouri Census*, lists no Hanly or Hanley in this region, but three Seely or Sealy households in central and east Jasper and west Lawrence counties with Missouri-born, farmer, heads-of-households who were young men in thirties as of 1864, with wives born in Tennessee or North Carolina, and small children at home.

54. *O.R.*, vol. 34, part 2, 89, 99–100; State of Missouri, Secretary of State's Office, Missouri State Archives, military service record of Private Hiram W. Cornogg, Company A, 72nd EMM, who enrolled at Ozark, Christian County, May 1,1864; United States Government, *1860 Missouri Census*, lists in Finley Township near the town of Ozark, Christian County, the household of Pennsylvania-born 47-year-old blacksmith F. H. Cornog, and his large family including Tennessee-born 15-year-old son H. W. Cornog.

55. *O.R.*, vol. 41, part 2, 10; State of Missouri, Secretary of State's Office, Missouri State Archives, military service record for Private Samuel C. Hoskins early in the war first in the Ozark County northern home guards in Ozark County and then in Springfield immediately followed by his service in Phelps Regiment Missouri Volunteers at Rolla. The latter unit record strangely shows that Haskins "died of disease 5 March 1862," but that could be an error; United States Government, *1860 Missouri Census*, lists in Falling Spring Township of Ozark County the small household of 27-year-old Tennessee-born farmer Samuel Haskins, a young wife and small child, but no other Haskins by that name in this region of Missouri or Arkansas.

56. *O.R.*, vol. 41, part 2, 149; Broadfoot, *Supplement to the O.R.*, part 2, vol. 35, 16th Missouri Cavalry, 815; Rose Mary Lankford, *The Encyclopedia of Quantrill's Guerrillas*, 319–20; (Author's note: Lankford compiled information from a variety of sources to indicate that Jacob Franklin Gregg joined Andy Blunt's guerrilla company with Frank James perhaps in 1863, and for a time joined regular Confederate service in Louisiana during the winter of 1863–1864 with John Jarette. This would indicate that these bushwhackers may have deserted regular Confederate service or were detailed to return to Missouri to recruit just prior to the time of their trip through southwest Missouri in July 1864.).

57. *O.R.*, vol. 41, part 1, 75; Dyer, *Compendium*, vol. 2, 811.

58. *O.R.*, vol. 41, part I, 75; Dyer, *Compendium*, vol. 2, 811.

59. Dyer, *Compendium*, vol. 2, 811.

60. Lizzie C. Gilmore, Papers, 1861–1865, letter written from Lebanon, Missouri, 9 August 1864, Rolla, Missouri: Western Historical Manuscripts Collection, Collection number R346, 1 folder.

61. *O.R.*, vol. 41, part 1, 240–1; part 2, 687; Broadfoot, *Supplement to the O.R.*, part 2, vol. 35, 16th Missouri *Cavalry*, 816; McGhee, *Guide to Missouri Confederate Units, 1861–1865*, 113–4.

62. Dyer, *Compendium*, vol. 2, 811.

63. Stanley, Wilson, and Wilson, *Death Records From Missouri Newspapers, January 1861–December 1865*, 183 (citing undated *Lebanon Union* as quoted later in the *Sedalia Advertiser*, Pettis County, of 3 September 1864; State of Missouri, Secretary of State's Office, Missouri State Archives, military service record of Private Isaac Whitson of Captain D. A. W. Morehouse' General Orders Number 107 unit of Laclede County Provisional Company EMM, which states only that he enlisted in the company at Lebanon 1 August 1864; United States Government, *1860 Missouri Census*, shows household of 41-year-old Tennessee-born farmer Isaac Whitson on page 286 of Osage Township, in east-central Laclede County.

64. *O.R.*, vol. 41, part 1, 301; part 2, 940 (the part 2 reference printed the contents of two letters from 10th Missouri Cavalry Quartermaster A. M. Lay, one of which was apparently addressed to inactive Rebel Brigadier General Warwick Hough); Broadfoot, *Supplement to the O.R.*, part 2, vol. 35, 16th Missouri Cavalry (USA), 816; Dyer, *Compendium*, vol. 2, 812; McGhee, *Guide to Missouri Confederate Units, 1861–1865*, 88–92 (McGhee lists Company A commander Captain John D. Brinker of Johnson County, mentioned by Lay in one of his two letters); State of Missouri, Secretary of State's Office, Missouri State Archives, military service records for southern Missouri State Guard Brigadier General Warwick Hough who served the southern cause in Missouri during 1861 (who evidently was the intended recipient for one of Quartermaster Lay's letters), and for a Captain John Pace of Company H, 3rd Missouri Infantry of Missouri State Guard, buried at the Springfield National Cemetery in Greene County (who may or may not be the Captain Pace of this episode); United States Government, *1860 Missouri Census*, lists all in Jefferson Township of north-central Cole County the households of 24-year-old U.S. District Attorney A. M. Lay; a 25-year-old clerk, James F. McHenry, in the J. B. McHenry household (probably the Jim McHenry mentioned in one of Lay's intercepted letters), and in the George W. Hough household, 23-year-old lawyer Warwick Hough.

FOURTEEN

1. "Trial of J.W. Terman," *St. Joseph Weekly Herald*, Buchanan County, 14 July 1864; *O.R.*, vol. 34, part 4, 314, 324.

2. *O.R.*, vol. 34, part 4, 272, 286, 314–5, 324, 328, 345–7, 371–4, 396–8, 436; National Historical Company, *History of Howard and Chariton Counties, Missouri*, St. Louis: National Historical Company, 1883, 538–40; "Trial of J.W. Terman," *St. Joseph Weekly Herald*, Buchanan County, 14 July, 21 July, 28 July, 4 August, and 11 August 1864 (trial transcripts list names of Chariton County men killed by Terman and his entourage to include John and Jathin Walker, George Veal, Peter Fox, Henry C. Jennings, Veach Starks, William Viers, and a Berve); "Bushwhacking in Chariton—Six Union Men Killed,"

Daily Missouri Republican, St. Louis, 10 January 1865; Edwards, *Noted Guerrillas, or the Warfare on the Border,* 307 (Edwards lists Howard County men killed by Terman and company as Sashel Carson, Oliver Rose, Tazewell Jones, John Stepp, John T. Marshall, and John Cooper); Stanley, Wilson, and Wilson, *Death Records From Missouri Newspapers, January 1861–December 1865,* 44, 57, 59, 86, 88, 163, 176; (Author's note: Local sources list additional men evidently killed by Terman and his supporters to include Abner Finnell, Moses Hurt, [first name unknown] Dejarnett, William R. Redding, James Stark Jr., [first name unknown] Pixley, Allen Farmer, and [first name unknown] Franklin.).

3. "Bushwhackers," *Missouri Statesman,* Columbia, Boone County, 3 June 1864, from the earlier *Fayette Advertiser,* Howard County.

4. *O.R.,* vol. 34, part 4, 224, 248; "Great Excitement in Chariton County," *Daily Missouri Democrat,* St. Louis, 9 June 1864, quoted from the *Central City and Brunswicker,* Brunswick, Chariton County, 6 June 1864; "Bushwhackers in Chariton County," *Liberty Tribune,* Clay County, 17 June 1864, from the earlier *Central City and Brunswicker,* Brunswick, Chariton County; "Guerrillas in Missouri," *Missouri Statesman,* Columbia, Boone County, 17 June 1864, taken from the earlier *Macon Gazette,* Macon County; "Raid on Keytesville," *Missouri Statesman,* Columbia, Boone County, 24 June 1864; Nichols, *Guerrilla Warfare in Civil War Missouri, Volume II, 1863,* 138 (for details about the 9th Cavalry MSM killing of Holtzclaw's father in August 1863).

5. *O.R.,* vol. 34, part 4, 350.

6. *O.R.,* vol. 34, part 4, 363, 375, 377–8 (These resources do not name the murdered men.); "Bushwhacking in Chariton—Six Union Men Killed," *Daily Missouri Republican,* St. Louis, 10 January 1865; Stanley, Wilson, and Wilson, *Death Records From Missouri Newspapers, January 1861–December 1865,* 88 (lists Charles Jenson as a retaliatory killing in Chariton County); United States Government, *1860 Missouri Census,* lists in Prairie Township of south-central Chariton County the households of both Lucius Salisbury, Jr., on page 213 and Charles Jinson on page 206; National Historical Company, *History of Howard and Chariton Counties,* 540 (lists as retaliatory murders Parkenhammer, Charles Jenson, [first name unknown] McDonald, and a black man "who worked at Hurt's tobacco factory"); State of Missouri, Secretary of State's Office, Missouri State Archives, military service record of First Sergeant Charles Jenson of Company A, 35th EMM who served 36 days active duty in Brunswick, southwest Chariton County, in November and December 1862.

7. *O.R.,* vol. 34, part 4, 437 (This source quotes Judge Salisbury as stating Charles Coleman and Charles Grotjohn are two of the four murdered men.); "Bushwhacking in Chariton—Six Union Men Killed," *Daily Missouri Republican,* St. Louis, 10 January 1865; Stanley, Wilson, and Wilson, *Death Records From Missouri Newspapers, January 1861–December 1865,* 34, 69 (lists a Coleman as a retaliatory killing in Chariton County, and a Grojohn as being killed by bushwhackers in Chariton County, both according to a Randolph County newspaper printed June 17); United States Government, *1860 Missouri Census,* lists in Keytesville Township of south Chariton County the households of Charles Coleman on page 234 and Charles Grotjohn on page 231.

8. *O.R.,* vol. 34, part 1, 1026–31; "A Raid on Laclede," *St. Joseph Weekly Herald,* Buchanan County, 24 June 1864; "Raid on Linneus [sic]," *Missouri Statesman,* Columbia, Boone County, 1 July 1864; Frank Moore, editor, *The Rebellion Record: A Diary of American Events, with Documents, Narratives, Illustrative Incidents, Poetry, etc.,* vol. 2 of 12 volumes, New York: G. P. Putnam, 1861–1868 and VanNostrand, 1862–1871, reprinted New York: Arno Press, 1977, 469 (hereinafter referred to as "Moore, *The Rebellion Record."* This account of the Laclede raid is actually most of the St. Joseph newspaper article cited above.); Henry Taylor and Company, *Compendium of History and Biography of Linn County, Missouri,* Chicago: Henry Taylor and Company, 1912, 78–80; Dyer, *Compendium,* vol. 2, 810; State of Missouri, Secretary of State's Office, Missouri State Archives, military service record of Private David A. Crowder, who enlisted at age 43 on 12 March 1862 at Laclede in Company F, 1st Cavalry MSM, and was discharged 10 April 1864 for disability.

9. "Bushwhackers," *Missouri Statesman,* Columbia, Boone County, 8 July 1864, from the earlier *Central City and Brunswicker,* Brunswick, Chariton County.

10. *O.R.,* vol. 34, part 4, 541.

11. *O.R.,* vol. 41, part 1, 10; "Guerrilla Fight in Howard County," *Daily Missouri Democrat,* St. Louis, 6 July 1864, quoting word for word part of the 2 July Federal report as printed in the *O.R.;* "Bushwhacking in Howard County," *Missouri Statesman,* Columbia, Boone County, 8 July 1864; "Guerrillas in Howard County Whipped," *Missouri Statesman,* Columbia, Boone County, 15 July 1864, which also quotes part of the 2 July Federal report as printed in the *O.R.* (The headline reflected wishful thinking, as this skirmish was a draw and not a victory or defeat for either side.); Dyer, *Compendium,* vol. 2, 810.

12. "Shot," *Daily Missouri Democrat,* St. Louis, 13 July 1864, quoting the earlier *Fayette Advertiser,* Howard County; "Guerrilla Operations in Missouri," "Shot," *Missouri Statesman,* Columbia, Boone County, 15 July 1864, (The same as the *Daily Missouri Democrat* article, and also quoting the earlier *Fayette Advertiser);* State of Missouri, Secretary of State's Office, Missouri State Archives, military service record for Private John Brashear who enrolled 10 September 1862 at Laclede, Linn County, in Company E, 62nd EMM, and performed 15 days of active duty service between that date and 7 November 1862 (This may or may not be the Brashear or Brashears murdered the evening of 3 July 1864. The Missouri State Archives shows two other men with this surname from Linn County in Union service who both died of disease before the date of the murder.); United States Government, *1860 Missouri Census,* lists in Richmond Township of central Howard County the household of laborer Robert Brashear. (Author's note: Robert Brashear is the name of the murdered man's relative the newspaper article stated the Linn County man visited. The county seat of Fayette is located in the center of Richmond Township.).

13. "Bushwhackers at Work," *Daily Missouri Democrat,* St. Louis, 12 July 1864, from *Boonville*

Monitor, Cooper County, 9 July 1864; "Guerrilla Operations in Missouri," *Missouri Statesman*, Columbia, Boone County, 15 July 1864, from earlier *Boonville Advertiser*, Cooper County; Way, *Way's Packet Directory, 1848–1994*, 441; United States Government, *1860 Missouri Census*, lists in Richmond Township of central Howard County, the household of Kentucky-born 44-year-old wealthy farmer William H. Stapleton with 16-year-old Missouri-born laborer Robert Stapleton in household; (Author's note: The village of Franklin in south Howard County is the present-day New Franklin.).

14. *O.R.*, vol. 41, part 2, 109; "Guerrilla Atrocities: The Scoundrels in Ambush for Gen. Fisk," *Daily Missouri Democrat*, St. Louis, 14 July 1864; "Fight with Guerrillas in Howard County," *Missouri Statesman*, Columbia, Boone County, 15 July 1864; "Fight With Guerrillas," *Howard County Advertiser*, Fayette, 15 July 1864.

15. United States Government, *1850 Missouri Census*, lists in Pike County that year the household of 56-year-old Maryland-born Edward W. Dorsey, including 16-year-old Missouri-born Caleb Dorsey.

16. Robert M. Crisler, "Missouri's 'Little Dixie,'" *Missouri Historical Review* 42, 2 (January 1948), 130–39.

17. Peterson, et al., *Price's Lieutenants*, 126, 128; Nichols, *Guerrilla Warfare in Civil War Missouri, Volume I, 1862*, 15, 197–8, 203; Nichols, *Guerrilla Warfare in Civil War Missouri, Volume II, 1863*, 136–7, 233.

18. *O.R.*, vol. 34, part 4, 338–9.
19. *O.R.*, vol. 34, part 4, 301.
20. *O.R.*, vol. 34, part 4, 524.
21. *O.R.*, vol. 34, part 4, 370.
22. *O.R.*, vol. 34, part 4, 492.
23. *O.R.*, vol. 34, part 1, 1024–5; part 4, 447–8; "An Escort Fired Into By Bushwhackers—Two Soldiers Wounded," *Missouri Statesman*, Columbia, Boone County, 24 June 1863; "An Escort Fired Into By Bushwhackers—Two Soldiers Wounded," *Daily Missouri Democrat*, St. Louis, quoting exactly the *Missouri Statesman* article of 24 June; (No headline), *Missouri Statesman*, Columbia, Boone County, 8 July 1864, quoting the earlier *State Times*, Jefferson City, Cole County; "Arrival of Arms," *Missouri Statesman*, Columbia, Boone County, 8 July 1864; Herschel Schooley, *Centennial History of Audrain County*, 83 (which states Captain Bryson was at the John Barnes home when he learned about the arms shipment); Dyer, *Compendium*, vol. 2, 810; United States Government, *1860 Missouri Census*, lists in Bourbon Township of northwest Boone County, the households of two John Barnes, both born in Kentucky.

24. "Shot By Bushwhackers," *Daily Missouri Democrat*, St. Louis, 27 June 1864, from the *Randolph Citizen*, Huntsville, of 24 June 1864.

25. *O.R.*, vol. 34, part 4, 525; Schooley, *Centennial History of Audrain County*, 83.

26. *O.R.*, vol. 34, part 4, 588–9 (Author's note: Exactly what Detective Stauber meant when he wrote that the guerrillas "abused" the wife of the absent Sanders will have to remain in the realm of conjecture. What constituted the abuse of a woman in 1864 covered a wider sweep of possible actions compared to what it means in present day parlance.).

27. "From Randolph County—Villainous Outrage on the Wife of a Union Soldier," *Daily Missouri Democrat*, St. Louis, 4 July 1864 (from a correspondent to that newspaper then in Randolph County); "Outrage in Randolph," *Missouri Statesman*, Columbia, Boone County, 8 July 1864, from an earlier edition of the *St. Louis Union*; "The Guerrilla War—Continued Outrages," *Daily Missouri Democrat*, St. Louis, 16 July 1864, quoting the *Kirksville Patriot*, Adair County, of 14 July 1864; (Author's note: The online military service records of the Missouri State Archives reveal no such name as "Armand Price" or anything similar in their records, Union or Confederate. These records are imperfect since they fail to reflect all of the Missouri service member records of the Civil War.); United States Government, *1860 Missouri Census*, lists in Sugar Creek Township of east Randolph County with post office at Allen, the household of 37-year-old Virginia-born physician J. B. Mitchel, which also contains 25-year-old Ohio-born female D. P. Mitchel and 23-year-old Ohio-born attorney A. F. Price—the only Price in Randolph County in the 1860 census. (Author's note: It would appear that A. F. Price was brother to Mrs. D. P. Mitchel since both were of similar age and both born in Ohio. Possibly, the single A. F. Price married after the 1860 census was taken, and the woman afflicted by the bushwhackers on 30 June 1864 was his new wife.).

28. "Guerrillas," *St. Joseph Weekly Herald*, Buchanan County, 7 July 1864; "Guerrilla Atrocities," *Daily Missouri Democrat*, St. Louis, 14 July 1864.

29. "Bushwhacking," *Daily Missouri Democrat*, St. Louis, 13 July 1864, from the *Howard County Advertiser*, Fayette, of 8 July 1864.

30. *O.R.*, vol. 41, part 2, 52–3; (No headline), *Missouri Statesman*, Columbia, Boone County, 1 July 1864.

31. National Historical Company, *History of Howard and Cooper Counties, Missouri*, 282–4; Western Historical Company, *History of Boone County*, St. Louis: Western Historical Company, 1882, 439; Edwards, *Noted Guerrillas, or the Warfare of the Border*, 292.

32. "Guerrilla Robberies," *Missouri Statesman*, Columbia, Boone County, 1 July 1864.

33. Nichols, *Guerrilla Warfare in Civil War Missouri, Volume II, 1863*, 238; "Missouri Items," *Daily Missouri Republican*, St. Louis, 7 October 1863 (which states Handcock is from Osage County, but mistakenly states the Ramseys are from Callaway County); Walter D. Kamphoefner, "Uprooted or Transplanted? Reflections on Patterns of German Immigration to Missouri," *Missouri Historical Review*, 103, 2 (January 2009), 71–89 (which verifies the large German-American populations of Osage and Franklin Counties of this period); United States Government, *1850 Missouri Census*, lists in the household of 38-year-old Virginia-born Rawley A. Hancock the 14-year-old Missouri-born William Hancock.

34. *O.R.*, vol. 34, part 4, 392.

35. *O.R.*, vol. 41, part 2, 74, 99, 135; "More Bushwhacking," *Daily Missouri Democrat*, St. Louis, 14 July 1864; "Affairs in Montgomery," *Daily Missouri Democrat*, St. Louis, 15 July 1864; "Rebels in Montgomery County," *Daily Missouri Democrat*, St. Louis, 16 July 1864; "From Montgomery County," *Daily Missouri Democrat*, St. Louis, 2 August 1864;

(Author's note: All four articles in the St. Louis newspapers were originated by correspondents in the field, who seemed to be mostly northern in sympathy, and not from other area newspapers); National Historical Company, *History of St. Charles, Montgomery, and Warren Counties*, 645–6.

36. National Historical Company, *History of St. Charles, Montgomery, and Warren Counties, Missouri*, 641–2; National Historical Company, *History of Callaway County, Missouri*, St. Louis: National Historical Company, 1884, 395; United States Government, *1860 Missouri Census*, household in Callaway County of 48-year-old South Carolina-born farmer James Brewer of moderate means, including his 37-year-old South Carolina-born wife Eliza and 13-year-old Virginia-born son James.

37. *O.R.*, vol. 34, part 4, 200; W. S. Burke, *Official History of Kansas Regiments (During the War for the Suppression of the Great Rebellion)*, Leavenworth, Kansas: W. S. Burke, 1870, reprinted Ottawa, Kansas: Kansas Heritage Press, 1994, 157 (hereinafter referred to as "Burke, *Official History of Kansas Regiments*"); (Author's note: See Chapter Eight notes for other sources about the Union District of Northern Missouri unofficially employing troopers of the 7th Kansas Cavalry to rid Pike County of certain southerners in late May 1864.).

38. "Jail Birds Loose," *Missouri Statesman*, Columbia, Boone County, 24 June 1864.

39. "Heavy Robbery," *Missouri Statesman*, Columbia, Boone County, 8 July 1864; "Guerrilla Operations in Missouri," *Missouri Statesman*, Columbia, Boone County, 15 July 1864, from the earlier *Louisiana Journal*, Pike County.

40. *O.R.*, vol. 34, part 4, 555; McGhee, *Guide to Missouri Confederate Units, 1861–1865*, 149–50 (McGhee mentioned a Confederate Major W. M. Shaw who recruited a battalion during Price's great Missouri raid, but McGhee was unable to provide much detail about him.); United States Government, *1850 Missouri Census*, listed in Pike County in a Turner household 25-year-old Virginia-born Mary Jane Shaw and four-year-old Missouri-born Jesse Webb Shaw; United States Government, *1860 Missouri Census*, lists in city of Louisiana in Pike County in John Turner household 28-year-old Virginia-born Mary Shaw and 14-year-old, Missouri-born male J. W. Shaw. Next door is 29-year-old Missouri-born Sidney Shaw whose occupation is listed as "negrotrader"; (Author's note: Although it is unlikely an 18 or 19 year old would hold the rank of major or be a battalion commander in Confederate service, this may be the mysterious Major Webb Shaw.).

41. *O.R.*, vol. 34 part 4, 523 (a troop disposition list of the activated EMM units showing Captain Hiram Baxter and 60 enlisted men of unnamed company of EMM activated in Louisiana June 17, but later "ordered relieved"), 555, 592–3.

42. *O.R.*, vol. 34, part 4, 599–600.

43. *O.R.*, vol. 34, part 2, 60–1; National Historical Company, *History of St. Charles, Montgomery, and Warren Counties, Missouri*, 645–6.

FIFTEEN

1. Hamp B. Watts, *The Babe of the Company*, Fayette, Missouri: the Democrat-Leader Press, 1913, 6–7.

2. Donald R. Hale, *They Called Him Bloody Bill*, Clinton, Missouri: The Printery, 1975, 1–2, 21–2; Albert Castel and Thomas Goodrich, *Bloody Bill Anderson: The Short, Savage Life of a Civil War Guerrilla*, Mechanicsburg, Pennsylvania: Stackpole Books, 1998, 45 (hereinafter referred to as "Castel and Goodrich, *Bloody Bill Anderson*.").

3. "Murder of Capt. M. H. Snyder," *Central City and Brunswicker*, Brunswick, Chariton County, 16 July 1864; "Great Excitement in Carroll County," *Daily Missouri Republican*, St. Louis, 21 July 1864; "More Bushwhacking Outrages," *Kansas City Daily Journal*, Jackson County, 21 July 1864; "Guerrilla Murders," *Missouri Statesman*, Columbia, Boone County, 22 July 1864, quoting exactly the *Central City and Brunswicker* of 16 July 1864; Stanley, Wilson, and Wilson, *Death Records From Missouri Newspapers, January 1861–December 1865*, 162; State of Missouri, *Annual Report of the Adjutant General of Missouri for the Year 1865*, 561 (which inaccurately states that Captain Snyder was "killed by bushwhackers July 12, 1864," since he was actually killed July 14); United States Government, *1860 Missouri Census*, lists in Prairie Township of south-central Chariton County, the household of M. H. Snyder including a wife and a number of children; Larry Wood, *The Civil War Story of Bloody Bill Anderson*, Austin, Texas: Eakin Press, 2003, 78.

4. *O.R.*, vol. 41, part 2, 209, 216–7; "The Guerrilla War: Guerrillas in Huntsville," *Daily Missouri Democrat*, St. Louis, 16 July 1864, from the *Randolph Citizen*, Huntsville, of 15 July 1864 (the same day as the raid); "Guerrilla Depredations: Huntsville, Missouri Robbed," *Daily Missouri Democrat*, St. Louis, 18 July 1864; "Telegraphic," *St. Joseph Weekly Herald*, Buchanan County, 21 July 1864 (word for word the same as the *Daily Missouri Democrat*, St. Louis, of 18 July 1864); "The Guerrilla Robbery of Huntsville," *Missouri Statesman*, Columbia, Boone County, 22 July 1864, from the earlier *Randolph Citizen*, Huntsville; "A Raid on Huntsville," *Missouri Statesman*, Columbia, Boone County, 29 July 1864, from the earlier *Randolph Citizen*, Huntsville; Hale, *They Called Him Bloody Bill*, 18–24; Castel and Goodrich, *Bloody Bill Anderson*, 45–7; Larry Wood, *The Civil War Story of Bloody Bill Anderson*, 78–82; Castel, *William Clarke Quantrill: His Life and Times*, 180–1; Brownlee, *Gray Ghosts of the Confederacy*, 204; Edwards, *Noted Guerrillas, or the Warfare of the Border*, 239; Birch, *Quantrell*, 187; Dyer, *Compendium*, vol. 2, 810 (Dyer also listed a skirmish July 16 on the "Fayette Road, near Huntsville," which probably refers to the running fight Captain Smith's 9th Cavalry MSM patrol had with Anderson's band an hour or so after the July 15 Huntsville raid. Dyer listed the Union units involved as 2nd Colorado Cavalry—actually two counties west of Randolph County at this time—and a detachment of the 4th Cavalry MSM—south of the Missouri River at this time.).

5. *O.R.*, vol. 41, part 1, 51, part 2, 244; Watts, *The Babe of the Company*, 6.

6. *O.R.*, vol. 41, part 2, 235; "The *War Eagle* Fired Into," *Daily Missouri Democrat*, St. Louis, 21 July 1864 (article written for this newspaper by a correspondent who was aboard the *War Eagle* when she was attacked at Rocheport); "Guerrilla Operations," *Missouri Statesman*, Columbia, Boone County, 22 July 1864 (article contains quotes from Rocheport

residents about the raid); Way, *Way's Packet Directory, 1848-1994*, 220, 323, 480; Wood, *The Civil War Story of Bloody Bill Anderson*, 82; Dyer, *Compendium*, vol. 3, 1032 (thumbnail history of 17th Illinois Cavalry); Brownlee, *Gray Ghosts of the Confederacy*, 204; Castel, *William Clarke Quantrill: His Life and Times*, 181.

7. *O.R.*, vol. 41, part 2, 273-4.

8. *O.R.*, vol. 41, part 1, 124-5; part 2, 364, 367, 490; "Guerrillas on North Mo. R. R.," *Kansas City Daily Journal*, Jackson County, 28 July 1864; "The Guerrilla War: A Skirmish on the N. M. R. R.," *St. Joseph Weekly Herald*, Buchanan County, 28 July 1864; "Guerrillas at Renick and Allen," and "Two Bushwackers Killed," *Missouri Statesman*, Columbia, Boone County, 29 July 1864; Wood, *The Civil War Story of Bloody Bill Anderson*, 83; Brownlee, *Gray Ghosts of the Confederacy*, 204; Castel, *William Clarke Quantrill: His Life and Times*, 181; Hale, *They Called Him Bloody Bill*, 25; Castel and Goodrich, *Bloody Bill Anderson*, 47; Dyer, *Compendium*, vol. 2, 811.

9. *O.R.*, vol. 41, part 1, 124-5, part 2, 490; "From Huntsville," *Daily Missouri Democrat*, St. Louis, 28 July 1864, from a Huntsville correspondent to this newspaper writing July 25; "Rebel Barbarity—Men Scalped," *Kansas City Daily Journal*, Jackson County, 10 August 1864; Dyer, *Compendium*, vol. 2, 811; Brownlee, *Gray Ghosts of the Confederacy*, 204-5; Castel, *William Clarke Quantrill: His Life and Times*, 181; Hale, *They Called Him Bloody Bill*, 25; Wood, *The Civil War Story of Bloody Bill Anderson*, 83-6.

10. Watts, *The Babe of the Company*, 9.

11. *O.R.*, vol. 41, part 1, 174; part 2, 24 (which mistakenly says the bridge was burned July 2), 409-12, 421-24, 441; "Raid on the H. and St. Joe R. R.," *Kansas City Daily Journal*, Jackson County, 28 July 1864; "Hannibal and St. Joe Railroad—Gen. Fisk," *Kansas City Daily Journal*, Jackson County, 31 July 1864; "Guerrillas on the Railroad!" *St. Joseph Weekly Herald*, Buchanan County, 4 August 1864; R. I. Holcombe, *History of Marion County, Missouri*, St. Louis: E. F. Perkins, 1884, 539; Dyer, *Compendium*, vol. 2, 811; Hale, *They Called Him Bloody Bill*, 25-6; Castel and Goodrich, *Bloody Bill Anderson*, 47-8; Wood, *The Civil War Story of Bloody Bill Anderson*, 86-7.

12. *O.R.*, vol. 41, part 2, 441.

13. *O.R.*, vol. 41, part 2, 479; "The Hanging of Judge Denney [sic]," *Missouri Statesman*, Columbia, Boone County, 18 November 1864, quoted from the earlier *Daily Missouri Democrat*, St. Louis; Castel and Goodrich, *Bloody Bill Anderson*, 48; Wood, *The Civil War Story of Bloody Bill Anderson*, 87-8.

14. Missouri Historical Company, *History of Carroll County, Missouri*, 348; National Historical Company, *History of Caldwell and Livingston Counties, Missouri*, St. Louis: National Historical Company, 1886, 208; S. K. Turner and S. A. Clark, *Twentieth Century History of Carroll County, Missouri*, 289; Castel and Goodrich, *Bloody Bill Anderson*, 48; Wood, *The Civil War Story of Bloody Bill Anderson*, 88.

15. *O.R.*, vol. 41, part 1, 71-2; part 2, 272-3; "Guerrilla Raid in Grundy Co.," *Daily Missouri Democrat*, St. Louis, 23 July 1864, from a 20 July letter by a correspondent to this newspaper in nearby Trenton, Grundy County; "A Fight in Grundy," *Kansas City Daily Journal*, Jackson County, 23 July 1864, from an earlier issue of the *St. Joseph Tribune*, Buchanan County; Birdsall and Dean, *The History of Linn County Missouri*, 352, 354-6; Gladys Wells Crumpacker, *The Complete History of Sullivan County, Missouri, Volume 1, 1836-1900*, Milan, Missouri: History Publications, 1977,460-1.

16. *O.R.*, vol. 41, part 1, 177-9; part 2, 424; Dyer, *Compendium*, vol. 2, 811; United States Government, *1860 Missouri Census*, lists the Nathaniel Butler household in Prairie Township of south-central Chariton County.

17. *O.R.*, vol. 41, part 2, 894-5; "More Murders," *Daily Missouri Republican*, St. Louis, 30 July 1864, from the earlier *Central City and Brunswicker*, Brunswick, Chariton County; United States Government, *1860 Missouri Census*, lists in Clark Township of northeast Chariton County in the Oldham household 17-year-old Missouri-born farm laborer Jesse Mason and the large family of 47-year-old Virginia-born farmer Lawrence D. Long, including his three teenage sons William, Robert, and Richard; State of Missouri, Secretary of State's Office, shows military service records for a William, a Robert, and a Richard Long in the 35th EMM with some active service at Brunswick in Chariton County.

18. *O.R.*, vol. 41, part 2, 564, 719; "Interesting Question—Are Missouri Guerrillas Commissioned Rebels?" *Missouri Statesman*, Columbia, Boone County, 12 August 1864, taken from the earlier *St. Louis Union*; "From Boonville," *Daily Missouri Democrat*, St. Louis, 16 August 1864, from a correspondent to the St. Louis newspaper at Boonville identified only as "L."; Bruce S. Allardice, *More Generals in Gray*, Baton Rouge: Louisiana State University Press, 1995, 187-8 (about Edwin Price's record in the war and controversies); Brownlee, *Gray Ghosts of the Confederacy*, 198; Castel, *General Sterling Price and the Civil War in the West*, 132-6 (details controversies about Edwin Price, but does not cover his interviews with southern leaders in 1864); (Author's note: It is noteworthy that Colonel Perkins accused Anderson and his band of committing depredations against southern residents, since William Quantrill in Jackson County during 1862 refused to operate with the guerrilla band there containing Bill and Jim Anderson and other Kansas exile bushwhackers for forcing residents to feed their horses and them without regard to the residents' loyalty. After this band's spectacular deep Kansas raid of early May 1863 Quantrill and his men overlooked this band's faults and accepted the survivors into their ranks.)

19. *O.R.*, vol. 41, part 1, 200; part 2, 452; Dyer, *Compendium*, vol. 2, 811.

20. *O.R.*, vol. 41, part 2, 490, 656-7; United States Government, *1860 Missouri Census*, recorded the household of John Earickson as the only Earickson or name of similar spelling listed in Glasgow Township of Howard County.

21. *O.R.*, vol. 41, part 2, 298; John Russell, MD, of Cape Girardeau, Missouri, assisted this author by researching the mysterious "Captain Holloway" and tentatively identified him as George T. Holloway. This person was listed in the 1850 Missouri census in Union Township of east Randolph County in the household of 41-year-old Kentucky-born shoemaker Jefre Holloway and 43-year-old Ken-

tucky-born Elizabeth Holloway as 14-year-old Missouri-born Thomas Holloway. By the 1860 Missouri census Elizabeth Holloway is listed as a 53-year-old domestic in the household of overseer Michael Myers in Glasgow Township, northwest Howard County, about twelve miles southwest of Roanoke. George Holloway apparently is not listed in the 1860 census; (Author's note: There is not much record of Holloway's southern service in the online Missouri State Archives in Jefferson City, but a record that the man served over 100 days active duty in the local Union 46th EMM in late 1862 and early 1863. Therefore, it appears George T. Holloway, like many other Missourians served on both sides of the war. After the war, this George T. Holloway moved his family to Maries County, Missouri, for a new start away from any recriminatory feelings of his former friends and neighbors of northeast Missouri.).

22. "One of 'Merrill's Horse' Captured by Bushwhackers," *Missouri Statesman*, Columbia, Boone County, 22 July 1864; "One of 'Merrill's Horse Murdered by Bushwhackers," *Missouri Statesman*, Columbia, Boone County, 29 July 1864; Western Historical Company, *History of Boone County*, 436.

23. O.R., vol. 41, part 2, 319.

24. O.R., vol. 41, part 2, 377; "Bushwhacker Killed," *Missouri Statesman*, Columbia, Boone County, 29 July 1864; "Missouri Items," *Daily Missouri Democrat*, St. Louis, 2 August 1864, taken word-for-word from the earlier *Missouri Statesman* article; United States Government 1860 *Missouri Census*, lists in Bourbon Township of northwest Boone County the household of 37-year-old Kentucky-born physician John M. Angell, his 25-year-old wife and their one-year-old son.

25. O.R., vol. 41, part 2, 375–6, 395; "Troubles in Audrain County," *Missouri Statesman*, Columbia, Boone County, 29 July 1864; Schooley, *Centennial History of Audrain County*, 84; United States Government, *1860 Missouri Census*, lists in Saling Township of west Audrain County, the household of 57-year-old Kentucky-born reform preacher D. B. Davis, including 22-year-old Missouri-born farm laborer J. H. Davis (actual census-taker's entry for this household is difficult to read); United States Government, *1860 Illinois Census*, lists in the 8th ward of Chicago, Cook County, the household of 24-year-old Massachusetts-born Isaac Gannett; State of Missouri, Secretary of State's Office, Missouri State Archives, contains military service record for Private F. J. Davis of Company G, 61st EMM, showing that at age 19 he enrolled at Mexico on 3 October 1862 and was mustered out on 8 October 1862; (Author's note: John Russell, MD, of Cape Girardeau assisted the author with research about First Lieutenant Gannett and the man's military service record in Company B, 7th Kansas Cavalry Regiment, and his postwar pension application probably for a war wound or injury.); (Author's note: Readers probably recognize "Mexican standoff" as a slang idiom for an instance when two equally equipped opponents mutually decide to forego combat with each other, but it applies well in this series of incidents at and near Mexico, Missouri, during July 1864.).

26. O.R., vol. 41, part 2, 440, 461.

27. O.R., vol. 41, part 2, 490; Way, *Way's Packet Directory, 1848–1994*, 428.

28. Barton, *Three Years With Quantrill*, 152; Eakin, *Warren Welch Remembers*, 12–13; Connelley, *Quantrill and the Border Wars*, 451; Elaine Derendinger, Melba Fleck, and LaVaughn Miller, editors, *Stories of Howard County Missouri*, publication place not stated: South Howard County Historical Society, 1996,119–20.

29. "Outrages in Randolph County," *Missouri Statesman*, Columbia, Boone County, 12 August 1864.

30. O. R., vol. 41, part 2, 540; "From the Jefferson City Times, 6th," *Missouri Statesman*, Columbia, Boone County, 12 August, from the *State Times*, Jefferson City, Cole County, 6 August 1864; "Negroes Killed By Bushwhackers," *Missouri Statesman*, Columbia, Boone County, 12 August 1864; "Missouri Items," *Daily Missouri Democrat*, St. Louis, 15 August 1864; United States Government, *1860 Missouri Census*, lists no Buffington households in Boone County, but in the *1870 Missouri Census* in Cedar Township of south Boone County is listed the households of 57-year-old Pennsylvania-born J. P. Buffington and that of 68-year-old Pennsylvania-born T. Buffington.

31. "Guerrilla Operations," *Missouri Statesman*, Columbia, Boone County, 5 August 1864.

32. O.R., vol. 41, part 2, 544; Edwards, *Noted Guerrillas or the Warfare of the Border*, 283, 353 (referring specifically to the Lafayette County council of war); Brownlee, *Gray Ghosts of the Confederacy*, 209 (referring specifically to the Lafayette County council of war).

33. O.R., vol. 41, part 1, 230–1; part 2, 610, 625; "Fight With Jim Anderson's Gang," *Missouri Statesman*, Columbia, Boone County, 19 August 1864; Hale, *They Called Him Bloody Bill*, 27–8; Dyer, *Compendium*, vol. 2, 811; United States Government, 1860 *Missouri Census*, lists the Robert Bagby household in Salt Springs Township of central Randolph County.

34. O.R., vol. 41, part 2, 609, 624; "Missouri Items," *Daily Missouri Democrat*, St. Louis, 12 August 1864.

35. "A Daring Act," *Daily Missouri Democrat*, St. Louis, 22 August 1864, from the earlier *Mexico Ledger*, Audrain County.

36. O.R., vol. 41, part 2, 859–60; Broadfoot, *Supplement to the O.R.*, part 2, vol. 19, 1st Iowa Cavalry, 47, 58; Dr. Charles H. Lothrop, *A History of the First Regiment Iowa Cavalry Veteran Volunteers*, Lyons, Iowa: Beers and Eaton, Printers, 1890, 185–7; United States Government, 1860 *Missouri Census*, lists in Prairie Township of north-central Howard County the household of 57-year-old Kentucky-born farmer Evan Price, with 24-year-old Missouri-born student Joseph H. Price; (Author's note: The author consulted John Russell, MD, Cape Girardeau, to identify "Pitney" the spy Williams named. Through genealogy research Dr. Russell eliminated all the Pitney men of military age of northeast Missouri except those of the Howard County area Pitneys who moved there from Ohio several years before the war. Several members of this family served in the Union 9th Cavalry MSM except Alexander Washington Pitney—born 1826 in Ohio—who was arrested in Randolph County as a Rebel private in early 1862 and spent time as a result in the St. Louis area military prisons, according to Eakins' *Missouri*

Prisoners of War. Some years after the war this same man lived in the Confederate Home at Higginsville, Missouri, according to his card in the Missouri State Archives. Perhaps he was also a Confederate recruiter in 1864, but there is no proof.).

37. *O.R.*, vol. 41, part 1, 259–60, 263; part 2,808; "War in Boone County," *Missouri Statesman*, Columbia, Boone County, 19 August 1864; "Fighting in Boone County," *Daily Missouri Democrat*, St. Louis, 22 August 1864, copied in part from the *Missouri Statesman* issue of 19 August; Western Historical Company, *History of Boone County*, 436–7 (also copied in part from the *Missouri Statesman* issue of 19 August 1864); Dyer, *Compendium*, vol. 2, 811.

38. Edwards, *Noted Guerrillas or Warfare of the Border*, 243; Hale, *They Called Him Bloody Bill*, 31.

39. *O.R.*, vol. 41, part 1, 255.

40. *O.R.*, vol. 41, part 2, 774.

41. *O.R.*, vol. 41, part 1, 259–60; part 2, 795, 808, 841, 880–1; "More Bushwhacking," *Missouri Statesman*, Columbia, Boone County, 26 August 1864 (This newspaper asserts Jim Anderson was leading part of the guerrillas in the Rocheport area this day.); Rose Mary Lankford, *The Encyclopedia of Quantrill's Guerrillas*, 250, 356 (regarding William Stewart); Eakin and Hale, *Branded as Rebels*, 414 (regarding William Stewart); Dyer, *Compendium*, vol. 2, 811; Wood, *Other Noted Guerrillas of the Civil War in Missouri*, 157–8 (Wood included details about Jim Anderson's men's antics in Rocheport that he obtained from the Moses Barth Papers in the Western Historical Manuscript Collection, University of Missouri, Columbia).

42. *O.R.*, vol. 41, part 2, 880–1; "Guerrilla Outrages," *Kansas City Daily Journal*, Jackson County, 30 August 1864, quoting the earlier *St. Louis Union* (this brief report tells only about the robbery of the store in Franklin); Edwards, *Noted Guerrillas or the Warfare of the Border*, 243 (Edwards must have obtained the details of this story from the surviving participants, as he spent considerable time after the war interviewing the remaining guerrillas for his book. Edwards' listing of all five names of the guerrilla participants and the time frame he provided matches Major Leonard's brief detail of killing two guerrillas near Franklin and the robbery of the Franklin store at this time.); Watts, *The Babe of the Company*, 12–14 (Watts in 1913 also named the guerrillas dining at the roadside house, but except for two, used different names than Edwards.).

43. *O.R.*, vol. 41, part 2, 808.

44. Neil Block, *Shades of Gray: Confederate Soldiers and Veterans of Randolph County, Missouri*, Shawnee Mission, Kansas: Two Trails Genealogy Shop, 1996, 86; Nichols, *Guerrilla Warfare in Civil War Missouri, Vol. II, 1863*, 151.

45. "Guerrillas in Macon County," *Daily Missouri Democrat*, St. Louis, 2 September 1864, from the *Courier*, Hannibal, Marion County of 29 August 1864 (Unfortunately, this vague newspaper article failed to identify the Union militia or even the brave lieutenant. There were so many other guerrilla activities at this time across this region, and there were several Union citizen guard and militia units in this area.).

46. *O.R.*, vol. 41, part 2, 823, 860.

47. *O.R.*, vol. 41, part 2, 857, 880; (No headline), *Kansas City Daily Journal*, Jackson County, 23 August 1864 (announcing the low water level of the Missouri River); "Guerrilla Outrages," *Kansas City Daily Journal*, Jackson County, 30 August 1864, from the earlier *St. Louis Union*.

48. *O.R.*, vol. 41, part 2, 840; "Another Steamer Fired Into," *Daily Kansas City Journal*, Jackson County, 28 August 1864; Way, *Way's Packet Directory, 1848–1994*, 163, 355; Wood, *The Civil War Story of Bloody Bill Anderson*, 97.

49. "More Cold-Blooded Murder," *Missouri Statesman*, Columbia, Boone County, 2 September 1864, taken from an earlier issue of the *Central City and Brunswicker*, Brunswick, Chariton County, which cited an August 25 letter from a correspondent at Keytesville; Stanley, Wilson, and Wilson, *Death Records From Missouri Newspapers, January 1861–December 1865*, 29; United States Government, *1860 Missouri Census*, lists the miller Beverly Hamner household and the William Carter household both in Prairie Township of south-central Chariton County, and in nearby Buffalo Lick Township the household of Martin C. Hurt; State of Missouri, Secretary of State's Office, Missouri State Archives, military service record of Private William Carter in Captain J. B. Stanley's Company B of 35th EMM reflecting 59 days of service since his enrollment in the unit 15 June 1864 with the notation that Carter was "Killed Aug 8th 1864 by Jim Jackson" (although that date is incorrect).

50. *O.R.*, vol. 41, part 2, 858; "Bushwhacker Shot," *Missouri Statesman*, Columbia, Boone County, 26 August 1864; "Bushwhacker Shot," *Daily Missouri Democrat*, St. Louis, 30 August 1864, taken word-for-word from the August 26 *Missouri Statesman*; United States Government, *1850 Missouri Census*, lists in Prairie Township of southeast Randolph County the household of 42-year-old Kentucky-born farmer William Perkins with 21-year-old Kentucky-born Caleb and 14-year-old son William; and in the *1860 Missouri Census* the same household but without Caleb and showing parents still living and farmer son William, 24, born in Missouri.

51. *O.R.*, vol. 41, part 2, 858; "Guerrillas Shot," *Daily Missouri Democrat*, St. Louis, 30 August 1864, from the earlier *Paris Mercury*, Monroe County.

52. *O.R.*, vol. 41, part 2, 914; Edwards, *Noted Guerrillas or The Warfare of the Border*, 308; "Outrages By Guerrillas," *Daily Missouri Democrat*, St. Louis, 5 September 1864 (regarding the three guerrillas robbing the Rocheport mail).

53. *O.R.*, vol. 41, part 1, 299–300; "Operations of Anderson's Band," *Missouri Statesman*, Columbia, Boone County, 2 September 1864; "Horrible Atrocities of the Guerrillas," *Kansas City Daily Journal*, Jackson County, 4 September 1864, from the earlier *St. Louis Union*; "Outrages By Guerrillas," *Daily Missouri Democrat*, St. Louis, 5 September 1864; "Horrible Atrocities of the Guerrillas," *St. Joseph Weekly Herald*, Buchanan County, 8 September 1864 (word-for-word the same as the Kansas City newspaper taken from the earlier *St. Louis Union*); Watts, *The Babe of the Company*, 12 (Hamp Watts may have participated in this fight in Anderson's band, and, although the basics he gives of the fight seem correct, his statistics about numbers of men doing this and that and casualty figures are incorrect.); Edwards, *Noted Guerrillas or The Warfare of the Border*, 243–4 (Edwards' account benefits from his interviews with

guerrilla participants of this fight. His descriptions of the terrain, details of the fight, inclusion of Bill Stewart's band of ten, and even giving the names of Clements' twelve men who conducted the feint provide valuable insight into this battle. The reader should ignore Edwards' casualty figures, the disparaging remarks about Captain Parke, and other histrionics.); National Historical Company, *History of Howard and Cooper Counties, Missouri*, St. Louis: National Historical Company, 1883, 769 (a solid, simply told account of the fight with the glaring error of the misidentification of the 4th Cavalry MSM as "Iowa cavalry"); E. J. Melton, *History of Cooper County, Missouri*, Columbia, Missouri: E. W. Stephens Publishing Company, 1937, 92 (short, concise account of the fight); Thoma, *This Cruel Unnatural War*, 103–4 (Thoma wrote a simple, direct narrative of the fight partly taken from an 1876 Cooper County history and a 10 September 1864 Sedalia, Pettis County, newspaper account not seen by this author.); Hale, *They Called Him Bloody Bill*, 33; Castel and Goodrich, *Bloody Bill Anderson*, 57–8; Wood, *The Civil War Story of Bloody Bill Anderson*, 98–9; Brownlee, *Gray Ghosts of the Confederacy*, 211; Castel, *William Clarke Quantrill: His Life and Times*, 181; Wood, *Other Noted Guerrillas of the Civil War in Missouri*, 145–6; State of Missouri, *Annual Report of the Adjutant General of Missouri for the Year Ending December 31, 1865*, 469 (showing the officer roll of the 4th Cavalry MSM with a notation beside Captain Joseph Parke's name that he resigned 28 September 1864).

54. O.R., vol. 41, part 2, 959; part 3, 8, 9, 30, 31; Charles Barth letter, 7 September 1864 from Rocheport to Moses Barth in St. Louis, Barth Papers, Western Historical Manuscripts Collection, University of Missouri Library, Columbia, Missouri, Collection Number C997; "Operations of Anderson's Band," *Missouri Statesman*, Columbia, Boone County, 2 September 1864; "Peace and Quiet in Missouri," *Daily Missouri Democrat*, St. Louis, 7 September 1864, from a correspondent in the interior of Missouri; "Letter From Rocheport," *Missouri Statesman*, Columbia, Boone County, 16 September 1864; Thoma, *This Cruel Unnatural War*, 105; Brownlee, *Gray Ghosts of the Confederacy*, 211–12; Castel and Goodrich, *Bloody Bill Anderson*, 58–9; Wood, *The Civil War Story of Bloody Bill Anderson*, 99.

55. "One of Captain Tallon's Men on a *Scout*," *Daily Missouri Democrat*, St. Louis, 9 September 1864 (The above newspaper account of this tale mentioned that Detective Murphy was a member of a "Captain Tallon's United States detective force." The online military service records in the Missouri State Archives contains one for a First Corporal Peter Tallon who on 27 April 1864 in St. Louis enrolled in Company C of the 83rd EMM, which was also designated in that record as "Captain Patrick's First U. S. Battalion." (Author's note: Perhaps the 83rd EMM, which the 1865 *Annual Report of the Adjutant General of Missouri* on page 617 indicates was formed in late April 1864 and was ordered disbanded later that year under Department of the Missouri Special Orders Number 236, was actually a unit of undercover detectives meant to infiltrate guerrilla units in Missouri's interior.).

56. O.R., vol. 41, part 2, 962–3.

57. O.R., vol. 41, part 1, 130; Stanley, Wilson, and Wilson, *Death Records From Missouri Newspapers, January 1861–December 1865*, 22; Dyer, *Compendium*, vol. 2, 811; United States Government, *1860 Missouri Census*, lists in Liberty Township of northwest Callaway County, the large, wealthy household of 54-year-old New York-born doctor-farmer James M. Martin. This gentleman does not appear in this area in the 1870 Missouri census; Eakins, *Missouri Prisoners of War*, contains several entries for guerrilla John L. Wright of Callaway County along with his capture, escape, and recapture involving several of the St. Louis area military prison facilities; Nichols, *Guerrilla Warfare in Civil War Missouri, Volume II, 1863*, 82 (John L. Wright), 239 (First Lieutenant Kempinski and Joe Cole).

58. O.R., vol. 41, part 2, 559.

59. "Arrested," *Missouri Statesman*, Columbia, Boone County, 12 August 1864; "Missouri Items," *Daily Missouri Democrat*, St. Louis, 15 August 1864 (this article discussing bushwhackers being arrested in the region said only that "two were arrested at Warrenton on the 6th."

60. O.R., vol. 41, part 3, 35 (Author's note: part 2, page 976 reveals that on 31 August 1864 Captain Campbell's company of 9th Cavalry MSM was stationed at Fulton, so these had to be the troops sent August 23 to deal with the guerrillas in the east part of that same county.); "Guerrilla Outrages," *Kansas City Daily Journal*, Jackson County, 30 August 1864; "Bushwhackers," *Missouri Statesman*, Columbia, Boone County, 2 September 1864, from the earlier issue of the *Fulton Telegraph*, Callaway County; (The 1860 Missouri census does not reveal a more detailed identity of "Dr. Wilkerson.").

61. O.R., vol. 41, part 2, 510.

62. "Missouri Items," *Daily Missouri Democrat*, St. Louis, 15 August 1864.

63. "Missouri Items," *Daily Missouri Democrat*, St. Louis, 2 August 1864; State of Missouri, Secretary of State's Office, Missouri State Archives, military service record for Sergeant J. Brashears, who enrolled and served 90 days active duty with Company B, 53rd EMM between late July and 1 November 1862.

64. O.R., vol. 41, part 2, 345, 366.

65. "Missouri Items," *Daily Missouri Democrat*, St. Louis, 6 August 1864, taken from the earlier *LaGrange American*, Lewis County; Stanley, Wilson, and Wilson, *Death Records From Missouri Newspapers, January 1861–December 1865*, 162.

66. "Missouri Items," *Daily Missouri Democrat*, St. Louis, 9 August 1864, taken from the earlier *Palmyra Spectator*, Marion County; (No headline), *Missouri Statesman*, Columbia, Boone County, 12 August 1864, also taken from the earlier *Palmyra Spectator*; Holcombe, *History of Marion County, Missouri*, 538–9; Frost, *Camp and Prison Journal*, 158–9 (The imprisoned Confederate Captain Frost's wife wrote to him about the death of Flannagan and Mallory, who had been killed near her father's home.); Stanley, Wilson, and Wilson, *Death Records from Missouri Newspapers*, January 1861–December 1865, 58, 116; United States Government, *1860 Missouri Census*, lists in Union Township of west-central Marion County the household of 42-year-old Virginia-born moderately successful farmer William C. Flannagan and his small family, and in Fabius Township of northeast Marion County the house-

hold of 50-year-old Virginia-born moderately successful farmer Edward Mallory and his large family. Among Mallory's children is listed 18-year-old Missouri-born student John W. Mallory; State of Missouri, Secretary of State's Office, Missouri State Archives, contains the military service record for John W. Mallory in the 2nd Division of the Missouri State Guard of this area during 1861 who took ill in southern service and returned to Palmyra where he was arrested and held for a time.

67. *O.R.*, vol. 41, part 2, 543–4.

68. "Guerrillas in Ralls County," *Daily Missouri Democrat*, St. Louis, 8 August 1864, from the *Hannibal Courier*, Marion County, of 5 August 1864.

69. *O.R.*, vol. 41, part 2, 598; "Guerrillas Near Hannibal," *St. Joseph Weekly Herald*, Buchanan County, 18 August 1864, from the earlier *Hannibal Courier*, Marion County; Hale and Eakin, *Branded as Rebels*, 220 (Hughes); McGhee *Guide to Missouri Confederate Units, 1861–1865*, 150–1 (Snider), 214–5 (Snider and Hughes); Peterson, et al., *Price's Lieutenants*, 119 (Harry Hughes early in the war); Nichols, *Guerrilla Warfare in Civil War Missouri, 1862*, 188–9 (Hayward operating in this region during 1862); State of Missouri, Secretary of State's Office, Missouri State Archives, military service records of Lieutenant Colonel Henry G. Snider, Lieutenant L. M. Frost, Captain Matthew Frost (these two Frosts may be the same person), and Major Harry H. Hughes (Author's note: The author could find no record or other mention of a Captain Kinkard or Kincaid, but the 1860 Missouri census lists a number of Kincaid and Kincade households in several counties in this immediate area.).

70. "Important Arrest," *Daily Missouri Democrat*, 51, St. Louis, 30 August 1864, from the earlier *Louisiana True Flag*, Pike County; United States Government, *1860 Missouri Census*, lists in Salt River Township of southwest Ralls County the household of 41-year-old Kentucky-born farmer Henry Utterback including 14-year-old Missouri-born Legran G. Utterback.

71. *O.R.*, vol. 41, part 2, 392–3, 425–7.

72. Goodspeed Publishing Company, *History of Lewis, Clark, Knox, and Scotland Counties, Missouri*, 390; United States Government, *1860 Missouri Census*, lists the household of 35-year-old Kentucky-born Samuel Dillard in Washington Township in the southeast corner of Clark County, and the household of 24-year-old Missouri-born George Standerford in Benton Township of north-central Knox County; State of Missouri, Secretary of State's Office, Missouri State Archives, lists the military service record of Private George W. Standifer, who enrolled in Company D, 50th EMM at Edina, county seat of Knox County, 30 April 1864, and remarks section of record states "rendered no service."

73. *O.R.*, vol. 41, part 2, 730; Joseph A. Mudd, *With Porter in North Missouri: A Chapter in the History of the War Between the States*, 447–8 (although Mudd mistakenly lists Mike McCully as Michael McCullough); Internet exchange between the author and McCully descendant Harold Dellinger, h.dellinger@yahoo.com, of Kansas City, early April 2009, regarding the research Dellinger and his mother Lois Dellinger performed over a number of years on the McCully men's contributions fighting for the South in northeast Missouri during the war; United States Government, *1860 Missouri Census*, listing in Salt River Township of southwest Schuyler County near Greentop of head-of-household 42-year-old Tennessee-born M. M. McCully and his large family.

Sixteen

1. Nichols, *Guerrilla Warfare in Civil War Missouri, 1862*, 311–3 (regarding formation of the "Paw Paw Militia" or 81st and 82nd EMM Regiments).

2. *O.R.*, vol. 34, part 4, 169, 170, 181–2, 200, 201; Paxton, *Annals of Platte County, Missouri*, 362 (provides only bare facts of the day's actions); "Matters in Platte County," *Kansas City Daily Journal*, Jackson County, 4 June 1864; "Guerrillas at Work," "Particulars of the Raid on New Market," "Four Men Were Murdered," and "Incendiarism," *St. Joseph Weekly Herald*, Buchanan County, 9 June 1864; "Guerrilla Operations," *Missouri Statesman*, Columbia, Boone County, 10 June 1864; Dyer, *Compendium*, vol. 2, 810.

3. "The Guerrillas," *St. Joseph Weekly Herald*, Buchanan County, 9 June 1864 (which wrote only that the Union troops involved were "Capt. Wood's men"); State of Missouri, *Annual Report of the Adjutant General of Missouri for the Year Ending December 31, 1865*, 316 (which identifies Captain W. T. Woods of Company D, 82nd EMM).

4. *O.R.*, vol. 34, part 1, 1005; State of Kansas, *Report of the Adjutant General of the State of Kansas*, 545 (for particulars about Private Bailey); Paxton, *Annals of Platte County, Missouri*, 366; "Guerrilla Operations," *St. Joseph Weekly Herald*, Buchanan County, 30 June 1864, from the earlier *Platte County Sentinel*; "Guerrilla Operations in Missouri: A Fiendish Crime," *Missouri Statesman*, Columbia, Boone County, 15 July 1864, from the earlier *Weston Times*, Platte County.

5. *O.R.*, vol. 34, part 4, 302, 313–4.

6. *O.R.*, vol. 34, part 1, 999–1000; part 4, 329, 348; "Guerrillas in Platte," *Kansas City Daily Journal*, Jackson County, 17 June 1864, (a detailed, rather complete account of the Ridgely fight); "Fight With Guerrillas," *Missouri Statesman*, Columbia, Boone County, 17 June 1864; "Fight at Ridgely," *Missouri Statesman*, Columbia, Boone County, 24 June 1864, from the earlier *St. Joseph News;* Jim Cummins, *Jim Cummins' Book, Written by Himself*, 39–40 (Cummins' version strays on details far from some respectable accounts, but as a participant, his input is unique and valuable.); National Historical Company, *History of Clay and Platte Counties, Missouri*, 727–29 (This southern-biased version of the fight reflects the "Lost Cause" movement then surging through former Confederate states. This account presents some evidently accurate aspects and details not found elsewhere, but also a strong dose of propaganda typical of that movement.) Harry Soltysiak, "Anarchy in Missouri: The Paw Paw Militia: Their Wild Record Told the Story," *Civil War Times Illustrated*, 31; United States Government, *1860 Missouri Census*, lists in Crawford Township, south-central Buchanan County the wealthy household of 47-year-old Kentucky-born Sanford Fielding including two of his sons, 19-year-old Missouri-born Thomas C. Fielding and 14-year-old Missouri-born George W. Fielding.

7. Paxton, *Annals of Platte County, Missouri*, 366.
8. *O.R.*, vol. 34, part 1, 1004–6, 1016–7; part 4, 338, 347, 352, 417, 446; Dyer, *Compendium*, vol. 2, 725, 810.
9. *O.R.*, vol. 34, part 4, 495; Paxton, *Annals of Platte County, Missouri*, 366; "Guerrilla Operations," *St. Joseph Weekly Herald*, Buchanan County, 30 June 1864, from the earlier *Platte County Sentinel* and *Weston Times*, Platte County; "Guerrilla Operations in Missouri," *Missouri Statesman*, Columbia, Boone County, 15 July 1864, from the earlier *Weston Times*.
10. Paxton, *Annals of Platte County, Missouri*, 366; "Guerrilla Operations," *St. Joseph Weekly Herald*, Buchanan County, 30 June 1864, from the earlier *Weston Times*, Platte County.
11. (No headline) *Kansas City Daily Journal*, Jackson County, 25 June 1864, quoting the earlier *St. Joseph Tribune*, Buchanan County.
12. "Words of Warning," *Daily Missouri Democrat*, St. Louis, 4 July 1864, from the *St. Joseph Weekly Herald*, Buchanan County, of 1 July 1864.
13. *O.R.*, vol. 41, part 2, 11.
14. Paxton, *Annals of Platte County, Missouri*, 367.
15. *O.R.*, vol. 41, part 1, 41; part 2, 44; "After Bushwhackers," *Daily Missouri Democrat*, St. Louis, 6 July 1864 (word for word the same as General Fisk's terse summary of the fight in the *O.R.*); "A Fight in Platte," *St. Joseph Weekly Herald*, Buchanan County, 7 July 1864 (also contains General Fisk's brief report with a short introductory paragraph with few additional details); "Fight with Bushwhackers Opposite Leavenworth!" *Kansas City Daily Journal*, Jackson County, 7 July 1864, from the earlier *Leavenworth Bulletin*; "Desperate Fight With Bushwhackers," *Missouri Statesman*, Columbia, Boone County, 15 July 1864, from the earlier *St. Louis Union*, that had a correspondent at Weston near the fight (This is the most detailed version from the Union viewpoint, since the correspondent interviewed several of the cavalry participants.); National Historical Company, *History of Clay and Platte Counties, Missouri*, 726–7 (This is a very detailed local southern version obviously obtained from a southern participant, although it displays much bias. See note #6 in this chapter regarding the source's bias.); Paxton, *Annals of Platte County, Missouri*, 362 (contains few details); Edwards, *Noted Guerrillas, or The Warfare of the Border*, 343–5 (The normally verbose Major Edwards seems to have greatly exaggerated this story more than most of his, the basis of which he must have obtained in one of the interviews he conducted with a large number of guerrillas just after the war.); Soltysiak, "Anarchy in Missouri," *Civil War Times Illustrated*, 32; Broadfoot, *Supplement to the O.R.*, part 2, vol. 35, 9th Cavalry MSM, 602 (few details); United States Government, *1860 Missouri Census*, lists in Lee Township of southwest Platte County, the household of 62-year-old Kentucky-born James F. Bradley, his 56-year-old wife, Nancy, and several children (see census report in note #6 above for information about Thomas C. Fielding).
16. "Mail Robbed," *Kansas City Daily Journal*, Jackson County, 13 July 1864, from the *St. Joseph Weekly Herald* of 8 July 1864; Paxton, *Annals of Platte County, Missouri*, 367.

17. *O.R.*, vol. 34, part 4, 248, 263, 351; "Escape from Jail," and "The Escaped Prisoners," *St. Joseph Weekly Herald*, Buchanan County, 9 June 1864 (This first article oddly states "at the request of the military authorities we refrain from giving the names or a description of any of them," and indeed, none of the other sources listed in this note and the next one name any of them either.); (No headline), *Kansas City Daily Journal*, Jackson County, 9 June 1864.
18. *O.R.*, vol. 34, part 1, 993; part 4, 284–5, 436; "The Escaped Prisoners Heard From," *St. Joseph Weekly Herald*, Buchanan County, 16 June 1864; "A Fatal Mistake," *Missouri Statesman*, Columbia, Boone County, 8 July 1864, from the earlier *Chillicothe Chronicle*, Livingston County; National Historical Company, *History of Caldwell and Livingston Counties, Missouri*, St. Louis: National Historical Company, 1886, 193–4; Dyer, *Compendium*, vol. 2, 810.
19. "To Be Shot," *Kansas City Daily Journal*, Jackson County, 18 May 1864, from an earlier *St. Joseph News*, Buchanan County; "To Be Shot," *Howard County Advertiser*, Fayette, 27 May 1864 (word for word the same as the Kansas City newspaper cited immediately above); "Joseph [sic] Lanier," *Kansas City Daily Journal*, Jackson County, 4 June 1864; "Shot to Death," *Kansas City Daily Journal*, Jackson County, 15 June 1864; "The Execution at Savannah," *St. Joseph Weekly Herald*, Buchanan County, 16 June 1864 (probably the most detailed account of Lanier's military tribunal findings and execution, although it contains a few errors); Goodspeed Publishing Company, *History of Andrew and DeKalb Counties, Missouri*, St. Louis: Goodspeed Publishing Company, 1888, 233; Stanley, Wilson, and Wilson, *Death Records From Missouri Newspapers, January 1861–December 1865*, 100; Eakin, *Missouri Prisoners of War*, entries for A. J. Lanier. (Author's Note: Sources differ as to whether the orphan A. J. Lanier should be called "Joseph" or "James.")
20. "Matters in the Country," *St. Joseph Weekly Herald*, Buchanan County, 24 June 1864; Nichols, *Guerrilla Warfare in Civil War Missouri, Volume II, 1863*, 188.
21. "Night Prowlers," *St. Joseph Weekly Herald*, Buchanan County, 30 June 1865.
22. "Matters at Taos," *St. Joseph Weekly Herald*, Buchanan County, 7 July 1864; United States Government, *1860 Missouri Census*, fails to identify Walter Bevins of Buchanan County under any of the various spellings of this surname; State of Missouri, Secretary of State's Office, Missouri State Archives, contains four or five military service records of Bevins and Bivins from Platte, Clay, and DeKalb Counties in this area who served in the Confederate 3rd and the 5th Missouri Infantry during the war; Second Lieutenant Thomas R. Ridge's record states he served on active duty with Company E, 87th EMM between 30 April and 4 September 1864 in and around St. Joseph; (Author's Note: Walter Bevins' information that Captain John R. Snyder's Company E, 87th EMM was disbanded was in error, as Union authorities disbanded Company A of the 87th in 1864, not Company E, according to the *Annual Report of the Adjutant General of Missouri for the Year Ending December 31, 1865*, 622.).
23. "An Outrage in Gentry," *St. Joseph Weekly Herald*, Buchanan County, 7 July 1864.
24. F. A. North, *The History of Jasper County, Mis-*

souri, Des Moines, Iowa: Mills and Company, 1883, reprinted in Duenweg, Missouri, by Jasper County Missouri Historical Society, 1979, 591–2 (detailing Taylor's background and successful postwar life in Jasper County operating lead mines and as a Missouri legislator); Nichols, *Guerrilla Warfare in Civil War Missouri, Volume II, 1863*, 105, 177, 290.

25. Lankford, *The Encyclopedia of Quantrill's Guerrillas*, 18 (James Bissett), 42–3 (Archie Clements), 50–2 (Jim Cummins), 119–24 (Frank and Jesse James), 144–5 (Peyton Long), 206–7 (Allen Parmer), 238 (Ferdinando Scott), 254–5 (Charles Fletcher "Fletch" Taylor).

26. O.R., vol. 34, part 4, 264, 272; (No headline), *Liberty Tribune*, Clay County, 10 June 1964 (regarding killings of Bond, Dagley, and Withers); National Historical Company, *History of Clay and Platte Counties, Missouri*, 247–8; W. H. Woodson, *History of Clay County, Missouri*, Topeka, Kansas: Historical Publishing Company, 1920, 135; Carolyn M. Bartels, *Clay County Missouri: The Civil War Years*, Vol. 1, Shawnee Mission, Kansas: Two Trails Publishing, 1993, 84; Cummins, *Jim Cummins' Book*, 54–5; Edwards, *Noted Guerrillas, or The Warfare of the Border*, 364–5; Stanley, Wilson, and Wilson, *Death Records from Missouri Newspapers, January 1861–December 1865*, 8.

27. National Historical Company, *History of Clay and Platte Counties, Missouri*, 248.

28. "Guerrilla Operations," *St. Joseph Weekly Herald*, Buchanan County, 30 June 1864.

29. "Bushwhacking: From Clinton County," *Daily Missouri Democrat*, St. Louis, 27 June 1864, from the *Kingston Banner*, Caldwell County, of 24 June 1864.

30. "Bushwhacking: From Clinton County," *Daily Missouri Democrat*, St. Louis, 27 June 1864, from the *Kingston Banner*, Caldwell County, 24 June 1864; Cummins, *Jim Cummins' Book*, 41–3; Lankford, *The Encyclopedia of Quantrill's Guerrillas*, 132–3 (Silas and Thomas King of Clay County), 234 (Doc Rupe of Clay County); Nichols, *Guerrilla Warfare in Civil War Missouri, 1862*, 155 (about guerrilla "Doctor Davis" in Daviess and Livingston Counties during August 1862); State of Missouri, Secretary of State's Office, Provost Marshal Files, File F1296 from 18 and 20 February 1862 about a Jethro Davis of Livingston and Daviess Counties raising a southern company, looking for guns, and attempting to ambush Union troops (a reference not used in Nichols' book about 1862 events); "Killed," *Central City and Brunswicker*, Brunswick, Chariton County, 4 September 1862, from the earlier *Chillicothe Chronicle*, Livingston County (describing the provost marshal's office at Chillicothe interrogating seven Grundy County men for belonging to the guerrilla band of a "Doctor Davis"; but not used in Nichols' book about 1862 events); Historical Publishing Company, *History of Daviess and Gentry Counties, Missouri*, Topeka, Kansas: Historical Publishing Company, 1922, 102 (This source relates how Druggist Baalis Davis was a pronounced secessionist of Gallatin, the Daviess County seat, whereas his son Druggist Harfield Davis was a pronounced advocate of the Union causing the elder Davis to move his business and residence to more pro-southern Chillicothe, Livingston County. Since pharmacists in Civil War times were often addressed as "Doctor," perhaps Baalis Davis, although in his 50s at this time according to the 1860 census, was the mysterious "Doctor Davis," and the man who guided the three Clay County guerrillas to raid in northeast Clinton County in June 1864.).

31. "Guerrilla Operations," *St. Joseph Weekly Herald*, 30 June 1864, from the earlier *Liberty Tribune*, Clay County.

32. "A Delegation from Clay County," *St. Joseph Weekly Herald*, 24 June 1864.

33. National Historical Company, *History of Clay and Platte Counties, Missouri*, 209.

34. (No headline), *Liberty Tribune*, Clay County, 1 July 1864 (regarding death of Coffman); "Brigand Killed," *Missouri Statesman*, Columbia, Boone County, 15 July 1864; "The Sainted Coffman," *Kansas City Daily Journal*, Jackson County, 17 July 1864, from the earlier *Liberty Tribune*, Clay County; National Historical Company, *History of Clay and Platte Counties, Missouri*, 248–9; Hale, *Branded As Rebels, Volume Two*, 63; Bartels, *Clay County, Missouri: The Civil War Years, Volume I*, 85–6; State of Missouri, Secretary of State's Office, Missouri State Archives, contains military service records for Gabriel and Thomas J. Pryor of Haynesville, southeast Clinton County, in Company C, 89th EMM, in late 1864, and Corporal Benjamin F. Pryor of Haynesville between March 1864 and January 1866 in Company D, 13th Missouri Cavalry; United States Government, *1860 Missouri Census*, contains in Jackson Township in southeast Clinton County, the household of Kentucky-born, wealthy farmer J. R. Coffman containing his 16-year-old Missouri-born son David; and the household of Virginia-born middle-income farmer Jefferson Pryor and his 14-year-old Kentucky-born son B. F. Pryor, and nearby the households of 27-year-old Kentucky-born Gabrel Pryor and 22-year-old Kentucky-born T. J. Pryor.

35. O.R., vol. 34, part 4, 566–7; vol. 41, part 2, 44–5; "Who Is Responsible—The Murders Still Continue," *St. Joseph Weekly Herald*, Buchanan County, 30 June 1864; (No headline) and "A Special Meeting of Clay Lodge No. 207," *Liberty Tribune*, Clay County, 1 July 1864 (regarding the killings of Coffman, the Bigelows, and Bailey); "Who Is Responsible—The Murders Still Continue," *Daily Missouri Democrat*, St. Louis, 2 July 1864, same as the above *St. Joseph Weekly Herald* article of 30 June 1864; "Letter from Taylor the Bushwhacker, to Kemper," *Liberty Tribune*, Clay County, 8 July 1864; "The Sainted Coffman," *Kansas City Daily Journal*, Jackson County, 17 July 1864, from the earlier *Liberty Tribune*, Clay County; "How to Secure Peace in Missouri," *Daily Missouri Democrat*, St. Louis, 18 July 1864 (Actually, this was guerrilla chieftain Charles Fletcher "Fletch" Taylor's letter addressed to local Union Captain Kemper, as printed originally in the Liberty newspaper cited above.); Cummins, *Jim Cummins' Book*, 57–8; Edwards, *Noted Guerrillas or The Warfare of the Border*, 338; National Historical Company, *History of Clay and Platte Counties, Missouri*, 248–50 (contains Taylor's letter); Bartels, *Clay County, Missouri: The Civil War Years, Volume 1*, 85–8 (contains Taylor's letter); Hale, *We Rode with Quantrill*, 83; State of Missouri, Secretary of State's Office, Missouri State Archives, military service records of Captain Solomon G. Bigelow from Haynesville in 48th EMM and of

Private Salmon G. Bigelow of Haynesville in Company C, 89th EMM with the remark that he was "Killed June 28th 1864 by Bushwhackers." (The Bigelow brothers were killed the night of 25/26 June 1864); United States Government, *1860 Missouri Census*, lists in Washington Township of northeast Clay County the households of 39-year-old Ohio-born schoolteacher Salmon G. Bigelow to include 9-year-old Ohio-born Elizabeth Bigelow; and that of 37-year-old Ohio-born schoolteacher John G. Bigelow.

36. *O.R.*, vol. 34, part 4, 567; vol. 41, part 2, 44–45; "Another Murder in Clay County," *Kansas City Daily Journal*, Jackson County, 30 June 1864; "A Fiendish Crime," *Liberty Tribune*, Clay County, 1 July 1864, from the earlier *Weston Times*, Platte County; Stanley, Wilson, and Wilson, *Death Records From Missouri Newspapers, January 1861–December 1865*, 6; Bartels, *Clay County Missouri: The Civil War Years, Volume I*, 75, 85; State of Missouri, Secretary of State's Office, Missouri State Archives, military service records of Private Bishop A. Baily in the 6th Cavalry MSM between January 1862 and March 1865; Private Henry C. Baily in the 6th Cavalry MSM between March 1862 and March 1864; and Private Henry C. Bailey in the 13th Missouri Cavalry between March 1864 and April 1866; United States Government, *1860 Missouri Census*, lists in Concord Township of central Clinton County the household of 53-year-old New Hampshire shoemaker Bishop A. Bailey of modest income including his teenage sons H. Clay, Lyman H. and Bishop A Bailey, all born in Missouri.

37. "Who Is Responsible—The Murders Still Continue," *Daily Missouri Democrat*, St. Louis, 2 July 1864, from the *St. Joseph Weekly Herald*, Buchanan County, of 30 June 1864; United States Government, *1860 Missouri Census*, lists several Biggerstaff households in central and northwest Clinton County.

38. "Rebel Soldier Hung at Cameron," *Kansas City Daily Journal*, Jackson County, 3 July 1864, from the earlier *St. Joseph Weekly Herald*, Buchanan County; "A Man Named Harpool," *Missouri Statesman*, Columbia, Boone County, 8 July 1864; National Historical Company, *History of Caldwell and Livingston Counties, Missouri*, 219–20; State of Missouri, Secretary of State's Office, Missouri State Archives, military service record for Private Absalom Harpold of Company I and then Company D, Confederate 3rd Missouri Infantry between December 1861 and sometime after August 1862; United States Government, *1860 Missouri Census*, lists in Blythe Township of central Caldwell County the household of Virginia-born 39-year-old farmer A. Harpold and his wife and nine children.

39. *O.R.*, vol. 41, part 2, 12–13; (No headline), *Kansas City Daily Journal*, Jackson County, 30 June 1864; "Clay County Bushwhackers," *Kansas City Daily Journal*, 2 July 1864.

40. *O.R.*, vol. 41, part 2, 44–5, 62–3; "A Fight in Clay County," *St. Joseph Weekly Herald*, Buchanan County, 7 July 1864; "Capt. Kemper," *Kansas City Daily Journal*, Jackson County, 9 July 1864; "Missouri Items," *Daily Missouri Democrat*, St. Louis, 11 July 1864, from the earlier *St. Joseph Weekly Herald*, Buchanan County; Broadfoot Publishing Company, *Supplement to the O.R.*, part 2, vol. 35, 9th Cavalry MSM, 611; Edwards, *Noted Guerrillas or The Warfare of the Border*, 340–1; National Historical Company, *History of Clay and Platte Counties, Missouri*, 250; Soltysiak, "Anarchy in Missouri," *Civil War Times Illustrated*, 32; Bartels, *Clay County Missouri: The Civil War Years, Volume 1*, 88–90; Dyer, *Compendium*, vol. 2, 810.

41. *O.R.*, vol. 34, part 4, 286, 351; State of Missouri, *Annual Report of the Adjutant General of Missouri For the Year Ending December 31, 1865*, 205 (shows Captain George K. Donnelley, I Company commander in 25th Missouri Infantry Regiment resigned his commission 1 July 1862).

42. National Historical Company, *History of Caldwell and Livingston Counties, Missouri*, 194–5.

43. "Two Bushwhackers Killed," *St. Joseph Weekly Herald*, Buchanan County 30 June 1864.

44. *O.R.*, vol. 34, part 4, 603; "Guerrilla Operations in Missouri: Camden Robbed," *Missouri Statesman*, Columbia, Boone County, 15 July 1864, from the earlier *Lexington Union*; (Author's Note: That the residents of Camden knew these boys by last name seems to indicate that these were local youths. The 1860 census reports for Lafayette, Clay, Jackson, and Ray Counties in the immediate vicinity of Camden do not clearly identify either of these teenagers under the surnames "Stevenson," "Stephenson," or "Thornton," although there are likely Thornton possibilities in Jackson County and likely Stephenson possibilities in the Liberty area of Clay County.).

45. *O.R.*, vol. 41, part 2, 51, 78; "Robbery," *Kansas City Daily Journal*, Jackson County, 6 July 1864; "Missouri Items," *Daily Missouri Democrat*, St. Louis, 11 July 1864.

46. *O.R.*, vol. 41, part 2, 51 (Inexplicably, on page 50 of this same source Brigadier General Brown, the district commander south of the river, on July 5 reported a movement of some guerrillas back south of the Missouri River, unless his information was incorrect.).

47. "Guerrillas Crossed to the North Side of the River," *St. Joseph Weekly Herald*, Buchanan County, 7 July 1864; "Missouri Items," *Daily Missouri Democrat*, St. Louis, 11 July 1864 (which refers to the St. Joseph article above with a one-sentence summary of that report).

48. Missouri Historical Company, *History of Carroll County, Missouri*, 342; Turner and Clark, *Twentieth Century History of Carroll County Missouri*, 283; Farley and Farley, *Missouri Rebels Remembered Si Gordon and John Thrailkill*, 75–6; State of Missouri, Secretary of State's Office, Missouri State Archives, lists many military service records of George Schmidts and Schmitts, but none for one in the 3rd Cavalry MSM as these two sources suggest, and not for a name such as this identifiable with Carroll County; United States Government, *1860 Missouri Census*, lists no such name as George Schmitt or Schmidt in or near Carroll County; (Author's Note: The two Carroll County histories claim Captain John Thrailkill's men robbed and killed Private Schmitt on July 5, but this author questions that assertion, and wonders if Confederate Captain Silas "Cy" Gordon of Platte County and his men, known to be in Carroll County about this time, may have been the culprits. Thrailkill passed through this area with a few companions

about this time after his 28 June escape from the Alton, Illinois, military prison. However, Thrailkill's reputation throughout the war for himself and his followers was to avoid depredations, whereas "Cy" Gordon did not always hold his men to that same standard. Of course, this is only conjecture.).

49. Missouri Historical Company, *History of Carroll County*, 341–2; Turner and Clark, *Twentieth Century History of Carroll County Missouri*, 282–3.

SEVENTEEN

1. *O.R.*, vol. 34, part 4, 430, 621–3.
2. "To Arms!" *Kansas City Daily Journal*, Jackson County, 7 June 1864 (although *O.R.*, vol. 41, part 3, 366 indicates that the rest of the 77th was called to active duty September 25).
3. *O.R.*, vol. 34, part 4, 237, 259; "Boats Fired Into," *Kansas City Daily Journal*, Jackson County, 12 June 1864; Way, *Way's Packet Directory, 1848–1994*, 377; Brownlee, *Gray Ghosts of the Confederacy*, 189–90.
4. *O.R.*, vol. 34, part 4, 222–3, 507–8; "Killed by Bushwhackers," and "The Condition of the Border," *Kansas City Daily Journal*, Jackson County, 4 June 1864; Nichols, *Guerrilla Warfare in Civil War Missouri, 1862*, 157–8 (narrative on the battle of Independence, August 11, 1862).
5. *O.R.*, vol. 34, part 4, 235–6; "Mail Robbed," *Kansas City Daily Journal*, Jackson County, 7 June 1864.
6. *O.R.*, vol. 34, part 4, 237, 259; "Boats Fired Into," *Kansas City Daily Journal*, Jackson County, 12 June 1864; Way, *Way's Packet Directory, 1848–1994*, 437–8; Brownlee, *Gray Ghosts of the Confederacy*, 189–90; Nichols, *Guerrilla Warfare in Civil War Missouri, Volume I, 1862*, 13 (for 1862 episode involving the *Sunshine*); Nichols, *Guerrilla Warfare in Civil War Missouri, Volume II, 1863*, 318 (for 1863 episode involving the *Sunshine*); (Author's Note: Further, in September 1861, southern troops moving to south Missouri captured this vessel briefly and used her to ferry themselves to the south bank of the Missouri River and in November 1861 Colonel Joseph O. Shelby with his band of irregulars raided the *Sunshine*, destroying or seizing Federal cargo on board the vessel. Chapter Twelve of this work describes the tragic end of the *Sunshine* at the levee in St. Louis July 15, 1864.).
7. *O.R.*, vol. 34, part 4, 299; Broadfoot, *Supplement to the O.R.*, part 2, vol. 34, 1st Cavalry MSM, 531.
8. *O.R.*, vol. 34, part 4, 281; (As narrated in Chapter Nine, Bill Anderson with about eighty riders arrived back in west Johnson County about May 22 after their long trek from the South.)
9. *O.R.*, vol. 34, part 4, 281–2.
10. *O.R.*, vol. 34, part 1, 969–70.
11. *O.R.*, vol. 34, part 4, 298–9; Nichols, *Guerrilla Warfare in Civil War Missouri, Volume II, 1863*, 199; Lankford, *The Encyclopedia of Quantrill's Guerrillas*, 23 (Brinker), 230 (Robinson), 250 (Stewart); Edwards, *Noted Guerrillas, or The Warfare of the Border*, 371 (giving detail regarding background of Gooly Robinson from Johnson County).
12. *O.R.*, vol. 34, part 1, 998, 1001–3; part 4, 326–7; vol. 41, part 2, 76 (Author's Note: Oddly, Corporal Parman's report of this incident mistakenly attributes guerrilla leadership to prewar freighter Richard Yeager or Yager of Westport, west Jackson County, but refers to the man as "Colonel Yeager, of the rebel army," and mentioned Anderson as assisting him. Perhaps this gaffe helped to motivate Bill Anderson to write to the Lexington paper to take proper credit for this fight. Yeager or Yager may have been present but only as a member of Anderson's band. Regarding what Bill Anderson wrote about 1st Cavalry MSM members being southern men, Colonel McFerran from Gallatin, Daviess County, was a moderate northern advocate and opposed the radical northern view of the war. The guerrillas of west-central Missouri knew of this from reading various accusations against McFerran in the more radically inclined press. During 1862 and 1863 Quantrill's men and others regarded prisoners from his regiment with less hostility than others and spared the lives of 1st Cavalry MSM men while killing prisoners of other regiments they regarded as more radical. Other than this, Anderson's diatribe about the 12 June 1864 fight near Kingsville is an odd mix of truth and hyperbole intended as propaganda.); "Twelve Soldiers Slaughtered Near Warrensburg," *Kansas City Daily Journal*, Jackson County, 16 June 1864 (Author's Note: The source of this article was a young man named Cooley associated with the nearby railroad construction who assisted Union forces recover the bodies using railroad carts. He also gave a graphic description of the stagecoach robbery scene a few miles away.); "Guerrilla Operations in Missouri," *Missouri Statesman*, Columbia, Boone County, 15 July 1864 from the earlier *Kingston Banner*, Caldwell County (which lists all twelve dead, partly since three of them were from Caldwell County. Vivian Kirkpatrick McLarty, ed., "The Civil War Letters of Colonel Bazel F. Lazear," *Missouri Historical Review*, 399–400 (Lieutenant Colonel Lazear of the 1st Cavalry MSM at Jefferson City wrote to his wife June 17 very upset that twelve men of his regiment were killed.); Edwards, *Noted Guerrillas, or The Warfare of the Border*, uncharacteristically omitted any mention of this guerrilla victory; Wood, *The Civil War Story of Bloody Bill Anderson*, 66–7. Hale, *They Called Him Bloody Bill*, 14–7. Castel and Goodrich, *Bloody Bill Anderson*, 41–4. Britton, *The Civil War on the Border*, vol. 2, 370–1; Brownlee, *Gray Ghosts of the Confederacy*, 189; Dyer, *Compendium*, vol. 2, 810.

13. *O.R.*, vol. 34, part 1, 996, 998.
14. "Mail Robbed," *Kansas City Daily Journal*, Jackson County, 15 June 1864.
15. "An Escort Attacked," *Kansas City Daily Journal*, Jackson County, 15 June 1864; "A Train Robbed," *Kansas City Daily Journal*, Jackson County, 16 June 1864, partly from the *Lawrence Tribune*, Douglas County, Kansas of 15 June 1864 (The Lawrence newspaper erroneously reported that 17 Union soldiers escorting this wagon were killed, which elicited a second article about the incident from the Kansas paper to clarify the misinformation.); "Telegraphic: Leavenworth, June 15," *St. Joseph Weekly Herald*, Buchanan County, 24 June 1864 (repeating the same error as the Lawrence paper with more added).
16. "The Bushmen," *Daily Missouri Democrat*, St. Louis, 27 June 1864; (No headline), *Missouri Statesman*, Columbia, Boone County, 1 July 1864;

United States Government, *1860 Missouri Census*, lists in Lexington Township the household of 62-year-old Virginia-born farmer and lawyer John F. Ryland and his several children in their twenties and teens; and in Lone Jack Township of southeast Jackson County the household of 46-year-old Kentucky-born farmer Gibson Wilhite including his son, farm laborer, Missouri-born 19-year-old Jefferson Wilhite.

17. *O.R.*, vol. 34, part 1, 996.

18. *O.R.*, vol. 34, part 4, 367; Dyer, *Compendium*, vol. 2, 810 (although Dyer placed this skirmish in Lafayette County in error); United States Government, *1860 Missouri Census*, lists in Fort Osage Township of northeast Jackson County the households of James and John Hambright, but no other households by that name in the county.

19. *O.R.*, vol. 34, part 1, 1007–8; vol. 41, part 2, 76 (Author's Note: Anderson's comment in his letter addressed to Colonel McFerrin showing disappointment that his men would have killed more of the men in this fight if they had "done their duty" may reflect Anderson missing several of his men that he permitted to operate for a few days north of the Missouri River in the Clay County area.); "Train Attacked By Guerrillas," *St. Joseph Weekly Herald*, Buchanan County, 30 June 1864, (Although this article correctly stated that nine Federals died, some of the other details it mentioned are not correct.); Broadfoot, *Supplement to the O.R.*, part 2, vol. 34, 1st Cavalry MSM, 531 (provides only brief sketch of this action from Company I records); Vivian Kirkpatrick McLarty, ed., "The Civil War Letters of Colonel Bazel F. Lazear," *Missouri Historical Review*, 399–400 (Lazear was far from the scene at Jefferson City); Edwards, *Noted Guerrillas, or The Warfare of the Border*, 237 (Edwards wrote a fanciful version in which Anderson's men killed 39 Federals and burned 22 wagons. He also wrote one of Anderson's men followed the Union officer four miles and killed the man with an impossible shot.); United States Government, *1860 Missouri Census*, lists in Washington Township of south-central Lafayette County the household of William Whitsell; Britton, *The Civil War on the Border*, vol. 2, 371–2; Brownlee, *Gray Ghosts of the Confederacy*, 189; Wood, *The Civil War Story of Bloody Bill Anderson*, 67; Hale, *They Called Him Bloody Bill*, 14–7; Castel and Goodrich, *Bloody Bill Anderson*, 41–4; Dyer, *Compendium*, vol. 2, 810.

20. *O.R.*, vol. 34, part 4, 433.

21. *O.R.*, vol. 34, part 1, 1008–9, 1017–24, 1032–3; part 4, 339, 352, 365, 380, 431; "A Successful Scout—Thirteen Bushwhackers Killed," *Kansas City Daily Journal*, Jackson County, 21 June 1864 (an overly optimistic survey of only the 2nd Colorado Cavalry portion of the expedition); "Bushwhackers Near Kansas City!" *St. Joseph Weekly Herald*, Buchanan County, 24 June 1864, from the *Leavenworth Bulletin* of 20 June 1864; Britton, *The Civil War on the Border*, Vol. 2, 372–4 (mostly from the Kansas cavalry point of view, which is understandable since Britton served in a Kansas regiment elsewhere at this time); Dyer, *Compendium*, vol. 2, 725, 810 (which mostly lists the Union troops involved down to company level).

22. "The Bushmen," *Daily Missouri Democrat*, St. Louis, 27 June 1864; (No headline), *Missouri Statesman*, Columbia, Boone County, 1 July 1864.

23. *O.R.*, vol. 34, part 1, 997, 999.

24. *O.R.*, vol. 34, part 1, 997, 999.

25. *O.R.*, vol. 34, part 1, 995, 997, 999.

26. *O.R.*, vol. 34, part 1, 997, 999; "Affairs in Lafayette [and other places]," *Missouri Statesman*, Columbia, Boone County, 8 July 1864, from the earlier *St. Louis Union*; (Author's Note: It seems hard to accept that about sixty Rebels would leave behind 55 firearms for only 23 Union troopers to capture in a stand-up fight, unless the Federals surprised them.).

27. "Affairs in Lafayette," *Missouri Statesman*, Columbia, Boone County, 8 July 1864, from the earlier *St. Louis Union*. Way, *Way's Packet Directory, 1848–1994*, 484; Brownlee, *Gray Ghosts of the Confederacy*, 190 (Brownlee mistakenly placed the *West Wind* attack on 26 June and one of the resources he cited was the *O.R.*, which had no mention of this incident.).

28. "Fired Into," *Kansas City Daily Journal*, Jackson County, 26 June 1864; "River News," *St. Joseph Weekly Herald*, Buchanan County, 30 June 1864; "Guerrillas on the River," *Missouri Statesman*, Columbia, Boone County, 22 July 1864; from the *Leavenworth Times* of 26 June 1864; Way, *Way's Packet Directory, 1848–1994*, 484; Brownlee, *Gray Ghosts of the Confederacy*, 190 (Brownlee mistakenly placed the West Wind attack on 26 June and one of the resources he cited was the *O.R.*, which had no mention of this incident.

29. *O.R.*, vol. 34, part 4, 536, 537; (Author's Note: Sergeant B. F. Poe at Knob Noster is not the same as the Captain Benjamin F. Poe who commanded a militia company at Plattsburg, Clinton County, at this same time three counties to the northwest and mentioned earlier in this chapter.).

30. *O.R.*, vol. 34, part 4, 536, 563; (Author's note: President Lincoln often intervened from time to time directly into the affairs of the Department of the Missouri.).

31. *O.R.*, vol. 34, part 4, 564; United States Government, *1860 Missouri Census*, lists in Clay Township of northeast Lafayette County the household of 37-year-old Pennsylvania-born shoemaker Davis K. Duck and his Illinois-born wife and five Missouri-born children; and in the Lexington area the household of 35-year-old Pennsylvania-born printer John A. Duck and his German-born wife and small Missouri-born child; there are in nearby Jackson County households of the name Ervin, Irvin, and Erwin.

32. *O.R.*, vol. 34, part 1, 1057–8; part 4, 572–3, 583–4, 588; vol. 41, part 2, 25; "The Guerrilla Outrages," *Daily Missouri Democrat*, St. Louis, 12 July 1864, from a Sedalia, Pettis County, correspondent to this newspaper who listed the two dead near Dunksburg as "G. McGuire" and "Bell"; Dyer, *Compendium*, vol. 2, 810; State of Missouri, Secretary of State's Office, Missouri State Archives, military service record of Kentucky-born Second Lieutenant George W. McGuire who enlisted at age 22 in Company B, 7th Cavalry MSM in Pettis County, was mustered in at Georgetown, and resigned 3 July 1862; United States Government, *1860 Missouri Census*, lists in Salt Pond Township of the southwest corner of Saline County, 29-year-old New York-born poor blacksmith David Bell (the only Bell within miles of Dunksburg); and also in the same township 21-year-old Kentucky-born laborer George

W. McGuire; and among the several Cooper families in Jefferson Township of southeast Johnson County is that of 50-year-old, Kentucky-born farmer Albert Cooper, who in 1860 had among his children 20-year-old Thomas, 12-year-old Isaac, and 10-year-old Albert Cooper. Except for the older generation, no other Cooper in the southeast corner of Johnson County had at least two sons who could pass as adults in June 1864. The 1860 census also contains as the only Peak in or near east Johnson County 33-year-old, Kentucky-born farmer Joseph Peak and his small family in Post Oak Township south of Warrensburg. (Author's note: Since several guerrillas frequented Post Oak Township during late May and June this year, if this Peak was the one who guided the bushwhackers around Knob Noster, his life, family, and farm would be in danger if he informed.).

33. "Missouri Items," *Daily Missouri Democrat*, St. Louis, 11 July 1864.

34. *O.R.*, vol. 41, part 2, 51; "The Steamer Live Oak Attacked By Guerrillas," *Kansas City Daily Journal*, Jackson County, 10 July 1864; "Looking For Kansas Men," *Liberty Tribune*, Clay County, 15 July 1864; from the earlier *Leavenworth Conservative*; "The Trouble of Navigation on the Missouri," *St. Joseph Weekly Herald*, Buchanan County, 14 July 1864; Wood, *The Civil War Story of Bloody Bill Anderson*, 69 (Wood found the details of the boat shooting at Waverly in the *Carrollton Democrat*, Carroll County, of 8 July 1864); Way, *Way's Packet Directory, 1848–1994*, 290, 376; Joanne Chiles Eakin, *The Little Gods: Union Provost Marshals in Missouri 1861–1865, Volume II, Central Western Border Area*, 1–4; Castel, *William Clarke Quantrill: His Life and Times*, 175; Nichols, *Guerrilla Warfare in Civil War Missouri, Volume II, 1863*, 271–2 (narrates how the 1859-built *Post Boy* was destroyed by Rebel arson at the St. Louis levee during 1863, but this *Post Boy* shooting incident 4 July 1864 involved a different *Post Boy* built in 1864).

35. *O.R.*, vol. 41, part 2, 50; "An Interesting Letter From our Warrensburg Correspondent," *Kansas City Daily Journal*, Jackson County, 6 July 1864, from a letter sent from Warrensburg to the newspaper June 29; (Author's note: Brigadier General Thomas Ewing, Jr., was Brown's predecessor as district commander of this area.).

36. *O.R.*, vol. 41, part 1, 49, 52; part 2, 73, 78, 85; "Skirmish With Bushwhackers—Capt Wagner and Six Men Killed!" *Kansas City Daily Journal*, Jackson County, 8 July 1864 (a short article with some inaccuracies); "Bushwhacking: Murders and Outrages in Howard and Jackson Counties," *Daily Missouri Democrat*, St. Louis, 13 July 1863, part from the Kansas City paper of 8 July 1864 cited immediately above; "The Death of Captain Wagoner," *Kansas City Daily Journal*, Jackson County, 23 July 1864 (a slightly longer and more accurate article than the July 8 version and includes a full list of the eight Union dead); Gregg, manuscript, 88–9 (In his 1909 memoir, William H. Gregg was in regular Confederate service in Arkansas during this fight, but quoted others to state this action took place at "Grinter's farm south of Independence," and complimented "the brave Wagoner and his sturdy, brave Coloradoans."); Eakin, *Warren Welch Remembers*, 6–7 (In this memoir evidently penned by Welch in the 1890s, he mentions that he was one of the three wounded and names the other two, that this fight took place near the "county farm," that a number of guerrilla horses were killed, complimented the fighting abilities of the 2nd Colorado troopers, but included a few inaccuracies about other details of the fight.); Barton, *Three Years With Quantrill*, 152–4 (In this 1914 memoir, John McCorkle mentioned Lieutenant Dick Yeager or Yager's role, complimented the bravery of the Colorado troopers, mentioned the killing of a number of guerrilla horses, stated that only one bushwhacker was wounded and named him [although this wounded man is not in Warren Welch's list], and described the clumsy Federal revolvers.); Castel, *William Clarke Quantrill: His Life and Times*, 176 (Castel quoted both the memoirs of McCorkle cited above and that of Frank Smith. Castel wrote that Smith's memoir complimented the bravery of the Colorado troopers, said the Coloradoans had fine horses, and mentioned the "inferior Savage pistols which tended to fire into the ground."); Brownlee, *Gray Ghosts of the Confederacy*, 196; (Author's note: See Note #39 of Chapter Nine addressing the problems of the Starr revolvers and carbines that plagued the 2nd Colorado Cavalry during 1864.); Internet discussion involving the author and others regarding the firearms problems of the 2nd Colorado Cavalry in "Civil War Arms and Equipment Message Board" during July 2008, http://history-sites.com/mb/cw/cwaemb/, and also included the 17 July 2008 input by John Hayward citing the Osprey book *The American Civil War in the Indian Territory* on page 20 that states that this regiment was equipped with a variety of pistols to include also a number of Lefaucheux revolvers from France. This seems to open the possibility that Captain Wagoner's men on 6 July 1864 could have been armed with Lefaucheux revolvers perhaps leading to John McCorkle's mention of the Yanks having "French Dragoon" revolvers. However, this particular revolver does not seem to match McCorkle's description of being "heavy at the muzzle."); Dyer, *Compendium*, vol. 2, 810 (Dyer wrote that only seven were killed.); United States Government, *1860 Missouri Census*, lists in Blue Township of central Jackson County, the G. N. or P. N. Grinter farm household with Kentucky and Missouri roots, and next up the road the county poor farm superintended by Washington Sales including Sales' own family and three paupers of varied backgrounds and nationalities. (Author's note: A problem inherent in the study of Quantrill's and Todd's operations in the Jackson County area throughout the war is that they repeatedly used the same ambush sites against different Union units causing even participant memoirs to scramble details of different fights. In fact, the bushwhackers fought so many similar actions that postwar survivors had problems telling them apart. Inaccurate reporting in period newspapers and official records resulted in other problems.).

37. *O.R.*, vol. 41, part 2, 75–7; "Miss Anne Fickle," *Kansas City Daily Journal*, Jackson County, 7 July 1864; Brownlee, *Gray Ghosts of the Confederacy*, 199–205; Castel, *William Clarke Quantrill: His Life and Times*, 179–80; Hale, *They Called Him Bloody Bill*, 14–19; Castel and Goodrich, *Bloody Bill Anderson: The Short Savage Life of a Civil War Guerrilla*, 42–4; Wood, *The Civil War Story of Bloody Bill Anderson*, 69–75.

38. *O.R.*, vol. 34, part 1, 967–8; part 4, 217, 235, 238–9, 299 (Union Colonel George H. Hall, commander of 4th Cavalry MSM, from intelligence gathering by his men identified two of the gang members as a Cranmer and a Warren, who had been staying near Knob Noster in east-central Johnson County just previous to this raid.); Historical Publishing Company, *History of Cooper County, Missouri*, 205–7 (which features the eyewitness narrative of Edward H. Harris, who accompanied William Mayo to the post office that day and was among the men lined up and robbed there on June 4); Melton, *History of Cooper County, Missouri*, 91; "Guerrillas in Missouri," *Missouri Statesman*, Columbia, Boone County, 17 June 1864, from the earlier *Macon Gazette*, Macon City, Macon County; Thoma, *This Cruel Unnatural War*, 93–5 (Thoma's detailed, careful synthesis of local resources enabled him to correctly identify the victims of this raid and also determine that Tom Cranmer's 1862 and 1863 guerrilla actions in Cooper County equipped him to guide Anderson's band there on 4 June 1864.); Wood, *The Civil War Story of Bloody Bill Anderson*, 65–6 (Wood also used an article from the 11 June 1864 issue of the *Boonville Weekly Monitor* of Cooper County and the Levens and Drake's 1876 *A History of Cooper County*, neither of which were available to this author. The latter source stated one of the two guerrillas Mayo shot at on 14 May 1864 was named Higby and for whom Anderson's men wanted revenge against Mayo.); Lankford, *The Encyclopedia of Quantrill's Guerrillas*, 273–4 (which mentioned that Tom Warren operated in southeast Lafayette County with Dave Poole in 1863, and in 1864 rode with Anderson); United States Government, 1860 *Missouri Census*, lists in Palestine Township of central Cooper County the households of: (1) 60-year-old Vermont-born wealthy farmer Nathaniel Leonard and his Missouri-born sons, 23-year-old law-student Leverett and 21-year-old college student Charles E.; (2) 66-year-old South Carolina-born wealthy farmer Henry Corum and his wife, 50-year-old, Kentucky-born Gilla; (3) 61-year-old Kentucky-born wealthy farmer James S. Hutchison and his wife, 45-year-old, Virginia-born Martha (the preceding three households are listed as close neighbors); (4) 45-year-old Virginia-born wealthy farmer W. H. Mayo; and in Pilot Grove Township of west-central Cooper County the households of: (1) 30-year-old Kentucky-born medium-income farmer E. H. Harris, a few households away from that of (2) 39-year-old Maryland-born blacksmith Samuel Roe, who local sources listed above tell us operated the Pilot Grove post office on his property at this time; (3) 42-year-old Virginia-born medium-income farmer Thomas Brownfield (who beside the 4 June 1864 raid on the Pilot Grove post office had other encounters during the war with local guerrilla leader Charles Brownlee); and in the town of Warrensburg, county seat of Johnson County, the household of 61-year-old Delaware-born family grocer William S. Cranmer, including 11-year-old Missouri-born son Thomas (The Historical Publishing Company's Cooper County history cited above includes as part of Edward H. Harris eyewitness testimony his memory that the guerrilla that personally took all the personal possessions from the men lined in front of the Pilot Grove post office was a fifteen- or sixteen-year-old boy. (Author's note: In all probability, this was 14-year-old Thomas Cranmer, already known for guerrilla actions in Cooper County earlier in the war.) ; Dyer, *Compendium*, vol. 2, 810; Stanley, Wilson, and Wilson, *Death Records From Missouri Newspapers, January 1861–December 1865*, 119.

39. *O.R.*, vol. 34, part 1, 987; part 4,280; "Guerrillas in Saline," *Missouri Statesman*, Columbia, Boone County, 24 June 1864; Turner, *Twentieth Century History of Carroll County, Missouri*, 282; Eakin, *Warren Welch Remembers*, 8–9 (In his memoir written about the 1890s Warren Welch of George Todd's guerrilla band seemed to indicate that he with J. Frank Gregg led sixteen others who may have conducted this raid, although he was confused about which Saline County village they robbed and the date. Welch's memoir specified his band defeated "Bingamon's" command there forcing them to cross by boat to the north bank of the Missouri River to escape, after which the guerrillas rode west to later raid the village of Miami in north-central Saline County. These details match the New Frankfort raid of June 7 since 71st EMM veteran Captain George W. Bingham's citizen guard company entered active duty in Saline County in late May and there were guerrillas reported at Miami the evening of June 23.); State of Missouri, *Annual Report of the Adjutant General of Missouri For the Year Ending December 31, 1865*, 630 (Captain George W. Bingham's General Orders Number 107 citizen guard company of men formerly of the 71st EMM, authorized by Department of the Missouri Special Orders Number 143 during late May 1864 in this source.); Lankford, *The Encyclopedia of Quantrill's Guerrillas*, 80 (contains detail of J. Frank Gregg's exploits that do not exclude being with Warren Welch in the 7 June 1864 raid on New Frankfort); Dyer, *Compendium*, vol. 2, 810.

40. *O.R.*, vol. 34, part 1, 994–5; Dyer, *Compendium*, vol. 2, 810; United States Government, *1860 Missouri Census*, shows in Miami village the household of 35-year-old Virginia-born tailor Max Haynie, his Virginia-born 24-year-old wife Mary, several children age 7 and younger, and 21-year-old Missouri-born Sylvia Haynie; in the nearby household of blacksmith Carroll Wright is 17-year-old Missouri-born Betsy Haney (These may or may not be the Haney ladies in Captain Parker's report, but these are the only women by similar names in this area.); (Author's note: Pinnacles of the Missouri River information is available at Van Meter State Park located near these notable geologic river bluffs of north-central Saline County and on the Internet.).

41. *O.R.*, vol. 34, part 4, 471; State of Missouri, Secretary of State's Office, Missouri State Archives, military service record of Private E. Keaton, in Captain George W. Bingham's Provisional Company H of General Orders Number 107 citizen guards of Saline County, enlisted 1 May 1864 at Marshall, mustered into active duty 25 August 1864 at Marshall, and captured at siege of Glasgow, 15 October 1864 having completed about 50 days of active duty.

42. "Guerrillas," *Missouri Statesman*, Columbia, Boone County, 1 July 1864, from the earlier *Carrollton Democrat*, Carroll County (also states that "Major Dale" led this expedition and listing among the prisoners Lawrence W. Haynie and David Fer-

ril); Broadfoot, *Supplement to the O.R.* part 2, vol. 35, 4th Cavalry MSM, 64–5 (This detailed itinerary of the regiment asserts that not Major Douglas Dale, but Second Lieutenant Columbus Dale took Company E from its Sedalia base June 23, scouted Pettis and Saline Counties, and returned June 28, having won a victory June 26 over guerrillas in Pettis County, killing three and wounding two. There is no mention of the fight near Miami as described in the above-cited newspapers.); United States Government, *1860 Missouri Census*, lists the household of 25-year-old Missouri-born farmer Lawrence Haney in the village of DeWitt of east-central Carroll County, and lists several Ferrill households in east Carroll County, but no David Ferrill or similar name; (Author's note: Considering the great difficulty the Union military was undergoing at this time fighting against overwhelming numbers of guerrillas and Confederate recruiting commands in this part of Missouri, it is uncharacteristic that the official records fail to note this victory in the records of General Egbert B. Brown's embattled District of Central Missouri, at a time when Brown was claiming much smaller successes to reassure General Rosecrans that his troops were winning.).

43. "Thieves," *Missouri Statesman*, Columbia, Boone County, from the earlier *Central City and Brunswicker*, Brunswick, Chariton County; Nichols, *Guerrilla Warfare in Civil War Missouri, Volume II, 1863*, 184–5, 193, 196, 316 (attesting to strong southern sympathy in the village of Miami and strong guerrilla presence in the Miami area during 1863).

44. *O.R.*, vol. 34, part 1, 1056–7; Broadfoot, *Supplement to the O.R.*, part 2, vol. 35, 4th Cavalry MSM, 64; Dyer, *Compendium*, vol. 2, 810.

45. United States Government, *1860 Missouri Census*, listing in Jefferson Township of north Cole County, the household of Wiley H. Shumate's Kentucky-born father, Nathan Shumate, along with other family members born in Indiana and Missouri; Internet exchanges between the author and Wiley Shumate descendant Glenn Hunt, googy@tx.rr.com, in October 2004, September 2006, April 2007, and February 2008 in which Mrs. Hunt passed along to this author details about Shumate's early life, military record, oral history of his war escapades, and information about his postwar life, death, and burial in Grayson County, Texas.

46. Clyde Lee Jenkins, *Judge Jenkins' History of Miller County*, Tuscumbia, Missouri: published by author, 1971, 433–4; United States Government, *1860 Missouri Census*, lists in Jim Henry Township of northeast Miller County the household of William Matthews.

47. Jenkins, *Judge Jenkins' History of Miller County*, 434–5; "Guerrilla Outrages in Miller County," *Kansas City Daily Journal*, Jackson County, 2 July 1864, from the earlier *St. Louis Union* (Judge Jenkins quoted this short article word-for-word in his history, but it contains few details of the raid.): State of Missouri, Secretary of State's Office, Missouri State Archives, military service record for John Bear who served first as a private in Captain Capps' company of the Osage Regiment Home Guards at Miller County between June and December 1861; then as a private in Captain Brumley's company of 47th EMM at Tuscumbia from 25 September 1862 until he was discharged for disability 1 February 1863; then as a sergeant in Captain Sayles or Brown's Miller County Provisional EMM, in which he enrolled 10 August 1864 at Tuscumbia, and served 199 days active duty between 25 August 1864 and 11 March 1865.

48. *O.R.*, vol. 41, part 2, 8–9; Jenkins, *Judge Jenkins' History of Miller County*, 437; "To Be Executed," *Daily Missouri Democrat*, St. Louis, 25 May 1864; State of Missouri, Secretary of State's Office, Missouri State Archives, Missouri Provost Marshal Papers, in file F1419, regarding "reports that a wounded bushwhacker named Wilcox escaped hospital"; Fellman, *Inside War*, 182–3, 296 (taken from diary of Charles C. Curtiss, eyewitness to Wilcox's public execution, kept at the Chicago Historical Society); United States Government, *1860 Missouri Census*, contains three separate John Wilcox entries in Cole and Miller Counties: 30-year-old, New York–born John Wilcox, an inmate in the state penitentiary at Jefferson City in Cole County, and in Equality Township of central Miller County near Tuscumbia household number 26 of 27-year-old Virginia-born farmer John V. Wilcox and his small family, and not far away in household number 40 of 44-year-old Virginia-born farmer William L. Wilcox, an 18-year-old, Missouri-born son John Wilcox (Author's note: Uncertain which John Wilcox is the one executed by the Federals in Jefferson City on 12 August 1864.).

Eighteen

1. *O.R.*, vol. 41, part 1, 57–8, 59–60; part 2, 77, 78, 79, 91, 101; "Parkville Sacked by Bushwhackers," *Kansas City Daily Journal*, Jackson County, 9 July 1864 (short article, containing few details of the raid); "Capture of Parkville by Guerrillas," *Daily Missouri Democrat*, St. Louis, 14 July 1864 (from an earlier detailed article from the *Leavenworth Times* written by Captain Thomas J. Wilson after he escaped from Parkville and sought refuge on the Kansas side; "Capture of Parksville [sic]," *Daily Missouri Democrat*, St. Louis, 15 July 1864, written with great detail to the *Democrat* by an anonymous correspondent on July 9 in Leavenworth; National Historical Company, *History of Clay and Platte Counties, Missouri*, 727; Edwards, *Noted Guerrillas, or the Warfare of the Border*, 342–3; Soltysiak, "Anarchy in Missouri," *Civil War Times Illustrated*, 32; State of Kansas, *Report of the Adjutant General of the State of Kansas, 1861–'65*, 548 (containing a brief ledger entry about Private Isaac Brink of Parkville, Missouri, who enlisted in Company F, 16th Kansas Cavalry 14 December 1863, was mustered into the regiment the following 21 January, and in remarks section states was "killed by guerrillas July 7, '64, Parkville, Mo."); State of Missouri, Secretary of State's Office, Missouri State Archives, military service records for both Captain Thomas J. Wilson and First Lieutenant George W. Noland of Company E, 82nd EMM.

2. Paxton, *Annals of Platte County, Missouri*, 367; United States Government, 1860 *Missouri Census*, lists in the town of Weston the household of 30-year-old Prussian-born laborer Peter Shaback, his Prussian-born wife, Rosina, and their four small children born in Prussia and Missouri; (Author's note: There does not appear to be any other house-

hold by this name or any similar surname in Platte County at this time.); State of Missouri, Secretary of State's Office, Missouri State Archives, military service records for Privates John and Peter Schabeck who both enlisted during December 1861 at Weston into Company H, 18th Missouri Infantry Regiment, and served together until mustered out 23 December 1864 at Savannah, Georgia.

3. "Missouri Items," *Daily Missouri Democrat*, St. Louis, 11 July 1864; State of Missouri, *Annual Report of the Adjutant General of Missouri for the Year Ending December 31, 1865*, 204 (containing the officer roster of the 25th Missouri Infantry Regiment).

4. *O.R.*, vol. 41, part 2, 100, 110.

5. *O.R.*, vol. 41, part 1, 58–9; part 2, 126–7, 133–4, 206–8; "Col. Coon Thornton-Platte City," *St. Joseph Weekly Herald*, Buchanan County, 14 July 1864 (a short, early report with a few details of the raid); "Guerrilla Atrocities; The Guerrilla Excitement," *Daily Missouri Democrat*, St. Louis, 14 July 1864, from the *St. Joseph Weekly Herald* of 12 July 1864; "Capture of Parksville [sic]," *Daily Missouri Democrat*, St. Louis, 15 July 1864, from this newspaper's special correspondent at Leavenworth, Kansas, as a July 11 postscript to his initial July 9 report; "Capture of Platte City," *Liberty Tribune*, Clay County, 15 July 1864 (a short article with a few key details); "Platte City Burned," *Daily Missouri Democrat*, St. Louis, 16 July 1864, taken from the *St. Joseph Weekly Herald* of July 16; "Coon Thornton's speech at Platte City," *St. Joseph Weekly Herald*, Buchanan County, 21 July 1864; "A Prisoner's Statement," *Kansas City Daily Journal*, Jackson County, 10 August 1864, (from the district provost marshal's office); Paxton, *Annals of Platte County, Missouri*, 367–8 (contains much precise detail); Woodson, *History of Clay County, Missouri*, 135–6 (sketchy version told from Clay County perspective); Edwards, *Noted Guerrillas or the Warfare of the Border*, 347–8 (Edwards' version on this corroborates closer with other sources than most of his book. "Fletch" Taylor's discourse with Colonel Thornton may be factual since Taylor survived the war and freely shared his war experiences afterward when he was a mine owner and legislator.); Dyer, *Compendium*, vol. 2, 810; Soltysiak, "Anarchy in Missouri," *The Civil War Times Illustrated*, 32–3; Scott A. Porter, "'Bashi-Bazouks' and Rebels Too: Action at Camden Point, July 13, 1864," *Missouri Historical Review*, 101, 2, (January 2007), 103–4; James L. Speicher, "The Battle at Camden Point, Missouri, July 13, 1864," *Confederate Veteran* (2001), no. 5, 34–7 (Speicher, as an active member of a local chapter of the Sons of Confederate Veterans, helps upkeep of the grounds at a monument of the battle and a few southern graves. He adds a southern viewpoint of the fight.); Nichols, *Guerrilla Warfare in Civil War Missouri, Volume II, 1863*, 190 (for Thrailkill's experiences in Missouri during 1863); United States Government, *1860 Missouri Census*, lists in Jackson Township of south-central Buchanan County, the household of 48-year-old Virginia-born farmer Charles Morris.

6. *O.R.*, vol. 41, part 2, 149, 152–62, 166, 174–80; Paxton, *Annals of Platte County, Missouri*, 368; Porter, "'Bashi-Bazouks' and Rebels Too: Action at Camden Point, July 13, 1864," *Missouri Historical Review*, 104–6.

7. *O.R.*, vol. 41, part 1, 49, 52, 53, 59, 63; part 2, 166, 178, 185, 187, 191, 251; "Rebel Flag Captured," *Kansas City Daily Journal*, Jackson County, 16 July 1864; "The Fight at Camden Point," *Daily Missouri Democrat*, St. Louis, 16 July 1864, from *St. Joseph Weekly Herald*, Buchanan County, 16 July 1864; "The Fight at Camden Point," *St. Joseph Weekly Herald*, Buchanan County, 21 July 1864 (long, very detailed account); "From Col. Ford's Command," *Liberty Tribune*, Clay County, 22 July 1864, from the earlier *Kansas City Daily Journal*; Paxton, *Annals of Platte County, Missouri*, 368; Edwards *Noted Guerrillas or the Warfare of the Border*, 347–8; Broadfoot, *Supplement* to the *O.R.*, part 2, vol. 21, 16th Kansas Cavalry, 493.

8. "From Col. Ford's Command," *Liberty Tribune*, Clay County, 22 July 1864; Paxton, *Annals of Platte County, Missouri*, 369–70; Soltysiak, "Anarchy in Missouri," *The Civil War Times Illustrated*, 34; Porter, "'Bashi-Bazouks' and Rebels Too: Action at Camden Point, July 13, 1864," *Missouri Historical Review*, 108–9.

9. *O.R.*, vol. 41, part 1, 54; part 2, 252; State of Missouri, Secretary of State's Office, Missouri State Archives, military service record of First Lieutenant John D. Page of Company F, 51st EMM out of Richmond, Ray County, with remark that he was killed July 8, 1864; and military service record of First Sergeant Robert F. H. Goode, of Company F, 51st EMM, out of Richmond, with notation that he was commissioned as second lieutenant July 14, 1864; Dyer, *Compendium*, vol. 2, 810.

10. *O.R.*, vol. 41, part 2, 178.

11. *O.R.*, vol. 41, part 1, 55; "Great Excitement in Carroll County, Mo." *Daily Missouri Republican*, St. Louis, 21 July 1864, from the earlier *Carrollton Democrat*, Carroll County, and the *Central City and Brunswicker*, Brunswick, Chariton County (lengthy, detailed article obtained from sources close to the events); "Guerrilla Murders," *Missouri Statesman*, Columbia, Boone County, 22 July 1864, from the earlier *Carrollton Democrat* and the *Central City and Brunswicker* (a more condensed version than the *Republican's*); "More Bushwhacking Outrages," *Kansas City Daily Journal*, Jackson County, 24 July 1864 (shorter version than the other newspapers that covered this); Missouri Historical Company, *History of Carroll County, Missouri*, 342–6 (guerrilla Jesse Hamlet, participant, provided many details to the writer for this county history); Turner and Clark, *Twentieth Century History of Carroll County Missouri*, 284–8 (nearly a copy of the 1881 version); Edwards, *Noted Guerrillas* or *The Warfare of the Border*, 238–9 (Edwards missed the mark on his short version of this story, perhaps because he was unable to interview any of the participants postwar as he had for many other events); Wood, *The Civil War Story of Bloody Bill Anderson*, 75–8 (Wood's is one of the better later accounts of Anderson's first Carroll County raid); Castel and Goodrich, *Bloody Bill Anderson*, 44–5; Hale, *They Called Him Bloody Bill*, 19 (Hale's short summary borrowed a couple of errors from Brownlee.); Brownlee, *Gray Ghosts of the Confederacy*, 203–4; Castel, *William Clarke Quantrill: His Life and Times*, 180.

12. *O.R.*, vol. 41, part 2, 187, 190–1, 199, 202–5; "To the Citizens of Northwest Missouri," *St. Joseph Weekly Herald*, Buchanan County, 21 July 1864; Way, *Way's Packet Directory, 1848–1994*, 376.

13. Edwards, *Noted Guerrillas or the Warfare on the Border*, 347–8; Soltysiak, "Anarchy in Missouri," *The Civil War Times Illustrated*, 34.

14. *O.R.*, vol. 41, part 2, 204.

15. *O.R.*, vol. 41, part 2, 246, 251(Colonel Ford on July 18 reporting General Curtis' pulling his Kansas troops from the expedition and back to Kansas); National Historical Company, *History of Clay and Platte Counties, Missouri*, 251, 725–6; "Ambush West of Liberty 90 Years Ago, Lives in Memory," *Liberty Tribune*, Clay County, 15 July 1954, in "Civil War in Missouri" vertical file at Missouri State Historical Society, University of Missouri Library, Columbia, Missouri; (No headline), *St. Joseph Weekly Herald*, Buchanan County, 28 July 1864 (attesting to the protest disbanding of Company I, 82nd EMM at Liberty earlier that month); Broadfoot, *Supplement to the O.R.*, part 2, volume 21, 16th Kansas Cavalry, 493 (mentioning Company C in actions between July 12 and 18 near Camden Point and near Liberty); Porter, "'Bashi-Bazouks' and Rebels Too: Action at Camden Point, July 13, 1864," *Missouri Historical Review*, 109; State of Kansas, *Report of the Adjutant General of the State of Kansas, 1861-'65*, 539–42 (Nowhere in the ledger pages of 15th or 16th Kansas Cavalry Regiment are any mentions of casualties from action near Liberty on or about 15–18 July 1864. There are individual soldier entries for departures of men deserting—four in Company C, 16th Kansas Cavalry—or for leaving the service on disability later in July and early August 1864, but this is not to suggest that these reported absences relate to specific actions in Platte or Clay County between July 12 and 18.); United States Government, *1860 Missouri Census*, lists in Liberty Township the household of 36-year-old Kentucky-born low-income farmer Abraham Estes and his large family; State of Missouri, Secretary of State's Office, Missouri State Archives, military service records for Private William H. Holt, Private Lafayette Thomas, Private William M. Thomas, and Sergeant Ferd V. Thompson, all enrolled 24 September 1863 at Liberty in Captain Thomason's Company I, 82nd EMM, and each performed varying amounts of active duty between that date and April 1864 at Liberty.

16. *O.R.*, vol. 41, part 1, 53–4; part 2, 245, 247, 250, 251, 252, 292; "A Desperate Fight with Guerrillas," *Kansas City Daily Journal*, Jackson County, 21 July 1864 (a detailed, mostly accurate account of the Fredericksburg fight); "From Clay County-Rumored Repulse of Federal Troops," *St. Joseph Weekly Herald*, Buchanan County, 21 July 1864 (an early, short report lacking details); "The Fredericksburg Fight," *Liberty Tribune*, Clay County, 22 July 1864 (Captain Moses' own account, which is omitted from the *O.R.* Moses' mentions of Captain Rouell's presence with the patrol as a volunteer attest to Rouell's unusual status with the regiment at this time.); "The Pursuit of Thornton," *Missouri Statesman*, Columbia, Boone County, 29 July 1864 (a short version with just a few details); Missouri Historical Company, *History of Ray County, Missouri*, St. Louis: Missouri Historical Company, 1881, 302 (short, mostly accurate local version); Edwards, *Noted Guerrillas, or the Warfare of the Border*, 349–51 (Edwards penned a long, rather accurate southern version of the Fredericksburg fight. He did exaggerate Union casualty figures and described the Coloradoans pillaging a house belonging to a "Conrow" family just before the fight. The 1860 Missouri census does include two Congus households and three Connor households in Fishing River Township where this fight took place, perhaps giving credence to Edwards' claim. He included a list of names of the guerrillas taking part, mentioned that they captured Captain Moses' hat, and accurately described the Yanks' pesky Starr carbines which were so troublesome.); Porter, "'Bashi-Bazouks' and Rebels Too: Action at Camden Point, July 13, 1864," *Missouri Historical Review*, 109; Soltysiak, "Anarchy in Missouri," *The Civil War Times Illustrated*, 34; United States Government, *Official Army Register of the Volunteer Force of the United States Army for the Years* 1861, '62, '63, '64, '65, vol. 8, 25 (which mentions that Captain Rouell was cashiered 30 May 1864); Wood, *Other Noted Guerrillas of the Civil War in Missouri*, 171; Castel, *William Clarke Quantrill: His Life and Times*, 178; Dyer, *Compendium*, vol. 2, 811.

17. National Historical Company, *History of Caldwell and Livingston Counties*, 196.

18. Missouri Historical Company, *History of Ray County, Missouri*, 302.

19. *O.R.*, vol. 41, part 2, 243, 247.

20. *O.R.*, vol. 41, part 2, 252; National Historical Company, *History of Caldwell and Livingston Counties*, 196; Soltysiak, "Anarchy in Missouri," *The Civil War Times Illustrated*, 34–5; State of Missouri, Secretary of State's Office, Missouri State Archives, military service records for Second lieutenant Jesse C. Turnage and Private John F. Shoemake, both of Company D, 51st EMM (This record only reflects their service during 1862 and 1863 and does not reflect their 1864 service which resulted in their deaths.).

21. *O.R.*, vol. 41, part 2, 251.

22. *O.R.*, vol. 41, part 2, 252; Wood, *Other Noted Guerrillas of the Civil War in Missouri*, 171; National Historical Company, *History of Caldwell and Livingston Counties*, 196; W. H. S. McGlumphy and Carrie Polk Johnston, *History of Clinton and Caldwell Counties, Missouri*, Topeka: Missouri Historical Publications Company, 1923, 270; State of Missouri, Secretary of State's Office, Missouri State Archives, military service record for Private Perry J. Wilson of Company A, 51st EMM (This record only reflects his service during 1862 and 1863 and omits the 1864 service which resulted in his death.).

23. *O.R.*, vol. 41, part 2, 252; "Guerrillas in Caldwell County," *Missouri Statesman*, Columbia, Boone County, 29 July 1864; National Historical Company, *History of Caldwell and Livingston Counties*, 197; McGlumphy and Johnston, *History of Clinton and Caldwell Counties, Missouri*, 270; Edwards, *Noted Guerrillas, or the Warfare of the Border*, 351 (Edwards only remarked that "Fletch" Taylor's band passed through Knoxville on their way toward Caldwell County, but gave no details.).

24. *O.R.*, vol. 41, part 1, 53–4; part 2, 245, 246; National Historical Company, *History of Caldwell and Livingston Counties*, 197; McGlumphy and Johnston, *History of Clinton and Caldwell Counties, Missouri*, 270–1; John Bartlett, *Familiar Quotations*, Boston: Little Brown and Company, 1955 (thirteenth edition), 11.

25. *O.R.*, vol. 41 part 2,300–1; "Guerrillas in Caldwell County," *Missouri Statesman*, Columbia, Boone County, 29 July 1864; National Historical Company, *History of Caldwell and Livingston Counties*, 198–200; McGlumphy and Johnston, *History of Clinton and Caldwell Counties, Missouri*, 271; Soltysiak, "Anarchy in Missouri," *The Civil War Times Illustrated*, 34–5.

26. *O.R.*, vol. 41, part 2, 270–1, 288, 297; National Historical Company, *History of Caldwell and Livingston Counties*, 198–200; McGlumphy and Johnston, *History of Clinton and Caldwell Counties, Missouri*, 271; Missouri Historical Company, *History of Carroll County, Missouri*, 346–7; Turner and Clark, *Twentieth Century History of Carroll County, Missouri*, 288–9.

27. *O.R.*, vol. 41, part 2, 271, 298, 299, 312; "The Guerrilla War," *St. Joseph Weekly Herald*, Buchanan County, 28 July 1864; "Guerrillas in Caldwell County," *Missouri Statesman*, Columbia, Boone County, 29 July 1864; National Historical Company, *History of Caldwell and Livingston Counties*, 201–5; McGlumphy and Johnston, *History of Clinton and Caldwell Counties, Missouri*, 271–3; Edwards, *Noted Guerrillas, or the Warfare of the Border*, 351; Wood, *Other Noted Guerrillas of the Civil War in Missouri*, 172–3; Soltysiak, "Anarchy in Missouri," *The Civil War Times Illustrated*, 35; Porter, "'Bashi-Bazouks' and Rebels Too: Action at Camden Point, July 13, 1864," *Missouri Historical Review*, 109.

28. *O.R.*, vol. 41, part 2, 311, 342 (Author's note: The usually accurate Union military records are rife with errors of Thornton's mobile campaign in Ray, Carroll, Livingston, Caldwell, and Clinton Counties during these days. Even some of the place names are confused, and the locations of telegraph stations where Union authorities made some reports can be confused to be the actual locations of some events. Only parts of these reports match other corroborating sources.); National Historical Company, *History of Caldwell and Livingston Counties*, 205; State of Missouri, Secretary of State's Office, Missouri State Archives, military service record for Private John H. Christopher first in the 48th EMM enrolled at nearby Cameron, southeast corner of DeKalb County in 1862 and early 1863, and then during late 1863 and 1864 in "Capt. Roger's Independent Company" of the 89th EMM with thirteen days of active duty during June 1864 at Liberty, Clay County, with the remark that he was "killed by bushwhackers at home July 21, 1864"; United States Government, *1860 Missouri Census*, lists in Shoal Township of northeast Clinton County the household of 23-year-old, Missouri-born farmer J. H. Christopher and his small family.

29. *O.R.*, vol. 41, part 1, 60–2; part 2, 312, 313, 316, 341; "The Guerrilla War" and "Judge Birch," *St. Joseph Weekly Herald*, Buchanan County, 28 July 1864; National Historical Company, *History of Caldwell and Livingston Counties*, 205–6; Edwards, *Noted Guerrillas, or the Warfare of the Border*, 351–2; Porter, "'Bashi-Bazouks' and Rebels Too: Action at Camden Point, July 13, 1864," *Missouri Historical Review*, 109–10; Wood, *Other Noted Guerrillas of the Civil War in Missouri*, 173–4; Dyer, *Compendium*, Vol. 2, 811.

30. *O.R.*, vol. 41, part 1, 54, 60–1; part 2, 312, 317, 318, 341; National Historical Company, *History of Caldwell and Livingston Counties*, 206; McGlumphy and Johnston, *History of Clinton and Caldwell Counties, Missouri*, 271, 272.

31. *O.R.*, vol. 41, part 1, 54, 61; part 2, 370 (Author's note: Some period and later sources state the fight near Union Mills on July 22 took place near Camden Point, which was on the other side of the Platte River and several miles from this action. This discrepancy can also cause confusion with the July 13 fight at Camden Point.); "Fight With Guerrillas in Platte County," *St. Joseph Weekly Herald*, Buchanan County, 28 July 1864; National Historical Company, *History of Caldwell and Livingston Counties*, 206–8; Edwards, *Noted Guerrillas, or the Warfare of the Border*, 356–60 (Edwards' version of the Union Mills fight has enough of the other accounts in it to corroborate each other, but his is fanciful, especially the large number of guerrilla casualties. He included the woman's warning, accurate overall numbers for both sides, and was in his way complimentary to the Union side of this tough fight.); Soltysiak, "Anarchy in Missouri," *The Civil War Times Illustrated*, 35; Wood, *Other Noted Guerrillas of the Civil War in Missouri*, 174; Dyer, *Compendium*, Vol. 2, 811.

32. *O.R.*, vol. 41, part 1, 51, 55; part 2, 374; "A Paw Paw at the Confessional," *St. Joseph Weekly Herald*, Buchanan County, 28 July 1864, quoting the prisoner's July 24 written statement; "The Pursuit of Thornton," *Missouri Statesman*, Columbia, Boone County, 29 July 1864, quoting the *St. Joseph Weekly Herald*, Buchanan County, of 23 July 1864.

33. *O.R.*, vol. 41, part 1, 60; part 2, 339, 340, 359, 360, 374, 376; National Historical Company, *History of Coldwell and Livingston Counties*, 209.

34. *O.R.*, vol. 41, part 1, 54; part 2, 312, 339, 340, 342, 343–4, 345, 358, 359, 360, 366, 374, 377,410.

35. *O.R.*, vol. 41, part 2, 344, 363, 427–8; "Missouri Items," *Daily Missouri Democrat*, St. Louis, 6 August 1864, based on a private letter sent to the newspaper from Laclede, Linn County; James Everett Ford, *A History of Grundy County*, Trenton, Missouri: News Publishing Company, 1908, 68–71 (This history's source was a participant in the Grundy County company of the 30th EMM in this expedition in Carroll County. He steadfastly refused the worst of the accusations, insisting that his company did no more harm than foraging for corn for their horses, and occasionally swapping a worn horse for a farmer's fresh one. Furthermore, the source insisted a number of the Grundy County company paid for their expenses in Carroll County out of their own pockets or left notes with the owners giving the militiaman's name and address for repayment later.); United States Government, 1860 *Missouri Census*, lists in Grand River Township of east Carroll County, served by the DeWitt Post Office, the household of Pennsylvania-born middle-income 54-year-old farmer David Gilbert and his wife and seven children; Nichols, *Guerrilla Warfare in Civil War Missouri, Volume II, 1863*, 314–5.

36. *O.R.*, vol. 41, part 1, 54, 63; part 2, 390; Soltysiak, "Anarchy in Missouri," *The Civil War Times Illustrated*, 35.

37. *O.R.*, vol. 41, part 2, 374–5.

38. *O.R*, vol. 41, part 2, 1020, 1023; Castel, *General Sterling Price and the Civil War in the West*, 199–200.

39. "Latest News from the Guerrillas," *St. Joseph Weekly Herald*, Buchanan County, 21 July 1864 (and this article was repeated word-for-word in the *Daily Missouri Republican* of St. Louis on 21 July 1864); Dyer, *Compendium*, vol. 2, 811.

40. "Bushwhackers in Buchanan," *Kansas City Daily Journal*, Jackson County, 27 July 1864, from the earlier *Atchison Free Press*, Atchison, Kansas.

41. *O.R.*, vol. 41, part 2, 248; National Historical Company, *History of Clay and Platte Counties, Missouri*, 731 (which lists the Union dead as Jefferson Ingram, Lewis Moore, and a Stanford; and the wounded to be Captain Fitzgerald and Thomas Able); State of Missouri, Secretary of State's Office, Missouri State Archives, military service records of Privates Jeff Ingram or Thomas Jefferson Ingram, Lewis Moore, Jr., and Thomas Able performed duty in Captain William J. Fitzgerald's Company C, 39th EMM during 1862 and/or 1863 in Platte County; State of Kansas, *Report of the Adjutant General of the State of Kansas, 1861-'65*, 545–6, shows records for service in late 1863 and in 1864 for Privates Jefferson Ingram, Lewis Moore, and Milton Stanford all in Captain Fitzgerald's Company C, 16th Kansas Cavalry. However, the Kansas record for Private Moore shows that he died at Leavenworth, Kansas, on 21 April 1864 and for Private Stanford that he died at Leavenworth, Kansas, on 4 June 1864, and does not state cause of death; (Author's note: Perhaps the local resident who related this episode to be included in the 1885 county history confused some of the names of the Union participants with other Platte County men who were then serving in the 16th Kansas Cavalry. As for James Rupe, there were several Rupe men who served the southern cause from the Platte and Clay County area in both the regular and guerrilla service. There is a Union military prison record for a guerrilla James Rupe of Colonel Gideon W. Thompson's 6th Missouri Cavalry captured in Platte County 1 October 1862, sent to Gratiot Street Prison, and transferred 4 March 1863 to Washington, D.C., for exchange, according to Eakin, *Missouri Prisoners of War*, Rupe entry; and Bartels, *The Forgotten Men*, 290.).

42. "Shooting Affair in Andrew," *St. Joseph Weekly Herald*, Buchanan County, 28 July 1864; State of Missouri, Secretary of State's Office, Missouri State Archives, military service record of Private A, R. Frogg, who was active in both the 81st and the 88th EMM at Savannah, county seat of Andrew County.

43. "The Guerrilla War," *St. Joseph Weekly Herald*, Buchanan County, 28 July 1864.

44. "Guerrillas in Gentry," *St. Joseph Weekly Herald*, Buchanan County, 4 August 1864.

45. *O.R.*, vol. 41, part 2, 409, 410; Wood, *Other Noted Guerrillas of the Civil War in Missouri*, 174–5; Wood, *The Civil War Story of Bloody Biff Anderson*, 88.

46. "Men Shot in Their Field," *St. Joseph Weekly Herald*, Buchanan County, 28 July 1864; State of Missouri, *Annual Report of the Adjutant General of Missouri for the Year Ending December 31, 1865*, 623 (identifying Colonel Bradshaw, mentioned in the article).

47. Nichols, *Guerrilla Warfare in Civil War Missouri, Volume II, 1863*, 179–81, 186–8, 189, 307–8, 310.

48. "Troubles in Missouri," *Missouri Daily Republican*, St. Louis, 30 July 1864, from the earlier *St. Joseph News*, Buchanan County, 27 July 1864; Paxton, *Annals of Platte County, Missouri*, 312 (affirming that a Chesnut recruited for the southern forces in Platte County in August 1861); Edwards, *Noted Guerrillas or the Warfare of the Border*, 283; Castel, *William Clarke Quantrill: His Life and Times*, 183; Castel, *General Sterling Price and the Civil War in the West*, 199; State of Missouri, Secretary of State's Office, Missouri State Archives, military service record of "Private John T. Chesnut" of Company A, Boyd's Battalion, Quartermaster Department, who participated in a 1902 Confederate reunion in St. Joseph; and of "Captain John Tully Chestnut" of Company A of Colonel John R. Boyd's regiment in United Daughters of the Confederacy records; United States Government, *1860 Missouri Census*, lists all in Crawford Township of south-central Buchanan County the households of 40-year-old Kentucky-born farmer Andrew C. Chesnut (containing also 20-year-old Kentucky-born farmhand John T. Chesnut); 29-year-old Tennessee-born farmer John Ferrell; and 36-year-old North Carolina–born farmer John Campbell (three of the slain southern men listed in the newspaper article referenced early in this note).

49. "Shot," *St. Joseph Weekly Herald*, Buchanan County, 4 August 1864; United State Government, *1860 Missouri Census*, lists the household of 37-year-old Missouri-born farmer Dowdle Roland in Platte Township of southeast Buchanan County, and two Meadows households in two other townships of south Buchanan County.

50. "The Work of Bushwhackers," *St. Joseph Weekly Herald*, Buchanan County, 4 August 1864 (The newspaper is using the term "bushwhacker" in the article headline in the most general sense without reference to northern or southern loyalty to denote an assassin who murders from ambush. Since the article clearly states both men were "decidedly disloyal in their sympathies," the writer implies the killers were northerners.); United States Government, *1860 Missouri Census*, lists in Tremont Township of central Buchanan County, the household of 64-year-old Kentucky-born farmer Ambrose McDaniel; and in Crawford Township of south-central Buchanan County, the household of 45-year-old Kentucky-born farmer Jeremiah Smith.

51. *O.R.*, vol. 41, part 2, 439, 443; Edwards, *Noted Guerrillas or the Warfare of the Border*, 338–9; National Historical Company, *History of Clay and Platte Counties, Missouri*, 251 (This short, local account mentions Clear Creek and individuals of "Fletch" Taylor's band, so may refer to the same incident as Colonel Catherwood and Edwards.); United States Government, *1860 Missouri Census*, lists in Washington Township of northeast Clay County only one Duncan: 52-year-old wealthy farmer David T. Duncan.

52. *O.R.*, vol. 41, part 2, 408, 445, 457, 460, 461, 462, 476, 477.

53. *O.R.*, vol. 41, part 2, 312, 409, 439, 445, 459; Soltysiak, "Anarchy in Missouri," *The Civil War Times Illustrated*, 35.

54. *O.R.*, vol. 41, part 2, 457.

55. *O.R.*, vol. 41, part 2, 461.

56. *O.R.*, vol. 41, part 2, 507 (Author's note: The Union military claimed these guerrillas belonged to

a band led either by Thrailkill, a Zeigler, or Shepherd. The author assumes this report concerns Taylor's guerrillas, since at this same time Thrailkill's band was very active in the northwest Clay County area about 25 miles away. The author has not encountered a guerrilla named Zeigler. George Shepherd and about six other guerrillas raided nearby Missouri City on 15 June, over six weeks earlier. It appears that the Union military was guessing the identity of the guerrilla leader.).

57. *O.R.*, vol. 41, part 2, 562–3; Wood, *Other Noted Guerrillas of the Civil War in Missouri*, 175 State of Missouri, Secretary of State's Office, Missouri State Archives, military service records for Private Thomas Marsh, who joined Company B, 89th EMM on 23 July 1864; and Private James Walker, who joined Company B, 89th EMM on 30 April 1864; United States Government, *1860 Missouri Census*, lists two James Walker households in Platte Township of northwest Clay County.

58. *O.R.*, vol. 41, part 2, 508.

Nineteen

1. *O.R.*, vol. 41, part 2, 527, 541 (On page 527 a Union official in distant Mexico, Audrain County, passed along a report August 2 that Anderson with 12 men headed west into Chariton County, but did not state when [on July 31]. The page 541 report is from a Union officer on board a riverboat in the Missouri River on August 3 that heard guerrillas were moving west and "they have killed a great many men within the last few days."); Missouri Historical Company, *History of Carroll County, Missouri*, 348–51 (This is by far the most detailed, authoritative history of Anderson's raid across north Carroll County on August 1 and 2, although there are minor faults with dates and precise names.); Turner and Clark, *Twentieth Century History of Carroll County Missouri*, 289–92 (This is really a copy of the 1881 county history cited above.); Edwards, *Noted Guerrillas or the Warfare of the Border*, 239 (Edwards lists all of Anderson's men present on this raid, which the above sources also use. This resource concentrates on the fight at Mary Mitchell's house, wrote that Anderson shot the woman "accidentally," and included John Maupin's barbarity to the guardsman.); Burch, *A True Story of Chas W. Quantrell*, 187–8 (Guerrilla Harrison Trow was not present on this raid, and merely quoted lines and phrases from Edwards' work.); Stanley, Wilson, and Wilson, *Death Records From Missouri Newspapers, January 1861–December 1865*, 49, 97 (citing the *Carrollton Democrat* of August 5 regarding the violent deaths of Isaac Dugan and John Kirker); Castel and Goodrich, *Bloody Bill Anderson: The Short, Savage Life of a Civil War Guerrilla*, 49–50; Wood, *The Civil War Story of Bloody Bill Anderson*, 88–91; State of Missouri, Secretary of State's Office, Missouri State Archives, military service records for Private Isaac W. Dugan of Company A, 65th EMM with 131 days active service in 1862, detailed in spring 1863 to 4th Provisional EMM Regiment, and lack of any 1864 record indicating he was probably inactive that year; also military service record for Private John W. Hudson in Captain Daniel Hoover's "Hoover's Carroll and Livingston Counties VMM" in spring 1865 with 99 days active duty in Carrollton, Carroll County (leaving open the possibility that he was active in a General Orders Number 107 citizen guards unit during 1864, although this is not reflected in this record); United States Government, *1860 Missouri Census*, lists in Hurricane Township of northeast Carroll County the households of Mary Mitchell with several teenage and older children, nearby the households of Stephen and Caroline Mitchell, and Jabes and Nancy A. Calvert; also in Hurricane Township the household of Isaac Dugan, John Hudson, and John Kirker; and in Grand River Township of east-central Carroll County the households of William A. Darr and a William T. Latham. (Author's note: Most of Bill Anderson's exploits during 1864 were recorded in great detail by local sources more than other guerrilla adventures in the same areas due to the horrific bloodlust displayed by his men.)

2. Missouri Historical Company, *History of Carroll County, Missouri*, 350–1; Turner and Clark, *Twentieth Century History of Carroll County Missouri*, 292–3 (a copy of the 1881 Carroll County history cited above); Castel and Goodrich, *Bloody Bill Anderson: The Short, Savage Life of a Civil War Guerrilla*, 50–1; Wood, *The Civil War Story of Bloody Bill Anderson*, 92–3; State of Missouri, Secretary of State's Office, Missouri State Archives, military service record of Corporal William Russell, who at age 18 in August 1862 enrolled at Richmond, Ray County, into Company E, 65th EMM, and then served 23 days active duty; his record remarks at the bottom "Enlisted in U.S. service." (There seems to be no way to prove this is Mr. Russell's son, presumably a Union officer home on leave, that Anderson and his men killed near Russellville, but he appears to be the William Russell indicated in the 1860 census report cited below.); United State Government, *1860 Missouri Census*, lists in Grape Grove Township of northeast Ray County, the household of Irish-born 50-year-old farmer William Russell of modest means, and among his three sons, 18-year-old Missouri-born farm laborer William Russell (Neither father nor son appear in this area in the *1870 Missouri Census*.); also in nearby Richmond Township is the household of Scottish-born 45-year-old farmer A. Oliphant, of comfortable means, and his 19-year-old Missouri-born farm laborer son Ralph.

3. Missouri Historical Company, *History of Carroll County, Missouri*, 351; Edwards, *Noted Guerrillas or the Warfare of the Border*, 239–40; John P. Burch, *A True Story of Chas W. Quantrell And His Guerrilla Band*, 188.

4. *O.R.*, vol. 41, part 2, 543; "Missouri Items," *Daily Missouri Democrat*, St. Louis, 8 August 1864, from the *Atchison Free Press*, Atchison County, Kansas of 3 August 1864.

5. "Missouri Items," *Daily Missouri Democrat*, St. Louis, 22 August 1864, from the earlier *Grand River News* of Albany, Gentry County.

6. "Missouri Items," *Daily Missouri Democrat*, St. Louis, 6 August 1864, taken either from the *St. Joseph Tribune*, Buchanan County, 4 August 1864 or the *St. Joseph Evening News* of about the same date (The St. Louis newspaper was vague about which St. Joseph paper originally printed this account.).

7. "Guerrillas About," *St. Joseph Weekly Herald*, Buchanan County, 4 August 1864; Eakins and Hale, *Branded as Rebels*, 74.

8. *O.R.*, vol. 41, part 2, 542.
9. *O.R.*, vol. 41, part 2, 543.
10. "Surrendered," *St. Joseph Weekly Herald*, Buchanan County, 11 August 1864; "Bushwhackers," *Missouri Statesman*, Columbia, Boone County, 12 August 1864, from the St. Joseph newspaper cited above.
11. *O.R.*, vol. 41, part 2, 562.
12. *O.R.*, vol. 41, part 2, 562, 563.
13. Edwards, *Noted Guerrillas or the Warfare of the Border*, 339–340; United States Government, *1860 Missouri Census*, lists in Fishing River Township that surrounds Missouri City in southeast Clay County only one Anderson family—that of Thomas Anderson.
14. "Missouri Items," *Daily Missouri Democrat*, St. Louis, 9 August 1864, perhaps from the *St. Joseph Weekly Herald*, Buchanan County, of August 6.
15. *O.R.*, vol. 41, part 2, 573.
16. *O.R.*, vol. 41, part 2, 576.
17. *O.R.*, vol. 41, part 2, 586, 595–6.
18. *O.R.*, vol. 41, part 2, 586, 595–6; (No headline), *St. Joseph Weekly Herald*, Buchanan County, 18 August 1864, from the earlier *Leavenworth Times*, Leavenworth, Kansas.
19. *O.R.*, vol. 41, part 2, 575; "Guerrillas and Their Operations," *St. Joseph Weekly Herald*, Buchanan County, 11 August 1864; "Liberty, Mo., August 5," *Liberty Tribune*, Clay County, 12 August 1864, quoting an earlier August 5 report by Colonel Catherwood; "Hunting Guerrillas," *Kansas City Daily Journal*, Jackson County, 13 August, from the St. Joseph newspaper cited above.
20. *O.R.*, vol. 41, part 2, 730.
21. *O.R.*, vol. 41, part 2, 610–1; "More Bushwhackers Captured," *St. Joseph Weekly Herald*, Buchanan County, 11 August 1864.
22. *O.R.*, vol. 41, part 2, 748; Edwards, *Noted Guerrillas or the Warfare of the Border*, 353.
23. Edwards, *Noted Guerrillas or the Warfare of the Border*, 352–3; Cummins, *Jim Cummins' Book*, 43.
24. *O.R.*, vol. 41, part 2, 608.
25. "Another Man Murdered," *Liberty Tribune*, Clay County, 12 August 1864; "Murder in Clay," *St. Joseph Weekly Herald*, Buchanan County, 18 August 1864 (This article, word-for-word, was repeated in the *Kansas City Daily Journal*, Jackson County, of 21 August; and the *Missouri Statesman* of Columbia, Boone County, of 26 August.); "Five Days, or the Uncertainty of Human Affairs in North-west Mo." *Liberty Tribune*, Clay County, 19 August 1864; National Historical Company, *History of Clay and Platte Counties, Missouri*, 252; State of Missouri, Secretary of State's Office, Missouri State Archives, military service record of Private Columbus Whitlock of Captain Anthony Harsell's Company D, 48th EMM, showing he enrolled 2 August 1862 at Liberty, served 244 days active duty, and was last mustered 30 April 1863 (There is no remark to indicate if Private Whitlock was discharged from the EMM.); United States Government, *1860 Missouri Census*, lists household of William Hall in Platte Township of northwest Clay County, and Collumbus Whitlock in Hardin Township of southwest Clinton County.
26. "A Fight With Chiles' Guerrillas," *St. Joseph Weekly Herald*, Buchanan County, 18 August 1864; State of Missouri, Secretary of State's Office, Missouri State Archives, military service record for Corporal John R. Snyder in Captain Drumheller's company of Joseph's Battalion Six Months Militia at St. Joseph between 24 September 1861 and 11 February 1862; commanding Company B of 25th EMM from 29 July 1862 until 23 March 1863 from St. Joseph on active duty; and active service in Company D, 3rd Provisional EMM from St. Joseph during 1863 (Apparently, there was no record for Snyder's service during August 1864.).
27. "Missouri Items," *Daily Missouri Democrat*, St. Louis, 12 August 1864; Edwards, *Noted Guerrillas or the Warfare of the Border*, 353–4.
28. "Bushwhackers," *Liberty Tribune*, Clay County, 12 August 1864. "Guerrillas and Their Operations," *St. Joseph Weekly Herald*, Buchanan County, 11 August 1864.
29. "Bushwhackers," *Liberty Tribune*, Clay County, 12 August 1864; "Guerrillas and Their Operations," *St. Joseph Weekly Herald*, Buchanan County, 11 August 1864.
30. *O.R.*, vol. 41, part 1, 250, 251, part 2, 689–90; National Historical Company, *History of Clay and Platte Counties, Missouri*, 253; "More Guerrilla Trouble," *St. Joseph Weekly Herald*, Buchanan County, 18 August 1864; "The Guerrilla War," *Daily Missouri Democrat*, St. Louis, 22 August 1864, from the *Caldwell County Banner*, Kingston, 19 August 1864; Edwards, *Noted Guerrillas or the Warfare of the Border*, 240; Britton, *The Civil War on the Border, Vol. 2, 1863–1865*, 376–7; Hale, *They Called Him Bloody Bill*, 28; Castel and Goodrich, *Bloody Bill Anderson: The Short Savage Life of a Civil War Guerrilla*, 54; Wood, *The Civil War Story of Bloody Bill Anderson*, 94; Dyer, *Compendium*, vol. 2, 811; State of Missouri, Secretary of State's Office, Missouri State Archives, military service records for Privates Smith and John Hutchings in Captain D. P. Whitmer's Company D, 48th EMM, and also in Captain Widmer's Company D, 4th Provisional EMM during 1863 (There are no remarks about the Hutchings' deaths on August 12 in these records.); There is also a military service record for Captain Patten Colley, Company E, 51st EMM, with the remark "Killed in Battle Aug 12, 64."
31. *O.R.*, vol. 41, part 2, 689; "The Guerrilla War," *Daily Missouri Democrat*, St. Louis, 22 August 1864, from the *Caldwell County Banner*, Kingston, 19 August 1864; Edwards, *Noted Guerrillas or the Warfare of the Border*, 240; Britton, *The Civil War on the Border, Vol. 2, 1863–1865*, 377; State of Missouri, Secretary of State's Office, Missouri State Archives, military service records for Privates Daniel H. Vinsant, Samuel Fortson, and James M. Maupin of Company G, 51st EMM; Fortson's record as explanation that he only served 19 days "actual service" after he enrolled 21 July 1864 in this unit states as a remark "Killed by Bushwhackers 1864 while carrying dispatches from Richmond to Knoxville"; Maupin's record states in remarks: "Killed Aug 13th 1864 by Anderson's Guerrillas while on furlough." United States Government, *1860 Missouri Census*, lists in Knoxville Township of northeast Ray County the record of the household of 30-year-old Tennessee-born moderate-income farmer James Maupin, his wife, and two small children.
32. *O.R.*, vol. 41, part 1, 251–2; "The Guerrilla

War," *Daily Missouri Democrat*, St. Louis, 22 August 1864, from the *Caldwell County Banner*, Kingston, 19 August 1864.

33. "More Bushwhacking," *Daily Missouri Democrat*, St. Louis, 20 August 1864, from the *Bethany Union*, Harrison County, 26 August 1864.

34. *O.R.*, vol. 41, part 1, 252; "Narrow Escape of Bill Anderson," *St. Joseph Weekly Herald*, Buchanan County, 18 August 1864 (repeated word-for-word a day or two later in the St. Louis *Daily Missouri Democrat);* "The Guerrilla War," *Daily Missouri Democrat*, St. Louis, 22 August 1864, from the *Caldwell Banner*, Kingston, 19 August 1864; "Bushwhackers in Carroll County," *Missouri Statesman*, Columbia, Boone County, 26 August 1864, from the earlier *Chillicothe Chronicle*, Livingston County; Missouri Historical Company, *History of Carroll County, Missouri*, 351–5 (about the best detailed version of the fight, although some of the guerrilla victims' names cannot be identified in the 1860 census); Turner and Clark, *Twentieth Century History of Carroll County Missouri*, 293–6; Missouri Historical Company, *History of Ray County, Missouri*, 303; National Historical Company, *History of Clay and Platte Counties, Missouri*, 254; Edwards, *Noted Guerrillas* or *the Warfare of the Border*, 240–3 (Edwards' mangled version of this fight seems accurate about one of the dead and naming the wounded; how they were treated by southern families in Chariton County; and Bill Anderson's wounds causing him to turn over band control to his brother Jim. Just about everything else he wrote on this topic is fanciful.); Britton, *The Civil War on the Border, Vol. 2, 1863–1865*, 377 (Britton's general account is okay, except he wrote that the guerrilla leader was Thrailkill and that he was seriously wounded in this fight.); Hale, *They Called Him Bloody Bill*, 29–31; Castel and Goodrich, *Bloody Bill Anderson: The Short Savage Life of a Civil War Guerrilla*, 55–6 (Castel and Goodrich had the guerrillas initiate the fight instead of the militia.); Wood, *The Civil War Story of Bloody Bill Anderson*, 96–7; Bartlett, *Familiar Quotations*, 399 (Napoleon Bonaparte's reference to his army's retreat from Moscow in 1812: "From the sublime to the ridiculous is but a single step.").

35. *O.R.*, vol. 41, part 2, 720–2, 751–2; "Reported Trouble in Atchison County," *Kansas City Daily Journal*, Jackson County, 20 August 1864, quoting the earlier *St. Joseph Tribune*, Buchanan County.

36. "Twenty-Five Horses Captured," *St. Joseph Weekly Herald*, Buchanan County, 18 August 1864.

37. "Bushwhackers in Carroll County," *Missouri Statesman*, Columbia, Boone County, 26 August 1864, from the earlier *Richmond Conservator*, Ray County.

38. (No headline), *Missouri Statesman*, Columbia, Boone County, 2 September 1864, from the earlier *Caldwell Banner*, Kingston; National Historical Company, *History of Caldwell and Livingston Counties, Missouri*, 220–1 (Author's note: There does not seem to be a record for Henry or Henry D. Whiteneck in the 1860 census. Perhaps the census-taker missed him or he moved into Caldwell County after the census. Both versions of this story have enough detail to appear genuine.).

39. (No headline), *St. Joseph Weekly Herald*, Buchanan County, 25 August 1864, from the earlier *Leavenworth Bulletin*, Leavenworth County, Kansas;

"The Guerrilla War," *Daily Missouri Democrat*, St. Louis, 30 August 1864, from the earlier *Weston Border Times*, Platte County; Paxton, *Annals of Platte County, Missouri*, 372; United States Government, *1860 Missouri Census*, lists in Lee Township of west-central Platte County, the households of moderately wealthy, Irish-born, farmers 34-year-old William Wallace and nearby 32-year-old James Wallace, as well as 70-year-old Kentucky-born John Vennaman.

40. *O.R.*, vol. 41, part 2, 762; "Narrow Escape of Sy Gordon," *St. Joseph Weekly Herald*, Buchanan County, 25 August 1864, repeated word-for-word the same day in the *Kansas City Daily Journal;* "Guerrillas in Platte County," *Missouri Statesman*, Columbia, Boone County, 2 September 1864, from a Weston, Platte County, letter published in the *Leavenworth Conservative*, Leavenworth County, Kansas; Wood, *Other Noted Guerrillas of the Civil War in Missouri*, 192; Farley and Farley, *Missouri Rebels Remembered Si Gordon and John Thrailkill*, first three chapters.

41. Eakin and Hale, *Branded As Rebels*, 169 (a pithy biography of Gordon with references); Paxton, *Annals of Platte County, Missouri*, 358–9; National Historical Company, *History of Clay and Platte Counties, Missouri*, 655–6, 695–8; Broadfoot, *Supplement to the O.R.*, part 2, vol. 38, 114 (documenting Gordon's desertion from his regiment); Wood, *Other Noted Guerrillas of the Civil War in Missouri*, 181–94; Farley and Farley, *Missouri Rebels Remembered Si Gordon and John Thrailkill*, 76.

42. *O.R.*, vol. 41, part 2, 787–8, 794; "The Guerrillas," *St. Joseph Weekly Herald*, Buchanan County, 25 August 1864; Farley and Farley, *Missouri Rebels Remembered Si Gordon and John Thrailkill*, 76; Wood, *Other Noted Guerrillas of the Civil War in Missouri*, 192–3.

43. *O.R.*, vol. 41, part 2, 824; Farley and Farley, *Missouri Rebels Remembered Si Gordon and John Thrailkill*, 77; Wood, *Other Noted Guerrillas of the Civil War in Missouri*, 193.

44. *O.R.*, vol. 41, part 2, 807; Farley and Farley, *Missouri Rebels Remembered Si Gordon and John Thrailkill*, 77–8.

45. *O.R.*, vol. 41, part 2, 841, 856; (No headline), *Kansas City Daily Journal*, Jackson County, 23 August 1864 (commenting on the falling water level of the Missouri River); "Guerrilla Crossing From Clay," *Kansas City Daily Journal*, Jackson County, 26 August 1864; Farley and Farley, *Missouri Rebels Remembered Si Gordon and John Thrailkill*, 116–7; Wood, *Other Noted Guerrillas of the Civil War in Missouri*, 176.

46. *O.R.*, vol. 41, part 1, 291–2; Paxton, *Annals of Platte County, Missouri*, 372; "Bushwhackers," *Kansas City Daily Journal*, Jackson County, 9 September 1864, from the earlier *Leavenworth Conservative*, Leavenworth County, Kansas; United States Government, *1860 Missouri Census*, shows the household of miller John L. Martin including his 19-year-old son James, also shown to be a miller, at or near the village of DeKalb in Bloomington Township of southwest Buchanan County.

47. "Man Murdered in Platte City," *St. Joseph Weekly Herald*, Buchanan County, 1 September 1864, repeated almost word-for-word in the *Missouri Statesman*, Columbia, Boone County, 9 September 1864; Paxton, *Annals of Platte County, Missouri*,

368, 372; Stanley, Wilson, and Wilson, *Death Records from Missouri Newspapers, January 1861–December 1865*, 177.

48. "More Guerrilla Trouble," *St. Joseph Weekly Herald*, Buchanan County, 18 August 1864; "A Fall Invasion of Missouri," *Missouri Statesman*, Columbia, Boone County, 26 August 1864, from the earlier *St. Louis Union;* "An Invasion of Missouri," *Kansas City Daily Journal*, Jackson County, 30 August 1864.

TWENTY

1. Eakin, *Warren Welch Remembers*, 11–12.
2. Fellman, "Emancipation in Missouri," *Missouri Historical Review*, vol. 83, (October 1988), 54–6; United States Government, *1860 Missouri Census*, lists in Washington Township of south-central Lafayette County the households of 63-year-old Kentucky-born farmer George Houx and his family and that of 37-year-old Missouri-born farmer Oliver Houx and his family (In neither household is a woman named "Fanny," but that name may be the nickname of one of the women shown by the census in these two families.).
3. Ford, *A History of Moniteau County, Missouri*, 46; United States Government, *1860 Missouri Census*, lists in Saline Township of northeast Cooper County near the Moniteau County line the household of Missouri-born 46-year-old poor farmer Caroline Lamb, including her 16-year-old Missouri-born son Sloan B. Lamb (The census shows several John Hunts in the area.).
4. *O.R.*, vol. 41 part 1, 65–7 (detailed Union account that agrees in the main with a southern version mentioned below in the Lafayette County history); "Bushwhackers Killed in Church," *Kansas City Daily Journal*, Jackson County, 20 July 1864, from the *Lexington Weekly Journal*, Lafayette County, of July 14; "Bushwhackers Killed," *Missouri Statesman*, Columbia, Boone County, 12 August 1864, from the same Lexington newspaper cited above; Young, *Young's History of Lafayette County, Missouri*, 132–3 (a detailed, accurate southern view of the skirmish told from a southern viewpoint of a witness who was fifteen years old at the time); Melton, *History of Cooper County, Missouri*, 95 (It is not clear why a history of Cooper County several miles east of the scene of this fight in Lafayette County would include this story.); Broadfoot, *Supplement to the O.R.*, part 2, vol. 35, 7th Cavalry MSM, 419 (not much detail); Eakin and Hale, *Branded as Rebels*, 359–60; Dyer, *Compendium*, vol. 2, 810; United States Government, *1860 Missouri Census*, shows in Westport of west Jackson County in household of Kentucky-born moderate-income farmer Gibson Wilhite, Kentucky-born 21-year-old laborer Emmitt A. Wilhite, and Missouri-born 19-year-old laborer Jefferson Wilhite (both said to have been in this fight in the Lafayette County history cited above), and in Clay Township of northwest Lafayette County the household of 36-year-old Kentucky-born farmer Joseph Warder and his large family, the household of 58-year-old wealthy Kentucky-born farmer Jesse Dean and his 18-year-old Missouri-born daughter Nettie Dean, and in the same neighborhood two different Estes families (all these also named in the Lafayette County history).

5. *O.R.*, vol. 41, part 2, 132.
6. *O.R.*, vol. 41, part 1, 65–7; Dyer, *Compendium*, vol. 2, 810.
7. *O.R.*, vol. 41, part 1, 50; part 2, 190.
8. *O.R.*, vol. 41, part 2, 178; Thoma, *This Cruel Unnatural War*, 97.
9. "From Boonville," *Daily Missouri Democrat*, St. Louis, 27 July 1864; Thoma, *This Cruel Unnatural War*, 98; The author also consulted with Missouri Civil War historian and author Terry E. Justice by telephone and email in early 2008 regarding the entry of "J. F. Gregg" as a first lieutenant in the roll of Company B, 12th Missouri Cavalry in Shelby's brigade; (Author's note: Ironically, some of those robbed by J. Frank Gregg's band near Pilot Grove were robbed in early June by Bill Anderson's band raiding through this same neighborhood.).
10. *O.R.*, vol. 41, part 2, 185, 188; "Another Guerrilla Outrage," *Kansas City Daily Journal*, Jackson County, 15 July 1864; "Kansas City, July 15," *Daily Missouri Democrat*, St. Louis, 16 July 1864 (repeated word-for-word in the *St. Joseph Weekly Herald*, Buchanan County, of 21 July 1864); (Author's note: The local Union decision not to react to the stagecoach robbery falls under the principle of war called "Economy of Force" in the United States military. This refers to careful husbanding of scarce resources, especially troops, using only what is needed in a certain instance, while other assets can be better used elsewhere.).
11. *O.R.*, vol. 41, part 2, 215; Eakin, *Warren Welch Remembers*, 8–9; (Author's note: There seems to be no other source to corroborate Welch's claim that Gregg's party killed four Union soldiers in the northeast corner of Saline County. However, by this time of the summer of 1864 there were so many guerrilla actions throughout this region that military records, period newspapers, and other sources failed to mention otherwise notable actions.)
12. "Bushwhacking," *Missouri Statesman*, Columbia, Boone County, 22 July 1864, from the *Boonville Monitor*, Cooper County, of 16 July 1864; "Bushwhackers at Arrow Rock," *Daily Missouri Democrat*, St. Louis, 26 July 1864, from the *Boonville Monitor* of 23 July 1864; Melton, *History of Cooper County, Missouri*, 91–2; Thoma, *This Cruel Unnatural War*, 98–9; United States Government, *1860 Missouri Census*, lists in Boonville Township of north Cooper County the household of 59-year-old Nassau-born middle-income farmer John H. Boller and his large family; although the census did not seem to have an entry for Cooper Countian Robert Sloan.
13. *O.R.*, vol. 41, part 2, 267; Eakin and Hale, *Branded As Rebels*, 351 (which states Dave's given name as "Francis Marion Poole"); United States Government, *1850 Missouri Census*, lists in Lafayette County the household of 50-year-old Virginia-born middle-income farmer Stephen Poole in which the third child listed is 12-year-old Missouri-born Francis M. Poole; and in the *1860 Missouri Census* Poole's older brother and father are residing in the same household in Washington Township of south-central Lafayette County.
14. *O.R.*, vol. 41, part 1, 51; part 2, 216; Broadfoot, *Supplement to the O.R.*, part 2, vol. 35, 7th Cavalry MSM, 479; Dyer, *Compendium*, vol. 2, 811; United States Government, *1860 Missouri Census*, lists in

Post Oak Township of south-central Johnson County the household of Tennessee-born middle-aged farmer James and Edith Stewart and their 21-year-old Missouri-born son William H. Stewart; and in neighboring Madison Township the small family of Kentucky-born 33-year-old farmer Lindsay Hutchinson and his small family.

15. *O.R.*, vol. 34, part 4, 518–9; Eakin, *Warren Welch Remembers*, 10.

16. *O.R.*, vol. 41, part 2, 241, 269–70.

17. *O.R.*, vol. 41, part 2, 267, 268, 289, 290–2.

18. *O.R.*, vol. 41, part 1, 51, 56; part 2, 307, 308, 309, 336, 337, 339–40, 360, 373, 388, 394; "Bushwhackers at Arrow Rock," *Daily Missouri Democrat*, St. Louis, 26 July 1864, from the *Boonville Monitor*, Cooper County, 23 July 1864; "Bushwhackers at Arrow Rock," *Missouri Statesman*, Columbia, Boone County, 29 July 1864 (Although the headline is the same as the newspaper citation immediately above, this is not a copy of the 29 July Boonville article.); "Missouri Items," *Daily Missouri Democrat*, St. Louis, 2 August 1864, from the *Boonville Monitor*, Cooper County, 30 July 1864; "Dick Yeager Killed Again," *Kansas City Daily Journal*, Jackson County, 5 August 1864, citing as source the *Boonville Monitor*, Cooper County, of 29 July (quoted word-for-word with headline in the *Liberty Tribune*, Clay County, of 12 August 1864); Eakin, *Warren Welch Remembers*, 6–7; Barton, *Three Years with Quantrill*, 155 (Guerrilla John McCorkle rode on this raid, but wrote in his memoir wrote more about Dick Yager's wound and treatment than the raid itself. This is one indicator of the great regard the guerrillas had for the former freighter from Westport.); Burch, *A True Story of Charles W. Quantrell*, 207 (Guerrilla Harrison Trow evidently did not participate in the Arrow Rock raid, as the fantasy he wrote bore no resemblance to what really happened.); Missouri Historical Company, *History of Saline County, Missouri*, 315–6 (short account with some errors, such as the wrong date, and the statement that Dick Yager was the commander of the guerrillas); Napton, *Past and Present of Saline County, Missouri*, 193 (mostly a copy of the 1881 county history account); Castel, *William Clarke Quantrill: His Life and Times*, 178–9; Dyer, *Compendium*, vol. 2, 811; (Author's Note: Although period sources spell Dick Yager's surname as "Yeager," his descendants in their input to "The Missouri in the Civil War Message Board" at http://history-sites.com/cgi-bin/bbs53x/mocwmb/webbbs_config.pl assert that "Yager" is the spelling the family used in the Civil War and in present times.).

19. "A Horrible Murder in Miller Co.," *Daily Missouri Democrat*, St. Louis, 2 August 1864; State of Missouri, *Annual Report of the Adjutant General of Missouri for the Year Ending December 31, 1865*, 573 (gives summary of Captain William Long's record in Company K of 47th Enrolled Missouri Militia).

20. Thoma, *This Cruel Unnatural War*, 100 (Thoma cited the *Boonville Monitor*, Cooper County, of 30 July 1864); United States Government, *1860 Missouri Census*, lists the wealthy farm of 36-year-old Kentucky-born farmer Elisha Warfield and his small family in Kelly Township of south-Central Cooper County.

21. *O.R.*, vol. 41, part 2, 311, 336; Stanley, Wilson, and Wilson, *Death Records from Missouri Newspapers, January 1861–December 1865*, 35, 77, 169 (who obtained their information from the *California Weekly News*, Moniteau County, 23 July 1864, and the *Daily Missouri Republican*, St. Louis, 24 July 1864); State of Missouri, Secretary of State's Office, Missouri State Archives, military service records of Private John F. Farmer of Company F, 43rd EMM, who served in California, Moniteau County, during 1862, and of Private Peter B. Thixton of Company G, 43rd EMM, who served during 1862 and 1863 at Tipton, and his record bears this remark "Killed by bushwhackers July 1864. No days of service credited. [for 1864]"; United States Government, *1860 Missouri Census*, lists in Moreau Township of east-central Morgan County the household of Peter Hays on page 671, that of Peter Thixton on page 672 and that of John Farmer on page 679.

22. *O.R.*, vol. 41, part 2, 368; "From Boonville," *Daily Missouri Democrat*, St. Louis, 27 July 1864, from a 23 July letter written by a correspondent in Boonville; "Missouri Item," *Daily Missouri Democrat*, St. Louis, 2 August 1864, from "Stage Driver Fired Upon," *Boonville Monitor*, Cooper County, 30 July 1864; Thoma, *This Cruel Unnatural War*, 100–1; State of Missouri, Secretary of State's Office, Missouri State Archives, military service record for Private Louis or Lewis P. Siceloff in Company A, 40th EMM, who served a long tour of active duty at or near Sedalia, Pettis County during 1862 and 1863, then was discharged in October 1863 with a disability; United States Government, *1860 Missouri Census*, lists in Blackwater Township of northwest Pettis County, the large household of wealthy 52-year-old North Carolina-born farmer A. D. Siceloff, including 18-year-old North Carolina-born student Lewis Siceloff or Chinard; (Author's Note: It appears that Lewis or Louis Siceloff had taken a year or two from his studies to serve in the 40th EMM, but after being discharged with a disability had returned to his studies when he was wounded riding on the stagecoach.).

23. *O.R.*, vol. 41, part 2, 388, 439, 446.

24. *O.R.*, vol. 41, part 1, 88; part 2, 373; Dyer, *Compendium*, vol. 2, 811 (lists large amount of Union patrol action with occasional inconclusive skirmishes between July 25 and August 3 involving the 7th Cavalry MSM and the 2nd Colorado Cavalry in Cass, Jackson, Johnson, and Lafayette Counties).

25. *O.R.*, vol. 41, part 2, 388.

26. (No headline), *Missouri Statesman*, Columbia, Boone County, 12 August 1864; Thoma, *This Cruel Unnatural War*, 101 (citing the *Boonville Monitor*, Cooper County, of 30 July and 6 August, 1864); State of Missouri, Secretary of State's Office, Missouri State Archives, military service record for Corporal Henderson Tally, who served between 3 August 1864 and 2 June 1865 for 120 days active duty in all in Lieutenant Julius Sombart's Cooper County Provisional EMM (founded under General Orders Number 107) at Boonville until he was discharged for "disability and old age"; Although local records state that the guerrillas robbed "Captain H. Meyers," there were several Henry Meyers, Meyer, Myers, or Myer who served in Union forces in this area. The only one that appears to have leadership experience was Sergeant Henry or G. W. Meyers of the 52nd EMM who served active service in Boonville during part of 1862; United States Govern-

ment, *1860 Missouri Census*, lists in Saline Township of northeast Cooper County the household of 49-year-old Virginia-born farmer Henson Tally and his large family; the household in Boonville Township of north-central Cooper County of 46-year-old Virginia-born wealthy farmer H. M. Myers; and in Blackwater Township of northwest Cooper County the household of wealthy 45-year-old Virginia-born farmer John Trigg and his large family.

27. *O.R.*, vol. 41, part 2, 407.

28. *O.R.*, vol. 41, part 1, 176–7; Dyer, *Compendium*, vol. 2, 811; United States Government, *1860 Missouri Census*, lists in Madison Township near Big Creek Post Office, the household of 46-year-old Kentucky-born farmer Louisa Pemberton.

29. *O.R.*, vol. 41, part 2, 437–8.

30. *O.R.*, vol. 41, part 2, 476, 477, 506.

31. *O.R.*, vol. 41, part 1, 182–3; part 2, 456; Dyer, *Compendium*, vol. 2, 811.

32. *O.R.*, vol. 41, part 2, 490; Way, *Way's Packet Directory, 1848–1994*, 428.

33. Privates Henry C. and William C. Crawford, 7th Cavalry MSM, letter, 5 August 1864, of H. C. and W. H. Crawford Letter Collection, 1857–1865, Western Historical Manuscripts Collection, University of Missouri Library, Columbia, Missouri, call number C239, folder 1; Nichols, *Guerrilla Warfare in Civil War Missouri, 1862*, 82, 89–91, 144–5, 210.

34. *O.R.*, vol. 41, part 2, 187, 476, 477 (the last two directing the 2nd Colorado Cavalry return to the District of Central Missouri to deal with 200 guerrillas in Jackson County); Dyer, *Compendium*, vol. 2, 811.

35. *O.R.*, vol. 41, part 2, 477 (regarding transfer of parts of 1st Cavalry MSM to Lexington); Missouri Historical Company, *History of Saline County, Missouri*, 305; Napton, *Past and Present of Saline County, Missouri*, 166–7.

36. *O.R.*, vol. 41, part 2, 525; "Guerrillas at Arrow Rock," *Kansas City Daily Journal*, Jackson County, 16 August 1864, from the *Boonville Monitor*, Cooper County, 6 August 1864.

37. *O.R.*, vol. 41, part 2, 541.

38. Nicholas P. Hardeman, "Bushwhacker Activity on the Missouri Border: Letters to Dr. Glen O. Hardeman," *Missouri Historical Review*, vol. 58, no. 3 (April 1964), 270–1.

39. *O.R.*, vol. 41, part 2, 541.

40. Thoma, *This Cruel Unnatural War*, 101; (Author's note: Thoma cited the *Boonville Monitor*, Cooper County, of August 6 as his source; but the 1860 census identifies John C. G. Goodwin's home as being in Kelly Township near present-day Bunceton in central Cooper County, which is several miles west of the location he cited. Perhaps Goodwin was the owner, but did not operate the store himself.).

41. *O.R.*, vol. 41, part 1, 232–3; part 2, 573, 578, 585, 623; Edwards, *Noted Guerrillas or the Warfare of the Border*, 283, 353; Brownlee, *Gray Ghosts of the Confederacy*, 209.

42. Hardeman, "Bushwhacker Activity on the Missouri Border: Letters to Dr. Glen O. Hardeman," *Missouri Historical Review*, 271.

43. *O.R.*, vol. 41, part 1, 219–20; "From Boonville," *Daily Missouri Democrat*, St. Louis, 16 August 1864, from a newspaper correspondent to this newspaper writing from Boonville, 11 August 1864; Missouri Historical Company, *History of Saline County, Missouri*, 305–6; Napton, *Past and Present of Saline County, Missouri*, 182–3 (more or less a copy of the above-cited 1881 county history account of this event); Vivian Kirkpatrick McLarty, "The Civil War Letters of Colonel Bazel F. Lazear," *Missouri Historical Review*, vol. 45 (October 1950), 49–51.

44. *O.R.*, vol. 41, part 2, 609, 653–4; "Murder and Burning at Frankfort, Mo." *Daily Missouri Democrat*, St. Louis, 17 August 1864, from the earlier *Central City and Brunswicker*, Brunswick, Chariton County; (No headline), *Missouri Statesman*, Columbia, Boone County, 19 August 1864; (No headline), *Kansas City Daily Journal*, 23 August 1864 (This article stated that the guerrilla brutality during this August 6 raid was in retaliation for the Union capture and execution of Jackson's lieutenant Durrett, but the Durrett execution and other killings by the 1st Cavalry MSM were after August 6.); (No headline), *St. Joseph Weekly Herald*, Buchanan County, 25 August 1864 (word-for-word the same as the Kansas City article cited above).

45. *O.R.*, vol. 41, part 1, 219–220; part 2, 588, 607, 609, 653.

46. *O.R.*, vol. 41, part 2, 585–6; "From the Jefferson City State Times, 6th," *Missouri Statesman*, Columbia, Boone County, 12 August 1864, from the *State Times*, Jefferson City, Cole County, 6 August 1864; Eakins, *Missouri Prisoners of War*, Blalock and Hall entries; Eakins, *Civil War Military Prisoners Sent to Missouri State Penitentiary*, 6 (which states that North Carolina-born Blalock was sentenced to ten years' imprisonment by a military tribunal on 1 December 1864); State of Missouri, Secretary of State's Office, Missouri State Archives, military service records for L. V. Hall of Shelby's Brigade "of Johnstown" who attended 1883 Confederate veterans meeting in Jefferson City; and for Thomas Blalock in Captain Mahan's Company F, 52nd EMM who served during 1863 at Boonville, and was later detailed into Charles E. Leonards' citizen guard company at Boonville during May 1865; (Author's note: The above military records seem to indicate there may have been two Thomas Blalocks in this area.).

47. *O.R.*, vol. 41, part 1, 200; Dyer, *Compendium*, vol. 2, 811; United States Government, *1860 Missouri Census*, lists in Madison Township near Holden of south-central Johnson County, the household of Kentucky-born 33-year-old farmer Lindsay Hutchinson and his wife and four children.

48. *O.R.*, vol. 41, part 1, 219–20; "From Boonville," *Daily Missouri Democrat*, St. Louis, 16 August 1864; "Bushwhackers Shot," *Missouri Statesman*, Columbia, Boone County, 19 August 1864, taken from the earlier *Boonville Advertiser*, Cooper County; Vivian Kirkpatrick McLarty, "The Civil War Letters of Colonel Bazel F. Lazear," *Missouri Historical Review*, 49–51; Missouri Historical Company, *History of Saline County, Missouri*, 305–7; Napton, *Past and Present of Saline County, Missouri*, 182–4; Stanley, Wilson, and Wilson, *Death Records from Missouri Newspapers, January 1861–December 1865*, page 72; Dyer, *Compendium*, vol. 2, 811; United States Government, *1860 Missouri Census*, lists in the M. B. Hall household near Tipton, twelve-year-old Missouri-born William H. Hall.

49. *O.R.*, vol. 41, part 2, 607; Vivian Kirkpatrick

McLarty, "The Civil War Letters of Colonel Bazel F. Lazear," *Missouri Historical Review*, 49–51 (This Lazear letter to his wife reveals General Pleasonton's detailing of Colonel McFerran to court-martial duty to Jefferson City leaving Lazear in command and free to conduct counter-guerrilla war in Saline County as he wished.).

50. *O.R.*, vol. 41, part 1, 219–20; "From Boonville," *Daily Missouri Democrat*, St. Louis, 16 August 1864; "Bushwhackers Shot," *Missouri Statesman*, Columbia, Boone County, 19 August 1864, taken from the earlier *Boonville Advertiser*, Cooper County; Vivian Kirkpatrick McLarty, "The Civil War Letters of Colonel Bazel F. Lazear," *Missouri Historical Review*, 49–51; Missouri Historical Company, *History of Saline County, Missouri*, 305–7; Napton, *Past and Present of Saline County, Missouri*, 182–4.

51. *O.R.*, vol. 41, part 1, 200; Dyer, *Compendium*, vol. 2, 811.

52. *O.R.*, vol. 41, part 2, 730; "Missouri Items," *Daily Missouri Democrat*, St. Louis, 15 August 1864.

53. *O.R.*, vol. 41, part 2, 622; "The Guerrillas in Rush Bottom," *Kansas City Daily Journal*, Jackson County, 10 August 1864 (repeated word-for-word in the weekly reprise *Kansas City Weekly Journal* of 13 August 1864); "Missouri Items," *Daily Missouri Democrat*, St. Louis, 16 August 1864; "News From the Brush," *Kansas City Daily Journal*, Jackson County, 19 August 1864; Edwards, *Noted Guerrillas or the Warfare of the Border*, 240, 353 (Edwards' narrative is highly accurate on this, so his many postwar interviews must have included "Fletch" Taylor.); National Historical Company, *History of Caldwell and Livingston Counties, Missouri*, 209; Brownlee, *Gray Ghosts of the Confederacy*, 199; Hale, *We Rode With Quantrill*, 149; Castel, *William Clarke Quantrill: His Life and Times*, 185; Wood, *Other Noted Guerrillas of the Civil War in Missouri*, 175–6.

54. "A Daring Outrage," *Kansas City Weekly Journal*, Jackson County, 13 August 1864; "Missouri Items," *Daily Missouri Democrat*, Jackson County, 16 August 1864; United States Government, *1860 Missouri Census*, lists in Kansas City the household of North Carolina-born 47-year-old tanner William Knight and his family of wife, son, and three teenage daughters, all born in Virginia.

55. "From Boonville," *Daily Missouri Democrat*, St. Louis, 16 August 1864.

56. "From Boonville," *Daily Missouri Democrat*, St. Louis, 16 August 1864; "Military Execution at Jefferson City," *Kansas City Daily Journal*, Jackson County, 18 August 1864, from the *State Times*, Jefferson City, Cole County, of 13 August 1864 "Bushwhacker Executed," *Missouri Statesman*, Columbia, Boone County, 19 August 1864.

57. *O.R.*, vol. 41, part 2, 242.

58. *O.R.*, vol. 41, part 2, 730.

59. *O.R.*, vol. 41, part 1, 254, 256; Missouri Historical Company, *History of Saline County, Missouri*, 306, 315–6; Napton, *Past and Present of Saline County, Missouri*, 193; Dyer, *Compendium*, vol. 2, 811.

60. Missouri Historical Company, *History of Saline County, Missouri*, 306; Napton, *Past and Present of Saline County, Missouri*, 182–3; United Daughters of the Confederacy, Missouri Division, *Reminiscences of the Women of Missouri During the Sixties*, 273–6.

61. "Bold and Diabolical Murder by Bushwhackers," *Missouri Statesman*, Columbia, Boone County, 26 August 1864, from the earlier *Lexington Weekly Union*, Lafayette County; "The Guerrilla War," *Daily Missouri Democrat*, St. Louis, 30 August 1864, from the same issue of the *Lexington Weekly Union*; United States Government, *1860 Missouri Census*, household of Daniel Williamson in the town Lexington.

62. *O.R.*, vol. 41, part 2, 747.

63. *O.R.*, vol. 41, part 1, 254, 257; Broadfoot, *Supplement to the O.R.*, part 2, vol. 35, 4th Cavalry MSM, 50; Dyer, *Compendium*, vol. 2, 811.

64. *O.R.*, vol. 41, part 1, 242; Dyer, *Compendium*, vol. 2, 811.

65. *O.R.*, vol. 41, part 1, 242; part 2, 747.

66. "Bushwhackers in Morgan County," *Missouri Statesman*, Columbia, Boone County, 9 September 1864, referring to the paper's interview with Lieutenant William Argo; Internet discourse between the author and Homer Fickas of HRFTX@aol.com between October 22 and 26, 2006 employing Homer's research of the Morgan County guerrillas including details of the Beanlands and Newkirks; Internet discourse between the author and Terry Justice of terrye.justice@sbcglobal.net between March and June 2008 including a roster he compiled of Company D, 12th Missouri Cavalry (Confederate) containing a service record of Private Robert R. Wilson in Company D during 1862, his desertion on 14 January 1863, his capture by unidentified Union troops in Miller County (just east of Morgan County) on 15 May 1863, his exchange as a regular Confederate POW at City Point, Virginia, on 23 July 1863; State of Missouri, Secretary of State's Office, Missouri State Archives, military service record of Lieutenant Charles Newkirk of Captain Dille's Company G, of 43rd EMM, including active duty through 25 November 1863 at Tipton, but no mention of further service or Newkirk's death during 1864; also military service record of Private J. E. Beauland (Confederate spelling of "Beanland") from Versailles, Morgan County, who at age 16 or 18 joined Company D, 2nd Regiment Missouri Infantry, Missouri State Guard 20 December 1861 at Osceola, St. Clair County, MO, served subsequently in unidentified Confederate unit, and deserted at Jackson, Mississippi 6 February 1863; United States Government, *1860 Missouri Census*, lists in Moreau Township of east-central Morgan County the households both on page 673 of Charles Newkirk and Pennsylvania-born farmer David Wilson, including 24-year-old Ohio-born schoolteacher Robert R. Wilson; and on page 660 the household of 26-year-old Tennessee-born farmer John N. Beanland and his small family, and on page 661 the household of 59-year-old Georgia-born farmer Leonard Beanland, containing two Missouri-born sons, William G. Beanland, 19, and Ephraim, 17 (the only Beanlands listed in the 1860 Missouri census), and in Mill Creek Township of northeast Morgan County, the household of 53-year-old Kentucky-born farmer Pat Mullins, including several teenage children, but no record for a teenage Patrick or Pat Mullins, who may have been working away from the family farm during the census.

67. *O.R.*, vol. 41, part 1, 257; Dyer, *Compendium*, vol. 2, 811.

68. *O.R.*, vol. 41, part 1, 254–5, 257.

69. Missouri Historical Company, *History of Saline County, Missouri*, 322; Napton, *Past and Present of Saline County, Missouri*, 199–200; United States Government, *1860 Missouri Census*, lists in Marshall Township, in the household of renter Samuel Shannon 42-year-old Kentucky-born poor wagon maker Charles Flanagan.

70. Eakin, *Warren Welch Remembers*, 7–8.

71. *O.R.*, vol. 41, part 1, 255–6; part 2, 822–3; Dyer, *Compendium*, vol. 2, 811; (Author's note: Tabo Creek is generally west and northwest of present day Higginsville, and Cottonwood Creek is generally north of Higginsville. Poole's family is said to have lived near present day Mayview, about three miles southwest of Higginsville.).

72. *O.R.*, vol. 41, part 1, 271–2; State of Missouri, Secretary of State's Office, Missouri State Archives, military service record of Private S. T. Stoner from Independence, Jackson County, in Colonel Thomas H. Rosser's Confederate battalion; United States Government, *1860 Missouri Census*, lists in Madison County of west-central Johnson County the households of farmer Benjamin L. Durritt and Taylor Francis Cowarden, both with Virginia origins; and lists a Stoner household in the Kansas City area of Jackson County.

73. "Female Rebels in Limbo," *Missouri Statesman*, Columbia, Boone County, 2 September 1864; Eakins, *Missouri Prisoners of War*, Fickel entry, which states Federal authorities sent her to the Missouri State Penitentiary in Jefferson City on 20 September 1864; United States Government, *1860 Missouri Census*, shows in the household of Virginia-born Henry H. Fickel of Clay Township of northwest Lafayette County a 21-year-old Missouri-born daughter, Anne E. Fickel.

74. Barton, *Three Years with Quantrill*, 156–8; Nichols, *Guerrilla Warfare in Civil War Missouri, 1862*, 101; United States Government, *1860 Missouri Census*, lists in Big Cedar Township of Jackson the household of Kentucky-born farmer John Wigginton and his 17-year-old Missouri-born daughter, Mary. (Author's Note: This family probably displaced to someplace in Lafayette County because of the notorious General Orders Number Eleven during autumn of 1863.).

75. *O.R.*, vol. 41, part 2, 823.

76. *O.R.*, vol. 41, part 1, 255–6; Barton, *Three Years with Quantrill*, 150–2; Robert W. Frizzell, "'Killed By Rebels': A Civil War Massacre and Its Aftermath," *Missouri Historical Review*, vol. 61, no. 4 (July 1977), 382–3 (Frizzell mistakenly wrote this raid took place on August 14, but stated another raid occurred on August 23.); Harry R. Voight, *Concordia, Missouri: A Centennial History*, Concordia, Missouri: Centennial Committee, 1960, 26, 32 (Voight did not learn the identity of the dead thirteen-year-old boy when he wrote his work in 1960.); State of Missouri, Secretary of State's Office, Missouri State Archives, military service Record of Captain C. H. Ehlers, who at age 32 enrolled into Company C, 71st EMM, on 9 August 1862, and was named as the captain; United States Government, *1860 Missouri Census*, listed in Freedom Township of southeast Lafayette County the large household of 30-year-old Hanover, Germany-born farmer Henry Ehlers, and nearby the small household of 26-year-old Hanover, Germany-born farmer Fred Ehlers.

77. *O.R.*, vol. 41, part 1, 292–3; part 2, 862; State of Missouri, Secretary of State's Office, Missouri State Archives, military service records of a few Palmers or Parmers who may be the mysterious Captain or Major Palmer in this case; United States Government, *1860 Missouri Census*, lists several Palmer or Parmer households both north and south of the Missouri River who may belong to the mysterious Confederate Officer who led this group of Lieutenant Colonel John C. Thornton's uprising refugees south toward the Confederate lines in Arkansas. (Author's note: The actual identity of Captain or Major Palmer or Parmer, if that is his true name, is not readily apparent from either the Missouri State Archives; the 1860 census; local sources in the western Missouri counties; or from lists of Missouri Confederate officers.).

78. *O.R.*, vol. 41, part 1, 271–2; part 2, 857.

79. Broadfoot, *Supplement to the O.R.*, part 2, vol. 35, 4th Cavalry MSM, 51.

80. *O.R.*, vol. 41, part 1, 293–4; Dyer, *Compendium*, vol. 2, 811; United States Government, *1860 Missouri Census*, lists in Davis Township of east Lafayette County the household of 40-year-old Kentucky-born farmer John T. Rutherford that includes also 17-year-old Missouri-born William G. Rutherford and 16-year-old Missouri-born E. F. Rutherford. (The next closest Rutherford households in the census were east in Saline County and north of the Missouri River in Clinton and DeKalb Counties.).

81. *O.R.*, vol. 41, part 1, 272.

82. Ibid.

83. *O.R.*, vol. 41, part 1, 290.

84. Ibid.

85. *O.R.*, vol. 41, part 2, 940.

86. Broadfoot, *Supplement to the O.R.*, part 2, vol. 35, 4th Cavalry MSM, 51.

87. *O.R.*, vol. 41, part 1, 272, 292.

88. *O.R.*, vol. 41, part 2, 945, 958.

89. Eakin, *Warren Welch Remembers*, 8.

90. "Peace and Quiet in Missouri," *Daily Missouri Democrat*, St. Louis, 7 September 1864 (little detail, but accurate, except for the poorly chosen headline); "Guerrilla Doings," *Missouri Statesman*, Columbia, Boone County, 9 September 1864, from the earlier *State Times* of Jefferson City, Cole County (This article has more accurate detail than the St. Louis version, and it seems to be the only known source of the Brazito store robbery and killings.); Goodspeed Publishing Company, *History of Cole, Moniteau, Morgan, Benton, Miller, Maries, And Osage Counties, Missouri*, 556; (This early Miller County history contains little detail, and mistakenly attributed the leadership of the guerrilla band to their early war leader, known only as "General Crabtree." Crabtree, or whatever his real name, was mortally wounded in a small action during autumn 1862 by local EMM who either failed to report Crabtree's demise or whose superiors failed to believe them.); Jenkins, *Judge Jenkins' History of Miller County*, 436–40 (This very detailed account of the Curtman Island incident is accurate except the judge repeated the earlier history's error about the deceased Crabtree still being in charge during 1864.); State of

Missouri, Secretary of State's Office, Missouri State Archives, military service records of First Lieutenant John P. Starling and Privates Stephen F. Christ, William Gibson, Farrah B. Long, Nathanial Hicks, Samuel McClure, and Yancy Roark, all of Babcoke's Miller County Provisional EMM (General Orders Number 107) Company at Mount Pleasant annotated in remarks section "Killed Aug 30th 1864 by Bushwhackers." Privates Hicks, Long, and Roark's records also attest to their membership in local companies of the 42nd EMM earlier.

91. Thoma, *This Cruel Unnatural War*, 104; Edwards, *Noted Guerrillas, or The Warfare of the Border*, 236; Castel, *William Clarke Quantrill: His Life and Times*, 108, 116; Nichols, *Guerrilla Warfare in Civil War Missouri, Volume II, 1863*, 50; United States Government, *1860 Missouri Census*, lists in Blue Springs Township of central Jackson County the household of 49-year-old Kentucky-born farmer of moderate income Jeptha M. Crawford, his 46-year-old Virginia-born wife, Elizabeth, and nine children, including 13-year-old son Riley.

92. *O.R.*, vol. 41, part 3, 47; "Outrages by Guerrillas," *Daily Missouri Democrat*, St. Louis, 5 September 1864; "Peace and Quiet in Missouri," *Daily Missouri Democrat*, St. Louis, 7 September 1864; Historical Publishing Company, *History of Cooper County, Missouri*, 210; Melton, *History of Cooper County, Missouri*, 93; Thoma, *This Cruel Unnatural War*, 105; United States Government, *1860 Missouri Census*, does not show the small household of Christian Krohn or that of his father-in-law, Johann E. Hoflander.

93. "Outrages By Guerrillas," *Daily Missouri Democrat*, St. Louis, 5 September 1864; "The Murder of the Germans at Pilot Grove," *Daily Missouri Democrat*, 4 November 1864; Historical Publishing Company, *History of Cooper County, Missouri*, 208–9; Melton, *History of Cooper County, Missouri*, 93; Thoma, *This Cruel Unnatural War*, 105; United States Government, *1860 Missouri Census*, lists in Pilot Grove Township of west-central Cooper County the household of 51-year-old Maryland-born wealthy farmer Otho Zeller including his seven children with the nine-year-old born in Maryland and the five-year-old born in Missouri, and the household of 53-year-old Pennsylvania-born poor farmer Jacob Mitzill including his six children all born in Ohio—the youngest being eight years old.

94. *O.R.*, vol. 41, part 3, 9.

95. Melton, *History of Cooper County, Missouri*, 97; United States Government, *1860 Missouri Census*, lists in Moniteau Township of southeast Cooper County three Boswell men all born in North Carolina, who fail to appear in the 1870 census of Cooper or neighboring Moniteau County: moderately wealthy 35-year-old farmer G. A. Boswell, his wife, and two small children; moderately wealthy 45-year-old single merchant John Boswell; and 19-year-old single R. C. Boswell, who lived on the farm of William Hunt, Jr.; (Author's note: There seems to be no existing online military service record for any Cooper County citizens guard officer named Boswell in the Missouri State Archives.).

Bibliography

Manuscript Material

Barth, Charles. Letter, 7 September 1864, from Rocheport, Missouri, to Moses Barth in St. Louis. Western Historical Manuscripts Collection, University of Missouri Library, Columbia. Barth Papers, collection number C997.

Brophy, Dixie V., and Patrick Brophy, eds. "Vernon County Confederates." Pamphlet. Nevada, MO: Bushwhacker Museum, 1993. 1–11.

Burns, D. Dennis. "William Wilson, a Missouri Guerrilla." Undated fourteen-page typescript. Western Historical Manuscripts Collection, University of Missouri Library, Columbia. collection number C995, vol. III, document 98.

"Civil War Years in Bates County." Pamphlet for third Butler re-enactment. Butler, MO: N.p., n.d. 1–17.

Crawford, William H., and H. C. Crawford. Letter dated 5 August 1864 from Warrensburg, Johnson County. Western Historical Manuscripts Collection, University of Missouri Library, Columbia. Collection number C239, folder 1.

Gentry, North Todd. "Some Incidents of the Civil War in Boone County," text of speech given 14 October 1931. Western Historical Manuscripts Collection, University of Missouri Library, Columbia. Collection number C49.

Gilmore, Lizzie C. Letters, written by Lizzie of near Lebanon, Laclede County, and other family during 1864 describing guerrilla activities. Western Historical Manuscripts Collection, University of Missouri Library, Columbia. Collection number R346, folder 1.

Goddard, John W. Diary. April–October 1864, near Hinch's in northeast Crawford County, while he was member of 63rd EMM. Private collection of descendant, Dottie Braunsdorf of St. Louis County.

Mayes, Jack F. "The Civil War in Iron County." Pamphlet. Ironton, MO: author, 1994, 109.

Smith, Frank. Unpublished guerrilla memoir manuscript. Transcribed copy from private collection of noted Missouri Civil War author Albert Castel. 1–18.

Gregg, William H. "A Little Dab of History Without Embellishment." Handwritten by Gregg in 1906. Western Historical Manuscripts Collection, University of Missouri Library, Columbia. Collection number C375, folder 1.

Seyffert, Wilhelm, and Augustus Seyffert. Notebook. Handwritten account of patrols and other activities of Company E, 13th Cavalry Regiment, Missouri State Militia, while stationed at Waynesville, October 1862-September 1864. Western Historical Manuscripts Collection, University of Missouri Library, Columbia. Collection number C2888, volume 2.

Civil War Era Newspapers Containing Missouri Articles

(Newspapers are assumed to be weekly unless stated as daily.)

Argus. Macon City, Macon County.
Atchison Free Press. Atchison County, Kansas.
Bethany Union. Harrison County.
Boonville Advertiser. Cooper County.
Boonville Monitor or *Boonville Weekly Monitor*. Cooper County.
Caldwell County Banner or *Kingston Banner*. Caldwell County.
California Weekly News. Moniteau County.
Carrollton Democrat. Carroll County.
Central City and Brunswicker. Brunswick, Chariton County.
Charleston Courier. Mississippi County.
Chicago Post. (Daily).
Chicago Tribune. (Daily).
Chillicothe Chronicle. Livingston County.
Chillicothe Constitution. Livingston County.
Cincinnati Commercial. (Daily).
Daily Kansas City Journal of Commerce or *Daily Kansas City Journal*. (Daily).
Daily Missouri Democrat. St. Louis (daily).
Daily Missouri Republican. St. Louis (daily).
Fayette Advertiser or *Howard County Advertiser*. Howard County.
Fort Scott Monitor. Bourbon County, Kansas.
Fulton Telegraph. Callaway County.
Gallatin Northwest Missourian. Daviess County.
Grand River News. Albany, Gentry County.
Hannibal Courier. Marion County.
Harper's Weekly. New York.
Howard County Advertiser or *Fayette Advertiser*.
Huntsville Citizen or *Randolph Citizen*. Randolph County.
Ironton Radical. Iron County.
Kansas City Daily Journal of Commerce or *West-*

ern *Journal of Commerce* or *Kansas City Daily Journal.* Jackson County (daily).
Kingston Banner or *Caldwell County Banner.* Caldwell County.
Kirksville Patriot. Adair County.
La Grange American or *National American.* La Grange, Lewis County.
Leavenworth Bulletin. Leavenworth County, Kansas.
Leavenworth Conservative. Leavenworth County, Kansas.
Leavenworth Times. Leavenworth County, Kansas.
Leslie's Illustrated Newspaper. New York.
Lexington Union or *Lexington Weekly Union.* Lafayette County.
Liberty Tribune or *Liberty Weekly Tribune.* Clay County.
Louisiana Journal. Pike County.
Louisiana True Flag or *Louisiana Flag.* Pike County.
Macon Gazette. Macon County.
Mexico Beacon. Audrain County.
Mexico Citizen. Audrain County.
Mexico Gazette. Audrain County.
Mexico Ledger. Audrain County.
Missouri State Times. Jefferson City, Cole County.
Missouri Statesman. Columbia, Boone County.
National American or *La Grange American.* La Grange, Lewis County.
Nevada Daily Mail, Vernon County (probably a weekly).
New York Daily Tribune. New York.
Northwest Conservator. or *Richmond Conservator.* Ray County.
Palmyra Spectator. Marion County.
Paris Mercury. Monroe County.
Perryville Union. Perry County.
Platte City Atlas. Platte County.
Platte County Sentinel. Weston.
Randolph Citizen or *Huntsville Citizen.* Randolph County.
Richmond Conservator or *Northwest Conservator.* Ray County.
Rolla Express. Phelps County.
St. Joseph Express. Buchanan County.
St. Joseph Herald or *St. Joseph Weekly Herald.* Buchanan County.
St. Joseph News. Buchanan County.
St. Joseph Tribune. Buchanan County.
St. Joseph Union. Buchanan County.
St. Louis Dispatch. (Daily).
Saint Louis News. (Daily).
St. Louis Republic. (Daily).
St. Louis Union. (Daily).
Savannah Plaindealer. Andrew County.
Sedalia Advertiser. Pettis County.
Shelbyville Herald. Shelby County.
Springfield Journal. Greene County.
Warrensburg Standard. Johnson County.
Warrensburg Tribune. Johnson County.
Warrenton Nonpareil. Warren County.
Washington County News. Potosi.
Western Journal of Commerce or *Kansas City Daily Journal of Commerce* or *Kansas City Daily Journal.* Jackson County (daily).
Weston Times or *Weston Border Times.* Platte County.

Post–Civil War Newspapers

Dallas Morning News. Dallas County, Texas, 1927 (daily).
Kansas City Star. Jackson County, 1969 (daily).
Warrensburg Daily Star-Journal. Johnson County, 1939, 1976.
Wayne County Journal-Banner. Piedmont, Wayne County, 2002.

Periodical Articles

Bird, Roy. "Jo Shelby and His Shadow." *America's Civil War* 8, no. 1 (March 1995): 26–32.
Bradbury, John F., Jr. "'Bushwhacker' Bill Wilson: Incidents on the Rolla-Salem Road." *Newsletter of the Phelps County Historical Society* new series, no. 5 (April 1992): 3–6.
———. "Hunting Bushwhackers for a Living." *Newsletter of the Phelps County Historical Society* 10, no. 1 (October 1994): 3–15.
Canan, Howard V. "The Missouri Paw Paw Militia of 1863–1864." *Missouri Historical Review* 62, no. 4 (July 1968): 431–8.
Collins, Andy. "To the Victor Belongs the Spoils." *Missouri Historical Review* 80, no. 2 (January 1986): 176–195.
Crisler, Robert M. "Missouri's Little Dixie." *Missouri Historical Review* 42, no. 2 (January 1948): 130–9.
Davis, Steve. "'I am a Rip-Squealer and My Name is Fight': M. Jeff Thompson of Missouri." *Blue & Gray* 4, no. 5: 28–39.
Dunn, Emma Comfort. "Civil War Era: The Diary of John W. Goddard." *Ozarks Mountaineer* (July-August 1982): 22–3.
Fannin, William. "Defenders of the Border: Missouri's Union Military Organizations in the Civil War." *Pioneer Times* 6, no. 3 (July 1982): 187–206.
Fellman, Michael. "Emancipation in Missouri." *Missouri Historical Review* 83, no. 1 (October 1988): 35–56.
Frizzell, Robert W. "'Killed By Rebels': A Civil War Massacre and Its Aftermath." *Missouri Historical Review* 71, no. 4 (July 1977): 369–95.
Geise, William B. "Missouri's Confederate Capital in Marshall, Texas." *Missouri Historical Review* 58, no. 1 (October 1963): 37–54.
Gerteise, Louis S. "An Outrage on Humanity, Martial Law and Military Prisons." *Missouri Historical Review* 96, no. 4 (July 2002): 315–21.
Hamilton, James A. "The Enrolled Missouri Militia: Its Creation and Controversial History." *Missouri Historical Review* 69, no. 4 (July 1975): 413–32.
Hardeman, Nicholas P. "Bushwhacker Activity on the Missouri Border: Letters to Dr. Glen O. Hardeman." *Missouri Historical Review* 58, no. 3 (April 1964): 265–77.
Herklotz, Hildegarde Rose. "Jayhawkers in Missouri, 1856–1863." *Missouri Historical Review* 17, no. 3 (April 1923): 266–84; 17, no. 4 (July 1923): 505–13; 18, no. 1 (October 1923): 64–101.

Hesseltine, W. B. "Military Prisons of St. Louis, 1861–1865." *Missouri Historical Review* 23, no. 3 (April 1929): 380–99.

Huff, Leo E. "Guerrillas, Jayhawkers and Bushwhackers in Northern Arkansas." *Arkansas Historical Quarterly* 24, no. 2 (summer 1965): 127–48.

Hulston, John K., and James W. Goodrich. "John Trousdale Coffee: Lawyer, Politician, Confederate." *Missouri Historical Review* 77, no. 3 (April 1983): 272–95.

Kamphoefner, Walter D. "Uprooted or Transplanted? Reflections on Patterns of German Immigration to Missouri." *Missouri Historical Review* 103, no. 2 (January 2009): 71–89.

Kirkpatrick, Arthur Roy. "Missouri's Secessionist Government, 1861–1865." *Missouri Historical Review* 45, no. 2 (January 1951).

Lee, Bill R. "Missouri's Fight over Emancipation." *Missouri Historical Review* 45, no. 3 (April 1951): 256–64.

McLarty, Vivian Kirkpatrick, ed. "The Civil War Letters of Colonel Bazel F. Lazear." *Missouri Historical Review* 44, no. 3 (April 1950); 254–73; 44, no. 4 (July 1950): 387–401; 45, no. 1 (October 1950): 47–63.

Melton, Senator Emory. "Civil War Days in Barry County." *White River Valley Historical Quarterly* 5, no. 1: 8–11.

Niepman, Ann Davis. "General Orders No. 11 and Border Warfare During the Civil War." *Missouri Historical Review* 66, no. 2 (January 1972): 185–210.

Porter, Scott A. "'Bashi-Bazouks' and Rebels Too: Action at Camden Point, July 13, 1864." *Missouri Historical Review* 101, no. 2 (January 2007): 99–114.

Soltysiak, Harry. "Anarchy in Missouri." *Civil War Times Illustrated* 24, no. 8 (December 1985): 26–35.

Speicher, James L. "The Battle of Camden Point, Missouri, July 13, 1864." *Confederate Veteran* 5 (2001): 34–7.

Interviews, Correspondence, Email, and Internet Sources

Barton, O. S., comp. *The Secret of the Key and Crossbar*. Memoir of Mary Carroll Brooks, electronic media pamphlet. Online in Cooper County Rootsweb Genealogy Website at http://www.rootsweb.com/~mocooper/military/The_Secret_of_the_Key_and_Crossbar.htm.

Braunsdorf, Dottie. Correspondence between Braunsdorf of St. Louis County with author in November 1992 with excerpts of diary written by her Civil War ancestor, John Goddard of Crawford County, about his encounters with guerrillas in his home area twice during 1864.

Dellinger, Harold. Email exchange between Dellinger at h.dellinger@yahoo.com of Kansas City and the author during April 2009 regarding Dellinger's and his mother's research about ancestor and guerrilla leader Mike McCully of Schuyler County, and his war adventures.

Ellis, Lloyd. Email exchange between Ellis of eaglevalley@gotrain.org of Cabool, Mo., and the author in March and April 2008 regarding Ellis' ancestor, Confederate Captain Bill Coats of south-central Missouri and his war history.

Fickas, Homer. Email exchange between Fickas at HRFTX@aol.com and the author between 22 and 26 October 2006 regarding his research of Morgan County guerrillas, especially Beanland and Newkirk; and again in late January 2007 regarding church death records of German-Americans of southeast Lafayette County killed by guerrillas.

Firearms problems of 2nd Colorado Cavalry. Internet exchange between the author and several others in the "Civil War Arms and Equipment Message Board" between 4 and 7 July 2008 at http://history-sites.com/mb/cw/cwaemb/ highlighting useful references to the author.

Hunt, Glenn. Email exchange between the author and Hunt in Texas at googy@tx.rr.com and googy@flash.net off and on between September 2004 and September 2010 regarding her ancestor, guerrilla chief Wiley Shumate of Cole County, Mo., and Grayson County, Texas.

Justice, Terry E. Email exchanges between Justice at terrye.justice@sbcglobal.net and the author during 2007 and early 2008 about several Rebel soldiers of General Jo Shelby's "Iron Brigade" who had a dual role as both Confederate regulars while with the army and guerrillas when back home in west-central Missouri; Justice also confirmed many of these Confederates had Sharp's breechloaders.

Moser, Arthur Paul. "A Directory of Towns, Villages, and Hamlets Past and Present." Internet geographical dictionary of Missouri at http://thelibrary.org/lochist/moser.html from Moser's research of many years.

Pearson, Thomas A. "Weapons Issued to Missouri Union Militia Organizations by the Missouri Quartermaster General, 1862–1865." Internet article August 2001, at http://www.slpl.lib.mo.us/libsrc/moquartermaster.htm in Pearson's capacity in the Special Collections Department, St. Louis Public Library.

Ramsay, Robert L. "Missouri Place Names File, 1928–1945." Internet geographical dictionary of Missouri at http://whmc.umsystem.edu/exhibits/ramsay/ramsay.html kept at the Western Historical Manuscripts Collection, Ellis Library, University of Missouri Campus in Columbia.

Reed, Casey. "William Francis Hadley, Missouri Guerrilla." Internet exchange with the author 16 June 2008 in "The Civil War in Missouri Message Board" with discussion by others through 21 June 2008 at http://history-sites.com/cgi bin/bbs53x/mocwmb2/webbs_config.pl.

Ripley, Thaddeus A. Internet exchange between the author, Ross Brooks, and Hugh Simmons

27–29 December 2006 about Ripley's arrest and imprisonment in "The Civil War in Missouri Message Board" at http://history-sites.com/cgi-bin/bbs53x/mocwmb2/webbs_config.pl.

Ross, Kirby. "Federal Militia in Missouri." Internet article in "Civil War in St. Louis" at http://ww.civilwarstlouis.com/militia/federalmilitia.htm, pp. 3–4.

Rule, George E., and Deb Rule. "Civil War St. Louis: The Boatburners." At http://www.civilwarstlouis.com/boatburners and "Tucker's War: Missouri and the Northwest Conspiracy," at http://www.civilwarstlouis.com/History2/tuckerswar.htm. Internet articles on the "Civil War in St. Louis" website at http://www.civilwarstlouis.com.

Russell, John, MD, of Cape Girardeau. Internet exchanges with the author from 2008 through 2012 at jrussell@clas.net regarding his historical and genealogical research about guerrilla chief Pete Smith of Bollinger County; the mysterious Rebel recruiters Captains Holloway and Pitney of northeast Missouri; the mysterious guerrilla leader "Dr Beck" of southwest Missouri; Union First Lieutenant Gannett of the 7th Kansas Cavalry in Audrain County; and a number of other Missouri Civil War guerrilla war topics.

Summers, Lynna. Internet exchange between Summers and the author on 8 July 2008 in the "Missouri in the Civil War Message Board," at http://history-sites.com/cgi-bin/bbs53x/mocwmb2/webbs_config.pl, regarding the bushwhacker "Pony Hill" of Vernon County, who Summers revealed was her husband's ancestor, and that "Pony Hill's" real name is James Napoleon "Pony" Hill.

Yeager or Yager, Richard. Internet exchange between Yager descendants and a variety of Missouri Civil War researchers from January 2007 through April 2012 in the "Missouri in the Civil War Message Board" at http://history-sites.com/cgi-bin/bbs53x/mocwmb2/webbs_config.pl on many topics about Dick Yeager or Yager, with emphasis that historic accounts spell Dick's name as "Yeager" while the descendants spell the family name as "Yager," leading the author to use both interchangeably.

Government Publications

State of Kansas. *Report of the Adjutant General of the State of Kansas, 1861–1865.* Vol. 1. Topeka: Kansas State Printing Company, 1896.

State of Missouri. *Annual Report of the Adjutant General of Missouri for the Year 1863.* St. Louis: Public Printer, 1864.

State of Missouri. *Annual Report of the Adjutant General of Missouri for the Year 1864.* Jefferson City: W. A. Curry, Public Printer, 1865.

State of Missouri. *Annual Report of the Adjutant General of Missouri for the Year 1865.* Jefferson City: Emory S. Foster, Public Printer, 1866.

State of Missouri. *Report of the Committee of the House of Representatives of the Twenty-Second General Assembly of the State of Missouri Appointed to Investigate the Conduct and Management of the Militia.* Jefferson City: W. A. Curry, Public Printer, 1864.

State of Missouri. Dr. Charles P. Williams, comp. *Geologic Survey of Missouri.* Jefferson City: Regan and Carter, State Printers, 1877.

State of Missouri. Secretary of State's Office. Missouri State Archives. Jefferson City: Secretary of State Building. Hard copy records and online military records at http://www.sos.mo.gov/archives/soldiers (for individual soldiers' records) and at http://www.sos.mo.gov/archives/provost (for Union provost marshal records).

U.S. Bureau of the Census. *Seventh Census of the United States, 1850: Population.* Washington, D.C.: Government Printing Office.

U.S. Bureau of the Census. *Eighth Census of the United States, 1860: Population.* Washington, D.C.: Government Printing Office, 1864.

U.S. Bureau of the Census. *Ninth Census of the United States, 1870: Population.* Washington, D.C.: Government Printing Office.

U.S. Department of War, Adjutant General's Office. *Official Army Register of the Volunteer Force of the United States Army for the Years 1861-'65.* Washington, D.C.: Adjutant General's Office. 8 vols., 1861–1865.

U.S. Department of War, Adjutant General's Office. *Organization and Status of Missouri Troops in Service During the Civil War.* Washington, D.C.: Government Printing Office, 1909.

U.S. Department of War. *The War of the Rebellion: A Compilation of the Official Records of Union and Confederate Armies.* 128 volumes. Washington, D.C.: Government Printing Office, 1880–1901.

U.S. Geologic Survey. 1:100,000 Intermediate Scale Topographic Quadrangle Maps, 30 X 60 Minute Series.

U.S. National Archives and Records Administration, periodical article by Musick, Michael P. "War in an Age of Wonders, Part 2, Civil War Arms and Equipment." *Prologue* 27, no. 4 (Winter 1995) (discussion of problems with firearms issued to First and Second Regiments, Colorado Cavalry in the second quarter of 1864).

Military Unit Histories and Memoirs

Anders, Leslie. *The Eighteenth Missouri.* Indianapolis: Bobbs-Merrill, 1968.

———. *The Twenty-First Missouri: From Home Guard to Union Regiment.* Westport, CT: Greenwood, 1975.

Arthur, George Clinton. *Bushwhacker: A Story of Missouri's Most Famous Desperado.* Rolla, MO: Rolla Printing, 1938.

Asbury, Ai Edgar. *My Experiences in the War, 1861*

to 1865: A Little Autobiography. Kansas City: Berkowitz and Company, 1894.

Banasik, Michael E. *Cavaliers of the Brush: Quantrill and His Men*. Iowa City: Camp Pope Bookshop, 2003.

Bartels, Carolyn M. *The Forgotten Men: Missouri State Guard*. Shawnee Mission, KS: Two Trails, 1995.

Barton, O. S., comp. *Three Years with Quantrill: A True Story Told by His Scout John McCorkle*. Armstrong, MO: Armstrong Herald Print, 1914. Reprint Norman: University of Oklahoma Press, 1992.

Boswell, Evault. *Quantrill's Raiders in Texas*. Austin, TX: Eakin, 2003.

Bradley, James. *The Confederate Mail Carrier*. Mexico, MO: published by the author, 1894.

Britton, Wiley. *Memoirs of the Rebellion on the Border, 1863*. Chicago: Cushing, Thomas, and Company, 1882. Reprint Florissant, MO: Inland Printer, 1986.

Broadfoot Publishing. *Supplement to the Official Records of the Union and Confederate Armies*. About 100 volumes divided into part 1, Addendum to Reports, and part 2, Records of Events (unit itineraries). Wilmington, NC: Broadfoot, 1994–2002.

Brophy, Patrick, ed. *"Found No Bushwhackers": The 1864 Diary of Sgt. James P. Mallery*. Nevada, MO: Vernon County Historical Society, 1988.

Burch, John P. *Charles W. Quantrell: A True History of His Guerrilla Warfare on the Missouri and Kansas Border During the Civil War of 1861 to 1865*. Vega, TX: published by author, 1923.

Burke, W. S. *Official History of Kansas Regiments (During the War for the Suppression of the Great Rebellion)*. Leavenworth, KS: W. S. Burke, 1870. Reprint Ottawa, KS: Kansas Heritage, 1994.

Castel, Albert. *William Clarke Quantrill: His Life and Times*. New York: Frederick Fell, 1962.

Castel, Albert, and Thomas Goodrich. *Bloody Bill Anderson: The Short, Savage Life of a Civil War Guerrilla*. Mechanicsburg, PA: Stackpole, 1998.

Connelley, William Elsey. *Quantrill and the Border Wars*. Cedar Rapids, IA: Torch, 1910. Reprint Ottawa, KS: Kansas Heritage, 1992.

Crute, Joseph H., Jr. *Units of the Confederate States Army*. Midlothian, VA: Derwent, 1987.

Cummins, Jim. *Jim Cummins' Book*. Denver: Reed, 1903. Reprint Provo, UT: Triton, 1988.

Eakin, Joanne C., ed. *A Civil War Guerrilla Goes on Trial: The Case of G. Byron Jones in 1864*. Shawnee Mission, KS: Two Trails, 1997.

Eakin, Joanne Chiles. *Warren Welch Remembers: A Civil War Guerrilla From Jackson County*. Shawnee Mission, KS: Two Trails Genealogy, 1997.

_____ and Donald R. Hale. *Branded as Rebels*. Independence, MO: Wee Print, 1993.

Edwards, John N. *Noted Guerrillas, or the Warfare of the Border*. St. Louis: H.W. Brand and Company, 1877.

Farley, James W., and John W. Farley. *Missouri Rebels Remembered: Si Gordon and John Thrailkill*. Independence, MO: Two Trails, 2005.

Frazier, Margaret Mendenhall, ed. *Missouri Ordeal, 1862–1864: Diaries of Willard Hall Mendenhall*. Newhall, CA: Carl Boyer III, 1985.

Frost, Griffin. *Camp and Prison Journal*. Quincy, IL: Quincy Herald Book and Job Office, 1867. Reprint Iowa City, IA: Camp Pope Bookshop, 1994.

Hale, Donald R. *Branded as Rebels, Vol. 2*. Lee's Summit, MO: published by author, 2003.

_____. *They Called Him Bloody Bill*. Clinton, MO: Printery, 1975.

_____. *We Rode with Quantrill*. Clinton, MO: Printery. 1974.

Houts, Joseph K., Jr. *Quantrill's Thieves*. Kansas City: Truman, 2002.

Lankford, Rose Mary. *The Encyclopedia of Quantrill's Guerrillas*. Evening Shade, AK: published by author, 1999.

Leslie, Edward E. *The Devil Knows How to Ride: The True Story of William Clarke Quantrill and His Confederate Raiders*. New York: Random House, 1996.

Lothrop, Dr. Charles H. *A History of the First Regiment Iowa Cavalry Veteran Volunteers*. Lyons, IA: Beers and Eaton, Printers, 1890.

Maddox, George T. *Hard Trials and Tribulations of an Old Confederate Soldier*. Van Buren, AK: The Argus office, 1897. Reprint Springfield, MO: Oak Hills, 1997.

McGhee, James E. *Guide to Missouri Confederate Units, 1861–1865*. Fayetteville: University of Arkansas Press, 2008.

McKee, Ivan N. *Lost Family—Lost Cause*. Freeman, SD: Pine Hill, 1978.

Monks, William A. *A History of Southern Missouri and Northern Arkansas; Being an Account of the Early Settlements, the Civil War, the Ku-Klux, and Times of Peace*. West Plains, MO: West Plains Journal, 1907. Reprint Fayetteville: University of Arkansas Press, 2003.

Mudd, Joseph A. *With Porter in North Missouri: A Chapter in the History of the War Between the States*. Washington, D.C.: National, 1909. Reprint Iowa City, IA: Camp Pope Bookshop, 1992.

Norton, Richard L., comp. and ed. *Behind Enemy Lines: The Memoirs and Writings of Brigadier General Sidney Drake Jackman*. Springfield, MO: Oak Hills, 1997.

Ozarks Genealogical Society. *Confederate Organizations, Officers and Posts, 1861–1865: Missouri Units*. Springfield, MO: Ozarks Genealogical Society, 1988.

Peterson, Paul R. *Quantrill of Missouri: The Forgotten Campaign*. Nashville: Cumberland House, 2007.

_____. *Quantrill of Missouri: The Making of a Guerrilla Warrior*. Nashville, TN: Cumberland House, 2003.

Peterson, Richard C., James E. McGhee, Kip A. Lindberg, and Keith I. Daleen. *Sterling Price's Lieutenants: A Guide to the Officers and Organization of the Missouri State Guard, 1861–1865*. Shawnee Mission, KS: Two Trails, 1995.

Ponder, Jerry. *A History of the 15th Missouri Cavalry Regiment, C.S.A.* Doniphan, MO: Ponder, 1994.
Quaife, Milo M, ed. *Absalom Grimes, Confederate Mail Runner.* New Haven, CT: Yale University Press, 1926.
Ross, Kirby, ed. *Autobiography of Samuel S. Hildebrand: The Renowned Missouri Bushwhacker.* Fayetteville: University of Arkansas Press, 2005.
Schmidt, Bob. *Veterans and Events in the Civil War in Southeast Missouri*, vol. 2. French Vilage, MO: published by author, 2000.
Schnetzer, Wayne. *More Forgotten Men.* Independence, MO: Two Trails. 2003.
Settle, William A., Jr. *Jesse James Was His Name.* Lincoln: University of Nebraska Press, 1966.
Sifakis, Stewart. *Compendium of the Confederate Armies: Kentucky, Maryland, Missouri, the Confederate Units and the Indian Units.* New York: Facts on File, 1995.
United Daughters of the Confederacy, Missouri Division. *Reminiscences of the Women of Missouri During the Sixties.* Jefferson City, MO: Hugh Stephens, 1913.
Watts, Hamp B. *The Babe of the Company.* Fayette, MO: The Democrat-Leader Press, 1913.
Williams, Mrs. Ellen. *Three Years and a Half in the Army; or History of the Second Colorados.* New York: Fowler and Wells Company, 1885.
Wood, Larry. *The Civil War Story of Bloody Bill Anderson.* Austin, TX: Eakin, 2003.
———. *Other Noted Guerrillas of the Civil War in Missouri.* Joplin, MO: Hickory, 2007.

County and Local Histories

Abbott, Clayton. *Historical Sketches of Cedar County, Missouri.* Stockton, MO: published by author, 1968.
Abbott, Clayton, and Lewis B. Hoff. *Missouri History in Cedar County.* Greenfield, MO: Vedette, 1971.
Bartels, Carolyn. *Clay County, Missouri: The Civil War Years*, vol. 1. Shawnee Mission, KS: Two Trails, 1993.
Bell, James E. *History of Early Reynolds County, Missouri.* Paducah, KY: Turner, 1986.
Birdsall and Dean. *The History of Linn County, Missouri.* Kansas City: Birdsall and Dean, 1882.
Block, William Neil. *Shades of Gray: Confederate Soldiers and Veterans of Randolph County, Missouri.* Shawnee Mission, KS: Two Trails, 1996.
Block, William Neil, and Merrill M. Brockman. *Records of Confederate Soldiers, POWS, and Southern Partisans from Howard County, Missouri During the War Between the States 1861–1865.* Huntsville, MO: published by the authors. 1995.
Bollinger County Bicentennial Committee. *Bollinger County: 1851–1976, A Bicentennial Commemorative.* Marceline, MO: Walsworth, 1977.
Bradbury, John F., Jr. *Phelps County in the Civil War.* Rolla, MO: published by author, 1997.
Brophy, Patrick. *Fire and Sword: A Missouri County in the Civil War.* Nevada, MO: Vernon County Historical Society, 2008.
Brown and Company. *History of Vernon County, Missouri.* St. Louis: Brown and Company, 1887.
Cedar County Historical Society. *Cedar County, Missouri: History and Families.* Paducah, KY: Turner, 1998.
Clay County Archives and Historical Library. *Missouri Pioneers of Clay County.* Bowling Green, MO: Info Tech, 1992.
Cockrell, Ewing. *History of Johnson County, Missouri.* Topeka: Historical, 1918.
Conard, Howard L., ed. *Encyclopedia of the History of Missouri: A Compendium of History and Biography for Ready Reference*, vol. 4 of 6 volumes. St. Louis: Southern History, 1901.
Cooper, Martha. *The Civil War and Nodaway County, Missouri.* Signal Mountain, TN: Mountain, 1989.
Cramer, Rose Fulton. *Wayne County, Missouri.* Cape Girardeau, MO: Ramfire, 1972.
Crumpacker, Gladys Wells. *The Complete History of Sullivan County, Missouri, vol. 1, 1836–1900.* Milan, MO: History, 1977.
Denslow, William Ray. *Centennial History of Grundy County, Missouri.* Trenton, MO: published by the author, 1939.
Derendinger, Elaine, Melba Fleck, and LaVaughn Miller, eds. *Stories of Howard County, Missouri.* N.p.: South Howard County Historical Society, 1996.
Ellinghouse, Cletis R., ed. *Old Bollinger: A Collection of Articles from "The Banner Press,"* six volumes. N.p., 1975.
Fairbanks, Jonathan, and Clyde Edwin Tuck. *Past and Present of Greene County, Missouri.* Indianapolis, IN: A. W. Bowen, 1915.
Farthing, C. M. *Chronicles of the Civil War in Monroe County.* Independence, MO: Two Trails, 1997.
Filbert, Preston. *The Half Not Told: The Civil War in a Frontier Town.* Mechanicsburg, PA: Stackpole, 2001.
Ford, James E. *A History of Grundy County.* Trenton, MO: News Publishing, 1908.
———. *A History of Moniteau County, Missouri.* California, MO: Marvin H. Crawford, 1936.
Forister, Robert H. *History of Stoddard County.* Bloomfield, MO: Stoddard County Historical Society, 1971.
Gerteis, Louis S. *Civil War in St. Louis.* Lawrence, KS: University Press of Kansas, 2001.
Goodspeed Publishing Company. *History of Adair, Sullivan, Putnam, and Schuyler Counties, Missouri.* Chicago: The Goodspeed Publishing Company, 1902.
———. *History of Andrew and DeKalb Counties, Missouri.* Chicago: The Goodspeed Publishing Company, 1888.
———. *History of Cole, Moniteau, Morgan, Benton, Miller, Maries, and Osage Counties, Missouri.* Chicago: The Goodspeed Publishing Company, 1889.
———. *History of Franklin, Jefferson, Washington, Crawford, and Gasconade Counties, Missouri.*

Chicago: The Goodspeed Publishing Company, 1888.

———. *History of Hickory, Polk, Cedar, Dade, and Barton Counties, Missouri*. Chicago: The Goodspeed Publishing Company, 1889.

———. *History of Laclede, Camden, Dallas, Webster, Wright, Texas, Pulaski, Phelps, and Dent Counties, Missouri*. Chicago: The Goodspeed Publishing Company, 1889.

———. *History of Lewis, Clark, Knox, and Scotland Counties, Missouri*. Chicago: The Goodspeed Publishing Company, 1887.

———. *History of Lincoln County, Missouri*. Chicago: The Goodspeed Publishing Company, 1888.

———. *History of Newton, Lawrence, Barry, and McDonald Counties, Missouri*. Chicago: The Goodspeed Publishing Company, 1888.

Historical Publishing Company. *History of Clay County, Missouri*. Topeka, KS: Historical, 1920.

———. *History of Cooper County, Missouri*. Topeka, KS: Historical, 1919.

———. *History of Daviess and Gentry Counties, Missouri*. Topeka, KS: Historical, 1922.

Hodges, Miss Nadine, and Mrs. Howard Woodruff, comps. *Genealogical Notes From the "Liberty Tribune" and 1858–1868.*, vol. 2. Liberty, MO: published by compilers, 1975.

Holcombe, R. I. *History of Marion County, Missouri*. St. Louis: E. F. Perkins. 1884.

Howard, Goldena Roland. *Ralls County, Missouri*. Marceline, MO: Walsworth, 1980.

Hurley, Lottie Sedwick. *History of Mt. Vernon and Lawrence County, Missouri, 1831–1931*. Mt. Vernon, MO: publisher not identified, 1931.

Iron County Historical Society. *Past and Present: A History of Iron County, Missouri, 1857–1994*, vol. 1. Marceline, MO: Heritage, 1995.

Jenkins, Clyde Lee. *Judge Jenkins' History of Miller County*. Tuscumbia, MO: published by author, 1971.

Johnson, J. B. *History of Vernon County, Missouri*. Chicago: C. F. Cooper, 1911.

Kansas City Historical Company. *The History of Johnson County, Missouri*. Kansas City, MO: Kansas City Historical Company, 1881.

———. *History of Pettis County, Missouri*. N.p., 1882. Reprint Clinton, MO: Printery, 1974.

Kuhn, Kate Ray. *A History of Marion County*. Hannibal, MO: Western, 1963.

Lang, Delta. *Along Old Gravois: A History of Northwest Jefferson County*. St. Louis: Beaumont Graphics, 1983.

Livingston, Joel T. *A History of Jasper County, Missouri*. Chicago: Lewis, 1912.

McGhee, James E., and James R. Mayo. *Stoddard Grays: Confederate Soldiers of Stoddard County, Missouri 1861–1865*. Shawnee Mission, KS: Two Trails, 1995.

McGlumphy, W. H. S., and Carrie Polk Johnson. *History of Clinton and Caldwell Counties, Missouri*. Topeka, KS: Missouri Historical, 1923.

Melton, E. J. *History of Cooper County, Missouri*. Columbia, MO: E. W. Stephens. 1937.

Miles, Kathleen White. *Bitter Ground: The Civil War in Missouri's Golden Valley*. Clinton, MO: Printery, 1971.

Mills and Company. *The History of Pike County, Missouri*. Des Moines, IA: Mills and Company, 1883.

Missouri Historical Company. *History of Carroll County, Missouri*. St. Louis: Missouri Historical Company, 1881.

———. *History of Howard and Chariton Counties, Missouri*. St. Louis: Missouri Historical Company, 1883.

———. *History of Lafayette County, Missouri*. St. Louis: Missouri Historical Company, 1881.

———. *History of Monroe and Shelby Counties, Missouri*. St. Louis: Missouri Historical Company, 1884.

———. *History of Ray County, Missouri*. St. Louis: Missouri Historical Company, 1881.

———. *History of Saline County, Missouri*. St. Louis: Missouri Historical Company, 1881.

Napton, William Barclay. *Past and Present of Saline County, Missouri*. Chicago: B.F. Brown, 1910.

National Historical Company. *History of Audrain County, Missouri*. St. Louis: National Historical Company, 1884.

———. *History of Caldwell and Livingston Counties, Missouri*. St. Louis: National Historical Company. 1886.

———. *History of Callaway County, Missouri*. St. Louis: National Historical Company, 1884.

———. *History of Carroll County, Missouri*. St. Louis: National Historical Company, 1881.

———. *The History of Cass and Bates Counties, Missouri*. St. Joseph, Missouri: National Historical Company, 1883.

———. *History of Clay and Platte Counties, Missouri*. St. Louis: National Historical Company. 1885.

———. *History of Henry and St. Clair Counties, Missouri*. St. Joseph, Missouri: National Historical Publishing Company. 1883.

———. *History of Howard and Chariton Counties, Missouri*. St. Louis: National Historical Company, 1883.

———. *History of Howard and Cooper Counties, Missouri*. St. Louis: National Historical Company, 1883.

———. *History of Lafayette County, Missouri*. St. Louis: National Historical Company, 1881.

———. *History of Monroe and Shelby Counties, Missouri*. St. Louis: National Historical Company, 1884.

———. *History of Randolph and Macon Counties, Missouri*. St. Louis: National Historical Company, 1884.

———. *History of St. Charles, Montgomery, and Warren Counties, Missouri*. St. Louis: Paul V. Cochran Company, 1885.

Newton County Historical Society. *Neosho: A City of Springs*. Neosho, MO: Newton County Historical Society, 1984.

North, F. A. *The History of Jasper County, Missouri*. Des Moines, IA: Mills and Company, 1883. Reprint Duenweg, MO: Jasper County Missouri Historical Society, 1979.

Oakley, Gene. *The History of Carter County*. Van Buren, MO: J-G, 1970.
Oliva, Leo E. *Fort Scott: Courage and Conflict on the Border*. Topeka, KS: Kansas State Historical Society, 1984.
Paxton, William M. *Annals of Platte County, Missouri*. Kansas City, MO: Hudson-Kimberly Publishing Company, 1897.
Pioneer Historical Company. *History of Dade County and Her People*. Greenfield, MO: Pioneer Historical, 1917.
Ponder, Jerry. *The Civil War in Ripley County, Missouri*. Doniphan, MO: Prospect-News, 1992.
Powell, Betty F. *History of Mississippi County: Beginning Through 1972*. N.p.: published by author, 1975.
Schooley, Herschel. *Centennial History of Audrain County*. Mexico, MO: McIntyre, 1937.
Schrantz, Ward L. *Jasper County, Missouri in the Civil War*. Carthage, MO: Carthage Press, 1923.
Schultz, Gerald A. *A History of Miller County, Missouri*. Jefferson City, MO: Midland, 1933.
Scotland County Bicentennial Committee and Historical Society. *Scotland County, Missouri, in Retrospect*. Memphis, MO: Scotland County Bicentennial Committee and Historical Society, 1977.
Selleck, Bessie Janet (Woods). *Early Settlers of Douglas County, Missouri*. Berkeley, CA: Professional, 1952.
Shrum, Edison. *The History of Scott County, Missouri Up to the Year 1880*. Sikeston, MO: Scott County Historical Society, 1984.
Simpson, Lewis A. W. *Oregon County's Three Flags Via the Horse and Buggy*. Thayer, MO: Thayer News, 1971.
Smith, Geraldine Sanders. *Civil War Soldiers of Madison County, Missouri (and Surrounding Counties)*. St. Louis: published by the author, 1997.
_____. *Civil War Times in Madison County, Missouri and Surrounding Counties*. St. Louis: published by the author, 1999.
Smyth-Davis, Mary F. *History of Dunklin County, Missouri*. St. Louis: Nixon-Jones Printing Company, 1896.
Sturges, J. A. *Illustrated History of McDonald County, Missouri*. Pineville, MO: N.p., 1897.
Tathwell, S. L. *The Old Settlers History of Bates County, Missouri*. Amsterdam, MO: Tathwell and Maxey, 1897.
Taylor, Henry, and Company. *Compendium of History and Biography of Linn County, Missouri*. Chicago: Henry Taylor, 1912.
_____. *General History of Macon County, Missouri*. Chicago: Henry Taylor, 1910.
Thoma, James F. *This Cruel Unnatural War: The American Civil War in Cooper County, Missouri*. Kingsport, TN: published by author, 2003.
Thompson, Henry C. *Our Lead Belt Heritage*. N.p.: published by author, 1955.
Turner, S. K., and S. A. Clark. *Twentieth Century History of Carroll County, Missouri*. Indianapolis: B. F. Bowen, 1911.
Union Historical Company. *The History of Jackson County, Missouri*. Kansas City, MO: Union Historical Company, 1881.
Vaughan, James R., J. J. Gideon, and W. H. Pollard. *History of Christian County*. Ozark, MO: E. E. Patterson Publishing Company, 1893.
Vienna Centennial Committee. *Maries County, Missouri, 1855–1955*. Vienna, MO: Vienna Centennial Committee, 1955.
Violette, E. M. *History of Adair County*. Kirksville, MO: Denslow History, 1911.
Voigt, Harry R. *Concordia, Missouri: A Centennial History*. Concordia, MO: Centennial Committee, 1960.
Western Historical Company. *History of Boone County*. St. Louis: Western Historical Company, 1882.
_____. *History of Greene County, Missouri*. St. Louis: Western Historical Company, 1883.
Wilcox, Pearl. *Jackson County Pioneers*. Independence, MO: published by author, 1975.
Winter, William C. *The Civil War in St. Louis: A Guided Tour*. St. Louis: Missouri Historical Society, 1994.
Woodson, W. H. *History of Clay County, Missouri*. Topeka, KS: Historical, 1920.
Young, William. *Young's History of Lafayette County, MO*. Indianapolis: B. F. Brown, 1910.

General Books

Allardice, Bruce S. *Confederate Colonels: A Biographical Register*. Columbia: University of Missouri Press, 2008.
_____. *More Generals in Gray*. Baton Rouge: Louisiana State University Press, 1995.
Bartels, Carolyn. *The Civil War in Missouri Day by Day 1861 to 1865*. Shawnee Mission, KS: Two Trails, 1992.
_____. *The Forgotten Men: Missouri State Guard*. Shawnee Mission, KS: Two Trails, 1995.
_____, transcriber. *Missouri Confederate Deaths Union Prisons and Hospitals*. Shawnee Mission, KS: Two Trails, 1996.
Bartlett, John. *Familiar Quotations*. Boston: Little, Brown, 1955.
Boatner, Mark M., III. *The Civil War Dictionary*, rev. ed. New York: David McKay, 1988.
Boman, Dennis K. *Lincoln and Citizens' Rights in Civil War Missouri: Balancing Freedom and Security*. Baton Rouge: Louisiana State University Press, 2011.
Britton, Wiley. *The Civil War on the Border*. New York: G. P. Putnam's Sons. 2 volumes, 1890–1891.
Brownlee, Richard S. *Gray Ghosts of the Confederacy: Guerrilla Warfare in the West 1861–1865*. Baton Rouge: Louisiana State University Press, 1958.
Castel, Albert. *General Sterling Price and the Civil War in the West*. Baton Rouge: Louisiana State University Press, 1993.
Chittenden, Hiram Martin. *History of Early Steamboat Navigation on the Missouri River: Life and Adventures of Joseph Labarge*, vol. 2. New York: Francis P. Harper, 1903.
Crist, Mark K. *Rugged and Sublime: The Civil War*

in Arkansas. Fayetteville: University of Arkansas Press, 1994.
Coates, Earl J., and Dean S. Thomas. *An Introduction to Civil War Small Arms*. Gettysburg, PA: Thomas, 1990.
Conard, Howard L., ed. *Encyclopedia of the History of Missouri: A Compendium of History and Biography for Ready Reference*. 6 volumes. St. Louis: Southern History, 1901.
Crute, Joseph H. Jr. *Units of the Confederate States Army*. Midlothian, VA: Derwent, 1987.
Daughters of Union Veterans of the Civil War, 1861–1865. *Missouri: Our Civil War Heritage*. St. Louis: Julia Dent Grant Tent no. 16 of Daughters of Union Veterans of the Civil War, 1861–1865, 1994.
Dyer, Frederick H. *A Compendium of the War of the Rebellion*. 3 volumes. New York: Sangamore, 1959.
Eakin, Joanne Chiles. *Civil War Military Prisoners Sent to Missouri State Penitentiary*. Independence, MO: published by the author, 1995.
_____. *Civil War Union Military Post Returns from Missouri*. Independence, MO: Print America, 1995.
_____. *The Little Gods: Union Provost Marshals in Missouri, 1861–1865*, vol. 1. Independence, MO: published by the author, 1996.
_____. *The Little Gods: Union Provost Marshals in Missouri, 1861–1865*, vol. 2. Shawnee Mission, KS: Two Trails Genealogy, 1996.
_____. *Missouri Prisoners of War From Gratiot Street Prison, St. Louis, MO and Alton Prison, Illinois Including Citizens, Confederates, Bushwhackers, and Guerrillas*. Independence, MO: published by the author, 1995.
Faust, Patricia, ed. *Historical Times Illustrated Encyclopedia of the Civil War*. New York: Harper and Row, 1986.
Fellman, Michael. *Inside War: The Guerrilla Conflict in Missouri During the American Civil War*. New York: Oxford University Press, 1989.
Gibson, Charles Dana, and E. Kay Gibson. *Dictionary of Transports and Combatant Vessels, Steam and Sail, Employed by the Union Army, 1861–1868*. The Army's Navy Series. Camden, ME: Ensign, 1995.
Gilmore, Donald L. *Civil War on the Missouri-Kansas Border*. Gretna, LA: Pelican, 2006.
Goodrich, Thomas. *Black Flag: Guerrilla Warfare on the Western Border, 1861–1865*. Bloomington: Indiana University Press, 1995.
Guralnik, David B., ed. *Webster's New World Dictionary of the American Language*. New York: World, 1970.
Hansen, Duncan E. *A Reunion in Death: Gravesites of the Men Who Ride with William Clarke Quantrill*, vol. 1. Independence, MO: Two Trails, 2002.
_____. *A Reunion in Death, Vol. II: Gravesites of the Men Who Rode with William Clarke Quantrill*. Independence, MO: Two Trails, 2003.
Haswell, A.M., ed. *The Ozarks Region*. Springfield, MO: Interstate Historical Society, 1917.
Ingenthron, Elmo. *Borderland Rebellion: A History of the Civil War on the Missouri-Arkansas Border*. Ozark Regional History Series, book 3. Branson, MO: Ozarks Mountaineer, 1980.
King, James B., Jr. *The Tilley Treasure*. Point Lookout, MO: School of the Ozarks Press, 1984.
Long, E. B., and Barbara Long. *The Civil War Day by Day: An Almanac, 1861–1865*. Garden City, NY: Doubleday, 1971.
Moore, Frank, ed. *The Rebellion Record: A Diary of American Events, with Documents, Narratives, Illustrative Incidents, Poetry, etc.* 12 volumes. New York: G. P. Putnam, 1861–1868, and Van-Nostrand, 1862–1871. Reprint New York: Arno, 1977.
Nichols, Bruce. *Guerrilla Warfare in Civil War Missouri, Volume I, 1862*. Jefferson, NC: McFarland, 2004.
_____. *Guerrilla Warfare in Civil War Missouri, Volume II, 1863*. Jefferson, NC: McFarland, 2007.
Oates, Stephen B. *Confederate Cavalry West of the River*. Austin: University of Texas Press, 1961. Reprinted by same, 1992.
Parrish, William E., ed. *The Civil War in Missouri: Essays From the Missouri Historical Review: 1906–2006*. Columbia: State Historical Society of Missouri, 2006.
Rader, Perry S. *The Civil Government of the United States and the State of Missouri and the History of Missouri*. Columbia, MO: E. W. Stephens, Publisher, 1898.
Shoemaker, Floyd C., ed. *Missouri—Day by Day*. 2 volumes. Columbia: State Historical Society of Missouri, 1943.
Siddali, Silvana R., ed. *Missouri's War: The Civil War in Documents*. Athens: Ohio University Press, 2009.
Warner, Ezra J. *Generals in Blue: Lives of the Union Commanders*. Baton Rouge: Louisiana State University Press, 1964.
_____. *Generals in Gray: Lives of the Confederate Commanders*. Baton Rouge: Louisiana State University Press, 1959.
Way, Frederick, Jr. *Way's Packet Directory, 1848–1994*. Athens: Ohio University Press, 1994.
Webb, W. L. *Battles and Biographies of Missourians, or the Civil War Period of Our State*. Kansas City, MO: Hudson-Kimberly, 1903.
Wilson, George F., Maryhelen Wilson, and Lois Stanley. *Death Records from Missouri Newspapers, January 1861–December 1865*. Decorah, IA: Anundson, 1983.

Index

Page numbers in *bold italics* indicate pages with illustrations.

Abbret, F. E. ("Albright," Northern) 75
abolitionists 7, 215
Abshire, John (Southern) 187
Adair County 251
Adams, Dr. W. C. (Southern) 103
Agency Ford, Buchanan County 328
Aker, Sylvester (Southern) 96–7
Alabama 132
Albany, Ray County 316, 331
Alder, 1st Lt. George N. (Northern) 105–6
Alexander, Surgeon Charles T. (Northern) 188–9
Alexandria, Clark County 120
Allen, Maj. Abraham (Northern) 148
Allen, Detective Benjamin F. (Northern) 126
Allen, Col. John D. (Northern) 107, 200–1
Allen, Randolph County 111, 113, 222, 233–4, 257
Allison, Thomas W. (Northern) 90, 400*n*2
Alton, Illinois 22
Alton, Illinois, Military Prison 24, 85, 86, 99, 165, 179, 187–9, 207, 308, 369, 370
Ames, Bishop Edward R. 61
Anders, Dr. Leslie (historian) 4, 122
Anderson, Garret A. (Southern) 36–7
Anderson, James "Jim" (Southern) *236*, 245, 247, 248, 249, 250, 333, 344, 391
Anderson, Capt. Morton (Northern) 205
Anderson, Mrs. 338
Anderson, Reverend (Northern) 237
Anderson, Pvt. Samuel M. (Southern) 12, 393*n*4
Anderson, William T. "Bill" (Southern) 241, *236*, 245, 247, 258, 294, 301, 316, 331–2, 350, 352, 356, 358, 364, 368, 388, 389, 390; back to Missouri from Texas (middle May–early June) 104–6, 136, 137; Carroll County first time (12 July) 311–2; Carroll County and Ray County second time (1–2 August) 333–6; Carroll County and Ray County third time (12–14 August) with defeat Wakenda Creek 340–4, 349; combined wounded Taylor's band with his (10–11 August) 339–44, 349, 372; Cooper County first time (4–5 June) 297–9; Cooper County second time (30 August) 384; council of war in Lafayette County (4–5 August) 327, 367; deposed Quantrill (late May–early June) *138*–40, 143–4, 264; first time northeast Missouri (13–31 July) 230–1, 232–7; manifesto (7 July) 295–7; operations Johnson and Lafayette Counties (June–early July) 279–80, 281, 283, 285–6, 287–8, 290, 292, 293; recuperating from wounds suffered at Carroll County (14–25 August) 249, 253; second time northeast Missouri (25–31 August) 253–7
Andrew County 145, 149, 270–1, 326, 328
Angell, Dr. John M. (Southern) 244
Arcadia, Iron County 75
Argo, Lt. William (Northern) 375–6
Arkansas River 100
Arkansas troops (Northern): 1st Arkansas Cavalry Regiment 203, 211; 2nd Arkansas Cavalry Regiment 211
Armstead, Joseph (Northern) 78–9
Army of the Cumberland (Northern) 56
Army of the Potomac (Northern) 60, 359

Arnold, Reverend Mose B. 125
Arnoldsville, Buchanan County 263, 265, 272, 348
Arrow Rock, Saline County 239, 299, 354, 362, 365, 366, 367, 370
Arrow Rock raid (20 July 1864) 357–9, 359–60, 373, 377, 381
Arsenal, U. S. 314
arson *15*, 16, 17, 20, 22, 45, 53, 76, 79, 94, *107*, 110, 113, 120, 122, 137, 138, 142, 148, 149, 153, 160, 163, 183–5, 193, 195, 199, 206, 212, 222, 261, *271*, 299, 307, 310, 320, 327, 335, 342, 356, 363, 367, 368, 372, 375, 384
artillery *see* cannon
Asbury, Maj. Ai Edgar (Southern) 168
"Ash Flats," (south-central Missouri) 12
assessment of penalty 256, 371, 373
Atchison, Kansas 336, 339
Atchison County 145, 345
Athens, Clark County 120
Atkinson, Mr. (Northern) 129
Atlantus, Gentry County 44
Audrain County 113, 189, 218, 220, 227, 229, 243, 244–5, 247, 259
Austin, Green (Southern) 352
Australia 268
axe 141, 187, 215
Axline, Capt. Jacob (Northern) 283

Bagby farm, Randolph County 247
Bailey, Bishop A. (Northern) 277
Bailey, Pvt. Thomas (Northern) 264, 266, 267
Baker, 1st Lt. James (Northern) 343
Baker, Capt. William P. (Northern) 369
Baker farm, Montgomery County 115

457

Ball, Capt. Jackson (Northern) 209
ball and chain restraints 27, 189
Ballew, Capt. Squire (Northern) 292
Ballew, Capt. William B. (Northern) 91
Ballinger, Capt. John (Northern) 136
Balltown, Vernon County 93, 202, 206
banishment 179, 251, 348
Baptist denomination 20, 78, 110, 169, 223, 301
Barkley, Sgt. John W. (Northern) 92–3
Barnes, Charles (Southern) 75–6, 399n17
Barnes, John (Southern) 220
Barnes, or Baines, Moses (Northern) 274
Barnesville, Kansas 203
Barr, Col. A. J. (Northern) 338
Barry, Platte County 331
Barry County 28, 95, 104, 190, 209
Bartlett, Maj. Solon A. C. (Northern) 244, 245
Barton County 90, 103, 105, 107, 193, 197–8, 200, 202
Basin Knob, Johnson County 383
Bates, 1st Lt. Uriah (Northern) 14, 15, 17
Bates County 33, 49, 50, 91, 92, 93–4, 98–9, 102–3, 130, 190, 195, 202, 205, 206, 208
Batesville, Arkansas 81, 167
Battle of Athens, Clark County (5 August 1861) 120
Battle of Baxter Springs, Kansas (6 October 1863) 127, 138
Battle of Captain Wagoner's patrol (6 July 1864) 294–5
Battle of Chickamauga, Georgia (September 1863) 56, 180, 291
Battle of Elkhorn Tavern see Battle of Pea Ridge
Battle of Independence, Jackson County (11 August 1862) 283
Battle of Lexington, Lafayette County (September 1861) 66
Battle of Lowe's Cabin, Jackson County (16 April 1862) 49
Battle of Newtonia, Newton County (September 1862) 127
Battle of Pea Ridge, Arkansas (March 1862) 44
Battle of Round Pond, Cape Girardeau County (1 August 1863) 18
Battle of Sibley, Jackson County (6 October 1862) 134
Battle of Springfield, Greene County (January 1863) 63
Battle of Stockton, Cedar County (11 July 1863) 199

Battle of Whitsell farm, Lafayette County (14 June 1864) 287–8
Battle of Wilson's Creek, Greene County (10 August 1861) 66, 209
battlefield acquisition see guerrilla logistics
Baugh family, Jackson County (Northern) 132
Baxter, Capt. Hiram (Northern) 226
Baxter, Lt. (Southern) 196–7
Baxter Springs, Kansas 195
Bazier, Jackson (Southern) 112
Beanland, John (Southern) 375–6
Bear, Sgt. John (Northern) 303, 433n47
Bear Creek, Taney County 95
Beaver Creek, Douglas County 208
Beck, Dr. (Southern) 205, 416n43
Bedford, Livingston County 146
Bee Branch, Chariton County 240
Bee Creek, Platte County 267
Bee Creek, Taney County 95
Bell, Mr. 292
Bell Air, Cooper County 142, 298
Bellefontaine Cemetery, St. Louis 59, *181*
Benecke, 1st Lt. Louis (Northern) 239–40
Benton, Scott County 70
Benton Barracks, St. Louis City 88
Benton County, Arkansas 93, 94, 100, 106, 140, 203, 207, 210, 354, 387
Bequette, Henry (Northern) 178
Bernard, Cpl. William W. T. (Northern) 207
Berryman, Col. Richard "Dick" (Southern) 154, 162, 175
Berryville, Arkansas 191
Berve, Mr. 417n2
Bethany Union, Harrison County 342
Beverage, Col. John L. (Northern) 75
Bevins, Walter (Southern) 272
Biddle's Store, Franklin County 83
Big Creek, Douglas County 208
Big Creek, Johnson and Henry Counties 363, 369, 381
Big Creek, Newton County 31
Big Drywood Creek, Vernon County 34–5
Big Muddy Creek, Johnson County 292
Big Piney River, southeast Missouri 16, 17, 164, 165, 166, 167
Big River, southeast Missouri 171
Big Spring, Montgomery County 224

Big Tavern Creek, Miller County 183
Bigelow family, Clay County (Northern) 276–7
Biggerstaff families 277
Biggs, or Briggs, Mr. (Southern) 278
Bingham, Capt. George W. (Northern) 355, 366
Bishop, William (Northern) 120
Bissett, James (Southern) 273
Black Oak, Caldwell County 318–9, 322
Black River, southeast Missouri 21, 78, 162, 174
"Blackfoot Neighborhood" see Perche Hills, Boone County
Blackwater River, northwest Missouri 54, 99, 285, 292, 301, 363
Blackwell, St. Francois County 170
Blair, Col. Charles W. (Northern) 106, 198, 200, 202, 204
Blair, Capt. William D. (Northern) 141, 298–9
Blalock, Thomas (Southern) 369, 443n46
Bledsoe, Bill (Southern) 98
blockhouse or stockade 362, 380
Bloomfield, Stoddard County 18, 70, 72, 73, 155, 156, 158, 161, 172
Bloomington, Buchanan County 327
Blue Cane Island, St. Francis River, Dunklin County 158
Blue River, Jackson County 135
Blue Springs, Jackson County 133, 294
Blunt, Andy (Southern) 48–9, 51, 387; actions of his men 52, 54, 126, 129; controversies after death 124–5, 129, 130–2, 143, 387; death 124, 143, 387; jailbreak attempt to free band member 54–5, 296; mysterious identity 48–9; operations mostly in Lafayette County 51, 126; remnant of his band moves operations to Henry County 92–3, 126
Blunt, Brig. Gen. James G. (Northern) 66
boats, small 146, 232, 258, 292–3, 303, 311, 345, 348, 351
Bogart's Mound, Carroll County 45
Bolin, John F. (Southern) 18, 72, 387
Bolin, Nathan (Southern) 18, 68, 69, 72, 73, 158–9, 387, 392
Bolivar, Polk County 34
Boller, John H. 356
Bollinger County 18, 69, 73, 74, 155, 171, 172, 175; Union Township 177

Bonaparte, Napoleon 6
Bond, Pvt. Brantley Y. (Northern) 274
Bond, Mrs. Sarah 80–1
Bond, Ruth, and Sarah (Miller County, Southern) 143
Bone Hill, Jackson County 127, 382
Boone County 109, 111, 114, 179, 213, 218, 220, 222, 223, 227, 229, 231, 233, 242, 243–4, 244, 245, 246, 247, 251–2, 253, 254, 256, 319
Boonsboro, Howard County 245
Boonville, Cooper County 48, 100, 110, 141, 142, 232, 249, 254, 354, 355–6, 361, 364, 366, 368, 373, 377, 384; newspaper 100, 367
"the Bootheel" 17–8, 68–73, 154, 161, 169, 174, 387
Boswell, Capt. (Northern) 385
Botts, Seth, Sr., and Jr. (Southern) 36
Bottsville Linn County 36
bounty 268
Bourbon County, Kansas 203, 204
Bourbose River, east-central Missouri 176
Bowen, Capt. (Southern) 159
Bowen, or Bones, John (Southern) 141
Bowie knife *133*
Bowling Green, Pike County 116, 226
Bowling Green Prairie, Chariton County 110
Bowman, Capt. (Southern) 412*n*50
boxcars 118–*119*, 164, 277
Boyd, J. W. (Northern) 177
Boyd, Lt. William F. (Northern) 15, 16
Boze, Dick (Southern) 75–6
Brackman Capt. Albert (Northern) 299
Bradbury, Dr. John F. (historian) 80
Bradford, 1st Sgt. Harvey (Northern) 149–50
Bradley, Lt. Hugh M. (Northern) 172
Bradley, Mrs. (Southern) 269–70
Bradshaw, Col. R. C. (Northern) 327
Bragg, General Braxton (Southern) 291
Bragg, Howard (Southern) 238
Branded as Rebels (book) 141
Brashears (Linn County, Northern) 216
Brashears, 2nd Lt. Lewis (Southern) 94–5
Brazito, Cole County 384
Breckenridge, Caldwell County 270, 278, 322

Bretz Mills, Buchanan County 149
Brewer, Col. James, and James, Jr. (Southern) 225
Bridgton, St. Louis County 174
Briggs, Mr. 110
Brink, Pvt. Isaac (Northern) 305
Brinker, John (Southern) 285
Briscoe, John F. (Southern) 114
Britton, Wiley (historian) 31, 104
Brookfield, Linn County 215, 240
Brookshire, Mrs. Ellen 17
Brown, Col. Buck (Southern) 194, 196
Brown, Brig. Gen. Egbert G. (Northern) *64*, 131, 134, 136, 283, 308, 312, 357, 362; Anderson's manifesto mentioning Brown (7 July 1864) 286, 295, 296–7; confused 52–3, 92, 232, 289, 291–2, 293–4; Curtis' advice 123–4, 151; fired as district chief (23 July 1864) 359–60, 370; innovations 63–5, 124, 283, 284–5, 387–8; insightful 130; Lincoln doubts Brown's ability (24 June 1864) 291; working with Curtis' Kansans 288
Brown, Peter 257
Brown, Tom (Southern) 9
Brownfield, Thomas 298
Brownlee, Charles (Southern) 141–2, 144, 352, 361
Brownsville, Saline County 132, 140–1, 298
Brunswick, Chariton County 110, 214, 215, 301
Brush Creek, Carter County 162
brush fighting 14, 20, 55, 82, 104, 147, *156*, 164, 192, 193, *196*, 196–7, 198, 239, 259, 285, 287, 301, 314–6, *316*, *322*, *334*, 340, 341, 343
Bryson, Capt. George W. (Southern) 218, 220, 221, 222
Buchanan County 41, 43, 140, 145, 148, 149, 152, 262, 263, 265–6, 268, 270, 272, 307, 311, 318, 324, 326, 327, 328, 332, 337, 340, 348, 349; Crawford Township 328; Jackson Township 149
Bucklin, Linn County 213, 252
buckshot *see* shotguns
Buffalo River, northwest Arkansas 162
Buffington (vessel) 256, 384
Buffington, Mr. (Northern) 246
Buffington, Boone County 246
buggy (or small passenger wagon) 40, 74, 130, *131*, 356
bullet-making or casting 125
Bunceton (present day), Cooper County 384

Burbridge, Col. John Q. (Southern) 86, 115
Burch, Capt. Milton (Northern) 29, 194
Burgess, Michael (Southern) 137
Burns, Pvt. John R. (Northern) 54
Burris, Lt. Col. John T. (Northern) 157–9, 172, 173
Burris, Capt. Milton (Northern) 55, 124, 125, 287–8, 289, 295–6
Burrus, Nancy (Southern) 203
Burton, George (Southern) 146
Burts, Capt. John H. (Northern) 346
Butler, Nathaniel 239–40
Butler County 20, 75, 161, 163, 171, 175
Butler's Creek, northwest Arkansas 108
Byrne, Lt. Harrison H. (Northern) 156

Cache Swamp, southeast Missouri 78
Cadet, Washington County 170
Caldwell County 119, 270, 278–9, 318–9, 321, 323, 329, 342, 345, 358; history of 1886 236; newspaper 342
Caledonia, Washington County 73
Calhoun, William (Southern) 238–9
Calhoun, Henry County 206
Calhoun County, Illinois 116, 227
Calhoun House, Calhoun, Henry County 206
California 40, 277
California, Moniteau County 352, 361, 362
California Gold Rush (1848–early 1850s) 166
California House Inn, Pulaski County 14, 16, 17, 81
Callaway County 40, 111, 113, 114, 218, 223–4, 225, 227, 257, 258
Calvert, Capt. D. A. (Northern) 343
Calvert, 1st Lt. Robert C. (Northern) 71
Cambridge, Saline County (present day Gilliam) 359, 366, 373
Camden, Arkansas 325
Camden, Ray County 146, 279, 290
Camden County 93, 100
Camden Point, Platt County 152, 153, 308–9, 312, 390
Cameron, Clinton County 275, 277
Campbell, Bill (Southern) 247
Campbell, Mr. (Southern) 12
Campbell, Mr. (bushwhacker, Southern) 95

Index

Campbell, Mrs. (Southern) 20
Campbell, Capt. Thomas L. (Northern) 258
Campbell, Vernon (Southern) 20, 68, 69, 387
Cane Creek, Taney County 210
Cane Island, St. Francis River, Dunklin County 155, 157
cannon 15, 204
Canton area, Lewis County 118
Canton Press, Canton, Lewis County 122
Canville Creek, Allen County, Kansas 31
Cape Girardeau, Cape Girardeau County 18, 155, 157–8, 160
Cape Girardeau County 18, 69, 70, 72, 73, 74–5, 171
Capitol building, Jefferson City, Cole County 180
carbines 50, 127, *135*, 160, 204, 377
Carlin, Col. John C. (Southern) 187, 414n15
Carpenter, Capt. Robert (Northern) 198, 200–1, 202
Carpenter's Store (present day Trimble), Clinton County 331
carriage (elegant passenger wagon) 212, 217
Carroll, J. M. (Northern) 177
Carroll County 44, 45, 229, 233, 249, 250, 278, 280, 301, 311–2, 319, 323, 324, 329, 333–6, 341, 324, 342, 347, 349, 350, 351, 355; history of 1881 335, 343; history of 1911 299; Hurricane Township 334, 349
Carrollton, Carroll County 44, 301, 319; newspaper 304, 343
Carson, Sashel (Southern) 418n2
Carter, Al (Southern) 355–6
Carter, Sgt. LeGrand (Northern) 83, *84*
Carter, William (Northern) 253
Carter County 20, 77, 161, 162
Carthage, Jasper County 100, 102, 107, 192, 193, 200
Cartnel, Robert (Southern) 125
Cass County 48, 50, 53, 124, 129, 131, 134, 136, 137, 141, 206, 281, 286, 288, 289, 291, 354, 347, 362, 365, 369, 375, 380–1, 383
Cassairt, Capt. Jacob (Northern) 207–8
Cassville, Barry County 104, 209
Castel, Albert (historian) 98–9, 128
Castle, Maj. Spell (Northern) 328
Castle, Theodore (Southern) 147
Castor Creek, Madison County 172

Castor River, southeast Missouri 69
Catherwood, Col. Edwin C. (Northern) 327, 328, 339, 340–1, 348
Catholic or Roman Catholic denomination 57, 72
Catron, John 124
cave 13, 84, 163, 164, 171, 197
Cave Springs, Greene County 107
Cave Springs, Jasper County 102, 193
Cavender, Sgt. Jeffrey (Northern) 106
C. E. Hillman (vessel) 73
Cedar County 33, 34, 196–7, 197–8, 199–200
Cedar Creek, Boone County 227
Cedar Creek, Vernon County 104
Centerville, or Centreville (present day Kearney), Clay County 277, 278 326
Centerville, Reynolds County 75
Centralia, Boone County 220
Chambers, Capt. B. (Southern) 79
Chapel Hill, Lafayette County 130, 137–8, 364, 375, 381, 381
Chariton County 109, 110, 112, 113, 187, 212, 214, 215, 216, 217, 230, 238–40, 240, 242, 248, 249, 255, 258, 301, 312, 319, 334, 344, 364, 365; Prairie Township 214, 253
Chariton River, north-central Missouri 37; forks of 239, 252, 256
Charleston, Mississippi County 20, 71, 72, 155, 156
Cherokee Bay Swamp, Butler County 21
Cherokee Indians (Southern) 192
Cherryville, Crawford County 176
Chesnut, Capt. John (Southern) 328, 367, 437n48
Chester, William E. (Northern) *381*
Chicago, Illinois 186, 244
Chiles, Christopher, and Rachel (Southern) 337
Chiles, William "Billy" H. (Southern) 332, 333, 337, 338, 340, 344, 345, 346, 348, 349
Chiles brothers, Kit and Dick (Southern) 337
Chilhowee, Johnson County 136, 137
Chillicothe, Livingston County 119, 319, 324
Chitwood, Capt. Richard C. (Northern) 209

Chitwood, Lt. W. T. (Northern) 17
Christian, John (Northern) 149–50, 264, 409n12
Christian Brothers Academy (or hospital), St. Louis 85
Christian County 95
Christopher, John H. (Northern) 320, 436n28
Christopher Bridge, Iron Mountain Railroad, Washington County 170
Cincinnati, Ohio 180, 232, 233, 245, 364
circle of violence 149, 167, 170, 193, 195, 214, 240, 296, 326, 348–9, 360, 383–4, 389, 392
circus 268
citizen guards 21, 61–3, 64, 129, 132, 136, 137, 147, 207, 211, 213, 220, 233, 236, 238, 242, 292, 295–6, 299, 303, 311, 321, 322, 326, 328, 335, 338, 339, 344, 345, 352, 353, 338, 339, 344, 345, 352, 353, 354, 355, 356, 358, 359, 360, 366, 368, 371, 383–4, 385, 388; see also Missouri Troops, Provisional EMM Companies
citizen posses 116, 118, 257, 279
City of Alton (vessel) 185
civil law / civil courts / civil rights 7, 121–2, 146, 209, 352, 388
Claggett, Capt. Milton M. (Northern) 345
Clardy, Maj. Martin Linn (Southern) 175
Clark (Southern) 143
Clark, Surgeon Augustus M. (Northern) 25, 26, 85–6
Clark, Col., Henry E. (Southern) 157–9
Clark, Maj. John M. (Northern) 306
Clark County 117, 120, 260–1
Clark's Station or Clarksburg, Moniteau County 362
Clarksville, Arkansas 100
Clarkton, Dunklin County 18, 156
Clay County 45, 47, 128, 134, 145, 146, 148, 187, 268, 273–8, 288, 298, 308, 312–16, 324, 325, 326, 328, 329, 330, 337–8, 339, 340, 345, 347–8, 357, 361, 390; history of 1885 313; Fishing River Township 275; Washington Township 274
Claycomb, John 69
Claysville, Boone County 252
Claysville, Clay County 274
Clear Creek, Clay County 328
Clear Creek, Vernon County 104, 202, 204
Clear Fork Creek, Johnson County 356

Index

Clements, Archibald "Little Archie" (Southern) 94, *234*, 254, 273, 311, 336, 344
Clements, Mr. (Southern) 93–4
Clemmons, Sgt. John F. (Northern) 187
Clifford, Capt. James (Northern) 183
Clinton, Henry County 92, 207
Clinton County 145, 148, 262, 265, 273, 275, 312, 318, 320, 324, 329, 338; Shoal Township 320
Cluteban *see* Cruteban
Coal Creek, Gasconade County 115
Coats, Bill (Southern) 16, 164, 411*n*36
Cobb, Alvin (Southern) 37, 40
Cockrell, Col. Jeremiah V. (Southern) 98, 103, 363–4
Cody, Mr. 122
Coffee, Col. John T. (Southern) 228
Coffman, David (Southern) 275–7
Coil, Mr. 45
Colclazier, Pvt. Joseph H. (Southern) 187, 414*n*15
Cole, Joe (Southern) 114, 257
Cole, Selaphian 172
Cole County 143, 144, 252, 297, 302–3, 360, 373, 384; Jefferson Township 211
Coleman, Charles (Northern) 418*n*7
Coleman, Capt. Charles F. (Northern) 53
Coleman, Col. William O. (Southern) 12, 163, 165, 393*n*5
Colley, Capt. Patten (Northern) 341, 343
Collier, James (Southern) 171, 172–3
Colony, Knox County 122, 261
Colorado Territory 49
Colorado Troops (Northern) 61, 64, 104; 2nd Colorado Artillery Battery 308; 2nd Colorado Cavalry Regiment ("Mountain Boomers") 49, 102, 125, 128, 129–30, 133, 134, 137, 206, 268, 281, 286, 288–9, 294, 308, 309, 314–6, 317, 318, 322, 323, 324, 329, 331, 338, 354, 356, 357, 362, 365, 381, 382, 387; 2nd Colorado Infantry Regiment 129; 3rd Colorado Infantry Regiment 129
Colson, Archibald (Northern) 92–3
Colt's revolvers *see* revolvers
Colt's revolving rifle *111*, 230
Colton, Pvt. William (Northern) 145
Columbia, Boone County 111, 220, 221, 243, *244*, 248, 252; newspaper 82, 232, 250, 258, 299
Columbus, Johnson County 52, 353, 364
Columbus, Kentucky 85
Colver, James *see* Collier, James
Combs, Lt. James L. (Northern) 371
Commissary-General of Prisoners (Northern) 185
A Compendium of the War of the Rebellion by Frederick Dyer (book) 3
Conan, Captain (Northern) 106
Confederate currency 44, 172, 183, 206, 311
Confederate recruiters: bold technique 219–20; stealth technique 218
Confederate regulars (or Confederate army) 142, 164, 167, 175, 200, 208, 290, 296, 304, 318, 328, 330, 339, 354, 361, 364, 366
Confederate uniforms 151, 153, 211, 219–20, 295, 307, 310
Connelley, William (historian) 96
Conrad, Esquire (Northern) 113
conscripting into military 77, 160, 168, 170, 204; *see also* drafting; Shelby
Conyers, Polk (Southern) 159
Cook, M. (Northern) 160
Coon Island, Butler County 21
Cooper, John (Southern) 418*n*2
Cooper, Joseph (Northern) 107
Cooper, Thomas (Southern) 385
Cooper brothers 292
Cooper County 48, 100, 101, 110, 141–3, 144, 256, 283, 287, 293, 297–9, 352, 354, 355–6, 357, 361, 362, 364, 365, 367, 368, 372, 377, 383, 384; Kelly Township 384
Copeland, Brig. Gen. Joseph T. (Northern) 88
"Copperhead" 120; *see also* Peace Democrats
corn, ripening of 241, 349
Cornelia, Johnson County 137, 249, 356
Cornogs, Hiram and F. H. (Northern) 209
"Corps de Belgique" 180
Corum, Mrs. 298
Cottonwood Creek, Lafayette County 377–8
Couch, 1st Lt. James (Northern) 52, 130–1
councils of war, Lafayette and Monroe Counties (early August 1864) 138, 236, 246–7, 327, 331, 333, 338, 339, 349, 363, 365, 366, 367, 369, 385, 391
county records hidden or destroyed 107, 205, 214
couriers or dispatch riders 9, 78, 79, 80, 194, 202, 341, *342*, 355
court martial 7, 370; *see also* tribunal and "drumhead"
Cow Creek, McGee County, Kansas 103, 202, 203, 204
Cow Island, St. Francis River, Butler County 163
Cowarden, Francis family of Johnson County 378
Cowen, Col. (Southern) 159
Cowskin Bottom, or Cowskin Prairie, McDonald County 29, 100
Cowskin Creek, McDonald County 196
Cox, Maj. Samuel P. (Northern) 321–3, 324, 329
Coy, Sgt. H. J. (Northern) 289, 365
Crab Orchard, Ray County 147
Crabtree, "General" (Southern) 143, 302
Craig, Joe (Southern) 16
Craig, Jones 115
Crandall, Col. Lee (Southern) 75
Crane Creek, Stone County 209
Cranmer, Tom (Southern) 298–9*m* 432*n*38
Cranor, Maj. David (Northern) 339
Crawford, Jeptha (Southern) 384
Crawford, Riley (Southern) 384
Crawford County 10, 81, 168, 176, 177–8
Crawford's Fork, Johnson County 369
Creve Coeur Lake, St. Louis County *182*, 183
Crews, Mr. (Southern) 394*n*51
Crisp's Mill, Johnson County 283
Crites, Daniel (Northern) 18
Crooked River, Clay County 327
Crowder, David M. (Northern) 215
Crowley's Ridge, northeast Arkansas 96
Cruteban, or Cluteban, Mr. (Southern) 160
Cuba, Crawford County 82
Cuivre River, northeast Missouri 227
Cummins, Jim (author) 147, 265, 273, 274, 275, 276, 340
Cunningham, Col. David B. (Southern) 247
Cunningham, Lieutenant 145
Current River, south-central Missouri 21, 162
Curtis, Capt. Orren A. (Northern) 363
Curtis, Maj. Gen. Samuel R. (Union Department of Kansas chief) *123*, 151, 345; advice and criticism for Missouri

commanders 123, 151–2, 306, 326; exchange with Brig. Gen. Brown 288; exchanges with Maj. Gen. Rosecrans 191, 267; permits Missouri operations in Kansas 339; sends Kansas troops into Missouri 268, 288, 308, 314, 329
Curtman's Island, Osage River, Miller County 383–4
Cushman, Mr. (Southern) 85, 400n42

Dade County 29, 98, 101–2, 141, 190, 196–7, 197–8, 200
Dagley, Sgt. Alvis (Northern) 274
Dale, 2nd Lt. Columbus (Northern) 301
Dale, Maj. Douglas (Northern) 301
Dallas, Bollinger County 18, 393n20
Dallas, Texas 247
Dallas County 31, 33
Damon, George 231
Danville, Montgomery County 115
Dare, William A. (Northern) 334–5
Darling (vessel) 71
Darling, Mr. (Northern) 168
Darnelle, Mr. (Southern) 159
David, Lt. (Northern) 203
Daviess County 51, 120, 275, 278, 321, 329
Davis, Reverend D. B. (Northern) 245
Davis, "Dr." (Southern) 275, 427n30
Davis, F. J. (Northern) 245
Davis, Capt. Frank (Southern) 218, 247, 253
Davis, Mr. 79
Davis, "Old One-Eyed" (Southern) 195
Davis Creek, Lafayette County 377–8
Dawson, John 47
Dayton, Cass County 129
Deal, Col. Henry J. (Northern) 71
Deardorff, Pvt. Reuben D. (Northern) 34
Deardorff, Lt. Samuel T. (Southern) 34
death sentence 85, 187; *see also* executions
Deer Creek, Bates County 94
Deer Ridge, Lewis County 261
Dejarnette, Mr. (Southern) 418n2
DeKalb, Buchanan County 148, 149, 326, 348
DeKalb County 145, 149, 312
Denison, Orville (Northern) 128
Denny, Col. Alexander F. (Northern) 236, 247

Denny, Judge David (Northern) 236
Dent County 9, 10, 12, 16, 154, 164, 165
Department of Kansas (Union) 123, 267, 268, 281, 288, 306, 326, 329–30, 339, 345
Department of the Missouri (Union) 56, 57, 58, 60, 96, 127, 179, 185, 186, 188, 213, 225, 232, 268, 284, 291, 330, 359
Department of War (Union) 57, 359
deserters 29, 31, 91, 110, 145, 165, 171, 175, 176, 209–10, 368, 388
DeSoto, Jefferson County 170, 172, 173, 174
detectives (Northern) 22, 27, 41, 53, 68, 88, 120, 126, 187, 212, 213, 221, 227, 256, 337
DeWitt, Carroll County 324
Diamond Grove, Newton County 191, 195
Dillard, Samuel (Southern) 261
Dillon, Phelps County 164
District of Central Missouri (Union) 57, 64–5, 92, 123, 254–5, 283, 291, 293, 303, 356, 357, 359, 362, 371, 374, 276, 377, 387
District of North Missouri (Union) 254
District of Northeast Missouri (Union) 121, 225, 241, 388
District of Southwest Missouri (Union) 209
District of St. Louis (Union) 58
District of the Border (Union) 32, 57
Dodson, Mr. 94
Doniphan, Ripley County 162
Donovan, Park (Southern) 274
Dorsey, Col. Caleb (Southern) 221, 225, 226, 229, 257; his operations 218, 258–9, 260; his versus Col. Perkins' methods 218–20; May 1864 expedition into Missouri 99–101, 115, 142, 212, 388
Douglas, William M. (Southern) 187, 414n15
Douglas, Kansas 128
Douglas County 16, 70, 95–6, 208, 210
Douglass, Brig. Gen. Joseph (Northern) 112, *243*, 245, 256–7, 261
Dover, Lafayette County 292, 351, 355, 376, 385
drafting into military 7–8; *see also* conscripting
Drake, Ire 174
Draper, Lt. Col. Daniel M. (Northern) 112, 117, 213, *269*, 308

Dripping Springs, Boone County 222–3, 248–9
"drumhead" (or on-the-spot court martial) 7; *see also* court martial and tribunal
Dry Creek, Jefferson County 174
Dry Creek, Vernon County 103
Dry Fork, Jasper County 105
Dry Wood, Vernon County 200
Drywood Creek, Vernon County 200
Duck, Postmaster (Northern) 242
Dugan, Isaac W. (Northern) 334–5
Dugon, Sgt. (Northern) 10
Duncan, David T. (Southern) 328
Dunklin County 18, 69, 70, 72, 73, 155, 156, 157–9
Dunksburg, Johnson County 292
Dunn, Charles F. 180, 182
Durbin, Benedict J. (Northern) 118
Duroc Ford of Osage River, Benton County 210, 354
Durrett, Benjamin 378
Durrett, Bill (Southern) 366
Durrett, Dick (Southern) 369
Duvall, "old" Mr. 82

Eads, Capt. William (Northern) 283
Eakins, Joanna Chiles (historian) 141
Earickson, John (Northern) 242
Eastman, Cpl. Michael (Northern) 145
Eazel, Mr. (Northern) 118
Edina, Knox County 122, 261
Edward F. Dix (vessel) 184
Edwards, Capt. James W. (Northern) 156
Edwards, Pvt. John M. (Southern) 207, 287
Edwards, John N. (historian) 48, 98, 99, 124, 130, 146, 213, 246–7, 249, 250, 253, 276, 305, 307, 315, 328, 336, 367; *see also* Noted Guerrillas
Ehlers, Friedrich (Northern) 380
Eisner, Mr. (Northern) 368
election, national (8 November 1864) 179, 211, 238, 261
Eleven Points River (south-central Missouri) 12, 75
Elizabeth, Pennsylvania 184
Elizabethtown, Monroe County 259
Elk Chute, Pemiscot County 159
Elk Creek, Chariton County 112
Elkhorn, Ray County 316, 341
Elliott, Capt. Benjamin F. (Southern) 188
Ellis, 2nd Lt. George M. (Northern) 93

Enfield rifles *290*; see also rifle-muskets
England 167, 273
Eppstein, Lt. Col. Joseph A. (Northern) 14, 33, 80
Erwin, Marion D. (Southern) 292, 296–7
Estes, Abraham (Southern) 314
Evans, Maj. Frank D. (Northern) 220
Evans, Capt. George W. (Southern) 12, 15, 16, 77, 79, 178
Eveningshade, Arkansas 168
Everett, Pvt. Riley (Southern) 27, 394n45
Everett, Boone County 223
Ewing, Capt. Charles (Northern) 129, 136
Ewing, Capt. James A. (Northern) 71
Ewing, Brig. Gen. Thomas Jr. (Northern) 58, 158, 160, 161, 170, 176, 293
exchange of POWs 157
executions 7, 49, 111, 119, 133, 134, 141, 155, 170, 171, 174, 303, 310, 313, 323, 330, 361, 369, 370, 383, 384, 391; *see also* circle of violence; death sentence
express wagon 215–6

Faber, Christopher 47
Fair Grove, Greene County 211
false alarms 47, 99–101, 106, 132, 133, 136, 142, 149, 192–3, 232, 248, 264, 285, 286, 291–2, 293, 331, 363, 378, 385
Fanny Ogden (vessel) 252, 366
Farley, Platte County 266–7, 331, 347
Farmer, Allen (Southern) 418n2
Farmer, Andrew (Northern) 146
Farmer, John (Southern) 361
Farmington, St. Francois County 74, 170
Farris, Capt. Seth C. (Southern) 178
Fayette, Howard County 214, 216, 242, 254; newspaper 214, 216, 222, 232, 361
Fear (Southern) 129
female prison in St. Louis 189, 203, 374
female prisoners 22, 23, 25, 55, 189, 203, 296–7, 299, 301, 352, 373–4
Ferman, Capt. F. W. (Northern) 124, 125
ferryboat 18, 100, 216, 224, 267, 292, *355*
Fickel, Annie (Southern) 54–5, 189, 296–7, 378, 415n22
Fickel, Joe (Southern) 54
Fielding, George (Southern) 263–4, 269
Fielding, Thomas (Southern) 269

Finley, George 44
Finnell, Abner (Southern) 418n2
Fire Prairie Creek, Jackson County 126, 286, 382
Fishing River, Ray County 147, 278, 279, 327, 328, 331, 338
Fisk, Brig. Gen. Clinton B. Fisk (Northern) 66–7, 213, 225, 226, 240, 242, 246, 261, 264, 266, 267, 274, 276, 308, 316, 324, 331, *337*; commander of District of North Missouri 149–50, 153, 159, 217, 243, 256, 259, 320, 324, 328, 331, 347, 388; commander of District of Northeast Missouri 117; commander of District of Southeast Missouri 75–6; Detective Terman's atrocities (late May–early June 1864) 213; hunter/killer team ordered 321; reply to Rosecrans regarding atrocities by Fisk's men (3 August 1864) 337; Thornton's insurgency (July 1864) 153, 323, 325, 329; warning of Price's invasion (23 June 1864) 159
Fitzgerald, Capt. William J. (Northern) 151, 263, 264, 265, 267, 268, 326, 329, 347
flags: Confederate flags 307, 326, 376; U.S. flags 61, 216, 257, 273, 307, 321, 380
Flanagan, Charles (Southern) 376
Flannagan, William C. (Southern) 259–60
Flannery, Ike (Southern) 373
Flannery, Miss Jennie (Southern) 373–4
Flat Creek, Pettis County 140
Flat River, St. Francois County 171
Floyd, Mr. 149
foot patrols 71–2, 127, 284, 285, 286, 287, 288, 295, 340, 381, 382, 388
foraging or forage 7, 18, 22, 31, 48, 77, 81, 90, 104, 129, 138, 140, 160, 194, 195, 216, 237, 351, 352, 373, 381, 384
Ford, Col. James H. (Northern) 64, 268, *288*, 294, 308, 312–8, 322–24, 325, 329, 331, 338, 354
Ford, Capt. L. A. (Northern) 338
Foreman, Capt. James (Northern) 118
Fornshill, Pvt. Moses (Southern) 88–9
Forsythe, Taney County 31, 208, 210
Fort Blair, Kansas 139
Fort Curtis, Balltown, Vernon County 203
Fort Gibson, Indian Nations 200, 202

Fort Leavenworth, Kansas 152, 153, 267, 283, 308, 314, 329, 338, 347
Fort Lincoln, near Bourbon County, Kansas 203
Fort Randall, South Dakota 184
Fort Scott, Kansas 31, 90, 98, 102, 104, 192, 198, 200, 202, 203, 204
Fort Smith, Arkansas 33, 104, 197
Foster, Capt. Melville U. (Northern) 363, 379, 380, 382
Fowkes, Capt. William E. (Northern) 253
Fox, Mr. (Northern) 343
Fox, Peter (Southern) 417n2
Francis, Capt. Lyon S. (Northern) 280
Frankford, Pike County 116
Franklin, Mr. (Southern) 418n2
Franklin and New Franklin, Howard County 216–7, 232, 250, 254
Franklin County 81, 82, 114, 175, 223
Frederick's Fork, Oregon County 12, 17
Fredericksburg, Ray County 314–6, 341, 343
"Free Stater" 212
"freebooters" 2; *see also* deserters; renegades
Freeman, Mrs. Martha 31
Freeman, Col. Thomas Roe (Southern) 10, 16, 393n5; operations in south-central Missouri in early months of 1864 12, 16–7, 21, 68, 75–6, 79, 96, 165, 387, 392; recruiting south of Arkansas border in spring and early summer 1864 154, 163, 167; returned to operations in south-central Missouri in August 1864 168
"French Dragoon" revolvers 294, *295*, 431n36
Fristoe, Col. Edward T. (Southern) 210–1
Frogg, Mr. (Southern, probably A. R. Frogg) 327
Frost, Capt. Griffin (Confederate POW and author) 27, 28, 85–9
Frost, Capt. L. M. "Matthew" (Southern) 260
Fuchs Bridge, Davis Creek, Lafayette County 380
Fulbright, Pvt. William W. (Southern) 94
Fuller, William (Northern) 226
Fulton, Callaway County 115, 219, 225; newspaper 115, 257, 258
furlough 70, 109–10; furloughed Union veterans abused hometown southerners 120, 121–2, 313; furloughed Union veter-

ans easy targets for guerrillas 55, 91, 132, 172, 243, 305, 306, 343

Gaines, Lewis 250
Gaines, Mr. (Southern) 370
Gainesville, Arkansas 78
Gamble, Provisional Missouri Governor Hamilton B. (Northern) 57, *58*, *59*, 387
Gamel, Mr. 174
Gann (Southern) 131–2
Gann, Benton 92–3, 94, 129
Gann, Oliver (Southern) 92–3, 129
Gannett, 1st Lt. Isaac (Northern) 186, 244–5
Garnett, Lewis (Southern) 44
Gasconade County 81, 82, 223, 224
Gasconade River, southeast Missouri 15
Gaugh, or Gaw, Bill (Southern) 147
Geary City, Kansas 41
Gee, Sgt. (Northern) 80
General Assembly of Missouri (legislative branch) 57, 58, 63–4
General Orders Number 11 32, 45, 48, 50, 58, 91, 124, 131, 206, 363, 378
General Orders Number 85 87
General Orders Number 107 62–3, 64, 217, 220, 222, 223, 228, 242, 258, 295–6, 303, 311, 313, 321, 326, 328, 335, 338, 339, 344, 345, 352, 353, 354, 355, 358, 359, 360, 366, 368, 371, 383–4, 385, 388; *see also* Missouri troops
General Orders Number 119 185
Gentry County 44, 273, 327
Gentryville, Gentry County 273
George, Nancy (Southern) 167
Georgia 210
German Americans 7, 74, 82, 114, 172, 223, 259, 299, 342, 352, 368, 379, 385
Germantown, Henry County 92, 93–4, 128
Gibler, E.: store, Franklin County 82
Gilbert, David (Northern) 324
Gilliam family (Southern) 373
Gilmore, Donald L. (historian) 140
Gilmore, James (Southern) 141
Gilmore, Mrs. Lizzie (Northern) 210, 211
Givens, Capt. Merrill (Northern) 270
Glasgow (vessel) 184
Glasgow, Howard County 101, 110, 159–60, 214, 232, 233, 238, 242, 243, 245, 248, 251, 252, 256, 257, 364, 366

Glaze, Capt. Henry S. (Northern) *217*, 218
Glover, Daniel T. (Northern) 45
Goddard, John (Northern) 82, 177–8, 399n35, 414n79
Goebel, Gert (Northern) 82–3
Golden City, Barton County 193
Gooch, Joseph (Southern) 238, 256
Goode, Lt. John R. (Southern) 190–191, 194, 195, 204
Goode, 1st Sgt. Robert (Northern) 311
Gooding, 2nd Lt. Albert L. (Northern) 128, 134
Goodwin, John C. G.: store, Cooper County 367
Goodwin's Mill, Monroe County 221
Goose Creek, Platte County 264
Goose Neck Bend of Platte River, Platte County 264, 306
Gordon, 2nd Lt. Carey H. (Northern) 275
Gordon, Lucretia (Southern) 347
Gordon, Capt. Silas "Cy" (Southern) 134, 152, 280, 332, 333, 344, 346–7, 349
Gosney, Mr. 276
Gosneyville, Clay County 322, 331, 338
Grady, Bob (Southern) 172, 175
Graham, Robert (Southern) 189
Graham, Holt County 44
Granby, Newton County 197
Grand River, northwest Missouri 312, 334, 344
Grand River, west-central Missouri 53, 103, 129, 131, 380
Grant, Samuel, and Mrs. Grant 176
Grant, Gen. Ulysses S. (Northern) 56, 359
Gratiot Street Military Prison (formerly McDowell Medical College) *24*, 25, 26, *85*, *185*, 186–9, 203, 242, 251, 271
Gravely, Col. Joseph J. (Northern) 196–7
Gray, Judge F. R. 125, 132
Green, Col. Clark H (Northern) 217, 219
"greenbacks" 83, 134, 222, 232, 279, 320
Greene, Asst. Adj. Gen. Oliver D. (Northern) 330
Greene County 27, 94–5, 106, 195, 209; Campbell Township 94; Clay Township 94
Greene County, Arkansas 70, 156, 158–9, 171, 172, 173
Greenfield, Dade County 98, 199
Green's Mills, Washington County 177
Greenton, Lafayette County 53, 54, 126, 284, 367, 378
Greenville, Clay County 275
Greenville, Wayne County 21

Greenwood, Bill (Southern) 384
"Greer," Mr. (Northern) 106
Gregg, Bill (Southern) 138
Gregg, J. Frank (Southern) 210, 354–5, 357, 391, 417n56
Gregory's Landing, Lewis County 118
Greiser, Henry 166
Griffith, Mr. 116
Grimes, Absalom (Southern) 185, 187
Grimes, Maj. John (Northern) 341, 342
Grinter G. N.: farm in Jackson County 294
Grosby, Pemiscot County 160
Grotjohn, Mr. 110, 418n7
Grubbville, Washington County 171
Grundy County 237–8, 275, 324
"Grundy County Militia" *see* Missouri troops, 30th Enrolled Missouri Militia
guerrilla logistics: battlefield acquisition to overcome shortages 295; sanctuary areas 65, 72
guerrilla tactics 96–9; abuse of women increased in 1864 69, 73, 76–7, 113, 132, 198, 221–2, 296–7, 298, 305, 335, 368, 372, 398n10; decoy enemies into ambush position 200, 254, 269, 294, *336*, 341; dispersing as a defense technique 52, 254; double back when followed 347; infiltrate past Union security at night 71, 72; masks, use of 142; mobile warfare 299, 311–2, 331–2, 333–6, 340–5, 359, 367, 377, 389, 390; moving through Union-controlled areas 96; returning to Missouri from the South each spring 66, 101–7; safe cracking 215, 217, 231, 259; superior intelligence network 63, 66, 75; torture 143, 236; using children 133, 135, 178, 351, 398n10; well-hidden camps *34*, 75; *see also* mutilation of the dead
guerrillas: embroidered guerrilla shirts *336*; incident or episodic nature of guerrilla warfare 3; influence of American Revolution as a precedent for using guerrilla warfare 7; meaning of "guerrilla" 1; motivations for guerrillas 7–8; uniforms 7
Guess, Hiram (Southern) *336*, 344
guides (voluntary and involuntary) 173, 210, 230, 355, 358
Guitar, Brig. Gen. Odon (Northern) 66, *121*, 177, *278*
Gum Slough (in "the Bootheel") 73

gunpowder 16, 88, 120, 141–2, 150
Guthrie, Capt. John H. (Southern) 155, 156, 158–9, 160, 410*n*2
G. W. Graham (vessel) 158

Hackberry Ridge, Andrew County 327
Hadley, Willard Francis (Southern) 134
Hale, Donald R. (historian) 141
Hale, Thomas 153
Hall, Col. George H. (Northern) 101, 231, 298
Hall, Lafayette (Southern) 369
Hall, Governor Willard P. (Northern) 58–9, 61–2, 213, 387
Halleck, Maj. Gen. Henry W. (Northern) 6, 123, *227*
Hallsville, Boone County 223, 243
Hambright family, Jackson County 287
Hamburg, Scott County 72
Hamilton, 1st Lt. Walter B. (Northern) 54
Hamilton, Caldwell County 278, 279
Hamlet, Jesse (Southern) 336
Hamner's Mill, Chariton County 253
Hancock, William (Southern) 223–4, 257–8
Hancock County, Illinois 120
Haney, Mrs. (Southern) 299
Hanly, Mr. (Southern) 209
Hannibal, Marion County 183, 259, 260; newspaper 251
Hannibal and St. Joseph Railroad, northern Missouri 235, 251, 318
Hansen, Pvt. Edward (diarist, Northern) 162
Hardeman, Dr. Glen O. (Northern) 366, 367
Hardesty, 1st Lt. William L. (Northern) 93–4
Hardin, or Harens, Miss Lizzie (Southern) 22, 394*n*36
Hardshell Baptist denomination 352
Harens, Mary, or Lizzie *see* Hardin, Mary Lizzie
Harpold, Pvt. Absalom (Southern) 277
Harris, Harrison "Doc" (Southern) 47
Harrison County 336
Harrisonville, Cass County 205–6, 286, 289, 363, 381
Hart, George (Northern) 170, 412*n*50
Hart, Joe (Southern) 148, 149
Hartle, Jefferson (Northern) 171
Hartville, Wright County 210–1

Haskins, Samuel C. (Northern) 209
Hastain, John (Northern) 207
Havana, Gentry County 327
Hay, John (Northern) 180
Hayes, G. M. (Northern) 160
Haynesville, Clay County 277, 321, 328
Hays, Pvt. Joseph (Northern) 125
Hays, Peter (Northern) 361
Hayward, Col. J. T. K. (Northern) 259, 260
Head, James (Northern) 239
Headlee, Capt. Samuel W. (Northern) 211
Hebard, Capt. William (Northern) 247–8, 249
Hebron Church, Macon County 245
Heinrichs, Maj. Gustav (Northern) 187
Helber, 1st Lt. Christian (Northern) 175
Hembree, 2nd Lt. Joel T. (Northern) 198–9, 200
Henderson, W. R. P. (Southern) 188, 415*n*19
Hendrick, Amelia (Northern) 141
Hendrick family, Miami Township, Saline County 141
Henry, 1st Lt. Brice (Northern) 195
Henry County 92–3, 94, 100, 103, 106, 125, 130, 136, 205, 207, 370, 375, 387; Bogart Township 103; Deepwater Township 92
Henslee, Capt. Murline C. (Northern) 352–3
Herder, Lt. Col. John N. (Northern) 75–6
Heren, Judge William (Northern) 152
Hermann, Gasconade County 82, 115, 224, 258, 399–400*n*36
Hermitage, Hickory County 91
Herold, George (Southern) 92–3, 94
Herring, Capt. George L. (Northern) 164
Hickman, William (Southern) 112
Hickman Mills, Jackson County 283, 286
Hickory County 91, 93, 207
Hickory Creek, Allen County, Kansas 31
Hickory Hill, Miller County 143
Hicks, Captain (Northern) 156, 410*n*5
High Point, Moniteau County 368
Highley, Bob (Southern) 175
Highley, John (Southern) 68, 74
Hightown, Mr. 90
Hildebrand, Sam (Southern) 68,
69, 73, 78, 154, 165, 387, 391–2; August and early September 1864 174–5; early weeks of 1864 18; June 1864 156, 159–60; July 1864 170–1, 172, 173; spring 1864 70, 74–5
Hill, James N., "Pony" (Southern) 93, 400–1*n*9
Hill, Capt. Jasper C. (Southern) 187
Hill, Dr. William H. 31
Hill, Woot (Southern) *336*
Hillard, Maj. Hiram (Northern) 347
Hiller, Maj. Hiram M. (Northern) 155, *160*
Hill's Landing, Carroll County 44, 343
Hillsboro, Jefferson County 174
Hinches, Crawford County 178
Hindman Maj. Gen. Thomas C. (Southern) 163
Hindricks, Mrs. 141
Hines, William (Southern) 112, 391; *see also* Hines brothers
Hines brothers (Southern) 391
Hinkson Creek, Boone County 114
Hinton, Otho (Southern) 53, 124
Hite, Reverend A. T. 110
Hoffman, Col. William (Northern) 185
Holcomb, E. A. (Northern) 214
Holcomb Island, St. Francis River 18
Holden, Johnson County 130, 136, 285, 287, 356, 363, 369, 373, 375, 378, 380, 381, 382, 383
Holder, Mancil (Southern) 163
Holland, Dr. Willis S. (Northern) 206
Holley, John (Northern) 145
Holloway, Capt. (Southern) 343
Holmes, Lawson (Northern) 307
Holmes, Maj. Gen. Theophilus (Southern) 59
Holt County 27, 43–4, 145, 308, 345
Holtzclaw, Clifton D. (Southern) 37, 109, 122, 212, 214, 222, 229, 232, 242, 245, 248, 252, 364, 365, 387; Bill Jackson's band joins Holtzclaw's band (19–28 July 1864) 239; Butler house fight in Chariton County (30 July 1864) 239–40; defeat forks of Chariton River (about 30–31 August 1864) 256; hiding in Linn County (winter of 1863–1864) 37, 45, 109; Howard County operations (1–9 July 1864) 216–8, 222; interview with Edwin Price (late July 1864) 240–1; Keytesville, Chariton County raid (3 June 1864) 214; Laclede, Linn County,

raid (18 June 1864), and pursuit to Chariton County 215–6; Lindley, Grundy County, raid (22 July 1864) 237–9; operations in Linn and Chariton Counties (8–11 April 1864) 112, 214; with Anderson and Stewart in Battle Rawlin's Lane, Howard County (28 August 1864) 254–5; with Tom Todd in Battle of Dripping Springs (15 and 16 August 1864) 248–9
Honey Creek, Johnson County 364, 375
Hopkins, Billy F. (Southern) 133, 135
Hopkins, Richard (Southern) 133, 135
Horn, Lt. Elisha (Northern) 364
Hornersville, Dunklin County 72
Horse Creek, Dade and Cedar Counties 98, 100, 199, 200
Horse Island, St. Francis River 73
Houston, Texas County 9–10, 12, 15, 17
"Houts' Guerrillas" of Illinois (Southern) 188
Houx, Fanny (Southern) 352
Houx family (Southern) 352
Howard County 37, 101, 106, 109, 110, 120, 140, 144, 213, 214, 216, 217, 218, 219, 222, 223, 229, 231 232, 233, 238, 239, 240, 242, 243, 244, 245, 248, 249, 253, 255, 258, 279, 293, 319, 327, 333, 355, 356, 364, 365, 367, 388; newspaper 116; Richmond Township 113
Howard County Poor Farm 216
Howell County 12, 16, 168
Hudson, John W. (Northern) 335
Hughes, Capt. Harry Horatio (Southern) 260, 425n68
Huiskamp, Capt. Herman J. (Northern) 78
Hull, Col. Edwin B. (Southern) *177*, 413–4n77
Humbard, Ab (Southern) 190, 193
Hunnewell, Shelby County 118
Hunt, Charles L. (Southern) 180, 182
Hunt, Elijah 94
Hunt, Maj. Robert H. (Northern) 267
Hunter, 1st Lt. Malcolm (Northern) 192, 195, 196, 198
Hunter, Capt. Samuel A. (Northern) 145
Hunter, Capt. William T. (Northern) 224–5, 258
"hunter/killer" teams (Northern) 127, 321
Huntress No. 58 (vessel, tinclad) 157–8

Huntsville, Randolph County 230–1, 236, 247, 252
Hurst, Pvt. (Northern) 174
Hurt, Martin C. 253
Hurt, Moses (Southern) 418n2
Hutchings, Pvt. Smith, and Pvt. John (Northern) 341
Hutchinson, James S. 298
Hutchinson, Lindsay (Southern) 356, 369, 370–1, 373, 375, 381
Hutchinson, Martha 298
Huzza Creek, Crawford County 178
Hynes, Lt. Col. Dennis J. (Northern) 233

Iatan (vessel) 233
Illinois 70, 73, 74, 115–6, 122, 173, 187, 225, 378–9; raid by Missouri Federal troops on Prairie du Rocher, Randolph County (6 April 1864) 74
Illinois officials 116–7
Illinois troops (Northern) 61, 317, 337; 13th Illinois Cavalry Regiment 88; 17th Illinois Cavalry Regiment 75, 233–4, 242, 248–9, 251, 257, 316, 324, 329, 338, 346, 347, 348; 135th Illinois Infantry Regiment 170; 138th Illinois Infantry Regiment 331
Imperial (vessel) 183
Independence, Jackson County 55, 132–3, 135, 148, 273, 294, 351, 354, 357, 365, 371
Indian Creek, Bourbon County, Kansas 203
Indian Creek, Newton County 98
Indian Creek, Stone County 108
Indian Creek, Washington County 177
Indian Nations (present day Oklahoma) 40, 98, 101, 104, 190
Indian Territory *see* Indian Nations
Indiana 103, 131, 187, 192, 222
Indians (Native Americans) 53, 339, 345
informants 17, 22, 77, 120, 124, 165, 177, 189, 269, 275, 286, 307, 352, 362, 363, 365, 367
Ingersoll, Joseph (Northern) 118
Ingram, or Ingraham, Capt. (Southern) 37, 395n4
Inman, John (Southern) 10
insurgency 43, 127, 151, 204, 269, 280, 293, 303, 304, 323, 324, 325, 329, 331, 339, 347, 349, 350, 351, 354, 356, 357, 358, 390
insurrection *see* insurgency
Iowa 236–7, 268
Iowa troops (Northern) 345; 1st Iowa Cavalry Regiment 242, 248, 249, 251–2, 316, 324,

327, 344; 7th Iowa Infantry Regiment 145; 37th Iowa Infantry Regiment 25
Ireland 346
"Iron Brigade" *see* Shelby's brigade
Iron County 21, 75, 78, 161, 162, 170, 172, 174
Iron Mountain Railroad, southeast Missouri 73, 81, 170
Irvin, Green (Southern) 110
Island No. 8, Mississippi River 158

Jackman, Col. Sidney D. (Southern) 37, 99–101, 109, 142, 208, 219, 401n27
Jack's Fork Creek, Shannon County 81
Jackson (Northern, Houx family slave) 352
Jackson, Bill S. (Southern) 239, 252, 365, 366, 367, 368, 369, 370
Jackson, Governor Claiborne F. 58, 239, 365
Jackson, Jim (Southern) 238, 239, 248, 252–3, 256, 391
Jackson, Mr. (Southern) 204
Jackson brothers (Southern) 176
Jackson County, Blue Township 45, 48, 49, 50, 103, 124, 126, 127, 128, 132, 133, 137, 143, 150, 273, 279, 281, 283, 286, 287, 288, 289, 291, 292, 293, 294, 312, 331, 337, 338, 350, 351, 352, 354, 356, 357, 359, 362, 363, 365, 369, 377, 381, 382, 382–3, 387
Jackson County Poor House 294
Jacksonport, Arkansas 81, 161, 162
jail (local) 116, 145–6, 151, 175 209, 226, 238, 270, 278–9, 338, 346
James, Jesse, and Frank (Southern) *147*, 273, 276, 344
James Bayou, Mississippi County 158
Jamison, James A. (Southern) 88, 165
Jarrett, John (Southern) 138
Jasper County 49, 90, 100, 102, 105, 107, 190, 192, 193, 195, 196–7, 200
jayhawkers 2, 7, 33, 41, 43, 45, 52–3, 91, 145, 153, 244, 262, 272, 313–4, 345, 390
"J. B" (Northern spy) 12
Jeans, Col. Beal G. (Southern) 127, 128
Jefferson Barracks, St. Louis County 86, 188
Jefferson City, Cole County 47, 57, 65, 83, 94, 100, 142, 143, 180, 189, 220, 244, 246, 256, 303, 370, 373, 383

Index

Jefferson City *State Times* newspaper 220
Jefferson County 73, 170, 171–2, 173–4; Plattin Township 174
Jelkyll, Capt. Ross (Northern) 170
Jenkins, Judge Clyde Lee (historian) 302
Jennings, Henry C. (Southern) 417*n*2
Jenson, Charles (Northern) 418*n*6
Jersey County, Illlinois 188
Johns, Capt. Abijah (Northern) 21, 75, 77–8
Johnson, Capt. Daniel W. (Northern) 54
Johnson, Capt. David (Southern) 150
Johnson, James A. (Southern) 140
Johnson, Mr. (Northern) 206–7
Johnson, Col. Rector (Southern) 196–7
Johnson County 51, 54, 55, 64, 99, 103, 105, 106, 128–31, 132, 133, '36, 137, 234, 249, 281, 283, 284, 285, 287, 288, 289, 290, 291, 292, 296, 297, 298, 299, 353, 355, 356, 362, 363, 364, 365, 369, 373, 375, 378, 380–1, 382–3
Johnston, Maj. Albert V. E. (Northern) 260
Johnston, Robert (Northern) 260
Johnstown, Bates County 130
Jones, Capt. A. D. (Southern) 92
Jones, G. Byron (Southern) 43
Jones, John H. 215
Jones, Tazewell (Southern) 418*n*2
Jones, William (Northern) 219
Jones Ferry, St. Francis River, Dunklin County 18
Joslyn, Col. John J. (Northern) 76
Judd, Mr. (Northern) 15

Kameyer, John (Northern) 380
Kansas 104, 110, 131, 134, 149, 192, 206, 262, 272, 286, 288–9, 293, 296, 305, 308, 339, 345, 370
Kansas City, Jackson County 45, 65, 135, 203, 204, 252, 268, 279, 280, 284, 286, 287, 289, 293, 306, 308, 317, 338, 372; newspaper 52, 125, 128, 133, 135, 152, 153, 160, 192, 198, 203–4, 258, 283, 286, 288, 293, 295, 306, 372
Kansas/Missouri border conflict of 1850s 8, 212, 363
Kansas troops 2, 57, 91, 104, 226, 329, 337; "Kansas First Guerrillas" (Southern) 297; 5th Kansas Cavalry Regiment (Northern) 31, 33, 288–9; 6th Kansas Cavalry Regiment (Northern) 29, 50, 55, 200; 7th Kansas Cavalry Regiment (Northern) 116–7, 175–6, 186, 225, 244, 389, 403–4*n*24, 420*n*37; 9th Kansas Cavalry Regiment (Northern) 50, 53; 10th Kansas Infantry Regiment (Northern) 27, 83, 86, 87–8, 157–9, 186–7, 400*n*37; 11th Kansas Cavalry Regiment (Northern) 45, 52–3, 288–9; 14th Kansas Cavalry Regiment (Northern) 145; 15th Kansas Cavalry Regiment (Northern) 202, 208, 267, 288–9, 308 310, 313, 363; 16th Kansas Cavalry Regiment (Northern) 151, 263, 264, 265, 267, 305, 308, 313, 326, 329, 347
Kavanaugh, Cortez (Southern) 132
Kearney, Clay County *see* Centerville
Keaton, Mr. E. 299
Keetsville, Barry County 105
Kelley, 1st Lt. R. (Northern) 21
Kelly, Maj. George W. (Northern) 375
Kelly, Mike (Northern) 167
Kelso, Capt. John R. (Northern) 108, 191, 196–7
Kelton, Pvt. F. L. (Northern) 15
Kemper, Capt. William B. (Northern) *145*, 151, 277–8
Kempinsky, 1st Lt. Abraham (Northern) 257
Kenner, John H. (Northern) 73
Kennett, Dunklin County 161
Kentucky 37, 118, 244, 334
Kerrick, Stephen (Southern) 27
Kessinger, 1st Lt. William (Northern) 279, 289, 293
Keytesville, Chariton County 214, 239, 240
Kidder, Caldwell County 270, 323
"kill list" 117, 225, 266
Kincaid, or Kindard, Capt. (Southern) 260
Kincaid, Col. George W. (Northern) 25
Kincaid, Sgt. John (Northern) 54
Kindrick, William (Northern) 116
King, Frank (Southern) 167
King, Kate (Southern) 138
King, Judge Richard M. (Northern) 136, 137, 140
King, Samuel (Southern) 175, 413*n*72
Kingston, Caldwell County 277, 278, 320, 322, 345
Kingsville, Johnson County 285–6
Kirby Smith, Lt. Gen. Edmund (Southern) 67, 325–6
Kirker, John (Northern) 335

Kishbaum, 2nd Lt. William (Northern) 259–60
Kitchen, Andrew J. "Dick" (Southern) 81, 164, 165, 168
Kitchen, Col. Solomon G. (Southern) 70, 78, 79, 157, 158
Knapp, 2nd Lt. Ebenezer (Northern) 233–4
Knight, William 372
Knights of the Golden Circle (KGC) *see* Order of American Knights (OAK)
Knob Noster, Johnson County 132, 284–5, 290, 292, 353, 381
Knox County 121–2, 260–1; Colony Township 122
Krohn, Christian (Northern) 384
Kuecker, Wilham (Northern) 380
Kuntz, Mr. 143

LaBelle, Lewis County 117–8
Laclede, Linn County 112, 214, 215–6
Laclede County 16, 31, 33, 122, 210, 211
Lafayette County 44, 51, 52, 96, 103, 124–5, 126, 127, 128–31, 132, 134, 136, 137, 143, 146, 148, 189, 210, 232, 236, 246, 247, 279, 281, 283, 286, 287–8, 291, 292, 293, 296, 297, 299, 311, 336, 339, 349, 350, 351, 352, 353, 354–5, 357, 358–9, 361, 362, 363, 365, 367, 368, 369, 372, 375–6, 377, 378, 381, 382, 383, 384, 385, 387, 391; Clay Township 52; Davis Township 125, 132; Freedom Township 379–80; Lexington Township 132; Washington Township 129, 356
LaGrange, Lewis County 259; *National American* newspaper 120
Lakenan, Shelby County 235, 341
Lamar, Barton County 90, 105, 107, 198–9, 201
Lamb, William (Southern) 16
Lamine, or LaMine, Cooper County 369
LaMine bridge, Cooper County 362
Lancaster, Capt. Albert (Northern) 262
Lane, Kansas Senator James (Northern) 319
Lane's Prairie, Maries County 83–4
Lanier, Joseph, or James (Southern) 185, 270–1
Latham, Mr. 335
Lavelle, Lt. Robert S. (Southern) 187, 415*n*16
Lawrence, Kansas 2, 47, 53, 128; newspaper 286; raid (21

August 1863) 57, 58, 61, 63, 126, 127, 128, 129, 134, 137, 141, 288
Lawrence County 29, 31, 90, 95, 105, 190, 192, 195, 209
Lawson's Station, Washington County 170
Lawther, Col. Robert (Southern) 211
Lazear, Lt. Col. Bazel F. (Northern) 52, 368, 369, 374, 376-7, 379, 380
Lea's Store, Crawford County 178
Leavenworth, Kansas 184, 232, 307, 338, 346, 349; *see also* Fort Leavenworth, Kansas
Lebanon, Laclede County 16, 17, 31, 32, 79, 210; newspaper 211
LeClair, Capt. Francis (Northern) 338
Lee County, Iowa 120
Leeper, Capt. William T. (Northern) 20, 21, 172
Leesville, Henry County 207
Lefaucheux pin-fire revolvers *see* "French Dragoon" revolvers
Lefever, 1st Lt. William C. (Northern) 143
Lenox, Bill (Southern) 164, 165, 168
Leonard, Capt. Charles (Northern) 298
Leonard, Leverett (Northern) 298
Leonard, Nathaniel (Northern) 298
Leonard, Maj. Reeves (Northern) 242, 249-*250*, 253, 243
Lepp, Matthias 170, 171-2
Lewis, Benjamin W. (Northern) 242
Lewis, Lt. David M. (Northern) 215-6
Lewis, John 177
Lewis, John T. (Southern) 110
Lewis, Mr. 81
Lewis, Solomon (Southern) 110
Lewis, Lt. William (Northern) 279
Lewis County 117, 122
Lewis families (two), Jackson County (Northern) 132
Lexington, Lafayette County 51, 52, 54, 55, 65, 103, 124, 126, 132, 136, 189, 279, 286, 287, 289, 292, 293, 296, 297, 316, 323, 338, 348, 371, 373, 374-5, 376, 378; newspaper 286, 287, 295-7, 351
Liberty, Clay County 45, 47, 277, 313-4, 317, 357; newspaper 47, 275, 313, 328, 339, 340, 341
Liberty School, Gentryville 273
Lincoln, President Abraham (Northern) 217; intervenes to determine Missouri overall commander 56; intervenes to mitigate Missouri Union military excesses 6, 56, 88, 180, 189, 217, 291, 378; intervenes to reduce military tribunal sentences in Missouri 6, 88, 189, 378; national election November 1864
Lincoln County 37, 116, 229, 258-9
Lindley, Grundy County 237-83
lines of communication 64, 73, 362
Linn County 36, 45, 109, 112, 121-2, 214, 215-6, 229, 238, 240, 252, 279; history of 1882 122
Linneus, Linn County 37, 45, 112
Little, Capt. Joseph H. (Northern) 92-3
Little, Thomas (Southern) 137
Little Beaver Creek, Phelps County 79
Little Blue River, Jackson County 284, 294
Little Bourbouse Creek, Gasconade and Franklin Counties 82
"Little Dixie" 218, 219, 220, 229
Little Piney Creek (and village), Phelps County 9, 80
Little River, southeast Missouri 69, 157
Little Rock, Arkansas 27, 28
Little Santa Fe, Jackson County 131
Live Oak (vessel) 293
Livingston, Maj. Thomas R. (Southern) 107, 192, 193, 194, 199
Livingston, William Jackson (Southern) 183
Livingston County 120, 145, 146, 270, 275, 318, 321, 324, 329
Lone Elm Prairie, Cooper County 385
Lone Jack, Jackson County 131, 292
Long, Capt. (Southern) 77
Long, Lawrence D. (Northern) 240
Long, Peyton (Southern) 147, 273
Long, Capt. William (Northern) 360
Long family, Bates County 92
Longacre, Mrs. (Southern) 285-6
Longwood, Pettis County 298
lookouts *see* pickets
"Lost Cause" movement (1870s and after) 425*n*6
Louisiana 349, 388
Louisiana, Pike County 116, 226; newspaper 226
Louisville, Kentucky 180
Love, Lt. Col. Joseph B. (Southern) 17
Lowe, D. I. 14
Lower, Henry 41
loyalty oath *see* oath of allegiance
Luthy, 1st Lt. Franklin (Northern) 152
Lynch's Slave Market, St. Louis *see* Myrtle Street Military Prison
Lyon County, Kansas 230

Macon City, Macon County 37, 111, 114, 213, 299
Macon County 36, 246, 251, 299
Macy, Joe (Southern) 312
Madison, Indiana 184
Madison County 73, 170, 171, 172
Magruder, Robert (Southern) 385
Mahan, Dr. David P. 142
mail, U.S. 16, 132, 136, 137, 269, 299, 361; *see also* Rebel mail network, secret
Majors, Capt. Elliott D. (Southern) 218, 247
malaria 188-9
Mallery, Sgt. James P. (diarist) 198
Mallory, Edward (Southern) 259-60, 424-5*n*66
Mammoth Springs, Arkansas 167, 168
Mandeville, Carroll County 319, 321, 324
Manly, Jacker (Northern) 103
Manwaring, Capt. Charles C. (Northern) 82
Marais des Cygnes River, southwest Missouri 206, 208
Marble Hill (present day village) *see* Dallas, Bollinger County
Marchbanks, Bob (Southern) 204
Marchbanks, Capt. William (Southern) 101, 102-3, 132, 190, 195, 197-8, 202, 204, 205, 206
Marcy, Inspector General Randolph B. (Northern) 62
Maries County 81, 83, 167, 176-7
Marion, General Francis ("Swamp Fox") 7
Marion County 117, 183, 187, 225, 259, 260; Warner Township 259
Marmaduke, Brig. Gen. John S. (Southern) 27, 63, 106, 110, 309; southwest Missouri raid, January 1863 63
Marr, 2nd Lt. Daniel V. (Northern) 375

Marshall, John T. (Southern) 418
Marshall, Sam (Northern) 150
Marshall, Saline County 47, 301, 359, 367, 370, 376
Marshall, Texas 160, 180
Marshfield, Webster County 192
Martin, Dr. James M. (Northern) 257
Martin, William (Southern) 141
Martin's Mill, Buchanan County 348
Martinsburg, Ripley County 21
Mary E. Forsyth (vessel) 185
Maryland 120
masks, use of *see* guerrilla tactics
Mason, Jesse (Northern) 240
masonic distress signal 320
Massachusetts 244
massacre 2
Mathews, James (Pulaski County, Northern) 81
Mathews, James T. (Jefferson County, Southern) 173
Matlack, Maj. Lucius C. (Northern) 242, 251, 252
Matthews, William (Northern) 302
Maupin, Lt. Col. Amos (Northern) 176
Maupin, James M. (Northern) 342
Maupin, John (Southern) 335
Maupin, Mr. (Southern) 118
Maxwell, Thomas (Northern) 80–1
Mayfield, Sallie, and Jennie (Southern) 203
Mayo, William H. (Northern) 142, 298–9
Mayview (present day village), Lafayette County 356, 373
McBride, Capt. (Northern) 207
McCalister, Thomas (Southern) 118
McCamey, Dr. M. C. (Southern) 278
McCarty, "old man" (Northern) 16
McCorkle, John (Southern, author) 98, 130, 295, 378–9
McCray, Col. Thomas H. (Southern) 155, 157
McCulloch, Capt. (Southern) 12
McCullough, Capt. Edward (Southern) 192, 194
McCullough, Capt. George W. (Northern) 338
McCully, John (Southern) 261
McCully, Mike (Southern) 261, 425n73
McDaniel, Ambrose (Southern) 328
McDaniel, Gabe (Southern) 107
McDaniel, Pvt. John H. (Southern) 88

McDermott, Maj. John (Northern) 248, 249, 251–2
McDonald, Capt. James (Northern) 149
McDonald, Mr. (Northern) 418n6
McDonald County 29, 100, 103, 104, 190, 192, 194, 195–7, 202
McDowell, Dr. Joseph (Southern) 25, 26, 85; *see also* Gratiot Street Military Prison
McElhannon, 2nd Lt. C. C. (Northern) 95
McElree's Ford, Carroll County *see* Simpson's Ford
McFadden, Rice (Southern) 122
McFerran, Col. James (Northern) 52, 136–7, 279, 286, 287–8, 289, 290, 295–6, 370
McGee, Blair, and Daniel (Southern) 163
McGee, 1st Sgt. David (Northern) 207
McGee, Lt. (Southern) 108
McGee, Thomas J. (Southern) 163
McGee, Wayne County 163
McGee's Grove, Cooper County 48
McGuire, Mr. G 292
McKee, Robert (Southern) 120
McKown, 2nd Lt. Isaac (Northern) 277
McMurry, Thomas A. (Southern) 122
McNeil, Brig. Gen. John (Northern) 70
McReynolds, Capt. Samuel H. B. (Northern) 338
McSpadden, Capt. James (Southern) 94
McVeigh, Capt. (Southern) 159
McWilliams, 1st Lt. George W. (Northern) 261
Meador, Capt. James D. (Northern) 351
Meador, T. M. (Southern) 187, 415n16
Meadows, Mr. (Southern) 328
Meloy, David (Northern) 78–9
Melville, Dade County 29, 199–200
Memphis, Tennessee 117
Meramec Ironworks, Phelps County *168*
Meramec River, southeast Missouri 178
Mercer County 324
Meredith, Capt. John D. (Northern) 260
Meredith, Capt. William (Northern) 373
Methodist Episcopal Church South denomination 61, 122
Mexican spurs 256
Mexican War (1846–1848) 212
Mexico, Audrain County 219, 220, 227, 244–5, 247, 256

Meyers, Capt. H (Northern) 362
Miami, Saline County 299, 301, 355, 366
Miami Creek, Bates County 206
Middle Grove, Monroe County 235, 246–7, 253, 367
Middlebrook, Iron County 172
Milan, Sullivan County 238
Miles Point, Carroll County 280, 343
Milks, Capt. Henry B. (Northern) 74, 174
mill, grist 35, 40, 73, 149, 155, *166*, 167, 171m, 174, 177, 206, 221, 253, 259, *271*, 283, 322, 348
Mill Creek, Stone County 108
Mill #1, Big Piney River, Texas County 167
Miller, 1st Lt. Benton (Northern) 376
Miller, Circuit Court Judge George W. 48
Miller, Henry 216
Miller, Hugh W. 48, 141
Miller, Mr. (Northern) 114–5
Miller County 143, 144, 167, 297, 302–3, 356–7, 360, 373, 383–4; history of 1971 302
Millersville, Cape Girardeau County 171
Milton, Randolph County 235
Minnehaha (vessel) 233
Minnesota 168
Minnesota troops (Northern) 61; 7th Minnesota Infantry Regiment 87; 9th Minnesota Infantry Regiment 64; 10th Minnesota Infantry Regiment 87
Minor, Blake 113
Mirabile, Caldwell County 320, 322, 345
Mississippi 134
Mississippi County 20, 68, 69, 71, 156, 158
Mississippi County, Arkansas 70, 158–9
Mississippi River 22, 68–9, 73, 86, 115, 116, 157, 173, 184, 185, 188, 227, 362, 388
Missouri Central Railroad, southeast Missouri 164, 176
Missouri City, Clay County 45, 47, 338
Missouri State Archives 94, 134
Missouri State Penitentiary, Jefferson City 189, 256, 368, 378
Missouri Troops, Northern: Northern "regular" cavalry units; 1st Missouri Cavalry Regiment 70, 76, 155, 157–9, 183; 2nd Missouri Cavalry Regiment ("Merrill's Horse") 45, 243; 3rd Missouri Cavalry Regiment 166; 4th Missouri Cavalry Regiment 187; 6th Missouri Cavalry Regiment

78, 158, 162, 173–4, 211; 11th Missouri Cavalry Regiment 80, 175, 176; 13th Missouri Cavalry Regiment 275; 15th Missouri Cavalry Regiment 194, 195, 199–200, 210; 16th Missouri Cavalry Regiment 194, 210, 211

Missouri Troops, Northern artillery units: 2nd Missouri Light Artillery Regiment 70, 162

Missouri Troops, Northern citizen guards (also called PEMM companies; spring 1864 through about spring 1865) 63, 103, 129, 130–1, 135, 136, 137, 147, 160, 207, 211, 213, 235, 283, 284, 290, 292, 295–6, 299, 303, 322, 326, 328, 335, 338, 339, 344; "Carroll County EMM" 343; "Cass County EMM" 363; "Chariton County Citizen Guards" 256; "Clinton County Militia" 338; "Linn County Citizen Guards" 279; "Livingston County Militia" 270, 344; "Luthy's Platte County Militia" 279

Missouri Troops, Northern Enrolled Missouri Militia (EMM) infantry regiments (often called by county of origin) 7, 57, 63, 115, 117, 164, 167, 204, 205, 235, 243, 283, 318, 322, 344; 25th EMM 259; 26th EMM 34, 402n50; 27th EMM 259; 30th EMM 237, 238, 324, 329; 31st EMM (also called "Gentry County Militia") 275, 276, 339; 32nd EMM 178; 33rd EMM 74, 270, 277, 278, 319, 322; 34th EMM 82; 35th EMM 113, 230, 239, 253; 38th EMM (also called "Railroad Regiment") 235 259; 39th EMM 151, 152, 308, 326, 346; 40th EMM 283, 284; 42nd EMM 384; 43rd EMM 361, 375; 46th EMM 111, 217, 233–4, 236, 247; 47th EMM 78–9, 360; 48th EMM 274, 276, 340, 341; 49th EMM 226; 50th EMM 260–1; 51st EMM 310, 316–7, 336, 338, 341, 343; 52nd EMM 142, 298, 299, 369; 53rd EMM 259, 260; 54th EMM 78–9; 56th EMM 18; 58th EMM 145; 60th EMM 99, 205, 206, 207, 253; 61st EMM 221, 245, 248–9; 63rd EMM 82, 178; 65th EMM 44, 119, 146, 280, 322, 324, 334, 385; 67th EMM 257; 68th EMM 170, 175; 69th EMM 259–60, 261; 70th EMM 118; 71st EMM 283, 366, 379–80; 72nd EMM 209; 73rd EMM 33, 210; 76th EMM 193, 194, 195, 402n43, 51, 55; 77th EMM 283, 351; 79th EMM 71, 158; 81st EMM ("Paw Paw" militia) 43, 262–3, 272, 304, 327, 345; 82nd EMM ("Paw Paw" militia) 43, 45, 47, 149, 150, 204, 262–3, 267, 268, 272, 277, 280, 304–5, 306, 308–10, 313–4, 316, 326, 328, 329–30, 331, 336, 338, 339, 349, 390; 87th EMM 149, 263–4, 272, 326, 327, 426n22; 88th EMM 328; 89th EMM 274, 275–6, 320, 321, 322

Missouri Troops, Northern home guards (1861 through early 1862) 210

Missouri Troops, Northern Missouri State Militia (MSM) units (cavalry and infantry active duty troops) 57, 343; 1st Cavalry Regiment MSM 52, 53, 55, 92, 93–4, 124–5, 127, 129, 130–1, 132, 133, 136, 279, 281, 284, 285–6, 287–8, 289, 290, 293, 295–7, 299, 321, 359–60, 365–6, 367, 368, 369, 370, 373, 376, 377, 381; 2nd Cavalry Battalion MSM 283; 2nd Cavalry Regiment MSM 18, 20, 70, 71, 72, 73, 155, 156, 157–9, 160; 3rd Cavalry Regiment MSM 18, 20, 21, 68, 74, 75, 76, 77, 78, 158–9, 162, 163, 164, 172, 173, 174–5, 224, 244, 248–9, 253, 258, 280; 4th Cavalry Regiment MSM 54, 55, 101, 136, 141, 142, 143, 145, 231–2, 249, 254–5, 283, 297, 298, 299, 301, 303, 356, 375, 381, 383; 5th Cavalry Regiment MSM (old) 384; 5th Cavalry Regiment MSM 10, 13, 14, 15, 16, 17, 33, 80, 164, 165–6, 167, 183, 313; 6th Cavalry Regiment MSM 131–2, 199–200, 274, 324, 327, 328, 329, 331, 337, 338, 339, 340; 7th Cavalry Regiment MSM 91, 93, 136, 137, 140, 141, 281, 285, 292, 297, 312, 316, 343, 348, 352–3, 356, 362, 363, 364, 365, 366, 369, 370, 373, 375–6, 380–1, 382, 383; 8th Cavalry Regiment MSM 17, 31, 33, 79, 95, 107–8, 190, 192, 194, 195, 196–7, 207, 208, 209; 9th Cavalry Regiment MSM 36–7, 110, 112, 145, 151, 213, 214, 216, 220, 222–3, 224, 231, 242, 247, 248–9, 250, 253, 254, 258, 269, 270, 275, 277–8, 299, 308, 318, 329, 340; 1st Infantry Regiment MSM 76, 82, 157–9, 170, 399n34

Missouri Troops, Northern Provisional Enrolled Missouri Militia (PEMM) infantry regiments (1863, some portions used through 1864): 1st PEMM Infantry Regiment 110; 2nd PEMM Infantry Regiment 260; 4th PEMM Infantry Regiment 274, 324; 5th PEMM Infantry Regiment 54; 6th PEMM Infantry Regiment 194, 209, 210; 7th PEMM Infantry Regiment 102, 103, 105, 107, 194, 195, 198, 200, 210, 402n43, 50, 51, 55

Missouri Troops, Northern "regular" infantry units: 7th Missouri Infantry Regiment 63; 18th Missouri Infantry Regiment 112, 121–2, 306, 389; 21st Missouri Infantry Regiment 120, 389; 23rd Missouri Infantry Regiment 36; 25th Missouri Infantry Regiment 146, 306; 26th Missouri Infantry Regiment 176; 39th Missouri Infantry Regiment 260; 44th Missouri Infantry Regiment 316; 47th Missouri Infantry Regiment 162, 175; 48th Missouri Infantry Regiment 142

Missouri Troops, Southern: Missouri State Guard (MSG) 1, 6, 37, 73, 102, 165, 179, 199, 219, 240

Missouri Troops, Southern cavalry units: Clardy's Cavalry Battalion 175; 3rd Missouri Cavalry Battalion 94; "Elliott's Guerrillas" (or "Elliott's Scouts," originally from Company I of 5th Missouri Cavalry Regiment of Shelby's Brigade, and later 9th Missouri Cavalry) 188; Freeman's Cavalry Regiment 10, 17; 1st Missouri Cavalry Regiment 88, 187, 347; 2nd Missouri Cavalry Regiment 34, 50; 5th Missouri Cavalry Regiment 72, 188; 7th Missouri Cavalry Regiment (also called "10th Regiment") 157; 10th Missouri Cavalry Regiment 187, 211; 12th Missouri Cavalry Regiment (also called "Jackson County Cavalry Regiment") 127, 354

Missouri Troops, Southern infantry units: Pindall's Sharpshooter Battalion 143, 302; 2nd Missouri Infantry Regiment 72; 3rd Missouri

Infantry Regiment 277; 7th Missouri Infantry Regiment 187; 10th Missouri Infantry Regiment 165; 11th Missouri Infantry Regiment 191, 195; 21st Missouri Infantry Regiment 120
Missouri Troops, Southern regiments not specified as cavalry or infantry: 4th Missouri Regiment 27; 7th Missouri Regiment 187; 10th Missouri Regiment 27
Mitchell, Mary, and Caroline 334–5
Mitchell, Mrs. George B. (Northern) 305
Mitchell, Maj. William B. (Northern) 199–200
Mitzell, Peter (Northern) 385
mob action 18, 20
mobile warfare 297, 299, 362; *see also* static defense
Mockbee, Pvt. Thomas (Northern) 55, 397*n*44
Molder, Judge Haly W., and Mrs. 69
Monaghan, James (editor) 117
Moniteau County 66, 101, 141–2, 297, 352, 361, 362, 364, 365, 368, 377, 383; High Point Township 361, 368
Monroe County 113, 218, 219–20, 229, 235, 246–7, 253, 260, 364, 367, 385
Monroe County Poor Farm 118, 391
Montana Territory 179, 184
Montevallo, Vernon County 198, 202, 203
Montgomery, Capt. R. H. (Northern) 173–4
Montgomery, Maj. Samuel (Northern) 162
Montgomery, Capt. William C. F. (Northern) 71
Montgomery County 40, 82, 86, 113, 115, 218, 223–4, 229, 257, 258; history of 1885 225
Monticello, Lewis County 118
Moonlight, Col. Thomas (Northern) 288–9
Moore, Capt. Calvin S. (Northern) 199–200
Moore, Capt. Henry B. (Northern) 192
Moore, Mr. 272
Moorhouse, Capt. William (Northern) 403–4*n*24
Moreau River, central Missouri 375
Morehouse, Capt. D. A. W. (Northern) 211
Morgan, Col. John Hunt (Southern) 118
Morgan, Maj. Wick (Northern) 199
Morgan County 141–2, 203, 297, 354, 357, 361, 362, 364, 375–6; Moreau Township 361
Morris, Reverend Charles (Northern) 307, 348–9
Morris, James (Southern) 99
Morris, John (Northern) 348–9
Morris, W. H. (Southern) 141
Morris family, Texas County (Southern) 165
Morris Mills, Jefferson County 174
Morristown, Cass County 380
Moseley, Capt. M. V. B. (Southern) 86, 400*n*45
Moses, Capt. Thomas (Northern) 314–5
Moss, Amasi (Southern) 177
Mound City, Kansas 203, 208, 380
"the Mounds," Lafayette County 372
Mount Hebron Church, Lafayette County 356
Mt. Hope, Lafayette County 137–8
Mount Pleasant, Miller County 383–4
Mt. Sterling, Brown County, Illinois 119–20
Mt. Vernon, Lawrence County 31, 105, 192, 195, 209
Mount Vernon Methodist Church, Pilot Grove, Cooper County 385
Mt. Zion Church, Boone County 249
Mountain Home, Douglas County 208
Muddy Creek, Livingston County 320
Muller, Capt. George (Northern) 167
Mullins, Maj. Alexander W. (Northern) 127, 129
Mullins, Patrick (Southern) 141, 361, 375
Murphy, Detective (Northern) 256
Murphy, Capt. Richard (Northern) 167, 168
Murray, Bennett (Northern) 171
muskets *see* rifle-muskets
Musselman, James 52
mutilation of dead 16, 107, 193, 207, 234, 254–5, 285, 295, 316, 319, 341, 342, 343, 389
Myrtle Street Military Prison, St. Louis (formerly Lynch's Slave Market) 22, 26, 85–6, 143, 185–9, 378

Napoleon 6
Native Americans *see* Indians
Nealyville, Butler County 21
Nebraska City, Nebraska Territory 43, 345
Nebraska Territory 43, 345
Nebraska Troops (Northern): 1st Nebraska Infantry Regiment 189
Nehmaha County, Nebraska 145
Neidergerte, Charles 224
Nemier, Mr. (Southern) 394*n*51
Neosho, Newton County 29, 105, 107, 108, 190, 192, 193, 194, 195
Neosho River, southwest Missouri 98
New Albany, Indiana 184
New Florence, Montgomery County 115
New Frankfort, Saline County 140, 141, 299, 301, 368, 373
New Hampshire 134, 176, 193, 277
New London, Ralls County 260
New Madrid, New Madrid County 70, 71, 72, 155, 157–8, 161
New Madrid County 69, 70, 155, 156, 158, 160, 187
New Market, Platte County 151, 263–4, 265, 268
New Mexico Territory 48
New Orleans, Louisiana 349
New York 56, 63, 257, 283
Newkirk, Lt. Charles (Northern) 375
newspapers 7, 21, 43, 50, 70, 122, 133, 339, 340, 359
Newton County 29, 31, 98, 103, 105, 107, 190, 191, 194, 195, 197, 198
Newtonia, Newton County 103, 105, 191
Nichols, James M. 142
Nichols, Mr. (Southern) 247
night riders 149, 272, 345
"no quarter" 2, 6–7, 10, 62, 96, 117, 138, 149, 155, 157, 162, 171, 172, 197–8, 216, 285, 307, 308
Noland, 1st Lt. George W. (Northern) 305
Norris, Milt (Southern) 193
Norris Creek, Johnson County 370
North Carolina 36
North Fork of the White River, southwest Missouri 208
North Missouri Railroad, northeast Missouri 114, 247, 248
Northern Methodist denomination 348
Northerner (vessel) 184
Noted Guerrillas 48, 213, 246; *see also* Edwards, John N.
notes, threatening 272; *see also* Jackson, Jim
Nowlin Store, Missouri City, Clay County 45

Oak Grove, Lafayette County 124, 125
oath of allegiance 44, 61, 67, 72,

74, 143, 203, 204, 240, 263, 271, 303, 374, 376
O'Fallon, St. Charles County 259
The Official Records of the Union and Confederate Armies (Official Records or *O. R.*) 3, 314
Offutt's Knob, Johnson County 130, 364
Ohio 56, 212, 273, 276
Ohio troops (Northern): 10th Ohio Cavalry Regiment 187
Oklahoma *see* Indian Nations
Old Bonhomme Road, St. Louis County 182
old Boonville Road, Vernon County 198
"Old West" 118
Oldham, Lt. John G. (Southern) 263–4
Oliphant, Ralph (Northern) 335
Olivette, St. Louis County 182
Omaha (vessel) 252
Order of American Knights (OAK) 120, 174, 179–83, 187, 213
Oregon 40
Oregon, Holt County 145
Oregon County 12, 15, 16, 17, 21, 75, 77, 79, 167, 168
Osage County 81, 223
Osage River, west and central Missouri 32, 98–9, 100, 102, 103, 106, 132, 205, 210, 223, 302–3, 354, 362, 383–4
Osborn, Clay County 274
Osceola, Arkansas 71, 159
Osceola, St. Clair County 205, 207
Otterville, Cooper County 141, 142
"our dear erring brethren" 404*n*25
Overlease, Abraham (Northern) 166
Overton, Capt. Holmes (Southern) 263–4
Ozark, Christian County 209
Ozark County 95, 96, 208, 209
Ozark Mountains or Hills 165, 208
Ozment, Ferd (Southern) 107

Pace, Capt. (Southern) 211
Pacific Railroad, central Missouri 47, 64, 81, 132–3, 285, 357, 362
pack animals 61, 206, 285
Paducah, Kentucky 293
Page, James 110
Page, 1st Lt. John D. (Northern) 310
Palmer, Allen *see* Parmer, Allen
Palmer, Col. (Southern) 192, 381, 445*n*77
Palmer, Pvt. James (Northern) 243

Palmer, Col. Ratliff B. (Northern) 33
Palmyra, Marion County 225
Panther Creek, Johnson County 363
Paola, Kansas 380
Papinsville, Bates County 98–9, 102–3, 206, 208
Paradise, Clay County *see* Gosneyville
Paragon (vessel) 153
Paris, Monroe County 113, 235, 253
Park, George S. (Northern) 347
Parke, Capt. Joseph (Northern) 232, 249, 254–*255*, 301, 356
Parkenhammer, Mr. (Northern) 418*n*6
Parker, Col. (Southern) 100
Parker, W. (Southern) 23
Parker, Capt. Wilson L. (Northern) 299, 301
Parkes, Mr. (Southern) 95
Parkville, Platte County 152, 267, 304–6, 313, 331, 338, 347, 390
Parman, Cpl. Joseph V. (Northern) 285–6, 296
Parmer, Allen (Southern) 273, *274*, 371
parole 305, 319, 322
"partisan rangers" 2, 10; *see also* guerrillas
Patterson, Wayne County 21, 75, 77–8, 162
Patton, Bollinger County 155
"Paw Paw militia" *see* Missouri troops
Paxton, William M. (historian) 268, 349
Payton, Capt. (Southern) 77
Peace Democrats 180, 182, 211; *see also* Copperheads
Peacher, Col. Quinton L. (Southern) 247
Peak, Mr. 292, 430–1*n*32
Pemberton, Louisa 363
Pemiscot County 69, 70, 73, 157–9, 160
Pendleton, Warren County 242
Penick, Col. William (Northern) 384
Pennsylvania 47, 246, 283, 284, 290, 293, 312
Perche Hills, Perche Township, Boone County (also called "Blackfoot Region") 219, 221, 222, 223, 227, 232
percussion caps 88, 378–*379*
Perkins, Buck (Southern) 74
Perkins, Col. Caleb (Northern) 110, 218, 251, 319; Boone County events 219, 232, 249, 256; brother William captured (24 August 1864) 253; interviewed by Edwin Price 241–2; operations 229, 232, 243, 248, 355; possible orders to Bill

Anderson 233; possibly conducted Monroe County war council (about 4–7 August 1864) 246–7; publicity stunt (June 1864) 219–20; Randolph County events 248; speech at Dripping Springs (late June 1864) 222–3
Perkins, William (Southern) 253
Perkins, Lt. William N. (Northern) 338
Perry, Charles A. 43
Perry County 73, 170
Perryville, Perry County 74, 170; newspaper 170
Petit Saline Creek, Cooper County 384
Pettis County 99, 125, 136, 140, 207, 297, 299, 301, 356, 365, 366; Heath's Creek Township 365
Phelps, F. (Northern) 182–3
Phelps County 9, 10, 13, 17, 68, 79, 88, 154, 163, 165, 168, 177
Philips, Edward 187, 415*n*16
Phillips, Elder C. M. W. (Northern) 113
Phillips, Col. John F. (Northern) 66
Phillips, 1st Lt. Joseph H. (Northern) 208
Phillips, Uri (Southern) 166
photographs 177, 292, 293
pickets or lookouts *14*, 167*m*, *191*, 195, 206, 213, 267, 335, 341, 343
Pickler, Maj. Jesse F. (Southern) 191–3, 194, 196, 199, 202–3
Piercey, Col. Andrew J. (Southern) 196–7
Pike County 37, 86, 99, 113, 115–7, 177, 218, 225, 227, 229, 259, 389
Pike Run, St. Francois County 74, 170–1
Pilot Grove, Cooper County 48, 141, 298, 354, 362, 385
Pilot Knob, Iron County 21, 75, 78, 111, 162, 163, 170, 172, 176
Pinckney, Warren County 224
Pineville, McDonald County 104, 192
Pink Hill, Jackson County 52
Pinnacles of the Missouri River, Saline County 399
Piper, John Will (Southern) 366
Piper, Marshall (Southern) 370
Pisgah, Cooper County 143
Pitney, Capt. Alexander (Southern) 248, 422–3*n*36
Pittsburg, Kansas 103
Pitzer, Dugeld 174
Pixley (Southern) 418*n*2
Plains City, Saline County 366
Platt River, northwest Missouri 149, 269, 306, 337
Platte City, Platte County 151,

Index

267, 268, 169, 270, 306–8, 325, 338, 346, 347, 348, 390
Platte County 41, 43, 120, 127, 134, 140, 145, 148, 150–3, 204, 262–70, 274, 277, 279, 280, 293, 304–10, 311, 312, 313, 321, 324–6, 329–31, 320, 321, 324, 325, 326, 328, 329, 330, 331, 332, 336, 337–8, 339, 345, 346, 348, 349, 351, 361, 367, 388, 390; history of 1885 326
Platte County Defensive Association 348
Plattsburg, Clinton County 148, 265, 321, 322, 338
Pleasant Gap, Bates County 102, 103
Pleasant Hill, Cass County 136, 292, 294, 357, 375, 381, 382
Pleasonton Maj. Gen. Alfred (Northern) 60, 359, 360; favored radical officers over conservative ones 362, 370, 377; mistakenly removed cavalry from Saline County 365; recommended firing local commander 255; replaced Brown as District of Central Missouri commander (23 July 1864) 359–60
Poag, Pvt. (Northern) 190–1
Pocahontas, Arkansas 77, 79, 165
Poe, Sgt. B. F. (Northern) 290, 430n29
Poe, Capt. Benjamin F. (Northern) 265–6, 321, 430n29
Point Pleasant, New Madrid County 160
Polk County 34, 36, 91, 107, 211
Poole, Francis Marion "Dave" (Southern) 138, 356, 380; established his territory (August 1864) 373, 377–8, 381; raid on German American community (23 August 1864) 379–80; raid to Cooper and Moniteau Counties with George Todd's band (Aug.–Sep. 1864) 383, 384, 385
Porche's Prairie, Chariton County 112, 230
Porter, Henry (Southern) 371
Porter, Col. Joseph C. (Southern) 260
Portland, Callaway County 114, 258
Post Boy (vessel) 293, 312m, 431n34
Post Oak Creek, Johnson County 136–7, 285
Potosi, Bourbon County, Kansas 203, 208
Potosi, Washington County 75
Potter, Mr. (Southern) 206
Powell, Bulge (Southern) 69, 70, 158

Prairie du Rocher, Randolph County, Illinois 68, 74
Prairie Home, Cooper County 385
Prairie Rose (vessel) 283
Prairieville, Pike County 226
press *see* newspapers
Preston, Jasper County 102, 201
Preutt, Capt. Valentine (Northern) 70
Price, Brig. Gen. Edwin W. "Stump" (Southern) 240–*242*, 421n18
Price, Capt. Joseph (Southern) 248
Price, Capt. Miles (Southern) 218, 242
Price, Mrs. Armand (Northern) 221–2
Price, Maj. Gen. Sterling (Southern) 59–60, 65–6, *325*; details of his Missouri invasion plans 159–60, 219; directs war councils to include guerrillas in operations 246–7, 339–40, 367, 385, 391; General Kirby Smith (Price wrote to him 23 July 1864) 325–6; Governor-in-exile Thomas C. Reynolds 160, 180, 325; hears of Lt. Col. Thornton's insurgency in progress (22 July 1864) 325–6; large numbers of regulars and recruiters infiltrate into Missouri to prepare for Price's army 212, 236, 239, 242, 302, 303, 307, 328; misconceptions and overoptimism of what to expect in Missouri 160, 180, 325–6; plan to come to Missouri when corn ripens 228; plan to influence National Election on 8 November by Missouri invasion 211, 261; plan to throw out Union occupation of his home state 261; plans of Missouri invasion invigorated by Union reverses in the region in spring 1864 388; rumors and threats of Price's coming 65, 112, 190, 208, 228, 229, 238, 243, 281; Sam Hildebrand as one of Price's scouts in the vanguard of the invasion 175; Thornton's insurgency timed with Price's original invasion plans 262, 304, 307, 312–3, 390; use of guerrillas planned into invasion 219, 242, 281, 385
Prig, Mr. (Southern) 114–5
prison and jail escapes 23, 26–8, 85–9, 185–9, 219 226, 271, 303, 308
prison inspections 24–6, 85–6, 87–8, 185–6, 187–9
prisons 7, 24–8, 85–9, 185–9;

see also Alton, Illinois; Gratiot Street; Myrtle Street
Pritchard, Maj. Jesse L. (Northern) 131, 317
Providence, Boone County 223, 246, 252
provost marshals (Northern) 7, 12, 22, 29, 82, 103, 111, 114, 116, 150, 153, 179, 219, 221, 244–5, 375
Pruitt, Mr. (Southern) 166
Prussia 306
Pryor, Benjamin (Northern) 275
Pryor, Jefferson (Northern) 275
Pugh, Maj. Andrew J. (Northern) 205
Pulaski County 9, 10, 14, 15, 16, 17, 33, 81, 164, 165
Pulliam, Capt. John D. (Southern) 37, 109, 387
Purcell, Capt. Young A. (Southern) 218, 221–2, 229, 251–2, 259, 260
Putnam County 121–2

Quantrill, William Clarke (Southern) 2, 31, 43, 47, 48, 49, 54, 55, 104, 123, 133, 141, 157, 210, 249, 273, 279, 297, 304, 307, 312, 329, 331, 337, 350, 354, 364, 387, 390; actions upon return to west central Missouri in April 1864 128–31, 143–4, 388; Andy Blunt left in charge for winter 1863–1864 124, 126, 387; false reports about 100, 132, 133, 264, 293, 363–4; George Todd and Bill Anderson depose Quantrill as chief (late May–early June 1864) 138–40; hard return trip to Missouri (April 1864) 96–9, 103, 105; Lawrence, Kansas, raid (21 August 1863) 61, 63, 127, 359; a no-show at early August 1864 Confederate councils of war for guerrillas 367; self-exile in Howard County after his lieutenants deposed him 140, 245, 364; Todd suffers shortage of percussion caps like Quantrill two years before 379
Quarantine Island, Mississippi River 188
Quartermaster Corps, U.S. Army 13, 95
Quincy, Hickory County 91, 207

Rabb, Maj. John W. (Northern) 70
Rader, William (Southern) 193
radical versus conservative northerners 20, 58, 212, 237, 240, 267, 276–7, 370
Rafter, John (Southern) 207

"Railroad Regiment" *see* Missouri troops, Northern, 38th EMM
railroad work crews 132–3, 357
railroads damaged by guerrillas *see* sabotage
Ralls County 116, 185, 259, 260
Ramsey, Barton J. (Southern) 114, 223, 358
Ramsey, Joel Franklin "Frank" (Southern) 114, 223, 257–8
Randolph County 101, 110, 113, 213, 218, 219, 220, 222, 229, 231, 233, 244, 245, 247, 248, 249, 251, 257, 258, 319, 327, 333; Prairie Township 220
Ratterman (village), Phelps County 164
"Ravenswood" (mansion), Cooper County 298
Rawlins Lane, near Rocheport 254–5
Ray County 132, 134, 145, 146, 147, 278–80, 310, 314–7, 321, 323, 330, 331, 334, 335–6, 337–8, 341, 345, 349, 361, 390
Raytown, Jackson County 294
Readsville, Callaway County 115
Rebel mail network, secret 23, 66, 78, 82, 87, 88, 174, 177, 185, 187, 192, 214, 299, 311
recognition signs 135, 180, 249, 301, 314
Red River, Louisiana 184
Red River, Texas 100
Red River Campaign, Louisiana (March–May 1864) 81, 212
Redding, William R. (Southern) 418*n*2
Reed, Lt. David (Southern) 175
Reed, Mrs. (Southern) 54–5
Reeves, Col. Timothy (Southern) 20, 21, 68, 75, 77–8, 154, 161, 387, 392
refugees 45, 50–*51*, 92, *95*, 373, 376, 377, 380
Remington revolvers 92–*93*, *231*
renegades 2, 41, 64, 91, 98, 145, 153, 176, 209, 295, 354, 375; *see also* deserters; "freebooters"
Renick, Jane 364
Renick, Strother 52
Renick, Randolph County 110, 113, 222, 231, 233–4, 247
Republic (present day village), Greene County 209
Republican Church, Lafayette County 129
Republican party 180, 182
"returned Rebels" 32, 49–53, 148, 150, 388
revenge *see* circle of violence
Revolution, American (1775–1783): and its influence on American guerrilla war 7
revolver cylinders (extra) 335
revolvers 71, *93*, 112, 113, 133, 150, 160, 173, 187, 221, 224, 230, *231*, 239, 242, 247, 249, 254, 256, 264, *265*, 267, 269, 270, 272, 273, 276, 283, 289, 293, 302, 303, 315, 335, 343, 346, 362, 364; large (.44 caliber) 40
Reynolds, Governor Thomas C. (Southern) 160, *180*, 325
Reynolds County 75, 77, 161, 162, 173, 175
Rhineland, Montgomery County 114, 115, 334, 225
Rice, Capt. H. A. (Northern) 162
Rice, Lt. John A. (Northern) 155
Richardson County, Nebraska 145
Richfield, Clay County 45, 345, 347
Richmond, Ray County 146, 277, 310, 316, 338, 341, 345
Richmond, Virginia 49
Richwoods, Washington County 176, 177
Rider, Jim *see* Ryder, Jim
Ridge, 2nd Lt. Thomas D. (Northern) 272
Ridgely, Platte County 265, 269, 326, 331, 345
Ridgeway, Pvt. John T. (Southern) 27, 394*n*45
Ridgway, Lt. John W. (Northern) 52–3
rifle-muskets 152, 200, *201*, 207, 242, 264, 266, 270, *290*, *302*, 303, 310, 322, 327, 335, 366, 373
Ripley, 1st Lt. Thaddeus A. (Southern) 86
Ripley County 20, 75, 77, 161, 162
Ritchey, Capt. James M. (Northern) 105, 195
Roanoke, Howard County 232, 243, 248
Roberts, Lt. James M. (Northern) 164
Roberts, Pvt. James W. (Southern) 167
Roberts, Lafayette "Pete" (Southern) 34, 141, 190, 192, 196–7, 199–200, 203
Roberts, Capt. Samuel E. (Northern) 195
Robinson, Capt. Alex (Northern) 363
Robinson, Marion "Gooly" (Southern) 137, 285
Robinson, Mr. (Northern) 167
Robinson, Mr. (Southern) 193–4
Robinson brothers 149
Rocheport, Boone County 214, 216–7, 223, 232, 249, 250, 251, 254, 255–6, 301, 356, 384
Rochester, Andrew County 271
Rock House Prairie, Buchanan County 272, 327, 337
Rockville, Bates County 92
Rocky Ford, Grand River, Chariton County 312, 344
Rocky Mountains 40
Rodgers family, Texas County (Southern) 167
Rogers, John (Northern) 200
Rogers, Col. John B. (Northern) 20, 72, 73, 155
Rohrer, Capt. Phillip (Northern) 105, 210
Roland, Jacob (Southern) 328
Rolla, Phelps County 9, 12, 13, 14, 17, 82, 83–4, 85, 94, 165, 166, 167, 175, 176, 208, 209; newspaper 79
Rolla and Springfield: main road between 9, 10, 14, 16, 17, 94, 165–6
"Root," Dave *see* Poole, Francis Marion "Dave"
Rose, Oliver (Southern) 418*n*2
Rose Hill, Johnson County 130, 363, 379, 381, 383
Rosecrans, Maj. Gen. William S. "Old Rosy" (Northern) 56–7, 101, 111, 117, 121, *127*, 142, 150, 151, 170, 187, 193, 226, 240, 244, 261, 266, 267, 268, *291*, 297, 308, 312, 317, 324, 337, 368, 387; ambitious start in Missouri (February and March 1864) 57–8, 60–3; bad plan allowing Detective Terman free rein killing prominent Rebels (May–June 1864) 213; citizens guards program (initiated 28 June 1864, with G.O. # 107) 62–3, 217, 313, 352; Curtis, Maj. Gen. Samuel, shared ideas 191; fixation with Order of American Knights (OAK) 180–1, 182; overconfidence 123; pleading for help 227, 242; powers granted by governor 57; problems intensify 127; problems with Brig. Gen. Brown as district chief 283–4, 291, 293–4, 358, 359–60; rebuffed in move to obtain new prisons 86; summation of his efforts 387–8
Ross, Frank (Northern) 202
Ross, Kirby (historian) 170, 173, 174
Rotten Rock, Jefferson County 173
Roubidoux Creek, Pulaski and Texas Counties 14, 15
Rouell, Capt. Lyman D. (Northern) 314–6, 435*n*16
Round Hill, Cooper County 141
Round Prairie, Jackson County 52

Rozier Mills, Perry County line 73
Ruark, Sgt. Josiah (Northern) 190–1
Ruark, Capt. Ozias (Northern) 191, 195
Rucker, Maj. John F. (Southern) 179, 414*n*1
Rudder (Southern) 394*n*51
Rulo, or Rue, family, Washington County 176
Rupe, James A. (Southern) 326
Rush Bottom, Holt County 145
Rush Bottom, Jackson County 371
Rush Tower, Jefferson County 173
Rushville, Buchanan County 41
Rusk, David (Southern) 190, 192, 194, 195, 196–7, 203
Russell, father, and son (Northern) 335
Russell, Lt. Col. Francis T. (Northern) 66
Russell, Sgt. P. (Northern) 129–30
Russellville, Ray County 335, 342
Rustin, Jacob (Southern) 10
Rutherford (Southern) 281
Rutledge (village), McDonald County 196
Ryder, or Rider, Jim (Southern) 391
Ryland, Judge John F. 287, 289

Sabins, Pvt. William (Northern) 54
sabotage: of railroads 6, 171, 182, 219, 233–4, 235, 247; of riverboats 22, 183–5, 283; *see also* arson
Sac River, southwest Missouri 200
Saddler, Pvt. Hollas (Southern) 72
St. Catherine, Linn County 37
St. Charles County 113, 119, 258–9
St. Charles Rock Road, St. Louis County 183
St. Clair County 98–9, 106, 205
St. Francis River 18, 68–9, 72, 155, 157, 158, 163, 172
St. Francisville, Clark County 120
St. Francois County 73, 74, 170–1, 172, 174, 175
St. James, Phelps County 164, 177
St. Joseph, Buchanan County 44, 58, 120, 145, 149, 150, 211, 213, 219, 243, 265, 274, 275, 276, 278, 308, 312, 320, 324, 327, 328, 337, 339; newspaper 41, 133, 149, 152, 222, 268, 272, 275, 277, 314, 323, 326, 327, 328, 337

St. Joseph Tribune, Buchanan County, newspaper 345
St. Joseph Weekly Herald, Buchanan County, newspaper 41, 268, 272–3, 279, 341
St. Louis city 18, 57, 68, 83, 86, 88, 117, 149, 160, 170, 173–4, 176, 179–89, 203, 217, 219, 225, 231, 242, 248, 251, 271, 289, 293, 330, 362; area Union military prisons 12, 34, 167, 171, 185–9, 207; great fire of 1849 *184*; levee and riverfront 179, 183–5; map of 1918 *181*; Union department headquarters 16, 324
St. Louis County 174, 182, 183
St. Louis Gas Light Company 180
St. Louis newspapers 50, 65, 84, 91, 103, 116, 117, 166, 171, 177, 183, 189, 198, 207, 250, 256, 259, 342; *Daily Missouri Democrat* 143, 384; *St. Louis Union* 170
St. Luke, Stoddard County 72
St. Paul, Minnesota 184
Ste. Genevieve, Ste. Genevieve County 74
Ste. Genevieve County 73
Salem, Dent County 16, 17, 164, 208
Saline City, Saline County 369, 370
Saline County 49, 110, 132, 140, 187, 216, 239, 252, 283, 297, 299–302, 354, 357, 363, 365, 366, 368, 369, 374, 376, 377, 385
Saline Creek, Miller County 302
Salisbury, Judge Lucius (Northern) 214
Salisbury, Chariton County 230
Sallee, Capt. James H. (Northern) 210
Sallee, Lt. Thomas (Northern) 206
Salt River, northeast Missouri 227, 235; railroad bridge, Shelby County 235
Sambo Slough, Carroll County 343
Samuel, Reuben 274
San Francisco (village), Carroll County 335
Sanborn, Brig. Gen. John B. (Northern) 16, 29, 31, 61, 100, 105, 107, 168, 193, 194, 198–9, 209
Sanders, Pvt. Elsy F. (Northern) 55, 397*n*44
Sanders, Maj. (Northern) 45
Sanders, Mr. (Northern) 221
Sanderson, Provost Marshal General J. P. (Northern) 88, 180, 182, 185–8
Santa Fe Trail 53
Santon, Dabney (Southern) 37

Sarcoxie, Jasper County 193
Savannah, Andrew County 149, 270–1; newspaper 149, 327
Scatterville, Arkansas 158–9
Schaback, William (Northern) 306
Schmitt, Pvt. George (Northern) 280
Schnabeck, John (Northern) 306
Schofield, Maj. Gen. John M. (Northern) 56, 61, 387
Schrantz, Ward L. (historian) 193
Schultz (Southern) 394*n*51
Schultz, Detective L. S. (Northern) 187
Schuyler County 260–1
Scotland County 260–1
Scott, Ferdinando (Southern) 273
Scott County 20, 70, 74
scouts *see* pickets
Sebring, Lt. William H. (Southern) 187
Sedalia, Pettis County 51, 136, 140, 205, 207, 299, 301
Seeley (Southern) 209
Seeley's Store, Round Hill, Cooper County 141
Selma, Jefferson County 173
Shaback, Peter (Northern) 306
Shackelford, Sgt. Matthew (Northern) 204, 287–8, 296
shackles *54*, 292
Shanghai, Johnson County 137, 356
Shanklin, Col. John H. (Northern) 329
Shannon County 12, 76, 168, 171
Sharp's breechloaders 49, *50*, 296, *331*, 396*n*24
Shattuck, 2nd Lt. Warren C. (Northern) 152
Shaw, Maj. Webb (Southern) 226, 420*n*40
Shelbina, Shelby County 235, 261, 341
Shelby, Brig. Gen. Joseph O. (Southern) 49, *91*, 188, 191, 199, 246, 387; concentrated on recruiting in north Arkansas (spring and summer 1864) 154–5, 159, 161, 163, 166–7, 203, 204, 208; false reports about 248, 293, 331; Lt. Col. Thornton's disappointment Shelby did not come to Thornton's rescue 256–7; order to subordinates to stop preying on civilian population (19 May 1864) 91; plans to raid ahead of Price's columns during the Missouri invasion 160, 219; southern recruiters of Boone County claim they were part of Shelby's command 256–7

Shelby County 118, 235, 261
Shelby's cavalry brigade 49, 50–1, 102, 127, 354, 368
Shelby's Missouri raid (October 1863) 66
Shelby's returned cavalrymen 49–51, 125, 126
Shepherd, George (Southern) *275*, 331
Shepherd, Oliver (Southern) *305*
Shibley, Capt. Samuel (Northern) 18, 70
Shirley, Edwin "Bud," and daughter Myra Shirley (Southern) 193
Shoal Creek, Newton County 190–1
Shoemake, Pvt. John F. (Northern) 316
shotguns 71, 78, 92, 112, 115, 146, 157, 158, *220*, 222, 224, 239, 249, 253, 254, 303, 335, 361, 364
Shousetown, Pennsylvania 184
Shumate, Lt. Daniel (Northern) 285
Shumate, Wiley H. (Southern) 143, 144, 297, 302–3, 356–7, 360, 373, 382, 383–4, 408*n*68, 433*n*45
Sibley, Jackson County 52, 135, 288, 293, 312, 338
Siceloff, Mr. 361
Sigel, Maj. Gen. Franz (Northern) 123–4
Sikeston, Scott County 72, 155
Silver Moon (vessel) 70
Simpson's Ford, Carroll County (also called "Flat Rock Ford" or "McElree's Ford") 343–4
Sioux City (vessel) 245, 364
Sioux Indian uprising in Minnesota (1862) 168
Six-Mile House Tavern, St. Louis County 183
Skinner, Capt. William A. (Northern) 111
Slash Valley, Platte County 326
slave catchers 41, 399–400*n*36
slave informants and help against Southerners 352, 354
Sloan, Robert (Southern) 355–6
smallpox 25, 86, 87, 188
Smith, Capt. Edward K. (Northern) 231
Smith, Frank (Southern) 14, 98–9, 387
Smith, George (Southern) 177
Smith, Jeremiah (Southern) 328
Smith, Joel 231
Smith, Pvt. John (Northern) 112
Smith, 2nd Lt. John T. (Northern) 191
Smith, 1st Lt. Marquis D. (Northern) 163
Smith, Mr. (Fishing River Township) 275

Smith, Mr. (shot by guerrillas) 90
Smith, Mr. (Southern) 177
Smith, Maj. J. Nelson (Northern) 324
Smith, Pete (Southern) 154, 171, 172, 175
Smith, 1st Sgt. R. W. (Northern) 200
Smith, Pvt. Vincent (Northern) 80
Smithville, Clay County 331, 338
smuggling 22, 78, 84–5, 87, 88, 173, 179, 182
Sni-A-Bar Creek, Lafayette County 352–3, 367, 383
Sni-A-Bar Hills, or Sni Hills 53, 55, 128, 129, 130, 132, 133, 134, 135, 286, 288–9, 291–2, 359
Snider, Maj. Henry (Southern) 260, 425*n*69
Snyder, Andrew (Southern) 118
Snyder, Capt. Henry (Northern) 230
Snyder, Capt. John R. (Northern) 272, 340
Sons of Confederate Veterans (SCV) 434*n*5
Sorrell, Wilhare (Northern) 220
South Carolina 225
Spalding, Thomas (Northern) 259
Sparrow, Pvt. Andrew (Northern) 80
Sparta, Buchanan County 272
Special Orders Number 141 (Union, District of Central Missouri, 1 July 1864) 303
speech, public 214, 215, 217, 240–1, 243, 307, 346
Spencerburg, Pike County 116
Spencer's Creek, Ralls County 259
spring, 1864 90, 97–8, 126, 388
Spring Creek, Oregon County 77
Spring Creek, Phelps County 79, 166
Spring Creek, Pulaski County 17
Spring River, southwest Missouri 105, 192
Springfield and Rolla: main road between 9, 10, 14, 16, 17, 94, 165–6
Springfield Plateau, southwest Missouri 31, 50, 94–6, 208
Springfield rifle-musket *302*; *see also* rifle-muskets
Springfield, Greene County 9, 16, 29, 31, 33, 94–6, 165, 207; newspaper 94, 98, 103, 105, 199, 209; prison or jail 209
spy 12, 16–7, 68, 86, 120, 128, 164, 166–7, 168, 174, 180, 183, 188, 207, 215, 219, 221, 237, 248, 252

stagecoach 9, 12, *13*, 15, 16, 17, 101, 131–2, 136, 137, 230, 234, 243, 254, 279, 284, 286, 287, 294–5, 316, 354, 361, 367, 371, 373, 375, 378, 380
Standerford, George (Southern) 261
Stanley, Capt. Joseph (Northern) 239, 241, 251, 253
Stanton, Union Secretary of War Edwin M. (Northern) *62*
Stapleton, Bob (Southern) 217
Starke, Dryden, and John, "Jack" 142
Starks, James, Jr. (Southern) 418*n*2
Starks, Veach (Southern) 417*n*2
Starling, Lt. John P. (Northern) 283–4
Starr, Belle *see* Shirley, Myra
Starr, Henry 49
Starr carbines and revolvers *135*, 206, 315, 416*n*42, 435*n*16
static defense 362; *see also* mobile warfare
Stauber, T. J. (Northern) 221, 227
Steakley, Sgt. James C. (Northern) 173
Steele, Maj. Gen. Frederick (Northern) 83; Camden Expedition in Arkansas 81
Steelville, Crawford County 168–9
Stemmons, Capt. T. J. (Northern) 102, 105, 107
Stephens, Capt. Bill (Southern) 251
Stepp, John (Southern) 418*n*2
Sterling, 1st Lt. James (Northern) 238
Stevenson, Mr. (Southern) 279
Stewart, Bill (Southern) 137, 249, 369, 371; in Boone County (mid-August 1864) 249; in Cooper County (15 July 1864) 355–6; in Howard County (16–28 August 1864) 254–5, 356; actions in Johnson County (16 July 1864) 137, 285; previous Stewart band member, Hutchinson 369, 371
Stewart, Rans 36
Stockton, Cedar County 34, 199
Stoddard County 18, 70, 72, 74, 78, 158, 172
Stone, Sgt. Solathel (Northern) 136, 137
Stone, 1st Lt. William (Northern) 317
Stone, William (Southern) 120
Stone County 95, 107–8, 209–10
Stoner family, Jackson County 378
Stonesport, Boone County 246

Story, Capt. George S. (Northern) 45
Stotts, Capt. Green C. (Northern) 102, 193
Sturgeon, Boone County 110, 179, 231, 234, 243, 253
subsistence 14, 18, 21, 22, 37, 48, 77, 81, 95, 103, 116, 164, 167, 202, 204, 207, 229, 230, 381, 384, 392
Suess, Maj. Henry (Northern) 316, 348, 366
Sullivan, Franklin County 174–5
Sullivan County 110, 121–2, 237, 238
Summers, Valentine P. (Southern) 176, 413n74
Sunshine (vessel) 184, 284
Supplement to the Official Records 3
Sutton, Dr. 156
Sutton family, Texas County (Southern) 165
Swain, Lt. Col. A. J. (Northern) 119–20
Sweet Springs, Saline County *see* Brownsville
Swift, Capt. Martin E. (Northern) 221
Swift, Samuel A. (Southern) 177
Switzler, Col. William F. (Northern) 111
Sylamore Mountains, northwest Arkansas 208

Taberville, St. Clair County 106
Tabo Creek, Lafayette County 355, 356, 377–8, 379–80, 381
Taggart, Capt. John (Northern) 136
Talifaro, Cpl. Wessel H. (Northern) 29
Talley, H. (Northern) 362
Taney County 31 95, 208, 210
Taneyville, Illinois 188
tanyard 108
Taos, Buchanan County 150, 270, 307, 326
Tatum 115
Taylor, Charles Fletcher "Fletch" (Southern) 236, *273*, 275, 276–7, 304, 323, 325, 327, 328–9, 330–1, 333, 338, 349, 350–1, 367, *371*, 390, 407n52, 427n35, 434n5, 444n53
Taylor, Capt. Henry (Southern) 93, 103–4, 107, 190, 195, 198, 200, 202, 204
Teague (Southern) 103
Teal, 2nd Lt. James E. (Northern) 133–4
telegram 112, 177, 268, 366
telegraph system and lines 14, 72, 96, 100, 118, 136, 155, 233, 252, 257, 284, 361, 373, 375, 378, 380
Tennessee 36, 167, 261

Terman, Detective J. W. (alias "Harry Truman," Northern) 212–3, 241, 389
Texas 12, 49, 96–9, 100, 103, 104, 105, 126, 129, 133, 136, 138, 139, 143–4, 171, 191, 212, 238, 252, 273, 388, 291
Texas County 9, 10, 12, 14, 16, 17, 79, 14, 164, 165, 167, 176, 211
Thannisch, George (Southern) 21
Thixton, Peter (Northern) 361
Thomason, Capt. John S. (Northern) 313
Thomasville, Oregon County 12, 15, 167
Thompson, Capt. A. Harrison (Northern) 101, 142
Thompson, L. A. (Northern) 114–5
Thornton, Lt. Col. John Calhoun, "Coon" (Southern) 140–1, 233, 263–5, 267–9, 280, 281, 304–10, 312–26, 327–32, 333, 337–8, 345, 347–8, 349, 350, 352, 354, 356, 357, 358, 361, 362, 363, 363, 367, 369, 375, 376, 377, 379, 380, 382–3, 388, 390
Thrailkill, Capt. John (Southern) 27, 187 (his St. Louis prison escape night of 27/28 June 1864), 307–8, 309–10, 312–16, 317–25, 327–31, 333, 338–9, 344, 347–8, 349, 350–1, 367, 371–2, 390, 415n16
Tiffin, Capt. Clayton (Northern) 277, 343
Tipton, Moniteau County 100, 141, 354, 361, 362, 367
T. L. McGill (vessel) 217
Todd, George (Southern) 49, 53, 104, 132, *139*, 281, 366; actions right after return from Texas (late April–early May) 103, 128–31, 132–3, 134–7; Anderson and Todd depose Quantrill (late May–early June) 138–40, 143–4, 245, 264, 279, 388; Arrow Rock raid (18–23 July) 356, 357, 358–9, 363–4, 367, 373; Cooper and Moniteau Counties raid (late August–early September) 377, 383, 384, 385; hard trip back to Missouri from Texas with Quantrill (April) 96–9, 126; helping refugees from Thornton's insurgency get started to Arkansas (late July–August) 323, 329, 350–1, 361, 377, 381, 382, 390; mobile warfare (Todd began August) 389; operations in Jackson and Lafayette Counties (June–early August) 279,

350–1, 361, 377, 381, 382, 390; percussion caps shortage (August) 378–9
Todd, Tom (Southern) 114, 218, 223, 229, 232, 248, 249, 251–2, 256
Todd's Mill, Montgomery County 40
Tompkins, Dr. Hyram A. 385
Toney, Lt. Harvey M. (Northern) 72
Totten, Brig. Gen. James (Northern) 232–3, 283, 291, 294
Tracy, Lt. Col. Jesse H. (Southern) 210–1
Tracy, Col. John Charles (Southern) 95–6
Trans-Mississippi West 157, 235
Trapp, Capt. William R. (Northern) 326
tribunal, military 7, 27, 37, 88, 117, 119, 141, 170, 171, 213, 271, 292, 361, 368, 378, 391; *see also* court martial; "drumhead"
Trigg, Judge John A. 362, 364, 367
Trow, Harrison (Southern and author) 93–4, 336
Troy, Lincoln County 259
True, John M. (Northern) 226
"Truman, Harry" *see* Terman, Detective J. W.
Tucker (Southern) 133
Tucker, Capt. (Southern) 21
Tucker, Frank (Southern) 170
Tucker Mill, Lewis County 259
Tufts and Miller Store, New Market, Platte County 151
Tunison, Maj. John (Northern) 331
Tunnage, 2nd Lt. Jesse C. (Northern) 316
Turkey Creek, Jasper County 194
Turley, Capt. James M. (Northern) 356
Turner, John (Southern) 150
Turney, Capt. John W. (Northern) 321
Tuscumbia, Miller County 302–3
Tuttle-Colony family, Phelps County (Northern) 168
Tyler, Col. John F. (Northern) 78–9, 170

"underground railroad" 120
Union Church, Chariton County 239
Union enrolling officer 153
"Union farm," Phelps County 168
Union League, Miller County 384
Union Mills, Platte County 322, 323, 324, 389–90

Union overcoats 92, 112, 237, 285, 298
Unionville, Putnam County 121
United States flag *see* flags
United States troops (Northern): 2nd United States Cavalry Regiment 48; 18th United States Colored Infantry 157–9
University City, St. Louis County 182
uprising *see* insurgency
Urbana, Dallas County 31
Ury, Lewis, and Josiah C. (Northern) 104
Utterback, Legan G. (Southern) 260
Utz, James M. (Southern) 174

Valle, Francis (Southern) 68, 73–4
Vance, Lt. John A. (Northern) 256
Vandevere, Louis (Southern) 148
Van Horn, Lt. Col. Robert T. (Northern) 306
Vaughan, 1st Sgt. Carmi B. (Northern) 205–6, 289
Vaughn, Brig. Gen. Richard C. (Northern) 52–3
Veal, George (Northern) 417n2
Venneman farm, Platte County 346
Vernon County 33, 34, 50, 91, 93, 98, 101, 102, 103, 190, 192, 195, 197–8, 200, 203–4, 205, 206; Dover Township 104
Versailles, Morgan County 354, 376
Vice, William D. (Northern) 112
Vicksburg, Mississippi: siege and surrender 28, 165, 220
Victoria, Jefferson County 174
Vida (present day village), Phelps County 79
Vienna, Maries County 83, 176–7
Viers, William (Southern) 417n2
Violette, Eugene M. (historian) 181
Virginia 12, 59, 232, 259, 362
Vittum, Capt. David S. (Northern) 202
Voges, Henry (Northern) 170

Wade, Robert W. (Northern) 12
Wagner 247
wagon trains or wagons 9, *10*, 14, 16, 18, 21, 22, 48, 52, 90–1, *110*, 120, 153, 160, *194*, 195, 200, 206, 209, 286–7, 287–8, 314, 351, 374
Wagoner, Capt. Seymour W. (Northern) *294*–295
Wainscot, Ira 36
Waitman (Southern) 108
Wakenda Creek, Carroll County 343–4, 389–90

Walker, John, and Jathan (Southern) 417n2
Walker, Dr. Joseph (Southern) 348–9
Wall, Thomas 174
Wallace, William, or James 346
Waller, James H. (Southern) 124, 126
Walnut Creek, Johnson County 379, 381
War Department of the U. S. 182
War Eagle (vessel) 232
Ward, Thomas 113
Warder, Joseph 352
Warder's Church fight (10 July 1864), Lafayette County 352–3
Warfield, Elisha 361
Warner, Pvt. Charles (Northern) 189
Warren, Pvt. James (Northern) 343
Warren, John Thomas (Southern) 298–9
Warren County 40, 113, 114, 223–4, 229, 242, 258
Warrensburg, Johnson County 52, 54, 55, 64, 65, 100, 103, 132, 133, 134, 136, 137, 193, 279, 283, 285, 287, 289, 291, 292, 293, 297, 356, 364, 365, 368, 371, 373, 374, 378, 380–1, 383
Warrenton, Warren County 258
Warsaw, Benton County 93, 106, 207
Washington, Jim 114
Washington, D. C. 60, 185
Washington County 73, 74–5, 161, 170, 171, 172, 173, 174, 176, 177, 187
Watie, Brig. Gen. Stand (Southern) 196–*197*
Watkins, Benjamin (Southern) 133–4
Watson, Capt. (Southern) 73
Watson, Dick (Southern) 165, 167, 176–7
Watts, Hamp B. (Southern, author) 230, 232, 234–5, 251
Waverly, Lafayette County 283, 293, 351, 355, 385
Wayne City, Jackson County 371
Wayne County 20, 69, 75, 77, 78, 161, 162, 163, 171, 175
Waynesville, Pulaski County 14, 15, 17, 33, 167
Wear, Lt. Oscar (Northern) 103
Webb, Capt. E. L. (Northern) 238
Webster, Washington County 172, 178
Webster County 210
Wedington, Pvt. Jacob, "Jake" (Southern) 50
Weems, Jonas (Southern) 98
Weer, Col. William (Northern) 27, 86, 87–8

Welch, Warren (Northern) 48–9, 407n52; Andy Blunt's corpse (Blunt killed 7 March) 125; Cooper and Moniteau Counties raid of Todd's band (mid-August–early September) 383, 385; Cooper and Moniteau Counties scout (early to middle August) 377; J. Frank Gregg's traveling band member (middle July) 354–5; Jackson County forage detail skirmish (January) 52; Jackson County operations (July–early August) 357; returned Rebel group member to Jackson County (October 1863 through January 1864) 49–51; Todd's band member (June or July) 351; Todd's band member on Arrow Rock raid (18–23 July 1864) 357–9
Welcome (vessel) 184
Weldon, Nicholas (Southern) 120
Wellington, Lafayette County 136, 284, 290, 292, 293, 351, 352, 372
Wells, C. C., and Ollie L. (Southern) 258
Wells, Capt. J. A. (Northern) 103
Wellsville, Montgomery County 40, 114
Wesly, Sgt. Thomas J. (Northern) 112, 213
West, Capt. George (Northern) 357
West, Kincheon (Southern) 31, 101–2
West, Mr. (Southern) 158
West Ely, Marion County 183, 260
West Fork of Dry Wood Creek, Kansas 104
West Fork of Post Oak Creek, Johnson County 292
West Point, or United States Military Academy 57
West Wind (vessel) 290, 351
Westlake, Mr. (Southern) 166
Weston, Platte County 43, 153, 264, 266, 267, 268, 269, 306, 308, 326, 331, 338, 347
Westover's Mill, St. Francois County 171
Westport, Jackson County 49, 55, 286
White, William O. (Southern) 86, 400n45
White Hare, Cedar County 199–200
White River, southwest Missouri 209
White Rock Prairie, McDonald County 105
Whiteneck, Henry D. (Southern) 345

Whitewater River, southeast Missouri 69, 70
Whitlock, Columbus (Northern) 340
Whitmer, Capt. David P. (Northern) 277, 316
Whitsell, William 287–8; *see also* Battle of Whitsell Farm
Whitson, Pvt. Harrison (Southern) 72
Whitson, Isaac (Northern) 211
Whybark, Capt. Levi E. (Northern) 16, 17, 164
Wigginton, John, and Mollie (Southern) 379
Wilborn, Capt. (Northern) 178
Wilcox, John (Southern) 143, 382
Wilcox, John P. (Southern) 303, 373, 383, 433n48
Wilhite, Jefferson "Jeff" (Southern) 129, 131–2, 287, 352–3
Wilhite, William (Southern) 141
Wilkenson, James W. (Southern) 125
Wilkerson, Dr. 258
Wilkie, Mr. (Southern) 113
Willard, John (Northern) 240
William Jewell College, Liberty, Clay County 313
Williams (Southern) 95
Williams, George (Northern) 248, 252
Williams, Col. John F. (Northern) 222–*223*
Williams, Miss (Southern) 299
Williamsburg, Callaway County 40, 114, 114–5, 258
Williamson, Daniel 374–5
Willsey, 1st Lt. Clark B. (Northern) 198
Wilson (Southern) 129
Wilson, Bill (Southern) 68, 79, 88, 153, 164, 165, 166, 399n24

Wilson, Bob (Southern) 352, 361, 362, 364, 367, 373, 375–6, 382, 444n66
Wilson, Capt. Hamilton S. (Northern) 149–30, 264, 409n13
Wilson, Maj. James (Northern) 77, 158, 174
Wilson, Napoleon (Northern) 80
Wilson, Pvt. Perry J. (Northern) 316
Wilson, Capt. Thomas J. (Northern) 305
Wilson, William P. (Southern) 188, 415n20
Winsell, William (Northern) 118
Winsett (Southern) 170
Winston, Col. John H. (Southern) 140–1, 151–*152*, 263, 268, 304, 388
Winters, Capt. Ezekiel L (Northern) 238
Wirt, Col. Samuel M. (Northern) 260–1
Wisconsin troops (Northern): 2nd Wisconsin Cavalry Regiment 9, 83–4; 3rd Wisconsin Cavalry Regiment 34–5, 93, 99, 102, 104, 176, 198, 200–1, 202, 203, 206
Withers, Hiram (Southern) 85, 400n42
Wolf Creek, St. Francois County 174
Wolfskill, Professor C. G. (author) 313
wood-cutting 152, 188, 267, 374–5
Woodland Diary, St. Louis County 183
Woodruff, 2nd Lt. D. C. (Northern) 258–9
Woods, Burt (Southern) 17

Woods, Capt. W. T. (Northern) 152, 264
Woodson, Col. Richard G. (Northern) 76
Woodson, Col. Samuel (Southern) 180
Woodson, Tom (Southern) 365–6, 367, 369, 370
Woodward's country store, Buchanan County 327
Wooten, Capt. W. H. (Southern) 133
Wright, Anthony (Southern) 165
Wright, John L. (Southern) 257
Wright, John P. (Southern) 155
Wright, Phineas (Southern) 180
Wright, Dr. Wm. A. (Southern) 88
Wright County 33, 210, 211
Wyandotte, Kansas 47

Yager, Miss Louisa (Southern) 373–*374*
Yager, or Yeager, Richard, "Dick" (Southern) 53, 126, 131, 294, 358–9, 363, 373, 377
Yates, Alfred (Southern) 171, 178, 187, 412n57, 414n15
Yates, Thomas (Southern) 165, 167
Yeager family, Jackson County *see* Yager, Richard
Young, Arthur G. 55
Youngblood, Asst. Surgeon J. M. (Northern) 189
Younger, Cole (Southern) 138
Younger, Jim (Southern) 276
Younger, Capt. John W. (Northern) 328

Zanesville, Ohio 273
Zeigler (Southern) 331
Zeller, Otho (Northern) 385
Zimmer, John (Northern) 170

www.ingramcontent.com/pod-product-compliance
Lightning Source LLC
Chambersburg PA
CBHW080935020526
44116CB00034B/2600